Stu
for
Mer
and
All
Boo
anot

N

4

9

TURN

76

2

36

Current perspectives in social psychology

Current perspectives

Second Edition

Readings with commentary

New York
OXFORD

in social psychology

Edited by

EDWIN P. HOLLANDER and RAYMOND G. HUNT

STATE UNIVERSITY OF NEW YORK AT BUFFALO

UNIVERSITY PRESS

London Toronto 1967

First Printing, March 1967
Second Printing, November 1967

Library of Congress Catalogue Card Number: 67-11758
Printed in the United States of America

Preface to the Second Edition

In this new edition, we have kept in mind the several goals of the first edition: to provide a current view and understanding of the various empirical problems studied under the banner of social psychology; to give a place and to pay due attention to the broadest range of prominent and productive viewpoints which characterize the field today; and to show the interrelationships as well as the divergencies which exist in these areas of social psychology.

The first edition's format and other features have been maintained while its scope has been considerably extended. Where it had fifty selections, this new edition has sixty-five selections. The eight original section headings have been retained and two more have been added—Organizational Processes and Intergroup Relations. Our hope thereby is to provide a greater coverage of the contemporary field and to update materials in the process: twenty-two selections, about a third of those in this new edition, appeared from 1963 onward.

We have not, however, sought newness for its own sake. In this edition we have retained thirty-two of the papers from the first edition. What we have aimed at is a balance between statements which served us well and newer ones which can help to enlarge a current view of the field.

Once again we have prefaced each section with a succinct chapter to provide a perspective of that area of social psychology and indicate the contribution the selections there make to its present character. We have also tried to emphasize the fundamental coherence of social psychology, even within the organization by sections. To compensate for unrealistic separations, we have as before cross-referenced extensively in the introduction to each of the ten sections. Ideally these introductions should be read in advance of the papers in a section so as to provide a needed backdrop to the ideas presented there. We also feel that using the book in sequence has some merit in building progressively toward a working acquaintance with the field. Furthermore, the cross-referencing of materials, together with the comprehensive bibliography and indexes at the end of the book, should provide the student with ready access to many related sources here and elsewhere.

In the selection and editing of papers our primary interest once again has been to include those which go beyond the presentation of a single study to a fuller representation of a point of view and range of research within the wider spectrum of the field. Thus we have sought out papers which reflect the major ideas and orientations of a whole line of investigation. Our selections are those which we feel achieve our goals, within our limitations of structure and scope, and with no judgment on our part as to the absolute merit of the many worthy contributions which could not be accommodated.

We have been fortunate again to have the wholehearted co-operation of our contributors and we are grateful especially for their willingness to have some abbreviations made to their papers, many of which were chapters of books, to bring them within manageable proportions for inclusion here. Our editing has not affected the internal content of material; we have not altered the sequence or flow of content whether we have "abridged" or "excerpted." Where these terms are used in the acknowledgment at the beginning of a paper, they signify in our usage distinct differences. *Abridgment* means the use of an entire paper with moderate deletions here and there of paragraphs, footnotes, and illustrative matter not affecting its total sense. *Excerption* means that one or more portions of a work have been republished to represent a particular point made there. Editing has therefore primarily involved moderate deletions with the sense of the selection still retained though usually in briefer form. Ellipses have *not* been employed to signify breaks in the material thus permitting each paper to be printed as an uninterrupted whole.

It is a pleasure to take this occasion again to publicly record our thanks to the contributors and to the publishers whose names appear in the acknowledgment at the beginning of each selection. Once again, in the name of all the contributors, the American Psychological Foundation shares in the royalties from this edition. We also wish to record our thanks to the Lockwood Library at the State University of New York at Buffalo for providing the resources needed for compilation of this edition. A special debt of gratitude is due to Leonore Ganschow, who has given us generous and steadfast assistance in all of the details associated with the preparation of the manuscript. For their considerable aid at many stages in this enterprise, we are delighted to thank our wives.

London, England and
Buffalo, New York
November 1966

E. P. H. & R. G. H.

Special note to the reader

The procedures adhered to in editing the selections in this volume are set out in the Preface. It should be emphasized again that, while some papers are republished virtually in their entirety, the specific omission of sentences, paragraphs, footnotes, illustrations, or tables is usually *not* indicated. Especially in those cases where excerption rather than abridgment of a paper is stated in the acknowledgment, readers would do well to consult the primary sources to find related information or the expansion of certain points.

Contents

X INTERGROUP RELATIONS

Current perspectives in social psychology

I BASIC ISSUES AND PROCESSES

Social psychology is a field of study which takes as its problem the understanding of social behavior. It seeks in particular to understand the nature of influence relationships between individuals, either in the person-to-person sense or with respect to larger groups, institutions, and society. The distinctiveness of social psychology arises from two features: first, its essential focus upon the *individual* as a participant in social processes; and second, its concern with the *analysis* of these processes, through appropriate empirical methods, to provide explanations rather than mere descriptions.

In recent years, the methodology of social psychology has grown increasingly experimental. Nonetheless, various research techniques, including observation, interviews, attitudinal and projective testing, sample surveys, content analysis, and sociometric measures, continue to be used, alone or in various combinations. Some works which present the methodological side of the field are those by Festinger and Katz (1953), Selltiz, *et al.* (1959), Lazarsfeld and Rosenberg (1955), and Hyman (1955). Whatever methodology is employed, however, its selection depends upon the particular concepts which guide research in the first place. The importance of research findings therefore depends quite relevantly on their theoretical sources and contributions to theory. This book emphasizes the conceptual side of research, not to the exclusion of empirical findings, but as a way of better understanding them.

In this section we hope to provide a brief introduction to the kinds of issues and processes with which social psychology is concerned. Our coverage will include historical guideposts as well as indications of significant contemporary thinking. These recent trends increasingly give special weight to the psychological processes of perception and motivation in determining the social behavior of individuals.

It is quite true to say that social psychology derives historically from psychology and sociology, but this often conveys a mistaken view of it in the sense of a literal melding. Many of the concepts in social psychology are clearly derivative of concerns which persist in these older disciplines. However, this does not mean that bits and pieces of each have been simply mixed together in a potpourri. The integrity of social psychology today comes from its steady movement toward a distinctive understanding of the psychology of the individual as an active agent in social situations.

Although it is a comparatively new field of study, one sees in current social psychology lines of emphasis that have origins in philosophical antiquity. In that sense, its heritage is dotted with problems centuries old. These include controversies surrounding "mind-body," "heredity-environment," "group mind," "mental elements," and the differences characterized by "phenomenological vs. behavioristic" approaches (see G. W. Allport, 1954). While not always resolved, or resolvable as stated, these concerns are now points of reference rather than lively preoccupations of the present scene. If there are important residues of emphasis discernible, these would more likely lie in the direction of how the course of behavior is conceived; illustrative of these would be rationalistic vs. nonrationalistic models of behavior, and attention to conscious vs. unconscious processes, and to personalistic vs. situational determinants.

This latter distinction, in particular, continues to bear upon approaches in the field, as one witnesses here notably in Sections III and VII. Indeed, the first two textbooks of social psychology, both published in 1908, dramatized this divergence. In his text, William McDougall, a major figure in psychology prominently identified with the "instinct" theory, though his position was far richer in its ramifications, gave heavy weight to dispositional "tendencies," which individuals bring to the situation, as determinants of social behavior. E. A. Ross, the noted sociologist, stressed situational determinants in his text and furthered especially the concepts of imitation and suggestion as explanations for social behavior.

In the more than half a century since these initial works laid out a difference in orientation to social behavior, social psychology has moved increasingly to a fusing of social and psychological variables. A vestige of this distinction remains, however, in connection with an emphasis on the individual's dispositions, including his past history and his intra-psychic processes, as against an emphasis on social forces in his immediate situation, such as social structure. The common ground for this development, as we shall be noting further, rests in the recognition that individuals perceive and thus define situations based upon their past experiences and present motivations.

In the first paper in this section, Zajonc provides an instructive view of the early work on social facilitation. This work commonly dealt with concepts like imitation or suggestion which enjoy a much diminished popularity today —e.g., see Allport's historical account in the *Handbook of Social Psychology* (Lindzey, 1954). The situational effects of the behavior of one individual upon the behavior of another were a basic concern in this research. As Zajonc notes, however, a distinction was required between two kinds of situations: the effect of an audience of onlookers, and the effect of other persons who were working side by side in a co-acting arrangement. He also indicates that performance and learning were differentially influenced by each of these situations. Thus, performance of something already well learned is facilitated by the presence of an audience, while initial learning is inhibited by having spectators present. As Zajonc notes: "The generalization which organizes these results is that the presence of others as spectators or as co-actors enhances the emission of dominant responses." The significant common feature which helps to explain these effects of social interaction is the hypothesis that the presence of other members of the same species tends to increase arousal. While the relevant physiological mechanisms are not completely understood, there is reason to believe that social interaction plays a vital preservative function for the individual.

In his treatment of social interaction, Zajonc draws on early human research, and on studies with animals (see Tolman & Wilson, 1965). The findings of such studies do not provide a view of how the individual perceives and is motivated to act in this situation, since only effects are observed. Greater attention is being given now to how the individual construes his world as a major determinant of his behavior, and increasingly social psychology is inclining toward a study of the nature and content of experience. This approach, which is associated with phenomenology (see MacLeod, 1951), emphasizes the necessity to get beneath the level of observable actions to an understanding of their psychological bases. This point is the essence of Asch's paper which follows in this section.

Asch considers that social psychology cannot develop without reference to experience. Furthermore, he contends that the distinction between behavior and experience is misleading. His point that the significance of actions can only be appreciated with reference to their meaning to the individual is basic to many of the "cognitive" approaches in social psychology today (see Sections III and VI, especially). In this respect, Asch argues for a focus on the individual as the primary actor whose perception of the world about him requires attention.

In varying ways, the two papers which follow in this section deal with the same fundamental issue. Drawing from the seminal work of Kurt Lewin (1936), Barker presents a detailing of the characteristics of "behavior settings" that act reciprocally to affect the behavior of individuals, as well as being affected by an individual's response. He says that situations that are defined in some commonly understood way produce certain characteristic behaviors, even on the part of different individuals. This is by way of noting that any situation will carry some culturally defined meaning to which the individual attaches importance, and to which he reacts. Thus, Barker's contribution lies in establishing a link between ecology, in the sense of the environment for action, and psychology, in the sense of the individual's premises for action in and on the environment. It is also noteworthy that Barker's concern with the psychological effects of behavior settings is well exemplified by Zajonc's report of the psycho-physiological stresses associated with crowding.

Lewin's attention to social perception is echoed here in the excerpt from Bruner's paper on perceptual readiness. Bruner's work with cognitive processes as a mediating influence on behavior has been of great significance. His conception of perceptual categories as devices for defining and interpreting "reality" is a key point of reference for a number of the papers here, e.g., Brown in Section IV, and Cantril and Steiner in Section V. With Osgood, he has been in the forefront of the movement toward understanding thought processes, whether under the heading of cognition or perception, as wellsprings for action through the mediation of meaning.

The other line of psychological emphasis has been directed toward motivation. There is, of course, a wide recognition today of the interrelated features of motivation and perception. In the past, however, motivation was seen in unitary terms as a pushing or pulling force. At the extreme, the instinctual viewpoint saw such forces as totally sovereign and largely unchanging. In his paper here, Beach reviews the concept of instinct to assess its place in the modern scene. He recaptures the flavor of Aristotelian tradition with its categories and the idea of "essences" to account for behavior. Such a system of classifying motives is outmoded and misleading, he says, because of its confining quality, and should be discarded in favor of greater attention to a study of the ongoing development of behavior and its relationship to genes. His discussion is a complement to considerations of the general nature of the person and, more directly, to socialization phenomena discussed in Section II.

A parallel break with the tradition of instinct is seen in the paper by White which follows. He presents a reconception of motivation in terms of "effectance," a movement toward efficacy or competence. Man, he says, is distinguished by his competence in handling the environment, and this has broad implications for an understanding of "human nature." White contends that this cannot be accounted for fully in terms of energy supplied by drives or instincts, but can be understood rather as the way humans assimilate the environment and relate to it. His formulations are part of the growing and widely based discontent with the deficiencies in traditional conceptualizations of primary drives as the major source of human action. He emphasizes exploratory and playful activities, as well as behaviors instigated by drives, as bases for the acquisition of competence. This conception has extensive implications for ideas about work and the functioning of organizations (see Section IX).

McClelland is represented by considerable work on social motivation, most importantly with achievement motivation (McClelland, *et al.*, 1953). A more recent work, *The Achieving Society* (1961), represents a novel analysis of the prevailing orientations within a society which incline its members toward achievement. His paper in this section, taken from that book, presents the essential features of the conception and measurement of achievement motivation. McClelland's work is in the tradition of social psychology's long-standing preoccupation with attitudes. In this respect his approach to achievement motivation reveals the underpinnings of attitudes and values.

In addition to the implications afforded by these papers for the perceptual and motivational dynamics of behavior, there is a counterpart development occurring in the study of physiological effects of the social environment upon the individual. A representation of this is seen in the work of Bovard (1959) referred to by Zajonc here. Drawing upon Selye's concept of stress (see *Stress,* 1950), Bovard considers that social stimuli may be stressors insofar as considerable symbolic content is conveyed by them as a function of past experience mediated through perception. Most relevant to social psychology is his contention that the presence of another member of the same species has a protective effect on the vertebrate organism under stress. Schachter's work (1959) on birth order also bears on this insofar as affiliation needs serve a protective function in reducing anxiety under threat, though in terms of an element of personal history varying in significance across individuals. Such findings add a new dimension to usual statements of the bases for group affiliation, considered in Section VII.

A larger view of human motivation is represented by Cantril's paper here from his recent book, *The Pattern of Human Concerns* (1965). His focus on the universals of "human nature" reveals a growing interest in the motivations for competence, mastery, and understanding that direct Man's actions. In this vein, Cantril's thinking is consistent with that of Goldstein (1940), Maslow (1954), Rogers (1959), and G. W. Allport (1955), all of whom stress human motivations toward "self-actualization," "self-realization," or "becoming" (see Section III). A parallel set of concepts is introduced by Gardner in his emphasis on commitment and meaning in Section II. Thus, Cantril signalizes the broadening trend away from heavily deterministic views of Man's action and toward a conception of the individual's interaction with the social environment and its meaning to him as central elements in social existence.

1 Social facilitation

ROBERT B. ZAJONC

Most textbook definitions of social psychology involve considerations about the influence of man upon man, or, more generally, of individual upon individual. And most of them, explicitly or implicitly, commit the main efforts of social psychology to the problem of how and why the *behavior* of one individual affects the behavior of another. The influences of individuals on each others' behavior which are of interest to social psychologists today take on very complex forms. Often they involve vast networks of interindividual effects, such as one finds in studying the process of group decision-making, competition, or conformity to a group norm. But the fundamental forms of interindividual influence are represented by the oldest experimental paradigm of social psychology: social facilitation. This paradigm, dating back to Triplett's original experiments on pacing and competition (1897), examines the consequences upon behavior which derive from the sheer presence of other individuals.

Research in the area of social facilitation may be classified in terms of two experimental paradigms: audience effects and co-action effects. The first experimental paradigm involves the observation of behavior when it occurs in the presence of passive spectators. The second examines behavior when it occurs in the presence of other individuals also engaged in the same activity. We shall consider past literature in these two areas separately.

Audience effects

Simple motor responses are particularly sensitive to social facilitation effects. Travis (1925) obtained such effects in a study in which he used the pursuit-rotor task. In this task the subject is required to follow a small revolving target by means of a stylus which he holds in his hand. If the stylus is even momentarily off target during a revolution, the revolution counts as an error. First each subject was trained for several consecutive days until his performance reached a stable level. One day after the conclusion of the training the subject was called to the laboratory, given five trials alone, and then ten trials in the presence of from four to eight upperclassmen and graduate students. They had been asked by the experimenter to watch the subject quietly and attentively. Travis found a clear improvement in performance when his subjects were confronted with an audience. Their accuracy on the ten trials before an audience was greater than on any ten previous trials, including those on which they had scored highest.

Dashiell, who, in the early 1930's, carried out an extensive program of research on social facilitation, also found considerable improvement in perform-

Abridged from **Science**, 1965, 149, No. 3681, 269–74, with permission of the author and the publisher.

ance due to audience effects on such tasks as simple multiplication or word association (1930). But, as is the case in many other areas, negative audience effects were also found. Pessin asked college students to learn lists of nonsense syllables under two conditions, alone and in the presence of several spectators (1933). When confronted with an audience, his subjects required an average of 11.27 trials to learn a seven-item list. When working alone they needed only 9.85 trials. The average number of errors made in the "audience" condition was considerably higher than the number in the "alone" condition. Husband found that the presence of spectators interferes with the learning of a finger maze (1931), and Pessin and Husband (1933) confirmed Husband's results. The number of trials which the isolated subjects required for learning the finger maze was 17.1. Subjects confronted with spectators, however, required 19.1 trials. The average number of errors for the isolated subjects was 33.7; the number for those working in the presence of an audience was 40.5.

The results thus far reviewed seem to contradict one another. On a pursuit-rotor task Travis found that the presence of an audience improves performance. The learning of nonsense syllables and maze learning, however, seem to be inhibited by the presence of an audience, as shown by Pessin's experiment. The picture is further complicated by the fact that when Pessin's subjects were asked, several days later, to recall the nonsense syllables they had learned, a reversal was found. The subjects who tried to recall the lists in the presence of spectators did considerably better than those who tried to recall them alone. Why are the learning of nonsense syllables and maze learning inhibited by the presence of spectators? And why, on the other hand, does performance on a pursuit-rotor, word-association, multiplication, or a vigilance task improve in the presence of others?

There is just one, rather subtle, consistency in the above results. It would appear that the emission of well-learned responses is facilitated by the presence of spectators, while the acquisition of new responses is impaired. To put the statement in conventional psychological language, performance is facilitated and learning is impaired by the presence of spectators.

This tentative generalization can be reformulated so that different features of the problem are placed into focus. During the early stages of learning, especially of the type involved in social facilitation studies, the subject's responses are mostly the wrong ones. A person learning a finger maze, or a person learning a list of nonsense syllables, emits more wrong responses than right ones in the early stages of training. Most learning experiments continue until he ceases to make mistakes —until his performance is perfect. It may be said, therefore, that during training it is primarily the wrong responses which are dominant and strong; they are the ones which have the highest probability of occurrence. But after the individual has mastered the task, correct responses necessarily gain ascendency in his task-relevant behavioral repertoire. Now they are the ones which are more probable—in other words, dominant. Our tentative generalization may now be simplified: audience enhances the emission of dominant responses. If the dominant responses are the correct ones, as is the case upon achieving mastery, the presence of an audience will be of benefit to the individual. But if they are mostly wrong, as is the case in the early stages of learning, then these wrong responses will be enhanced in the presence of an audience, and the emission of correct responses will be postponed or prevented.

There is a class of psychological processes which are known to enhance the emission of dominant responses. They are subsumed under the concepts of drive, arousal, and activation (e.g., see Dufy, 1962; Spence, 1956; Zajonc & Nieuwenhuyse, 1964). If we could show that the presence of an audience has arousal consequences for the subject, we would be a step further along in trying to arrange the results of social-facilitation experiments into a neater package. But let us first consider another set of experimental findings.

Co-action effects

The experimental paradigm of co-action is somewhat more complex than the paradigm involved in the study of audience effects. Here we observe individuals all simultaneously engaged in the same activity and in full view of each other. One of the clearest effects of such simultaneous action, or co-action, is found in eating behavior. It is well known that animals simply eat more in the presence of others. For instance, Bayer had chickens eat from a pile of wheat to their full satisfaction (1929). He waited some time to be absolutely sure that his subject would eat no more, and then brought in a companion chicken who had not eaten for 24 hours. Upon the introduction of the hungry co-actor, the apparently sated chicken ate two-thirds again as much grain as it had already eaten. Recent work by Tolman and Wilson fully substantiates these results (1965). In an extensive study of social-facilitation effects among albino rats, Harlow found dramatic increases in eating (1932). In one of his experiments, for instance, the rats, shortly after weaning, were matched in pairs for weight. They were then fed alone and in pairs on alternate days. It is clear that considerably more food was consumed by the animals when they were in pairs than when they were fed alone. James (1953, 1960; and James & Cannon, 1956), too, found very clear evidence of increased eating among puppies fed in groups.

Perhaps the most dramatic effect of co-action is reported by Chen (1937). Chen observed groups of ants working alone, in groups of two, and in groups of three. Each ant was observed under various conditions. In the first experimental session each ant was placed in a bottle half filled with sandy soil. The ant was observed for 6 hours. The time at which nest-building began was noted, and the earth excavated by the insect was carefully weighed. Two days afterward the same ants were placed in freshly filled bottles in pairs, and the same observations were made. A few days later the ants were placed in the bottles in groups of three, again for 6 hours. Finally, a few days after the test in groups of three, nest-building of the ants in isolation was observed.

There is absolutely no question that the amount of work an ant accomplishes increases markedly in the presence of another ant. In all pairs except one, the presence of a companion increased output by a factor of at least 2. The effect of co-action on the latency of the nest-building behavior was equally dramatic. The solitary ants of session 1 and the final session began working on the nest in 192 minutes, on the average. The latency period for ants in groups of two was only 28 minutes. The effects observed by Chen were limited to the immediate situation and seemed to have no lasting consequences for the ants. There were no differences in the results of session 1, during which the ants worked in isolation, and of the last experimental session, where they again worked in solitude.

If one assumes that under the conditions of Chen's experiment nest-building *is* the dominant response, then there is no reason why his findings could not be embraced by the generalization just proposed. Nest-building is a response which Chen's ants have fully mastered. Certainly, it is something that a mature ant need not learn. And this is simply an instance where the generalization that the presence of others enhances the emission of dominant and well-developed responses holds.

The experiments on social facilitation performed by Floyd Allport (1920) and continued by Dashiell (1930), both of whom used human subjects, are the ones best known. Allport's subjects worked either in separate cubicles or sitting around a common table. When working in isolation they did the various tasks at the same time and were monitored by common time signals. Allport did everything possible to reduce the tendency to compete. The subjects were told that the results of their tests would not be compared and would not be shown to other staff members, and that they themselves should refrain from making any such comparisons.

Among the tasks used were the following: chain word association, vowel cancellation, reversible perspective, multiplication, problem solving, and judgments of odors and weights. The results of Allport's experiments are well known: in all but the problem-solving and judgments test, performance was better in groups than in the "alone" condition. How do these results fit our generalization? Word association, multiplication, the cancellation of vowels, and the reversal of the perceived orientation of an ambiguous figure all involve responses which are well established. They are responses which are either very well learned or under a very strong influence of the stimulus, as in the word-association task or the reversible-perspective test. The problem-solving test consists of disproving arguments of ancient philosophers. In contrast to the other tests, it does not involve well-learned responses. On the contrary, the probability of wrong (that is, logically incorrect) responses on tasks of this sort is rather high; in other words, wrong responses are dominant. Of interest, however, is the finding that while intellectual work suffered in the group situation, sheer output of words was increased. When working together, Allport's subjects tended consistently to write more. Therefore, the generalization proposed in the previous section can again be applied: if the presence of others raises the probability of dominant responses, and if strong (and many) incorrect response tendencies prevail, then the presence of others can only be detrimental to performance. The results of the judgment tests have little bearing on the present argument, since Allport gives no accuracy figures for evaluating performance. The data reported only show that the presence of others was associated with the avoidance of extreme judgments.

There are experiments which show that learning is enhanced by the presence of other learners (Gurnee, 1939; Welty, 1934), but in all these experiments, as far as I can tell, it was possible for the subject to *observe* the critical responses of other subjects, and to determine when he was correct and when incorrect. In none, therefore, has the co-action paradigm been employed in its pure form. That paradigm involves the presence of others, and nothing else. It requires that these others not be able to provide the subject with cues or information as to appropriate behavior. If other learners can supply the critical individual with such cues, we are dealing not with the problem of co-action but with the problem of imitation or vicarious learning.

The presence of others as a source of arousal

The generalization which organizes these results is that the presence of others, as spectators or as co-actors, enhances the emission of dominant responses. We also know from extensive research literature that arousal, activation, or drive all have as a consequence the enhancement of dominant responses (see Spence, 1956). We now need to examine the hypothesis that the presence of others increases the individual's general arousal or drive level.

The evidence which bears on the relationship between the presence of others and arousal is, unfortunately, only indirect. But there is some very suggestive evidence in one area of research. One of the more reliable indicators of arousal and drive is the activity of the endocrine systems in general, and of the adrenal cortex in particular. Adrenocortical functions are extremely sensitive to changes in emotional arousal, and it has been known for some time that organisms subjected to prolonged stress are likely to manifest substantial adrenocortical hypertrophy (Selye, 1946). Recent work (Nelson & Samuels, 1952) has shown that the main biochemical component of the adrenocortical output is hydrocortisone (17-hydroxycorticosterone). Psychiatric patients characterized by anxiety states, for instance, show elevated plasma levels of hydrocortisone (Bliss, *et al.*, 1953; Board, *et al.*, 1956).

While there is a fair amount of evidence that adrenocortical activity is a reliable symptom of arousal, similar endocrine manifestations were found to be associated with increased population density. Crowded mice, for instance, show increased amphetamine toxicity—that is, susceptibility to the excitatory effects of amphetamine—against which they can be protected by the administration of phenobarbital, chlorpromazine, or reserpine (Lasagna & McCann, 1957). Mason and Brady (1964) have recently reported that monkeys caged together had considerably higher plasma levels of hydrocortisone than monkeys housed in individual cages. Thiessen (1964) found increases in adrenal weights in mice housed in groups of 10 and 20 as compared with mice housed alone. The mere presence of other animals in the same room, but in separate cages, was also found to produce elevated levels of hydrocortisone.

Needless to say, the presence of others may have effects considerably more complex than that of increasing the individual's arousal level. The presence of others may provide cues as to appropriate or inappropriate responses, as in the case of imitation or vicarious learning. Or it may supply the individual with cues as to the measure of danger in an ambiguous or stressful situation. Davitz and Mason (1955), for instance, have shown that the presence of an unafraid rat reduces the fear of another rat in stress. Bovard (1959) believes that the calming of the rat in stress which is in the presence of an unafraid companion is mediated by inhibition of activity of the posterior hypothalamus. But in their experimental situations (that is, the open field test) the possibility that cues for appropriate escape or avoidance responses are provided by the co-actor is not ruled out. We might therefore be dealing not with the effects of the mere presence of others but with the considerably more complex case of imitation. The animal may not be calming *because* of his companion's presence. He may be calming *after* having copied his companion's attempted escape responses. The paradigm which I have examined in this article pertains only to the effects of the mere presence of others, and to the consequences for the arousal level. The exact parameters involved in social facilitation still must be specified.

2 The data of social psychology

SOLOMON E. ASCH

The place of experience in human social psychology has been settled in a purely practical way. It is not possible, as a rule, to conduct investigation in social psychology without including a reference to the experiences of persons. The investigator must, for example, take into account what the person under observation is saying; and such utterances have to be treated in terms of their meaning, not as auditory waves, or sounds, or "verbal behavior." One can hardly take a step in this region without involving the subject's ideas, feelings, and intentions. We do this when we observe people exchanging gifts, engaging in an economic transaction, being hurt by criticism, or taking part in a ritual. The sense of these actions would disappear the moment we subtracted from our description the presumed mental operations that they imply. This requirement to include mental happenings in an account of human activities, one which the social disciplines generally must observe, should have spurred an examination of the systematic properties of experience and their relations to action. Instead we find that the situation has been accepted half-heartedly, and that its implications have not been explored with care.

To see how the problem of experience arises in this area, let us consider how we follow the actions of persons. The first observation we make is that persons

Excerpted from "A Perspective on Social Psychology" in Volume 3 of S. Koch (Ed.), **Psychology: A Study of a Science** (Copyright © 1959 by McGraw-Hill, Inc.), New York: McGraw-Hill, 1959, pp. 374–9, with permission of the author and the publisher.

invariably describe the doings of others (and their own doings) in *psychological* terms. We say that a person sees, hears, prefers, demands. This is also the way we describe happenings between persons; thus we say that one person helped another, or distrusted him. These are the ways in which we order the actions of persons whom we observe to be living and conscious.

An organism that relates itself to the environment in this manner is observed to act in it in a special way. Heider (1944) has pointed out that we observe persons to produce effects intentionally. They relate themselves to the environment by wanting, by being interested, by liking, by understanding. In the case of persons, a cause is not merely a preceding state of affairs; it is a state of affairs as known or understood by the actor. An effect is not merely a later state of affairs; persons make things happen, or intend them. The movements of persons thus gain the status of actions.

With these is connected the most significant property of persons: that we experience them as capable of responding to *us*. They alone can understand our thoughts and feel our needs. Therefore they become the adequate objects of praise and blame. It is only to beings having these properties that we can relate ourselves by cooperation and competition, by affection and hatred, by admiration and envy. It is in these terms that we follow the actions of a friend, the happening in a play of Sophocles or in the life of a primitive society. Events of this kind form much of the content of the mutually relevant fields of persons.

From the standpoint of a powerful tradition there is something suspect about these everyday observations. The main charge is that they do not speak the language of science. They refer, of course, to what the other person does, but they are not simply descriptions of the movements he carries out; they are not simply statements of the geometrical displacements of persons and things. At this point the temper of one theory in general psychology recommends the wholesale dismissal of the layman's concepts and language when we turn to investigation. His accounts are, it is said, contaminated by the inclusion of subjective conditions that are not observable because they are not describable in terms of physical operations. This formulation, although it has not originated in social psychology and would, if taken seriously, drastically curb further inquiry in this field, has nevertheless left a strong impress upon it.

The following illustration may clarify the point at issue and the difficulties it raises. Among his prescriptions for a psychological utopia, Skinner includes the training of children to tolerate frustration, and proposes an ingenious procedure (Skinner, 1953). He would occasionally have the children in his utopia come to their meals, but delay their eating for a few minutes while they watch some delicious specialties that had been prepared for them. Gradually he would extend the period of deprivation, the intention being to instill self-control without injurious consequences. As Skinner describes the procedure, it is exclusively an affair of timing responses to given physical conditions. One may be permitted to wonder whether the children, however carefully reared, might not take a different view of the proceedings. Are they not likely to wonder what their caretakers are up to? And will not the outcome depend on the answers the caretakers give? If it should come into the children's heads that the caretakers are malicious, it might go ill with the effects of the scheduling. On the other hand, if the children trusted their mentors, and particularly, if they credited the caretakers with the meritorious motive of instilling self-control without injurious consequences, the discipline might prove more successful. The elimination of any reference to these internal events amounts to a failure to describe the relevant conditions with any adequacy.

The problem arises whenever we refer to action between persons. A determined effort to treat the relation of frustration to aggression in nonexperiential terms could not avoid defining frustration as damage attributed to a particular instigator (Dollard, *et al.*, 1939). In a recent discussion, while again insisting that we give priority in psychological investigation to action, on the ground that it alone is public, Sears uses the following example: ". . . if a child wants to be kissed good-night, his mother must lean toward him affectionately and kiss him. He, in turn, must slip his arms around her neck and lift his face to her receptively" (Sears, 1951, p. 480). This sentence is surely not an unadulterated description of geometrical displacements; it does not supply the kinematics of affection, or even of slipping, lifting, or leaning.

The sources of disagreement about the place of experience in psychological investigation are too deep-seated to be dealt with summarily. We will consider only a few points most relevant to this discussion. In the first place, there are certain misconceptions to be noted. It is often asserted that actions are public but experiences are private, and that therefore the latter have no place in science. Surely there is an error here. The observation of actions is part of the observer's experience. Indeed, the same writers who make the first assertion as a rule subscribe to the second. There is thus no ground for calling actions objective and experience in general subjective. This confusion has been discussed by Köhler (1929); it is not necessary to repeat it in full.

There is another, seemingly more substantial reason for the difference in status accorded to behavior and experience. We can, it is asserted, arrive at a high degree of consensus about behavior, but not about our respective experiences. (In the light of the preceding point, this assertion claims that some kinds of experience produce consensus superior to others.) In particular, the conclusion is drawn that the positions and displacements of objects in space provide the only dependable consensus.

This conclusion will not withstand scrutiny. There is often, indeed, excellent consensus about events which, according to the preceding view, are unobservable or incommunicable. The size of an afterimage, or the experience of a causal connection, can be described with a lawfulness that permits the study of their dependence on inner and outer conditions. This suffices to qualify the data of experience as data of science. Instead of pursuing this fruitful direction, the physicalistic doctrine has attempted to demonstrate that the data of experience can be treated as verbal behavior. It can be shown, though, that the occurrence of an experience is not the occurrence of a verbal response.

It is not probable that the preceding formal arguments are actually responsible for the efforts to eliminate all reference to experience from human investigation. To locate the sources of difficulty we must look elsewhere. Perhaps the most decisive assumption is that the data of experience are not functionally connected with, and provide no help toward understanding, other concurrent events in the individual. This belief is contrary to what we know about the relations of mental and physical events. The physicalistic program also derives from the elementaristic assumption that the properties of action can be exhaustively described in terms of component movements. Were this the case, it might indeed follow that the data of experience have a limited place. But human actions are extended spatio-temporal events having a definite form, and we cannot describe them without reference to goals, and to means related to goals. These characteristics of actions are lost from view when we concentrate on their most minute components one at a time, just as we lose the quality of a form or a melody when we attend only to its smallest components. It has been convincingly shown that the most consistently behavioristic procedures do not actually deal with stimulus and response in these elementaristic terms (Koch, 1954). Behaviorism must and does include action; it grants in practice all that is needed when it speaks of "running toward a goal," or of "pushing" and "pulling."

What is the relation of the distinction we have tried to draw between movement and extended action to the data of experience? First, the data of experience point to, and thus help identify, the conditions in the environment to which we are responsive. Second, the data of experience provide hints concerning the internal events that steer action.

Those who dream of an objectivistic social psychology fail to realize that such a program can be pursued only if the data of experience are taken into account openly. We are today far from able to describe the most obvious and the most significant social acts except in the language of direct experience. What are the event-sequences corresponding to such data as "the mother praised the child," or "the boy refused to heed the teacher"? And how much more difficult is it to describe the actions of "keeping a promise" or "telling the truth"? Not only are we at a loss to report adequately the actual sequences of such events; there is often no fixed set of actions corresponding to them from occasion to occasion. How, then, could we go about locating and identifying the relevant action patterns unless we were guided to them by the distinctions of direct experience? Even if we succeeded in such a description, it would remain a foreign language until it was translated back into the terms we ordinarily employ. At this point the categories of the layman are actually in advance of those that formal psychology today has at its command. He has, without the benefit of a psychological education, identified some of the conditions and consequences of action. To be sure, these categories are descriptive, not explanatory. Also, everyday thinking identifies them in a shorthand, summary manner, which must be replaced with far more detailed description. But to counsel their abandonment is to give up the prospect of social understanding, and to bar the very advance toward which we aim.

Throughout this discussion we have noted the prevalence of the assumption that one can move directly from a few selected notions, derived mainly from the study of lower organisms, to an account of human actions, and that the latter require no concepts appropriate to them. Actually, concepts such as conditioning, stimulus generalization, extinction, response strength, secondary reinforcement, and reinforcement itself have as a rule been extrapolated to social settings without a serious effort to demonstrate their relevance under the new conditions. In this passage the terms lose the relatively clear sense they initially have. The extrapolations become largely verbal; we are not the wiser when the translation has been accomplished. This procedure, instead of increasing objectivity, often conceals distinctions long familiar to ordinary observation. It discourages the exploration of those differences between persons and things, between living and dead, that are at the center of the subject. It creates the curious presumption that hardly anything new remains to be discovered in a field that has barely been studied.

The conclusion we have reached could have been arrived at more simply. Every field of inquiry must begin with the phenomena that everyday experience reveals, and with the distinctions it contains. Further inquiry may modify our understanding of them, but the phenomena themselves will never be displaced. In social psychology the phenomena with which we begin are qualitatively diverse and the description of them prior to formal investigation is consequently of particular importance. Let us, for the purpose of this discussion, assume that concepts such as "role," or "internalizing of values," have a place in social psychology. They must then be shown to apply to the ways in which the actors, who are often innocent of these notions, see their situation. The latter act in terms of conceptions and emotions peculiar to them—in terms of envy and trust, hope and suspicion. The concepts must be relevant to this world of appearances, which are among the indispensable data of the field. Those who avoid this initial phase of investigation run the danger of placing themselves in the position of the hero in Greek mythology who was shorn of his power the moment he lost contact with mother earth.

Having said this, it is necessary to add that a psychology based on phenomenal data alone must remain incomplete. The latter are always part of a wider field of events within the individual; any order they may reveal will be partial unless completed by a more comprehensive knowledge of psychological functioning. We need, therefore, an objective psychology that will account for the structure of experience. It also follows that the examination of experience should not become either an aimless or an endless occupation. It should strive to issue in inductive inquiry and, where possible, experimentation.

These conclusions should not hide the difficulties that face investigation in social psychology. In one area of psychology, that of perception, the reliance on phenomenal data has proceeded fruitfully. Such investigation possesses one indisputable advantage: phenomenal events are studied in their dependence on stimulus conditions which are describable in terms of well-understood physical operations, and in relation to internal processes that are also described in terms of natural science categories. This advantage deserts us in most parts of social psychology. Here we must abandon, at least for the foreseeable future, the yardsticks of physics, and describe both the stimulus conditions and the effects they produce in psychological terms. Since the dimensions of these events are frequently complex and only vaguely known, the prospect of discovering clear functional relations may arouse skepticism. It would be misleading to minimize the difficulties, but it would also be premature to prejudge the outcome. This is a challenge social psychology must accept.

3 On the nature of the environment

ROGER G. BARKER

The essence of science for Lewin was a system of explicitly stated concepts by means of which exceptionless derivations could be made. Since, in this view, the concepts of physics, biology, and sociology are incommensurable with those of psychology, he concluded that only probabilistic, empirical relations could be discovered between variables of psychology and those of other sciences. It was impossible, as he saw it, to make derivations to behavior from the nonpsychological environment, to use his own term, or the preperceptual or ecological environment, to use Brunswik's terms. It was this that made it essential for Lewin to limit psychology to an encapsulated system of purely psychological constructs. But he saw very clearly that an adequate applied behavioral science requires bridges between psychology and ecology, and much of his effort was preoccupied with it. Sometimes he approached the psychological-ecological breach directly and explicitly, as in his gatekeeper theory of the link between food habits and food technology and economics; sometimes he approached it obliquely and implicitly, as in his attempt to treat the social field as a psychological construct.

It seems to me that, as psychologists, we are all confronted with the same dilemma today. Who can doubt that changes in our environment ranging from new levels of radiation, to increased numbers of people, to new kinds of medicines, and new kinds of social organizations, schools, and governments are inexorably changing our behavior, and that our new behavior is, in turn, altering our environment? Can this total eco-behavioral system be incorporated within an explanatory science? Can we understand and control the total array and flow of what is happening to us, or must the couplings between the environment and behavior always be dealt with fragmentally, probabilistically, empirically, and *post hoc?* It would appear desirable to examine the ecological environment as it exists before being received, coded, and programmed. Egon Brunswik wrote, in this connection:

> . . . both organism and environment will have to be seen as systems, each with properties of its own, yet both hewn from basically the same block. Each has surface and depth, or overt and covert regions . . . the interrelationship between the two systems has the essential characteristic of a "coming-to-terms." And this coming-to-terms is not merely a matter of the mutual boundary or surface areas. It concerns equally as much, or perhaps even more, the rapport between the central, covert layers of the two systems. It follows that, much as psychology must be concerned with the texture of the organism or of its nervous processes and must investigate them in depth, it also must be concerned with the texture of the environment as it extends in depth away from the common boundary (1957, p. 5).

I raise the question then: What is the

Abridged, and adapted with the author's assistance, from the **Journal of Social Issues, 1963, 19, 17–38,** and reprinted with the permission of the author and the Society for the Psychological Study of Social Issues.

texture of the ecological environment? To answer this, we must have a unit of behavior. One cannot study the environment of behavior in general.

The environment of behavior episodes

Psychology has been so busy selecting from, imposing upon, and rearranging the behavior of its subjects that it has until very recently neglected to note behavior's clear structure when it is not molested by tests, experiments, questionnaires and interviews. Following the basic work on behavior structure by Herbert F. Wright (Barker & Wright, 1955), Dickman (1963) has shown that people commonly see the behavior continuum in terms of the units (or their multiples) which Wright identified, namely, behavior episodes. Here, for example, are descriptive titles of consecutively occurring episodes from the behavior stream of six-year-old Belinda Bevan during a 10-minute period beginning at 2:22 p.m., on July 18, 1957 (Barker, *et al.*, 1961):

Watching bigger girls form a pyramid (gymnastic)
Taking off her shoes
Going closer to the big girls
Putting on her shoes
Admiring bracelet on Alice
Poking Alice
Looking at Winifred's ladybug
Following Alice
Watching boys
Looking into porch of schoolroom
Closing door of schoolroom
Watching girls play hopscotch
Giving Harry his shoe
Getting bracelet from Alice
Interfering in Delia's and Winifred's fight
Admiring bracelet on Alice.

Behavior episodes, such as these, are not arbitrarily imposed divisions of the behavior continuum in the way that microtome slices of tissue and mile-square sections of the earth's surface are imposed divisions. They are, rather, natural units of molar behavior (Barker, 1963) with the attributes of constancy of direction, equal potency throughout their parts, and limited size-range. Like crystals and cells which also have distinguishing general attributes and limited size-ranges, behavior episodes have as clear a position in the hierarchy of behavior units as the former have in the physical and organic hierarchies. It makes sense, therefore, to ask what units of the ecological environment encompass behavior episodes.

Consider, for example, Belinda's behavior episode, Looking at Winifred's Ladybug, from the series just given.

The record of this episode of Belinda's behavior stream reads as follows:

Belinda ran toward Winifred from Miss Groves' room.
Winifred had found a ladybug and was walking around with this ladybug saying, "Ladybug, ladybug, fly away home."
Belinda went up to Winifred.
She pulled Winifred's arm down so she could see the ladybug better.
She smiled as she watched the beetle. She watched the ladybug for 10 or 15 seconds.

The environing unit in which this episode occurred was easily identified. It extended in depth away from the junction points between Belinda and Winifred-with-the-ladybug with a characteristic pattern of people, behavior, and objects which abruptly changed at a surrounding physical wall, and at temporal beginning and end points (Barker & Wright, 1955, pp. 45–83). The environmental unit was Afternoon Break, Yoredale County School Playground,

North Yorkshire, England, 2:22–2:31 p.m., July 18, 1957.

We have studied many behavior episodes, and we have always found them within ecological units like the one surrounding the episode Looking at Winifred's Ladybug. We have called these ecological units *behavior settings*. Our work in Midwest, Kansas, and Yoredale, Yorkshire, has demonstrated that behavior settings can be identified and described reliably without an explicit theory and by means of a variety of survey techniques. This is of some importance, we think, as an indication that behavior settings are tough, highly visible features of the ecological environment.

There is only a beginning of a scientific literature on behavior settings. Except in their applied phases, the biological and physical sciences have eschewed ecological units with human behavior as component elements. They have stopped with man-free ponds, glaciers, and lightning flashes; they have left farms, ski-jumps, and passenger trains to others. And psychology and sociology, have, for the most part, shied in the other direction; they have avoided whole, unfractionated ecological units with physical objects as well as people and behavior as component parts. So behavior-setting-type units have almost completely fallen between the bio-physical and the behavioral sciences, and this has been a source of serious trouble for the eco-behavioral problem: there have been no solid empirical ecological units. Unbounded, demi-theoretical, demi-empirical units do not provide the firm base an empirical science must have. Floyd Allport (1961) has persuasively pointed to one difficulty of such demi-entities: they disappear when the attempt is made to touch them, as is essential if they are to be studied; in their place one encounters individuals. And there is another difficulty: a universal attribute of the environment of a person, whatever its other characteristics may be, is a univocal position in time and space. The units of an eco-behavioral science must have time-space loci. Behavior settings fulfill both of these requirements: they can be encountered, qua environmental units, and re-encountered; and they can be exactly located in time and space.

It is not often that a lecturer can present to his audience an example of his phenomena, whole and functioning *in situ*—not merely with a demonstration, a description, a preserved specimen, a picture, or a diagram of it. I am in the fortunate position of being able to give you, so to speak, a real behavior setting.

If you will change your attention from me to the next most inclusive, bounded unit, to the assembly of people, behavior episodes, and objects before you, you will see a behavior setting. It has the following structural attributes which you can observe directly:

1. It has a space-time locus: 3:00–3:50 p.m., September 2, 1963, Clover Room, Bellevue-Stratford Hotel, Philadelphia, Pennsylvania.
2. It is composed of a variety of interior entities and events: of people, objects (chairs, walls, a microphone, paper), behavior (lecturing, listening, sitting), and other processes (air circulation, sound amplification).
3. Its widely different components form a bounded pattern that is easily discriminated from the pattern on the outside of the boundary.
4. Its component parts are obviously not a random arrangement of independent classes of entities; if they were,

how surprising, that all the chairs are in the same position with respect to the podium, that all members of the audience happen to come to rest upon chairs, and that the lights are not helter-skelter from floor to ceiling, for example.

5. The entity before you is a part of a nesting structure; its components (e.g., the chairs and people) have parts; and the setting, itself, is contained within a more comprehensive unit, the Bellevue-Stratford Hotel.
6. This unit is objective in the sense that it exists independently of anyone's perception of it, qua unit.

This, then, is a behavior setting; within it is displayed, for you to see, the finer-grained texture of the environment as it extends around and away from the behavior occurring here. What is this texture and how does it affect behavior? This leads us to the more dynamic characteristics of behavior settings.

It does not require systematic research to discover that the patterns of behavior settings do not inhere in the people or the objects within them. It is common observation that the *same* people and objects are transformed into different patterns as they pass from one variety of setting to another. This is exemplified by numerous pairs of behavior settings in Midwest and Yoredale with essentially the same people and objects as component parts but with quite different patterns. For example:

Church Service—Church Wedding
High School Senior Class Play—Senior Graduation
School Playground: Recess—May Fete on School Playground

It is common observation, too, that *different* sets of people and objects exhibit the same pattern within the same variety of behavior setting. This is exemplified by the almost complete turnover of persons each year in academic behavior settings, with the patterns of the settings remaining remarkably stable. One of the striking features of communities is how, year after year, they incorporate new people, despite the idiosyncratic behavior and personality traits of these people, into the characteristic patterns of their stable behavior settings: of Rotary Club meetings, of doctors' offices, of garages, of bridge clubs. Obviously, whatever it is that impresses the characteristic array and flow of behavior settings upon their interior entities and events is largely independent of the persons who participate in them.

A considerable number of investigators have made quantitative studies of the differences in the behavior of the same persons in different behavior settings (Goffman, 1963; Gump, *et al.*, 1957, 1963; Gump & Sutton-Smith, 1955; Jordan, 1963; Rausch, *et al.*, 1959a, 1959b, 1960; Soskin & John, 1963). I shall not survey this rather extensive body of research; the findings are in general agreement on the issue of importance to us here, and they are represented by the research of Rausch, Dittmann and Taylor. Working within a therapeutic milieu with disturbed boys, these investigators found that on the behavior dimensions hostility-friendliness and dominance-passivity there was as much variation between behavior settings, with boys constant, as between boys with settings constant.

Altogether, then, there is abundant evidence that behavior settings, like many bio-physical entities, are strongly self-regulated systems which regulate the behavior episodes within them as molecules regulate atoms, as organs regulate cells, and as structures regulate the beams of which they are constructed (Barker & Wright, 1955; Barker & Barker, 1961). To the extent that this is true, it means that the ecological environment of behavior is not passive, is not directionless, is not chaotic or probabilistic.

The regulation of behavior settings

But how do behavior settings regulate themselves, including the behavior episodes within them? How does "the texture of the environment as it extends in depth away from the common boundary" influence individual behavior?

One can ask, of course, why one should bother with the distal texture of behavior settings. Whatever this texture may be, it ultimately has to be translated into input at the junction points with particular persons. Why not, therefore, get down to brass tacks at these junction points, i.e., at the sensory surfaces?

There are a number of reasons why this cannot be done. For one thing, behavior settings have so many richly interconnected elements that their tremendous complexity at the sensory surfaces of all inhabitants concurrently cannot, at the present time, be dealt with conceptually or practically. Behavior settings are often very large systems, and simplification is necessary. But what may appear to be the most obvious simplification, namely, dealing with the input to single inhabitants, or to a sample of inhabitants, does not reveal behavior settings. It is not only in perception that the attributes of parts differ from those of the whole. In any system with interdependent parts the order obtaining at a point of the system varies with the portion of the total system within which the part is considered. It is easy to overlook how greatly attributes vary with context. Take, for example, a visual target, a spot on the tire of an automobile moving forward at a road speed of 50 miles per hour. The spot will display simultaneously the following motions: (1) a random vertical vibratory motion within the field of a stroboscope focused on the spot at a single point in the wheel's revolution; (2) a uniform circular motion of about 1000 RPM within the context of the wheel; and (3) a cyclical forward motion varying from zero to 100 miles per hour within the context of the auto-highway traction system. The same state of affairs occurs in a behavior setting. Suppose one were to study input and output of a second baseman in a ball game. By careful observation, all incoming and outgoing balls could be tallied, timed, and their speeds and directions recorded. The input itself would be without a sensible order, and there would be no relation between baseball inputs and outputs. But within the behavior setting, baseball game, the record would be sensible, orderly and lawful. It is important to note that it is not the player who converts this into order, it is the game, the behavior setting. The player acts as the game's agent and is able to receive and throw the ball in an orderly way because the rules (the program) of the game, and all information about the momentary state of the game available to him through a variety of inputs, guide his actions. However, all the inputs and outputs of a single player, of a sample of the players, or of all the players if considered outside the context of "the game" would be without sensible order. It is important to note, too, that a much greater quantity of information would be required to discover "the game" from the inputs and outputs at the junction points with the individual players than is contained in the program of "the game" itself (Maruyama, 1963).

A special difficulty with the ecological input at the junction points with individuals arises from the difference in the temporal dimensions of the inputs at these points, i.e., of the stimuli, and the behavior output with which we are concerned, i.e., behavior episodes. Stimuli are very short units occurring in unpredictable sequences during the period of any episode, while episodes are much longer units with direction and interdependence from their points of origin. However, episodes are not determined by their internal states alone; they are guided in their details by the ecological environment. To predict a behavior episode it is necessary to know the prevailing conditions throughout its entire course, but the ecological input of stimuli during an episode can only be known at the completion of the episode. What is needed as an ecological anchor for behavior episodes is a stable unit with at least as long duration as episodes. Behavior settings, whole and undismantled, fulfill this minimal requirement; they are episode-sized ecological units. And behavior episodes are setting-sized behavior units.

Behavior settings do have unitary textured properties which can be dealt with as bridge builders deal with the span of a bridge rather than with its atoms. One such property is number of inhabitants. In the remainder of this paper, I shall present some evidence that this ecological variable influences individual behavior and some ideas as to how it does so.

Behavior setting size and individual behavior

There is evidence, some of which I have presented to you, for each of the following statements, but I shall consider them, here, as hypotheses that were investigated by the research to be reported. Behavior settings are bounded, self-regulated entities involving forces which form and maintain the component inhabitants and objects of settings in functioning patterns with stable attributes. One of the stable attributes of a setting is its functional level, and another is the optimal number of inhabitants for maintenance of this level. The optimal number of inhabitants may be precisely specified by the setting (a bridge game requires four inhabitants), or may fall within a range (a First Grade reading class in Midwest functions well with 15 to 25 pupils). When the number of inhabitants of a behavior setting is below the optimal number (within limits), the homeostatic controls of the setting maintain the total complement and pattern of the setting's forces essentially intact, and this produces differences, in comparison with an optimally populated setting, that ramify to the level of individual behavior. The differences reach the level of individual inhabitants by two main routes, one a rather direct route involving behavior setting structure and dynamics, the other more indirect via control mechanisms. I shall consider the more direct route first.

Behavior settings with fewer than optimal inhabitants are less differentiated, and their networks of forces are interconnected through fewer junction points than otherwise equivalent settings with optimal numbers of inhabitants. It follows from this that on the level of individual dynamics, the inhabitants (i.e., the junction points) of the former, or "underpopulated," settings are points of application of more behavior setting forces with wider ranges of direction than are inhabitants of the latter, or optimally populated, settings. Behavior setting forces cause participation in behavior settings, and persons and objects which receive more forces in more varied directions will participate with greater forcefulness in more varied ways. On the level of particular activities, far-reaching differences will result, all characterized by stronger motivation, greater variety, and deeper involvement in the settings with less than the optimal number of inhabitants. When people are more than optimally abundant in behavior settings, the differences noted will be reversed (see Barker, 1960).

The derivations from behavior setting size to individual behavior were investigated recently at the Midwest Psychological Field Station in the behavior settings of high schools. The settings were equivalent in all respects except number of inhabitants, which ranged from below to above optimal. Prototypes of the settings that were studied are the Junior Class Play of a small high school where each of the 22 members of the class participated in presenting the play to an audience of about 350 persons and the Junior Class Play of a large high school where about 100 (14 per cent) of the 700 members of the class had some part in presenting the play to an audience of about 2000 persons. Only behavior settings where attendance was voluntary were included in the studies.

The data showed that the students of the small high schools, in comparison with those of the large school:

entered the same number of behavior settings (although there were fewer available),
held important, responsible, and central positions in a greater number of the settings,
experienced more attractions and more pressures toward participation in the settings,
entered a wider variety of behavior settings, and
held important, responsible, and central positions in a wider variety of the settings.

These differences were not slight. Over the 17 week period of the study, the students of the small high schools participated in central, responsible positions (as members of play casts, as officers of organizations, as members of athletic teams, as soloists, etc.) in over three-and-a-half behavior settings per student, on the average (3.7), while students of the large high school participated in these important roles in 16 per cent as many settings, i.e., in just over one-half setting per student (0.6). The students of the small schools held central, responsible, and important positions in twice as many *varieties* of behavior settings as the students of the large school (Gump & Friesen, 1964). In short, these data showed, as the theory predicted, that the students of the small high schools (with fewer than optimal inhabitants per setting) were more strongly motivated, engaged in more varied activities, and were more responsibly involved than the students of the large school (with more than optimal inhabitants per setting). These are direct symptoms of the predicted differences in the strength and range of direction of forces. There is much additional evidence from research in industry that supports the predictions (Willems, 1964), and the investigations and theories of Calhoun (1956, 1963) on population density and behavior velocity in animals are in general accord with the predictions.

There are less direct consequences of behavior setting population differences. When the participants in behavior settings fall below the optimal number and become points of application of more forces, they have increased functional importance within settings, and the situation may be reached where everyone is a key person for the stability, and even for the survival of settings. These are ecological facts. To the degree that the inhabitants are aware of their own behavior in behavior settings their experiences will pertain to their own efforts, achievements, and contributions to the functioning of settings. In fact, Gump and Friesen (1964) found that the students of the small schools exceeded those of the large schools in satisfying experiences related to the development of competence, to being challenged, to engaging in important activities, and to being involved in group activities. When the number of inhabitants of behavior settings are greater than optimal, when there is a surplus of people, and people are the points of application of fewer forces, the functional importance of all inhabitants is reduced on the average, and the situation will be reached where almost no one will be crucially missed as a contributor to the functioning of settings. Under these circumstances, it is to be expected that the inhabitants' experiences will pertain to behavior settings as detached, independent phenomena, to the performances of others, and to their own standings in comparison with others. In fact, the students of the large school exceeded those of the small schools in number of satisfying experiences related to the vicarious enjoyment of others' activities, to being affiliated with a large institution, to learning about the school's people and affairs, and to gaining "points via participation." These data may be summarized in terms of Dembo's distinction between *asset* values and *comparative* values (1956). The small schools more frequently generated in their students self-valuations based upon how adequately the students saw themselves contributing to behavior settings, i.e., being assets to settings. The large schools more frequently generated in their students self-valuations based upon the students' perception of their standing in comparison with others. These are fundamental differences: in terms of asset values, everyone in a behavior setting can be important and successful; in terms of comparative values, only a few can be important and successful.

I shall turn next to the connection between behavior setting population and individual behavior via the regulatory systems.

The inhabitants of a behavior setting always have the potentiality, and usually the active tendency, to exhibit a greater variety of behavior than the setting requires or can tolerate. The behavior setting control mechanism reduces this variety to the amount appropriate to the setting, and maintains it within an acceptable range of values. One type of control mechanism found in connection with behavior settings is a direct, deviation-countering servo-mechanism that counteracts any deviation beyond the acceptable values; a restaurant hostess who supplies coatless patrons with "appropriate" jackets functions as a deviation-countering homeostat and exemplifies this type of control. Another frequent behavior setting control is a vetoing-type mechanism that provides just two states with respect to the variables it governs: *in* and *out* of the setting (member-nonmember, pass-fail, alive-dead, permitted-not permitted, free-trapped) (Ashby, 1956). A restaurant hostess who refuses admission to coatless, aspiring patrons exemplifies this control mechanism. In general, deviation-countering controls are more efficient, but they are more difficult to devise and more expensive to operate than vetoing regulators. The latter are abundant in nature, e.g., vetoing the "unfit."

The regulation of behavior settings is usually a complex process, involving alternative mechanisms, and the continual selection of the most effective regulators for the conditions obtaining. In other words, regulation operates directly on behavior setting patterns and indirectly via the regulators themselves. In general, behavior settings with fewer than the optimal number of inhabitants must use deviation-countering control mechanisms, or they will perish; inhabitants are functionally too important to be vetoed out. I have seen a four-man baseball game of nine-year-olds tolerate and nurse along with carefully applied deviation-countering controls a four-year-old participant, or even a mother. In this case one outfielder, even an inefficient and inapt one, is likely to produce a better-functioning game than a game with no outfielder. On the other hand, if there are 30 candidates for players in the game, a better game will result with less fuss and bother if all four-year-olds, mothers, and other inapt players are vetoed out. And nine-year-olds have ways of doing this, and they regularly do it. Those vetoed out become substitutes, bat-boys, and spectators. In behavior settings with more than the optimal numbers of inhabitants, efficiency usually moves behavior settings toward veto-type control mechanism.

Both deviation-countering and vetoing controls, insofar as they are effective in stabilizing the functioning of behavior settings, apply their differing influences more frequently to marginal inhabitants, likely to engage in deviant behavior, than to focal, conformable inhabitants, unlikely to engage in deviant behavior.

In the case of the high school study we expected that deviation-countering control measures would be more frequent in the small than in the large schools, and that this excess frequency would be greater among the academically unpromising than among the academically promising students. Willems's data bear upon these issues. He called the deviation-countering influences *pressures;* they included all the forces toward participation which the subjects reported as originating outside themselves, e.g., "My friend asked me to go"; "Band players were expected to come," etc. Over all, students of the small schools received two times as many deviation-countering influences as the students of the large school, and academically marginal students of the small schools (i.e., students without academically favorable abilities and motivation) received almost five times as many deviation-countering measures as marginal students of the large school.

Both deviation-countering and vetoing control mechanisms produce uniformity of behavior, but with very different consequences for people. In settings where people are at a premium, uniformity is necessarily achieved as we have seen, by the regulating *behavior,* without limiting the interests, abilities, and motives of inhabitants. In settings where people are surplus, uniformity is achieved to a considerable degree by vetoing, not behavior, but inhabitants who exhibit deviant behavior; and this amounts, in effect, to selecting inhabitants for conformity and uniformity with respect to personality characteristics (interests, abilities, motives). There are secondary resultants of these control processes which cannot be considered here; but it is immediately clear that the settings with fewer than optimal inhabitants, within which behavioral uniformity is ingrafted upon personality diversity, are desegregated, egalitarian, functionally tolerant settings, while settings that veto the unfit and retain the fit are segregated, uniform, specialized settings.

Data were not secured upon details of the vetoing control processes in the schools. But the consequences were apparent: students who did not participate on a responsible level in any voluntary school activity, i.e., that were vetoed out of all but spectator participation, constituted 2 per cent of the students of the small schools, and 29 per cent of the students in the large school. It is from the nonparticipating students that great numbers of school "drop-outs" come (Willems, 1964).

The conceptual breach between psychological and ecological phenomena is, of course, not closed by behavior settings, it is as great as ever. But within the behavior setting context, the problem is restated so that breach can be by-passed on certain levels: the approach is re-directed from the sublime but millennial goal of developing a single conceptual system, and also from the discouraging prospect of mere empiricism, probabilism, and fractionated micro-sciences, to the more modest and hopeful goal of discovering general principles of eco-behavioral organization and control without regard for the conceptual or substantive content of the phenomena regulated.

Behavior settings have their roots in Kurt Lewin's conceptions of quasi-stable equilibria, in his treatment of parts and wholes, in his concern for the total situation, in his teaching that theory always must defer to data, and in his preoccupation with the eco-behavioral problem. How greatly the plant that has grown from these roots would have benefitted from his cultivation and pruning! Whether or not behavior settings prove to be a fruitful approach to the eco-behavioral problem, they serve at least to continue Lewin's multi-directional approach to it, and to emphasize the crucial importance of the eco-behavioral problem for the science of psychology (see Sells, 1963).

4 On perceptual readiness

JEROME S. BRUNER

On the nature of perception

Perception involves an act of categorization. Put in terms of the antecedent and subsequent conditions from which we make our inferences, we stimulate an organism with some appropriate input and he responds by referring the input to some class of things or events "That is an orange," he states, or he presses a lever that he has been "tuned" to press when the object that he "perceives" is an orange. On the basis of certain defining or criterial attributes in the input, what are usually called cues although they should be called clues (Harper, 1948), there is a selective placing of the input in one category of identity rather than another. The category need not be elaborate: "a sound," "a touch," "a pain," are also examples of categorized inputs. The use of cues in inferring the categorial identity of a perceived object, most recently treated by Bruner, Goodnow, and Austin (1956) and by Binder (1955), is as much a feature of perception as the sensory stuff from which percepts are made. What is interesting about the nature of the inference from cue to identity in perception is that it is in no sense different from other kinds of categorial inferences based on defining attributes. "That thing is round and nubbly in texture and orange in color and of such-and-such size—therefore an orange; let me now test its other properties to be sure." In terms of process, this course of events is no different from the more abstract task of looking at a number, determining that it is divisible only by itself and unity, and thereupon categorizing it in the class of prime numbers. So at the outset, it is evident that one of the principal characteristics of perceiving is a characteristic of cognition generally. There is no reason to assume that the laws governing inferences of this kind are discontinuous as one moves from perceptual to more conceptual activities. In no sense need the process be conscious or deliberate. A theory of perception, we assert, needs a mechanism capable of inference and categorizing as much as one is needed in a theory of cognition.

Let it be plain that no claim is being made for the utter indistinguishability of perceptual and more conceptual inferences. In the first place, the former appear to be notably less docile or reversible than the latter. I may know that the Ames distorted room that looks so rectangular is indeed distorted, but unless conflicting cues are put into the situation, as in experiments to be discussed later, the room still looks rectangular. So too with such compelling illusions as the Müller-Lyer: in spite of knowledge to the contrary, the line with the extended arrowheads looks longer than the equal-length one with those inclined inward. But these differences, interesting in themselves, must not lead us to overlook the common feature of in-

Excerpted from the **Psychological Review**, 1957, 64, 123–52, with permission of the author and the American Psychological Association.

ference underlying so much of cognitive activity.

Is what we have said a denial of the classic doctrine of sense-data? Surely, one may argue (and Hebb (1949) has done so effectively) that there must be certain forms of primitive organization within the perceptual field that make possible the differential use of cues in identity categorizing. Both logically and psychologically, the point is evident. Yet it seems to me foolish and unnecessary to assume that the sensory "stuff" on which higher order categorizations are based is, if you will, of a different sensory order than more evolved identities with which our perceptual world is normally peopled. To argue otherwise is to be forced into the contradictions of Locke's distinction between primary and secondary qualities in perception. The rather bold assumption that we shall make at the outset is that all perceptual experience is necessarily the end product of a categorization process.

And this for two reasons. The first is that all perception is generic in the sense that whatever is perceived is placed in and achieves its "meaning" from a class of percepts with which it is grouped. To be sure, in each thing we encounter, there is an aspect of uniqueness, but the uniqueness inheres in deviation from the class to which an object is "assigned." Analytically, let it be noted, one may make a distinction, as Gestalt theorists have, between a pure stimulus process and the interaction of that stimulus process with an appropriate memory trace—the latter presumably resulting in a percept that has an identity. If indeed there is a "pure stimulus process," it is doubtful indeed that it is ever represented in perception bereft of identity characteristics. The phenomenon of a completely unplaceable object or event or "sensation"—even unplaceable with respect to modality—is sufficiently far from experience to be uncanny. Categorization of an object or event—placing it or giving it identity—can be likened to what in set theory is the placement of an element from a universe in a subset of that universe of items on the basis of such ordered dimensional pairs, triples, or *n*-tuples as man-woman, mesomorph-endomorph-ectomorph, or height to nearest inch. In short, when one specifies something more than that an element or object belongs to a universe, and that it belongs in a subset of the universe, one has categorized the element or object. The categorization can be as intersecting as "this is a quartz crystal goblet fashioned in Denmark," or as simple as "this is a glassy thing." So long as an operation assigns an input to a subset, it is an act of categorization.

More serious, although it is "only a logical issue," is the question of how one could communicate or make public the presence of a nongeneric or completely unique perceptual experience. Neither language nor the tuning that one could give an organism to direct any other form of overt response could provide an account, save in generic or categorial terms. If perceptual experience is ever had raw, i.e., free of categorial identity, it is doomed to be a gem serene, locked in the silence of private experience.

Various writers, among them Gibson (1950), Wallach (1949), and Pratt (1950), have proposed that we make a sharp distinction between the class of perceptual phenomena that have to do with the identity or object-meaning of things and the attributive or sensory world from which we derive our cues for inferring identities. Gibson, like

Titchener (1916) before him, urges a distinction between the visual field and the visual world, the former the world of attributive sense impressions, the latter of objects and things and events. Pratt urges that motivation and set and past experience may affect the things of the visual world but not the stuff of the visual field. And Wallach too reflects this ancient tradition of his Gestalt forebears by urging the distinction between a stimulus process pure and the stimulus process interacting with a memory trace of past experience with which it has made a neural contact on the basis of similarity. The former is the stuff of perception; the latter the finished percept. From shirtsleeves to shirtsleeves in three generations: we are back with the founding and founded content of the pre-Gestalt Gestalters. If one is to study the visual field freed of the things of the visual world, it becomes necessary —as Wallach implies—to free oneself of the stimulus error: dealing with a percept not as an object or as a thing with identity, but as a magnitude or a brightness or a hue or a shape to be matched against a variable test patch.

If we have implied that categorizing is often a "silent" or unconscious process, that we do not experience a going-from-no-identity to an arrival-at-identity, but that the first hallmark of *any* perception is some form of identity, this does not free us of the responsibility of inquiring into the origin of categories. Certainly, Hebb (1949) is correct in asserting like Immanuel Kant, that certain primitive unities or identities within perception must be innate or autochthonous and not learned. The primitive capacity to categorize "things" from "background" is very likely one such, and so too the capacity to distinguish events in one modality from those in others—although the phenomena of synesthesia would suggest that this is not so complete a juncture as it might seem; e.g., von Hornbostel (1926). The sound of a buzz saw does rise and fall phenomenally as one switches room illumination on and off. The full repertory of innate categories—a favorite topic for philosophical debate in the 19th century—is a topic on which perhaps too much ink and too little empirical effort have been spilled. Motion, causation, intention, identity, equivalence, time, and space, it may be persuasively argued, are categories that must have some primitive counterpart in the neonate. And it may well be, as Piaget (1951) implies, that certain primitive capacities to categorize in particular ways depend upon the existence of still more primitive ones. To identify something as having "caused" something else requires, first, the existence of an identity category such that the two things involved each may conserve identity in the process of "cause" producing "effect." Primitive or unlearned categories—a matter of much concern to such students of instinctive behavior as Lashley (1938) and Tinbergen (1951)—remain to be explicated. In what follows, we shall rather cavalierly take them for granted. As to the development of more elaborated categories in terms of which objects are placed or identified, it involves the process of learning how to isolate, weigh, and use criterial attribute values, or cues for grouping objects in equivalence classes. It is only as mysterious, but no more so, than the learning of any differential discrimination, and we shall have occasion to revisit the problem later.

A second feature of perception, beyond its seemingly categorial and inferential nature, is that it can be described as varyingly veridical. This is what has classically been called the "representative function" of perception: what is perceived is somehow a representation of the external world—a metaphysical hodgepodge of a statement but one which we somehow manage to understand in spite of its confusion. We have long since given up simulacral theories of representation. What we generally mean when we speak of representation or veridicality is that perception is predictive in varying degrees. That is to say, the object that we *see* can also be *felt* and *smelled* and there will somehow be a match or a congruity between what we see, feel, and smell. Or, to paraphrase a younger Bertrand Russell, what we see will turn out to be the same thing should we take a "closer look" at it. Or, in still different terms, the categorial placement of the object leads to appropriate consequences in terms of later behavior directed toward the perceived object: it appears as an apple, and indeed it keeps the doctor away if consumed once a day.

Let it be said that philosophers, and notably the pragmatist C. S. Peirce, have been urging such a view for more years than psychologists have taken their urgings seriously. The meaning of a proposition, as Peirce noted in his famous essay on the pragmatic theory of meaning (1878), is the set of hypothetical statements one can make about attributes or consequences related to that proposition. "Let us ask what we mean by calling a thing *hard*. Evidently, that it will not be scratched by many other substances" (White, 1955). The meaning of a thing, thus, is the placement of an object in a network of hypothetical inference concerning its other observable properties, its effects, and so on.

All of this suggests, does it not, that veridicality is not so much a matter of representation as it is a matter of what I shall call "model building." In learning to perceive, we are learning the relations that exist between the properties of objects and events that we encounter, learning appropriate categories and category systems, *learning to predict and to check what goes with what.* A simple example illustrates the point. I present for tachistoscopic recognition two nonsense words, one a O-order approximation to English constructed according to Shannon's rules, the other a 4-order approximation: YRULPZOC and VERNALIT. At 500 milliseconds of exposure, one perceives correctly and in their proper place about 48 per cent of the letters in O-order words, and about 93 per cent of the letters in 4-order words. In terms of the amount of information transmitted by these letter arrays, i.e., correcting them for redundancy, the subject is actually receiving the same information input. The difference in reportable perception is a function of the fact that the individual has learned the transitional probability model of what goes with what in English writing. We say that perception in one case is more "veridical" than in the other—the difference between 93 per cent correct as contrasted with 48 per cent. What we mean is that the model of English with which the individual is working corresponds to the actual events that occur in English, and that if the stimulus input does not conform to the model, the resulting perception will be less veridical. Now let us drop the image of the model and adopt a more sensible terminology. Perceiving accurately under substandard conditions consists in being able to refer stimulus inputs to appropriate coding systems;

where the information is fragmentary, one reads the missing properties of the stimulus input from the code to which part of the input has been referred. If the coding system applied does not match the input, what we read off from the coding system will lead to error and nonveridical perception. I would propose that perceptual learning consists not of making finer and finer discriminations as the Gibsons (1955) would have us believe, but that it consists rather in the learning of appropriate modes of coding the environment in terms of its object character, connectedness, or redundancy, and then in allocating stimulus inputs to appropriate categorial coding systems.

The reader will properly ask, as Prentice (1954) has, whether the notion of perceptual representation set forth here is appropriate to anything other than situations where the nature of the percept is not "clear"—perceptual representation under peripheral viewing conditions, in tachistoscopes, under extreme fatigue. If I am given a very good look at an object, under full illumination and with all the viewing time necessary, and end by calling it an orange, is this a different process from one in which the same object is flashed for a millisecond or two on the periphery of my retina with poor illumination? In the first and quite rare case the cues permitting the identification of the object are superabundant and the inferential mechanism operates with high probability relationships between cues and identities. In the latter, it is less so. The difference is of degree. What I am trying to say is that under *any* conditions of perception, what is achieved by the perceiver is the categorization of an object or sensory event in terms of more *or* less abundant and reliable cues. Representation consists of knowing how to utilize cues with reference to a system of categories. It also depends upon the creation of a system of categories-in-relationship that fit the nature of the world in which the person must live. In fine, adequate perceptual representation involves the learning of appropriate categories, the learning of cues useful in placing objects appropriately in such systems of categories, and the learning of what objects are likely to occur in the environment, a matter to which we will turn later.[1]

Conclusions

We have been concerned in these pages with a general view of perception that depends upon the construction of a set of organized categories in terms of which stimulus inputs may be sorted, given identity, and given more elaborated, connotative meaning. Veridical perception, it has been urged, depends upon the construction of such category systems, categories built upon the inference of identity from cues or signs. Identity, in fine, represents the range of inferences about properties, uses, and consequences that can be predicted from the presence of certain criterial cues.

Perceptual readiness refers to the relative accessibility of categories to afferent stimulus inputs. The more accessible a category, the less the stimulus input required for it to be sorted in terms of the category, given a degree of match between the characteristics of the input and the specifications of the category. In rough form, there appear to

1 For an extension of these and associated points, omitted here, the reader is referred to pp. 127–48 of the original.—Eds.

be two general determinants of category accessibility. One of them is the likelihood of occurrence of events learned by the person in the course of dealing with the world of objects and events and the redundant sequences in which these are imbedded. If you will, the person builds a model of the likelihood of events, a form of probability learning only now beginning to be understood. Again in rough terms, one can think of this activity as achieving a minimization of surprise for the organism. A second determinant of accessibility is the requirements of search dictated by need states and the need to carry out habitual enterprises such as walking, reading, or whatever it is that makes up the round of daily, habitual life.

Failure to achieve a state of perceptual readiness that matches the probability of events in one's world can be dealt with in one of two ways: either by the relearning of categories and expectancies, or by constant close inspection of events and objects. Where the latter alternative must be used, an organism is put in the position of losing his lead time for adjusting quickly and smoothly to events under varying conditions of time pressure, risk, and limited capacity. Readiness in the sense that we are using it is not a luxury, but a necessity for smooth adjustment.

The processes involved in "sorting" sensory inputs to appropriate categories involve cue utilization, varying from sensorially "open" cue searching under relative uncertainty, to selective search for confirming cues under partial certainty, to sensory "gating" and distortion when an input has been categorized beyond a certain level of certainty.

Four kinds of mechanisms are proposed to deal with known phenomena of perceptual categorizing and differential perceptual readiness: *grouping and integration, access ordering, match-mismatch signal utilization,* and *gating.* The processes are conceived of as mediators of categorizing and its forms of connectivity, the phenomena of differential threshold levels for various environmental events, the guidance of cue search behavior, and lastly, the phenomena of sensory inhibition and "filtering."

Finally, we have considered some of the ways in which failure of perceptual readiness comes about—first, through a failure to learn appropriate categories for sorting the environment and for following its sequences, and second, through a process of interference whereby more accessible categories with wide acceptance limits serve to mask or prevent the use of less accessible categories for the coding of stimulus inputs. The concept of "perceptual defense" may be re-examined in the light of these notions.

In conclusion, it seems appropriate to say that the ten years of the so-called New Look in perception research seem to be coming to a close with much empirical work accomplished—a great deal of it demonstrational, to be sure, but with a promise of a second ten years in which hypotheses will be more rigorously formulated and, conceivably, neural mechanisms postulated, if not discovered. The prospects are anything but discouraging.

5 The achievement motive

DAVID C. McCLELLAND

Assessing human motives

At least from the time of Plato and the Bhagavad-Gītā, Western philosophers have tended to see reason and desire as two distinctly different elements in the human mind. There would be little point here in giving a history of the various ways in which the "desiring" element has been conceived in the last 2,000 years, but suffice it to say that it always represented a kind of "motivational force" often opposed to but ultimately controllable by reason. At about the dawn of modern scientific psychology, in the middle of the nineteenth century, the relationship between these two psychic elements took on a very specific meaning largely under the influence of Darwin and the wide interest he and others aroused in the theory of evolution. Man was conceived as an animal engaged in a struggle for survival with nature. It was an obvious corollary to assume that because man struggled he had a desire or wish to survive. Biologists and psychologists were quick to point out how such a desire was mechanically controlled by the organism, since unmet physiological needs ordinarily triggered certain danger signals which would irritate or disturb the organism until the needs were satisfied.

The most obvious example is the hunger need. If the organism does not get food, it does not survive; therefore, it is equipped with danger signals (controlled perhaps by contractions of the empty stomach) which would be activated in the absence of food and so cause the organism to be active until it obtains food. The more or less "intelligent" activities of the organism, representing the old reasoning element in man, were conceived as originated and guided by the hunger drive, not in the teleological sense that the organism "knows" it needs food, but purely in the mechanical sense that hunger keeps the organism going until it manages to find some food substance which shuts off the danger signals. The most important theoretical advance made by psychologists who thought of human adaptation in these terms was the conceptual distinction they ultimately made between eating and hunger (the desire to eat). Common-sense psychology might suggest that the more a man eats, the more he wants to eat, in exactly the same sense that the more a man achieves, the more he must *want* to achieve. If, in fact, the two variables are so closely connected that desire to eat can be inferred without error from eating activity, then there is no need for the motive concept at all.

Since science is a parsimonious enterprise using as few concepts as it possibly can to explain what it tries to explain, it can get along without a variable which is always perfectly associated with another. But what behavioral scientists did at this juncture in history was to estab-

Excerpted from Chapter 2 of **The Achieving Society** (Copyright © 1961 by D. Van Nostrand Co., Inc.), Princeton: D. Van Nostrand, 1961, pp. 36–62, with permission of the author and the publisher.

lish an *independent set of operations* for defining the strength of the hunger drive—independent that is, of the activity of eating. They defined the strength of the hunger drive in terms of the number of hours of food deprivation. They assumed that the longer an organism had been without food, the hungrier it would be, and they could then go about determining how different strengths of the hunger drive, as independently measured in this way, would influence various types of behavior, including even eating. They found, not too surprisingly, that when the strength of hunger was measured by hours of deprivation, it did not correlate at all perfectly with the tendency to eat. There were, and are, many disagreements, of course, as to the best method of measuring the hunger drive, but the only point of real significance here is that the way was opened to measure motivation independently of consummatory action. So psychologists have tended by and large to distinguish between motivation and action—between hunger and eating, and between the desire to achieve and actual achievement.

Nevertheless, much remained to be done. There was as yet no interest in the unique effects of particular drives. It is true that American psychologists studied not only the hunger drive, but also the thirst drive, the pain-avoidance drive, and other basic drives. Yet all these were conceived as functionally equivalent forces acting to energize human behavior until the organism managed to remove them by something it did. As might also be expected, there was no particular interest in individual differences in the strength of various motives. In fact the model of the hunger drive suggested that motive potentialities might be pretty much alike in all people and that their actual strength was primarily determined by changes in the external environment (e.g., lack of food). There was not much interest in the possibility that some particular person might have an especially strong hunger drive either because of biological endowment or because of some special learning experiences that had reinforced it. It remained for those more directly interested in human behavior and social motives to fill out the picture somewhat.

Many of them took their cue from Freud. Oddly enough he, too, had been strongly influenced by Darwin. He recognized the importance of survival needs like hunger, but concentrated his attention on the force that perpetuated the species—namely, sexual love. His general "model of motivation" remained not unlike the one adopted by the American psychologists of the functional school. A general motive force—the libido—drives man to invent through reason a variety of techniques or stratagems for diverting or satisfying it. But while the general model stayed the same, he made important empirical contributions that markedly influenced the direction research was to take.

For one thing he destroyed forever (except, perhaps, in the minds of economic theorists) the notion that motives are rational or can be rationally inferred from action. By concentrating his attention on notable irrationalities in behavior—slips of the tongue, forgetting of well-known facts, dreams, accidents, neurotic symptoms—he demonstrated over and over again that motives "are not what they seem." In fact they might be just the opposite. It could no longer be safely assumed that a man walks across the street because he wants to get to the other side. He might, in fact, want just the opposite—to enter a tavern on this side, a desire revealed indirectly by his exaggerated avoidance behavior. Since Freud, psychologists have accepted the fact that a simple act may be variously motivated. In the economic sphere, advertisers have long since taken advantage of Freud's findings in recognizing that a man doesn't buy a car just because he "needs" one in a rational sense, but because the possession of a particular kind of car may satisfy other motives—for power, prestige, or even sexual display. But how is one to know exactly what these other motives are? Here again, Freud provided us with an important clue in the method he himself used for discovering certain motives. He searched in dreams and free associations—in short, *in fantasy*—for clues to irrational motives. The limitation of his method was that it was always *ad hoc*. He proceeded, like the doctor he was, to analyze each symptom, for each person, or each dream as it came along, but did not provide scientists with measures of particular motives that would (1) enable different observers to agree what motives were operating with the degree of consensus necessary for science, (2) permit individuals to be compared as to the strength of a given motive, and (3) provide at least crude estimates of group levels or differences in human motives that would be of use to economists and other social theorists in dealing with the behavior of large groups of people.

Measuring the achievement motive

The next step was to develop a method of measuring individual differences in human motivation firmly based on the methodology of experimental psychology and on the psychoanalytic insights of Freud and his followers. How this was accomplished might just as well be illustrated by reviewing briefly the history of the development of a measure of the achievement motive, since we are to study its connection with economic growth throughout the rest of the book. The procedure, which has been described in full elsewhere (McClelland, *et al.*, 1953), may be briefly summarized as follows. First the achievement motive was aroused in a group of subjects to see what its effects on behavior might be. In this way we could avoid the mistake of assuming *a priori* that the strength of the achievement motive may be inferred simply and directly from some particular type of behavior. For example, actual achievement cannot be considered a safe index of the strength of the *need* to achieve any more than eating can be considered a safe measure of the strength of the hunger drive. In fact actual achievement is controlled by many more forces than eating—desires for social approval, power, or knowledge—to say nothing of ability factors, so that it is far less a reliable index of the need to achieve than eating is of hunger.

Instead we need some more unique index of the presence of an aroused desire for achievement. Ideally, of course, we might favor something like a "psychic X-ray" that would permit us to observe what was going on in a person's head in the same way that we can observe stomach contractions or nerve discharges in a hungry organism. Lacking such a device, we can use the next best thing—a sample of a person's spontaneous thoughts under minimum external restraints, in short, of his waking fantasies and free associations, as already used by Freud and many others to assess human motives. The question then narrows down quite specifically to: What "unique" effects on fantasy does an aroused state of achievement motivation have? If we can discover any, we can use these effects to infer the strength of "inner concerns" for achievement in subsequent studies.

Deciding how to arouse the achievement motive already involves to a certain extent at least a rough definition of the motive being investigated. It is therefore important to report just how it was done. The subjects initially were all male college students who were given a series of tasks to perform that were introduced in the following way:

> The tests which you are taking directly indicate a person's general level of intelligence. These tests have been taken from a group of tests which were used to select people of high administrative capacity for positions in Washington during the past war. Thus, in addition to general intelligence, they bring out an individual's capacity to organize material, his ability to evaluate crucial situations quickly and accurately—in short, these tests demonstrate whether or not a person is suited to be a leader. (McClelland, Atkinson, Clark & Lowell, 1953, p. 105.)

The important point about these instructions is that they stress the fact that the individual is about to be evaluated in terms of standards of excellence—intelligence and leadership capacity—which are ordinarily of considerable importance to men in American culture. It is assumed that such instructions will arouse in most of the people to whom the tests were given a desire to do well, a desire to appear intelligent and demonstrate some leadership capacity. It is, of course, unnecessary to assume that these motives were conscious, or even present, in all of the subjects tested. It is only necessary to assume that consciously or unconsciously a motive to do well was aroused in more of the subjects to whom the instructions were given than in a comparable group of subjects to whom the tests and instructions were not given. Any differences in the subsequent fantasy behavior of the two groups might then be attributed to the difference in the level of arousal of the achievement motive in the two groups.

After the above tests had been completed, samples of the subjects' fantasies were collected by having them write brief five-minute stories suggested by pictures flashed on a screen for a few seconds. The pictures represented a variety of life situations centering particularly around work, because it was not known in advance exactly what associations would be most likely to be affected by arousing the achievement motive. In non-technical language, the stories represented short samples of the things people are most likely to think about or imagine when they are in a state of heightened motivation having to do with achievement. It may be worth considering for a moment why fantasy as a type of behavior has many advantages over any other type of behavior for sensitively reflecting the effects of motivational arousal. In fantasy anything is at least symbolically possible—a person may rise to great heights, sink to great depths, kill his grandmother, or take off for the South Sea Islands on a pogo stick. Overt action, on the other hand, is much more constrained by limits set by reality or by the person's abilities. Furthermore, fantasy is more easily influenced than other kinds of behavior. Contrast it with problem-solving, for example. One might assume that how hard a person works would directly reflect the strength of his achievement motive. Yet how hard a person works is not easy to influence experimentally. Apparently most people develop a problem-solving "set" which is sufficient to keep them working at a more or less constant rate despite wide variations in feeling, such as those induced by extreme fatigue. In producing work, one motive can substitute for another so that even though the achievement motive may be weak in some people, their output may well be the same as somebody else's because of a stronger desire to please the experimenter.

This points to a third advantage of fantasy over any "overt" behavioral measure—namely, the way in which it gives clues as to *what motive* is aroused. Even if working behavior were more sensitive to experimental influences, one could not determine from the mere fact that a person was working harder what his motive was in working harder. It might be the achievement motive, or it might be the need for social approval, or the desire to get out of a situation as fast as possible and do something else. It is the fantasies of the person, his thoughts and associations, which give us his real "inner concerns" at the time he is working.

The next step was to compare the stories written by subjects whose achievement motives had presumably been aroused with those written by subjects under normal conditions. Certain differences immediately became apparent. The stories written under "aroused" conditions contained more references to "standards of excellence" and to doing well, or wanting to do well, with respect to the standards. A couple of actual stories will illustrate the point best. One of the pictures frequently used shows a boy sitting at a desk with a book open in front of him. Under normal conditions, it evokes a story like this one:

> A boy in a classroom who is daydreaming about something. He is recalling a previously experienced incident that struck his mind to be more appealing than being in the classroom. He is thinking about the experience and is now imagining himself in the situation. He hopes to be there. He will probably get called on by the instructor to recite and will be embarrassed.

Nothing in this story deals with achievement or with standards of excellence, but compare it with the following story:

> The boy is taking an hour written. He and the others are high-school students. The test is about two-thirds over and he is doing his best to think it through. He was supposed to study for the test and did so. But because it is factual, there were items he saw but did not learn. He knows he has studied the answers he can't remember and is trying to summon up the images and related ideas to remind him of them. He may remember one or two, but he will miss most of the items he can't remember. He will try hard until five minutes is left, then give up, go back over his paper, and be disgusted for reading but not learning the answers.

Obviously, here the boy is concerned about doing his best on the examination ("he is doing his best to think it through" and he is "disgusted for reading but not learning the answers"). Furthermore, there are a number of aspects of an achievement sequence specifically mentioned such as the fact that it is his fault that he is not doing well ("he saw but did not learn") and that he is trying out various ways of solving his problem ("trying to summon up the images and related ideas to remind him of them"). The fact that he is not successful in his achievement efforts is *not* taken to mean that the student who composed this story has a weaker achievement motive than someone who wrote a story in which his problem-solving activities were successful. In fact, the precise advantage of the experimental method adopted is that it makes it unnecessary to make such decisions on "rational" grounds. One might make a case *a priori* for regarding images of success as more likely to be indicative of a strong and successful achievement drive than images of failure. One might also make a good *a priori* case for the exact opposite conclusion—that people who daydream about success are the very ones whose achievement motive is too weak to engage in actual attempts to do something in real life. To decide such a question on the grounds of what is most reasonable would be to fall into the error that plagued the psychology of economists and philosophers in the 19th century. The experimental approach makes *no* assumptions as to how the achievement motive is going to affect fantasy in advance: it simply takes whatever differences appear in fact between stories written under "aroused" and normal conditions so long as they make some kind of theoretical sense, and uses them as a means of detecting the presence of the achievement motive.

For example, it was thought in advance that arousal of the achievement motive might affect the outcome of the story, perhaps producing more successful or unsuccessful outcomes as compared with vague or indecisive ones. But in fact there were no differences in the frequency of various types of outcomes of the stories written under "aroused" conditions as compared with those written under normal conditions. So the outcome of the story, or of the achievement sequence in it, cannot be considered a sign of the presence of heightened achievement motivation, no matter how good an *a priori* case might be made for using it in this way. The point cannot be stressed too much. It was not logic that decided what aspects of fantasy would reflect achievement motivation. It was experimental fact. There is no need to list and define here the several different aspects of fantasy that did change under the influence of achievement arousal in college students, since they have been fully described elsewhere (McClelland, *et al.*, 1953; Atkinson, 1958). It might be questioned though how general these effects would be. Perhaps an aroused achievement motive would influence the thoughts of Chinese, or Ancient Greeks, or Navaho Indians in quite different ways. Are the results obtained restricted to the male college population on which they were obtained? Ancient Greeks have not, of course, been tested, but Navahos have and their stories change in exactly the same ways under the influence of achievement arousal (McClelland, *et al.*, 1953). So do those written by Brazilian students (Angelini, 1955), or high-school students in our culture from more unselected socioeconomic backgrounds. There may be cultural differences, but the data to date point to major similarities—inducing achievement motivation increases in all types of subjects thoughts of doing well with respect to some standard of good performance, of being blocked in the attempt to achieve, of trying various means of achieving, and of reacting with joy or sadness to the results of one's efforts.

The next step was to obtain a score for an individual by assuming that the more such thoughts he had under normal conditions, the stronger his motive to achieve must be, even in the absence of special instructions and experiences designed to arouse it. What the experiments had demonstrated was what channels peoples' thoughts turned to under achievement pressure. But suppose a person's thoughts run in those same channels without any external pressure. It seems reasonable to infer that he has a strong "inner concern" with achievement. Under normal testing conditions, the pictures used to elicit stories are sufficiently ambiguous to evoke a variety of ideas. If someone, however, in writing his stories consistently uses achievement-related ideas of the same kind as those elicited in everyone under achievement "pressure," then he would appear to be someone with a "bias," a "concern," or a "need" for achievement. So it was decided that a simple count of the number of such achievement-related ideas in stories written under normal testing conditions could be taken to represent the strength of a man's concern with achievement. The count has been called the score for *n* Achievement (abbreviation for "need for Achievement"), in order to have a technical term which points unmistakably to the fact that the measure was derived in a very particular way, and has an operational meaning quite distinct from estimates one might arrive at by inferring the strength of a person's achievement motive from his actual successful achievements, or from his frequent assertions that he is interested in getting ahead in the world. It remains only to say that the method just described for deriving the *n* Achievement measure can be applied to measuring *n* Affiliation, *n* Power (see Atkinson, 1958), and any other motive that an experimenter can demonstrate influences fantasy in regular and predictable ways.

But of what use are such measures? What good does it do us to know that a person's *n* Achievement score is high? The answer lies in dozens of research projects which have contrasted the behavior of subjects with high and low *n* Achievement scores. American males with high *n* Achievement come more often from the middle class than from the lower or upper class, have better memory for incompleted tasks, are more apt to volunteer as subjects for psychological experiments, are more active in college and community activities, choose experts over friends as working partners, are more resistant to social pressure, cannot give accurate reports of what their "inner concern" with achievement is, etc. (McClelland, *et al.*, 1953; Atkinson, 1958). It is not necessary to review the many such findings in detail here, but it is directly relevant to consider how subjects with high *n* Achievement actually perform when confronted with a working situation.

Figure 1 presents an early result obtained by Lowell. Obviously the subjects with high *n* Achievement scores, while they start at about the same level of performance as the subjects with low *n* Achievements scores, do progressively better as they proceed with the rather complex task of unscrambling words. In common-sense language, they appear to be concerned enough about doing the task well to learn how to do it better as they go along. It might, therefore, be assumed that such subjects—the "highs"—would always do better at any kind of task under any circumstances. Such is not the case. They do not ordinarily do better at routine tasks like canceling the number of "e's" and "o's" in a long string of unrelated letters where no standard of improvement with respect to the performance itself is present. That is, one can really not do such a task "better"—only faster. Furthermore, the "highs" perform better only when performance has achievement significance for them. The point can best be made with the results in Table 1 as adapted from an experiment by French (1955).

In the "relaxed" experimental condition, the subjects with high *n* Achievement did not do significantly better at a decoding task, presumably because the experimenter removed all achievement

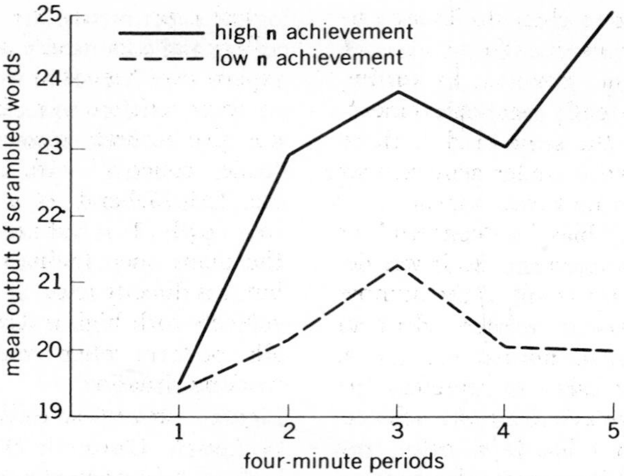

Figure 1. Mean output of scrambled words per four-minute period for subjects with high and low **n** Achievement scores.

significance from what they were doing with the following instructions: "We are just experimenting today and we appreciate your cooperation very much. We want to find out what kinds of scores people make on these tests." Other research has suggested that appealing for cooperation leads those in the group who have strong *n* Affiliation to work harder, rather than those with high *n* Achievement.

In the "task" experimental condition, the subjects were told that the test "measures a critical ability—the ability to deal quickly and accurately with unfamiliar material. It is related to general intelligence, and will be related to your future career. Each man should try to perform as well as possible." Under these instructions, the subjects with high *n* Achievement as measured some months earlier, performed significantly better than those with low *n* Achievement. Finally, in the "extrinsic" experimental condition, the subjects were told that "we want to see how fast it is possible to work on a code test . . . without making errors. . . . The five men who make the best scores in five minutes will be allowed to leave right away—as soon as I can check the papers. The others will have more practice periods and more tests." These instructions introduced specific pressure for speed with the extra incentive of time off from work for those who get through as fast as possible. Under these conditions, again the subjects with high *n* Achievement do not perform better than those with low *n* Achievement. If anything, the "lows" do a little better on the average, suggesting that the possibility of getting out of the working situation appeals to them the most!

All of these facts together suggest that high *n* Achievement will lead a person to perform better when achievement in the narrow sense is possible. If the task is just routine, or if finishing it sooner implies cooperating with someone or getting some special reward like time off from work or a money prize (Atkinson & Reitman, 1958), subjects with other motives will perform better. The achieve-

TABLE 1
MEAN PERFORMANCE SCORES AS A FUNCTION OF INITIAL MOTIVATION LEVEL AND EXPERIMENTAL CONDITIONS (*After French, 1955*)

	EXPERIMENTAL CONDITIONS		
	Relaxed orientation	Task orientation	Extrinsic reward
Initial motivation:			
High *n* Achievement	17.73	29.80	18.20
Low *n* Achievement	15.40	16.66	22.47
Correlations with initial motivation	.03	.48*	.02

* A correlation this large could have arisen by chance less than 1 out of 100 times ($p < .01$).

ment motive is apparently not strongly "engaged" under such conditions. Furthermore, we might legitimately expect that people with strong achievement motives would seek out situations in which they could get achievement satisfaction. They ought to be the kind of people who set achievement standards for themselves rather than relying on extrinsic incentives provided by the situation, and they should try harder and more successfully to reach the standards they set for themselves. It does not take a great stretch of imagination to assume further that if a number of people with high *n* Achievement happened to be present in a given culture at a given time, things would start to hum. They might well start doing things better, as in Fig. 1, or what is even more important, they might start doing them differently by trying to get achievement satisfaction out of what they were doing. What had been done out of a desire to please, to make money, or to get time off from work, might now be converted into an activity in which standards of excellence were defined and pursued in their own right. Viewed in this light it would not be at all surprising to imagine that an increase in *n* Achievement should promote economic or cultural growth.

6 The descent of instinct

FRANK A. BEACH

"The delusion is extraordinary by which we thus exalt language above nature:—making language the expositor of nature, instead of making nature the expositor of language" (Alexander Brian Johnson, *A Treatise on Language*).

The basic ideas underlying a concept of instinct probably are older than recorded history. At any rate they are clearly set forth in the Greek literature of 2,500 years ago. They have been controversial ideas and they remain so today. Nevertheless, the instinct concept has survived in almost complete absence of empirical validation. One aim of the present article is to analyze the reasons for the remarkable vitality of a concept which has stood without objective test for at least two millenia. A second objective is to evaluate the concept as it relates to a science of behavior.

Origins in philosophy and theology

The concept of instinct evolved in relation to the broad problems of human destiny, of Man's place in nature, and his position in this world and the next. From the beginning, instinct has been defined and discussed in terms of its relation to reason and, less directly, to the human soul.

During the fourth century B.C. the Greek philosopher Heraclitus declared that there had been two types of creation. Men and gods were the products of rational creation, whereas irrational brutes comprised a separate category of living creatures. Heraclitus added the observation that only gods and men possess souls. The close relation between rational powers and possession of a soul has been reaffirmed time and again during the ensuing 2,500 years. Heraclitus did not advance the concept of instinct but he laid the groundwork for its development.

Stoic philosophers of the first century A.D. held that men and gods belong to one natural community, since they are rational beings. All animals were specifically excluded since they are not creatures of reason and even their most complex behavior takes place "without reflection," to use the words of Seneca. This stoical taxonomy was both flattering and convenient since, according to the tenets of this school, members of the natural community were forbidden to harm or enslave other members.

It is significant that neither Heraclitus nor the Stoics based their conclusions upon objective evidence. Their premises concerning the psychology of animals were not derived from empirical observation; they were demanded by assumption of the philosophical position that animals lack a rational soul.

Aristotle, who was more of an observer than a philosopher, was of a different mind. In *Historia Animalium* Man is placed at the top of Scala Natura (directly above the Indian ele-

Reprinted from the Psychological Review, 1955, 62, 401–10, with permission of the author and the American Psychological Association.

phant), and is accorded superior intellectual powers, but none qualitatively distinct from those of other species.

In the thirteenth century Albertus Magnus composed *De Animalibus*, based chiefly upon the writings of Aristotle but modifying the Aristotelian position where necessary to conform to Scholastic theology. Albertus removed Man from the natural scale, holding that he is unique in possessing the gift of reason and an immortal soul. Animals, lacking reason, "are directed by their natural instinct and therefore cannot act freely."

St. Thomas Aquinas, student of Albertus, supported his teacher's distinction between men and animals. Animals possess only the sensitive soul described by Aristotle. The human embryo is similarly endowed, but the rational soul is divinely implanted in the fetus at some time before birth.[1] The behavior of man therefore depends upon reason, whereas all animals are governed by instinct. Like the Stoic philosophers, the Scholastics were unconcerned with factual evidence. Their emphasis upon instinctive control of animal behavior was dictated by a need of the theological system, and in this frame of reference instinct was a useful concept.

Roughly four centuries after the time of St. Thomas Aquinas, René Descartes and his followers aggressively restated the existence of a man-brute dichotomy. The bare facts of the Cartesian position are common knowledge, but for the purpose of the present argument it is important to ask why Descartes felt so strongly about the matter—felt compelled to hold up man as the Reasoner, at the same time insisting that all other living creatures are only flesh-and-blood machines. The explanation stands out in the following quotation:

> After the error of atheism, there is nothing that leads weak minds further astray from the paths of virture than the idea that the minds of other animals resemble our own, and that therefore we have no greater right to future life than have gnats and ants (René Descartes, *Passions of the Soul*).

From Albertus to Descartes the argument runs clear. The theological system posits a life after death. Hence the postulation of the soul. But mere possession of a soul is not enough. Each man must earn the right of his soul's salvation. This in turn depends upon reason, which man exercises in differentiating good from evil, behavior which is sinful from that which is not. An afterlife is man's unique prerogative; no animals share it. They have no souls and therefore no need to reason. But how are the complex and adaptive reactions of subhuman creatures to be explained if not by reason, foresight, volition? They are comfortably disposed of as products of instincts with which the Creator has endowed all dumb brutes.

That the thirteenth-century point of view persists today is shown by the following quotation:

> In animals there are only instincts, but not in man. As St. Thomas points out, there cannot be any deliberation in a subrational being (even though we may get the impression that there is). . . . Instincts in animals seem to operate according to the pattern of physical forces, where the stronger always prevails; for animals are utterly devoid of the freedom which characterizes man. . . . That is why when one studies human behavior one must rise above the purely animal pattern and concentrate upon those two faculties, intellect and will,

[1] It is not irrelevant to point out that weighty disputation concerning the exact age at which the soul enters the fetus retarded the advancement of embryological knowledge during its seventeenth century beginnings.

which separate man from animal (Msgr. Fulton J. Sheen, *Peace of Soul*).

To summarize what has been said thus far, it appears that the descent of the instinct concept can be traced from early philosophies which set man apart from the rest of the living world and sought for him some divine affinity. This was achieved by claiming for man alone the power of reason. By a process of elimination the behavior of animals was ascribed to their natural instincts. During the Middle Ages this dichotomous classification became a part of Church doctrine, with the result that possession of reason and of a soul were inextricably linked to the hope of eternal life. Prescientific concepts of instinct were not deduced from the facts of nature; they were necessitated by the demands of philosophical systems based upon supernatural conceptions of nature.

Early scientific usage

When biology emerged as a scientific discipline, there was a general tendency to adopt the prescientific point of view regarding instinct. Some exceptions occurred. For example, Erasmus Darwin's *Zoonomia* expressed the theory that all behavior is a product of experience, but this point of view was subsequently disavowed by the grandson of its sponsor. Charles Darwin made the concept of instinct one cornerstone of his theory of evolution by means of natural selection.

To bridge the gap of the Cartesian man-brute dichotomy, and thus to establish the evolution of mind as well as structure, Darwin and his disciples amassed two types of evidence. One type purported to prove the existence of human instincts; the other pertained to rational behavior in subhuman species. The idea of discontinuity in mental evolution was vigorously attacked, but the dichotomy between instinct and reason was never challenged.

The nineteenth-century literature on evolution shows plainly that the concept of instinctive behavior was accepted because it filled a need in the theoretical system, and not because its validity had been established by empirical test.

Contemporary psychologists such as Herbert Spencer were influenced by the evolutionary movement, and the idea of an instinctive basis for human psychology became popular. William James, in Volume II of his *Principles,* insisted that man has more instincts than any other mammal. McDougall's widely read *Social Psychology* listed human instincts of flight, repulsion, parental feeling, reproduction, self-abasement, etc. Woodworth, Thorndike, and other leaders agreed that much of human behavior is best understood as an expression of instinctive drives or needs.

One of the difficulties with such thinking is that it often leads to the nominal fallacy—the tendency to confuse naming with explaining. Some psychological writers were guilty of employing the instinct concept as an explanatory device, and the eventual result was a vigorous revolt against the use of instinct in any psychological theory.

The anti-instinct revolt

Dunlap's 1919 article, "Are there any instincts?" was one opening gun in the battle, but the extreme protests came from the most radical Behaviorists as represented by Z. Y. Kuo, who wrote on the subject, "A psychology without heredity" (1924). For a while the word "instinct" was anathema, but the revolt was abortive, and there were three principal reasons for its failure.

First, Kuo denied instinct but admitted the existence of unlearned "units of reaction." By this phrase he meant simple reflexes, but in using it he set up a dichotomy of learned and unlearned behavior which was fatal to his basic thesis. It merely shifted the debate to arguments as to the degree of complexity permissible in an unlearned response, or the proportion of a complex pattern that was instinctive. The second error consisted essentially of a return to the position taken by Erasmus Darwin at the close of the eighteenth century. Having averred that the only unlearned reactions consist of a few simple reflexes, the opponents of the instinct doctrine invoked learning to explain all other behavior. This forced them into untenable positions such as that of maintaining that pecking behavior of the newly-hatched chick is a product of head movements made by the embryo in the shell, or that the neo-natal infant's grasp reflex depends upon prenatal exercise of this response. The third loophole in the anti-instinct argument derived from a dualistic concept of the hereditary process. Admitting that genes can affect morphological characters, and simultaneously denying that heredity influences behavior, opponents of instinct were hoist by their own petard. If the physical machinery for behavior develops under genetic control, then the behavior it mediates can scarcely be regarded as independent of inheritance.

It is important to note that this war over instinct was fought more with words and inferential reasoning than with behavioral evidence. It is true that a few individuals actually observed the behavior of newborn children or of animals, but most of the battles of the campaign were fought from the armchair in the study rather than from the laboratory.

Current thought in psychology

Although there are militant opponents of the instinct doctrine among present-day psychologists, it is undoubtedly correct to say that the concept of instincts as complex, unlearned patterns of behavior is generally accepted in clinical, social, and experimental psychology. Among experimentalists, Lashley suggested that instinctive behavior is unlearned and differs from reflexes in that instincts depend on "the pattern or organization of the stimulus," whereas reflexes are elicited by stimulation of localized groups of sensory endings (1938).

Carmichael (1947) expressed agreement with G. H. Parker's statement that human beings are "about nine-tenths inborn, and one-tenth acquired." Morgan (1947) studied food-hoarding behavior in rats, and concluded, "since it comes out spontaneously without training, it is plainly instinctive." The following quotation reveals that some modern psychologists not only embrace the concept of instinctive behavior, but consider it a useful explanatory device.

"Of the theories of hoarding which have been advanced, the most reasonable one in terms of recent data is that the behavior is instinctive . . ." (Waddell, 1951).

At least three serious criticisms can be leveled against current treatment of the problem of instinctive behavior. The first is that psychologists in general actually know very little about most of the behavior patterns which they confidently classify as instinctive. In his paper, "The experimental analysis of instinctive activities," Lashley mentions the following 15 examples:

1. Eating of Hydra by the Planarian, Microstoma.
2. Nest-building, cleaning of young and retrieving by the primiparous rat.
3. Restless running about of the mother rat deprived of her litter.
4. Homing of pigeons.
5. Web-weaving of spiders.
6. Migratory behavior of fishes.
7. Nest-building of birds, including several species.
8. Mating behavior of the female rat in estrus.
9. Dancing reactions of the honeybee returning to the hive laden with nectar.
10. Visual reactions of rats reared in darkness.
11. Responses of the sooty tern to her nest and young.
12. Reactions of the seagull to artificial and normal eggs.
13. Sexual behavior of the male rat.
14. Mating responses in insects.
15. Mating responses in domestic hens.

It is a safe guess that most American psychologists have never observed any of these patterns of behavior. At a conservative estimate, less than half of the reactions listed have been subjected to even preliminary study by psychologically trained investigators. The significance of this criticism lies partly in the fact that those psychologists who *have* worked in the area of "instinctive" behavior tend to be more critical of the instinct concept than are those who lack first-hand knowledge of the behavioral evidence.

Relevant to the criticism of unfamiliarity is the fact that the degree of assurance with which instincts are attributed to a given species is inversely related to the extent to which that species has been studied, particularly from the developmental point of view. Before the development of complex behavior in human infants had been carefully analyzed, it was, as we have seen, a common practice to describe many human instincts. Longitudinal studies of behavior have reduced the "unlearned" components to three or four simple responses not much more complex than reflexes (Dennis, 1941).

The second criticism is that despite prevailing ignorance about the behavior which is called instinctive, there is strong pressure toward premature categorization of the as yet unanalyzed patterns of reaction. The history of biological taxonomy shows that the reliability of any classificatory system is a function of the validity of identification of individual specimens or even populations. Unless the systematist is thoroughly familiar with the characteristics of a given species, he cannot determine its proper relation to other groups. Similarly, until psychologists have carefully analyzed the salient characteristics of a given pattern of behavior, they cannot meaningfully classify or compare it with other patterns.

The third criticism of current treatment of instinctive behavior has to do with the classificatory scheme which is in use. When all criteria which supposedly differentiate instinctive from acquired responses are critically evaluated, the only one which seems universally applicable is that instincts are unlearned (Munn, 1938). This forces psychology to deal with a two-class system, and such systems are particularly unmanageable when one class is defined solely in negative terms, that is, in terms of the absence of certain characteristics that define the other class. It is logically indefensible to categorize any behavior as unlearned unless the characteristics of learned behavior have been thoroughly explored and are well known. Even the most optimistic "learning psychologist" would not claim that we have reached this point yet. At present, to prove that behavior is unlearned is equivalent to proving the null hypothesis.

Perhaps a more serious weakness in the present psychological handling of instinct lies in the assumption that a two-class system is adequate for the classification of complex behavior. The implication that all behavior must be determined by learning or by heredity, neither of which is more than partially understood, is entirely unjustified. The final form of any response is affected by a multiplicity of variables, only two of which are genetical and experiential factors. It is to the identification and analysis of all of these factors that psychology should address itself. When this task is properly conceived and executed there will be no need nor reason for ambiguous concepts of instinctive behavior.

Genes and behavior

Experimental investigation of relationships between genetical constitution and behavior was exemplified by the pioneering studies of Yerkes (1913), Tryon (1929), and Heron (1935). Interest in this area has recently increased, and a large number of investigations have been summarized by Hall (1951) who anticipates a new interdisciplinary science of psychogenetics.

As Hall points out, the psychologist interested in examining gene-behavior relations has several approaches to choose from. He can compare the behavior of different inbred strains of animals currently available in the genetics laboratory. He can cross two strains and study the behavior of the hybrids. Selective breeding for particular behavioral traits is a well-established technique. The behavioral effects of induced mutations have as yet received very little attention but should be investigated.

It is known that selective breeding can alter the level of general activity (Rundquist, 1933), maze behavior (Heron, 1935), emotionality (Hall, 1938), and aggressiveness (Keeler & King, 1942) in the laboratory rat. Inbred strains of mice differ from one another in temperature preference (Herter, 1938), aggressiveness (Scott, 1942), and strength of "exploratory drive" (Thompson, 1953).

Various breeds of dogs exhibit pronounced differences in behavioral characteristics. Some are highly emotional, unstable and restless; whereas others are phlegmatic and relatively inactive (Fuller & Scott, 1954). Special breeds have been created by selective mating to meet certain practical requirements. For example, some hunting dogs such as the foxhound are "open trailers." While following a fresh trail they vocalize in a characteristic fashion. Other dogs are "mute trailers." The F_1 hybrids of a cross between these types are always open trailers although the voice is often that of the mute trailing parent (Whitney, 1929).

Inbreeding of domestic chickens for high egg production has produced behavioral deficiencies of various kinds. Although hens of some lines are excellent layers, they have almost totally lost the normal tendency to brood the eggs once they have been laid (Hurst, 1925). The maternal behavior of sows of different inbred lines of swine is strikingly different. Females of one line are so aggressively protective of their young that they cannot be approached during the lactation period. Sows of a second genetical line possess such weak maternal interest that they frequently kill their litters by stepping or lying on the young (Hodgson, 1935).

Study of the effects of controlled breeding cast doubt upon the validity of any classificatory system which describes one type of behavior as genetically determined and another as experientially determined. For example, by manipulating the genotype it is possible to alter certain types of learning ability. As far as present evidence can show, the influence of genes on learning is as important as any genetical effect upon other behavior patterns commonly considered instinctive. There is no reason to assume that so-called instinctive reactions are more dependent upon heredity than noninstinctive responses; hence genetical determination is not a differentiating criterion.

The meaning of genetical determination

Behavior which is known to vary with the genotype is often incorrectly defined as "genetically determined" behavior. Although we can show a correlation between certain genes and particular behavior patterns, this is of course no proof of a causal relationship. Many other genes and nongenic factors are always involved in such correlations. This point is nicely illustrated by a series of experiments on audiogenic seizures in mice.

Susceptibility to fatal seizures is high in some inbred strains and low in others (Hall, 1947). When a high-incidence and low-incidence strain are crossed, the susceptibility of the F_1 generation is intermediate between those of the parental strains. So far the evidence strongly supports the conclusion that seizure incidence is genetically determined. However, the incidence of seizures can be altered without changing the genetic constitution.

This is accomplished by modifying the prenatal environment. Fertilized eggs recovered from the tubes or uterus of a female of one strain and introduced into the uterus of a female of a different strain will sometimes implant normally and produce viable young. This has been done using seizure-suspectible females as donors and seizure-resistant females as hosts. Under such conditions the genetical characteristics of the young are unaltered, but their susceptibility to fatal seizures is lower than that of their own genetic strain and higher than that of the "foster" mothers in whose uteri they developed (Ginsburg & Hovda, 1947).

Studies of this sort emphasize the important but often neglected fact that postnatal behavior is affected by factors acting upon the organism before birth. As Sontag has pointed out, this is true of human beings as well as lower species.

> Fetal environment may play a part in determining characteristics of the physiological behavior of any newborn infant. We are too often inclined to neglect this source of modification of physiological potential. Too frequently we think of the individual as beginning life only at birth. Yet because it is during the period of intrauterine life that most of the cells of the vital organs are actually formed, it is during this period that "environmental" factors such as nutrition, oxygen, mother's hormones, etc. are most important in modifying their characteristics (Sontag, 1950, p. 482).

Another fundamental principle illustrated by the results of transplanting fertilized ova is that the uniformity of behavior which characterizes highly inbred strains of animals cannot be ascribed solely to homozygosity, but depends as well upon *minimal variability of the prenatal environment*. More broadly conceived, this principle implies that behavioral similarities and differences observable at birth are in part a product of intrauterine effects.

If forced to relinquish the criterion of genetical control, proponents of the instinct doctrine fall back upon the criterion of the unlearned nature of instinctive acts. Now learning is a process occurring through time, and can only be studied by longitudinal analysis. If instinctive acts are unlearned, their developmental history must differ in some significant fashion from that of a learned response.

The ontogeny of behavior

No bit of behavior can ever be fully understood until its ontogenesis has been described. Had psychologists always recognized this fact, much of the fruitless debate about unlearned behavior could have been avoided.

Perhaps the most widely cited psychological experiment on development and instinctive behavior is that of Carmichael, who studied the swimming behavior of larval amphibians (1927). He reared embryos in a solution which paralyzed the striped muscles but permitted normal growth. Animals that were thus prevented from practicing the swimming response were nevertheless capable of normal swimming when placed in pure water. These findings are often offered as proof of the claim that swimming is instinctive. However, to demonstrate that practice is not essential for the appearance of a response is only the beginning of the analysis. This point is clearly illustrated by certain observations of insect behavior.

Gravid female moths, *Hyponomenta padella*, lay their eggs on the leaves of the hackberry plant and die shortly thereafter. The eggs hatch, the larvae eat the leaves and eventually become mature. Females of this new generation in turn select hackberry leaves on which to deposit their eggs. Another race of moths prefers apple leaves as an oviposition site. The difference between the two races has been perpetuated, generation after generation, for many centuries. It would appear to be the example par excellence of a genetically controlled behavior trait. But such an explanation is insufficient.

When eggs of the apple-preferring type are transferred to hackberry leaves, the larvae thrive on the new diet. Thirty per cent of the females developing from these larvae show a preference for hackberry leaves when it comes time for them to deposit their eggs (Imms, 1931).

The evidence is of course incomplete. Why only 30 per cent of the insects show a reversal of preference is not clear. It would be illuminating if the same experimental treatment could be repeated on several successive generations. Nevertheless it appears likely that the adult moth's choice of an oviposition site is influenced by the chemical composition of the food consumed during the larval period (Emerson, 1943). If this interpretation is correct, the data illustrate the fact that a complex behavior pattern may be "unlearned" and still depend upon the individual's previous history.

Comparable examples can be found in the behavior of vertebrates. Stereotyped patterns of behavior appear with great regularity in successive generations under conditions in which practice plays no obvious role. Nonetheless such "species-specific" responses may be dependent upon previous experience of the organism.

The maternal behavior of primiparous female rats reared in isolation is indistinguishable from that of multiparous individuals. Animals with no maternal experience build nests before the first litter is born, clean the young, eat the placenta, and retrieve scattered young to the nest (Beach, 1937). However, pregnant rats that have been reared in cages containing nothing that can be picked up and transported do not build nests when material is made available. They simply heap their young in a pile in a corner of the cage. Other females that have been reared under conditions preventing them from licking and grooming their own bodies fail to clean their young at the time of parturition (Riess, 1950).

There are undoubtedly many adaptive responses which appear *de novo* at the biologically appropriate time in the absence of preceding practice, but the possibility remains that component parts of a complex pattern have in fact been perfected in different contexts. Whether or not this is the case can only be determined by exhaustive analysis of the ontogeny of the behavior under examination. Nonetheless, to define behavior as "unlearned" in the absence of such analysis is meaningless and misleading.

Summary and conclusions

The concept of instinctive behavior seems to have originated in antiquity in connection with attempts to define a clear-cut difference between man and all other animals. Human behavior was said to be governed by reasoning, and the behavior of animals to depend upon instinct. In his possession of the unique power of reason, man was elevated above all other creatures, and, incidentally, his use of them for his own purposes was thus morally justified.

Christian theologians adopted this point of view and averred that man was given the power of reason so that he could earn his own salvation. Similar privileges could not logically be accorded to lower animals. Therefore they were denied reason and their behavior was explained as a product of divinely implanted instincts. In both sacred and secular philosophies the concept of instinct served a practical purpose, although in no instance was there any attempt to validate it by examination of the empirical evidence.

The concept gained a central position in scientific thinking as a result of the Darwinian movement. Proponents of the evolutionary theory accepted uncritically the assumption that all behavior must be governed by instinct or by reasoning. Their aim was to demonstrate that animals can reason and that men possess instincts. The same dichotomy has persisted in experimental psychology. Attempts to eliminate the instinct concept were unsuccessful because those who made the attempt accepted the idea that all behavior is either acquired or inherited.

No such classification can ever be satisfactory. It rests upon exclusively negative definitions of one side of the dichotomy. It obscures the basic problems involved. It reflects an unnaturally narrow and naïve conception of factors shaping behavior.

To remedy the present confused situation it is necessary first to refrain from premature classification of those kinds of behavior that are currently defined as unlearned. Until they have been systematically analyzed it will remain impossible to decide whether these numerous response patterns belong in one or a dozen different categories.

The analysis that is needed involves two types of approach. One rests upon determination of the relationships existing between genes and behavior. The other consists of studying the development of various behavior patterns in the individual, and determining the number and kinds of factors that normally control the final form of the response.

When these methods have been applied to the various types of behavior which today are called "instinctive," the concept of instinct will disappear, to be replaced by scientifically valid and useful explanations.

7 Motivation reconsidered: the concept of competence

ROBERT W. WHITE

When parallel trends can be observed in realms as far apart as animal behavior and psychoanalytic ego psychology, there is reason to suppose that we are witnessing a significant evolution of ideas. In these two realms, as in psychology as a whole, there is evidence of deepening discontent with theories of motivation based upon drives. Despite great differences in the language and concepts used to express this discontent, the theme is everywhere the same: Something important is left out when we make drives the operating forces in animal and human behavior.

The chief theories against which the discontent is directed are those of Hull and of Freud. In their respective realms, drive-reduction theory and psychoanalytic instinct theory, which are basically very much alike, have acquired a considerable air of orthodoxy. Both views have an appealing simplicity, and both have been argued long enough so that their main outlines are generally known. In decided contrast is the position of those who are not satisfied with drives and instincts. They are numerous, and they have developed many pointed criticisms, but what they have to say has not thus far lent itself to a clear and inclusive conceptualization. Apparently there is an enduring difficulty in making these contributions fall into shape.

Excerpted from the **Psychological Review**, 1959, 66, 297–334, with permission of the author and the American Psychological Association.

In this paper I shall attempt a conceptualization which gathers up some of the important things left out by drive theory. To give the concept a name I have chosen the word *competence*, which is intended in a broad biological sense rather than in its narrow everyday meaning. As used here, competence will refer to an organism's capacity to interact effectively with its environment. In organisms capable of but little learning, this capacity might be considered an innate attribute, but in the mammals and especially man, with their highly plastic nervous systems, fitness to interact with the environment is slowly attained through prolonged feats of learning. In view of the directedness and persistence of the behavior that leads to these feats of learning, I consider it necessary to treat competence as having a motivational aspect, and my central argument will be that the motivation needed to attain competence cannot be wholly derived from sources of energy currently conceptualized as drives or instincts. We need a different kind of motivational idea to account fully for the fact that man and the higher mammals develop a competence in dealing with the environment which they certainly do not have at birth and certainly do not arrive at simply through maturation. Such an idea, I believe, is essential for any biologically sound view of human nature.[1]

Effectance

The new freedom produced by two decades of research on animal drives is of great help in this undertaking. We are no longer obliged to look for a source of energy external to the nervous system, for a consummatory climax, or for a fixed connection between reinforcement and tension-reduction. Effectance motivation cannot, of course, be conceived as having a source in tissues external to the nervous system. It is in no sense a deficit motive. We must assume it to be neurogenic, its "energies" being simply those of the living cells that make up the nervous system. External stimuli play an important part, but in terms of "energy" this part is secondary, as one can see most clearly when environmental stimulation is actively sought. Putting it picturesquely, we might say that the effectance urge represents what the neuromuscular system wants to do when it is otherwise unoccupied or is gently stimulated by the environment. Obviously there are no consummatory acts; satisfaction would appear to lie in the arousal and maintaining of activity rather than in its slow decline toward bored passivity. The motive need not be conceived as intense and powerful in the sense that hunger, pain, or fear can be powerful when aroused to high pitch. There are plenty of instances in which children refuse to leave their absorbed play in order to eat or to visit the toilet. Strongly aroused drives, pain, and anxiety, however, can be conceived as overriding the effectance urge and capturing the energies of the neuromuscular system. But effectance motivation is persistent in the sense that it regularly occupies the spare waking time between episodes of homeostatic crisis.

In speculating upon this subject we must bear in mind the continuous nature of behavior. This is easier said than done; habitually we break things down in order to understand them, and such units as the reflex arc, the stimulus-response sequence, and the

[1] For an elaboration of these points, omitted here, the reader is referred to pp. 297–321 of the original.—Eds.

single transaction with the environment seem like inevitable steps toward clarity. Yet when we apply such an analysis to playful exploration we lose the most essential aspect of the behavior. It is constantly circling from stimulus to perception to action to effect to stimulus to perception, and so on around; or, more properly, these processes are all in continuous action and continuous change. Dealing with the environment means carrying on a continuing transaction which gradually changes one's relation to the environment. Because there is no consummatory climax, satisfaction has to be seen as lying in a considerable series of transactions, in a trend of behavior rather than a goal that is achieved. It is difficult to make the word "satisfaction" have this connotation, and we shall do well to replace it by "feeling of efficacy" when attempting to indicate the subjective and affective side of effectance.

It is useful to recall the findings about novelty: the singular effectiveness of novelty in engaging interest and for a time supporting persistent behavior. We also need to consider the selective continuance of transactions in which the animal or child has a more or less pronounced effect upon the environment—in which something happens as a consequence of his activity. Interest is not aroused and sustained when the stimulus field is so familiar that it gives rise at most to reflex acts or automatized habits. It is not sustained when actions produce no effects or changes in the stimulus field. Our conception must therefore be that effectance motivation is aroused by stimulus conditions which offer, as Hebb (1949) puts it, difference-in-sameness. This leads to variability and novelty of response, and interest is best sustained when the resulting action affects the stimulus so as to produce further difference-in-sameness. Interest wanes when action begins to have less effect; effectance motivation subsides when a situation has been explored to the point that it no longer presents new possibilities.

We have to conceive further that the arousal of playful and exploratory interest means the appearance of organization involving both the cognitive and active aspects of behavior. Change in the stimulus field is not an end in itself, so to speak; it happens when one is passively moved about, and it may happen as a consequence of random movements without becoming focalized and instigating exploration. Similarly, action which has effects is not an end in itself, for if one unintentionally kicks away a branch while walking, or knocks something off a table, these effects by no means necessarily become involved in playful investigation. Schachtel's (1954) emphasis on focal attention becomes helpful at this point. The playful and exploratory behavior shown by Laurent is not random or casual. It involves focal *attention* to some object—the fixing of some aspect of the stimulus field so that it stays relatively constant—and it also involves the focalizing of *action* upon this object. As Diamond (1939) has expressed it, response under these conditions is "relevant to the stimulus," and it is change in the *focalized* stimulus that so strongly affects the level of interest. Dealing with the environment means directing focal attention to some part of it and organizing actions to have some effect on this part.

In our present state of relative ignorance about the workings of the nervous system it is impossible to form a satisfactory idea of the neural basis of effectance motivation, but it should at least be clear that the concept does not refer to any and every kind of neural action. It refers to a particular kind of activity, as inferred from particular kinds of behavior. We can say that it does not include reflexes and other kinds of automatic response. It does not include well-learned, automatized patterns, even those that are complex and highly organized. It does not include behavior in the service of effectively aroused drives. It does not even include activity that is highly random and discontinuous, though such behavior may be its most direct forerunner. The urge toward competence is inferred specifically from behavior that shows a lasting focalization and that has the characteristics of exploration and experimentation, a kind of variation within the focus. When this particular sort of activity is aroused in the nervous system, effectance motivation is being aroused, for it is characteristic of this particular sort of activity that it is selective, directed, and persistent, and that instrumental acts will be learned for the sole reward of engaging in it.

Some objection may be felt to my introducing the word *competence* in connection with behavior that is so often playful. Certainly the playing child is doing things for fun, not because of a desire to improve his competence in dealing with the stern hard world. In order to forestall misunderstanding, it should be pointed out that the usage here is parallel to what we do when we connect sex with its biological goal of reproduction. The sex drive aims for pleasure and gratification, and reproduction is a consequence that is presumably unforeseen by animals and by man at primitive levels of understanding. Effectance motivation similarly aims for the feeling of efficacy, not for the vitally important learnings that come as its consequence. If we consider the part played by competence motivation in adult human life we can observe the same parallel. Sex may now be completely and purposefully divorced from reproduction but nevertheless pursued for the pleasure it can yield. Similarly, effectance motivation may lead to continuing exploratory interests or active adventures when in fact there is no longer any gain in actual competence or any need for it in terms of survival. In both cases the motive is capable of yielding surplus satisfaction well beyond what is necessary to get the biological work done.

In infants and young children it seems to me sensible to conceive of effectance motivation as undifferentiated. Later in life it becomes profitable to distinguish various motives such as cognizance, construction, mastery, and achievement. It is my view that all such motives have a root in effectance motivation. They are differentiated from it through life experiences which emphasize one or another aspect of the cycle of transaction with environment. Of course, the motives of later childhood and of adult life are no longer simple and can almost never be referred to a single root. They can acquire loadings of anxiety, defense, and compensation, they can become fused with unconscious fantasies of a sexual, aggressive, or omnipotent character, and they can gain force because of their service in producing realistic results in the way of income and career. It is not my intention to cast effectance in the star part in adult motivation. The acquisition of motives is a complicated affair in which simple and sovereign theories grow daily more obsolete. Yet it may be that the satisfaction of effectance contributes significantly to those feelings of interest which often sustain us so well in day-to-day actions, particularly when the things we are doing have continuing elements of novelty.

The biological significance of competence

The conviction was expressed at the beginning of this paper that some such concept as competence, interpreted motivationally, was essential for any biologically sound view of human nature. This necessity emerges when we consider the nature of living systems, particularly when we take a longitudinal view. What an organism does at a given moment does not always give the right clue as to what it does over a period of time. Discussing this problem, Angyal (1941) has proposed that we should look for the general pattern followed by the total organismic process over the course of time. Obviously this makes it necessary to take account of growth. Angyal defines life as "a process of self-expansion"; the living system "expands at the expense of its surroundings," assimilating parts of the environment and transforming them into functioning parts of itself. Organisms differ from other things in nature in that they are "self-governing entities" which are to some extent "autonomous." Internal processes govern them as well as external "heteronomous" forces. In the course of life there is a relative increase in the preponderance of internal over external forces. The living system expands, assimilates more of the environment, transforms its surroundings so as to bring them under greater control. "We may say," Angyal writes, "that the general dynamic trend of the organism is toward an increase of autonomy. . . . The human being has a characteristic tendency toward self-determination, that is, a tendency to resist external influences and to subordinate the heteronomous forces of the physical and social environment to its own sphere of influence." The trend toward increased autonomy is characteristic so long as growth of any kind is going on, though in the end the living system is bound to succumb to the pressure of heteronomous forces.

Of all living creatures, it is man who takes the longest strides toward autonomy. This is not because of any unusual tendency toward bodily expansion at the expense of the environment. It is rather that man, with his mobile hands and abundantly developed brain, attains an extremely high level of competence in his transactions with his surroundings. The building of houses, roads and bridges, the making of tools and instruments, the domestication of plants and animals, all qualify as planful changes made in the environment so that it comes more or less under control and serves our purposes rather than intruding upon them. We meet the fluctuations of outdoor temperature, for example, not only with our bodily homeostatic mechanisms, which alone would be painfully unequal to the task, but also with clothing, buildings, controlled fires, and such complicated devices as self-regulating central heating and air conditioning. Man as a species has developed a tremendous power of bringing the environment into his service, and each individual member of the species must attain what is really quite an impressive level of competence if he is to take part in the life around him.

We are so accustomed to these

human accomplishments that it is hard to realize how long an apprenticeship they require. At the outset the human infant is a slow learner in comparison with other animal forms. Hebb (1949) speaks of "the astonishing inefficiency of man's first learning, as far as immediate results are concerned," an inefficiency which he attributes to the large size of the association areas in the brain and the long time needed to bring them under sensory control. The human lack of precocity in learning shows itself even in comparison with one of the next of kin: as Hebb points out, "the human baby takes six months, the chimpanzee four months, before making a clear distinction between friend and enemy." Later in life the slow start will pay dividends. Once the fundamental perceptual elements, simple associations, and conceptual sequences have been established, later learning can proceed with ever increasing swiftness and complexity. In Hebb's words, "learning at maturity concerns patterns and events whose parts at least are familiar and which already have a number of other associations."

This general principle of cumulative learning, starting from slowly acquired rudiments and proceeding thence with increasing efficiency, can be illustrated by such processes as manipulation and locomotion, which may culminate in the acrobat devising new stunts or the dancer working out a new ballet. It is especially vivid in the case of language, where the early mastery of words and pronunciation seems such a far cry from spontaneous adult speech. A strong argument has been made by Hebb (1949) that the learning of visual forms proceeds over a similar course from slowly learned elements to rapidly combined patterns. Circles and squares, for example, cannot be discriminated at a glance without a slow apprenticeship involving eye movements, successive fixations, and recognition of angles. Hebb proposes that the recognition of visual patterns without eye movement "is possible only as the result of an intensive and prolonged visual training that goes on from the moment of birth, during every moment that the eyes are open, with an increase in skill evident over a period of 12 to 16 years at least."

On the motor side there is likewise a lot to be cumulatively learned. The playing, investigating child slowly finds out the relationships between what he does and what he experiences. He finds out, for instance, how hard he must push what in order to produce what effect. Here the S-R formula is particularly misleading. It would come nearer the truth to say that the child is busy learning R-S connections—the effects that are likely to follow upon his own behavior. But even in this reversed form the notion of bonds or connections would still misrepresent the situation, for it is only a rare specimen of behavior that can properly be conceived as determined by fixed neural channels and a fixed motor response. As Hebb has pointed out, discussing the phenomenon of "motor equivalence" named by Lashley (1942), a rat which has been trained to press a lever will press it with the left forepaw, the right forepaw, by climbing upon it, or by biting it; a monkey will open the lid of a food box with either hand, with a foot, or even with a stick; and we might add that a good baseball player can catch a fly ball while running in almost any direction and while in almost any posture, including leaping in the air and plunging forward to the ground. All of these feats are possible because of a history of learnings in which the main lesson has been the effects of actions upon the stimulus fields that represent the environment. What has been learned is not a fixed connection but a flexible relationship between stimulus fields and the effects that can be produced in them by various kinds of action.

One additional example, drawn this time from Piaget (1952), is particularly worth mentioning because of its importance in theories of development. Piaget points out that a great deal of mental development depends upon the idea that the world is made up of objects having substance and permanence. Without such an "object concept" it would be impossible to build up the ideas of space and causality and to arrive at the fundamental distinction between self and external world. Observation shows that the object concept, "far from being innate or readymade in experience, is constructed little by little." Up to 7 and 8 months the Piaget children searched for vanished objects only in the sense of trying to continue the actions, such as sucking or grasping, in which the objects had played a part. When an object was really out of sight or touch, even if only because it was covered by a cloth, the infants undertook no further exploration. Only gradually, after some study of the displacement of objects by moving, swinging, and dropping them, does the child begin to make an active search for a vanished object, and only still more gradually does he learn, at 12 months or more, to make allowance for the object's sequential displacements and thus to seek it where it has gone rather than where it was last in sight. Thus it is only through cumulative learning that the child arrives at the idea of permanent substantial objects.

The infant's play is indeed serious business. If he did not while away his time pulling strings, shaking rattles, examining wooden parrots, dropping pieces of bread and celluloid swans, when would he learn to discriminate visual patterns, to catch and throw, and to build up his concept of the object? When would he acquire the many other foundation stones necessary for cumulative learning? The more closely we analyze the behavior of the human infant, the more clearly do we realize that infancy is not simply a time when the nervous system matures and the muscles grow stronger. It is a time of active and continuous learning, during which the basis is laid for all those processes, cognitive and motor, whereby the child becomes able to establish effective transactions with his environment and move toward a greater degree of autonomy. Helpless as he may seem until he begins to toddle, he has by that time already made substantial gains in the achievement of competence.

Under primitive conditions survival must depend quite heavily upon achieved competence. We should expect to find things so arranged as to favor and maximize this achievement. Particularly in the case of man, where so little is provided innately and so much has to be learned through experience, we should expect to find highly advantageous arrangements for securing a steady cumulative learning about the properties of the environment and the extent of possible transactions. Under these circumstances we might expect to find a very powerful drive operating to insure progress toward competence, just as the vital goals of nutrition and reproduction are secured by powerful drives, and it might therefore seem paradoxical that the interests of competence should be so much entrusted to times of play and leisurely exploration. There is good reason to suppose, however, that a strong drive would be precisely the wrong arrangement to secure a flexible, knowledgeable power of transaction with the environment. Strong drives cause us to learn certain lessons well, but they do not create maximum familiarity with our surroundings.

This point was demonstrated half a century ago in some experiments by Yerkes and Dodson (1908). They showed that maximum motivation did not lead to the most rapid solving of problems, especially if the problems were complex. For each problem there was an optimum level of motivation, neither the highest nor the lowest, and the optimum was lower for more complex tasks. The same problem has been discussed more recently by Tolman (1948) in his paper on cognitive maps. A cognitive map can be narrow or broad, depending upon the range of cues picked up in the course of learning. Tolman suggests that one of the conditions which tend to narrow the range of cues is a high level of motivation. In everyday terms, a man hurrying to an important business conference is likely to perceive only the cues that help him to get there faster, whereas a man taking a stroll after lunch is likely to pick up a substantial amount of casual information about his environment. The latent learning experiments with animals, and experiments such as those of Johnson (1953) in which drive level has been systematically varied in a situation permitting incidental learning, give strong support to this general idea. In a recent contribution, Bruner, Matter, and Papanek (1955) make a strong case for the concept of breadth of learning and provide additional evidence that it is favored by moderate and hampered by strong motivation. The latter "has the effect of speeding up learning at the cost of narrowing it." Attention is concentrated upon the task at hand and little that is extraneous to this task is learned for future use.

These facts enable us to see the biological appropriateness of an arrangement which uses periods of less intense motivation for the development of competence. This is not to say that the narrower but efficient learnings that go with the reduction of strong drives make no contribution to general effectiveness. They are certainly an important element in capacity to deal with the environment, but a much greater effectiveness results from having this capacity fed also from learnings that take place in quieter times. It is then that the infant can attend to matters of lesser urgency, exploring the properties of things he does not fear and does not need to eat, learning to gauge the force of his string-pulling when the only penalty for failure is silence on the part of the attached rattles, and generally accumulating for himself a broad knowledge and a broad skill in dealing with his surroundings.

8 The human design

HADLEY CANTRIL

With the mounting discussion of "existentialist" and "humanistic" psychology on both sides of the Atlantic, together with the search of political scientists for a psychological interpretation useful for their level of analysis, it seems appropriate to try to spell out what seem to be the demands human beings impose on any society or political culture because of their genetically built-in design. Furthermore, in bringing together recently in summary form the conclusions of a cross-national study of 13 different countries (Cantril, 1965), I kept realizing anew that in describing differences found among people, it is all too easy to neglect basic functional uniformities which take diverse forms and to leave the accounting or explanation at that level. Differences are often dramatic and easier to detect than the similarities they may obscure. Here I shall try to orchestrate the diversities of mankind found in different societies into some systematic unity.

The aspects of "human nature" differentiated here are those that seem to me to be pointed to by the data of psychology and by the observations sensitive observers have made of the way people live their lives in a variety of circumstances. I shall try to use a level of accounting appropriate both to an understanding of people and to an understanding of social and political systems. In doing this some of the absurdities may be avoided that result when a single man-made abstraction, usually devised to account for some single aspect of behavior, is the sole theme song. As the different characteristics of the human design are reviewed here, it must be recognized and emphasized that they all overlap, intertwine and are interdependent. One must differentiate artificially in order to focus and describe.

1. *Man requires the satisfaction of his survival needs.* Any listing of the characteristics of any living organism must begin here. Neurophysiologists have located and described in a most general way two built-in appetitive systems found in higher animals: one system propelling them to seek satisfying and pleasurable experiences, the other protecting them from threatening or unpleasant experiences (Cantril & Livingston, 1963). These two systems together can be thought of as the basic forces contained within all human beings which not only keep them and the species alive as their simple survival needs for food, shelter and sex are gratified, but that are involved in the desire for life itself.

These appetitive systems of course become enormously developed, refined and conditioned, especially in man, as new ways are learned to achieve satisfactions and avoid dangers and discomforts. It has often been noted that unless the survival needs are satisfied, a person devotes himself almost exclusively to a continued attempt to fulfill them, a preoccupation which pre-empts his energies and

Reprinted from the **Journal of Individual Psychology**, 1964, 20, 129–36, with permission of the author and the publisher.

repels any concern for other activities. Most people in the world today are still concerned with living a type of life that constitutes well-being on a relatively simple level with what amenities their cultures can provide.

2. *Man wants security both in its physical and its psychological meaning to protect gains already made and to assure a beachhead from which further advances may be staged.* Man wants some surety that one action can lead to another, some definite prehension which provides an orientation and integration through time. People invariably become embittered if they nurse a dream for what they regard as a long time with no signs of it becoming a reality.

In this connection it should be recalled that the story of evolution seems to tell us that members of every species stake out some territory for themselves within which they can provide for their needs and carry on their living, the extent of this territory being dependent on what is required for the survival of the species and being extended if it will contribute to such survival. In the present era the territories human beings stake out for themselves are largely bounded by the nation-state, a territorial unit rapidly replacing narrower geographical and psychological identifications but doing so just at the time when it is becoming more and more apparent that the concept of nation itself limits and threatens man's development in an age of increasing interdependence and highly developed weaponry.

3. *Man craves sufficient order and certainty in his life to enable him to judge with fair accuracy what will or will not occur if he does or does not act in certain ways.* People want sufficient form and pattern in life to be sure that certain satisfactions already enjoyed will be repeatable and will provide a secure springboard for take-offs in new directions.

The conflict of old loyalties with emerging new loyalties in the case of developing people is bound to create uncertainties, doubts and hesitations. If people become frustrated and anxious enough, they will do almost anything in a desperate attempt to put some order into apparent chaos or rally around new symbols and abstractions that enable them to identify with a new order that promises to alleviate the uncertainties experienced in the here and now.

In stressing process and change, the desire of people to preserve the status quo when it has proved satisfying and rewarding and to protect existing forms against alteration must never be overlooked. And the craving for certainty would include the satisfactions that come from the sense of stability provided by our habitual behavior—including much of our social and political behavior.

4. *Human beings continuously seek to enlarge the range and to enrich the quality of their satisfactions.* There is a ceaseless quest impelling man to extend the range and quality of his satisfactions through the exercise of his creative and inventive capacities. This is, of course, a basic reason why order of any kind is constantly being upset. Whitehead expressed the point eloquently and repeatedly, for example, in his statements that "The essence of life is to be found in the frustrations of established order" (1938, p. 119) and that "The art of progress is to preserve order amid change, and to preserve change amid order" (1929, p. 515).

The distinguished British philosopher John Macmurray has used the phrase *The Self as Agent* as the title of his book

(1957) analyzing the role of action in man's constant search for value-satisfactions. And in a companion volume he has noted that "Human behavior cannot be understood, but only caricatured, if it is represented as an adaptation to environment" (1961, p. 46). The search for an enlargement of satisfactions in the transactions of living can also be phrased as the *desire for development in a direction*, the desire to do something which will bring a sense of accomplishment as we experience the consequences of successfully carrying out some intention, and thereby have an occasional feeling that our lives are continuous creations in which we can take an active part. During a conversation in Beirut, a wise man once remarked to me that "people are hungry for new and good experiences."

It seems worthwhile to differentiate this search for value-satisfactions into two varieties: (a) value-satisfactions that are essentially new, different, more efficient, more reliable, more pleasurable or more status-producing results of activity along familiar and tried dimensions, and (b) value-satisfactions that are new in the sense of being emergent, a new quality a person discovers or creates himself for the first time as does the child who tries out and relishes new experiences as his own developmental pattern unfolds. The former variety, like the growth on the limb of a tree, builds people out and extends their range, while the latter, like the new growth at the top of the tree, lets them attain new heights and see new vistas. The satisfactions sought by a newly developing people are at first most likely to be of the former type.

The particular value-satisfactions man acquires are the result of learning. Some of the values learned will serve as the operative ideals of a people, others will be chiefly instrumental. People in rich countries have learned to want and to expect many aspects of a good life that less favored people have not yet learned are possibilities. From this point of view one might say that the competition between social and political systems is a competition in teaching people what to want, what is potentially available to them and then proving to them in their own private experience that these wants are best attainable under the system described.

5. *Human beings are creatures of hope and are not genetically designed to resign themselves.* This characteristic of man stems from the characteristic just described: that man is always likely to be dissatisfied and never fully "adapts" to his environment.

Man seems continually to hope that the world he encounters will correspond more and more to his vision of it as he acts within it to carry out his purposes, while the vision itself continuously unfolds in an irreversible direction. The whole process is a never-ending one. It is characteristic of man in his on-going experience to ask himself "Where do I go from here?" Only in his more reflective moods does a person ask "Where did I come from?" or "How did I get this way?" Most of the time, most people who are plugged into the changing world around them are future-oriented in their concerns.

6. *Human beings have the capacity to make choices and the desire to exercise this capacity*. Any mechanical model of man constructed by a psychologist or by anyone else is bound to leave out the crucially important characteristic of man as an "appetitive-perceptive agency." Perceptions are learned and utilized by people to provide prognoses or bets of a variety of kinds to weigh alternative

courses of action to achieve purposes. Consciously or without conscious awareness, people are trying to perceive the probable relation between their potential acts and the consequences of these acts to the intentions that constitute their goals.

The human nervous system, including the brain, has the capacity to police its input, to determine what is and what is not significant for it and to pay attention to and to reinforce or otherwise modify its behavior as it transacts in the occasions of living (Cantril & Livingston, 1963). In this sense, the human being is a participant in and producer of his own value-satisfactions: people perceive only what is relevant to their purposes and make their choices accordingly.

7. *Human beings require freedom to exercise the choices they are capable of making.* This characteristic of man related to freedom is deliberately worded as it is, rather than as a blanket statement that "Human beings require freedom," since the freedom people want is so relative to their desires and the stage of development they have attained. Human beings, incidentally, apparently require more freedom than other species of animals because of their much greater capacity to move about and to engage in a much wider variety of behavior.

While it seems true that maximum freedom is a necessary condition if a highly developed individual is to obtain maximum value-satisfaction, it is equally true, as many people have pointed out, that too much freedom too soon can be an unbearable burden and a source of bondage if people, like children, are insufficiently developed to know what to do with it. For freedom clearly involves a learning of responsibility and an ability to take advantage of it wisely.

The concept of freedom is essentially a psychological and not a political concept. It describes the opportunity of an individual to make his own choices and act accordingly. Psychologically, freedom refers to the freedom to experience more of what is potentially available, the freedom to move about and ahead, to be and to become. Freedom is thus less and less determined and more of a reality as man evolves and develops; it emerges and flowers as people learn what it can mean to them in terms of resolving some frustrations under which they are living.

The authoritarian leadership sometimes required to bring about man's awakening and to start him on the road to his definition of progress appears to go against the grain of the human design once man is transformed into a self-conscious citizen who has the desire to exercise the capacity latent within him. The definition of freedom in the Soviet dictionary, *Ushakov*, as "the recognition of necessity" is limited to those periods in the life of an individual or a people when they are willing to let others define what is necessary and to submerge their own individuality.

8. *Human beings want to experience their own identity and integrity,* more popularly referred to as the need for *personal dignity.* Every human being craves a sense of his own self-constancy, an assurance of the repeatability of experience in which he is a determining participant. He obtains this from the transactions he has with other individuals.

People develop significances they share with others in their membership and reference groups. If the satisfaction and significance of participation with others ceases to confirm assumptions or to enrich values, then a person's sense of self-constancy becomes shaken or insecure, his loyalties become formalized and empty or are given up altogether. He becomes alienated or seeks new significances, new loyalties that are more operationally real.

9. *People want to experience a sense of their own worthwhileness.* This differentiation is made from the desire for personal identity and integrity to bring out the important relationship between this search for identity and the behavior and attitudes of others toward us. A human being wants to know he is valued by others and that others will somehow show through their behavior that his own behavior and its consequences make some sort of difference to them in ways that give him a sense of satisfaction. When this occurs, not only is a person's sense of identity confirmed, but he also experiences a sense of personal worth and self-respect. The process of extending the sense of Self both in space and in time appears also to involve the desire that one's "presence" shall not be limited merely to the here and now of existence but will extend into larger dimensions.

People acquire, maintain, and enrich their sense of worthwhileness only if they at least vaguely recognize the sources of what personal identity they have: from their family, their friends and neighbors, their associates or fellow workers, their group ties or their nations. The social, religious, intellectual, regional, or national loyalties formed play the important role of making it possible for individuals to extend themselves backward into the past, forward into the future and to identify themselves with others who live at more or less remote distances from them. This means the compounding of shared experiences into a bundle that can be conceptualized, felt, or somehow referred to in the here and now of daily living, thus making a person feel a functional part of a more enduring alliance. Man accomplishes such feats of self-extension largely through his capacity to create symbols, images, and myths which provide focal points for identification and self-expansion. After reviewing the lessons from history, Herbert Muller noted as one of the "forgotten simplicities" the fact that "Men have always been willing to sacrifice themselves for some larger cause, fighting and dying for their family, tribe, or community, with or without hope of eternal reward" (1954, p. 392).

10. *Human beings seek some value or system of beliefs to which they can commit themselves.* In the midst of the probabilities and uncertainties that surround them, people want some anchoring points, some certainties, some faith that will serve either as a beacon light to guide them or a balm to assuage them during the inevitable frustrations and anxieties living engenders.

People who have long been frustrated and who have searched for means to alleviate their situations are, of course, particularly susceptible to a commitment to a new system of beliefs or an ideology that they feel holds promise of effective action.

Beliefs are confirmed in so far as action based on them brings satisfying consequences and they are denied with growing skepticism if disastrous results consistently occur because they are followed.

Commitment to a value or belief system becomes more difficult among well-informed and sophisticated people who self-consciously try to reconcile what they believe with what they know and what they know with what they believe. In such circumstances, beliefs become more and more secular and less important as personal identifications.

11. *Human beings want a sense of surety and confidence that the society of which they are a part holds out a fair degree of hope that their aspirations will be fulfilled.* If people cannot experience the effectivity of social mechanisms to accomplish some of the potential goals they aspire to, then obviously their frustrations and anxieties mount, they search for new means to accomplish aims. On the other hand, they make any sacrifice required to protect a society they feel is fulfilling their needs but appears seriously threatened.

It cannot be stressed too strongly that any people will become apathetic toward or anxious about ultimate goals they would like to achieve through social organizations if they continually sense a lack of reliability in the means provided to accomplish these goals. Obviously any society that is to be viable must satisfy basic survival needs, must provide security, must insure the repeatability of value-satisfactions already attained and provide for new and emerging satisfactions. The effective society is one that enables the individual to develop personal loyalties and aspirations which overlap with and are congenial to social values and loyalties, and which at the same time take full account of the wide range of individual differences that exist.

Such a social organization must, too, become the repository of values, must provide symbols for people's aspirations, must comprise and contain customs, institutions, laws, economic arrangements and political forms which enable an individual in various ways to give concrete reference to his values in his day-to-day behavior. If the gap between what his society actually provides in terms of effective mechanisms for living and what it purports to provide becomes too great, the vacuum created will sooner or later engender the frustrations that urge people on to seek new social patterns and new symbols. Whitehead wrote:

> The major advances in civilization are processes which all but wreck the societies in which they occur—like unto an arrow in the hand of a child. The art of free society consists first in the maintenance of the symbolic code; and secondly in fearlessness of revision, to secure that the code serves those purposes which satisfy an enlightened reason. Those societies which cannot combine reverence to their symbols with freedom of revision, must ultimately decay either from anarchy, or from the slow atrophy of a life stifled by useless shadows (1927, p. 88).

Every social and political system can be regarded as an experiment in the broad perspective of time. Whatever the experiment, the human design will in the long run force any experiment to accommodate it. This has been the case throughout human history. And few would deny that the varied patterns of experiments going on today hold out more promise of satisfying the human condition for a greater number of people than ever before.

II CULTURE, LEARNING, AND GROUP IDENTIFICATION

Most human behavior occurs through contact with an ever-present environment. The fact that people populate this environment insures that much behavior will emerge from processes generally labeled social learning (see Bandura & Walters, 1963). As the person behaves and develops in a social world, his performances become increasingly tied to the social-cultural milieu of which he is a part. The cultural agents with whom he interacts, the symbols he encounters, and the particular groups with which he comes to be identified, all work, however subtly and unconsciously, to mold and control his actions. As Cooley (1922) and Mead (1934), among others, have shown, the controlling features of the social-cultural environment are gradually internalized by the person in the form of habits, beliefs, values, and other dispositions. Even in the absence of direct influence by others, therefore, his conduct is directed by symbolic representations of the social world.

The varied processes by which these normative controls become internalized are generally summarized by the term socialization. The groups with which a person is associated and the individuals with whom he interacts in the course of a lifetime are the "agents" of socialization.

All this is well known, of course. The importance of group identifications has long been recognized, and psychologists, anthropologists, and sociologists have extensively documented interpersonal diversities linked with different group affiliations (see Kluckhohn, 1954). What a person is and does can be seen as proceeding, very largely, from the features of groups, real or imagined, to which he belongs, refers himself, or aspires. While not always used so broadly, the concept of the reference group is a useful tool for comprehending these matters. In his paper in this section, Shibutani demonstrates its utility as a vehicle for illuminating phenomena of social control in a pluralistic society.

In such a society, a variety of groups are available to the person for reference. Consequently, his behavior is unlikely to come under the exclusive sway of any single group. Which perspectives are chosen and which, of those chosen, have greater significance, vary with the person's attraction and sentiments relative to given groups and their members. Shifts in reference are likely, as Shibutani points out here and elsewhere (1961, 1962), as the conditions for attraction and sentiment shift, although certain early and enduring identifications doubtless play major parts in a person's life.

With regard to socialization, it follows that no single agent will be totally responsible for the whole process, though some, such as parents, will be more important than others. One may also expect changes in the salience of agents in the face of changing circumstances, as, for instance, when the adolescent turns from his parents to his peer group as a normative reference.

Whatever may be its specific attributes and membership, the reference group is a primary source of a person's "premises for action" and these premises or perspectives, as Shibutani calls them, regulate his behavior. Whether the group be a family, a neighborhood gang, a social class, or a society, the individual's behavior is organized with reference to the group's perspectives and these perspectives, in turn, are based in the group's "culture."

Care must be taken, however, to avoid the error of many social theorists, among whom Freud was not the least, who have pictured the relation between culture and the person as basically negative. According to such views culture operates mainly as a barrier to expressions of Man's egocentric predilections. By contrast, Gardner offers a different conception here of Man's nature that permits description of the interrelation of society and the individual in terms of the positive contributions of culture to human life.

For Gardner, Man in his nature is a rationalizing, if not a rational being. The theme of human existence, in his eyes, is a continuing quest for meaning, a search for identity, growing from a fundamental personal need for a serviceable definition of reality and an understanding of relations between self and world. Culture, with its perspectives, is an indispensable guide to, and source of, the meanings essential to sentient Men.

From a distinctively humanistic posture, then, Gardner emphasizes the central value of the individual. Yet, Man at the same time is a social being possessed of responsibilities extending beyond himself, though still aware of and sometimes troubled by his individuality. In contrast with traditional Man, embedded in his culture and indistinguishable from it, Gardner perceives modern Man caught in the perplexing cross-currents of self and non-self. Often the resolution of Man's need for a stable identity takes the form of an alienation from society. But Gardner can discern a basis for a mature conception of self as a component of society leading to a creative appreciation of culture as a means to human ends.

Some of these points will be treated further in Section III, and it might be said that many of the thinkers represented in this volume share, in its essentials, Gardner's view of the human condition and predicament. Cantril and White in Section I, Allport in Section III, Festinger in Section VII are a few of them. At any rate, with the evident dependence of individual behavior upon group characteristics it is hardly surprising that social psychologists often refer to culture in their attempts to account for social behavior. Despite the concept's widespread use, however, it has not always been clear exactly what culture is. The paper here by Murdock addresses itself to this issue in the form of a characterization of the nature of culture and how it changes in time.

First of all, Murdock asserts, cultures are learned. They constitute "systems of collective habits" and are dynamic in form, changing in response to both internal and external functional requirements. Moreover, with time and circumstance, cultures tend to differentiate themselves into variant- or sub-cultures reflecting different conditions of life within the compass of the larger system.

Whether culture is to be thought of as "real" or only as an abstraction is not at issue in Murdock's paper, although it is a subject for lively debate among anthropologists, as a reading of Leslie White's article on the concept of culture (1959) or his book, *The Science of Culture* (1949), will reveal. However, Murdock does treat as problematic the "social sharing of habits" and to account for it he invokes the socialization process dealt with at length in the three remaining papers of this section. In doing so, he draws an important distinction between culture and social behavior. Culture, he points out, is found not in behavior itself, but in the "collective habits" underlying it.

Actual behavior, however, is critical to cultural change for change arises from persistent deviations of behavior from existing norms. Murdock provides a discussion of several processes of cultural change, emphasizing the phenomenon of cultural borrowing through contact, and indicates the various conditions under which it proceeds. After a discussion of "cultural lag"—the disjunction between the acceptance of an innovation and its integration into the cultural pattern—he ends by underscoring the adaptive functions of culture and its linkage with "conditions of existence."

In this view cultures do not exist in isolation; rather, they represent, partly anyway, techniques by which people accommodate themselves to the demands of their environments, including technological, economic, and other facets of them. The "present-time orientation" of the American lower class, as one example, may be a cultural characteristic directly tied to emphases upon immediate gratification fostered by comparative economic insecurity.

These ideas have significant implications for social learning and socialization that are frequently overlooked. Among other things, it has been suggested (Hunt, 1961) that specific socialization practices may be a function of particular conditions of life such that they are not "chosen," but are required by situational demands. Whether this be the case or not, it is true that most analyses of social learning and socialization rarely attempt to connect these processes with environmental factors. As the anthropologist David Aberle (1961) has observed, studies of socialization commonly stop with efforts to show the impact of child-rearing on personality. Child-rearing practices are usually taken as causes and personality as an effect (cf. Whiting & Child, 1953; and Sears, Maccoby, & Levin, 1957). However, it is equally useful, he suggests, to examine the causes of socialization practices themselves. The query he poses is, "Why do members of a particular system show uniformities in socialization rather than randomness?" The answer obviously must reside in controlling conditions common to many learning situations—a community or culture. Socialization and psychological representations of culture thus may be conceptualized as *dependent* variables changing in response to variations in cultural independent variables. The fact that often, as psychologists, we choose simply to take the latter as "givens" does not alter this progression.

In either event, socialization practices may be studied in relation to themselves and other cultural-environmental circumstances or in relation to personality and behavior. By the same token, processes of learning may be considered as independent variables controlling behavior, or as dependent variables contingent upon other antecedent cultural and extra-cultural factors. With varying emphases, the three remaining papers in this section look at socialization in both these ways.

Gordon is mainly concerned with cultural responses to "environmental" events in the form of extensive immigration by culturally alien groups, such as took place in nineteenth- and early twentieth-century America. In this context socialization has to do with the processes by which such persons and groups achieve assimilation of and to an existing social-cultural pattern. It becomes clear from Gordon's treatment that the details of such processes depend upon the nature of the prevailing pattern and the relations between it and the properties of the immigrant culture.

Seven variables are identified by Gordon as involved in the assimilation process, and he uses them to identify types or stages of assimilation. Applying his seven-variable model to the analysis of four American "minority" ethnic groups, he shows that the American experience has been primarily one of their gradual, if uneven and incomplete, adaptation to a prevailing Anglo-Saxon core society. The fabled American melting pot apparently did little melting and produced no real blending of "old" and "new" cultural forms; instead it worked effectively to "transmute" the latter into the former.

The fact that America today displays a variety of sub-societies, Gordon attributes, for one thing, to a slower and more difficult absorption of and by immigrants of existing Anglo-Saxon structural patterns as compared with cultural ones. A major consequence of this is the pluralism to which Shibutani gives prominence.

Along with the ethnic, religious and similar sub-societies featured in Gordon's writing are others, some of which are associated with the so-called vertical organization of society. It is with these that the papers by Himmelweit and Bronfenbrenner are chiefly concerned.

The heart of Himmelweit's paper has to do with socialization as a function of socio-economic classification, although she also touches upon matters pertinent to notions of national character (see Kardiner, *et al.*, 1945). The social classes that figure so prominently in Himmelweit's work, and in Bronfenbrenner's too, can each be thought of as cultures or reference groups at least partly different from other groups with which they may be socially and/or geographically contiguous. Their agents will tend to employ socialization practices consistent with the group's culture and will convey similarly consistent behavioral standards. What these standards and practices are in relation to particular groups is basic to Himmelweit's theme. Her discussion of "upward mobility" is an excellent illustration of the reference group in action, making plain that a socializing agency may dispense perspectives associated with groups other than the nominal membership group. In the groups studied by Himmelweit and her associates this happenstance apparently had favorable ramifications, but there are probably other circumstances where it may lead to conflict (see Gursslin, Hunt, & Roach, 1959).

Where Himmelweit concentrates on generalities in socialization, Bronfenbrenner puts his stress upon the formulation of theoretical propositions having to do with dimensions of the immediate socialization relationship. In underscoring the general patterning of parent-child relations by practices prevailing in the community, he brings into focus the effects upon the object of socialization of variations in the practices employed. Thus, the specific practices of given agents may be analyzed in relation to a matrix of social-biological factors (e.g., age, sex, social class, etc.) and evaluated in terms of a constant set of psychological criteria. Bronfenbrenner's paper also directs attention to what can be called "by-products" of socialization, i.e., more general and individualized psychological effects upon the person of interaction with specific persons engaging in specific modes of behavior in specific familial contexts.

Bronfenbrenner's survey of current directions in socialization raises provocative questions about modern child-rearing practices. Presently popular psychological methods of discipline, permissive socialization climates, and love-oriented training techniques seem to yield a mixed bag of consequences when these are measured against our prevailing values. Bronfenbrenner stresses the structure of socialization and the role of fathers in its context. He describes some of the apparent ambivalent results for personality development of shifts toward more mother-centered families (a matter of vital interest to Pettigrew in Section III), and the emergence of "democratic" family structures.

Looking into the future, Bronfenbrenner cites Miller and Swanson's work (1958) with "bureaucratic" and "entrepreneurial" families and discusses their suggestion that contemporary American societal trends are in the bureaucratic direction. The social values most salient in such systems have to do with "getting along" in contrast with the entrepreneurial zeal for "getting ahead." Therefore, if Miller and Swanson are correct, we should be witness to the appearance of more equalitarian families and the increased production of the organization men whom we shall discuss further in Section IX. Bronfenbrenner, however, fortunately or not as one might choose, sees reason to temper Miller and Swanson's forecast. He points to apparently opposite tendencies toward familial processes calculated to maximize the achievement drives discussed by McClelland in Section I. Whatever its predictive value, Bronfenbrenner's analysis serves well in providing an orientation to the interplay of culture, family structure, socialization, and personality.

In sum, this section presents some prominent thought apropos the effects upon the person of his social-cultural surroundings. What is talked about is commonly represented under the rubric of personality and culture or, more recently, personality-in-culture. It is probably a fair statement that the guiding perspective of this rubric sees behavior under the rule of personality which, in turn, represents features of culture (cf. Kluckhohn & Mowrer, 1944; Kluckhohn & Murray, 1953; Child, 1954; Whiting, 1961; Hsu, 1961). This section and the next one dealing more directly with treatments of personality as a "variable" in psychological theory are, therefore, interlocking. Whatever personality may be thought to be, it has an inescapable social-culture basis.

9 Reference groups as perspectives

TAMOTSU SHIBUTANI

Although Hyman coined the term scarcely more than a decade ago, the concept of reference group has become one of the central analytic tools in social psychology, being used in the construction of hypotheses concerning a variety of social phenomena. The inconsistency in behavior as a person moves from one social context to another is accounted for in terms of a change in reference groups; the exploits of juvenile delinquents, especially in interstitial areas, are being explained by the expectations of peer-group gangs; modifications in social attitudes are found to be related to changes in associations. The concept has been particularly useful in accounting for the choices made among apparent alternatives, particularly where the selections seem to be contrary to the "best interests" of the actor. Status problems—aspirations of social climbers, conflicts in group loyalty, the dilemmas of marginal men—have also been analyzed in terms of reference groups, as have the differential sensitivity and reaction of various segments of an audience to mass communication. It is recognized that the same generic processes are involved in these phenomenally diverse events, and the increasing popularity of the concept attests to its utility in analysis.

As might be expected during the exploratory phases in any field of inquiry, however, there is some confusion involved in the use of this concept, arising largely from vagueness of signification. The available formal definitions are inconsistent, and sometimes formal definitions are contradicted in usage. The fact that social psychologists can understand one another in spite of these ambiguities, however, implies an intuitive recognition of some central meaning, and an explicit statement of this will enhance the utility of the concept as an analytic tool. The literature reveals that all discussions of reference groups involve some identifiable grouping to which an actor is related in some manner and the norms and values shared in that group. However, the relationship between these three terms is not always clear. Our initial task, then, is to examine the conceptions of reference group implicit in actual usage, irrespective of formal definitions.

One common usage of the concept is in the designation of that group which serves as the point of reference in making comparisons or contrasts, especially in forming judgments about one's self. In the original use of the concept Hyman spoke of reference groups as points of comparison in evaluating one's own status, and he found that the estimates varied according to the group with which the respondent compared himself. Merton and Kitt, in their reformulation of Stouffer's theory of relative deprivation, also use the concept in this manner; the judgments of rear-echelon soldiers overseas concerning their fate

Reprinted from the **American Journal of Sociology**, 1955, 60, 562–70, with permission of the author and the University of Chicago Press.

varied, depending upon whether they compared themselves to soldiers who were still at home or men in combat. They also propose concrete research operations in which respondents are to be asked to compare themselves with various groups. The study of aspiration levels by Chapman and Volkmann, frequently cited in discussions of reference-group theory, also involves variations in judgment arising from a comparison of one's own group with others (Hyman, 1942; Merton, *et al.*, 1950; and Chapman, *et al.*, 1939). In this mode of application, then, a reference group is a standard or check point which an actor uses in forming his estimate of the situation, particularly his own position within it. Logically, then, *any* group with which an actor is familiar may become a reference group.

A second referent of the concept is that group in which the actor aspires to gain or maintain acceptance: hence, a group whose claims are paramount in situations requiring choice. The reference group of the socially ambitious is said to consist of people of higher strata whose status symbols are imitated. Merton and Kitt interpret the expressions of willingness and felt readiness for combat on the part of inexperienced troops, as opposed to the humility of battle-hardened veterans, as the efforts of newcomers to identify themselves with veterans to whom they had mistakenly imputed certain values. Thus, the concept is used to point to an association of human beings among whom one seeks to gain, maintain, or enhance his status; a reference group is that group in which one desires to participate.

In a third usage the concept signifies that group whose perspective constitutes the frame of reference of the actor. Thus, Sherif speaks of reference groups as groups whose norms are used as anchoring points in structuring the perceptual field (1953), and Merton and Kitt speak of a "social frame of reference" for interpretations (1950). Through direct or vicarious participation in a group one comes to perceive the world from its standpoint. Yet this group need not be one in which he aspires for acceptance; a member of some minority group may despise it but still see the world largely through its eyes. When used in this manner, the concept of reference group points more to a psychological phenomenon than to an objectively existing group of men; it refers to an organization of the actor's experience. That is to say, it is a structuring of his perceptual field. In this usage a reference group becomes any collectivity, real or imagined, envied or despised, whose perspective is assumed by the actor.

Thus, an examination of current usage discloses three distinct referents for a single concept: (1) groups which serve as comparison points; (2) groups to which men aspire; and (3) groups whose perspectives are assumed by the actor. Although these terms may be related, treating together what should be clearly delineated as generically different can lead only to further confusion. It is the contention of this paper that the restriction of the concept of reference group to the third alternative —that group whose perspective constitutes the frame of reference of the actor —will increase its usefulness in research. Any group or object may be used for comparisons, and one need not assume the role of those with whom he compares his fate; hence, the first usage serves a quite different purpose and may be eliminated from further consideration. Under some circumstances, however, group loyalties and aspirations are related to perspectives assumed, and the character of this relationship calls for further exploration. Such a discussion necessitates a restatement of the familiar, but, in view of the difficulties in some of the work on reference groups, repetition may not be entirely out of order. In spite of the enthusiasm of some proponents there is actually nothing new in reference-group theory.

Culture and personal controls

Thomas pointed out many years ago that what a man does depends largely upon his definition of the situation. One may add that the manner in which one consistently defines a succession of situations depends upon his organized perspective. A perspective is an ordered view of one's world—what is taken for granted about the attributes of various objects, events, and human nature. It is an order of things remembered and expected as well as things actually perceived, an organized conception of what is plausible and what is possible; it constitutes the matrix through which one perceives his environment. The fact that men have such ordered perspectives enables them to conceive of their ever changing world as relatively stable, orderly, and predictable. As Riezler puts it, one's perspective is an outline scheme which, running ahead of experience, defines and guides it.

There is abundant experimental evidence to show that perception is selective; that the organization of perceptual experience depends in part upon what is anticipated and what is taken for granted. Judgments rest upon perspectives, and people with different outlooks define identical situations differently, responding selectively to the environment. Thus, a prostitute and a social worker walking through a slum area notice different things; a sociologist should perceive relationships that others fail to observe. Any change of perspectives—becoming a parent for the first time, learning that one will die in a few months, or suffering the failure of well-laid plans—leads one to notice things previously overlooked and to see the familiar world in a different light. As Goethe contended, history is continually rewritten, not so much because of the discovery of new documentary evidence, but because the changing perspectives of historians lead to new selections from the data.

Culture, as the concept is used by Redfield, refers to a perspective that is shared by those in a particular group; it consists of those "conventional understandings, manifest in act and artifact, that characterize societies" (Redfield, 1941; Mandelbaum, 1949). Since these conventional understandings are the premises of action, those who share a common culture engage in common modes of action. Culture is not a static entity but a continuing process; norms are creatively reaffirmed from day to day in social interaction. Those taking part in collective transactions approach one another with set expectations, and the realization of what is anticipated successively confirms and reinforces their perspectives. In this way, people in each cultural group are continuously supporting one another's perspectives, each by responding to the others in expected ways. In this sense culture is a product of communication.

In his discussion of endopsychic social control Mead spoke of men "taking the role of the generalized other," meaning by that that each person approaches his world from the standpoint of the culture of his group. Each perceives, thinks, forms judgments, and controls himself according to the frame of reference of the group in which he is participating. Since he defines objects, other people, the world, and himself from the perspective that he shares with others, he can visualize his proposed line of action from this generalized standpoint, anticipate the reactions of others, inhibit undesirable impulses, and thus guide his conduct. The socialized person is a society in miniature; he sets the same standards of conduct for himself as he sets for others, and he judges himself in the same terms. He can define situations properly and meet his obligations, even in the absence of other people, because, as already noted, his perspective always takes into account the expectations of others. Thus, it is the ability to define situations from the same standpoint as others that makes personal controls possible (Mead, 1925, 1934; Parsons, 1952). When Mead spoke of assuming the role of the generalized other, he was not referring to people but to perspectives shared with others in a transaction.

The consistency in the behavior of a man in a wide variety of social contexts is to be accounted for, then, in terms of his organized perspective. Once one has incorporated a particular outlook from his group, it becomes his orientation toward the world, and he brings this frame of reference to bear on all new situations. Thus, immigrants and tourists often misinterpret the strange things they see, and a disciplined Communist would define each situation differently from the non-Communist. Although reference-group behavior is generally studied in situations where choices seem possible, the actor himself is often unaware that there are alternatives.

The proposition that men think, feel, and see things from a standpoint peculiar to the group in which they participate is an old one, repeatedly emphasized by students of anthropology and of the sociology of knowledge. Why, then, the sudden concern with reference-group theory during the past decade? The concept of reference group actually introduces a minor refinement in the long familiar theory, made necessary by the special characteristics of modern mass societies. First of all, in modern societies special problems arise from the fact that men sometimes use the standards of groups in which they are *not* recognized members, sometimes of groups in which they have never participated directly, and sometimes of groups that do not exist at all. Second, in our mass society, characterized as it is by cultural pluralism, each person internalizes several perspectives, and this occasionally gives rise to embarassing dilemmas which call for systematic study. Finally, the development of reference-group theory has been facilitated by the increasing interest in social psychology and the subjective aspects of group life, a shift from a predominant concern with objective social structures to an interest in the experiences of the participants whose regularized activities make such structures discernible.

A reference group, then, is that group whose outlook is used by the actor as the frame of reference in the organization of his preceptual field. All kinds of groupings, with great variations in size, composition, and structure, may become reference groups. Of greatest importance for most people are those groups in which they participate directly—what have been called membership groups—especially those containing a number of persons with whom one stands in a primary relationship. But in some transactions one may assume the perspective attributed to some social category—a social class, an ethnic group, those in a given community, or those concerned with some special interest. On the other hand, reference groups may be imaginary, as in the case of artists who are "born ahead of their times," scientists who work for "humanity," or philanthropists who give for "posterity." Such persons estimate their endeavors from a postulated perspective imputed to people who have not yet been born. There are others who live for a distant past, idealizing some period in history and longing for "the good old days," criticizing current events from a standpoint imputed to people long since dead. Reference groups, then, arise through the internalization of norms; they constitute the structure of expectations imputed to some audience for whom one organizes his conduct.

The construction of social worlds

As Dewey emphasized, society exists in and through communication; common perspectives—common cultures—emerge through participation in common communication channels. It is through social participation that perspectives shared in a group are internalized. Despite the frequent recitation of this proposition, its full implications, especially for the analysis of mass societies, are not often appreciated. Variations in outlook arise through differential contact and association; the maintenance of social distance—through segregation, conflict, or simply the reading of different literature—leads to the formation of distinct cultures. Thus, people in different social classes develop different modes of life and outlook, not because of anything inherent in economic position, but because similarity of occupation and limitations set by income level dispose them to certain restricted communication channels. Those in different ethnic groups form their own distinctive cultures because their identifications incline them to interact intimately with each other and to maintain reserve before outsiders. Different intellectual traditions within social psychology—psychoanalysis, scale analysis, *Gestalt*, pragmatism—will remain separated as long as those in each tradition restrict their sympathetic attention to works of their own school and view others with contempt or hostility. Some social scientists are out of touch with the masses of the American people because they eschew the mass media, especially television, or expose themselves only condescendingly. Even the outlook that the *avant-garde* regards as "cosmopolitan" is culture-bound, for it also is a product of participation in restricted communication channels—books, magazines, meetings, exhibits, and taverns which are out of bounds for most people in the middle classes. Social participation may even be vicarious, as it is in the case of a medievalist who acquires his perspective solely through books.

Even casual observation reveals the amazing variety of standards by which Americans live. The inconsistencies and contradictions which characterize modern mass societies are products of the multitude of communication channels and the ease of participation in them. Studying relatively isolated societies, anthropologists can speak meaningfully of "culture areas" in geographical terms; in such societies common cultures have a territorial base, for only those who live together can interact. In modern industrial societies, however, because of the development of rapid transportation and the media of mass communication, people who are geographically dispersed can communicate effectively. Culture areas are coterminous with communication channels; since communication networks are no longer coterminous with territorial boundaries, culture areas overlap and have lost their territorial bases. Thus, next-door neighbors may be complete strangers; even in common parlance there is an intuitive recognition of the diversity of perspectives, and we speak meaningfully of people living in different social worlds—the academic world, the world of children, the world of fashion.

Modern mass societies, indeed, are made up of a bewildering variety of social worlds. Each is an organized outlook, built up by people in their interaction with one another; hence, each communication channel gives rise to a separate world. Probably the greatest sense of identification and solidarity is to be found in the various communal structures—the underworld, ethnic minorities, the social elite. Such communities are frequently spatially segregated, which isolates them further from the outer world, while the "grapevine" and foreign-language presses provide internal contacts. Another common type of social world consists of the associational structures—the world of medicine, of organized labor, of the theater, of café society. These are held together not only by various voluntary associations within each locality but also by periodicals like *Variety*, specialized journals, and feature sections in newspapers. Finally, there are the loosely connected universes of special interest—the world of sports, of the stamp collector, of the daytime serial—serviced by mass media programs and magazines like *Field and Stream*. Each of these worlds is a unity of order, a universe of regularized mutual response. Each is an area in which there is some structure which permits reasonable anticipation of the behavior of others, hence, an area in which one may act with a sense of security and confidence (Riezler, 1950; Landgrebe, 1940; Schuetz, 1944). Each social world, then, is a culture area, the boundaries of which are set neither by territory nor by formal group membership but by the limits of effective communication.

Since there is a variety of communication channels, differing in stability and extent, social worlds differ in composition, size, and the territorial distribution of the participants. Some, like local cults, are small and concentrated; others, like the intellectual world, are vast and the participants dispersed. Worlds differ in the extent and clarity of their boundaries; each is confined by some kind of horizon, but this may be wide or narrow, clear or vague. The fact that social worlds are not coterminous with the universe of men is recognized; those in the underworld are well aware of the fact that outsiders do not share their values. Worlds differ in exclusiveness and in the extent to which they demand the loyalty of their participants. Most important of all, social worlds are not static entities; shared perspectives are continually being reconstituted. Worlds come into existence with the establishment of communication channels; when life conditions change, social relationships may also change, and these worlds may disappear.

Every social world has some kind of

communication system—often nothing more than differential association—in which there develops a special universe of discourse, sometimes an argot. Special meanings and symbols further accentuate differences and increase social distance from outsiders. In each world there are special norms of conduct, a set of values, a special prestige ladder, characteristic career lines, and a common outlook toward life—a Weltanschauung. In the case of elites there may even arise a code of honor which holds only for those who belong, while others are dismissed as beings somewhat less than human from whom bad manners may be expected. A social world, then, is an order conceived which serves as the stage on which each participant seeks to carve out his career and to maintain and enhance his status.

One of the characteristics of life in modern mass societies is simultaneous participation in a variety of social worlds. Because of the ease with which the individual may expose himself to a number of communication channels, he may lead a segmentalized life, participating successively in a number of unrelated activities. Furthermore, the particular combination of social worlds differs from person to person; this is what led Simmel to declare that each stands at that point at which a unique combination of social circles intersects. The geometric analogy is a happy one, for it enables us to conceive the numerous possibilities of combinations and the different degrees of participation in each circle. To understand what a man does, we must get at his unique perspective—what he takes for granted and how he defines the situation—but in mass societies we must learn in addition the social world in which he is participating in a given act.

Loyalty and selective responsiveness

In a mass society where each person internalizes numerous perspectives there are bound to be some incongruities and conflicts. The overlapping of group affiliation and participation, however, need not lead to difficulties and is usually unnoticed. The reference groups of most persons are mutually sustaining. Thus, the soldier who volunteers for hazardous duty on the battlefield may provoke anxiety in his family but is not acting contrary to their values; both his family and his comrades admire courage and disdain cowardice. Behavior may be inconsistent, as in the case of the proverbial office tyrant who is meek before his wife, but it is not noticed if the transactions occur in dissociated contexts. Most people live more or less compartmentalized lives, shifting from one social world to another as they participate in a succession of transactions. In each world their roles are different, their relations to other participants are different, and they reveal a different facet of their personalities. Men have become so accustomed to this mode of life that they manage to conceive of themselves as reasonably consistent human beings in spite of this segmentalization and are generally not aware of the fact that their acts do not fit into a coherent pattern.

People become acutely aware of the existence of different outlooks only when they are successively caught in situations in which conflicting demands are made upon them, all of which cannot possibly be satisfied. While men generally avoid making difficult decisions, these dilemmas and contradictions of status may force a choice between two social worlds. These conflicts are essentially alternative ways of defining the same situation, arising from several possible perspectives. In the words of William James, "As a man I pity you, but as an official I must show you no mercy; as a politician I regard him as an ally, but as a moralist I loathe him." In playing roles in different social worlds, one imputes different expectations to others whose differences cannot always be compromised. The problem is that of selecting the perspective for defining the situation. In Mead's terminology, which generalized other's role is to be taken? It is only in situations where alternative definitions are possible that problems of loyalty arise.

Generally such conflicts are ephemeral; in critical situations contradictions otherwise unnoticed are brought into the open, and painful choices are forced. In poorly integrated societies, however, some people find themselves continually beset with such conflicts. The Negro intellectual, children of mixed marriages or of immigrants, the foreman in a factory, the professional woman, the military chaplain—all live in the interstices of well-organized structures and are marginal men (cf. Hughes, 1945; Stonequist, 1937). In most instances they manage to make their way through their compartmentalized lives, although personal maladjustments are apparently frequent. In extreme cases amnesia and dissociation of personality can occur.

Much of the interest in reference groups arises out of concern with situations in which a person is confronted with the necessity of choosing between two or more organized perspectives. The hypothesis has been advanced that the choice of reference groups—conformity to the norms of the group whose perspective is assumed—is a function of one's interpersonal relations; to what extent the culture of a group serves as the matrix for the organization of perceptual experience depends upon one's relationship and personal loyalty to others who share that outlook. Thus, when personal relations to others in the group deteriorate, as sometimes happens in a military unit after continued defeat, the norms become less binding, and the unit may disintegrate in panic. Similarly, with the transformation of personal relationships between parent and child in late adolescence, the desires and standards of the parents often become less obligatory.

It has been suggested further that choice of reference groups rests upon personal loyalty to significant others of that social world. "Significant others," for Sullivan, are those persons directly responsible for the internalization of norms. Socialization is a product of a gradual accumulation of experiences with certain people, particularly those with whom we stand in primary relations, and significant others are those who are actually involved in the cultivation of abilities, values, and outlook (1947). Crucial, apparently, is the character of one's emotional ties with them. Those who think the significant others have treated them with affection and consideration have a sense of personal obligation that is binding under all circumstances, and they will be loyal even at great personal sacrifice. Since primary relations are not necessarily satisfactory, however, the reactions may be negative. A person who is well aware of the expectations of significant others may go out of his way to reject them. This may account for the bifurcation of orientation in minority groups, where some remain loyal to the parental culture while others seek desperately to become assimilated in the larger world. Some who withdraw from the uncertainties of real life may establish loyalties to perspectives acquired through vicarious relationships with characters encountered in books (Grinker, *et al.*, 1945; Shils, *et al.*, 1948).

Perspectives are continually subjected to the test of reality. All perception is hypothetical. Because of what is taken for granted from each standpoint, each situation is approached with a set of expectations; if transactions actually take place as anticipated, the perspective itself is reinforced. It is thus the confirming responses of other people that provide support for perspectives (Mead, 1938; Postman, 1951). But in mass societies the responses of others vary, and in the study of reference groups the problem is that of ascertaining *whose* confirming responses will sustain a given point of view.

The study of mass societies

Because of the differentiated character of modern mass societies, the concept of reference group, or some suitable substitute, will always have a central place in any realistic conceptual scheme for its analysis. As is pointed out above, it will be most useful if it is used to designate that group whose perspective is assumed by the actor as the frame of reference for the organization of his perceptual experience. Organized perspectives arise in and become shared through participation in common communication channels, and the diversity of mass societies arises from the multiplicity of channels and the ease with which one may participate in them.

Mass societies are not only diversified and pluralistic but also continually changing. The successive modification of life-conditions compels changes in social relationships, and any adequate analysis requires a study of these transformational processes themselves. Here the concept of reference group can be of crucial importance. For example, all forms of social mobility, from sudden conversions to gradual assimilation, may be regarded essentially as displacements of reference groups, for they involve a loss of responsiveness to the demands of one social world and the adoption of the perspective of another. It may be hypothesized that the disaffection occurs first on the level of personal relations, followed by a weakening sense of obligation, a rejection of old claims, and the establishment of new loyalties and incorporation of a new perspective. The conflicts that characterize all persons in marginal roles are of special interest in that they provide opportunities for cross-sectional analyses of the processes of social change.

In the analysis of the behavior of men in mass societies the crucial problem is that of ascertaining how a person defines the situation, which perspective he uses in arriving at such a definition, and who constitutes the audience whose responses provide the necessary confirmation and support for his position. This calls for focusing attention upon the expectations the actor imputes to others, the communication channels in which he participates, and his relations with those with whom he identifies himself. In the study of conflict, imagery provides a fertile source of data. At moments of indecision, when in doubt and confusion, who appears in imagery? In this manner the significant other can be identified.

An adequate analysis of modern mass societies requires the development of concepts and operations for the description of the manner in which each actor's orientation toward his world is successively reconstituted. Since perception is selective and perspectives differ, different items are noticed and a progressively diverse set of images arises, even among those exposed to the same media of mass communication. The concept of reference group summarizes differential associations and loyalties and thus facilitates the study of selective perception. It becomes, therefore, an indispensable tool for comprehending the diversity and dynamic character of the kind of society in which we live.

10 Individuality, commitment, and meaning

JOHN W. GARDNER

Estrangement for all

If one had to select a single conception that is central to the consensus in our own society, it would be the idea of the dignity and worth of the individual. The individual is not just so many pounds of assorted chemicals plus a bucket of water. He is not just a link in a genetic chain or an element in a biological-social system. He is not just a "resource" (as in the phrase "human resources") that may be used to strengthen the social group. There is not only something important about him, there is something inviolable. At the most basic level this involves a right to life and to security of person; but it involves much more. There are limits beyond which his privacy should not be invaded, his individuality not threatened, his dignity not impaired.

Yet man is a social being, and to talk about individuality without talking about the social system that makes it possible is to talk nonsense. It will be useful for us to examine more closely the relationship of the individual to the group.

Most human beings who have trod the earth have been rather completely embedded in the culture of their tribe or community. The testimony of historians on earlier periods and of anthropologists on contemporary primitive societies agrees on this point. The man embedded in a traditional society hardly thinks of himself as separate or separable from his group. He is engulfed by his culture. He accepts the traditions, beliefs and way of life of his group so completely that he is not even aware that he is accepting them. He is a culturally defined man.

For such a man, his community is for all practical purposes "the world." Daniel Lerner (1958) found that when

Turkish villagers were asked, "If you could not live in Turkey, where would you want to live?" they could not answer the question because they could not imagine living anywhere else. They could more easily imagine destroying the self ("I would rather die") than separating that self from its familiar context (p. 148).

Although such embeddedness places severe limits on individuality and freedom as we think of them, the men and women involved are not conscious of these limits. It is said that the last thing a fish would be conscious of would be water. Embedded man swims just as innocently in the culture of his community.

Such embeddedness cannot exist unless the community enjoys some degree of insulation from other cultures. Even in the ancient world there were relatively cosmopolitan centers in which a good many individuals were by no means embedded in their culture. One need only call to mind Plato, who viewed his society with the cool eye of a physician studying a difficult patient.

In the light of these facts it is not strictly accurate to say—as some writers do—that "the emergence of the individual" came with the Renaissance. What does date from the Renaissance is the appearance of men who made a considerable point about their individuality—who were even, one might say, rather theatrical about it. The men of the Renaissance found that it was exciting not only to be an individual but to talk about it, to preen one's self on it and to build a life around it.

The premonitions of modern individualism in the Renaissance were amply confirmed in the course of the next three centuries. The Reformation, the rise of science, the Enlightenment, the Industrial Revolution—each in its way contributed powerfully to the dissolution of embeddedness as a social norm. Only as this process gained ground did it become possible to think of the free society as we conceive it today—a society in which every man is encouraged and expected to become a free and morally responsible individual.

By the nineteenth century the stage was set for some of the more extreme manifestations of the modern cult of the individual. We encounter on a wide scale the individual who is intensely conscious of—even preoccupied with—his individuality. Kierkegaard said, ". . . if I were to desire an inscription for my tombstone, I should desire none other than 'That individual'" (1859). We encounter the individual who harbors an intense and explicit hostility toward his own society, the individual who is capable of the deepest feelings of alienation with respect to his community.

The rebellious individualists of the nineteenth century paved the way for an army of followers. The circumstances of modern life are highly favorable to the achievement of certain kinds of individual detachment and autonomy. Mobility is one such circumstance; traditions are apt to be strongly linked to family and locality, and cannot maintain their strength among a transient population. Urbanization and modern communications produce a confrontation of differing traditions. In the resulting confusion of voices, the hold of all traditions is weakened. Under such conditions the authority of the church diminishes, as does the authority of parents. In addition, a powerful literature of rebellion and dissent has accumulated and is available to all young people.

By the time the nineteenth century

was finished, any young man intelligent enough and literate enough to know his own tradition could rebel in the grand manner. Today it doesn't even require intelligence or education. The opportunity for estrangement has been fully democratized.

Escape from what?

Against this background, any observer at the beginning of the twentieth century might easily have believed that the path was leading on to ever loftier heights of individual autonomy. But he would have been wrong. Two major developments of the twentieth century forced us to re-examine that view. First, it became apparent that modern mass society was placing new restraints on the individual, a subject we have already discussed. Second, new totalitarian forms emerged and enjoyed devastating success. Most contemporary discussions of the individual and the group are attempts to cope with one or the other of these developments.

It is not easy for young people today to comprehend the shocking impact on free men everywhere of the rise of modern totalitarianism. During the eighteenth, nineteenth and early twentieth centuries, the notion had become more and more widespread that man was indeed progressing toward freedom. It was believed that slowly but surely he was liberating himself from benighted traditions, tyrannical social institutions and power-hungry rulers. Then in the face of twentieth-century totalitarianism the ideology of freedom that had grown into such a sturdy plant over the centuries appeared to wither. The depressing thought occurred to many observers that there might be something in human nature that was not, after all, antagonistic to tyranny; perhaps even something that welcomed it.

That this is not strictly a modern phenomenon is emphasized by E. R. Dodds (1957) in describing the rising vogue of astrology in Greece in the second century B.C.:

> . . . For a century or more the individual had been face to face with his own intellectual freedom, and now he turned tail and bolted from the horrid prospect—better the rigid determinism of the astrological Fate than that terrifying burden of daily responsibility (p. 246).

In short, it is necessary to examine the capacity of the individual to accept the responsibility of freedom and the conditions under which he will sacrifice his freedom to gain other objectives. These were the questions, among others, that concerned Erich Fromm in *Escape from Freedom* (1941). In that memorable book, Fromm was particularly interested in discovering why the Nazi and Fascist movements of the 1930's found it so easy to win adherents. He explained it by pointing out that the man who submits willingly to an authoritarian regime relieves himself of the anxieties and responsibilities of individual autonomy. Eric Hoffer, in *The True Believer* (1951), explored the same thesis.

Before we comment further on that view, it might be well to pause for some common-sense reflections on individual autonomy. One frequently encounters the romantic notion that the individual can be master of himself and his fate, divested of all hampering ties, a free-soaring bird. Such notions create grave confusion. Complete individual autonomy is unthinkable. The dictum of Theocritus, "Man will ever stand in need of man," is borne out by all of modern psychology and anthropology. Man's social character is fixed in his biological nature. For at least the first half dozen years of his life the human infant is utterly dependent on his elders. By the time those years have passed he possesses deeply rooted social habits. And beyond that, all that makes us most human—communication, self-awareness, sympathy, conscience—is dependent on interaction with other beings of our own kind. So, although we cannot accept the totalitarian notion that man's highest fulfillment is to become a faceless member of the group, neither can we accept romantic notions of complete individual autonomy.

For two generations now we have seen (but have not always understood) that when modern civilization loosens the ties that bind the individual to his tradition and family, it may result in greater freedom or it may result in alienation and loss of a sense of community. Similarly, when the individual seeks autonomy he may achieve freedom and moral responsibility or he may achieve only aggrandizement of the self, with all the accompanying disorders of self-regard: cancerous pride, uncontrolled inflation of his self-evaluations, unfulfillable self-expectations.

Most human beings *are* capable of achieving the measure of autonomy and mature individuality required by our conceptions of individual dignity and worth. But certain kinds of separation of *the self* from *all that is beyond the self* are inherently destructive and intolerable to human beings.

It is important to keep these facts in mind when we use the phrase "escape from freedom." Unless we specify what the individual is running away from and what form the running away takes, we may conceal under one label a wide range of distinctive behavior patterns.

It makes a great deal of difference whether the individual is really running away from freedom—i.e., from the moral responsibility of individual choice—or from the meaningless isolation that modern life so often thrusts on us and the arid egocentrism into which we are so often driven by romantic notions of individualism. If it is the latter, then the flight is justifiable, and the only question is what the individual chooses to run *to*. He may make the catastrophic mistake of submerging his individuality in mindless conformity to a cause or group. Or he may be wise enough to relate himself—as a free and morally responsible individual—to the larger social enterprise and to values that transcend the self. This will be difficult, of course, if the larger social enterprise is so fragmented or decayed that he cannot in fact relate himself to it.

The mature person must achieve a considerable measure of independence if he is to meet the standards implicit in our ideals of individual freedom and dignity; but at the same time he must acknowledge the limitations of the self, come to terms with his membership in the society at large and give his allegiance to values more comprehensive than his own needs.

Some modern intellectuals have not been at all helpful in clarifying these paradoxical facts. Oppressed by the threats to individuality inherent in our modern highly organized society and frightened by the specter of the organization man, they have tended to resent any hint that the individual is not sufficient to himself.

A meaningful relationship between the self and values that lie beyond the self is not incompatible with individual freedom. On the contrary, it is an essential ingredient of the inner strength that must characterize the free man. The man who has established emotional, moral and spiritual ties beyond the self gains the strength needed to endure the rigors of freedom. Let us not doubt that those rigors exist and that the strength is needed. Learned Hand was correct when he said that freedom is a burden to all but the rare individual (1952).

Paul Tillich, who has explored these relationships more profoundly than any other contemporary thinker, points out that the seemingly contradictory requirements of self-affirmation and commitments beyond the self are most nearly resolved when man sees himself as reflecting a larger harmony, as a bearer of the creative process of the universe, as a microcosmic participant in the creative process of the macrocosm (1958).

Individual commitment

The mature individual, then, makes commitments to something larger than the service of his "convulsive little ego," to use William James' memorable phrase—religious commitments, commitments to loved ones, to the social enterprise and to the moral order.

One can accept this fact without at the same time under-rating the pleasant things in life. One is rightly suspicious of those who tell poor people that they should be content with poverty, or hungry people that hunger is ennobling. Every human being should have the chance to enjoy the comforts and pleasures of good living. All we are saying here is that they are not enough. If they were, the large number of Americans who have been able to indulge their whims on a scale unprecedented in history would be deliriously happy. They would be telling one another of their unparalleled serenity and bliss instead of trading tranquilizer prescriptions.

It is widely believed that man in his natural state will do only what is required to achieve strictly physical satisfactions; but, as every anthropologist can testify, this is not true. Primitive man is intensely committed to his social group and to the moral order as he conceives it. Man has to be fairly well steeped in the artificialities of civilization before he is able to imagine that indulgence of physical satisfactions might be a complete way of life.

Anyone with eyes in his head can see that most men and women are prepared to (and do) undergo hardship and suffering in behalf of a meaningful goal. Indeed, they often actually court hardship in behalf of something they believe in. "Virtue will have naught to do with ease," wrote Montaigne. "It seeks a rough and thorny path."

This is not to say that the aims that man conceives beyond the needs of the self are necessarily ones that would win our admiration. They may be characterized by the highest idealism or they may be crude, even vicious. That is a salient feature of the problem. If we make the mistake of imagining that only man's material wants need be satisfied and offer him no significant meanings, he is likely to seize upon the first "meanings" which present themselves to him, however shallow and foolish, committing himself to false gods, to irrational political movements, to cults and to fads. It is essential that man's hunger for dedication be directed to worthy objects.

It would be wrong to leave the implication that man is a selfless creature who only wishes to place himself at the service of some higher ideal. Having rejected the oversimplified view of man's nature as wholly materialistic and selfish, we must not fall into the opposite error. Man is a complex and contradictory being, egocentric but inescapably involved with his fellow man, selfish but capable of superb selflessness. He is preoccupied with his own needs, yet finds no meaning in his life unless he relates himself to something more comprehensive than those needs. It is the tension between his egocentrism and his social and moral leanings that has produced much of the drama in human history.

Hunger for meaning

Man is in his very nature a seeker of meanings. He cannot help being so any more than he can help breathing or maintaining a certain body temperature. It is the way his central nervous system works.

In most societies and most ages, however primitive they may have been technologically, man's hunger for meaning was amply served. Though some of the religions, mythologies, and tribal superstitions with which the hunger for meaning was fed were crude and impoverished, they did purport to describe a larger framework in terms of which events might be interpreted.

With the arrival of the modern age many misguided souls conceived the notion that man could do without such nourishment. And for a breath-taking moment it did seem possible in view of the glittering promises which modern life offered. Under the banner of a beneficial modernity, the individual was to have security, money, power, sensual gratification and status as high as any man. He would be a solvent and eupeptic Walter Mitty in a rich and meaningless world.

But even (or especially) those who came close to achieving the dream never got over the nagging hunger for meaning.

At one level, man's search for meanings is objectively intellectual. He strives to organize what he knows into coherent patterns. Studies of perception have demonstrated that this tendency to organize experience is not an afterthought or the result of conscious impulse but an integral feature of the perceptual process. At the level of ideas, his tendency to organize meaningful wholes out of his experience is equally demonstrable. He tries to reduce the stream of experience to orderly sequences and patterns. He produces legends, theories, philosophies.

To an impressive degree, the theories of nature and the universe which man has developed are impersonal in the sense that they take no special account of man's own aspirations and status (though they are strictly dependent on his conceptualizing power and rarely wholly divorced from his values). Out of this impersonal search for meaning has come modern science.

But man has never been satisfied to let it go at that. He has throughout history shown a compelling need to arrive at conceptions of the universe *in terms of which he could regard his own life as meaningful.* He wants to know where *he* fits into the scheme of things. He wants to understand how the great facts of the objective world relate to *him* and what they imply for his behavior. He wants to know what significance may be found in his own existence, the succeeding generations of his kind and the vivid events of his inner life. He seeks some kind of meaningful framework in which to understand (or at least to reconcile himself to) the indignities of chance and circumstance and the fact of death. A number of philosophers and scientists have told him sternly that he must not expect answers to that sort of question, but he pays little heed. He wants, in the words of Kierkegaard, "a truth which is true for me" (1835). He seeks conceptions of the universe that give dignity, purpose and sense to his own existence.

When he fails in this effort he exhibits what Tillich describes as the anxiety of meaninglessness—"anxiety about the loss of an ultimate concern, of a meaning which gives meaning to all meanings" (1952). As Erikson has pointed out, the young person's search for identity is in some respects this sort of search for meaning (1956). It is a search for a framework in terms of which the young person may understand his own aims, his relation to his fellow man and his relation to larger purposes. In our society every individual is free to conduct this search on his own terms and to find, if he is lucky, the answer that is right for him.

Meaning, purpose and commitment

There are those who think of the meaning of life as resembling the answer to a riddle. One searches for years, and then some bright day one finds it, like the prize at the end of a treasure hunt. It is a profoundly misleading notion. The meanings in any life are multiple and varied. Some are grasped very early, some late; some have a heavy emotional component, some are strictly intellectual; some merit the label *religious*, some are better described as *social*. But each kind of meaning implies a relationship between the person and some larger system of ideas or values, a relationship involving obligations as well as rewards. In the individual life, meaning, purpose and commitment are inseparable. When a man succeeds in the search for identity he has found the answer not only to the question "Who am I?" but to a lot of other questions too: "What must I live up to? What are my obligations? To what must I commit myself?"

So we are back to the subject of commitment. As we said earlier, a free society will not specify too closely the kinds of meaning different individuals will find or the things about which they should generate conviction. People differ in their goals and convictions and in the whole style of their commitment. We must ask that their goals fall within the moral framework to which we all pay allegiance, but we cannot prescribe the things that will unlock their deepest motivations. Those earnest spirits who believe that a man cannot be counted worthy unless he burns with zeal for civic affairs could not be more misguided. And we are wrong when we follow the current fashion of identifying moral strength too exclusively with fighting for a cause. Nothing could be more admirable nor more appealing to a performance-minded people such as ourselves. But such an emphasis hardly does justice to the rich variety of moral excellences that man has sought and occasionally achieved in the course of history.

A good many of the most valuable people in any society will never burn with zeal for anything except the integrity and health and well-being of their own families—and if they achieve those goals, we need ask little more of them. There are other valuable members of a society who will never generate conviction about anything beyond the productive output of their hands or minds—and a sensible society will be grateful for their contributions. Nor will it be too quick to define some callings as noble and some as ordinary. One may not quite accept Oliver Wendell Holmes' dictum—"Every calling is great when greatly pursued"—but the grain of truth is there.

11 How culture changes

GEORGE PETER MURDOCK

It is a fundamental characteristic of culture that, despite its essentially conservative nature, it does change over time and from place to place. Herein it differs strikingly from the social behavior of animals other than man. Among ants, for example, colonies of the same species differ little in behavior from one another and even, so far as we can judge from specimens embedded in amber, from their ancestors of fifty million years ago. In less than one million years man, by contrast, has advanced from the rawest savagery to civilization and has proliferated at least three thousand distinctive cultures.

The processes by which culture changes are by now reasonably well known to science. They cannot be understood, however, without a clear comprehension of the nature of culture.

Culture is the product of learning, rather than of heredity. The cultures of the world are systems of collective habits. The differences observable among them are the cumulative product of mass learning under diverse geographic and social conditions. Race and other biological factors influence culture only in so far as they affect the conditions under which learning occurs, as when the presence of people of markedly different physique operates as a factor in the development of race prejudice.

Culture is learned through precisely the same mechanism as that involved in all habit formation. Hunger, sex, fear, and other basic drives, as well as acquired motivations, impel human beings to act. Actions encounter either success or failure. With failure, especially when accompanied by pain or punishment, an action tends to be replaced by other behavior, and its probability of recurring under similar conditions is diminished. Success, on the other hand, increases the tendency of responses to occur when the same drive is again aroused in a like situation. With repeated success, responses are established as habits, and are progressively adapted to the situations in which they are appropriate.

A culture consists of habits that are shared by members of a society, whether this be a primitive tribe or a civilized nation. The sharing may be general throughout the society, as is normally the case with language habits. Often, however, it is limited to particular categories of people within the society. Thus persons of the same sex or age group, members of the same social class, association, or occupational group, and persons interacting with others in similar relationships commonly resemble one another in their social habits, though diverging behaviorally from persons in other categories.

The social sharing of habits has several causes. The fact that the situations under which behavior is acquired are similar for many individuals conduces in itself to parallel learning. Even more im-

Reprinted from Chapter 11 of H. L. Shapiro (Ed.), **Man, Culture, and Society,** New York: Oxford University Press, 1956, pp. 247–60, with permission of the author and the publisher.

portant is the fact that each generation inculcates on the next, through education, the cultural habits which it has found satisfying and adaptive. Finally, the members of any society exercise pressure upon one another, through formal and informal means of social control, to conform to standards of behavior which are considered right and appropriate. This is particularly true of behavior in interpersonal relationships, where the success or failure of an action depends upon the reaction of another person to it, rather than, for example, upon its adaptiveness to the innate qualities of natural objects. Once one has acquired a limited number of stereotyped patterns of social behavior one is equipped to cope successfully with widely diversified social situations, and one is also provided with a body of reliable expectations regarding the probable responses of others to one's own behavior. This gives confidence and spares the individual an immense amount of individualized learning, which is ever a painful process. It is with good reason, therefore, that every society lays great stress on social conformity.

The habits that are variously shared within a society, and which constitute its culture, fall into two major classes, namely, habits of action and habits of thought. These may be termed, respectively, "customs" and "collective ideas." Customs include such readily observable modes of behavior as etiquette, ceremonial, and the techniques of manipulating material objects. Collective ideas are not directly observable but must be inferred from their expression in language and other overt behavior. They include such things as practical knowledge, religious beliefs, and social values. Moreover, they embrace a mass of rules or definitions, which specify for each custom the persons who may and may not observe it, the circumstances in which it is and is not appropriate, and the limits and permissible variations of the behavior itself. Collective ideas also include a body of social expectations—anticipations of how others will respond to one's own behavior, especially of the sanctions, i.e., social rewards and punishments that can be expected from conformity and deviation. With every custom and with every organized cluster of customs, such as a "culture complex" or "institution," there is ordinarily associated a mass of collective ideas.

Actual social behavior, as it is observed in real life, must be carefully distinguished from culture, which consists of habits or tendencies to act and not of actions themselves. Though largely determined by habits, actual behavior is also affected by the physiological and emotional state of the individual, the intensity of his drives, and the particular external circumstances. Since no two situations are ever exactly alike, actual behavior fluctuates considerably, even when springing from the same habit. A description of a culture is consequently never an account of actual social behavior but is rather a reconstruction of the collective habits which underlie it.

From the point of view of cultural change, however, actual or observable behavior is of primary importance. Whenever social behavior persistently deviates from established cultural habits in any direction, it results in modifications first in social expectations, and then in customs, beliefs, and rules. Gradually, in this way, collective habits are altered and the culture comes to accord better with the new norms of actual behavior.

Changes in social behavior, and hence in culture, normally have their origin in some significant alteration in the life conditions of a society. Any event which changes the situations under which collective behavior occurs, so that habitual actions are discouraged and new responses are favored, may lead to cultural innovations. Among the classes of events that are known to be especially influential in producing cultural change are increases or decreases in population, changes in the geographical environment, migrations into new environments, contacts with peoples of differing culture, natural and social catastrophes such as floods, crop failures, epidemics, wars, and economic depressions, accidental discoveries, and even such biographical events as the death or rise to power of a strong political leader.

The events which produce cultural change by altering the conditions under which social behavior proves adaptive, i.e., is or is not rewarded, are invariably historical, i.e., specific with respect to time and place. Events occurring at different places and times may resemble one another, however, and exert parallel influences upon different cultures. It is thus possible to view changes in culture either in relation to their spatial and temporal setting or in relation to comparable events wherever and whenever they have occurred. The former or "historical" approach answers such questions as what? when? and where? The latter or "scientific" approach, by illuminating the processes by which change occurs, answers the question how? Both approaches are valid and completely complementary.

Historical anthropologists commonly discuss particular traits of culture, such as the use of tobacco, the wheel, the domesticated horse, the alphabet, or money, treating of their "invention" at specific times and places and of their "diffusion" from the points of origin to other parts of the world. Since our problem is to describe *how* culture changes, we must abandon the bird's-eye view of the historian and examine the processes within societies by which all changes, and not merely particular ones, take place. These processes may be conveniently grouped under the terms "innovation," "social acceptance," "selective elimination," and "integration."

Cultural change begins with the process of *innovation*, the formation of a new habit by a single individual which is subsequently accepted or learned by other members of his society. An innovation originates through the ordinary psychological mechanism of learning, and differs from purely individual habits only in the fact that it comes to be socially shared. It is nevertheless useful to distinguish several important variants of the process.

An innovation may be called a *variation* when it represents a slight modification of pre-existing habitual behavior under the pressure of gradually changing circumstances. The slow evolution in the forms of manufactured objects over time usually represents an accumulation of variations. In the same manner, tattooing can be extended over a wider area of the body, additional barbs may be added to a harpoon, skirts may be lengthened or shortened, folk tales may grow by accretion, or ceremonial may become increasingly elaborate and formalized. Variation occurs in all cultures at all times. The individual increments of change are often so slight as to be almost imperceptible, but their cumulative effect over long periods may be immense.

When innovation involves the transfer of elements of habitual behavior from one situational context to another, or their combination into new syntheses, it is called *invention.* At least some degree of creativeness is always present. Most of the important technological innovations are of this type. Thus the invention of the airplane involved the synthesis of such elements as the wings of a glider, an internal-combustion engine from an automobile, and an adaptation of a ship's propeller. Though less well known, inventions are equally common in the non-material aspects of culture. The city-manager plan, for example, represents an obvious transfer of techniques of business management to the sphere of local government, and most forms of religious worship are modeled on behavior toward persons of high social status, e.g., sacrifice upon bribery, prayer upon petitions, laudation upon flattery, ritual upon etiquette.

Since invention always involves a new synthesis of old habits, it is dependent upon the existing content of the culture. A synthesis cannot occur if the elements which it combines are not present in the culture. It is for this reason that parallel inventions so rarely occur among unconnected peoples of differing culture. With the exception of such simple and obvious combinations as the hafting of tools, anthropologists know of only a handful of genuine inventions that have been arrived at independently by historically unrelated peoples. Among them perhaps the most famous are the fire piston, invented by the Malays and a French physicist, and the dome, developed by the ancient Romans from the arch and independently invented by the Eskimos for their snow igloos.

Among peoples of the same or related cultures, on the other hand, parallel inventions are extraordinarily common. The culture provides the same constituent elements to many people, and if one person does not achieve the synthesis others are likely to do so. The Patent Office furnishes thousands of examples. In one famous instance, the telephone, applications for a patent were received on the same day from two independent inventors, Bell and Gray. Another noted case is the independent formulation of the theory of natural selection by Darwin and Wallace. So common is this phenomenon that scientists often live in dread of the anticipation of their discoveries by rivals. Parallel invention thus appears to be frequent and almost inevitable among peoples of similar culture, though so rare as to be almost non-existent among peoples of different culture.

A third type of innovation may be called *tentation.* Unlike the previous types, which merely modify or recombine elements of habit already in existence, tentation may give rise to elements that show little or no continuity with the past. The mechanism by which these are acquired is that which psychologists call "trial-and-error learning." Tentation may occur in any situation in which established habits prove ineffective and individuals are so strongly motivated that they try out other modes of behavior in a search for an adequate solution to their problems. They will ordinarily try out first a number of variations and recombinations of existing habitual responses, but if all of these fail they will resort to "random behavior," in the course of which they may accidentally hit upon some novel response which solves the problem and thereby becomes established as a new cultural element.

Crises are particularly conducive to tentation. In a famine, for instance, people try out all sorts of things that they have never eaten before, and if some of them prove nutritious and tasty they may be added to the normal diet. An epidemic similarly leads to a search for new medicines, and both primitive and civilized peoples have discovered useful remedies in this way. War also leads to improvisation, as do economic crises. The New Deal in the recent history of the United States, for example, reveals numerous instances of tentation. Scientific experimentation, it should be pointed out, is often a form of controlled tentation, as when a new series of chemical compounds are systematically put to test. The saying that "necessity is the mother of invention" applies more forcefully to tentation than to invention proper.

When accidental discoveries lead to cultural innovations, the process is commonly that of tentation. The origin of the boomerang in aboriginal Australia will serve as an example. Over much of that continent the natives used curved throwing sticks to kill or stun small animals, and in a limited part of the area the true boomerang was used for this purpose. Almost certainly the first boomerang was produced by sheer accident in the attempt to fashion an ordinary throwing stick. Observing the unique behavior of the particular stick in flight, the maker and his fellows doubtless attempted to duplicate it. They must have resorted to tentation, or trial-and-error behavior, until they eventually succeeded, and thereby established boomerang manufacture as a habit. The history of modern "inventions" is full of such instances, the discovery of the photographic plate by Daguerre being one of the most familiar examples.

Tentation also accounts for a type of cultural parallel which is distinct from genuine independent invention. There are certain universal problems which every people must solve and for which there are a limited number of easy and obvious solutions, so that peoples in different parts of the world have often hit upon the same solution quite independently. Rules of descent provide a good illustration. In all societies, each individual must be affiliated with a group of relatives to whom he regards himself as most closely akin and to whom he can turn for aid in time of need. There are only three possibilities: patrilineal descent, which relates an individual to kinsmen in the male line; matrilineal descent, which affiliates him with relatives through females; and bilateral descent, which associates him with a group of his closest relatives irrespective of their line of descent. Every society must choose one of these alternatives or some combination thereof, and, since the possibilities are limited to three, many peoples have, of necessity, arrived independently at the same cultural solution. Funeral customs present another example, since there are only a limited number of feasible ways of disposing of a dead body. In all such instances, if a society is compelled for any reason to abandon its previous custom it will inevitably, through tentation, arrive at an alternative solution which other peoples have independently adopted.

The fourth and last type of innovation is *cultural borrowing*, which is what the historical anthropologist, with his bird's-eye view, calls "diffusion." In this case the innovator is not the originator of a new habit, but its introducer. The habit has previously been part of the culture of another society; the innovator is merely the first member of his social group to adopt it. From the point of view of psychology, cultural borrowing is merely a special case of the learning process known as "imitation." The innovator, faced with a situation in which the shared habits of his own society are not fully satisfactory, copies behavior which he has observed in members of another society, instead of resorting to variation, invention, or tentation to solve his problem.

Of all forms of innovation, cultural borrowing is by far the most common and important. The overwhelming majority of the elements in any culture are the result of borrowing. Modern American culture provides a good illustration, as can be shown by a few random examples. Our language comes from England, our alphabet from the Phoenicians, our numerical system from India, and paper and printing from China. Our family organization and system of real property derive from medieval Europe. Our religion is a composite of elements largely assembled from the ancient Hebrews, Egyptians, Babylonians, and Persians. Metal coinage comes from Lydia, paper money from China, checks from Persia. Our system of banking, credit, loans, discounts, mortgages, et cetera, is derived in its essentials from ancient Babylonia, with modern elaborations from Italy and England. Our architecture is still largely Greek, Gothic, Georgian, et cetera. Our favorite flavors in ice creams, vanilla and chocolate, are both borrowed from the Aztecs of Mexico and were unknown to Europeans before the conquest by Cortez. Tea comes from China, coffee from Ethiopia, tobacco from the American Indians. Our domesticated animals and plants, virtually without exception, are borrowed. If the reader were to make a list of absolutely everything he eats during the next week, analysis would probably show that one third are products that were already cultivated in Neolithic times and that at least two thirds were being raised at the time of Christ, and it would be surprising if the list contained any item that was not cultivated for food somewhere in the world when Columbus sailed for America.

Our own culture is not unique in this respect, for it is doubtful whether there is a single culture known to history or anthropology that has not owed at least ninety per cent of its constituent elements to cultural borrowing. The reason is not far to seek. Any habit that has become established in a culture has been tried out by many people and found satisfactory. When a society finds itself in a dilemma, therefore, the chances that an element already present in the culture of another people will turn out to be an adequate solution to its own problem are vastly greater than those of any random and untested innovation of another type. Cultural borrowing is thus highly economical, and most peoples tend to ransack the cultural resources of their neighbors for adaptive practices before they resort to invention or tentation.

Cultural borrowing depends upon contact. Obviously the opportunity for borrowing is lacking in the case of a completely isolated society. Other factors being equal, the extent to which one culture will borrow from another is proportionate to the intensity and duration of the social intercourse between their bearers. Contact need not always be face-to-face, however, for there are numerous instances of cultural borrowing at a distance through the medium of written language or through copying of articles received by trade. By and large, however, societies borrow mainly from their immediate neighbors, with the result that the products of diffusion are ordinarily clustered in geographically contiguous areas.

Trade, missionary enterprise, and political conquest create conditions conducive to cultural borrowing. Peculiarly important, however, is intermarriage, for this brings individuals of differing culture together within the family, where children can learn from both parents. Diffusion then proceeds through the socialization process, which produces far more perfect copying than does cultural borrowing on the adult level. The American "melting pot" operates largely through this mechanism. Primitive peoples practicing local exogamy, i.e., requiring individuals to obtain spouses from another village or band, commonly reveal considerable cultural uniformity over wide areas, as in aboriginal Australia and among the Indians of the Northwest Coast. By contrast, in areas like Melanesia and Central California where marriage normally takes place within the community, even villages a few miles apart may differ strikingly in dialect and customs. In the one case culture is diffused through the same process by which it is transmitted; in the other, even adult contacts tend to be restricted to a minimum.

Incentive—a need or drive—is as essential in cultural borrowing as in other types of innovation. A people rarely borrows an alien cultural element when they already possess a trait which satisfactorily fills the same need. Thus the blubber lamp of the Eskimos was not borrowed by the Indians to the south, who had plenty of wood for fires to heat and light their dwellings. On the other hand, the extraordinarily rapid diffusion of tobacco over the earth after the discovery of America reflected the general absence of competing traits. It has been observed that the first individuals in a society to borrow alien customs are likely to be the discontented, underprivileged, and maladjusted. Thus in India Christian missionaries have made many more converts among the "untouchables" than in the higher strata of society, and in our own country fascism and communism attract an unduly high proportion of unsuccessful and neurotic people.

The presence in a receiving society of some of the habit elements involved in a new trait greatly facilitates borrowing. It is for this reason that diffusion occurs most readily among peoples of similar culture, who already share many elements of habit. Thus Englishmen and Americans borrow more frequently and easily from each other than from Russians, Chinese, or Hottentots. Conversely, aboriginal peoples are greatly handicapped in taking over the complex technology of modern civilization. They cannot, for example, begin to manufacture the steel products which they want without also taking over such things as blast furnaces and rolling mills.

Cultural borrowing will occur only if the new habit is demonstrably rewarding. The native quickly adopts steel knives and axes from the white man because their superiority to his former stone implements becomes immediately apparent. On the other hand, Europeans were slow to borrow paper manufacture from the Chinese because the advantages of paper over parchment appeared very slight at first. The Chinese and Japanese have not yet adopted the alphabet from western civilization because, however great its ultimate advantages, it would impose heavy burdens and discomforts upon all literate persons during the necessary period of readjustment. Geographic and climatic factors may prevent diffusion by withholding or reducing the possibilities of reward, and social prejudices such as ingrained conservatism may counterbalance potential advantages by inflicting disapprobation upon innovators.

Borrowing need not be exact. Oftentimes, indeed, all that is borrowed is the external "form" of a custom and not its "meaning," i.e., the collective ideas associated with it. The familiar caricature of the cannibal chief wearing a silk hat provides a good illustration. Frequently an imperfect copy is quite adequate. Thus when the Plains Indians took over horses and riding equipment from the Spaniards they omitted the horseshoe, which was quite unnecessary on the prairie. Sometimes changes are imposed by the conditions of the geographical environment. When the Iroquois Indians adopted the birchbark canoe from their Algonkian neighbors, for example, they altered the material to elm bark because of the scarcity of birch trees in their habitat. Frequently cultural factors favor a modification. The original Phoenician alphabet lacked characters for vowels, the nature of their language being such that consonant signs sufficed for the identification of words. Since this was not true of the Greek language, when the Greeks borrowed the Phoenician alphabet they converted characters for which they had no need into symbols for vowels.

Modifications are so common in cultural borrowing that authorities like Malinowski have regarded the process as scarcely less creative than other forms of innovation. Often, indeed, it is inextricably blended with invention or tentation. This is well illustrated in instances of "stimulus diffusion," in which only the general idea of an alien cultural trait is borrowed, the specific form being supplied by improvisation. Thus a famous Cherokee chief named Sequoyah, though an illiterate man, had noticed that white men could somehow understand messages from pieces of paper on which peculiar marks were inscribed, and he came to the conclusion that this would be a useful skill for his own people to acquire. He therefore set himself the task of devising a system of marks by which the Cherokee language could be written. Inventing some signs of his own and copying some from pieces of printed matter —numbers and punctuation marks as well as letters, upside down or on their sides as often as upright—he produced a novel form of writing, a syllabary rather than an alphabet, which his tribesmen learned and still use to this day.

The second major process in cultural change is *social acceptance*. So long as an innovation, whether original or borrowed, is practiced by the innovator alone in his society, it is an individual habit and not an element of culture. To become the latter it must be accepted by others; it must be socially shared. Social acceptance begins with the adoption of a new habit by a small number of individuals. From this point it may spread until it becomes part of the subculture of a family, clan, local community, or other sub-group, or until it becomes a "specialty" characteristic of persons belonging to a particular occupational, kinship, age-graded, or other status category, or until it becomes an "alternative" widely but optionally practiced. Eventually it may even become a "universal," shared by all members of the society. The term "degrees of cultural saturation" has been proposed for the various steps in social acceptance.

The learning mechanism involved in social acceptance is imitation, as in the case of cultural borrowing, but the model whose behavior is copied is a member of one's own rather than another society.

So similar are the two processes that the term "diffusion" is often applied to both; social acceptance is called "internal" or "vertical" diffusion to differentiate it from cultural borrowing, which is termed "external" or "horizontal" diffusion. With minor exceptions, most of what has previously been stated about the latter process applies equally to the former. Since close contact and similarity of culture can be taken for granted, however, copying is usually far more exact, and this is accentuated by social control.

A factor of considerable importance in social acceptance is the prestige of the innovator and of the group who are first to imitate him. Changes advocated by an admired political or religious leader are readily adopted, whereas few will follow an unpopular or despised innovator. Clothing styles accepted by "the four hundred" quickly diffuse throughout the masses, but the "zoot suit" does not spread from the taxi dance hall to the ballroom. Women imitate men more readily than *vice versa*. In our own society, for example, many women have adopted masculine garments, smoking and drinking habits, and occupations, but there appears to be no concerted movement among men to wear skirts, use cosmetics, or apply for positions as nurses, governesses, or baby-sitters.

Selective elimination constitutes a third major process of cultural change. Every innovation that has been socially accepted enters, as it were, into a competition for survival. So long as it proves more rewarding than its alternatives a cultural habit will endure, but when it ceases to bring comparable satisfactions it dwindles and eventually disappears. The process superficially resembles that of natural selection in organic evolution. It should be noted, however, that cultural traits do not compete directly with one another but are competitively tested in the experience of those who practice them. Oftentimes the competition is carried on between organized groups of people with contrasting customs and beliefs, as between nations, political parties, religious sects, or social and economic classes, and the issue is decided indirectly by the victory of one group over the other. By and large, the cultural elements that are eliminated through trial and error or social competition are the less adaptive ones, so that the process is as definitely one of the survival of the fittest as is that of natural selection.

Few of the genuine gains of culture history—the achievements of technology, of science, of man's control over nature—have ever been lost. The so-called "lost arts of antiquity" are largely mythical. To be sure, particular peoples have declined in civilization, but not until they have passed on their contributions to others. What man has lost, in the main, is a mass of maladaptive and barbarous practices, inefficient techniques, and outworn superstitions. New errors arise, of course, in each generation, but it is comforting to realize that the mortality of error is vastly greater than that of truth.

It is the genuine achievements of man that anthropologists have in mind when they say that culture is cumulative, comparing culture history to the growth of a snowball as it is rolled down a hill. Even achievements that are superseded rarely disappear. Today the electric light has proved superior to earlier methods of lighting, but the gas mantle, the kerosene lamp, and the tallow candle still survive in out-of-the-way places or under special conditions. Survival is often assured through a change in function. The use of outmoded weapons has been preserved, for example, in athletic sports like fencing and archery and in boyhood toys such as the sling and the peashooter. Other ancient usages survive in legal, religious, and academic ceremonial. Written records, of course, preserve much of the culture of the past from oblivion. Our libraries bulge with the puerilities as well as the achievements of history.

The fourth and last important process of cultural change is that of *integration.* The shared habits that constitute a culture not only fluctuate in their degree of social acceptance, and compete for survival, but they also become progressively adapted to one another so that they tend to form an integrated whole. They exhibit what Sumner has called "a strain toward consistency." Every innovation alters in some respect the situations under which certain other forms of habitual behavior occur, and leads to adaptive changes in the latter. Similarly it must, in its turn, be adjusted to modifications elsewhere in the culture. While each such change is in itself, of course, an innovation, their reciprocal interaction and cumulative effect deserve special recognition as an integrative process.

The history of the automobile during the present century in our own culture provides an excellent example. The changes brought about by this technological invention are described by Professor Leslie Spier (1956). A similar story could be told for other modern innovations such as the telephone, the airplane, the radio, and electrical household gadgets, and all of them pale before the potentialities of atomic energy.

Certain anthropologists have erroneously assumed that the elements of any culture are in a state of nearly perfect integration, or equilibrium, at all times. Actually, however, perfect equilibrium is never achieved or even approached. The adjustment of other elements of culture to an innovation, and of it to them, requires time—often years or even generations. In the meantime other innovations have appeared and set in motion new processes of integration. At any given time, therefore, a culture exhibits numerous instances of uncompleted integrative processes as well as examples of others which have been carried through to relatively satisfactory completion. What we always encounter is a strain toward internal adaptation, never its full realization.

The period of time which must elapse between the acceptance of an innovation and the completion of the integrative readjustments which follow in its train Ogburn has aptly called "cultural lag." During such a period of lag people attempt, through variation, invention, tentation, and cultural borrowing, to modify old customs and ideas to accord with the new, and to adjust the new to the old, so as to eliminate inconsistencies and sources of friction and irritation. In a modern democratic society, politics is a major scene of such efforts.

The net effect of the various processes of cultural change is to adapt the collective habits of human societies progressively over time to the changing conditions of existence. Change is always uncomfortable and often painful, and people frequently become discouraged with its slowness or even despair of achieving any genuine improvement. Neither history nor anthropology, however, gives grounds for pessimism. However halting or harsh it may appear to participants, cultural change is always adaptive and usually progressive. It is also inevitable, and will endure as long as the earth can support human life. Nothing—not even an atomic war—can destroy civilization.

12 The nature of assimilation and the theory of the melting pot

MILTON M. GORDON

Let us, first of all, imagine a hypothetical situation in which a host country, to which we shall give the fictitious name of "Sylvania," is made up of a population all members of which are of the same race, religion, and previous national extraction. Cultural behavior is relatively uniform except for social class divisions. Similarly, the groups and institutions, i.e., the "social structure," of Sylvanian society are divided and differentiated only on a social class basis. Into this country, through immigration, comes a group of people who differ in previous national background and in religion and who thus have different cultural patterns from those of the host society. We shall call them the Mundovians. Let us further imagine that within the span of another generation, this population group of Mundovian national origin (now composed largely of the second generation, born in Sylvania) has taken on completely the cultural patterns of the Sylvanians, has thrown off any sense of peoplehood based on Mundovian nationality, has changed its religion to that of the Sylvanians, has eschewed the formation of any communal organizations made up principally or exclusively of Mundovians, has entered and been hospitably accepted into the social cliques, clubs, and institutions of the Sylvanians at various class levels, has intermarried freely and frequently with the Sylvanians, encounters no prejudice or discrimination (one reason being that they are no longer distinguishable culturally or structurally from the rest of the Sylvanian population), and raises no value conflict issues in Sylvanian public life. Such a situation would represent the ultimate form of assimilation—complete assimilation to the culture and society of the host country. Note that we are making no judgment here of either the sociological desirability, feasibility, or moral rightness of such a goal. We are simply setting it up as a convenient abstraction—an "ideal type"—ideal not in the value sense of being most desirable but in the sense of representing the various elements of the concept and their interrelationships in "pure," or unqualified, fashion (the methodological device of the "ideal type" was developed and named by the German sociologist, Max Weber).

Looking at this example, we may discern that seven major variables are involved in the process discussed—in other words, seven basic subprocesses have taken place in the assimilation of the Mundovians to Sylvanian society. These may be listed in the following manner. We may say that the Mundovians have

1. changed their cultural patterns (including religious belief and observance) to those of the Sylvanians;
2. taken on large-scale primary group

Excerpted from Chapters 3 and 5 of **Assimilation in American Life,** New York: Oxford University Press, 1964, with permission of the author and the publisher.

relationships with the Sylvanians, i.e., have entered fully into the societal network of groups and institutions, or societal structure, of the Sylvanians;
3. have intermarried and interbred fully with the Sylvanians;
4. have developed a Sylvanian, in place of a Mundovian, sense of peoplehood, or ethnicity;
5. have reached a point where they encounter no discriminatory behavior;
6. have reached a point where they encounter no prejudiced attitudes;
7. do not raise by their demands concerning the nature of Sylvanian public or civic life any issues involving value and power conflict with the original Sylvanians (for example, the issue of birth control).

Each of these steps or subprocesses may be thought of as constituting a particular stage or aspect of the assimilation process. Thus we may, in shorthand fashion, consider them as types of assimilation and characterize them accordingly. We may, then, speak, for instance, of "structural assimilation" to refer to the entrance of Mundovians into primary group relationships with the Sylvanians, or "identificational assimilation" to describe the taking on of a sense of Sylvanian peoplehood. For some of the particular assimilation subprocesses there are existing special terms, already reviewed. For instance, cultural or behavioral assimilation is what has already been defined as "acculturation." The full list of assimilation subprocesses or variables with their general names, and special names, if any, is given in Table 1.

Not only is the assimilation process mainly a matter of degree, but, obviously, each of the stages or subprocesses distinguished above may take place in varying degrees.

In the example just used there has been assimilation in all respects to the society and culture which had exclusively occupied the nation up to the time of the immigrants' arrival. In other instances there may be other subsocieties and subcultures already on the scene when the new group arrives but one of these subsocieties and its way of life is dominant by virtue of original settlement, the preemption of power, or overwhelming predominance in numbers. In both cases we need a term to stand for the dominant subsociety which provides the standard to which other groups adjust or measure their relative degree of adjustment. We have tentatively used the term "host society"; however, a more neutral designation would be desirable. A. B. Hollingshead, in describing the class structure of New Haven, has used the term "core group" to refer to the Old Yankee families of colonial, largely Anglo-Saxon ancestry who have traditionally dominated the power and status system of the community, and who provide the "master cultural mould" for the class system of the other groups in the city (1952; 1958). Joshua Fishman has referred to the "core society" and the "core culture" in American life, this core being "made up essentially of White Protestant, middle-class clay, to which all other particles are attracted" (1961). If there is anything in American life which can be described as an over-all American culture which serves as a reference point for immigrants and their children, it can best be described, it seems to us, as the middle-class cultural patterns of, largely, white Protestant, Anglo-Saxon origins, leaving aside for the moment the question of minor reciprocal influences on this culture exercised by the cultures of later entry into the United States, and ignoring also, for this purpose, the distinction between the upper-middle class and the lower-middle class cultural worlds.

There is a point on which I particularly do not wish to be misunderstood. I am not for one moment implying that the contribution of the non-Anglo-Saxon stock to the nature of American civilization has been minimal or slight. Quite the contrary. The qualitative record of achievement in industry, business, the professions, and the arts by Americans whose ancestors came from countries and traditions which are not British, or in many cases not even closely similar to British, is an overwhelmingly favorable one, and with reference to many individuals, a thoroughly brilliant one. Taken together with the substantial quantitative impact of these non-Anglo-Saxon groups on American industrial and agricultural development and on the demographic dimensions of the society, this record reveals an America in mid-twentieth century whose greatness rests on the contributions of many races, religions, and national backgrounds (see Handlin & Handlin, 1955). My point, however, is that, with some exceptions, as the immigrants and their children

TABLE 1
THE ASSIMILATION VARIABLES

Subprocess or condition	Type or stage of assimilation	Special Term
Change of cultural patterns to those of host society	Cultural or behavioral assimilation	Acculturation [1]
Large-scale entrance into cliques, clubs, and institutions of host society, on primary group level	Structural assimilation	None
Large-scale intermarriage	Marital assimilation	Amalgamation [2]
Development of sense of peoplehood based exclusively on host society	Identificational assimilation	None
Absence of prejudice	Attitude receptional assimilation	None
Absence of discrimination	Behavior receptional assimilation	None
Absence of value and power conflict	Civic assimilation	None

1 The question of reciprocal cultural influence will be considered later.

2 My use of the term here is not predicated on the diversity in race of the two population groups which are intermarrying and interbreeding. With increasing understanding of the meaning of "race" and its thoroughly relative and arbitrary nature as a scientific term, this criterion becomes progressively less important. We may speak of the "amalgamation" or intermixture of the two "gene pools" which the two populations represent, regardless of how similar or divergent these two gene pools may be.

have become Americans, their contributions, as laborers, farmers, doctors, lawyers, scientists, artists, etc., have been made *by way* of cultural patterns that have taken their major impress from the mould of the overwhelmingly English character of the dominant Anglo-Saxon culture or subculture in America, whose dominion dates from colonial times and whose *cultural* domination in the United States has never been seriously threatened. One must make a distinction between influencing the cultural patterns themselves and contributing to the progress and development of the society. It is in the latter area that the influence of the immigrants and their children in the United States has been decisive.

Accordingly, I shall follow Fishman's usage in referring to middle-class white Protestant Americans as constituting the "core society," or in my terms, the "core subsociety," and the cultural patterns of this group as the "core culture" or "core subculture." I shall use Hollingshead's term "core group" to refer to the white Protestant element at any social class level.

Let us now, for a moment, return to our fictitious land of Sylvania and imagine an immigration of Mundovians with a decidedly different outcome. In this case the Sylvanians accept many new behavior patterns and values from the Mundovians, just as the Mundovians change many of their ways in conformance with Sylvanian customs, this interchange taking place with appropriate modifications and compromises, and in this process a new cultural system evolves which is neither exclusively Sylvanian nor Mundovian but a mixture of both. This is a cultural blend, the result of the "melting pot," which has melted down the cultures of the two groups in the same societal container, as it were, and formed a new cultural product with standard consistency. This process has, of course, also involved thorough social mixing in primary as well as secondary groups and a large-scale process of intermarriage. The melting pot has melted the two groups into one, societally and culturally.

Whether such a process as just described is feasible or likely of occurrence is beside the point here. It, too, is an "ideal type," an abstraction against which we can measure the realities of what actually happens. Our point is that the seven variables of the assimilation process which we have isolated can be measured against the "melting pot" goal as well as against the "adaptation to the core society and culture" goal. That is, assuming the "melting pot" goal, we can then inquire how much acculturation of both groups has taken place to form such a blended culture, how much social structural mixture has taken place, and so on.[3] We now have a model of assimilation with seven variables which can be used to analyze the assimilation process with reference to either of two variant goal-systems: (1) "adaptation to the core society and culture," and (2) the "melting pot." Theoretically, it would be possible to apply the analysis model of variables with reference to carrying out the goal-system of "cultural pluralism" as well. However, this would be rather premature at this point since the concept of cultural pluralism is itself so meagerly understood.

Let us now apply this model of assim-

[3] I am indebted to Professor Richard D. Lambert of the University of Pennsylvania for pointing out to me that my array of assimilation variables must be applied with reference to the basic assimilation goal. In my original scheme of presentation I had implicitly applied it only to the goal-system of "adaptation to the core society and culture."

ilation analysis in tentative fashion to selected "minority" ethnic groups on the American scene. The applied paradigm presented in Table 2 allows us to record and summarize a great deal of information compactly and comparatively. We shall deal here, for illustrative purposes, with four groups: Negroes, Jews, Catholics (excluding Negro and Spanish-speaking Catholics), and Puerto Ricans. The basic goal-referent will be "adaptation to core society and culture." The entries in the table cells may be regarded, at this point, as hypotheses. Qualifying comments will be made in the footnotes to the table. The reader may wish to refer back to Table 1 for definitions of each column heading.

One of the tasks of sociological theory is not only to identify the factors or variables present in any given social process or situation, but also to hypothesize how these variables may be related to each other. Let us look at the seven assimilation variables from this point of view. We note that in Table 2, of the four ethnic groups listed, only one, the Puerto Ricans, are designated as being substantially unassimilated culturally. The Puerto Ricans are the United States' newest immigrant group of major size. If we now examine the entries for the Negro, one of America's oldest minorities, we find that assimilation has not taken place in most of the other variables, but with allowance for social class factors, *has* taken place culturally. These two facts in juxtaposition should give us a clue to the relation of the cultural assimilation variable to all the others. This relationship may be stated as follows: (1) *cultural assimilation, or acculturation, is likely to be the first of the types of assimilation to occur when a minority group arrives on the scene; and* (2) *cultural assimilation, or acculturation, of the minority group may take place even when none of the other types of assimilation occurs simultaneously or later, and this condition of "acculturation only" may continue indefinitely.*

If we examine the history of immigration into the United States, both of these propositions are seen to be borne out. After the birth of the republic, as each succeeding wave of immigration, first from Northern and Western Europe, later from Southern and Eastern Europe and the Orient, has spread over America, the first process that has occurred has been the taking on of the English language and American behavior patterns, even while the creation of the immigrant colonies sealed off their members from extensive primary contacts with "core society" Americans and even when prejudice and discrimination against the minority have been at a high point. While this process is only partially completed in the immigrant generation itself, with the second and succeeding generations, exposed to the American public school system and speaking English as their native tongue, the impact of the American acculturation process has been overwhelming; the rest becomes a matter of social class mobility and the kind of acculturation that such mobility demands. On the other hand, the success of the acculturation process has by no means guaranteed entry of each minority into the primary groups and institutions—that is, the subsociety—of the white Protestant group. With the exception of white Protestant immigrant stock from Northern and Western Europe—I am thinking here particularly of the Scandinavians, Dutch, and Germans—by and large such structural mixture on the primary level has not taken place. Nor has such acculturation success eliminated prejudice and discrimination or in many cases led to large-scale intermarriage with the core society.

The only qualifications of my generalizations about the rapidity and success of the acculturation process that the American experience suggests are these: (1) If a minority group is spatially isolated and segregated (whether voluntarily or not) in a rural area, as is the case with the American Indians still on reservations, even the acculturation process will be very slow; and (2) Unusually marked discrimination, such as that which has been faced by the American Negro, if it succeeds in keeping vast numbers of the minority group deprived of educational and occupational opportunities and thus predestined to remain in a lower-class setting, may indefinitely retard the acculturation process for the group. Even in the case of the American Negro, however, from the long view or perspective of American history, this ef-

TABLE 2
PARADIGM OF ASSIMILATION
APPLIED TO SELECTED GROUPS IN THE UNITED STATES—
BASIC GOAL REFERENT: ADAPTATION TO CORE SOCIETY AND CULTURE

Group	Type of assimilation						
	Cultural[4]	Structural	Marital	Identificational	Attitude Receptional	Behavior Receptional	Civic
Negroes	Variation by class[5]	No	No	No	No	No	Yes
Jews	Substantially Yes	No	Substantially No	No	No	Partly	Mostly
Catholics (excluding Negro and Spanish-speaking)	Substantially Yes	Partly (variation by area)	Partly	No	Partly	Mostly	Partly
Puerto Ricans	Mostly No	No	No	No	No	No	Partly

[4] Some reciprocal cultural influences have, of course, taken place. American language, diet, recreational patterns, art forms, and economic techniques have been modestly influenced by the cultures of non-Anglo-Saxon resident groups since the first contacts with the American Indians, and the American culture is definitely the richer for these influences. However, the reciprocal influences have not been great. See George R. Stewart (1954) and our subsequent discussion (Gordon, 1964, Ch. 4). Furthermore, the minority ethnic groups have not given up all their pre-immigration cultural patterns. Particularly, they have preserved their non-Protestant religions. I have thus used the phrase "Substantially Yes" to indicate this degree of adaptation.

[5] Although few, if any, African cultural survivals are to be found among American Negroes, lower-class Negro life with its derivations from slavery, post-Civil War discrimination, both rural and urban poverty, and enforced isolation from the middle-class white world, is still at a considerable distance from the American cultural norm. Middle- and upper-class Negroes, on the other hand, are acculturated to American core culture.

fect of discrimination will be seen to have been a delaying action only; the quantitatively significant emergence of the middle-class Negro is already well on its way.

Before we leave specific examination of the acculturation variable and its relationships, it would be well to distinguish between two types of cultural patterns and traits which may characterize any ethnic group. Some, like its religious beliefs and practices, its ethical values, its musical tastes, folk recreational patterns, literature, historical language, and sense of a common past, are essential and vital ingredients of the group's cultural heritage, and derive exactly from that heritage. We shall refer to these as *intrinsic* cultural traits or patterns. Others, such as dress, manner, patterns of emotional expression, and minor oddities in pronouncing and inflecting English, tend to be products of the historical vicissitudes of a group's adjustment to its local environment, including the present one (and also reflect social class experiences and values), and are in a real sense, external to the core of the group's ethnic cultural heritage. These may conveniently be referred to as *extrinsic* cultural traits or patterns (cf. Vickery & Cole, 1943, pp. 43–4). To illustrate, the Catholicism or Judaism of the immigrant from Southern or Eastern Europe represent a difference in *intrinsic culture* from the American core society and its Protestant religious affiliation. However, the greater volatility of emotional expression of the Southern and Eastern European peasant or villager in comparison with the characteristically greater reserve of the upper-middle class American of the core society constitutes a difference in *extrinsic culture*. To take another example, the variant speech pattern, or argot, of the lower-class Negro of recent southern background, which is so widespread both in the South and in northern cities, is a product of external circumstances and is not something vital to Negro culture. It is thus an *extrinsic* cultural trait. Were this argot, which constitutes such a powerful handicap to social mobility and adjustment to the core culture, to disappear, nothing significant for Negro self-regard as a group or the Negro's sense of ethnic history and identity would be violated. While this distinction between intrinsic and extrinsic culture is a tentative one, and cannot be uniformly applied to all cultural traits, it is still a useful one and may help cast further light on the acculturation process, particularly in its relationship to prejudice and discrimination.

As we examine the array of assimilation variables again, several other relationships suggest themselves. One is the indissoluble connection, in the time order indicated, between structural assimilation and marital assimilation. That is, entrance of the minority group into the social cliques, clubs, and institutions of the core society at the primary group level inevitably will lead to a substantial amount of intermarriage. If children of different ethnic backgrounds belong to the same play-group, later the same adolescent cliques, and at college the same fraternities and sororities; if the parents belong to the same country club and invite each other to their homes for dinner; it is completely unrealistic not to expect these children, now grown, to love and to marry each other, blithely oblivious to previous ethnic extraction. Communal leaders of religious and nationality groups that desire to maintain their ethnic identity are aware of this connection, which is one reason for the proliferation of youth groups, adult clubs, and communal institutions which tend to confine their members in their primary relationships safely within the ethnic fold.

If marital assimilation, an inevitable by-product of structural assimilation, takes place fully, the minority group loses its ethnic identity in the larger host or core society, and identificational assimilation takes place. Prejudice and discrimination are no longer a problem, since eventually the descendants of the original minority group become indistinguishable, and since primary group relationships tend to build up an "in-group" feeling which encloses all the members of the group. If assimilation has been complete in all intrinsic as well as extrinsic cultural traits, then no value conflicts on civic issues are likely to arise between the now dispersed descendants of the ethnic minority and members of the core society. Thus the remaining types of assimilation have all taken place like a row of tenpins bowled over in rapid succession by a well placed strike. We may state the emergent generalization, then, as follows: *Once structural assimilation has occurred, either simultaneously with or subsequent to acculturation, all of the other types of assimilation will naturally follow.* It need hardly be pointed out that while acculturation, as we have emphasized above, does not necessarily lead to structural assimilation, structural assimilation inevitably produces acculturation. Structural assimilation, then, rather than acculturation, is seen to be the keystone of the arch of assimilation. The price of such assimilation, however, is the disappearance of the ethnic group as a separate entity and the evaporation of its distinctive values.

There are a number of other crucial hypotheses and questions which can be phrased by the manipulation of these variables. One of the most important, of course, is whether "attitude receptional" and "behavior receptional" assimilation—that is, elimination of prejudice and discrimination—may take place when acculturation, *but not structural assimilation,* occurs. This can be shown to be one of the key questions in the application of our analytical model to "cultural pluralism." Another interesting question is whether prejudice and discrimination are more closely related to differences between the core group and the ethnic minority in intrinsic culture traits or extrinsic culture traits. I would hypothesize that, at least in our era, differences in extrinsic culture are more crucial in the development of prejudice than those of an intrinsic nature (cf. Vickery & Cole, 1943, p. 45). Differences in religious belief, *per se,* are not the occasion for bitter acrimony in twentieth-century America,[6] particularly when these differences occur in middle-class Americans of native birth whose external appearance, speech patterns, and manner are notably uniform. On the other hand, the gap in extrinsic cultural traits between the zoot-suited side-burned slum juvenile and the conservatively clothed and behaving middle-class American distinctly gives the signal for mutual suspicion and hostility. This is not to say that differences in intrinsic values among ethnic groups in America, particularly as these differences spill over into demands on the shaping of American public life, may not result in power conflict. But one must make a distinction between irrational ethnic prejudice,

[6] Cf. R. M. McIver's statement: "But we do not find sufficient reason to regard religion **by itself** as of crucial importance in provoking the tensions and cleavages manifested in the everyday relationships of American society." (1948, p. 12; italics in original.)

in what might be called the old-fashioned sense, and the conflict of groups in the civic arena over issues based on opposing value-premises, sincerely held in each case.

We shall forgo additional manipulation of the variables in the analytical model at this point [7] since the preceding discussion should have clarified its potential use. We now have an analytical scheme—a set of conceptual categories—which allows us to appreciate the true complexity of the assimilation process, to note the varying directions it may take, and to discern the probable relationships of some of its parts. This set of analytical tools should serve us well as we consider the theories of assimilation and minority group life which have arisen historically in America.

Partisans of the idea of America as one huge melting pot, like adherents of Anglo-conformity, have provided no systematic delineation of their views. Indeed, the concept is one which singularly lends itself to expression in vague rhetoric which, however, noble its aims, gives minimal clues as to the exact implications of the term for the manifold spheres of societal organization and behavior. Nevertheless, certain logical inferences can be made, and one feature appears to be envisaged in all the statements of the idea: a complete mixture of the various stocks through intermarriage—in other words, marital assimilation, or amalgamation.

With regard to cultural behavior, the most characteristic implication is that the cultures of the various groups will mix and form a blend somewhat different from the cultures of any one of the groups separately. However, a neglected aspect of this model of cultural intermixture is whether all groups will make an equally influential contribution to the boiling pot, or whether there is to be a *proportionate* influence depending upon the size, power, and strategic location of the various groups. If, to illustrate hypothetically and simply, there are 100,000 Sylvanians occupying their own country, and 2000 Mundovians enter as immigrants, under the melting pot model of cultural interpenetration will the resulting blend—assuming some rough measurement were possible—consist of equal parts of Sylvanian and Mundovian culture, or will the Sylvania cultural contribution be fifty times as important and pervasive as the Mundovian contribution? The answer to this question obviously has significant consequences for the contributing societies, in relation to the questions of both objective cultural survival and group psychology.

Indeed, at one extreme of interpretation—a loose and illogical one, to be sure—the melting pot concept may envisage the culture of the immigrants as "melting" completely into the culture of the host society without leaving any cultural trace at all. It would appear that some exponents of the idea came close to feeling that this was the proper role for Southern and Eastern European im-

[7] The question, of great contemporary interest to social scientists and others concerned with problems of intergroup relations, of whether the objective behavioral phenomenon of discrimination can be reduced or eliminated prior to the reduction or elimination of the subjective attitudinal phenomenon of prejudice may be considered within this framework; thus, can "behavior receptional" assimilation take place prior to "attitude receptional" assimilation? The Supreme Court ban on racial segregation in the public schools, and state and municipal anti-discrimination legislation constitute, of course, a test of the hypothesis that legal curbs on discrimination may be successful even though prejudice still exists, and that such legal curbs may actually result in the reduction of prejudice. See Robert K. Merton (1949), David W. Petegorsky (1951), Arnold M. Rose (1951), John P. Roche and Milton M. Gordon (1957).

migrants to play in the American melting process. In this form, of course, the melting pot concept embraces a view of acculturation which is hardly distinguishable in nature from that of Anglo-conformity, except that the conformity is to be exacted toward a cultural blend to which the cultures of immigrant groups from Northern and Western Europe have been conceded an earlier contribution.

With regard to the remaining assimilation variables, the analysis may proceed as follows: If large-scale intermarriage is to have taken place, then obviously the immigrants must have entered the cliques, clubs, other primary groups, and institutions of the host society and, in addition, placed their own impress upon these social structures to some extent. Thus the process of structural assimilation must somehow reflect a blending effect, also. Identificational assimilation takes place in the form of all groups merging their previous sense of peoplehood into a new and larger ethnic identity which, in some fashion, honors its multiple origins at the same time that it constitutes an entity distinct from them all. Prejudice and discrimination must be absent since there are not even any identifiably separate groups to be their target, and "civic assimilation" will have taken place since disparate cultural values are assumed to have merged and power conflict between groups would be neither necessary nor possible. This, then, is the "ideal-typical" model of the melting pot process. With this analysis and the previous discussion in mind, let us take a quick look at the American experience to see how well the model applies.

While no exact figures on the subject are attainable, it is safe to say that a substantial proportion of the descendants of the non-English immigrants of colonial times and the first three-quarters of the nineteenth century (with the exception of the Irish Catholics and the German Jews) have by now been absorbed into the general white "sociological Protestant" sector of American life. That is to say, they do not live in communal subsocieties which are lineal descendants of those which their immigrant ancestors created, and so far as they understand it, are simply "Americans" who may be vaguely conscious of an immigrant forebear here and there from a non-English source but for whom this has little current meaning. This would include many descendants of the Scotch-Irish, German Protestants, Swedes, and Norwegians, among other groups from Northern and Western Europe, as well as, in all probability, a few with colonial Jewish ancestry whose early American progenitors converted to Christianity (not to mention occasional individuals who have a mulatto ancestor who, at some time, "passed" into the white group).[8] This does not mean that communal societies with appropriate institutions representing most of these ancestral groups do not still exist, but that, in relation to the total number of ethnic descendants, they become increasingly thinly manned as the third and fourth generation leave their rural or small town (occasionally urban) enclaves and venture forth into the broader social world.

The burden of our point should now be clear. Entrance by the descendants of these immigrants into the social struc-

[8] Estimates of the number of very light Negroes who "pass" permanently into the white group range from 2000 to 30,000 annually, although the practice is obviously so shrouded in secrecy that even these limits may not include the true figure. (See Maurice R. Davie, 1949; also Gunnar Myrdal, 1944.)

tures of the existing white Protestant society, and the culmination of this process in intermarriage, has not led to the creation of new structures, new institutional forms, and a new sense of identity which draws impartially from all sources, but rather to immersion in a subsocietal network of groups and institutions which was already fixed in essential outline with an Anglo-Saxon, general Protestant stamp. The prior existence of Anglo-Saxon institutional forms as the norm, the pervasiveness of the English language, and the numerical dominance of the Anglo-Saxon population made this outcome inevitable.

If we turn to the cultural realm, we find much the same result. The tremendous contributions of non-English immigrants—of both the "Old" and "New" varieties—to American civilization collectively in the form of agricultural and industrial manpower, as sources of population growth, as bearers of strategic new crafts and skills, and as patrons of the developing fine arts is not here in question. Nor is the brilliant record achieved by countless individual immigrants and their descendants in the business, professional, scientific, and artistic life of the nation. All this has been mentioned before. The question at issue is rather the alteration of cultural forms. Here we would argue that, in great part, rather than an impartial melting of the divergent cultural patterns from all immigrant sources, what has actually taken place has been more of a transforming of the later immigrant's specific cultural contributions into the Anglo-Saxon mould. As George Stewart has put it, a more accurate figure of speech to describe the American experience would be that of a "transmuting pot" in which "as the foreign elements, a little at a time, were added to the pot, they were not merely melted but were largely transmuted, and so did not affect the original material as strikingly as might be expected" (1954, p. 23). Will Herberg echoes this view. "The enthusiasts of the 'melting pot' . . . ," he writes, "were wrong . . . in regard to the cultural aspect of the assimilative process. They looked forward to a genuine blending of cultures, to which every ethnic strain would make its own contribution and out of which would emerge a new cultural synthesis, no more English than German or Italian and yet in some sense transcending and embracing them all. In certain respects this has indeed become the case: our American cuisine includes antipasto and spaghetti, frankfurters and pumpernickel, filet mignon and french fried potatoes, borsch, sour cream, and gefüllte fish, on a perfect equality with fried chicken, ham and eggs, and pork and beans. But it would be a mistake to infer from this that the American's image of himself—and that means the ethnic group member's image of himself as he becomes American—is a composite or synthesis of the ethnic elements that have gone into the making of the American. It is nothing of the kind: the American's image of himself is still the Anglo-American ideal it was at the beginning of our independent existence. The 'national type' as ideal has always been, and remains, pretty well fixed. It is the *Mayflower*, John Smith, Davy Crockett, George Washington, and Abraham Lincoln that define the American's self-image, and this is true whether the American in question is a descendant of the Pilgrims or the grandson of an immigrant from southeastern Europe. . . . Our cultural assimilation has taken place not in a 'melting pot,' but rather in a [citing Stewart] 'transmuting pot' in which all ingredients have been transformed and assimilated to an idealized 'Anglo-Saxon' model" (Herberg, 1955, pp. 33–4).

Both structurally and culturally, then, the "single melting pot" vision of America has been something of an illusion—a generous and idealistic one, in one sense, since it held out the promise of a kind of psychological equality under the banner of an impartial symbol of America larger than the symbols of any of the constituent groups—but one which exhibited a considerable degree of sociological naïveté. Given the prior arrival time of the English colonists, the numerical dominance of the English stock, and the cultural dominance of Anglo-Saxon institutions, the invitation extended to non-English immigrants to "melt" could only result, if thoroughly accepted, in the latter's loss of group identity, the transformation of their cultural survivals into Anglo-Saxon patterns, and the development of their descendants in the image of the Anglo-Saxon American.

Culturally, this process of absorbing Anglo-Saxon patterns has moved massively and inexorably, with greater or lesser speed, among all ethnic groups. Structurally, however, the outcome has, so far, been somewhat different, depending on whether we are considering white Protestant descendants of the "Old" immigration, white Catholics and Jews of both periods of immigration, or the racial and quasi-racial minorities. Here, then, is where the "triple melting pot" hypothesis of Kennedy and others becomes applicable. While Protestant descendants of Germans and Scandinavians can, if they wish, merge structurally into the general white Protestant subsociety with relative ease, Jews, Irish Catholics, Italian Catholics, and Polish Catholics cannot do so without either formal religious conversion or a kind of sociological "'passing"—neither process being likely to attract overwhelmingly large numbers. Negroes, Orientals, Mexican-Americans, and some Puerto Ricans are prevented by racial discrimination from participating meaningfully in either the white Protestant or the white Catholic communities. Nationality background differences within the white population, however, appear to be more amenable to dissolving influences. The passing of the "nationality" communities may be slower than Kennedy and Herberg intimate and the rate of Catholic-Protestant intermarriage has been shown to be substantially higher in the country as a whole than in New Haven. However, a vastly important and largely neglected sociological point about mixed marriages, racial, religious, or national, apart from the rate, is *in what social structures the intermarried couples and their children incorporate themselves*. If Catholic-Protestant intermarried couples live more or less completely within either the Catholic social community or the Protestant social community, the sociological fact of the existence of the particular religious community and its separation from other religious communities remains.

The result of these processes, structurally speaking, is that American society has come to be composed of a number of "pots," or subsocieties, three of which are the religious containers marked Protestant, Catholic, and Jew, which are in the process of melting down the white nationality background communities contained within them; others are racial groups which are not allowed to melt structurally; and still others are substantial remnants of the nationality background communities manned by those members who are either of the first generation, or who, while native born, choose to remain within the ethnic enclosure. All of these constitute the ethnic subsocieties which we have described earlier, with their network of primary groups, organizations, and institutions within which a member's life may be comfortably enclosed except for secondary contacts with "outsiders" in the process of making a living and carrying out the minimal duties of political citizenship, if he so desires. Another pot besides the religious containers which is actually doing some structural melting is labeled "intellectuals." All these containers, as they bubble along in the fires of American life and experience are tending to produce, with somewhat differing speeds, products which are culturally very similar, while at the same time they remain structurally separate. The entire picture is one which, with the cultural qualifications already noted, may be called a "multiple melting pot." And so we arrive at the "pluralism" which characterizes the contemporary American scene.

13 Socio-economic background and personality

HILDE T. HIMMELWEIT

During the last four years, my colleagues [1] and I have carried out a series of inquiries into the psychological aspects of social differentiations. There is not sufficient time to present a systematic account of these studies. Instead I shall concentrate on findings in four areas which I think are of more general theoretical interest.

The first set of findings relate to the area of *tensions*. Allison Davis and others in this country suggest that a kind of adaptive socialized anxiety is generated more readily as a result of middle class as compared with working class methods of upbringing. While many of the differences between middle and working class child rearing were also found in England, there was no evidence of differences in the amount of overt or covert anxiety shown. By relating the differences to the total process of parent-child interaction, we arrived at a rather different interpretation of the consequences of these variations in upbringing for the personality of the child—an explanation which we think would account for the absence of greater anxiety in the middle class child despite the very real pressures which are put upon him.

The second area concerns a problem

Abridged from the **International Social Science Bulletin**, 1955, 7, 29–35, with permission of the author and of **UNESCO**.

[1] Eve Bene, H. A. Halsey, and A. N. Oppenheim.

central to the field of social pyschology, namely that of *the transmission of values*. Warner and others have tried to explain the relatively poorer integration into school of the working class child as the result, in part, of conflict in the child's mind between one set of values which he is taught at home and another at school. Such integration into school, Warner suggests, is made much easier for the middle class child, in whose case values taught at home and those taught at school reinforce one another. By obtaining data from both parents and children covering their value systems, we find that the conflict interpretation is too simplified and that certain other important variables need to be taken into account.

The third set of findings relate to *the teacher's role in this process of socialization.*

The last area is that of *cross national comparison*. Some tentative findings will be presented to show the feasibility of such cross national studies, and the extent to which they can serve as a first useful step in understanding national character.

I will begin by giving a brief outline of the main inquiry, in which over 600 13–14 year old boys served as subjects.

We had several objectives in planning research in this field. First, we wanted to ascertain the degree to which the Davis hypotheses could be confirmed in England, using, not the relatively extreme and selected samples of middle and lower lower class subjects on which he based his findings, but rather more representative samples ranging from middle middle, lower middle via upper working to lower working class groups.

Secondly, we wanted to extend our inquiry beyond those areas where previous research had shown social class differences to obtain. Exclusive concentration on those areas alone, we believed, might well lead to an overestimation of their significance in the total picture of the child's development. Consequently, we aimed, as far as it was possible by group techniques of inquiry, to arrive at the kind of data normally collected for case studies—data which would then make it possible to place the social class differences found in their appropriate context.

The areas on which we obtained information were:

1. The boy's activities at home, at school and in his leisure time.
2. His school performance, his attitude to and his anxiety about school.
3. His vocational and educational aspiration and his perception of his parents' aspiration for him.
4. His value system—the things he considers good or bad things to do—his hierarchy of values.
5. His awareness of social class differences and of social class indices within his society, with special reference to his assessment of the prestige of occupations.
6. His perception of his relations with parents, and with peers.
7. Some indications of the nature of his tensions and of his mode of reacting to frustration.
8. His performance on personality tests.

Each boy was tested for several sessions, seven hours in all. An aspect on which we wanted to obtain information was studied by a variety of techniques ranging from closed questions of the yes, no or agree-disagree scale variety, via questions in which the child was presented with a verbal problem situation and given multiple choice answers, to open-ended questions such as "a good father is one who . . . ; home is a place where . . ." Projective techniques were used to obtain measures of the child's aggression and anxiety.

Each area of inquiry was sampled by the variety of techniques described above. In this way we obtained the boy's spontaneous frame of reference as well as his reactions to questions which were placed in a more adult frame of reference, and to which he could respond by accepting or rejecting the values stated.

The study was restricted to London. All boys in the third grade of 11 state schools were included (equivalent to American seventh grade). The boys were assigned to a given social class on the basis of the prestige of their father's occupation. As our inquiry was restricted to state schools, it included no upper and very few upper middle class boys. Since the results for the two subgroups within each class were relatively similar, to make reporting easier I shall contrast the two social class groups only.[2]

Results. We confirmed several of the Davis and Warner hypotheses. We found middle class children more concerned about how well they do at school, more integrated into school, and with higher educational and vocational aspirations. The parents supervise their schoolwork more closely and are in their turn more concerned about the boys' school performance. Their supervision extends also, to a more marked degree than in the working class, to the boy's activities at home and to his leisure activities. The middle class children, showed a more rigid value system, not only with regard to school values but generally considered more things bad things to do, and believed more strongly that infringement of rules required punishment. They also showed relatively less interest in the opposite sex. Despite so many confirmatory results as to the greater pressure to which the middle class child is subjected, both externally by the parents and internally by his more rigid superego and more intropunitive technique of handling frustrations, no evidence of greater overall anxiety or tension was obtained.

We believe that this is due to the far greater *child-centredness* of middle class homes. On all questions dealing with family relationship, the middle class child felt more accepted, he said more often than the working class boy that he could discuss things with his parents, that he could confide in them, and that they shared his interests. It would appear then that pressure exerted in a protected, cushioned environment can be tolerated without undue anxiety.

It seems to us that too many studies have concentrated upon external happenings, upon differences in acceleratory or supervisory handling in early years, and on differences in pressure exerted to do well, and have placed too little emphasis upon the emotional context in which they occur. According to our findings, the working class child, while less pushed, is emotionally left more to fend for himself. Dr. Frenkel-Brunswik suggests that the working class child's need for dependence may be less well satisfied compared with that of the middle class child. It would be important then to map all the regions in which tensions are aroused in the adolescents

[2] At the age of eleven, children are placed into one of three types of secondary schools: the grammar school, the technical school, or the secondary modern school. Selection tends to be made on the basis of intelligence and attainment test results. Approximately the top 20 per cent of each age group with I.Q.'s of 115 and over are selected for grammar schools. The grammar school curriculum is academic; its pupils tend to enter white-collar jobs or to go on to University. A working class boy accepted for a grammar school is, therefore, already beginning his upward social mobility.

of the two classes—regions which may well differ from one another—rather than to assume that because a child is pushed educationally, he ought to be more anxious than another child where pressure in this particular area is less strong.

The second set of findings I wanted to discuss was that concerned with the transmission of values. We interviewed a random sample of the parents of the boys, giving them some of the questionnaires for which we had already answers from the boys.

One of the hypotheses we had was that the upwardly socially mobile working class boy would try to become like his middle class co-pupil and that his answers would be markedly different from the working class boy who was not upwardly mobile. We further predicted that in the case of the middle class the two school groups would not differ markedly. Our results were as follows: First, the differences between the school groups both in the middle and in the working class were so marked, and so very much more marked than any difference between classes within the same school, that this is likely to reflect in large measure differences in educational and intellectual level. This underscores the need for taking account of intelligence in social class studies of this kind. Secondly, we found that the difference between the two working class groups was the most marked. This provides suggestive evidence that the upwardly mobile boy is trying to adopt the new middle class values. We further predicted that in the case of the parents, middle and working class parents would give different answers, but that the two middle class and the two working class groups would be very similar in their outlook. If this were found to be true, it would support the hypothesis that the socially mobile boy is acquiring a different hierarchy of values as a result of contact with the school ethos.

The results were however quite different. Of all our groups, the parents of the upwardly socially mobile boys had a much more middle class set of values than any other group, including the two middle class parental groups. Thus, far from coming from a home where the values held conflict with those taught at school, these boys tend to come from homes of over-conformers to middle class values. It is likely in fact that this may have been initially responsible for the successful passing of examinations at the age of 11. Why is it then that, despite the pressure and support from home, the working class boy is less well integrated into school and subscribes less to the prevailing school ethos. I suggest here that two further variables need to be taken into account. First, the working class boys with whom he is in contact out of school may well act as an antidote to the grammar school outlook. Secondly, there is the attitude of the teacher, which may be based on stereotypes about the capacity, personality and value system of working class parents and their children, whom in recent years he has had to accept into his school in ever increasing numbers.

This brings me to the third aspect which I wanted to discuss, namely, that of the role of the teacher in the process of social mobility. In the adolescent study, we asked the teachers of each form to make a series of separate assessments, i.e., to pick out for each of the following characteristics the five best and the five worst boys. Eleven teachers took part, each assessing the children of whom he was in charge. They were asked to assess scholastic performance and then in turn such characteristics as industriousness, sense of responsibility, interest in school affairs, good behaviour, good manners and popularity with other boys. The teachers did not know the purpose of our investigation, and once they had given the names of the boys we classified them in accordance with their socio-economic background. All the comparisons concerning personality characteristics showed that more middle class boys were chosen by each of the 11 teachers as being the five best. In the teachers' eyes, then, the middle class child is better mannered, more responsible, more mature—and yet also more popular with the other boys. This, despite the fact that the sociometrics which the boys did themselves showed no such class typed picture. Whilst for other characteristics no independent assessment could be obtained, the evidence appears suggestive as to the ambivalent attitude of the teachers. This was further confirmed by the second inquiry to which I referred earlier, namely that in which a random sample of 400 teachers were interviewed. Questions were included to investigate their attitude to this new pressure for equal educational opportunity. In part the teachers' attitude reflected official political party views, but within each party, the sharply upwardly mobile were the ones who said more often that the system permitted the wrong type of child to get into the grammar school. This, despite the fact that—or probably because—the teacher himself had used this process to achieve his present status. Further, sharply upwardly mobile teachers tended to be more authoritarian in their outlook. There is not time to enlarge further on this problem. These pointers indicate, however, the need for studying much more the subtle process of identification and projection which operates in the teacher and which is likely to be an important factor in preventing adequate integration of the working class child into school.

The feasibility of cross national comparison. Mr. J. Montague, Associate Professor of Sociology of State College, Washington, joined our research group in London and repeated part of the inquiry using the same questionnaires on 700 13–14 years old boys in Spokane, Washington. Preliminary comparative analysis has shown that while in certain matters national rather than class differences are more pronounced, in others the English and American middle classes have more in common with one another than either the English working and the English middle class or the American middle or working classes: these matters concern severity of moral code, conformity with school values, and a closeness of affectional ties between parents and children which I have just mentioned. While none of this is perhaps in any way surprising, it is a field in which generalizations abound and one in which precise documentation is important. It is important to study in particular the hierarchy of values in given groups in the various countries, e.g., the strength of their "need achievement" drive, the areas in which this need achievement operates most strongly and the goal seeking mechanisms developed by the various groups as well as the defensive mechanisms used. I suggest that such studies should not be carried out on random samples, but on stratified samples, stratified by social class and other relevant variables. Using stratified samples the kind of comparison I have just described can be carried out. For example, if the leaders of one country are drawn primarily from a section of the population different from that from which the leaders of the other country are drawn, then we can describe and predict their behaviour far better if we can place their reactions in the appropriate cultural as well as subcultural setting. Such studies, in the present era of misunderstanding—misunderstanding both of motives and of mechanisms—are of value and it is my belief that social psychologists have now the tools and the experience to make a very real contribution in this field.

14 The changing American child

URIE BRONFENBRENNER

A question of moment

It is now a matter of scientific record that patterns of child rearing in the United States have changed appreciably over the past twenty-five years (Bronfenbrenner, 1958). Middle class parents especially have moved away from the more rigid and strict styles of care and discipline advocated in the early twenties and thirties toward modes of response involving greater tolerance of the child's impulses and desires, freer expression of affection, and increased reliance on "psychological" methods of discipline, such as reasoning and appeals to guilt, as distinguished from more direct techniques like physical punishment. At the same time, the gap between the social classes in their goals and methods of child rearing appears to be narrowing, with working class parents beginning to adopt both the values and techniques of the middle class. Finally, there is dramatic correspondence between these observed shifts in parental values and behavior and the changing character of the attitudes and practices advocated in successive editions of such widely read manuals as the Children's Bureau bulletin on *Infant Care* and Spock's *Baby and Child Care* (1946). Such correspondence should not be taken to mean that the expert has now become the principal instigator and instrument of social change, since the ideas of scientists and professional workers themselves reflect in part the operation of deep-rooted cultural processes. Nevertheless, the fact remains that changes in values and practices advocated by prestigeful professional figures can be substantially accelerated by rapid and widespread dissemination through the press, mass media of communication, and public discussion.

Given these facts, it becomes espe-

Reprinted with slight abridgment from the **Journal of Social Issues**, 1961, 17, 6–18, with permission of the author and the Society for the Psychological Study of Social Issues.

cially important to gauge the effect of the changes that are advocated and adopted. Nowhere is this issue more significant, both scientifically and socially, than in the sphere of familial values and behavior. It is certainly no trivial matter to ask whether the changes that have occurred in the attitudes and actions of parents over the past twenty-five years have been such as to affect the personality development of their children, so that the boys and girls of today are somewhat different in character structure from those of a decade or more ago. Or, to put the question more succinctly: has the changing American parent produced a changing American child?

A strategy of inference

Do we have any basis for answering this intriguing question? To begin with, do we have any evidence of changes in the behavior of children in successive decades analogous to those we have already been able to find for parents? If so, we could take an important first step toward a solution of the problem. Unfortunately, in contrast to his gratifying experience in seeking and finding appropriate data on parents, the present writer has, to date, been unable to locate enough instances in which comparable methods of behavioral assessment have been employed with different groups of children of similar ages over an extended period of time. Although the absence of such material precludes any direct and unequivocal approach to the question at hand, it is nevertheless possible, through a series of inferences from facts already known, to arrive at some estimate of what the answer might be. Specifically, although as yet we have no comparable data on the relation between parental and child behavior for different families at successive points in time, we do have facts on the influence of parental treatment on child behavior at a given point in time; that is, we know that certain variations in parental behavior tend to be accompanied by systematic differences in the personality characteristics of children. If we are willing to assume that these same relationships obtained not only at a given moment but across different points in time, we are in a position to infer the possible effects on children of changing patterns of child rearing over the years. It is this strategy that we propose to follow.

The changing American parent

We have already noted the major changes in parental behavior discerned in a recent analysis of data reported over a twenty-five year period (Bronfenbrenner, 1958). These secular trends may be summarized as follows:

1. Greater permissiveness toward the child's spontaneous desires
2. Freer expression of affection
3. Increased reliance on indirect "psychological" techniques of discipline (such as reasoning or appeals to guilt) vs. direct methods (like physical punishment, scolding, or threats)
4. In consequence of the above shifts in the direction of what are predominantly middle class values and techniques, a narrowing of the gap between social classes in their patterns of child rearing.

Since the above analysis was published, a new study has documented an additional trend. Bronson, Katten, and Livson (1959) have compared patterns of paternal and maternal authority and affection in two generations of families from the California Guidance Study. Unfortunately, the time span surveyed overlaps only partially with the twenty-five year period covered in our own analysis, the first California generation having been raised in the early 1900's and the second in the late twenties and early thirties. Accordingly, if we are to consider the California results along with the others cited above, we must make the somewhat risky assumption that a trend discerned in the first three decades of the century has continued in the same direction through the early 1950's. With this important qualification, an examination of the data cited by Bronson *et al.* (1959) points to still another, secular trend—a shift over the years in the pattern of parental role differentiation within the family. Specifically:

5. In succeeding generations the relative position of the father vis-à-vis the mother is shifting with the former becoming increasingly more affectionate and less authoritarian, and the latter becoming relatively more important as the agent of discipline, especially for boys.

"Psychological" techniques of discipline and their effects

In pursuing our analytic strategy, we next seek evidence of the effects on the behavior of children of variations in parental treatment of the type noted in our inventory. We may begin by noting that the variables involved in the first three secular trends constitute a complex that has received considerable attention in recent research in parent-child relationships. Within the last three years, two sets of investigators, working independently, have called attention to the greater efficacy of "love-oriented" or "psychological" techniques in bringing about desired behavior in the child (Sears, Maccoby, & Levin, 1957; Miller & Swanson, 1958, 1960). The present writer, noting that such methods are especially favored by middle class parents, offered the following analysis of the nature of these techniques and the reasons for their effectiveness:

> Such parents are, in the first place, more likely to overlook offenses, and when they do punish, they are less likely to ridicule or inflict physical pain. Instead, they reason with the youngster, isolate him, appeal to guilt, show disappointment—in short, convey in a variety of ways, on the one hand, the kind of behavior that is expected of the child; on the other, the realization that transgression means the interruption of a mutually valued relationship. . . .
>
> These findings [of greater efficacy] mean that middle class parents, though in one sense more lenient in their discipline techniques, are using methods that are actually more compelling. Moreover, the compelling power of these practices is probably enhanced by the more permissive treatment accorded to middle class children in the early years of life. The successful use of withdrawal of love as a discipline technique implies the prior existence of a gratifying relationship; the more love present in the first instance, the greater the threat implied in its withdrawal (Bronfenbrenner, 1958).

It is now a well-established fact that children from middle class families tend to excel those from lower class in many characteristics ordinarily regarded as desirable, such as self-control, achievement, responsibility, leadership, popularity, and adjustment in general (see Mussen & Conger, 1956). If, as seems plausible, such differences in behavior are attributable at least in part to class-linked variations in parental treatment, the strategy of inference we have adopted would appear on first blush to lead to a rather optimistic conclusion. Since, over the years, increasing numbers of parents have been adopting the more effective socialization techniques typically employed by the middle class, does it not follow that successive generations of children should show gains in the development of effective behavior and desirable personality characteristics?

Unfortunately, this welcome conclusion, however logical, is premature, for it fails to take into account all of the available facts.

Sex, socialization, and social class

To begin with, the parental behaviors we have been discussing are differentially distributed not only by socio-economic status but also by sex. As we have pointed out elsewhere (Bronfenbrenner, 1961), girls are exposed to more affection and less punishment than boys, but at the same time are more likely to be subjected to "love-oriented" discipline of the type which encourages the development of internalized controls. And, consistent with our line of reasoning, girls are found repeatedly to be "more obedient, cooperative, and in general better socialized than boys at comparable age levels." But this is not the whole story.

> . . . At the same time, the research results indicate that girls tend to be more anxious, timid, dependent, and sensitive to rejection. If these differences are a function of differential treatment by parents, then it would seem that the more "efficient" methods of child rearing employed with girls involve some risk of what might be called "over-socialization" (Bronfenbrenner, 1961).

One could argue, of course, that the contrasting behaviors of boys and girls have less to do with differential parental treatment than with genetically-based maturational influences. Nevertheless, two independent lines of evidence suggest that socialization techniques do contribute to individual differences, *within the same sex*, precisely in the types of personality characteristics noted above. In the first place, variations in child behavior and parental treatment strikingly similar to those we have cited for the two sexes are reported in a recent comprehensive study of differences between first and later born children (Schachter, 1959). Like girls, first children receive more attention, are more likely to be exposed to "psychological" discipline, and end up more anxious and dependent, whereas later children, like boys, are more aggressive and self-confident.

A second line of evidence comes from our own current research. We have been concerned with the role of parents in the development of such "constructive" personality characteristics as responsibility and leadership among adolescent boys and girls. Our findings reveal not only the usual differences in adolescents' and parents' behaviors associated with the sex of the child, but also a striking contrast in the relationship between parental and child behaviors for the two sexes. To start on firm and familiar ground, girls are rated by their teachers as more responsible than boys, whereas the latter obtain higher scores on leadership. Expected differences similarly appear in the realm of parental behavior: girls receive more affection, praise, and companionship; boys are subjected to more physical punishment and achievement demands. Quite unanticipated, however, at least by us, was the finding that both parental affection and discipline appeared to facilitate effective psychological functioning in boys, but to impede the development of such constructive behavior in girls. Closer examination of our data indicated that both extremes of either affection or discipline were deleterious for all children, but that the process of socialization entailed somewhat different risks for the two sexes. Girls were especially susceptible to the detrimental influence of over-protection; boys to the ill effects of insufficient parental discipline and support. Or, to put it in more colloquial terms: boys suffered more often from too little taming, girls from too much.

In an attempt to account for this contrasting pattern of relationships, we proposed the notion of differential optimal levels of affection and authority for the two sexes.

The qualities of independence, initiative, and self-sufficiency, which are especially valued for boys in our culture, apparently require for their development a somewhat different balance of authority and affection than is found in the "love-oriented" strategy characteristically applied with girls. While an affectional context is important for the socialization of boys, it must evidently be accompanied by and be compatible with a strong component of parental discipline. Otherwise, the boy finds himself in the same situation as the girl, who, having received greater affection, is more sensitive to its withdrawal, with the result that a little discipline goes a long way and strong authority is constricting rather than constructive (Bronfenbrenner, 1960).

What is more, available data suggest that this very process may already be operating for boys from upper middle class homes. To begin with, differential treatment of the sexes is at a minimum for these families. Contrasting parental attitudes and behaviors toward boys and girls are pronounced only at lower class levels, and decrease as one moves up the socio-economic scale (Kohn, 1959; Bronfenbrenner, 1960). Thus our own results show that it is primarily at lower middle class levels that boys get more punishment than girls, and the latter receive greater warmth and attention. With an increase in the family's social position, direct discipline drops off, especially for boys, and indulgence and protectiveness decrease for girls. As a result, patterns of parental treatment for the two sexes begin to converge. In like manner, we find that the differential effects of parental behavior on the two sexes are marked only in the lower middle class. It is here that girls especially risk being overprotected and boys not receiving sufficient discipline and support. In upper middle class the picture changes. Girls are not as readily debilitated by parental affection and power; nor is parental discipline as effective in fostering the development of responsibility and leadership in boys.

All these trends point to the conclusion that the "risks" experienced by each sex during the process of socialization tend to be somewhat different at different social class levels. Thus the danger of overprotection for girls is especially great in lower class families, but lower in upper middle class because of the decreased likelihood of overprotection. Analogously, boys are in greater danger of suffering from inadequate discipline and support in lower middle than in upper middle class. But the upper middle class boy, unlike the girl, exchanges one hazard for another. Since at this upper level the more potent "psychological" techniques of discipline are likely to be employed with both sexes, the boy presumably now too runs the risk of being "oversocialized," of losing some of his capacity for independent aggressive accomplishment.

Accordingly, if our line of reasoning is correct, we should expect a changing pattern of sex differences at successive socio-economic levels. Specifically, aspects of effective psychological functioning favoring girls should be most pronounced in the upper middle class; those favoring boys in the lower middle. A recent analysis of some of our data bears out this expectation. Girls excel boys on such variables as *responsibility* and *social acceptance* primarily at the higher socio-economic levels. In contrast, boys surpass girls on such traits as *leadership, level of aspiration,* and *competitiveness* almost exclusively in lower middle class. Indeed, with a rise in a family's social position, the differences tend to reverse themselves with girls now excelling boys. These shifts in sex difference with a rise in class status are significant at the 5% level of confidence (one-tailed test).

Trends in personality development: a first approximation

The implications for our original line of inquiry are clear. We are suggesting that the "love-oriented" socialization techniques, which over the past twenty-five years have been employed in increasing degree by American middle class families, may have negative as well as constructive aspects. While fostering the internalization of adult standards and the development of socialized behavior, they may also have the effect of undermining capacities for initiative and independence, particularly in boys. Males exposed to this "modern" pattern of child rearing might be expected to differ from their counterparts of a quarter century ago in being somewhat more conforming and anxious, less enterprising and self-sufficient, and, in general, possessing more of the virtues and liabilities commonly associated with feminine character structure (see Green, 1946).

At long last, then, our strategy of inference has led us to a first major conclusion. The term "major" is appropriate since the conclusion takes as its points of departure and return four of the secular trends which served as the impetus for our inquiry. Specifically, through a series of empirical links and theoretical extrapolations, we have arrived at an estimate of the effects on children of the tendency of successive generations of parents to become progressively more permissive, to express affection more freely, to utilize "psychological" techniques of discipline, and, by moving in these directions to narrow the gap between the social classes in their patterns of child rearing.

Family structure and personality development

But one other secular trend remains to be considered: what of the changing pattern of parental role differentiation during the first three decades of the century? If our extrapolation is correct, the balance of power within the family has continued to shift with fathers yielding parental authority to mothers and taking on some of the nurturant and affectional functions traditionally associated with the maternal role. Again we have no direct evidence of the effects of such secular changes on successive generations of children, and must look for leads to analogous data on contemporaneous relationships.

We may begin by considering the contribution of each parent to the socialization processes we have examined thus far. Our data indicate that it is primarily mothers who tend to employ "love-oriented" techniques of discipline and fathers who rely on more direct methods like physical punishment. The above statement must be qualified, however, by reference to the sex of the child, for it is only in relation to boys that fathers use direct punishment more than mothers. More generally, . . . the results reveal a tendency for each parent to be somewhat more active, firm, and demanding with a child of the same sex, more lenient and indulgent with a child of the opposite sex . . . . The reversal is most complete with respect to discipline, with fathers being stricter with boys, mothers with girls. In the spheres of affection and protectiveness, there is no actual shift in preference, but the tendency to be especially warm and solicitous with girls is much more pronounced among fathers than among mothers. In fact, generally speaking, it is the father who is more likely to treat children of the two sexes differently (Bronfenbrenner, 1960).

Consistent with this pattern of results, it is primarily the behavior of fathers that accounts for the differential effects of parental behavior on the two sexes and for the individual differences within each sex. In other words, it is paternal authority and affection that tend especially to be salutary for sons but detrimental for daughters. But as might be anticipated from what we already know, these trends are pronounced only in the lower middle class; with a rise in the family's social status, both parents tend to have similar effects on their children, both within and across sexes. Such a trend is entirely to be expected since parental role differentiation tends to decrease markedly as one ascends the socio-economic ladder. It is almost exclusively in lower middle class homes that fathers are more strict with boys and mothers with girls. To the extent that direct discipline is employed in upper middle class families, it tends to be exercised by both parents equally. Here again we see a parallelism between shifts in parental behavior across time and social class in the direction of forms (in this instance of family structure) favored by the upper middle class group.

What kinds of children, then, can we expect to develop in families in which the father plays a predominantly affectionate role, and a relatively low level of discipline is exercised equally by both parents? A tentative answer to this question is supplied by a preliminary analysis of our data in which the relation between parental role structure and adolescent behavior was examined with controls for the family's social class position. The results of this analysis are summarized as follows: . . . Both responsibility and leadership are fostered by the relatively greater salience of the parent of the same sex . . . . Boys tend to be more responsible when the father rather than the mother is the principal disciplinarian; girls are more dependable when the mother is the major authority figure . . . . In short, boys thrive in a patriarchal context, girls in a matriarchal . . . . The most dependent and least dependable adolescents describe family arrangements that are neither patriarchal nor matriarchal, but equalitarian. To state the issue in more provocative form, our data suggest that the democratic family, which for so many years has been held up and aspired to as a model by professionals and enlightened laymen, tends to produce young people who "do not take initiative," "look to others for direction and decision," and "cannot be counted on to fulfill obligations" (Bronfenbrenner, 1960).

In the wake of so sweeping a conclusion, it is important to call attention to the tentative, if not tenuous character of our findings. The results were based on a single study employing crude questionnaire methods and rating scales. Also, our interpretation is limited by the somewhat "attenuated" character of most of the families classified as patriarchal or matriarchal in our sample. Extreme concentrations of power in one or another parent were comparatively rare. Had they been more frequent, we suspect the data would have shown that such extreme asymmetrical patterns of authority were detrimental rather than salutary for effective psychological development, perhaps even more disorganizing than equalitarian forms.

Nevertheless, our findings do find some peripheral support in the work of others. A number of investigations, for example, point to the special importance of the father in the socialization of boys (Bandura & Walters, 1959; Mussen & Distler, 1959). Further corroborative evidence appears in the growing series of studies of effects of paternal absence (Bach, 1946; Sears, Pintler & Sears, 1946; Lynn & Sawrey, 1959; Tiller, 1958). The absence of the father apparently not only affects the behavior of the child directly but also influences the mother in the direction of greater overprotectiveness. The effect of both these tendencies is especially critical for male children; boys from father-absent homes tend to be markedly more submissive and dependent. Studies dealing explicitly with the influence of parental role structure in intact families are few and far between. Papanek (1957), in an unpublished doctoral dissertation, reports greater sex-role differentiation among children from homes in which the parental roles were differentiated. And in a carefully controlled study, Kohn and Clausen (1956) find that "schizophrenic patients more frequently than normal persons report that their mothers played a very strong authority role and the father a very weak authority role." Finally, what might best be called complementary evidence for our inferences regarding trends in family structure and their effects comes from the work of Miller, Swanson, and their associates (1958, 1960) on the differing patterns of behavior exhibited by families from *bureaucratic* and *entrepreneurial* work settings. These investigators argue that the entrepreneurial-bureaucratic dichotomy represents a new cleavage in American social structure that cuts across and overrides social class influences and carries with it its own characteristic patterns of family structure and socialization. Thus one investigation (Gold & Slater, 1958) contrasts the exercise of power in families of husbands employed in two kinds of job situations: (a) those working in large organizations with three or more levels of supervision; (b) those self-employed or working in small organizations with few levels of supervision. With appropriate controls for social class, equalitarian families were found more frequently in the bureaucratic groups; patriarchal and, to a lesser extent, matriarchal in the entrepreneurial setting. Another study (Miller & Swanson, 1958) shows that, in line with Miller and Swanson's hypotheses, parents from these same two groups tend to favor rather different ends and means of socialization, with entrepreneurial families putting considerably more emphasis on the development of independence and mastery and on the use of "psychological" techniques of discipline. These differences appear at both upper and lower middle class levels but are less pronounced in higher socio-economic strata. It is Miller and Swanson's belief, however, that the trend is toward the bureaucratic way of life, with its less structured patterns of family organization and child rearing. The evidence we have cited on secular changes in family structure and the inferences we have drawn regarding their possible effects on personality development are on the whole consistent with their views.

Looking forward

If Miller and Swanson are correct in the prediction that America is moving toward a bureaucratic society that emphasizes, to put it colloquially, "getting along" rather than "getting ahead," then presumably we can look forward to ever increasing numbers of equalitarian families who, in turn, will produce successive generations of ever more adaptable but unaggressive "organization men." But recent signs do not all point in this direction. In our review of secular trends in child rearing practices we detected in the data from the more recent studies a slowing up in the headlong rush toward greater permissiveness and toward reliance on indirect methods of discipline. We pointed out also that if the most recent editions of well-thumbed guidebooks on child care are as reliable harbingers of the future as they have been in the past, we can anticipate something of a return to the more explicit discipline techniques of an earlier era. Perhaps the most important forces, however, acting to redirect both the aims and methods of child rearing in America emanate from behind the Iron Curtain. With the firing of the first Sputnik, Achievement began to replace Adjustment as the highest goal of the American way of life. We have become concerned—perhaps even obsessed—with "education for excellence" and the maximal utilization of our intellectual resources. Already, ability grouping, and the guidance counsellor who is its prophet, have moved down from the junior high to the elementary school, and parents can be counted on to do their part in preparing their youngsters for survival in the new competitive world of applications and achievement tests.

But if a new trend in parental behavior is to develop, it must do so in the context of changes already under way. And if the focus of parental authority is shifting from husband to wife, then perhaps we should anticipate that pressures for achievement will be imposed primarily by mothers rather than fathers. Moreover, the mother's continuing strong emotional investment in the child should provide her with a powerful lever for evoking desired performance. It is noteworthy in this connection that recent studies of the familial origins of need-achievement point to the matriarchy as the optimal context for development of the motive to excel (Strodtbeck, 1958; Rosen & D'Andrade, 1959).

The prospect of a society in which socialization techniques are directed toward maximizing achievement drive is not altogether a pleasant one. As a number of investigators have shown (Baldwin, Kalhorn & Breese, 1945; Baldwin, 1948; Haggard, 1957; Winterbottom, 1958; Rosen & D'Andrade, 1959), high achievement motivation appears to flourish in a family atmosphere of "cold democracy" in which initial high levels of maternal involvement are followed by pressures for independence and accomplishment. Nor does the product of this process give ground for reassurance. True, children from achievement-oriented homes excel in planfulness and performance, but they are also more aggressive, tense, domineering, and cruel (Baldwin, Kalhorn & Breese, 1945; Baldwin, 1948; Haggard, 1957). It would appear that education for excellence if pursued single-mindedly may entail some sobering social costs.

As we look ahead to the next twenty-five years of human socialization, let us hope that the "optimal levels" of involvement and discipline can be achieved not only by the parent who is unavoidably engaged in the process, but also by the scientist who attempts to understand its working, and who—also unavoidably—contributes to shaping its course.

III PERSONALITY AND SOCIETY

Because social behavior is a function of a person in an environment, a concept of personality has always been basic to social psychological thought. Much effort has gone into assessment of personality attributes and examinations of their relations with social processes (see Mann, 1959). Yet, personality theory (see Hall & Lindzey, 1957) and social psychological theory have developed essentially in parallel as partly independent, though mutually relevant, domains. Personality has commonly entered social psychology from the outside, so to speak, as a generalized representation of the "organismic" behavioral tendencies brought to the situation by the individual, acting with the properties of the setting to produce behavior.

Exactly how much relative weight to allocate to personality and how much to the situation has been a matter for much theoretical argument among social psychologists reflecting their part in the long-standing dispositional-situational debate. Although more often than not personality has been conceived as something constant which people have inside them to govern their actions regardless of circumstances, it appears unduly arbitrary to consider the individual as categorically separate from his social surroundings. Indeed, the matters discussed in the preceding section, and later in Section V, indicate that personality must find a place within general theory in social psychology (see Sanford, 1963). Developments in the analysis of comparative cultures (see Kroeber, 1953) and direct investigation of social processes (see Hare, 1962) all emphasize the blending of the person and the social situation, as do the works of pioneering theorists like Emile Durkheim (1950); Max Weber (1946, 1947); Charles Cooley (1922); George Herbert Mead (1934); Abram Kardiner (1939); Erich Fromm (1941); and Ralph Linton (1945), to name a few.

Speaking in a general way to these same matters, but with more empirical evidence, J. McV. Hunt begins this section with a forceful challenge to traditional modes of thought about personality. He identifies five widespread and fundamental beliefs about personality which we take very much for granted. In the light of the evidence which he surveys, each of them proves to be dubious. He therefore presses for the adoption of a more cognitive point of view in contrast with the emotion-centered focus of the older post neo-Freudian theories. In Hunt's line of thought, meaning and information are key concepts. As touchstones of human conduct, they are significant determiners of the *relations* between persons and social situations. However, Hunt's viewpoint is an especially notable one for its stress on the idea that both meaning and information are components of these relations. They are not an exclusive feature of either one or the other. His thinking clearly leads in the direction of a closer scrutiny of the person and his environment, especially in its social aspects. Thus, Hunt questions the traditional intra-personal emphases in personality theory, preferring instead an emphatically interactional outlook.

In his paper here, Gordon Allport presents an incisive discussion of many of these same points and some others as well, in terms of "open" and "closed" social systems. He brings into focus the ideas and issues fundamental to an integration of personality and social concepts, a task he characterizes as "the knottiest problem in social science," and provides a glimpse of modern systems theory (see Scott in Section IX).

Allport is well known as the foremost champion of an idiographic case history approach to personality theory, holding the unique individual to be the only proper final unit of analysis (see also Rosenzweig, 1958, and for a statement of the opposing "nomothetic" position, Eysenck, 1954). Few have argued so effectively as he has the difficulties associated with fixed-trait, psychometric, and past-oriented approaches to personality. Yet, traits, tests, and the historical analysis have all found places in his research and writing, but always interwoven with conceptions of potential, growth, and change (see especially, Allport, 1937, 1954, 1960, 1961, 1966).

Allport's thinking pivots on a view of personality as "becoming." The person is not simply transformed by his environment, he continuously deals creatively with it, and Allport is openly critical of "integumented" constructions of personality as "closed systems." The relation between personality and the social environment, he maintains, is open, even if not totally so. Openness, in Allport's usage, carries a sense of two systems (person and environment) that merge into one another through mutually permeable boundaries. But there are boundaries. Man is conceived as a social being through and through, yet also as an integral biological-psychological system, and social behavior is thought by Allport to be patterned in and by the person as an active agent.

The shaping of personality by social forces, especially the self-concept in its core, is vividly portrayed by Pettigrew in the excerpt reprinted here from his *Profile of the Negro American* (1964). He brings to sharp awareness the baneful effects of prejudice and discrimination upon the white as well as the Negro (see Allport, Section X). Both the blunt and the subtle interplay between social roles, social attitudes, and the individual's developing self-concept are revealed in his analysis. These are matters to which we shall turn again in Section V.

Taking the person's concept of self as a central feature of personality functioning, Pettigrew shows how the roles and social categories to which an individual is allocated cause the person and the structure of society to become inextricably entwined. He describes the successive "identity crises" imposed upon the Negro by his position of subservience and by his immersion in a family which may be chronically disorganized. It is no wonder that these conditions may conspire to produce disfunctional social patterns including alienation and with it crime, delinquency, and mental illness. In short, Pettigrew points up how being a Negro involves a great deal more than being colored; it signifies relationships between the person and the society's norms which are lived out in direct social interaction.

Along with Allport's contribution, the remaining papers in this section describe varying points on a spectrum of views of personality, its components, and its relations to social systems. They range from Rokeach's classic dispositional model at one end, to Secord and Backman's highly provocative interaction model at the other, with Allport's appraisal of personality and its relationship to social systems somewhere near the middle.

By implication at least, Rokeach's paper treats personality largely as a complex of enduring "integumented" tendencies of a person which make a difference in his behavior across widely varied situations. In this sense, personality is an *intra*-personal structure with behavior being "pre-programmed" in the form of relatively constant dimensions or dispositions that account for continuities in the person and his behavior in the face of environmental flux.

Social and general environmental factors enter into personality mainly in the course of development, i.e., via learning, especially during childhood. This point is clearly made by Rokeach and is characteristic of psychological interpretations of personality. He differentiates the *development* of personality traits, like dogmatism, as a problem apart from their functioning. Suggested by this is the assumption, explicit in the case of Freud (1920), that personality and its components become progressively less sensitive to immediate forces in the social environment and that personality and behavior are firmly tied to the person's past.

It is also noteworthy that Rokeach's work, more extensively reported in his book *The Open and Closed Mind* (1960), illustrates a popular approach to personality in terms of psychometric dimensions; Cattell's (1957) and Eysenck's (1953) factor analysis approaches are other illustrations of this. Both as a trait model and because of its psychometric predilections, Rokeach's efforts are right in the classic lines of thought regarding personality proceeding in essential continuity from McDougall's early (1908, 1923, 1937) personalistic formulations. However, in a significant sense, Rokeach reveals a substantial contemporary interest in belief systems in personality, and his work accordingly bears upon approaches to the study of attitudes seen in Section VI. He represents, therefore, an updated, more sophisticated trait theory, cognitive in emphasis and less intrapersonal and mechanistic than has often been true of such theories.

Whereas traditionally personality theory, especially of the trait variety, tended to emphasize stability and historical determinants, change and the influence of immediate situational forces are central threads in Sears's searching analysis and reformulation here. The nexus of his approach is to bring about a closer co-ordination between personality theory and social psychological theory. Manifestly, Sears has in mind a theoretical synthesis different from most previous attempts. Starting from some of the same points elucidated by Hunt and by Allport, he argues that individual and group phenomena are so intermixed that both must be encompassed by a single theory—a theory systematically fed from psychological, sociological, and anthropological sources. The implications of his position are really broader, but one may take it as a plea for a personality theory that is at one and the same time a social psychological theory.

To accomplish this, Sears maintains that both situational factors and phenomena of change must be taken into account. This requires a dynamic *inter*personal model for personality that considers the person in interaction with his surroundings. In this respect, writing from an early vantage point, he anticipates a number of developments revealed in later papers here, especially those in Sections V and VII. He, too, vigorously challenges purely personalistic fixed-trait theories, proposing that personality is both a cause and consequence of behavior. In Sears's more situational view, no trait or disposition exists apart from its activating conditions (cf. Hollander, 1960b). Instead of conceptualizing personality in terms of dispositions that are distributed differentially *between* individuals, but that are essentially constant *within* persons and across situations, he thinks of personality characteristics as varying, in some degree, with the settings in which the person interacts.

The most thoroughly interactional-situational view among the papers presented in this section is that set forth by Secord and Backman. They advance an analysis of personality in which stability and change are accorded equal emphasis and are embraced by the same principles. In concert with Sears, they adopt a diadic interactional unit of analysis and argue that the person strives to maintain a sort of equilibrium among elements in any interaction (cf. Osgood's and Festinger's papers in Section VI). The person's characteristics and patterns of behavior are held to remain stable to the degree that this system is in equilibrium.

In short, *intra*-personal structures, as well as behavior, will be maintained only so long as such maintenance is consistent with an ongoing interaction process which is in a state of balance. Thus, Secord and Backman integrate the person and his situation into a unitary interactional system without any rigid segregation of independent-dependent variable relations.

One conclusion is probably inescapable from the contributions comprising this section; consensus relative to the *form* and *content* of any theory of personality and to relations between personality and larger social psychological systems is something less than complete. Effective integrating theories are needed, as Sears points out, and toward that end some distinctive contributions have been presented here. In the light of the unsettled state of the art, Allport's injunction that we maintain open minds in the matter is quite obviously to the point. However, it has become increasingly evident that future developments in thinking about personality will need to go beyond mere allowance for societal influences. What is required is a more adequate set of propositions to conceptualize the essential interactional melding of the person and the situation.

15 Traditional personality theory in the light of recent evidence

J. McVICKER HUNT

Although science does ultimately yield a body of relatively definitive knowledge about a domain, it is in essence less this definitive knowledge that is science than the dynamic, self-corrective process of ongoing inquiry. This process of science, to quote Conant (1947, p. 37), consists in the "development of [I would prefer the phrase *creating of*] conceptual schemes" where the relative validity of competing concepts is tested against concept-directed observations so that "new concepts arise from . . . these observations [and experiments]." It has been common for many critics to contend that the failure of this dynamic yeast of science to get underway within our knowledge of persons result from the vagueness of the conceptual schemes which pass for personality theory. I wish to counter that any beliefs definite enough to make observed phenomena surprising or incredible constitute a suitable starting point. Moreover, a majority of personologists have been sharing a number of beliefs which are sufficiently definite to render a good many of the observations made since World War II, and some made earlier, very surprising and so incredible that they call for revision of these beliefs. My purpose in this paper is to state five of these beliefs and to synopsize some of the observations which they make surprising.

Are personality traits the major source of behavioral variance?

According to the first of these beliefs, the source of most of the variation in behavior resides within persons. Psychoanalysts, clinicians generally, personologists, and students of individual differences have shared this belief. Moreover, they have shared it in opposition to those social psychologists—their thought rooted in the work of C. H. Cooley (1902), George Herbert Mead (1934), and W. I. Thomas (see Volkart, 1951)—who have contended that the major source of the variation in behavior resides in the "situation."

In this context, individual differences have been conceived typically after the fashion of static dimensions and have been called traits. Those who have attempted to measure personality traits, however, have all too often found even the reliability and validity coefficients of their measures falling within a range of 0.2 and 0.5. If one takes the square of the coefficient of correlation as a rough, "rule-of-thumb" index of the proportion of the variance attributable to persons, it would appear to be limited to somewhere between 4 and 25% of the total. This is incredibly small for any source which is considered to be *the* basis of behavioral variation, but we personologists have blamed our instruments rather than

Abridged from **American Scientist,** 1965, 53, 80–96, with permission of the author and the publisher.

our belief in the importance of static dimensional traits. Such results, when coupled with the opposition of the social psychologists, suggest the desirability of a direct attempt to determine the relative amounts of common-trait variance attributable to persons, to the modes-of-response which serve as indicators of the traits, and to situations.

Norman Endler and Alvin Rosenstein, two of my former students, and I have attempted this for the trait of *anxiousness* (Endler, Hunt, & Rosenstein, 1962). We asked our subjects to report the degree (on a five-step scale) to which they had manifested a sample of 14 modes-of-response which are commonly considered indicative of anxiety. These included, for instance, "Heart beats faster," "Get an 'uneasy feeling,'" "Emotions disrupt action," "Feel exhilarated and thrilled," "Need to urinate frequently," "Mouth gets dry," "Seek experiences like this," "Experience nausea," and "Have loose bowels." We asked our subjects to report the degree to which they had manifested each of these modes-of-response in each of a sample of 11 specified situations. This sample of situations included, for instance, "Going to meet a [blind] date," "Crawling along a ledge high on a mountain side," "Getting up to give a speech before a large group," "Sailing a boat on a rough sea," "Being alone in the woods at night," "Going into an interview for a very important job," and "Entering a final examination in an important course."

When we made a three-way analysis of variance of these quantified reports of response, the largest main source came from the modes-of-response. This finding in itself is trivial, for one might expect an individual to "get an 'uneasy feeling'" to an extreme degree in many situations without ever having "loose bowels" in any. Far from trivial, however, is the fact that the second largest main source came from the situations. In one sample of Illinois sophomores, with the middle 70% on a measure of anxiousness removed, the mean square for situations (152) was 3.8 times that for persons (40); and in another sample of unselected Penn State freshmen, the mean square for situations (244) was somewhat more than 11 times that for persons (21).

When we have recited these facts to our colleagues, some of them have criticized our comparing of mean squares. Nevertheless, they have typically paid us the compliment of staring in disbelief. Such a reaction implies that personality theory has contained at least one proposition sufficiently definite to be the basis for incredibility of observational evidence. The compliment derives from the implication that we have apparently found evidence, the inappropriateness of comparing mean squares notwithstanding, which is sufficiently relevant to the belief in static trait-dimensions to be surprising. We admitted that the generality of our findings could not be inferred from comparing mean squares. Rather, the generality of our findings would have to derive from their reproducibility with other samples of modes-of-response, with other samples of situations, with other samples of subjects, and with other personality traits. If these results should prove to be reproducible in general, as I have defined general, they imply that our brethren from social psychology have had a conceptual slant which is more nearly congruent with reality than has been the slant of us personologists.

On the other hand, like many disputes in the history of science, this one is based on what is, in a sense, a pseudo-question. Behavioral variance is due primarily to neither persons nor situations. Although a comparison of mean squares for situations and for subjects may have surprise or shock value, actually the mean square for the situational source is a composite of the variances from situations *per se*, from the interaction of situations-by-subjects, from the interaction of situations-by-modes-of-response, from the triple interaction, and from the residual. Also, the mean square for subjects is a similar composite. If one employs the equations of Gleser, Cronbach, and Rajaratnam (1961) to partition these various sources properly, one finds that the modes-of-response do contribute about one-fourth of the variance, again a trivial point. But one also finds that neither situations nor subjects contribute substantially. Typically, neither contributes 5% of the total, and for subjects this is what would be expected from the reliability and validity coefficients for tests of personality traits. The simple interactions contribute nearly a third of the total variance (about 10% each), and the triple interaction with residual contributes about the final third. Thus, main sources, simple interactions, and triple interaction with residual each contribute about a third of the total variance (Endler & Hunt, 1964). Three-way analyses of variance for some 15 samples of subjects with three forms of the S-R Inventory have served to indicate that the percentages of total variance from these various main sources and interactive sources are quite stable. While increasing the variability of situations increases the percentage of variance from situations, the increase is only one from something of the order of 2 or 5% to something of the order of 7 or 8%. Thus, it is neither the individual differences among subjects, *per se*, nor the variations among situations, *per se*, that produce the variations in behavior. It is, rather, the interactions among these which are important.

In the words of a Vermont farmer once quoted by Henry A. Murray, "people is mostly alike, but what difference they is can be powerful important." I am now guessing to be "powerful important" the variations in the meanings of situations to people and the variations in the modes-of-response they manifest. These results imply that, for either understanding variations of behavior or making clinical predictions, we should be looking toward instruments that will classify people in terms of the kinds of responses they make in various categories of situations. Osgood has provided us with the Semantic Differential, an important method of assessing the interaction between people and situations (Osgood, Suci, & Tannenbaum, 1957). Perhaps our own approach may also be helpful.

Is all behavior motivated?

The second belief which I wish to confront with evidence from recent investigation concerns personality dynamics or, particularly, motivation. It has most commonly taken the form of the assertion that "all behavior is motivated." In this form, which either originated with or was popularized by Freud, the assertion is indeed too vague to provide a basis for observational surprise, but Freud (1900, 1915), such physiologists as Cannon (1915), and such modern behavior theorists as Hull (1943), Miller and Dollard (1941), and Mowrer (1960), have all shared in filling out the statement so that it has come to say, "all behavior is motivated by painful stimulation, homeostatic need, sexual appetite, or by acquired drives, i.e., originally neutral stimuli which have been associated with painful stimuli, homeostatic need, or sex in the organism's past experience."

This is the well-known drive-reduction theory. According to this theory, the aim or function of every instinct, defense, action, habit, or phantasy is to reduce or to eliminate either stimulation or excitation within the nervous system. Once the assertion gets this form, it can readily provide the basis for observational surprise, for it implies that, in the absence of such motivation, organisms will become quiescent.

They do not become quiescent. I have reviewed these surprising observations elsewhere (1960, 1963a). It has been contended that I have reviewed them *ad nauseam,* so let me be brief here. These observations derive from the studies of play in children by Bühler (1928) and in animals by Beach (1945) and others, the studies of monkeys and chimpanzees manipulating puzzles by Harlow (1950) and by Harlow, Harlow, and Meyer (1950), the studies of spatial exploration in rats by Berlyne (1960) and by Nissen (1930), the studies of spontaneous alternation of rats in a T-maze by Montgomery (1953, 1955), the finding that monkeys will learn various things merely to get a peek at a new scene by Butler (1953), the studies of human beings under conditions of homogeneous input by Bexton, Heron, and Scott (1954), and the now classic studies by Hebb (1946) which found that fear in chimpanzees will occur with encountering something familiar in an unfamiliar guise.

Such evidence, however, has recently been given theoretical recognition in several unfortunate fashions. One of these is drive-naming. The literature is now full of drives (manipulative, exploratory, curiosity, etc.) and of needs (stimulus, change, etc.). This naming of new motives which merely describe the activities they are designed to explain, helps little. Moreover, in motive-naming, we are revisiting the instinct-naming which McDougall (1908) popularized early in this century but which was discredited just after World War I. We should know better.

A second unfortunate fashion of theoretical recognition is naming motives in terms of their telic significance. I refer to the "urge to mastery" promulgated by Ives Hendrick (1943) and to the concept of "competence motivation" proposed by Robert White (1959) in his excellent review of the evidence concerned. Unfortunately, concepts of telic significance seem to me to provide no means of developing hypotheses about antecedent-consequent relationships that can be tested against observations.

A third unfortunate fashion of theoretical recognition has consisted of postulating spontaneous activity. Some activity can be said to be spontaneous, from a descriptive standpoint, as Hebb has pointed out to me. But this does not make spontaneity a useful explanation, and I am indebted to my colleague, L. I. O'Kelly, for noting that postulating spontaneous activity as an explanation may be just as useless as postulating a list of instincts and drives, and for precisely the same reasons.

As I see it, these various lines of evidence combine to indicate that a system and a mechanism of motivation inheres within the organism's informational interaction with its environmental circumstances. I have described this mechanism elsewhere (Hunt, 1963a). The news of its existence was, I believe, one of the implicit messages of that now classic book entitled *The Organization of Behavior* (Hebb, 1949). This message has since been made explicit, and it has been confirmed by various lines of evidence.

Whatever the essential character of this informational organism-environment interaction and its relationship to arousal turns out to be, there appears to be an optimum amount of it for each organism at any given time. I suspect that this optimum is to a considerable degree a function of experience, and that it may obey Helson's (1959) notion of the adaptation level. When a situation offers too much, i.e., when the inputs from a situation are too incongruous with the information already coded and stored, the organism withdraws as illustrated by Hebb's (1946) fearful chimpanzees, and by some of the human beings whom Festinger (1957) has found to be avoiding or discrediting information dissonant with their commitments and plans. On the other hand, when a situation offers too little incongruity, i.e., when the inputs from a situation are too similar to the information already in storage, boredom results, and the organism withdraws from that situation to seek another one offering more incongruity, stimulus-change, novelty, dissonance, uncertainty, or what-have-you. It is this seeking of incongruity which is apparently illustrated by the college students in the McGill experiments of Bexton, Heron, and Scott (1954) who refused to remain under conditions of homogeneous input even though they were paid $20 a day. It is this seeking of incongruity which is also illustrated by the fact that Butler's (1953) monkeys will learn merely in order to get a peek at the world outside their monotonous cage-situations, and by that early study of Nissen's (1930) in which rats left their familiar nests and crossed an electrified grid (one of Worden's obstructions) to get to a Dashiell maze filled with objects fresh and novel to them. This work of Nissen's never got into the textbooks, probably because it was too dissonant with the traditional propositions about motivation presented therein.

This line of conceptualizing has still largely unacknowledged implications for our traditional notions of both psychodynamics and psychological development. Both Sigmund Freud (1926) and Anna Freud (1936) conceived of the mechanisms of defense as serving to protect a person from anxiety. Sigmund Freud, at least in his later days when he came to see repression as a consequence of anxiety rather than as its source, saw anxiety originating from castration threats, Oedipal anxieties, and other overwhelmingly intense experiences of painful stimulation. The fact that Hebb (1946) has found chimpanzees withdrawing from sources of input which could never have been associated with painful stimulation (by virtue of the fact that the infants had been reared under observation in the Yerkes Laboratory), coupled with the fact that Festinger (1957) and his students have found human subjects utilizing various strategies to avoid dissonant information, and coupled again with the fact that evidence dissonant with prevailing theories—like that of Nissen's early study—seldom gets into the textbooks, suggest that the mechanism of defense may sometimes, or may even typically, function chiefly to protect individuals from information too incongruous with that which they already have coded in the storage or with that already involved in their commitments and plans. Probably the most important category of stored information for this theoretical context is that concerning the self, as the theorizing of Hilgard (1949) and as the clinical observations and theorizing of Rogers (1951) and George Kelly (1955) would indicate. I dare not take the time to elaborate; here it must be enough to point a direction.

Are emotional factors so much more important than cognitive factors in psychological development?

The third belief which I wish to discuss in the light of recently uncovered evidence is also motivational and dynamic, but it is developmental as well. Freud probably did more to emphasize the importance of infantile experience in psychological development than anyone else in the history of thought. Freud's (1905) theory of psychosexual development put the emphasis on the fate of the instinctive modes of infantile pleasure-striving, i.e., sucking, elimination, and genitality. Freud's influence has led to the very widespread belief among personologists that these extrinsic motivational or emotional factors are much more important in development than are cognitive factors. This minimization of the importance of cognitive and perceptual factors in early infantile, or preverbal, development has been abetted, moreover, by the beliefs in fixed intelligence and predetermined development so widely held among the earlier students of individual differences in intelligence.

Recent evidence indicates, perhaps, that just about the opposite should hold. Reviews of those relatively objective studies of the effects of the emotional factors pointed up in the theory of psychosexual development have generally tended to depreciate the importance of those factors (see Child, 1954; Hunt, 1946, 1956; Orlansky, 1949). Every study finding significant effects can be matched with another which does not. Moreover, the better controlled the study, the less likely is it to have found significant effects. Similarly, while infantile feeding-frustration in rats appeared to increase eating speed and hoarding in adulthood (Hunt, 1941; Hunt, *et al.*, 1947), thereby lending support to the importance of extrinsic motivational factors, these studies have not always been reproducible so far as the effect on hoarding is concerned (Marx, 1952; McKelvey & Marx, 1951). Moreover, having done the first of these studies, perhaps I should admit that I probably misinterpreted the facts anyway. Of course, it is still true that painful stimulation can inhibit eating and drinking and that prolonged failure to eat and drink can kill an organism. On the other hand, the studies of the effects of variations in the richness of early perceptual experience in animals have regularly shown (Forgays & Forgays, 1952; Forgus, 1954, 1955a, 1955b; Hymovitch, 1952) substantial effects on adult problem-solving. These studies have stemmed from Hebb's theorizing, and the first of the kind (Hebb, 1947) compared the performances of pet-reared rats with those of cage-reared rats in the Hebb-Williams (1946) test of animal intelligence. The pet-reared animals proved much superior to their cage-reared litter-mates. Thompson and Heron (1954) have made a similar experiment with dogs, and the evidence of the superiority of the pet-reared dogs over their cage-reared litter-mates is even more striking than that for rats. The fact that the evidence from dogs is stronger than that from rats suggests that the importance of early experience, and particularly the importance of early cognitive or perceptual experience, probably increases up the phylogenetic scale as that portion of the brain without direct connection to sensory input or motor outlet increases relative to the portion which does have direct sensory and/or motor connections (i.e., with the size of what Hebb [1949] has termed the A/S ratio). Moreover, there is direct evidence that such effects can be generalized from animal subjects to human beings in studies by Goldfarb (see 1955 for summary) which indicate that being reared in an orphanage, where the variety of circumstances encountered is highly restricted, results at adolescence in lower intelligence, less ability to sustain a task, less attentiveness, and more problems in interpersonal relations than being reared in a foster home. Moreover, those findings of Dennis (1960) that 60% of the two-year-olds in a Teheran orphanage, where changes in ongoing stimulation were minimal, were not yet sitting up alone and that 85% of the four-year-olds were not yet walking alone, serve to dramatize how very much the factor of variety of circumstances encountered in infancy can affect the rate of development—even the rate of development of posture and locomotion.

As I see it, these various lines of evidence combine to indicate that cognitive experience—or, more precisely, the organism's informational interaction with the environment—can be as important for psychological development as emotions based on the fate of instincts, and perhaps it is typically more important. In corollary fashion, these same bits of evidence would also appear to indicate that we have been wrong in our widespread belief that it is the intellectual characteristics of a person which are most nearly fixed by the genotype and that the emotional characteristics of a person are highly subject to substantial environmental influence. Although the life history is of considerable importance in the development of both types of characteristics, it appears that it may be the intellectual variety which is the more subject to substantial effects of environmental encounters, particularly those coming in early infancy.

Must emotional attachments derive from gratification of libidinal or homeostatic needs?

According to a fourth belief commonly held by personologists, the emotional attachments to objects, persons, and places—called cathexes in psychoanalytic terminology—derive from their association with the gratification of libidinal or homeostatic needs. In his *Three Contributions to the Theory of Sex,* Freud (1905) not only assumed a separation of libidinal from nutritional needs, but he also attributed all object-cathexes to libidinal energy (see p. 553, p. 611, and p. 743 footnote 2). These points, coupled with Freud's (1915) conception of instinct, appear to indicate that he attributed all emotional attachments to libidinal gratification, as he defined it. As I (Hunt, 1946) pointed out nearly 20 years ago, any such generalization is contradicted by the wide variety of studies in which preference for objects, persons, and places has been changed by association with food reward (see, e.g., Mowrer, 1960; Razran, 1938a, 1938b; Williams, 1929; Williams & Williams, 1943) or by association with success in goal-achievement (see Mierke, 1933; Nowlis, 1941; Rosenzweig, 1933).

More recently, it has been generally believed that such emotional attachment derives from the association of objects, persons, and places with homeostatic gratification. And so it is sometimes, but Harlow's (1958) work indicates that association with homeostatic gratification is far from the whole story. In his studies, you will recall, monkey babies, when frightened, went for solace to the soft surrogate-mothers covered with padded terry-cloth rather than to the wire surrogate-mothers on which they had sucked to gratify their need for food.

Nor can softness of contact be the whole story, for behavioral criteria defining emotional attachment appear to have another basis. Infants of various species appear to approach, to seek, and to take delight in objects which are becoming recognizably familiar in the course of repeated encounters (see Hunt, 1963b), and they show varying degrees of distress as these objects escape their perceptual ken. Piaget (1936) has described how his children came to make what is clearly an "intentional effort" to keep interesting spectacles within perceptual range. Anyone who has ever jounced an infant on his knee and stopped his motion only to find the infant starting a similar motion of his own, is familiar with this intentional effort of the infant to hold on to an interesting spectacle. One gathers from Piaget's (1936) observations that these interesting spectacles very commonly consist of objects or persons that are becoming familiar through repeated encounters. In an exploratory study of this phenomenon, Dr. Ina Uzgiris and I have got evidence consonant with this idea that the young human infant prefers a mobile which has been hanging over his crib to another mobile which he has never encountered before (Hunt & Uzgiris, 1966). Here, the term *prefers* is based on looking time. When the familiar mobile has been withdrawn for a time and is then returned with another unfamiliar one beside it, the infant looks more at the familiar than at the unfamiliar one. Similar phenomena of emotional attachment are to be found in animals. Since it is following an object and distress at its escape from perceptual ken that characterizes the one major component of what the ethnologists (Heinroth, 1910; Lorenz, 1935; Thorpe, 1944) call "imprinting," it intrigues me to consider that this effort to follow and to keep interesting spectacles within view and the distress at losing them in lower mammals and birds may be a special case of this more general principle of emotional attachment deriving from recognitive familiarity. If this be sensible, and I believe it is, one can then relate the marked variation in the number of encounters required to establish such recognitive emotional attachments to Hebb's A/S ratio. There appears to be a progression in the number of encounters or in the amount of exposure time required, from two or three hours in the grey-leg goose, through two or three days in the sheep or deer, some two weeks in the monkey infant, and some six or so weeks in the chimpanzee infant, to some six or so months in the human infant. Maternal attachment appears to be another special case of this same principle, but it is well contaminated also with skin contacts and with the gratification of homeostatic need. In all probability, fear of strangers is a direct derivative comparable to the fear of the familiar in an unfamiliar guise found in adult chimpanzees by Hebb (1946) and already mentioned.

But following is alone no indication of emotional delight. Evidence of the delight comes from the infant's smile and laugh of recognition. Spitz (1946) and others have considered smiling to be a social response, one based, presumably, on the fact that the human face is repeatedly associated with homeostatic gratification, but Piaget's (1936) observations and those of my colleague, Dr. Uzgiris, indicate that the infant will smile and show laughing delight at the appearance of various objects which are merely becoming familiar with repeated encounters (Hunt, 1963b; Hunt & Uzgiris, 1966).

Such observations and considerations strongly suggest that recognitive familiarity is in itself a source of emotional attachment, and this attachment is attested further by the fact that separation grief always concerns familiar objects and persons and by the fact that such grief is but transient in infants too young to have established object permanence. In a sense, this is a further elaboration of the importance of that intrinsic system of motivation which inheres in the organism's informational interaction with the environment.

Do encounters with painful stimulation in infancy result in sensitivity and proneness to anxiety?

According to a fifth belief, which we may call the "trauma theory of anxiety," encounters with painful stimulation or strong homeostatic need inevitably leave a young child or a young animal prone to be sensitive and anxious in most situations. This trauma theory assumes the conditioning conception of fear. Thus, it is presumed that the various sources of inputs present immediately before and during encounters with painful stimulation will acquire the capacity to evoke the autonomic and central emotional features incorporated within the total response to painful stimulation.

In spite of Hebb's (1946) strong evidence to the contrary, most clinicians of all professions act as if *the only source* of anxious emotional disturbance were this association of originally neutral sources of input with pain. Recently, however, another source of evidence dissonant with this widely held belief has been the investigations of the effects of shocking infant animals before they are weaned. Although there may well be both species and strain differences in some of these effects, as indicated by reports—based on studies using mice as subjects—which deviate from those which I am about to mention (see Hall, 1934; Lindzey, *et al.*, 1960), rats shocked in infancy have been repeatedly found as adults to be less fearful than rats which have been left unmolested in the maternal nest. This is to say that they urinated less and defecated less in, were less hesitant to enter, and were more active in unfamiliar territory than were rats which had been left unmolested in the maternal nest (see Deneberg, 1962; Levine, 1959, 1961).

In two other investigations, moreover, rats shocked before weaning, with sufficient intensity to keep them squealing continually for three minutes each day, have been found as adults to require stronger shocks to instigate escape-activity than do rats left unmolested (Goldman, 1964; Griffiths, 1960). Finally, in a very recent study by Salama, one of my own students, rats shocked daily from their 11th through their 20th day were found to show much less "fixative effect" of shock after the choice-point in a T-maze than did rats left unmolested in the maternal nest or than did rats either gentled or handled for this same period (Salama & Hunt, 1964).

Let me explain this last experiment briefly. Some 16 years ago, Farber (1948) reported a study of "fixation" which showed that rats intermittently shocked just after the choice-point on their way to one of the goal-boxes in a T-maze, where they were fed, required substantially more unrewarded trials to give up going to that goal-box than did rats merely given food-reward in it. Salama (1962) has replicated this finding and found the mean number of unrewarded trials to be 20.7 for the shocked animals but only 2.8 for those merely given food-reward. He has gone further; he has compared the number of unrewarded trials required for rats shocked in infancy to give up the goal-box with the numbers required by rats gentled and handled. The means for those gentled (21.4) and for those handled (17.58) differed little from the mean for those left unmolested in the maternal nest (20.7), but the mean for those shocked (9) approximates only half the means for these other groups, and it differs significantly ($p < 0.001$) from these and from the unmolested group not shocked after the choice-point.

It is very interesting in connection with these studies that Holmes (1935) has found the children of lower-class backgrounds from a day-care center to be less fearful than children of an upper-middle-class background from a nursery school. Holmes's study was conducted in 1935, right in the midst of the Great Depression, when children of lower-class parents could be expected to have encountered more painful stimulation and homeostatic need than children of the upper-middle class. This result suggests that the findings from these animal studies may well generalize to human beings.

It is clear from the evidence that all of these studies tend to disconfirm the present formulation of the trauma theory of anxiety based on the conditioning principle as the only experiential basis for anxiousness. They also suggest that encounters with painful stimulation may serve instead to raise what Helson (1959) calls the adaptation level for painful stimulation and thereby to reduce its aversiveness. The force of such evidence is hardly yet sufficient to warrant—and certainly not sufficient to call for—a change in child-rearing practices, for trauma is also a fact. There are varieties of early experience that leave infants prone to be sensitive and anxious, but we cannot yet clearly specify their nature. Perhaps it should be remembered in connection with this evidence, however, that the Spartan culture survived for several centuries while holding to a belief that infants should be exposed to cold and to painful stimulation to prepare them to bear the dire exigencies of later life.

16 The open system in personality theory

GORDON W. ALLPORT

The concept of system

Until a generation or so ago science, including psychology, was preoccupied with what might be called "disorganized complexity." Natural scientists explored this fragment and that fragment of nature; psychologists explored this fragment and that fragment of experience and behavior. The problem of interrelatedness, though recognized, was not made a topic for direct inquiry.

What is called system theory today—at least in psychology—is the outgrowth of the relatively new organismic conception reflected in the work of von Bertalanffy, Goldstein, and in certain aspects of gestalt psychology. It opposes simple reaction theories where a virtual automaton is seen to respond discretely to stimuli as though they were pennies-in-the-slot. Interest in system theory is increasing in psychology, though perhaps not so fast as in other sciences.

Now a system—any system—is defined merely as a complex of elements in mutual interaction. Bridgman (1959), as might be expected of an operationist, includes a hint of method in his definition. He writes, a system is "an isolated enclosure in which all measurements that can be made of what goes on in the system are in some way correlated" (p. 188).

Systems may be classified as closed or open. A closed system is defined as one that admits no matter from outside itself and is therefore subject to entropy according to the second law of thermodynamics. While some outside energies, such as change in temperature and wind may play upon a closed system, it has no restorative properties and no transactions with its environment, so that like a decaying bridge it sinks into thermodynamic equilibrium.

Now some authors, such as von Bertalanffy (1952b), Brunswik (1955), and Pumpian-Mindlin (1959), have said or implied that certain theories of psychology and of personality operate with the conception of closed systems. But in my opinion these critics press their point too far. We had better leave closed systems to the realm of physics where they belong (although even here it is a question whether Einstein's formula for the release of matter into energy does not finally demonstrate the futility of positing a closed cgs system even in physics). In any event it is best to admit that all living organisms partake of the character of open systems. I doubt that we shall find any advocate of a truly closed system in the whole range of personality theory. At the same time current theories do differ widely in the amount of openness they ascribe to the personality system.

If we comb definitions of open systems we can piece together four criteria: there is intake and output of both matter and energy; there is the achievement and maintenance of steady (homeostatic) states, so that the intrusion

Abridged from the **Journal of Abnormal and Social Psychology**, 1960, 61, 301–11, with permission of the author and the American Psychological Association.

of outer energy will not seriously disrupt internal form and order; there is generally an increase of order over time, owing to an increase in complexity and differentiation of parts; finally, at least at the human level, there is more than mere intake and output of matter and energy: there is extensive transactional commerce with the environment.[1]

While all of our theories view personality as an open system in some sense, still they can be fairly well classified according to the varying emphasis they place upon each of these criteria, and according to how many of the criteria they admit.

CRITERION 1

Consider the first criterion of material and energy exchange. Stimulus-response theory in its purest form concentrates on this criterion to the virtual exclusion of all the others. It says in effect that a stimulus enters and a response is emitted. There is, of course, machinery for summation, storage, and delay, but the output is broadly commensurate with the intake. We need study only the two poles of stimulus and response with a minimum of concern for intervening processes. Methodological positivism goes one step further, saying in effect, that we do not need the concept of personality at all. We focus attention on our own measurable manipulations of input and on the measurable manipulations of output. Personality thus evaporates in a mist of method.

CRITERION 2

The requirement of steady state for open systems is so widely admitted in personality theory that it needs little discussion. To satisfy needs, to reduce tension, to maintain equilibrium, comprise, in most theories, the basic formula of personality dynamics. Some authors, such as Stagner (1951) and Mowrer (1959), regard this formula as logically fitting in with Cannon's (1932) account of homeostasis.[2] Man's intricate adjustive behavior is simply an extension of the principle involved in temperature regulation, balance of blood volume, sugar content, and the like, in the face of environmental change. It is true that Toch and Hastorf (1955) warn against overextending the concept of homeostasis in personality theory. I myself doubt that Cannon would approve the extension, for to him the value of homeostasis lay in its capacity to free man for what he called "the priceless unessentials" of life (1932, p. 323). When biological equilibrium is attained the priceless unessentials take over and constitute the major part of human activity. Be that as it may, most current theories clearly regard personality as a *modus operandi* for restoring a steady state.

[1] von Bertalanffy's definition explicitly recognizes the first two of these criteria as present in all living organisms. A living organism, he says, is "an open system which continually gives up matter to the outer world and takes in matter from it, but which maintains itself in this continuous exchange in a steady state, or approaches such steady state in its variations in time" (1952a, p. 125). But elsewhere in this author's writing we find recognition of the additional criteria (1952a, p. 145; 1952b, p. 34).

[2] In a recent review Mowrer (1959) strongly defends the homeostatic theory. He is distressed that the dean of American psychologists, Robert Woodworth (1958) has taken a firm stand against the "need-primacy" theory in favor of what he calls the "behavior-primacy" theory. With the detailed merits of the argument we are not here concerned. What concerns us at the moment is that the issue has been sharply joined. Need-primacy which Mowrer calls a "homeostatic" theory does not go beyond our first two criteria for an open system. Woodworth by insisting that contact with, and mastery of, the environment constitute a pervasive principle of motivation, recognizes the additional criteria.

Psychoanalytic theories are of this order. According to Freud the ego strives to establish balance among the three "tyrants"—id, superego, and outer environment. Likewise the so-called mechanisms of ego defense are essentially maintainers of a steady state. Even a neurosis has the same basic adjustive function.[3]

To sum up: most current theories of personality take full account of two of the requirements of an open system. They allow interchange of matter and energy, and recognize the tendency of organisms to maintain an orderly arrangement of elements in a steady state. Thus they emphasize stability rather than growth, permanence rather than change, "uncertainty reduction" (information theory), and "coding" (cognitive theory) rather than creativity. In short, they emphasize being rather than becoming. Hence, most personality theories are biologistic in the sense that they ascribe to personality only the two features of an open system that are clearly present in all living organisms.

There are, however, two additional criteria, sometimes mentioned but seldom stressed by biologists themselves, and similarly neglected in much current personality theory.

TRANSATLANTIC PERSPECTIVE

Before examining Criterion 3 which calls attention to the tendency of open systems to enhance their degree of order, let us glimpse our present theoretical situation in cross-cultural perspective.

Most men, the Hindus say, have four central desires. To some extent, though only roughly, they correspond to the developmental stages of life. The first desire is for pleasure—a condition fully and extensively recognized in our Western theories of tension reduction, reinforcement, libido, and needs. The second desire is for success—likewise fully recognized and studied in our investigations of power, status, leadership, masculinity, and need-achievement. Now the third desire is to do one's duty and discharge one's responsibility. (It was Bismarck, not a Hindu, who said: "We are not in this world for pleasure but to do our damned duty.") Finally, the Hindus tell us that in many people all these three motives pall, and they then seek intensely for a grade of understanding—for a philosophical or religious meaning—that will liberate them from pleasure, success, and duty (Smith, 1958).

Now we retrace our steps from India to modern Vienna and encounter the existentialist school of logotherapy. Its founder, Viktor Frankl, emphasizes above all the central place of duty and meaning, the same two motives that the Hindus place highest in their hierarchy of desire. Frankl reached his position after a long and agonizing incarceration in Nazi concentration camps. With other prisoners he found himself stripped to naked existence (1959a). In such extremity what does a person need and want? Pleasure and success are out of the question. One wants to know the meaning of his suffering and to learn how as a responsible being he should acquit himself. Should he commit suicide? If so, why; if not, why not? The search for meaning becomes supreme.

Neither Hindu psychology nor Frankl

[3] When we speak of the "function" of a neurosis we are reminded of the many theories of "functionalism" current in psychology and social science. Granted that the label, as Merton (1957) has shown, is a wide one, still we may safely say that the emphasis of functionalism is always on the usefulness of an activity in maintaining the "steady state" of a personality or social or cultural system. In short, "functional" theories stress maintenance of present direction allowing little room or none at all for departure and change.

underestimates the role of pleasure and success in personality. Nor would Frankl abandon the hard won gains reflected in psychoanalytic and need theory. He says merely that in studying or treating a person we often find these essentially homeostatic formulations inadequate. A man normally wants to know the whys and wherefores. No other biological system does so; hence, man stands alone in that he possesses a degree of openness surpassing that of any other living system.

CRITERION 3

Returning now to our main argument, we encounter a not inconsiderable array of theories that emphasize the tendency of human personality to go beyond steady states and to strive for an enhancement and elaboration of internal order even at the cost of considerable disequilibrium.

I cannot examine all of these nor name all the relevant authors. One could start with McDougall's proactive sentiment of self-regard which he viewed as organizing all behavior through a kind of "forward memory" (to use Gooddy's apt term—1959). Not too dissimilar is the stress that Combs and Snygg place on the enhancement of the phenomenal field. We may add Goldstein's conception of self-actualization as tending to enhance order in personality; also Maslow's theory of growth motives that supplement deficiency motives. One thinks of Jung's principle of individuation leading toward the achievement of a self (a goal never actually completed). Some theories, Bartlett and Cantril among them, put primary stress on the "pursuit of meaning." Certain developments in post-Freudian "ego psychology" belong here. So too does existentialism with its recognition of the need for meaning and of the values of commitment. (The brain surgeon, Harvey Cushing, was speaking of open systems when he said: "The only way to endure life is to have a task to complete.")

No doubt we should add Woodworth's recent advocacy of the "behavior primacy" theory as opposed to the "need" theory, Robert White's emphasis on "competence," and Erikson's "search for identity."

Now these theories are by no means identical. The differences between them merit prolonged debate. I lump them here simply because all seem to me to recognize the third criterion of open systems, namely, the tendency of such systems to enhance their degree of order and become something more than at present they are.

We all know the objection to theories of this type. Methodologists with a taste for miniature and fractionated systems complain that they do not lead to "testable propositions" (cf. Roby, 1959). The challenge is valuable in so far as it calls for an expansion of research ingenuity. But the complaint is ill-advised if it demands that we return to quasiclosed systems simply because they are more "researchable" and elegant. Our task is to study what is, and not what is immediately convenient.

CRITERION 4

Now for our fourth and last criterion. Virtually all the theories I have mentioned up to now conceive of personality as something integumented, as residing within the skin. There are theorists (Kurt Lewin, Martin Buber, Gardner Murphy, and others) who challenge this view, considering it too closed. Murphy says that we overstress the separation of man from the context of his living. Experiments on sensory deprivation Hebb (1955) has interpreted as demonstrations of the constant dependence of inner stability on the flow of environmental stimulation. Why Western thought makes such a razor-sharp distinction between the person and all else is an interesting problem. Probably the personalistic emphasis in Judeo-Christian religion is an initial factor, and as Murphy (1958, p. 297) has pointed out the industrial and commercial revolutions further accentuated the role of individuality. Shinto philosophy, by contrast, regards the individual, society, and nature as forming the tripod of human existence. The individual as such does not stick out like a raw digit. He blends with nature and he blends with society. It is only the merger that can be profitably studied.

As Western theorists most of us, I dare say, hold the integumented view of the personality system. I myself do so. Others rebelling against the setting of self over against the world, have produced theories of personality written in terms of social interaction, role relations, situationism, or some variety of field theory. Still other writers, such as Talcott Parsons (1951) and F. H. Allport (1955), have admitted the validity of both the integumented personality system and systems of social interaction, and have spent much effort in harmonizing the two types of systems thus conceived.

This problem, without doubt, is the knottiest issue in contemporary social science. It is the issue which, up to now, has prevented us from agreeing on the proper way to reconcile psychological and sociocultural science.

In this matter my own position is on the conservative side. It is the duty of psychology, I think, to study the person-system, meaning thereby the attitudes, abilities, traits, trends, motives, and pathology of the individual—his cognitive styles, his sentiments, and individual moral nature and their interrelations. The justification is twofold: (*a*) there is a persistent though changing person-system in time, clearly delimited by birth and death; (*b*) we are immediately aware of the functioning of this system; our knowledge of it, though imperfect, is direct, whereas our knowledge of all other outside systems, including social systems, is deflected and often distorted by their necessary incorporation into our own apperceptions.

At the same time our work is incomplete unless we admit that each person possesses a *range* of abilities, attitudes, and motives that will be evoked by the different environments and situations he encounters. Hence, we need to understand cultural, class, and family constellations and traditions in order to know the schemata the person has probably interiorized in the course of his learning. But I hasten to warn that the study of cultural, class, family, or any other social system does not automatically illumine the person-system, for we have to know whether the individual has accepted, rejected, or remained uninfluenced by the social system in question. The fact that one plays the role of, say, teacher, salesman, or father is less important for the study of his personality than to know whether he likes or dislikes, and how he defines, the role. And yet at the same time unless we are students of sociocultural systems we shall never know what it is the person is accepting, rejecting, or redefining.

The provisional solution I would offer is the following: the personality theorist should be so well trained in social science that he can view the behavior of an individual as fitting any system of interaction; that is, he should be able to cast this behavior properly in the culture where it occurs, in its situational context, and in terms of role theory and field theory. At the same time he should not lose sight—as some theorists do—of the fact that there is an internal and subjective patterning of all these contextual acts. A traveler who moves from culture to culture, from situation to situation, is none the less a single person; and within him one will find the nexus, the patterning, of the diverse experiences and memberships that constitute his personality.

Thus, I myself would not go so far as to advocate that personality be defined in terms of interaction, culture, or roles. Attempts to do so seem to me to smudge the concept of personality, and to represent a surrender of the psychologist's special assignment as a scientist. Let him be acquainted with all systems of interaction, but let him return always to the point where such systems converge and intersect and are patterned—in the single individual.

Hence, we accept the fourth (transactional) criterion of the open system, but with the firm warning that it must not be applied with so much enthusiasm that we lose the personality system altogether.

Some examples

I suggest that we regard all sharp controversies in personality theory as probably arising from the two opposed points of view—the quasiclosed and the fully open.

The principle of reinforcement, to take one example, is commonly regarded as the cement that stamps in a response, as the glue that fixes personality at the level of past deeds. Now an open-system interpretation is very different. Feigl (1959, p. 117), for instance, has pointed out that reinforcement works primarily in a prospective sense. It is only from a *recognition* of consequences (not from the consequences themselves) that the human individual binds the past to the future and resolves to avoid punishment and to seek rewards in similar circumstances, provided, of course, that it is consonant with his interests and values to do so. Here we no longer assume that reinforcement stamps in, but that it is one factor among many to be considered in the programing of future action (Allport, 1946). In this example we see what a wide difference it makes whether we regard personality as a quasiclosed or open system.

The issue has its parallels in neurophysiology. How open is the nervous system? We know it is of a complexity so formidable that we have only an inkling as to how complex it may be. Yet one thing is certain, namely, that high level gating often controls and steers lower level processes. While we cannot tell exactly what we mean by "higher levels" they surely involve ideational schemata, intentions, and generic personality trends. They are instruments for programing, not merely for reacting. In the future we may confidently expect that the neurophysiology of programing and the psychology of proaction will draw together. Until they do so it is wise to hold lightly our self-closing metaphors of sowbug, switchboard, giant computer, and hydraulic pump.

Finally, an example from motivation theory. Some years ago I argued that motives may become functionally autonomous of their origins. (And one lives to regret one's brashness.)

Whatever its shortcomings the concept of functional autonomy succeeds in viewing personality as an open and changing system. As might be expected, criticism has come chiefly from those who prefer to view the personality system as quasiclosed. Some critics say that I am dealing only with occasional cases where the extinction of a habit system has failed to occur. This criticism, of course, begs the question, for the point at issue is why do some habit systems fail to extinguish when no longer reinforced? And why do some habit systems that were once instrumental get refashioned into interests and values having a motivational push?

The common counterargument holds that "secondary reinforcement" somehow miraculously sustains all the proactive goal-seeking of a mature person. The scientific ardor of Pasteur, the religio-political zeal of Gandhi, or for that matter, Aunt Sally's devotion to her needlework, are explained by hypothetical cross-conditioning that somehow substitutes for the primary reinforcement of primary drives. What is significant for our purposes is that these critics prefer the concept of secondary reinforcement, not because it is clearer, but because it holds our thinking within the frame of a quasiclosed (reactive) system.

Now is not the time to re-argue the matter, but I have been asked to hint at my present views. I would say first that the concept of functional autonomy has relevance even at the level of quasiclosed systems. There are now so many indications concerning feedback mechanisms, cortical self-stimulation, self-organizing systems, and the like (Chang, 1950; Hebb, 1949; Olds & Milner, 1954) that I believe we cannot deny the existence of self-sustaining circuit mechanisms which we can lump together under the rubric "perseverative functional autonomy."

But the major significance of the concept lies in a different direction, and presupposes the view that personality is an expanding system seeking progressively new levels of order and transaction. While drive motives remain fairly constant throughout life, existential motives do not. It is the very nature of an open system to achieve progressive levels of order through change in cognitive and motivational structure. Since in this case the causation is systemic we cannot hope to account for functional autonomy in terms of specific reinforcements. This condition I would call "propriate functional autonomy."

Both perseverative and propriate autonomy are, I think, indispensable conceptions. The one applies to the relatively closed part-systems within personality; the other to the continuously evolving structure of the whole.

A last example. It is characteristic of the quasiclosed system outlook that it is heavily nomothetic. It seeks response and homeostatic similarities among all personality systems (or, as in general behavior systems theory, among *all* systems). If, however, we elect the open system view we find ourselves forced in part toward the idiographic outlook. For now the vital question becomes "what makes the system hang together in any one person?" (cf. Taylor, 1958). Let me repeat this question, for it is the one that more than any other has haunted me over the years. *What makes the system cohere in any one person?* That this problem is pivotal, urgent, and relatively neglected, will be recognized by open-system theorists, even while it is downgraded and evaded by those who prefer their systems semi-closed.

Final word

If my discourse has seemed polemical I can only plead that personality theory lives by controversy. In this country we are fortunate that no single party line shackles our speculations. We are free to pursue any and all assumptions concerning the nature of man. The penalty we pay is that for the present we cannot expect personality *theory* to be cumulative—although, fortunately, to some extent personality *research* can be.

Theories, we know, are ideally derived from axioms, and if axioms are lacking, as in our field they are, from assumptions. But our assumptions regarding the nature of man range from the Adlerian to the Zilborgian, from the Lockean to the Leibnitzian, from the Freudian to the Hullian, and from the cybernetic to the existentialist. Some of us model man after the pigeon; others view his potentialities as many splendored. And there is no agreement in sight.

Nils Bohr's principle of complementarity contains a lesson for us. You recall that he showed that if we study the position of a particle we cannot at the same time study its momentum. Applied to our own work the principle tells us that if we focus on reaction we cannot simultaneously study proaction; if we measure one trait we cannot fix our attention on pattern; if we tackle a subsystem we lose the whole; if we pursue the whole we overlook the part-functioning. For the single investigator there seems to be no escape from this limitation. Our only hope is to overcome it by a complementarity of investigators and of theorists.

While I myself am partisan for the open system, I would shut no doors. (Some of my best friends are quasi-closed systematists.) If I argue for the open system I plead more strongly for the open mind. Our condemnation is reserved for that peculiar slavery to fashion which says that conventionality alone makes for scientific respectability. We still have much to learn from our creative fumblings with the open system. Among our students, I trust, there will be many adventurers. Shall we not teach them that in the pastures of science it is not only the sacred cows that can yield good scientific milk?

17 Negro American personality: the role and its burdens

THOMAS PETTIGREW

Playing the role of "Negro"

Like all human interactions, discriminatory encounters between whites and Negroes require that both parties "play the game." The white must act out the role of the "superior"; by direct action or subtle cue, he must convey the expectation that he will be treated with deference. For his part, the Negro must, if racist norms are to be obeyed, act out the role of the "inferior"; he must play the social role of "Negro." And if he should refuse to play the game, he would be judged by the white supremacist as "not knowing his place," and harsh sanctions could follow.

The socially-stigmatized role of "Negro" is the critical feature of having dark skin in the United States. "It is part of the price the Negro pays for his position in this society," comments James Baldwin, "that, as Richard Wright points out, he is almost always acting" (1955, p. 68). At the personality level, such enforced role adoption further divides the individual Negro both from other human beings and from himself. Of course, all social roles, necessary as they are, hinder to some extent forthright, uninhibited social interaction. An employer and employee, for example, may never begin to understand each other as complete human beings unless they break through the formality and constraints of their role relationship, unless they "let their hair down." Likewise, whites and Negroes can never communicate as equals unless they break through the role barriers. As long as racial roles are maintained, both parties find it difficult to perceive the humanity behind the façade. Many whites who are by no means racists confuse the role of "Negro" with the people who must play this role. "Negroes are just like that," goes the phrase, "they are born that way." Conversely, many Negroes confuse the role of "white man" with whites. "Whites are just like that, they are born thinking they should be boss."

Intimately associated with this impairment of human relatedness is an impairment of the individual's acceptance and understanding of himself. Both whites and Negroes can confuse their own roles as being an essential part of themselves. Whites can easily flatter themselves into the conviction that they are in fact "superior"; after all, does not the deferential behavior of the role-playing Negro confirm this "superiority"? And Negroes in turn often accept much of the racists' mythology; for does not the imperious behavior of the role-playing white confirm this "inferiority"?

These are not mere speculations of existentialist philosophy. A large body of psychological research convincingly dem-

Abridged from Chapter 1 of **A Profile of the Negro American** (Copyright © 1964 by D. Van Nostrand Company, Inc.), Princeton: D. Van Nostrand, 1964, pp. 3–23, with permission of the author and the publisher.

onstrates the power of role-playing to change deeply-held attitudes, values, and even conceptions of self. Moreover, these remarkable changes have been rendered by temporary role adoptions of an exceedingly trivial nature when compared to the life-long role of "Negro." Imagine, then, the depth of the effects of having to play a role which has such vast personal and social significance that it influences virtually all aspects of daily living. Indeed, the resulting confusion of self-identity and lowering of self-esteem are two of the most serious "marks of oppression" upon Negro American personality.

Self-identity and self-esteem

The quest for self-identity is the search for answers to the all-important questions: Who am I? What am I like as a person? And how do I fit into the world? These are not easy questions for anyone to answer in our complex, swiftly-changing society. Yet they offer even greater difficulties for Negro Americans.

We learn who we are and what we are like largely by carefully observing how other people react to us. But this process is highly structured for the Negro by the role he is expected to play. When he attempts to gain an image of himself on the basis of his typical contacts with white America and the general culture, he often receives a rude jolt. While he is totally American in every conceivable meaning of the term, he finds that most Americans are white and that somehow the mere color of his skin puts him into a unique and socially-defined inferior category. And when the Negro looks around him—except in the spheres of athletics and entertainment—he discovers very few Americans with his skin color who hold important positions in his society. Save for the mass media expressly tailored for Negro audiences, he sees only white models in advertisements and only whites as heroes of stories (Berelson & Salter, 1946; Logan, 1954; Shuey, *et al.*, 1953; Writer's War Board, 1945). When he does see Negroes in the general mass media, they are likely to be cast in low-status roles and appear as "amusingly ignorant." Little wonder, then, that the question, who am I?, raises special difficulties for him.

Identity problems are unusually acute during certain periods in a person's life. These periods, these identity-crises, often occur in the preschool years, later in adolescence, and again in young adulthood. All three of these periods impose additional stress on Negroes. Negro parents confess to great anxiety and ambivalence over telling their preschool children what it means to be a Negro in American society. Should youngsters be shielded from the truth as long as possible? Or should they be prepared early for blows that are sure to come?

The importance of identity problems for young Negro children has been demonstrated by a series of ingenious investigations. Following the classical work of Kenneth and Mamie Clark (1963, 1947), these researches have utilized a wide assortment of techniques in a variety of segregated Southern and integrated Northern nursery and school settings and have consistently arrived at the same critical conclusions (Goodman, 1952; Landreth & Johnson, 1953; Morland, 1958; Stevenson & Stewart, 1958; Trager & Yarrow, 1952). Racial recognition in both white and Negro children appears by the third year and rapidly sharpens each year thereafter. Of special significance is the tendency found in all of these studies for Negro children to prefer white skin. They are usually slower than white children to make racial distinctions, they frequently prefer white dolls and white friends, and they often identify themselves as white or show a tense reluctance to acknowledge that they are Negro. Moreover, young children of both races soon learn to assign, realistically, poorer houses and less desirable roles to Negro dolls. This early "mark of oppression" is illustrated by the behavior of a small Negro boy who participated in one of these studies conducted in Lynchburg, Virginia. Asked if he were white or colored, he hung his head and hesitated. Then he murmured softly, "I guess I'se kinda colored." (Morland, 1958, p. 137)

Some of this direct manifestation of "self-hate" disappears in later years (Koch, 1946), though similar studies of older Negro children find residual symptoms (Johnson, 1941; Seeman, 1946). One investigation of children aged eight to thirteen years in an interracial summer camp found that Negroes tended at first to be oversensitive to unfavorable behavior of their Negro peers and to avoid choosing other Negroes as friends (Yarrow, 1958). A successful experience in an egalitarian, interracial setting, however, can alleviate these inclinations. In this study, a two-week experience in interracial camping is shown to have significantly modified these expressions of self-hate in the young Negro campers.

In the teens, sex becomes an acute issue. This is a period of great strain for most American adolescents, but for the Negro child in the North who has close friendships with white children, it frequently means a sudden parting of paths. After puberty, the Negro child is no longer invited to his white friends' parties, for at this time the deep racist fears of miscegenation harbored by many white parents enter on the scene. For the majority of Negro youth of this age who have no white friends, the early teens introduce their own version of identity-crisis. From his teachers, his peer group, his contacts with the white world beyond his immediate neighborhood, the Negro teenager encounters new shocks. The full awareness of his social devaluation in the larger society in addition to the sharp strains felt by all teenagers in a complex society can assume the dimensions of a severe emotional stress-situation (Milner, 1953).

If the ambitious Negro has successfully weathered these earlier crises, he must face yet another series of identity-shocks in young adulthood. Employment discrimination may keep him from the job for which he trained, and housing segregation may restrict him from securing the type of housing he wants for his family. Who am I? What am I like as a person? And how do I fit into the world? The old questions from childhood continue to require answers when he is refused a job for which he is qualified and a house for which he has the purchase price.

These identity problems are inextricably linked with problems of self-esteem. For years, Negro Americans have had little else by which to judge themselves than the second-class status assigned them in America. And along with this inferior treatment, their ears have been filled with the din of white racists egotistically insisting that Caucasians are innately superior to Negroes. Consequently, many Negroes, consciously or unconsciously, accept in part these assertions of their inferiority. In addition, they accept the American emphases on "status" and "success." But when they employ these standards for judging their own worth, their lowly positions and their relative lack of success lead to further self-disparagement. Competition with successful whites is especially threatening. Laboratory experimentation demonstrates that even when Negroes receive objective evidence of equal mental ability in an interracial situation they typically feel inadequate and respond compliantly (Katz & Benjamin, 1960).

The sweeping changes of recent years, however, have begun to alter this situation. The old wounds of confused identity and damaged self-esteem have not sufficiently healed, but recent events are potent medicines. Supreme Court decisions, in particular, brought new hope. A 1963 *Newsweek* national poll found that two-thirds of all Negroes credited the Supreme Court for their biggest breakthroughs. "It started the ball rolling," voiced one respondent. And another added, "The Supreme Court gave us heart to fight." (*Newsweek*, 1963, p. 27) Moreover, the Negro's own protests and assertion of civil rights, his increasing educational and economic opportunities, the findings of social science, and the emergence of proud new African nations all have salved the old wounds.

It is difficult for white Americans to grasp the full personal significance of these events for Negro Americans. But imagine how a Negro feels today. All of his life he has been bombarded with white-supremacy ideas and restrictions. Moreover, he has shared much of the naive conception of Africa as the dark continent of wild and naked savages. Now he is greeted with evidence from all sides that the white supremacists are wrong. On television, he sees segregationists desperately defying his national government in their losing battle to maintain Jim Crow, he sees his President conferring with black chiefs of state with full pomp and circumstance, and he sees his nation's representatives wooing the all-important black delegates to the United Nations. He sees all this, and his wounds begin to heal. The special role of "Negro" remains, but is undergoing drastic change.

The hostile environment

Another widespread reaction to racism is a generalized perception of the world as a hostile, threatening place. Horace Cayton considers this a critical feature of the "oppression phobia" experienced by many Negro Americans: an expectancy of violent mistreatment combined with a feeling of utter helplessness (Cayton, 1951). Negroes questioned in *Newsweek's* national poll groped for words to describe this phobia: "the feeling of being choked," said one; "feels like being punished for something you didn't do," said another (*Newsweek*, 1963, p. 18). Such feelings are also experienced by other minority groups. Many Jews, for instance, have reported a preoccupation with anti-Semitism and a vague sense of impending doom, of haunting anxiety, hovering over them (Allport, 1954).

Reality testing is involved here, of course, for the world *is* more often a treacherous, threatening place for Negroes. Consider the social scars of discrimination throughout Negro American history that make this true. Slavery cast the longest shadow. Compared with the institution in Latin America, slavery in the United States had an unusually crushing impact upon Negro personality, because it did not recognize the slave as a human being (Elkins, 1959; Tannenbaum, 1947). Spain and Portugal had centuries of experience with slavery prior to the founding of the New

World, hence Iberian law had evolved a special place for the slave as a human being with definite, if limited, rights. By contrast, England had no previous involvement with the "peculiar institution," and so its law, adopted by the American colonies, treated the slave as mere property—no different legally from a house, a barn, or an animal (Tannenbaum, 1947).

Recently, one historian ventured a parallel between Southern slavery on the large, cotton plantations and the concentration camps of Nazi Germany (Elkins, 1959). Both were closed systems, with little chance of manumission, emphasis on survival, and a single, omnipresent authority. The profound personality change created by Nazi internment, as independently reported by a number of psychologists and psychiatrists who survived, was toward childishness and total acceptance of the SS guards as father-figures—a syndrome strikingly similar to the "Sambo" caricature of the Southern slave. Nineteenth-century racists readily believed that the "Sambo" personality was simply an inborn racial type. Yet no African anthropological data have ever shown any personality type resembling Sambo; and the concentration camps molded the equivalent personality pattern in a wide variety of Caucasian prisoners. Nor was Sambo merely a product of "slavery" in the abstract, for the less devastating Latin American system never developed such a type (Elkins, 1959).

Extending this line of reasoning, psychologists point out that slavery in all its forms sharply lowered the need for achievement in slaves (McClelland, 1961, pp. 376–377). Negroes in bondage, stripped of their African heritage, were placed in a completely dependent role. All of their rewards came, not from individual initiative and enterprise, but from absolute obedience—a situation that severely depresses the need for achievement among all peoples. Most important of all, slavery vitiated family life (Bastide, 1950, pp. 240–247; Frazier, 1957). Since many slaveowners neither fostered Christian marriage among their slave couples nor hesitated to separate them on the auction block, the slave household often developed a fatherless, matrifocal (mother-centered) pattern.

Strong traces of these effects of slavery, augmented by racial discrimination, have persisted since Emancipation because of bitter poverty and the uprooted life of migrants far from home. Poverty is not limited to Negroes, of course, but it takes on a special meaning when due in part to the color of one's skin. Though a substantial number of Negroes have improved their status economically, a much greater percentage of Negroes than whites comprise the nation's most destitute citizens. For these Negroes, poverty means living in the degraded slums of our largest cities in close proximity to the worst centers of the nation's vice and crime. Poverty means less education, less opportunity, and less participation in the general culture. And it means less ability to throw off the effects of past oppression.

Furthermore, Negro Americans are often lonely, recent arrivals to huge metropolitan areas, strangers detached from their home moorings. Between 1950 and 1960, over one-and-a-half million Negroes left the South and came to cities in the North and West; others came to Southern cities from the farms. These migrants are frequently ill prepared for the demands of urban life, with only an inferior Southern rural education and few if any job skills. Consequently, they must fit onto the lowest rungs of the occupational ladder and hope for economic survival in an age when automation is dramatically reducing the number of jobs for unskilled workers. Small wonder such individuals come to view the world as a hostile place.

Family disorganization and personality

Both poverty and migration also act to maintain the old slave pattern of a mother-centered family. Not only does desperate poverty disturb healthy family life through dilapidated housing, crowded living conditions, restricted recreational facilities, and direct contact with the most corrupting elements of urban disorganization, but it makes the ideal American pattern of household economics practically impossible. Employment discrimination has traditionally made it more difficult for the poorly-educated Negro male to secure steady employment than the poorly-educated Negro female. In many areas of the nation, North as well as South, this is still true, with Negro females always able to obtain jobs as domestics if nothing else is available. When the unskilled Negro male does manage to secure a job, he generally assumes an occupation that pays barely enough to support himself—much less a family. Such conditions obviously limit the ability of lower-class Negroes to follow the typical American pattern—that is, a stable unit with the husband providing a steady income for his family.

The Negro wife in this situation can easily become disgusted with her financially-dependent husband, and her rejection of him further alienates the male from family life. Embittered by their experiences with men, many Negro mothers often act to perpetuate the mother-centered pattern by taking a greater interest in their daughters than their sons. For example, more Negro females graduate from college than Negro males, the reverse of the pattern found among white Americans.

Family stability also suffers from the effects of migration, with its tensions over relocation and its release of the migrant from the sanctions of his home community. When all of these factors are considered, the prevalence of divorce, separation, and illegitimacy among poor Negroes should not come as a surprise. For when American society isolates the lower-class Negro from contact with the general norms and prevents him from sharing in the rewards which follow from abiding by these norms, it guarantees the emergence of a ghetto subculture with different standards of conduct, motivation, and family life.

Census data for 1960 illustrate the depth of this family disorganization among Negroes: over a third (34.3 per cent) of all non-white mothers with children under six years of age hold jobs as compared with less than a fifth (19.5 per cent) of white mothers with children under six (U.S. Bureau of the Census, 1962); only three-fourths (74.9 per cent) of all non-white families have both the husband and the wife present in the household as compared with nine-tenths (89.2 per cent) of white families (U.S. Bureau of the Census, 1962); and only two-thirds (66.3 per cent) of non-whites under eighteen years of age live with both of their parents as compared with nine-tenths (90.2 per cent) of such whites (U.S. Bureau of the Census, 1962). These data do not cancel out the effects of social class differences between the two groups; rough comparisons between the lower classes of each race, however, still reveal a greater prevalence of father-absence among Negroes. The scar of slavery upon Negro family life, perpetuated through poverty and migration, is still evident.

Recent psychological research vividly demonstrates the personality effects upon children of having been raised in a disorganized home without a father. One such study reveals that eight-and-nine-year-old children whose fathers are absent seek immediate gratification far more than children whose fathers are present in the home. For example, when offered their choice of receiving a tiny candy bar immediately or a large bar a week later, fatherless children typically take the small bar while other children prefer to wait for the larger bar (Mischel, 1961c). This hunger for immediate gratification among fatherless children seems to have serious implications. Regardless of race, children manifesting this trait also tend to be less accurate in judging time, less "socially responsible," less oriented toward achievement, and more prone toward delinquency (Mischel, 1961a; 1961b). Indeed, two psychologists maintain that the inability to delay gratification is a critical factor in immature, criminal, and neurotic behavior (Mowrer & Ullman, 1945).

The reasons for these characteristics of father-absent children seem clear. Negro girls in such families model themselves after their mothers and prepare to assume male as well as female responsibilities. And various investigations have demonstrated the crucial importance of the father in the socialization of boys (Bandura & Walters, 1959; Mussen & Distler, 1959). Mothers raising their children in homes without fathers are frequently overprotective, sometimes even smothering, in their compensatory attempts to be a combined father and mother. Burton and Whiting persuasively contend that the boys whose fathers are not present have initially identified with their mothers and must later, in America's relatively patrifocal society, develop a conflicting, secondary identification with males (1961). In other words, they must painfully achieve a masculine self-image late in their childhood after having established an original self-image on the basis of the only parental model they have had—their mother.

The "psychologically vulnerable" Negro, crippled by weak ego development from earlier family disorganization, is more likely to fall prey to mental illness, drug addiction, or crime, depending on his particular life history. He has few personality resources to withstand the gale winds of discrimination that strike him full force in adolescence. Thus, segregation has its most fundamental influence on Negro personality in the manner in which it affects Negro family functioning (Jones & Arrington, 1945).

18 The nature and meaning of dogmatism

MILTON ROKEACH

In this paper we will attempt to provide the theoretical groundwork for a research project on the phenomenon of dogmatism in various spheres of human activity—political, religious, and scientific. Our main purpose is to present a detailed theoretical statement of the construct of dogmatism which is guiding the research.

A second purpose stems from the fact that our construct of dogmatism involves the convergence of three highly interrelated sets of variables: closed cognitive systems, authoritarianism, and intolerance. By virtue of this convergence it will be possible to examine certain assumptions underlying previous research on authoritarianism and intolerance (Adorno, *et al.*, 1950) with the aim of achieving a possibly broader conceptualization of these phenomena.

It is not within the scope of this paper to inquire into the social or personal conditions which give rise to dogmatism. This is considered to be an independent theoretical problem. Having defined the problem of dogmatism and its representation at the cognitive level—the main purpose of this paper—one can then seek explanations according to one's theoretical orientation.

A basic assumption guiding the present formulation is that despite differences in ideological content, analysis will reveal certain uniformities in the structure, the function, and, to some extent, even the content of dogmatism. Accordingly, attention will be directed to both political and religious dogmatism and, within each area, to diverse and even opposed dogmatic orientations.

The problem of dogmatism, however, is not necessarily restricted to the political and religious spheres. It can be observed in other realms of intellectual and cultural activity—in philosophy, the humanities, and the social sciences. To take some examples from psychology, it is possible to observe expressions of dogmatic Freudianism and dogmatic anti-Freudianism, dogmatic learning theory and dogmatic antilearning theory, dogmatic gestalt theory and dogmatic anti-gestalt theory, and so forth.

Dogmatism, furthermore, need not necessarily involve adherence to this or that group-shared, institutionalized system of beliefs. It is conceivable that a person, especially one in academic circles, can be dogmatic in his own idiosyncratic way, evolving a unique rather than institutionalized integration of ideas and beliefs about reality. The present formulation will attempt to address itself to noninstitutional as well as institutional aspects of dogmatism.

General setting for a cognitive representation of dogmatism

To conceptualize dogmatism adequately

Reprinted with slight abridgment from the **Psychological Review,** 1954, 61, 194–205, with permission of the author and the American Psychological Association.

at the cognitive level it is first necessary to employ a set of conceptual tools in terms of which all cognitive systems, varying in degree of dogmatism, may be represented.

ORGANIZATION INTO BELIEF AND DISBELIEF SYSTEMS

Objective reality can be assumed as being represented within a person by certain beliefs or expectations which to one degree or another are accepted as true, and other beliefs or expectations accepted as false. For the sake of analysis this can be formalized by conceiving of all cognitive systems as being organized into two interdependent parts: a belief system and a disbelief system. This belief-disbelief system can further be conceived as varying in terms of its structure and content as follows:

Structure. The total structure of a belief-disbelief system can be described as varying along a continuum from open to closed. This continuum, in turn, may be conceived as a joint function of: (*a*) The degree of interdependence among the parts within the belief system, within the disbelief system, and between belief and disbelief systems (Kounin, 1948; Krech, 1949; Lewin, 1951; Rokeach, 1951a). (*b*) The degree of interdependence between central and peripheral regions of the belief-disbelief system (Lewin, 1951). (*c*) The organization of the belief-disbelief system along the time perspective dimension (Crossman, 1949; Frank, 1939; Hoffer, 1951; Lewin, 1942).

Content. One can further describe all belief-disbelief systems in terms of the formal content of centrally located beliefs, especially those having to do with beliefs about authority and people in general.

A cognitive representation of dogmatism

In line with the above considerations we will now define dogmatism as (*a*) a relatively closed cognitive organization of beliefs and disbeliefs about reality, (*b*) organized around a central set of beliefs about absolute authority which, in turn, (*c*) provides a framework for patterns of intolerance and qualified tolerance toward others. A cognitive organization is considered to be closed to the extent that there is (*a*) isolation of parts within the belief system and between belief and disbelief systems, (*b*) a discrepancy in the degree of differentiation between belief and disbelief systems, (*c*) dedifferentiation within the disbelief system, (*d*) a high degree of interdependence between central and peripheral beliefs, (*e*) a low degree of interdependence among peripheral beliefs, and (*f*) a narrowing of the time perspective.

More specifically, in the relatively closed belief-disbelief system there is assumed to be a relation of relative isolation among the various parts of the belief system and between belief and disbelief systems. The latter, in turn, is composed of a series of disbelief subsystems, each arranged along a gradient of similarity to the belief system, the most similar disbelief subsystems being represented as regions most adjacent to the belief system. Each of these disbelief subsystems is conceived, to the extent that it is part of a closed system, as being relatively less differentiated than the belief system and, the farther away their positions from the belief system, as increasingly dedifferentiated with respect to each other.

Belief-disbelief systems can also be represented along a central-peripheral dimension. The more closed the system the more the central part corresponds to absolute beliefs in or about authority, and the more the peripheral part corresponds to beliefs and disbeliefs perceived to emanate from such authority.

With respect to the time perspective dimension, increasingly closed systems can be conceived as being organized in a relatively future-oriented or past-oriented direction rather than in terms of a more balanced orientation of past, present, and future.

With regard to the content of dogmatism, while the specific content of both central and peripheral parts may vary from one particular ideological system to another, it is possible to specify that in general the formal content of the central part of the system, to the extent it is closed, has to do with absolute beliefs in and about positive and negative authority, either external or internal, and related beliefs representing attempts on the part of such authority to perpetuate itself. Furthermore, the central part can be conceived to provide a framework for the organization of other beliefs representing patterns of rejection and qualified acceptance of people in general according to their patterns of agreement and disagreement with the belief-disbelief system.

Dogmatism distinguished from rigidity

Before going on to elaborate further on our conceptual definition of dogmatism, it may be illuminating first to distinguish the construct of dogmatism in a general way from that of rigidity. Both dogmatism and rigidity refer to forms of resistance to change, but dogmatism is conceived to represent a relatively more intellectualized and abstract form than rigidity. Whereas dogmatism refers to total cognitive *organizations* of ideas and beliefs into relatively closed ideological systems, rigidity, when genotypically conceived, refers solely to the degree of isolation between regions (Krech, 1949; Rokeach, 1951a) or to a "property of a functional boundary which prevents communication between neighboring regions" (Kounin, 1948, p. 157); when phenotypically conceived, rigidity is defined in terms of the way a person or animal attacks, solves, or learns *specific* tasks and problems (Rokeach, 1948). Thus, dogmatism is seen as a higher-order and more complexly organized form of resistance to change. While dogmatism may well be hypothesized to lead to rigidity in solving specific problems, the converse is not necessarily the case. Rats, the feebleminded, and the brain-injured, for example, can be characterized as rigid (also compulsive, fixated, perseverative, inflexible) but hardly as dogmatic.

Furthermore, whereas rigidity refers to person-to-thing or animal-to-thing relationships, dogmatism is manifested almost necessarily in situations involving person-to-person communication. Thus, we speak of a person as tying his shoelaces or solving an arithmetic problem rigidly, but of a professor, a politician, an orator, a theoretician, or an art critic as expressing himself to others dogmatically.

A final differentiation, closely related to the preceding, is that dogmatism has a further reference to the authoritarian and intolerant manner in which ideas and beliefs are communicated to others. Thus, the range of behavior considered under the rubric of dogmatism is considerably broader than rigidity and at the same time of possibly more intrinsic interest to the sociologist, the political scientist, and the historian, as well as the psychologist.

Postulates involving the cognitive structure of dogmatism

To the extent that the belief-disbelief system is closed, it is subjected to continual stresses and strains from objective and social reality. Reality can be coerced into congruence with the belief-disbelief system by virtue of the arrangement of parts within the belief-disbelief systems, within and between the central and peripheral regions thereof, and by virtue of its organization along the time perspective dimension.

A. ISOLATION WITHIN AND BETWEEN BELIEF AND DISBELIEF SYSTEMS

The greater the dogmatism the greater are the assumed degree of isolation or independence between the belief and disbelief systems and the assumed degree of isolation among the various parts of the belief system. On the basis of these considerations we introduce the following postulates:

1. *Accentuation of differences between belief and disbelief systems.* The greater the dogmatism the more will the belief system be perceived as different in content or aim from the disbelief system (e.g., Catholicism and Protestantism; the United States and the USSR; fascism and communism; psychoanalysis and behaviorism).

2. *The perception of irrelevance.* The greater the dogmatism the more will ideological arguments pointing to similarities between belief and disbelief systems be perceived as irrelevant.

3. *Denial.* The greater the dogmatism the greater the denial of events contradicting or threatening one's belief system (e.g., on grounds of "face absurdity," that the true facts are not accessible, that the only available sources of information are biased because they are seen to emanate from the disbelief system, etc.).

4. *Coexistence of contradictions within the belief system.* In line with the assumption that in increasingly closed cognitive organizations there is relatively more isolation among subparts of the belief system, as well as between belief and disbelief systems, it is postulated that the degree of adherence to contradictory beliefs will vary directly with the degree of dogmatism. Some examples of contradictory beliefs are an abhorrence of violence together with the belief that it is justifiable under certain conditions; expressions of faith in the intelligence of the common man and at the same time the belief that the masses are stupid; a belief in democracy and along with this the belief that our country can best be run by an intellectual elite; a belief in freedom for all but at the same time the belief that freedom for certain groups should be restricted; a belief that science makes no value judgments about "good" and "bad" but also that scientific criteria are available for distinguishing "good" theory from "bad" theory, and "good" experiment from "bad" experiment (Rokeach, 1951b).

B. THE DISBELIEF GRADIENT

We have already indicated that in relatively closed systems there is relative isolation between belief and disbelief systems. However, the various disbelief subsystems cannot all be assumed to be equally isolated from the belief system. Rather, degree of isolation can further be conceived as varying with the degree of perceived similarity of the various disbelief subsystems to the belief system. Those disbelief subsystems most similar to the belief system can be represented as regions most adjacent to the belief region and, hence, in relatively greater communication or interaction with the belief system than less similar disbelief subsystems.

1. *Strength of rejection of various disbelief subsystems.* The greater the dogmatism the more will the disbelief subsystem most similar to the belief system (factional or "renegade" subsystems) be perceived as threatening the validity of the belief system and hence the greater the tendency to exert effort designed to reject this subsystem and the adherents thereof. For example, with an increase in dogmatism there will be an increasingly militant rejection of Protestantism by the Catholic, of reformed Judaism by the more conservative Jew, of Trotskyism and Titoism by the Communist, and vice versa. In the academic realm, too, the greater the dogmatism the more antagonism there will be among representatives of divergent views within a single discipline as compared with related disciplines.

2. *Willingness to compromise.* Even though a person or group may reject a disbelief system it is often necessary, for the sake of achieving political or religious aims, to form working alliances with other individuals or groups. It is here postulated that such compromising varies inversely with dogmatism: the greater the dogmatism the less compromise there will be with adherents to the disbelief subsystem closest to the belief system.

C. RELATIVE DEGREES OF DIFFERENTIATION OF BELIEF AND DISBELIEF SYSTEMS

In our cognitive representation of dogmatism we have assumed that the greater the dogmatism the more differentiated the belief system will be as compared with the disbelief system. Moreover, various disbelief subsystems have been assumed to become relatively more dedifferentiated with respect to each other the farther away their positions from the belief system. The following postulates are based upon these considerations:

1. *Relative amount of knowledge possessed.* The greater the dogmatism the greater the discrepancy between degree of knowledge of facts, events, ideas, and interpretations stemming from the belief system and any one of the disbelief subsystems. Thus, for example, with an increase in dogmatism there will be an increasing discrepancy in the Freudian's knowledge of classical psychoanalysis as compared with Adlerian psychology or learning theory.

2. *Juxtaposition of beliefs and disbeliefs.* Under special conditions, however, e.g., social or personal conditions which lead to disillusionment with the belief system and thence to conversion wherein beliefs and disbeliefs become juxtaposed, it is conceivable that one of the disbelief subsystems will be more differentiated than the belief system. It is therefore postulated that as a function of the reversal of belief and disbelief systems, the greater the dogmatism the greater the discrepancy between degrees of differentiation of belief and disbelief systems in favor of the latter.

3. *Dedifferentiation within the disbelief system.* The greater the dogmatism the more will two or more disbelief subsystems represented as positions relatively far away from the belief system along the disbelief gradient be perceived as "the same" (e.g., that communism and socialism are the same, that the Democrats and Republicans are both run by Wall Street, etc.).

D. RELATION BETWEEN CENTRAL AND PERIPHERAL PARTS

We have assumed further that, to the extent we are dealing with closed systems, the central part corresponds to beliefs in and about absolute authority and the peripheral part to beliefs and disbeliefs perceived to emanate from such authority. Thus, the more closed the system the greater the assumed degree of communication between central and peripheral beliefs and, at the same time, the less the assumed degree of communication among the various peripheral beliefs. From these considerations it follows also that any given change in the peripheral part represents an isolated change in cognitive content without concomitant changes either in cognitive structure or in *over-all* ideological content.

It is this interrelation between central and peripheral parts which gives the relatively closed system its integrated and systematic character.[1] Specific peripheral beliefs and disbeliefs are organized together not so much by intrinsic logical connections as by virtue of their perceived origination with positive and negative authority, respectively. Whatever characterizes the authority's ideology, as represented by the central part, will be mirrored "gratuitously" in the closed system. If the authority is logical, the closed system will appear logical; if the authority is illogical, the closed system will appear illogical. The more closed the system the more will it reflect *in toto* the authority's own system with its logic or illogic, its *manifest* intellectualism or anti-intellectualism, and so forth.

1. *"Party-line" changes.* It is commonly observed that relatively dogmatic views on specific issues are stubbornly resistant to change by logical argument or objective evidence. One possible reason for this becomes apparent in the light of the preceding considerations. The greater the dogmatism the more will there be a change in a given peripheral belief (e.g., about birth control) if it is preceded by a perceived corresponding change by the authority (e.g., the Catholic Church). Moreover, the greater the dogmatism the less will any given change in a peripheral belief effect changes in other peripheral beliefs (e.g., about divorce, federal aid to education, etc.).

2. *Assimilation.* Further considerations regarding the relation between central and peripheral parts lead also to the following postulate: The greater the dogmatism the greater the assimilation of facts or events at variance with either the belief or disbelief system by altering or reinterpreting them such that they will no longer be perceived as contradictory.

3. *Narrowing.* Assuming, as we have, that the central region is crucial in determining what aspects of reality will be represented within the peripheral region, it follows that it will also be crucial in determining what aspects of reality will *not* be represented (Rokeach, 1951a). The greater the dogmatism the more the avoidance of contact with stimuli—people, events, books, etc.—which threaten the validity of the belief system or which proselyte for competing disbelief systems.

Cognitive narrowing may be mani-

1 This is illustrated very nicely by the following, which we believe is from Sholom Aleichem: "I did not borrow your pot; besides it was broken when you lent it to me; besides I have already returned it to you." Despite its illogical character, the statement is nevertheless systematic. While each of the beliefs expressed is contradictory to the others, they all reinforce each other to serve the end of protecting the central authority (in this case, the person speaking) against threat.

fested at both institutional and noninstitutional levels. At the institutional level, narrowing may be manifested by the publication of lists of taboo books, the removal and burning of dangerous books, the elimination of those regarded as ideological enemies, the omission of news reports in the mass media unfavorable to the belief system or favorable to the disbelief system, and the conscious and unconscious rewriting of history (Orwell, 1951).

At the noninstitutional level, narrowing may become apparent from the systematic restriction of one's activities in order to avoid contact with people, books, ideas, social and political events, and other social stimuli which would weaken one's belief system or strengthen part of one's disbelief system. Relevant here are such things as exposing oneself only to one point of view in the press, selectively choosing one's friends and associates solely or primarily on the basis of compatibility of belief systems, selectively avoiding social contact with those adhering to different belief systems, and avoiding those who formerly believed as one does.

In academic circles cognitive narrowing over and above that demanded by present day specialization may be manifested by a selective association with one's colleagues and selective subscription, purchase, and reading of journals and books such that one's belief system becomes increasingly differentiated while one's disbelief system becomes increasingly dedifferentiated or "narrowed out."

E. TIME PERSPECTIVE

1. *Attitude toward the present.* The greater the dogmatism the more will the present be perceived as relatively unimportant in its own right—as but a passageway to some future utopia. Furthermore, with an increase in dogmatism there will be a concomitant increase in the perception of the present as unjust and as full of human suffering.

2. *Belief in force.* Such a disaffected conception of the present can readily lead to the belief that a drastic revision of the present is necessary. Thus, we are also led to the following postulate: The greater the dogmatism the greater the condonement of force.

3. *Knowing the future.* Another aspect of time perspective has to do with one's understanding of the future. With an increase in dogmatism there will be the following variations: an increasing confidence in the accuracy of one's understanding of the future, a generally greater readiness to make predictions, and a decreasing confidence in the predictions of the future made by those adhering to disbelief systems.

Postulates involving the cognitive content of dogmatism

We have already pointed out that while the specific content of beliefs and disbeliefs varies from one system to another, it is nevertheless possible to point to certain uniformities in the formal content of centrally located beliefs which, to the extent that they are part of a closed system, form the cognitive bases for authoritarianism and intolerance.

A. AUTHORITARIANISM

At the center of the belief-disbelief system, to the extent it is closed, is assumed a set of absolute beliefs about positive and negative authority and other closely related beliefs representing attempts by such authority to reinforce and perpetuate itself.

1. *Positive and negative authority.* With an increase in dogmatism there will be not only increasing admiration or glorification of those perceived in positions of positive authority but also increasing fear, hatred, and vilification of those perceived in positions of authority opposed to positive authority.

2. *The cause.* With an increase in dogmatism there will be an increasing strength of belief in a single cause and concomitantly a decreasing tendency to admit the legitimacy of other causes. Manifestations of strength of belief in a single cause might be making verbal references to "the cause," expressing oneself as "feeling sorry" for those who do not believe as one does, believing that one should not compromise with one's ideological enemies, perceiving compromise as synonymous with appeasement, believing that one must be constantly on guard against subversion from within or without, and believing that it is better to die fighting than to submit.

3. *The elite.* With an increase in dogmatism there will be an increase in strength of belief in an elite (political, hereditary, religious, or intellectual).

B. INTOLERANCE

Beliefs in positive and negative authority, the elite, and the cause all have to do with authority as such. Coordinated with such beliefs are others representing organizations of people in general according to the authorities they line up with. In this connection there may be conceived to emerge, with increasing dogmatism, increasingly polarized cognitive distinctions between the faithful and unfaithful, orthodoxy and heresy, loyalty and subversion, Americanism and un-Americanism, and friend and enemy. Those who disagree are to be rejected since they are enemies of God, country, man, the working class, science, or art. Those who agree are to be accepted but only as long as and on condition that they continue to do so. This sort of qualified tolerance is, to our mind, only another form of intolerance. That it can turn quickly into a frank intolerance is often seen in the especially harsh attitude taken toward the renegade from the cause.

It is in this way that the problem of acceptance and rejection of people can become linked not only with authoritarianism but also with the acceptance and rejection of ideas. Perhaps the most clear-cut single behavioral manifestation of this linkage is the employment of opinionated language in communicating beliefs and disbeliefs to others. Opinionation is a double-barrelled sort of variable which refers to verbal communications involving acceptance or rejection of beliefs in an absolute manner and, at the same time, acceptance or rejection of others according to whether they agree or disagree with one's beliefs.

1. *Opinionated rejection.* This refers to verbal statements which imply absolute rejection of a belief and at the same time rejection of persons who accept it. The following examples illustrate this: "Only a simple-minded fool would think that . . . ," "A person must be pretty stupid to think . . . ," "The idea that . . . is pure hogwash (or [redacted]cock, nonsense, silly, preposterous, absurd, crazy, insane, ridiculous, piddling, etc.)."

The preceding considerations lead us to postulate that opinionated rejection will vary directly with dogmatism.

2. *Opinionated acceptance.* This refers to an absolute acceptance of a belief and along with this a qualified acceptance of those who agree with it. Some examples are: "Any intelligent person knows that . . . ," "Plain common sense tells you that . . . ."

Opinionated acceptance will also vary directly with dogmatism.

Some implications for further theory and research on authoritarianism and intolerance

Through the pioneering research of Adorno *et al.* (1950) significant theoretical and empirical advances have been made recently in understanding the phenomena of authoritarianism and intolerance. Since our construct of dogmatism also involves a representation of these phenomena, it is proper to ask: To what extent is the present formulation of the problem of dogmatism consonant with the work on the authoritarian personality?

To be noted first is a historical fact. The research on the authoritarian personality was launched at a time when the problem of fascism and its attendant anti-Semitism and ethnocentrism was of overriding concern to both social scientist and layman. Given this social setting as a point of departure, it was almost inevitable that the general problem of authoritarianism would become more or less equated with the problems of adherence to fascist ideology and ethnic intolerance. Thus, the personality scale designed to tap underlying predispositions toward authoritarianism was called the F (for fascism) Scale and was found to correlate substantially with measures of ethnic intolerance.

It is widely recognized, however, that authoritarianism is also manifest among radicals, liberals, and middle-of-the-roaders as well as among conservatives and reactionaries. Furthermore, authoritarianism can be recognized as a problem in such areas as science, art, literature, and philosophy, where fascism and ethnocentrism are not necessarily the main issues or may even be totally absent as issues. As pointed out in this paper, dogmatism, which is assumed to involve both authoritarianism and intolerance, need not necessarily take the form of fascist authoritarianism or ethnic intolerance.

It is thus seen that the total range of phenomena which may properly be regarded as indicative of authoritarianism is considerably broader than that facet of authoritarianism studied so intensively by the authors of *The Authoritarian Personality.* On theoretical grounds, we are in accord with the view that authoritarianism has a greater affinity to leanings to ideologies which are antidemocratic in content. But it need not be conceived as *uniquely* connected with such ideologies. If a theory of authoritarianism is to be a general one, it should also be capable of addressing itself to the fact that to a great extent authoritarianism cuts across specific ideological orientations. As we have tried to suggest, dogmatic authoritarianism may well be observed within the context of any ideological orientation, and in areas of human endeavor relatively removed from the political or religious arena.

One way to test the validity of the above considerations is to demonstrate that scores on the F Scale are related substantially to measures of dogmatism independently of liberalism-conservatism, or of the kinds of attitudes held toward such groups as Jews and Negroes. The results of one study, already reported (Rokeach, 1952), show that dogmatism and authoritarianism correlate over .60 when ethnocentrism or political-economic conservatism is held constant. Corroborative findings from several studies will be presented in a more detailed future report (see Rokeach, 1960).

Consider further the way the problem of intolerance has been conceived in social-psychological research (Adorno, *et al.*, 1950; Jahoda, *et al.*, 1951). Parallel to the more or less rough equating of authoritarianism with fascism, and perhaps for similar reasons, intolerance too can be said to have become more or less equated with one aspect of intolerance, namely, ethnic intolerance. Examination reveals that such concepts as intolerance, discrimination, bigotry, social distance, prejudice, race attitudes, and ethnocentrism are all defined operationally in much the same way—by determining how subjects feel or act toward Jews, Negroes, foreigners, and the like.

It is reasonable to assume that there are persons who, although they would validly score low on measures of ethnocentrism or similar scales presently in use, would nevertheless be characteristically intolerant of those whose belief-disbelief systems are at odds with their own.

It has already been suggested that while dogmatic authoritarianism may "attach" itself to any ideology, it is probably more closely related to those having antidemocratic content. A similar point may well be made in connection with dogmatic intolerance. Preliminary data already available suggest that measures of dogmatic intolerance (opinionation) and ethnic intolerance are, as expected, related to each other to a significant degree. At the same time they are also found to cut across each other in a relatively independent fashion.

The preceding considerations point to other aspects of man's intolerance to man, in addition to ethnic intolerance, which deserves scientific attention. And, as we have tried to point out in discussing the problem of authoritarianism, here too we think there is a need for a more comprehensive conceptualization of the problem of intolerance.

19 A theoretical framework for personality and social behavior

ROBERT R. SEARS

I wish to consider some systematic aspects of personality and social psychology, and to indicate what seem to me the directions further development of these fields is likely to take. Partly these directions are dictated by more general developments in psychology and the social sciences; but partly they are matters of choice, and of estimate as to what will provide us with the most effective science of human behavior.

Perhaps the most impressive thing about both these fields is the extent to which, in recent years, they have become empirical. The opinion poll, small group observational procedures, and attitude scales have contributed notably to the precision with which the actions of groups can be measured and their future behavior predicted. Similarly, in the field of personality and motivation, such devices as the TAT, doll play, behavior unit observations, and standardized interviews have become more and more effective for providing objective and quantified statements about significant variables.

From a practical standpoint, some of these methods have been extraordinarily valuable. Market surveys, studies of morale in the military services, diagnostic analyses of disturbed children, and comparative studies of techniques of teaching have yielded findings that have much improved the quality of human output. In effect, the past decade has put in the hands of any competent technician procedures which permit the empirical discovery of facts and principles that hitherto had been the province of so-called men of wisdom. For many areas of human action, intuitively skillful lucky guessing has given way to precise and replicable investigation.

Theory

This empirical progress has been accompanied by the construction of but a minimal amount of theory. Perhaps it could not have been otherwise. Theory does not grow in the absence of data, and until the last two decades, the data of social psychology have been meager and those of personality limited mainly to clinical observations.

Yet it is clear that further development in these fields will require an adequate theory. By a *theory* I mean a set of variables and the propositions that relate them to one another as antecedents and consequents. This involves such logical impedimenta as definitions, postulates, and theorems. And it requires the following of certain rules, such as that the definitions of variables must be mutually exclusive; that intervening variables must ultimately be reducible to operations; that the reference events specified as the consequents in theorems must be measured independently of the antecedents

Reprinted with slight abridgment from the **American Psychologist,** 1951, 6, 476–84, with permission of the author and the American Psychological Association.

from which they are derived, and so on. The general procedure of theory construction is sufficiently standard that it needs no explication here.

The *findings* to be integrated are those that describe consistent relationships between behavior (or its products) and some other events. Essentially, these are the descriptive behavioral relationships that comprise the disciplines of individual and social psychology, sociology, and anthropology. Individual and group behavior are so inextricably intertwined, both as to cause and effect, that an adequate behavior theory must combine both in a single internally congruent system.

There are two main advantages of a good theory that make such a development urgent. First, it is economical in the sense that it permits many observed relationships to be subsumed under a single systematic proposition. And second, it permits the use of multiple variables and their relating principles, in combination, for the prediction of events.

These virtues have long been recognized. Several psychologists have constructed conceptual frameworks within which the facts of either social psychology or personality could be theoretically formulated. McDougall (1908), Floyd Allport (1924), and Kurt Lewin (1944) provided them for social psychology; Freud (1920), G. V. Hamilton (1925), Lewin (1935), Gordon Allport (1937), and H. A. Murray (1938) have done the same for personality. Examples of the application of theory construction to problems important in social psychology and personality are to be found in Festinger's work on communication (1950), Miller's studies of displacement (1948), and our own analyses of the projective process in parent-child relationships (Sears, 1948, 1950, 1951b).

Action

Every theory must have a subject-matter. It must be a theory about something, obviously. A certain class of events must be selected for explication. These are the reference events, the consequents for which antecedents are discovered. The basic events to which behavior theory has reference are *actions*. This follows from the very nature of our interest in man. It is his behavior, the things he does, the ends he accomplishes, that concern us.

From a logical standpoint, a theory is of value to the extent that it orders a set of observations. There are many kinds of observations that can be and have been made of social and individual behavior. Some of these have involved inferred traits or needs; others have related to perceptions or to states of consciousness. By the criterion of logic, a theory that takes any of these phenomena as its basic reference events is acceptable.

But there is another criterion to be considered, the practical one. It is reasonable to ask what kind of events are important to us. On this score, action is clearly more significant than perception or traits. The clinician must make judgments about personality that will permit predictions of behavior. Will the patient attempt suicide? Will his performance at intellectual tasks continue to deteriorate? Will his level of social problem-solving improve under an anxiety-reduction therapy? Likewise, the teacher and the parent undertake methods of rearing a child with expectations that his actions will change in a particular direction. They want him to add more accurately, or paint more freely, or cry less violently when he is disappointed; even those changes commonly interpreted as perceptual, such as art or music appreciation, are evidenced in the form of choices as to where to go, what to look at, what to listen to.

The situation is even clearer with respect to social behavior. The social engineer is concerned with such questions as whether a certain parent-child relationship will establish habitually dependent behavior in the child, whether the eventual marriage of a courting couple will terminate in divorce or in the social facilitation of their mutual labors, whether citizens will buy bonds or vote for a Congressman, whether a group will be shattered or solidified by external opposition, i.e., whether there will be an increase or decrease in cooperative efforts and in-group aggression.

Aside from the fact that a behavior science, rather than a *need* or *perceptual* science, is of the greatest use to us, there is an evident practical advantage. Human beings deal with one another in terms of actions. The teacher has direct observation of the performance of her pupils. The parent or the husband or the foreman or the Congressman can have only inferential knowledge of the ideas or desires of those with whom he interacts. But he can describe the conditions that impinge on people and he can take note of the behavioral consequences. To put the argument briefly: actions are the events of most importance, and actions are most available to observation and measurement.

This is not to say that needs or motives, perceptions, traits, and other such internalized structures or processes are irrelevant. Any scientific system must contain both operational and intervening variables that are independent of the reference events forming the subject-matter of the system. But the choosing of such variables must depend on their contribution to a theory that will predict actions. There is no virtue in a descriptive statement that a person or a class of persons possesses such and such a trait or need unless that statement is part of a larger one that concludes with a specification of a kind of action to be performed. To describe a person as having *high emotionality* or *low sensitivity* or *diffuse anxiety* is systematically acceptable only if other variables are added that will, together with these internal personal properties, specify what kind of behavior can be expected from him under some specific circumstances.

Dynamics

By definition a theory of action is dynamic; i.e., it has to do with force or energy in motion. The term *dynamic* has been so abused by psychologists during the last half century, however, that its meaning is no longer clear. Perhaps it never was. But with successive "dynamic psychologies"—those of Freud, Morton Prince, Woodworth, Lewin, and a host of contemporary theorists—its meaning has been more obfuscated than ever. Sometimes it refers to a motivational approach, sometimes to a developmental, sometimes to an emphasis on unconscious processes. Mostly, I suspect, it merely means the theorist is revolting against what seem to him the stultifying, structuralistic, unhuman inadequacies of his predecessors. It boils down to a self-attributed accolade for virtue, a promise to deal with important characteristics of real live people rather than dry and dusty processes.

This is a waste of a good word. By no means all modern psychological systems are dynamic; some are trait-based and some are need-based. No one would deny that combinations of habit structures do exist and do provide a kind of integrated consistency in a person's behavior. Likewise, no one would attempt to order the events of human action without variables that relate to motivation, including those kinds of motivation that cannot be verbally reported by the person himself. But there is more to dynamics than motivation. There is *change*.

Changes in behavior are of two kinds. For a theory to be dynamic, both must be systematized, separately but congruently. One is ongoing action, or *performance*, and the other is learning, or *acquisition*. Obviously, no predictive statement can be made about ongoing action unless certain things are known about the person's *potentialities for action*. He has certain properties that determine what kind of behavior he will produce under any given set of circumstances. His motivation is weak or strong, he is frustrated or not in various goal-directed sequences, he has expectancies of the consequences of his behavior. Unless these are known, it is impossible to have any systematization of ongoing action. And unless the *changes* in potentialities for action are systematically ordered, there is no possibility of constructing an ongoing action theory that will enable one to predict beyond the termination of any single sequence of behavior.

The combining of these two approaches to behavior has not yet been fully accomplished. The most elaborate theory of performance, or ongoing action, is that of Kurt Lewin (1935), but his field theory has never been developed to care adequately for problems of personality development (learning). Similarly, the developmental theory of G. V. Hamilton (1925) gave an excellent account of the acquisition of potentialities for response but did not cover so effectively the problems of ongoing action.[1]

Monadic and diadic units

I have already made reference to the desirability of combining individual and social behavior into a single theoretical system. The reasons are obvious. In any social interaction, the interests, motives, habits or other psychological properties of the acting individuals determine to some degree the kind of interaction that will occur. The shy youngster is likely to have less stimulating learning experiences with his teacher than is a bolder one; the traveller in a foreign land who knows the language forms different kinds of friendships than the one who uses an interpreter. Conversely, the social milieu, the interpersonal relationships, within which a person acts determine his psychological properties. A man in a subordinate role cannot act as a leader; a child reared

[1] A simple behavior sequence is shown in Figure 1. The various potentialities for action are specified by S_D (motivation) and S_{cog} (cognitive structures). In large part these characteristics are a product of learning. The successful completion of a behavior sequence is a reinforcement, and this modifies the drives and habit structures of the person in certain lawful ways, these laws being part of the body of the laws of learning. In other words, there is a change in the person's potentialities for action. It is to be noted, therefore, that although Figure 1 describes a single behavior sequence, there are two ways of ordering the events that compose it. Both refer to changes, to energy in motion. To be dynamic, a theory of behavior must encompass both.

as the younger of two develops differently from one reared as the elder of two. Whether the group's behavior is dealt with as antecedent and the individual's as consequent, or vice versa, the two kinds of event are so commonly mixed in causal relationships that it is impractical to conceptualize them separately.

To wish for a combining theoretical framework is one thing, but to get it from psychologists is quite another. Sociologists have been more accustomed to think in such terms. The theoretical analyses of Cottrell (1942) and of Parsons (1951) have emphasized particularly the interactive processes. Among psychologists, Newcomb (1950), with his exposition of role expectancy, and Festinger (1950), in his studies of group cohesiveness, clearly exemplify the trend toward combination. In the main, however, in spite of their long prepossession with social influences on the individual, psychologists think monadically. That is, they choose the behavior of one person as their scientific subject matter. For them, the universe is composed of individuals. These individuals are acted upon by external events, to be sure, and in turn the external world is modified by the individuals' behaviors. But the universal laws sought by the psychologist almost always relate to a single body. They are monadic laws, and they are stated with reference to a monadic unit of behavior.

The main variables that compose such systems have been presented diagrammatically in many ways. Some are so well known as virtually to represent signatures for the theorists who devised them. There are Tolman's schematic sow-bug, Hull's behavior sequence, Lewin's field structure, and Miller and Dollard's learning paradigm. These diagrams differ considerably in the kinds of variables they incorporate. Some emphasize reward and reinforcement; others do not. Some are time-oriented; others are descriptive of a non-temporal force field. All specify antecedent stimulus conditions and consequent actions, but in very different ways and with quite different systematic constructs. But there is one thing in common among them—they are all monadic.

But if personality and social behavior are to be included in a single theory, the basic monadic unit of behavior must be expandable into a diadic one. A diadic unit is one that describes the combined actions of two or more persons. A diadic unit is essential if there is to be any conceptualization of the *relationships* between people, as in the parent-child, teacher-pupil, husband-wife, or leader-follower instances. To have a science of interactive events, one must have variables and units of action that refer to such events. While it is possible to systematize some observations about individuals by using monadic units, the fact is that a large proportion of the properties of a person that compose his personality are originally formed in diadic situations and are measurable only by reference to diadic situations or symbolic representations of them. Thus, even a monadic description of a person's action makes use of diadic variables in the form of social stimuli.

This is exemplified in Figure 1, a diagram of a monadic behavior sequence that, as will be seen, can be expanded into a diadic sequence. One aspect of this figure deserves comment, the *environmental event*. This concept refers to the changes produced in the environment by the instrumental activity; these are the changes necessary for the occur-

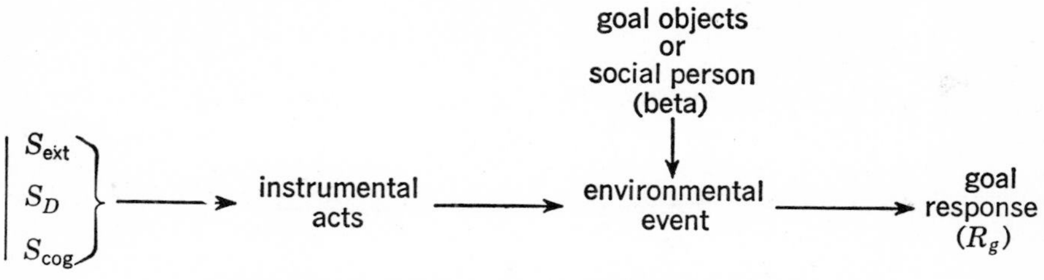

Figure 1. The monadic instigation-action sequence

rence of the goal response. The teacher trying to increase participatory activity in a class of children, for example, gets her reward when the youngsters spontaneously start a team game at recess. She makes her goal response—she has achieved her aim—when the environment changes, i.e., when the children play a team game. Or a boy is seeking approbation from his father; he hits a three-bagger; his father grins with satisfaction. The grin is the boy's environmental event in his monadically conceived action sequence.

This concept achieves importance in the present context, because it is the necessary connecting link between a monadic and diadic systematization of behavior. The framework for such a description is shown in Figure 2. For convenience the two persons are labelled Alpha and Beta. A diadic situation exists whenever the actions of Beta produce the environmental events for Alpha, and vice versa. The behavior of each person is essential to the other's successful completion of his goal directed sequence of action. The drives of each are satisfied only when the motivated actions of the other are carried through to completion. The nurturant mother is satisfied by the fully-loved child's expression of satiety, and the child is satisfied by the expressions of nurturance given by his mother.

It must be made clear in this connection that environmental events are *only those changes in environment produced by the behavior of the person under consideration*. The stroke of lightning that splits a log for the tired woodcutter is not in this category, nor is the food given the newborn infant by his mother, nor the empty taxi that providentially appears when the rain is at its worst. These are certainly char-

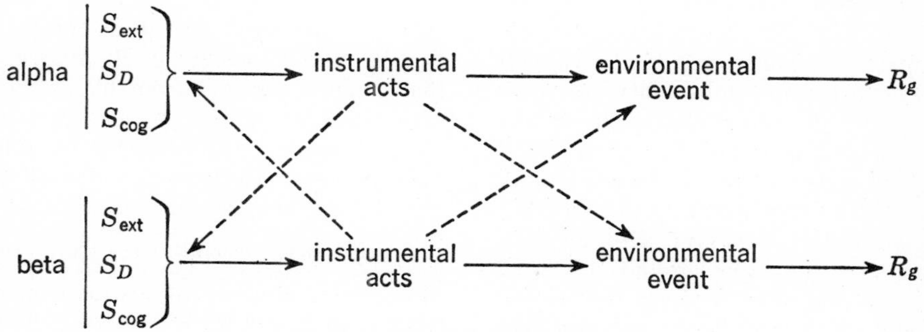

Figure 2. The diadic sequence

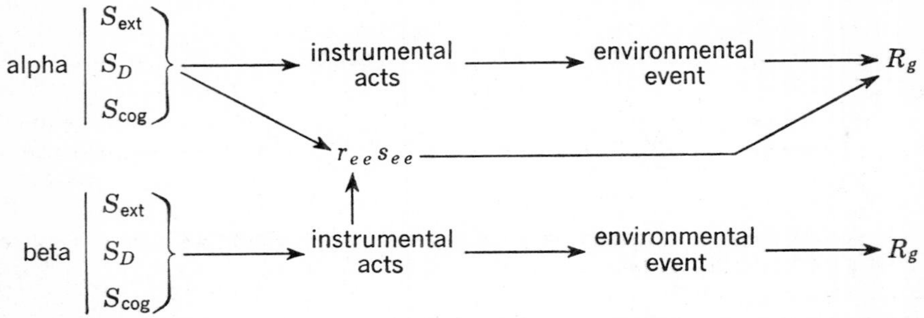

Figure 3. The diadic sequence with anticipatory responses to the environmental event

acteristics of the environment, manipulanda that govern in some ways the future behavior of Alpha, but they are not environmental events in the sense that the term is used here. They were not induced by any action of Alpha.

This is an important distinction. Unless the interaction of Alpha and Beta is based on something other than the fortuitously useful conjunction of their individual actions, there is no interdependence of each on the other. There is, in effect, no diadic system, only a piling up of parallel monadic sequences.

The factor responsible for maintaining stability of the diadic unit is exhibited in Figure 3. It is the *expectancy* of the environmental event, diagrammed in a notation similar to that used by Hull for the anticipatory goal response (1931). In the present case, the anticipatory response is a fractional part of the reactions Alpha makes to those behaviors of Beta that constitute the environmental event. For example, if a child wants to be kissed good-night, his mother must lean toward him affectionately and kiss him. He, in turn, must slip his arms around her neck and lift his face to hers receptively. These latter movements are the ones that fractionate and become anticipatory in Alpha's behavior sequence. And as in the case of the anticipatory goal response, they elicit response-produced stimuli ($r_{ee}s_{ee}$) that become integrated into the total stimulus constellation which serves to instigate this behavior sequence on future occasions.

These anticipatory reactions to Beta's behavior are the *expectancies* that make the behavior of the two people truly interdependent. They provide the mechanism, at least within the framework of one conceptualization of the learning process, by which a diadic behavior unit can be derived from the combining of two or more monadic units.

One can only speculate as to what variables, and what general principles, will eventually compose a diadic behavior theory.[2] Some of them will probably be discovered in the attempt to analyze those psychological processes that apparently result from highly particularized constellations of interpersonal relations. Identification is one such process. Reciprocal cathexis is another. A third is the process of sec-

[2] The reader should note that since 1951, when this paper originally appeared, a variety of diadic models actually have been developed, several of which are included in this volume, including for example the quite recent paper by Secord and Backman following.—Eds.

ondary drive formation, as in the early childhood development of aggression and dependency. Other variables will likely be devised in the study of small groups. Festinger's concept of cohesiveness is a big step forward in this direction.

One way of approaching the problem would be to examine the various possibilities of reward and nonreward or punishment for Alpha and Beta. If a diad exists on the basis of reciprocal rewards, as in the mother-child relationship, there are nevertheless possibilities of mutual interference. That is, while the diad is held together by powerful continuing motivations and expectancies of reciprocal support, each member has the potentiality of frustrating the other. One major source of frustration is the absence of the partner, Beta, at times when Alpha needs him. Such absences would be expected to occur partly (but by no means entirely, of course) because Beta was also the partner in diadic relationships with other people. Now, since in young children aggression and dependency are two of the major reactions to frustration, one might reach some such hypothesis as this: that the amount of aggression and dependency that characterize a mother-child interaction will be a positive function of the number of diadic relationships in which each is a member. Or to put it in a more testable form: everything else being held constant, a child's dependency and aggressiveness toward his mother will vary with the amount of role conflict the mother has.

Personality

In this monadic-diadic framework, personality is a description of those properties of a person that specify his potentialities for action. Such a description must include reference to motivation, expectations, habit structure, the nature of the instigators that activate instrumental behavior, and the kinds of environmental events that such actions will produce. Furthermore, all these factors must be described in terms of the diadic aspects of the behavior that occurs. That is, the kinds of Betas who can serve as instigators for particular responses must be specified, and the environmental events that Beta creates for Alpha must be described not only as they fit into Alpha's activity but also as they fit into the whole motivational sequence of Beta.

In behavior science, personality is sometimes treated as antecedent and sometimes as consequent. As antecedent, it is part of the total matrix that must be known in order to account for either individual or diadic action. In recent years various approaches to personality have too much depended on assumptions of fixed traits and fixed needs. This has led to measurement procedures that do not include reference to the social stimulus conditions under which the traits or needs will be expressed. As Fillmore Sanford has said, in connection with a study of leadership, there is no trait independent of the conditions that elicit it. Leadership is a quality in a person's behavior only if there are followers who react to him as a leader. Most behavior with which the personality psychologist is concerned is either directly diadic or is in response to symbolic representation of the diad. Therefore, any conceptualization of the person's properties must be done with consideration of the properties of the various Betas with whom Alpha is interactive.

A simple example of the measurement

problem created by these considerations arose in connection with some data on aggressive behavior collected in our laboratory (Sears, 1948, 1950, 1951b). Forty preschool children were the subjects. Two main measures of aggressiveness were secured. One was overt and socially directed aggression. This measure was obtained both by teachers' rating scales and by direct observation. The other was projective or fantasy aggression displayed in doll play. By a fixed trait or need assumption, one would expect these two measures to correspond somewhat. They did—somewhat! The correlation was +.13!

An analysis in terms of learning and action makes the meaning of this relationship clear. These children's mothers were interviewed concerning their methods of handling the youngsters' aggression at home. On the basis of this information it was possible to divide the children into three subgroups which had had different degrees of severity of punishment for aggression.

While the "mild" and "moderate" groups show a correspondence in amount of aggressive behavior of the two kinds [overt and fantasy aggression], there is a radical disagreement in the "severe" punishment subgroup. These latter children, on the average, behaved rather non-aggressively in preschool, but in their doll play fantasies there was an abundance of aggression. One could ask whether these children are very aggressive or very non-aggressive. Do they have strong need for aggression or weak?

Even if these questions could be sensibly answered, which they cannot, the answers would be of little help in predicting the future aggressive behavior of these children. To accomplish the latter, which is our aim, there must be an analysis of the social stimulus conditions under which the future behavior is to be observed.

The minimum specification would be as to whether the behavior would be observed in a nursery school or in a permissive doll play experiment. With a conceptualization of the diadic variables involved, however, it is possible to make a statement that goes beyond the narrow confines of these two measuring situations. In this instance, the more general statements can be made that, first, the amount of aggression will be a negative function of severity of punishment, and second, with severity of punishment held constant, the amount of aggression will vary positively with dissimilarity of the diadic situation to the original punishment situation in the home. These are strictly monadic statements, but they assume the prior existence of diadic experiences.

The systematization of personality development requires a different approach. When personality factors are considered as antecedents to individual or group behavior, the laws of ongoing action are involved. But when personality development is the matter for study, the laws of learning are the bases. What is needed in this case is a set of principles that will describe the way in which the child's potentialities for action—that is, his drives, habits, cognitive structures, and expectancies—are changed by the experiences he has throughout his life.

This is a difficult problem, both logically and empirically. Personality is partly the product of a life-time of diadic action which has modified the individual's potentiality for further action. The changed potentiality is therefore partly a product of his own actions. For example, in the data concerning child aggression and severity of maternal punishment for aggression, the mother's actions in punishing the child were doubtless influenced in part by the amount and kind of aggression exhibited toward her by the child. Thus, the behavior that served as an antecedent to the differential display of overt and fantasy aggression by the child was contributed to by the child himself.

Logically, and practically, a good theory requires that antecedents and consequents be entirely independent of one another. It would be most satisfactory if the child did not influence the mother's behavior, and if we could then say something about the effect of severity of punishment on later behavior. One solution to this problem appears to be a careful measurement of the child's contribution to the diadic relationship and a partialling out of that influence in the comparison of antecedent mother behavior with consequent child behavior.

The variables that appear most promising in the study of personality development come from two main sources. One is the set of definitions and postulates that compose the laws of learning. Whether the particular formulations used by Tolman, Hull, Guthrie, or Skinner are selected seems of little importance at the moment. Those of Hull and Tolman have certain *a priori* advantages, but the main point is the use of whatever laws of learning will best serve to account for changes in potentiality for action. The theoretical formulation of the research in our own laboratory stems from Hull through Miller and Dollard.

The second source of variables lies in the conceptualization of those secondary motivational systems that arise universally as a product of the diadic relationship between mother and child (Sears, 1948). These include aggression, dependency, self-reliance, responsibility, the anxieties, competition, and status-seeking, as well as the various consequences of the training inherent in socialization of the primary drives of hunger, sex, fatigue, and elimination. The exact forms of behavior potentiality created in each of these motivational areas are different from child to child and culture to culture. But the biological nature of man, coupled with his universal gregariousness, gives rise to various learning experiences that every human child endures in one fashion or another.

20 Personality theory and the problem of stability and change in individual behavior: an interpersonal approach

PAUL F. SECORD and CARL W. BACKMAN

Clinical psychologists, personality theorists, and most other students of individual behavior commonly assume that a person gradually forms characteristic behavior patterns which become more and more resistant to change with the passage of time. These patterns are usually thought of as reflections of intra-individual structures or mechanisms: e.g., habits, needs, cognitive structures, or traits. Because these intrapersonal determinants of behavior are, in effect, accepted as givens, observable consistency over a period of time tends to remain unexplained—it is simply a manifestation of these structures. From this point of view, a person behaves as he does because of what he is.

Thus, Allport (1937), Cattell (1950), and Eysenck (1953) attribute enduring structure to personality, a structure in which the concept of trait is central. Murray (1938) conceives of personality as an organizing and integrating force having a neural locus in the organism. In spite of his field emphasis, Lewin (1935) conceives of personality structure as characterized by certain differentiations and articulations of regions, which correspond to aspects of personal character. Murphy (1947) includes physiological dispositions, canalizations, conditioned responses, and cognitive and perceptual habits as components of personality. Two cognitive orientations are those of Rogers (1951), and Combs and Snygg (1959), who conceive of behavior as organized around and guided by a relatively enduring self-concept. Finally, almost all forms of personality assessment are based upon the assumption that the individual undergoing appraisal has a stable personality structure which the investigator is attempting to describe, in part or in whole.

For all of these theorists, then, personality has a certain stability of structure which in turn maintains continuity in behavior over time. This is not to assert that behavior is viewed by these theorists as unchanging or unresponsive to varying stimulus situations. On the contrary, many of these personologists often give careful attention to stimulus situations as modifiers of behavior. But, sometimes explicitly and sometimes implicity, they do appear to make the assumption that when behavioral stability occurs, it is a function of stability in personality structure. A closely related assumption is that personality structure has a strong resistance to change; in the absence of special change-inducing forces or conditions, it remains constant.

These assumptions have two conse-

Reprinted with slight abridgment from the **Psychological Review**, 1961, 68, 21–33, with permission of the authors and the American Psychological Association.

quences. The first is that continuity in individual behavior is not a problem to be solved; it is simply a natural outcome of the formation of stable structure. The second is that either behavioral change is not given systematic attention, or change is explained independently of stability. Whereas behavioral stability is explained by constancy of structure, change tends to be explained by environmental forces and fortuitous circumstances. A more parsimonious approach would be to account for both stability and change by means of a single set of explanatory principles. The following theoretical statement abandons the assumption that internal stabilizing mechanisms are inherently resistant to change and are the sole source of stability in individual behavior.

The present paper places the locus of stability and change in the interaction process rather than in intrapersonal structures. At the same time, the importance of habit, cognitive structure, and similar concepts is not denied, but these mechanisms do not by themselves establish necessary conditions for behavioral stability. Stable patterns in the interaction process, which constitute the essential condition for consistency in individual behavior, may be thought of as deriving from two major sources. One source is the cultural, normative, and institutional forces which stabilize the behavior of persons with whom a particular individual interacts, as well as his behavior toward them. With this important source the present paper is not concerned; social psychologists, sociologists, anthropologists, and others have analyzed these forces in extensive detail.

The other source of stability, although it has been given some attention by social psychologists, has been relatively neglected by students of individual behavior. It has been customary to think of two classes of behavioral determinants: cultural and normative forces, and those forces stemming from the individual. The present paper attempts to identify a third class of determinants, which have their locus neither in the individual nor the culture, but in the interaction process itself. In a general sense this third class may be characterized as the tendencies of the individual and the persons with whom he interacts to shape the interaction process according to certain requirements, i.e., they strive to produce certain patterned relations. As will be seen, the principles governing this activity are truly interpersonal; they require as much attention to the behavior of the other as they do to the behavior of the individual, and it cannot be said that one or the other is the sole locus of cause.

Because of limitations of space and in the interests of clarity, the theory will be presented without attempting to specifically examine the empirical evidence, but those familiar with the literature will recognize that much supporting evidence exists. For definitive support, however, an extensive research program guided by the theory needs to be carried out.

Sources of stability in individual behavior

DEFINITION OF INTERPERSONAL MATRIX AND MATRIX CONGRUENCY

The locus of behavioral stability and change lies in the interpersonal matrix, which has three components: an aspect of the self-concept of the subject (*S*), *S*'s interpretation of those elements of his behavior related to that aspect, and S's perception of related aspects of the other person (O) with whom he is interacting. An interpersonal matrix is a recurring functional relation between these three components. The behavior of a particular person is episodic in character, in that he shifts from one matrix to another over varying periods of time. A matrix is referred to as the same if, on two or more occasions, the same self-component, S-behavior, and O-component are present in the same functional relation. The present theoretical treatment focuses mainly on the discussion of single matrices. Also, only aspects of self and behavior which are valued by *S* are dealt with, and these are assumed to maintain relatively constant values.

S strives to achieve congruency[1] among the components of the matrix. Congruency is a cognitive phenomenon: i.e., each component enters into a state of congruency only as a perceptual cognitive experience on the part of S. All three components of the matrix are in a state of congruency when the behaviors of S and O imply definitions of self congruent with relevant aspects of the self-concept. In a nurturant-dependent relation, for example, a dependent *S* has conceptions of self containing elements of inadequacy and need for support. His behavior is consistent with these aspects of cognitive structure, for it is hesitant and compliant, reaffirming his self-definition. Since the behavior of O is perceived as providing assistance and as reassuring and decisive, it implies a matching definition of S's self-concept and behavior. In the above example, S's interpretation of his behavior is congruent with a relevant aspect of the self, S's perception of O is congruent with the self-aspect, and S's interpretation of his behavior is congruent with his perception of O. Thus, any two components of a matrix may be congruent with each other, with the third either congruent with both of them, or not congruent with either.

Implications for self-definitions may take three forms: *S* may perceive O's behavior as directly confirming a component of self, O's behavior may enable *S* to behave in ways that would confirm a component of self, O's behavior may (by comparison) lead other Os to confirm a comparison of S's self-concept. Examples of each form are:

An *S* who regards himself as mature and responsible perceives that Os respect him for these characteristics.

An *S* who regards himself as nurturant encounters an O in need of help; this allows him to behave toward O in a manner which supports his nurturant aspect of self.

A girl who regards herself as popular and well-liked keeps company with an unpopular girl; Os are viewed by her as judging her favorably by contrast.

Reality-oriented vs. cognitively distorted matrices. A matrix is reality-oriented if the S-behavior component and O-component are correctly interpreted or perceived. On the other hand, a matrix which involves misinterpretation of S's behavior or misperception of O is not reality-oriented; it involves some form of cognitive distortion. It is obvious that congruency

[1] Congruency as used here has some similarities to the following: Abelson's (1958) resolution of belief dilemmas, Cartwright and Harary's (1956) concept of structure balance, Festinger's (1957) theory of cognitive dissonance, Heider's (1958) theory of balance, and Osgood and Tannenbaum's (1955) concept of congruence.

would sometimes be achieved by means of cognitive distortion. Presumably a congruency achieved by this means would be less stable than a reality-oriented congruency. At least this would be true if there were forces tending to produce accurate interpretations and perceptions. On the other hand, *in*congruencies which might be made congruent simply by correcting cognitive distortions to fit reality are not regarded as particularly stable or significant, and thus are not further discussed.

The tendency to achieve and maintain congruent states. A number of general principles may be presented concerning the maintenance of congruent states. In many instances these will be elaborated later.

1. *S* tends to repeat and perpetuate those interpersonal relations which were previously characterized by congruency.

2. An *S* involved in a matrix which is not in a state of congruency will tend to modify the matrix in the direction of greater congruency.

3. The engagement of *S* and O in congruent interaction develops mutual affect toward each other, which tends to perpetuate the interaction.

4. Because of the tendency to establish congruent matrices, *S* gradually builds up an increasingly greater repertory of such matrices.

5. The more the O-component of a congruent matrix is valued, the greater the tendency of the matrix to be perpetuated.

Relations among matrices and the perpetuation of congruent states. A given matrix may be considered *relevant* to those matrices which contain one or more of the same or similar components as the given matrix. For example, for an *S* who considers himself to be a kind person, there will be many S-behaviors and O-behaviors which are perceived as forming congruencies and incongruencies with this aspect of self. The various matrices formed by distinctive S-behaviors and O-behaviors in connection with the aspect of self, kindness, are all considered relevant to each other.

A relevant matrix may be either *supportive* or *nonsupportive* with respect to a given matrix. Supportiveness between two matrices is determined by whether or not the component(s) common to them has the same relation (one of congruency or one of incongruency) to the other unique components in each matrix. If the common component has the same relation in both matrices, they are said to be supportive.

For example, suppose a woman regards herself as unattractive to men. Her mother continually calls her attention to the fact that women in her family were seldom noted for their attractiveness. Our *S* also finds that a man she likes at work avoids her as much as possible. In the one matrix, unattractiveness is congruent with her mother's direct definition of her as unattractive and, in the other, the avoidance behavior of the man leads her to perceive his behavior as defining her as unattractive. Thus, one matrix supports the other. On the other hand, if her mother perceived many good features in her appearance and stressed these, and the man professed admiration for her, both matrices would be incongruent with her notion of self as unattractive. These two matrices would also support each other—they agree in denying an aspect of self. These might be termed incongruent supportive matrices, and the former type, congruent supportive matrices.

A statement may now be made with respect to the role of a complex of matrices in perpetuating a given matrix. Matrices vary with respect to *centricality*. The centricality of a matrix is a function of the number of other matrices which stand in a supportive relation to it, and the value of the O-components in these matrices. The greater the centricality of a matrix, the more resistant it is to change, and, should it change, the greater the resultant shifts in other matrices.

INTERPERSONAL PROCESSES CONTRIBUTING TO CONGRUENT STATES

Congruency is continually threatened by the changing nature of interpersonal relations due to: (*a*) normative patterns of change, which result in changes in the behavior of others towards S, e.g., changes in the behavior of others as the child grows older, or as a person changes occupations, gets married; (*b*) fortuitous changes, e.g., death of a parent, loss of a friend, induction into the military; and (*c*) the fact that O's means of establishing congruency for himself often create incongruencies for S. A number of interpersonal processes may be suggested which counter these pressures for change and which perpetuate previous matrices.

The first five interpersonal processes restore congruency through some transformation of the O-component of the matrix:

1. *Selective interaction with Os.* S tends to maximize engagement in congruent patterns of interpersonal behavior by selecting and interacting with those Os whose behavior requires a minimum change from previously congruent interpersonal situations in which S has engaged. For example, if S regards himself as especially intelligent, he tends to interact frequently with Os who respect his intelligence or who allow him to exercise it, or he interacts in such a way as to make himself appear intelligent by comparison.

2. *Selective evaluation of Os.* S tends to maximize congruency by altering the evaluation of selected Os in a positive or negative direction, depending upon whether they are behaving congruently or incongruently with certain aspects of self. The more an O is valued by S, either positively or negatively, the more important his role is in maintaining congruency. This provides a means of increasing the effects of congruency or reducing the effects of incongruency. Thus, S tends to increase his liking for Os who behave toward him in a congruent fashion, and to decrease his liking for those who behave in an incongruent manner.

3. *Selective comparison with aspects of O.* S tends to maximize congruency by selectively attending to behaviors of O which are congruent, and selectively ignoring those which are incongruent. For example, a patient in therapy particularly notes those behaviors on the part of the therapist which confirm aspects of his self-concept and behavior, and tends to ignore those which are incongruent.

4. *Evocation of congruent responses from O.* S develops techniques for eliciting from O behavior which will be congruent with components of his self-concept and behavior. For example, a feminine woman plays a helpless role in order to elicit dominance from men.

5. *Misperception of O.* S may misperceive O's behavior so as to achieve

congruency with aspects of his behavior and self-concept. Thus, an *S* has a high regard for himself as a lover and perceives other women as more interested in him than they really are.

The sixth and seventh interpersonal processes restore congruency by a transformation of the S-behavior component of the matrix:

6. *Selective behavior-matching.* In interacting with a particular O, *S* tends to maximize congruency by selecting from his total behavioral repertory those behaviors which are most congruent with his perception of O. This principle reflects William James' (1890, Vol. 1, p. 294) notion that each person has as many "social selves" as there are classes of persons whose opinion he cares about.

7. *Misinterpretation of own behavior.* *S* may misinterpret his behavior so as to achieve maximum congruency with an aspect of his self-concept and his perception of O. For example, a dutiful mother spanks her child because of anger and frustration, but convinces herself that she is doing it for the child's own good.

Certain combinations of these principles may sometimes operate under a single rubric. For example, an individual may select a *social role* which enables him to achieve maximum congruency among the three components. This involves interaction with selected Os who will engage in certain desired reciprocal behavior, and also permits behaviors which validate the self. Thus, a woman who regards herself as intelligent, independent, and ambitious may reject the marital role in favor of a career role. A second example is found in *circular interaction systems.* In these, response evocation tends to become an activity mutual to two persons: the actions of *S* give rise to behavior on the part of O which in turn evoke further actions of the type initially displayed by the individual. For example, aggressive actions on the part of the mother, initiated in the attempt to control or eliminate undesirable aggressive behavior in her child, raise his frustration level, which in turn gives further impetus to his tendency to respond in aggressive ways.

Forces toward change and the resolution of these forces

STATES OF INCONGRUENCY AND THEIR CONSEQUENCES

Any theory of stability in self and behavior must also be able to explain change. There are three steps leading to change: the creation of an incongruency, the formation of a new congruent matrix which involves a different component of self or behavior from that existing prior to the change, and the adjustment of relevant matrices which have been affected by the changes made in resolving the incongruent matrix. As mentioned earlier, incongruencies arise from several sources: from cultural, normative, and institutional forces, from fortuitous factors, and from O's attempts to establish congruency for himself. Incongruencies occur frequently, but are often followed by restoration of a congruent matrix which does not involve a change in self or behavior. Whether or not change occurs, resolution of the newly formed incongruency occurs through utilization of one or more of the interpersonal processes previously discussed. Thus, a single set of interpersonal processes are presumed to underlie both behavioral stability and the directior of behavioral change.

Four types of incongruency are identified in the following discussion. Of considerable interest and importance is the manner in which the various types of incongruency may be resolved. As already noted, there are two general classes of resolution. One of these results in restoration of the original matrix, leaving self and behavior unchanged (although cognitive distortions may occur), and the other leads to a new matrix in which self or behavior are changed. In order to avoid being tedious, only a brief, informal discussion of the forms of resolution will be presented. Table 1, however, presents in symbolic form a complete set of resolutions for the first three types of incongruency. The fourth is omitted since it is mainly of academic interest and is probably quite rare.

Type I. The behavior of O is perceived as incongruent with a component of self and with *S*'s behavior, the latter two elements being congruent with each other.

For example, *S*, an alcoholic, who regards himself as a "weak," inadequate person, neglects his family by going on extensive binges, implying a definition of self as inadequate. O, his wife, behaves toward *S* as if he were capable of controlling his drinking.

In this type of incongruency, *S* may employ any one of the first five interpersonal processes to transform the incongruent O-component, and thereby maintain self and behavior unchanged. Thus, he may reduce interaction with his wife, may devaluate her, may avoid selective comparison by declaring her opinion irrelevant, may evoke new responses from her, or may falsely perceive her as trying to give him a pep talk.

Other forms of achieving congruency require a change in self or behavior. *S* may change both components, or he may change self but not behavior by misinterpreting his behavior.

Type II. An aspect of self is incongruent with *S*'s behavior and with the perceived behavior of O, the latter two elements being congruent with each other.

TABLE 1

RESOLUTION OF BASIC TYPES OF INCONGRUENCY

Let E represent the self-component of matrix
B represent S-behavior as a reality-oriented matrix component
O represent O-behavior as a reality-oriented matrix component
B′ represent a matrix component based on misinterpretation of S-behavior
O′ represent a matrix component based on misperception of O-behavior
$\bar{X}$ represent an incongruent form of a component *X*
X_c represent a change in a component *X*

	Type of resolution			
Type of incongruency	Maintenance of self and behavior	Change in self-concept	Change in behavior	Change in self-concept and behavior
I. $SB\bar{O}$	SB SB SBO_c SBO_c SBO′	$S_cB'O$	not applicable	S_cB_cO
II. $\bar{S}BO$	SB′ SB′ $SB'O_c$ $SB'O_c$ SB′O′	S_cBO	SB_c SB_c SB_cO_c SB_cO_c SB_cO'	not applicable
III. $S\bar{B}O$	SB′O	S_cB S_cB S_cBO_c S_cBO_c S_cBO'	SB_cO	not applicable

Note: Resolutions involving O are listed in order of the five interpersonal processes which apply to O: (*a*) reduced interaction—SB, (*b*) devaluation—SB, (*c*) O-behavior selection—SBO_c, (*d*) response evocation—SBO_c, and (*e*) misperception—SBO′.

For example, a woman behaving seductively gets matching responses from O, but regards herself as morally conservative.

One form of resolution involves maintenance of self and behavior. Since behavior is incongruent, it would have to be misinterpreted if self is to be maintained, and in addition, the five interpersonal processes which transform the incongruent O-component would be employed here. For example, behavior is misinterpreted if *S* regards her behavior as casually flirtatious, or as "not me" because she had been drinking, and, with respect to O, *S* might reduce interaction with him, regard his behavior as harmless flirtation, or she might make her own behavior irrelevant by defining him as a man who would try to seduce any woman, etc.

A simple change in self would result in a congruent matrix. Or, finally, *S* might change her behavior and transform the O-component.

Type III. *S*'s behavior is incongruent with a component of self and with the perceived behavior of O, the latter two elements being congruent with each other.

For example, a wife regards herself as loving, but realizes that she is often hostile toward her husband. Her husband fails to recognize much of the hostility and behaves toward her as if he perceives her as loving.

If, in this instance, *S* changes her self-concept to match her unchanged behavior, she may employ the five interpersonal processes to transform the O-component. Thus, she may leave her husband, devaluate him, emphasize occasions on which he has been angry with her, evoke hostility from him, or think that he secretly does recognize her hostility. If she maintains self-concept and behavior, she must necessarily misinterpret her behavior in order to achieve congruency.

Type IV. All three matrix components are incongruent with each other. Two general forms of resolution are: (*a*) any two of the components may be changed to match the third; (*b*) all three may be modified to achieve a new matrix congruency. Type IV incongruency is thought to be rare and is not discussed further.

FACTORS GOVERNING THE PROBABLE DIRECTION OF RESOLUTION

The various forms of resolution of incongruent matrices are not equally probable. Which ones are more likely to occur is in part a matter for empirical study. In the meantime, however, a number of factors relating to the probability of change in the various components may be identified. In the first place, O's behavior toward *S* may be systematic and consistent because it stems from certain factors external to the dyad, such as role expectations—e.g., O may be *S*'s therapist, or he may be a parent socializing his child. An obvious second consideration is the ease with which *S* may leave the dyad. A patient may readily leave therapy, but a child cannot usually leave his family. A third condition pertains to the extent to which an individual's congruent relations are reality-oriented, i.e., to what degree misinterpretation and misperception are required for congruency. Matrix components which are not reality-oriented tend to be less stable. A fourth point is that the greater the number and value of supportive congruent matrices which are relevant to a component, the more resistant is that component to change. Finally, it may be postulated that the individual learns to utilize selectively the various modes of resolution. For a particular individual, certain types of component-transformation are more practiced and are preferred to others.

Discussion

An important difference between the present approach and earlier ones should be re-emphasized. Such traditional concepts as cognitive structure, self-concept, trait, and habit are products of earlier social interaction. But the assumption is *not* made that persons strive to maintain either their self-concept or various habitual behaviors by virtue of some inherent "gyroscopic" force residing in these dispositions. Maintenance of intrapersonal structure occurs only when such maintenance is consistent with an ongoing interaction process which is in a state of congruency. That most individuals do maintain intrapersonal structure is a function of the fact that the behavior of others toward the individuals in question is normally overwhelmingly consistent with such maintenance. This fact has often been overlooked. It should be made clear that the concept of structure continues to have a place in the present theory. Matrices are structures; they are aspects of perceptual-cognitive experience. Unlike habit and trait, however, they tend to be more integrated with certain behaviors of O. Even the self-concept, employed in the present theory as a matrix component, is always tied to certain behaviors of S and O.

The interpersonal environment is not always stable and familiar. The present approach predicts that were the interpersonal environment to suddenly undergo drastic change, with others uniformly behaving toward the individual in markedly new and strange ways, an individual held in such an environment would rapidly modify his own behavior and internal structure to produce a new set of congruent matrices. As a result, he would be a radically changed person. This prediction is consistent with the experiences of some soldiers imprisoned and "brainwashed" by Chinese communists. Some investigators have emphasized as a key factor in successful brainwashing the isolation of the individual from his normal interpersonal relations. Marked changes in an individual may also occur as a result of shifts in a single matrix, if that matrix involves a highly valued O, e.g., a therapist. As noted earlier, there are complexes consisting of matrices relevant to each other because they contain at least one common component, and a shift in one highly valued matrix may have ramifications throughout the structure of relevant matrices. In a word, the differences in emphasis between the present and previous approaches to behavioral stability is that the individual strives to maintain interpersonal relations characterized by congruent matrices, rather than to maintain a self, habits, or traits. Some of the advantages of this approach are the following:

1. The approach provides a place in theory for the variability of individual behavior in different interpersonal situations. For example, it does not make the questionable assumption that an individual belongs at fixed points with respect to each of a variety of personality traits in all interpersonal situations. A given individual is unlikely to be equally aggressive in interaction with every other person or in every situation involving the same person. Yet, a typical personality appraisal instrument yields a single score on "aggressive" for

an individual. In the present view, trait behaviors such as aggressiveness tend to appear only when they are congruent with certain O-behaviors and certain components of self. This idea calls for an overhaul of our traditional methods of personality assessment.

2. While self-theory emphasizes that self emerges out of social interaction, it is rather vague on details. In fact it implies that the only role of the behavior of others in supporting the self is that expressed by the first type of congruent O-behavior, namely, behavior which directly defines an *S*-component of *S* in the same way as *S* does. Moreover, the organism is often assumed to be passive in this process. For example, the fact that *S* may actively seek out those who support components of self, may evoke certain responses on the part of the other, etc., is often ignored.

3. The interpersonal framework makes the process of individual change less mysterious and less difficult to explain. Individual behavior is always linked to the behavior of others, and the key to deliberate change lies in creating shifts in the perception of the behavior of Os toward *S*. This is accomplished either through bringing about actual changes in the behavior of Os toward S, or by blocking various techniques that *S* uses to distort or to evoke certain O-behaviors which tend to support his current perceptions. Socialization and psychotherapy will shortly be discussed in order to illustrate the application of the theory to problems of change.

4. It is believed that variables on the perceptual-cognitive level are more directly assessable in view of the ability of *S*s to directly describe their self-concept, their behavior, and the behavior of Os. In addition, the question of cognitive distortion can be checked by obtaining information by direct observation of the interaction, or by obtaining descriptive information from O. In contrast, such concepts as need, habit, and trait must be inferred, and there has been considerable controversy over the validity of various procedures of inference in regard to these variables. Another advantage stems from the fact that, in the experience of the present investigators, matrix variables are readily manipulable when using conventional experimental procedures in social psychology. For example, an incongruency can be readily created in the laboratory by false test protocol reports to *S*s concerning aspects of self and behavior, or by placing *S* in the laboratory with an O who has been instructed by the experimenter to behave in an incongruent fashion.

5. The present point of view should be helpful in integrating concepts of personality with those of social psychology. At present there is a tendency to conceptualize each of these disciplines in such a way as to make difficult, if not impossible, the simultaneous application of concepts from both areas to consideration of any particular behavioral phenomenon. Dyadic relations will be briefly touched upon to indicate how a rapprochement between these areas might be initiated. Also, by examining the role of culture in establishing congruencies and incongruencies, light may be thrown on variations in individual strain from culture to culture, and on a source of cultural change, namely, the attempt of individuals to resolve such strains.

Socialization and psychotherapy. The process of socialization involves those changes occurring as a result of movement through the social structure. Psychotherapy has a less systematic relation to social structure, and may be thought of as a process of change resulting from highly significant interaction between patient and therapist. Both socialization and psychotherapy may be examined briefly to determine whether or not the process of change can be conceptualized in terms of the present interpersonal theory.

Socialization may be viewed as a process in which the person moves through a succession of changing patterns of O-behaviors over a long period of time. These changing patterns are culturally induced, and create incongruencies for *S*. In this process there is a certain amount of resistance to change on the part of *S*, arising out of the fact that typically the changing behavior of Os toward him requires continual reorganization of previously established matrices. Behaviors which previously led readily to congruent matrices now bring forth incongruent reactions from O. Take, for example, the small child who has an overprotective mother. Here self-cognitions are rudimentary and limited, but if existing components were phrased in adult language, they might include the following: "I am the baby of the family." "Daily family life revolves around me." "I can get most anything I want." When this child moves out of his mother's sphere of control, however, and plays with other children, he meets many responses incongruent with these components of self. Other children are likely to thwart his needs rather than meet them; he is unlikely to be the center of play activities. These incongruencies force change in self-components and behavior. To the extent that an overprotective mother limits a child's contacts with other children, and reduces the extent to which other children are valued, components of self inappropriate to interaction outside the family develop in the child.

Normal development in the socialization process involves removing incongruency by changing components of self and behavior so that they correspond with the definitions made by significant Os. Because of the difficulty of changing S-components which are relevant to an increasingly larger number of congruent matrices, however, the individual also learns to use other ways of handling incongruency: e.g., misperception, misinterpretation, response evocation, changing valuations of others, etc. These latter actions delay or prevent changes in self or behavior. It is probable that early adjustment to incongruency involves changing the self-concept and behavior, but as the individual develops these other techniques, he frequently handles incongruency by means of them. Disturbances of the developmental sequence may frequently occur as a result of overuse of modes of reducing incongruency which involve distortion of reality instead of change in self or behavior. This may be expected to result in the establishment of a somewhat precarious stability of self at a low level of maturity. This is a social psychological interpretation of the Freudian phenomenon of fixation.

The interpersonal theory as outlined also seems to point to a crucial process in psychotherapy. The modes of reducing incongruency spelled out in an earlier section suggest that the primary problem facing a psychotherapist is the necessity for blocking all modes which permit the maintenance of the undesirable aspects of self and behavior, and facilitating those which involve change in these components. The advantage of a systematic theory providing an exhaustive classification of the various forms of reducing incongruency is that it allows the therapist to anticipate various ways in which the individual may fail to change. There are two directions, however, in which the theory must be further elaborated. One involves spelling out the behaviors required of the change agent for successful facilitation of modes of resolution leading to desired changes in the self-concept and behavior of the *S*. The other requires the elaboration of techniques for blocking those modes leading to maintenance of undesirable aspects of self and behavior.

Dyadic relations. So far the focus has been on stability and change in *individual* behavior. Emphasis has been placed on the point that stability and change in individual behavior is in part a product of a reciprocal process having its locus in the interactions between the individual and those around him. This reciprocal process may also be applied to an understanding of both members of the dyad. The instability of adolescent love relations would appear to be initiated by the confronting of the adolescent with marked and frequent changes in the behavior of peers and adults which are incongruent with components of self and his behavior. These changes lead to shifts in self-concept and behavior, and in turn new relations are sought to establish congruency with these modified aspects of self and behavior. The disruptive effect of separation on a friendship or a marriage is another case in point. The new interpersonal environment contains Os who define the individual's self and behavior differently, and he gradually changes so as to establish congruency in this new interpersonal situation. On the other hand, old relations become less congruent, and consequently progressively weaker in affect. These changes are dramatically illustrated by the disappointment so often experienced at the renuion after long separation of boyhood friends or ex-army buddies. In a similar fashion, induced changes in personality, such as those which occur in psychotherapy, and fortuitous ones which arise as a result of entering a new job, obtaining more formal education, etc., may well result in drastic shifts in dyadic relations.

IV LANGUAGE AND COMMUNICATION

Subhuman species regularly emit and respond to vocal stimuli, often with appropriately differentiated behavior. This "passive" language, as Klineberg calls it (1954), is widely distributed among animals. "Active" language—the use of sounds made by animals themselves as means for controlling others—is, however, sharply limited in distribution and, at best, is only rudimentary even at phylogenetic levels adjacent to man; consequently, the communicative capabilities necessary to support variegated social patterns exist only at the human level. Furthermore, what Korzybski has called the "time-binding" (1941) aspect of communicative modalities, referring to accumulations and transmissions from the past to the present and on to the future, is crucial to the existence of culture, and, so far as we know, is unique to man. Both as a vehicle and as a condition for social behavior, language and communication, therefore, are major objects for scientific investigation. Osgood and Sebeok make this evident in their descriptive schema reprinted here.

Social psychological interest in problems of language and communication has a long history (see Osgood & Sebeok, 1954, Ch. 2; Carroll, 1955). Aspects of communicative interaction have been extensively studied—the selections in Section V directly or indirectly attest to that—and, especially in recent years, increasing investigations of the modalities (notably language) by which these interactions progress, and of verbal behavior in general, can be noted.

Since communication entails processes of transmitting "coded" messages its comprehensive understanding requires an understanding of the "nature" of the message. For convenience the problem can be partitioned in two; first, the *content* or meaning of the message and its units can be considered and, second, the *structure* of the message, the properties of the "code," can be considered separately. In fact, analyses of behavior in relation to language necessarily assume prior description of language units. Early research in language-behavior relations suffered from the unavoidable primitiveness and naïveté of the means for description and analysis of linguistic codes. Today, however, thanks largely to development of the social science of descriptive or structural linguistics, a well-developed theory and set of procedures guide direct analyses of language, as Markel shows in his overview published in this section. Furthermore, linguistic theory and methods have served as models for the examination of non-vocal communications systems (see Osgood & Sebeok, 1954, p. 84), and Markel suggests that the framework of descriptive linguistics may prove a productive model for the analysis of other aspects of behavior. Hall (1959) has already demonstrated its potential usefulness for the understanding of non-linguistic cultural patterns. Nevertheless, the paramount application of descriptive linguistic theory and method is to the *structure* of spoken language.

Another well-known approach to the structural analysis of messages—information theory—is mentioned by Osgood and Sebeok, and a comprehensive, relatively non-technical account may be found in an excellent paper by G. A. Miller (1953). Based in mathematical probability theory and drawn originally from the study of inanimate communication systems, information theory is really a theory of information transmission, providing a useful methodology for examining organizational properties in a communication system. The theory has sometimes been applied as a general model for human behavior, but more frequently it has been used selectively in connection with communication processes. Now generally recognized as inadequate as a general schema for human behavior, and even oversimple as a model for human communication (see Toda, 1956), information theory is nevertheless appropriately applied to partial aspects of these processes. Its overall value to social psychology, however, remains uncertain.

Neither information theory nor descriptive linguistics has much to say about the *content* of messages. Meaning is handled in descriptive linguistics mainly in the limited sense of the equivalences of linguistic usage, illustrated by Markel's discussion of morphemes. It is obvious, however, that relations between language and behavior are fully comprehensible only with reference to the contents of messages. Standard psychological stipulations hold that behavior is not a function of "stimulus" units *per se*, but of the meanings attached to them. Yet, in spite of wide-ranging scholarly interest, the "meaning of meaning" has only recently begun to emerge from the metaphysical mists that had long enveloped it.

Of the contemporary specialties devoted to the study of meaning, *general semantics* is possibly most widely known. Departing from the somewhat eccentric theory of "sign processes" advanced by Korzybski (1941), S. I. Hayakawa, currently the leading figure in the movement, has concerned himself with broad constructions of meaning (1951). For the most part general semantics has tended to be rather focused in its interests and, following Korzybski's lead, has emphasized imprecisions in sign-significate relations and relativities of meaning associated with communication breakdowns, and even pathological states. However, the selection from Hayakawa's writing reprinted here reflects a broad interest in language and its uses.

In this excerpt from his book *Language in Thought and Action* (1964), Hayakawa is occupied with relations between "words and the world," with uses of language as a means for controlling events and influencing social processes. As he develops his ideas about the "directive uses of language," their wider relevance to social behavior becomes clear. In addition to meaning, *per se*, his approach pertains to matters such as conformity, leadership, and mass media effects, including attitude change—in fact to a whole gamut of issues and problems discussed at various points in this book under such headings as social influence or social organization.

Hayakawa notes that in order for language to function directively it must be "interesting." It must seize attention. To accomplish this, he suggests, emotional loadings are attached to words and often, for further emphasis, language is supplemented with non-verbal signs such as gestures, rituals, etc. Hayakawa describes the operation of these devices, and their effects and ends, by pointing out that because directive uses of language are in the nature of promissory notes, some care should be taken to insure that the promises are understood and kept. In this sense, his approach to language bears directly on the focus on social interaction in the next section.

An approach to meaning that overlaps Hayakawa's in many ways is C. E. Morris's comprehensive theory of signs (1946). Morris's views (along with those of some others) are discussed more fully by Osgood in his enormously influential paper, "The nature and measurement of meaning," a selection from which is included here. Osgood's own theory of meaning begins with a distinction between denotative and connotative meanings and goes on to develop a conception of the latter based in Hull-type learning theory. Modeled after his more general "mediation hypothesis" (Osgood, 1953), meaning is treated by Osgood as a perceptual process built up by conditioning and resting in "antedating" fragments of larger instrumental responses, comparable to Hull's fractional antedating goal responses. These fractional response components are presumed to be evoked in the course of behavior and, in turn, produce internal stimuli which serve as representations (signs) of larger behavioral complexes. The meaning of an object or an event, thus, becomes a "perception" *mediated* by internal representational fragments conditioned by previous experiences and aroused by the current situation. Since Osgood places connotative meaning at an "ideational"or cognitive level which is not directly observable he has developed a scaling technique, involving factor analytic procedures, called the "semantic differential." With this "indirect" device, meaning can be specified quantitatively as a point in a multidimensional "semantic space" (see also, Osgood, *et al.*, 1957).

With reference to language, Osgood reasons that representational mediation processes become conditioned to "linguistically coded stimuli" (e.g., the English language system), thereby accomplishing an organization in which either may be produced by the other in processes of "encoding" and "decoding" messages. Essentially arbitrary signs come to be labels for "concept classes" that derive their meanings from mediational processes, including conditions of prior reinforcement.

The psycholinguistic discussion presented here by Brown is directly related to these matters in terms of the acquisition of language and with the function of "names." Brown points out that in learning referents (meanings) the words presented by the child's "tutors" will tend to be the most common ones relevant. These words then come to control the child's behavior in reference to the objects and events named.

In effect, what Brown is describing is the relevance, in language learning, of the practices of the "verbal community," the construct so effectively developed by Skinner in the Appendix, reprinted here, to his book *Verbal Behavior*. The question is raised by Brown, for example, whether it is simply arbitrary that one word is more common than another. He makes the point that the name *denotes* behavioral equivalences, but equivalences differentiated from other reference categories. How one is expected to behave toward the reference object is differentiated and signaled by the label. In sum, the kinds of behaviors appropriate to given situations are acquired and a system of signals is also acquired which serve as "cues" for the differential identification of conditions appropriate to particular behavior patterns.

Names, in other words, can be thought of as generics. By denoting equivalences they tend to control behavior with reference to nominally different objects. Moreover, the transmission of names from parent to child amounts also to a process of transmitting cognitive structures and so has great relevance to socialization practices, discussed in Section II. Learning names may be a primary device by which cultural practices are transmitted from individual to individual. Shibutani's emphasis in Section II, upon the importance to behavior and cognition of the varying "communication channels" in which persons participate, is closely related to these ideas.

Implicit in Brown's offering and in his book, *Words and Things* (1958), is an important departure beyond language as such. He shows in some detail correspondences between linguistic and non-linguistic practices and, by suggesting that names are categories people use in ordering their worlds, feeds directly into what has come to be popularly called the *Whorfian hypothesis* (Whorf, 1956). In its general form this hypothesis asserts that, inasmuch as people behave and think in terms of the classifications they use to lend meaning to features of the world, language may not only be a vehicle by which people interact, it may also be an *active* determiner of what they perceive and think and, therefore, of what they interact about. This hypothesis is founded upon the idea that the *forms* of a linguistic system place finite limits upon the range of available "categories" (see

Bruner in Section I) and hence upon the kinds of perceptual differentiations and equivalences that can and will be made.

In "The Verbal Community," Skinner concentrates on the broad conditions regulating verbal behavior and offers a *denotational* definition of meaning as the *conditions* under which a response is characteristically reinforced. He comments that the languages studied by linguists are, therefore, the reinforcing practices of verbal communities. In studying these practices, the linguist (among others) has not broached what Skinner calls *verbal behavior*. For Skinner, the verbal community is a *given;* the question to which he directs his much more general analysis has to do with psychological mechanisms by which individuals behave within this community.

In his book *Verbal Behavior* (1957), Skinner, from an operant conditioning model, centers attention upon what happens when a person speaks or responds to speech. Speech is treated as part of the total behavior of the speaker and may be studied as such, as Skinner does, or as an "objective" fact apart from the speaker, as when a linguist studies a recording of speech. In Skinner's usage, verbal behavior is behavior reinforced through the mediation of other persons; it includes speech, but much more. To all intents and purposes, verbal behavior becomes coincident with general social behavior and its analysis is, therefore, social psychology. Further, Skinner's assertion that verbal behavior is governed by a verbal environment, makes his concept, the verbal community, a label for society and culture, one aspect of which is language.

Superficially Skinner's treatment of verbal behavior as a "dependent" variable seems to stand in opposition to the Whorfian hypothesis and its active view of verbal elements. Actually there is no necessary contradiction. Language may be an independent variable defining certain features of the verbal environment (as Whorf suggests), but the verbal behavior of the *individual* is always a function of these antecedent conditions. Whether verbal elements are viewed as independent or as dependent variables depends upon where one looks.

The final paper in this section, by George Miller, ranges over a variety of large issues vital to an understanding of language, its functions and its human context. The chief thrust of his essay is to depict the complexity of language and of meaning at the level of the sensible utterance. What Miller grapples with is the phenomenon of "understanding" and the problems and challenges it offers the student of language. In doing so, he sketches the meaning of "psycholinguistics" (see also, Osgood, 1963) and makes plain his exacting view of the psycholinguistic task, giving some illustrations of attempts to get on with that task.

Miller delves into relations between speakers and listeners and is led to a description of a "generative" theory of speech perception and performance that encompasses both. In this he stresses the importance of expectancies and cognitive processes and builds a case against motor-behavioristic accounts of language (Skinner's being an obvious case-in-point). To Miller, such accounts fail to treat adequately the original combination of linguistic elements, and this "combinatorial productivity" he sees as both fundamental and specific to the human species. Stressing the significance of rules and the ability of persons to follow them, Miller voices serious doubt about prospects for reducing these phenomena to behavioral "principles" derived from studies of infra-humans. He goes on to speak of linguistic universals and the evidence they provide for a biological basis of language. The point of Miller's message is clear enough: Language must be studied at the human level and such study must concentrate on the mental as well as the social processes that underlie it.

The next section focuses on detailed aspects of social interaction. Communication is a vital part, perhaps the essence, of such interaction, as many of the papers included there maintain and as we have mentioned here. The present section, therefore, serves as an essential complement to it by specifying the components, conditions, and complications of communicative modalities. In another sense, the present section is *inseparable* from the next, for linguistic codes are fundamental ingredients in the perceptual processes that direct interaction.

21 Communication and psycholinguistics

CHARLES E. OSGOOD and THOMAS A. SEBEOK

I Models of the communication process

In the most general sense, we have communication whenever one system, a *source*, influences another system, a *destination*, by manipulation of the alternative signals which can be carried in the *channel* connecting them. The information source is conceived as producing one or more messages which must be transformed by a *transmitter* into signals which the channel can carry; these signals must then be transformed by a *receiver* back into messages which can be accepted at the destination. This minimal system, borrowed from Shannon's discussion (1949) of the theory of information and diagrammed in Figure 1, has been applied, with great generality, to information transmission in electrical, biological, psychological and social systems as well as language communication in the strict sense. In a telephone communication system, for example, the messages produced by a speaker are in the form of variable sound pressures and frequencies which must be transformed into proportional electrical signals by the transmitter; these signals are carried over wire (channel) to a receiver which transforms them back into the variable sound pressures and frequencies which constitute the message to be utilized by the listener. The activity of the transmitter is usually referred to as *encoding* and that of the receiver as *decoding*. Anything that produces variability at the destination which is unpredictable from variability introduced at the source is called *noise*.

This model of the communication process, developed in connection with engineering problems, was not intended to provide a satisfactory picture of human communication. For one thing, it implies a necessary separation of source and destination, of transmitter and receiver, which is usually true of mechanical communication systems but not of human ones. The individual human functions more or less simultaneously as a source and destination and as a transmitter and receiver of messages—indeed, he is regularly a decoder of the messages he himself encodes through

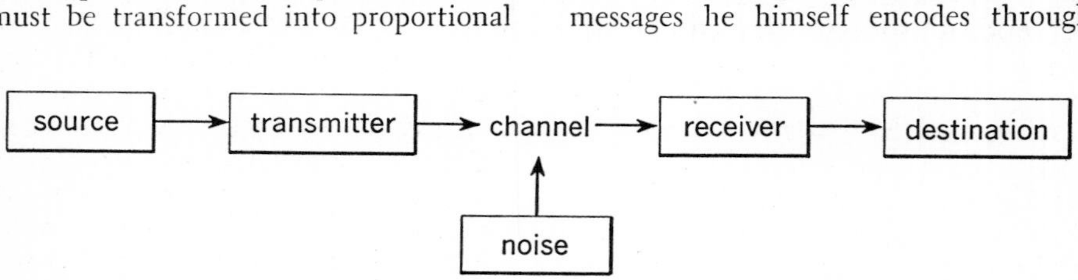

Figure 1

Excerpted from **Psycholinguistics: A Survey of Theory and Research Problems.** Supplement to the **Journal of Abnormal and Social Psychology,** 1954, 49, No. 4, Part 2, with permission of the authors, the American Psychological Association, and the Trustees of Indiana University.

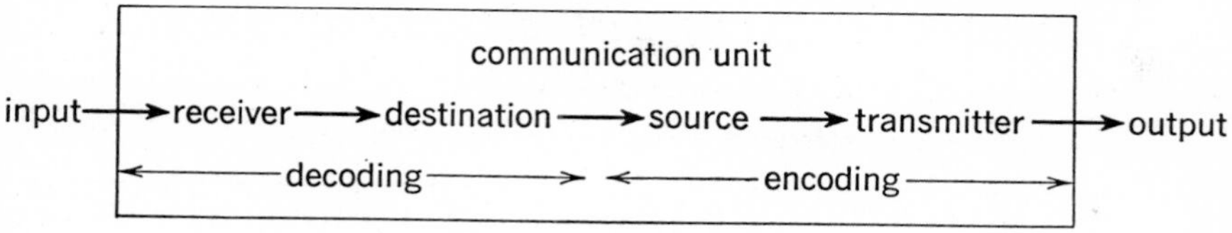

Figure 2

various feedback mechanisms. Each individual in a speech community may be conceived as a more or less self-contained communicating system, encompassing in his nervous apparatus, from receptors to effectors, all of the components shown in Figure 1. If we rearrange the components in Shannon's model in the fashion shown in Figure 2, what might be called a *communication unit* is described, equipped to both receive and send messages. In the process of human decoding, input of some form of physical energy, linguistically or otherwise coded, is first recoded into sensory neural impulses, operated upon by receiving apparatus, and finally "interpreted" at the destination (presumably as some pattern of activity in the higher centers). In the process of human encoding, an "intention" of the source (presumably some pattern of activity in the same centers) is operated upon by transmitting apparatus in the motor areas, is recoded into physical movements, and becomes the output of this unit. Translating into traditional psychological language, *input* becomes equivalent to "stimulus," *receiver* becomes "reception" and "perception," *destination* and *source* become "cognition" (meaning, attitude, and the like), *transmitter* becomes "motor organization and sequencing," and *output* becomes "response."

Another insufficiency of engineering models for human communication purposes is that they are not designed to take into account the *meaning* of signals, e.g., their significance when viewed from the decoding side and their intention when viewed from the encoding side. The research generated by such models has dealt almost exclusively with relations between transmitter and receiver, or with the individual as a single system intervening between input and output signals. This has not been because of lack of awareness of the problem of meaning or its importance, but rather because it is admittedly difficult to be rigorous, objective, and quantitative at this level. Nevertheless, one of the central problems in psycholinguistics is to make as explicit as possible relations between message events and cognitive events, both on decoding and encoding sides of the equation.

Human communication is chiefly a social affair. Any adequate model must therefore include at least two communicating units, a *source unit* (speaker) and a *destination unit* (hearer). Between any two such units, connecting them into a single system, is what we may call the *message*. For purposes of this report, we will define message as that part of the total output (responses) of a source unit which simultaneously may be a part of the total input (stimuli) to a destination unit. When individual A talks to individual B, for example, his postures, gestures, facial expressions and even manipulations with objects (e.g., laying down a playing

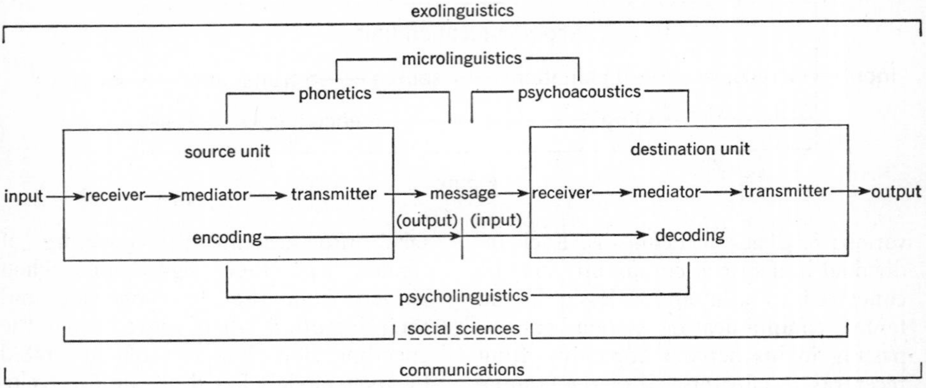

Figure 3

card, pushing a bowl of food within reach) may all be part of the message, as of course are events in the sound wave channel. But other parts of A's total behavior (e.g., breathing, toe-wiggling, thinking) may not affect B at all and other parts of the total stimulation to B (e.g., sensations from B's own posture, cues from the remainder of the environment) do not derive from A's behavior—these events are not part of the message as we use the term. These R-S message events (reactions of one individual that produce stimuli for another) may be either *immediate* or *mediate*—ordinary face-to-face conversation illustrates the former and written communication (along with musical recordings, art objects, and so forth) illustrates the latter.

Figure 3 presents a model of the essential communication act, encoding of a message by a source unit and decoding of that message by a destination unit. Since the distinction between source and destination within the same communicator (as shown in Figure 2) seems relevant only with respect to the direction of information exchange (e.g., whether the communicator is decoding or encoding), we substitute the single term *mediator* for that system which intervenes between receiving and transmitting operations. The ways in which the various sciences concerned with human communication impinge upon and divide up the total process can be shown in relation to this figure.

II Disciplines concerned with human communication

Microlinguistics (or linguistics proper) deals with the structure of messages, the signals in the channel connecting communicators, as events independent of the characteristics of either speakers or hearers. Once messages have been encoded and are "on the air," so to speak, they can be described as objective, natural science events in their own right. In an even stricter sense, the linguist is concerned with determining the *code* of a given signal system, the sets of distinctions which are significant in differentiating alternative messages. The term *exolinguistics* (sometimes called metalinguistics) has been used rather loosely by linguists to cover all those other aspects of language study which concern relations between the characteristics of messages and the characteristics of individuals who produce and receive them, including both their behavior and culture. Whether or not the grammatical structure of a language influences the thinking of those who speak it is thus an exolinguistic problem. The *social sciences* in general, and psychology, sociology, and anthropology in particular, are concerned with the characteristics of human organisms and societies which influence the selection and interpretation of messages—attitudes, meanings, social roles, values, and so forth. The rather new discipline coming to be known as *psycholinguistics* (paralleling the closely related discipline termed *ethnolinguistics*) is concerned in the broadest sense with relations between messages and the characteristics of human individuals who select and interpret them. In a narrower sense, psycholinguistics studies those processes whereby the intentions of speakers are transformed into signals in the culturally accepted code and whereby these signals are transformed into the interpretations of hearers. In other words, *psycholinguistics deals directly with the processes of encoding and decoding as they relate states of messages to states of communicators.* The terminal aspect of human speech encoding, production of speech sounds, is the special province of *phonetics*. Similarly, the initial aspect of human speech decoding, whereby sound pressures and frequencies are transformed into impulses in auditory nerve fibers and relayed to the cortex, is a special field of *psychoacoustics*. Finally, the science of *human communication* would be concerned with relations between sources who select messages and destinations who interpret and are affected by them. In the broadest sense, therefore, human communications as a science includes the other disciplines that have been mentioned; in a narrower sense—and one more in keeping with contemporary activities—students of communications research have usually worked at grosser levels of analysis, concerning themselves with sources such as radio and the newspaper and destinations such as the mass audience, members of another culture, and so on.

22 The basic principles of descriptive linguistic analysis

NORMAN N. MARKEL

Introduction

In the western world the Greek generalizations about language were not improved upon until about 1700. The ancient Greeks took it for granted that the structure of their language embodied universal forms of human thought. They further believed that the origin and true meanings of words could be traced in their shape, and the pursuance of this study they called *etymology*. A Greek etymologist working today on the English language would, for example, note that *goose* is part of *gooseberry*, or that *dog* reversed is *god*, and consider it his proper task to discover the relationship between these words. In their search for universal truths, the Greeks observed their language and discovered its parts of speech and syntactic constructions. But subject and predicate, genders, numbers, cases, persons, tenses and modes were classes defined in terms which were to tell their meaning.

The Romans constructed Latin grammars on the Greek model, and the medieval scholars saw in this classical Latin the logically normal form of human speech, which embodied universally valid canons of logic. An outgrowth of this conception of grammar was that the grammarians, after ascertaining the logical basis of a language, could prescribe how people *ought* to speak. When the students of language came in contact with exotic tongues they proceeded to distort the facts of these languages in order to fit them into the frame of Latin grammar.

It wasn't until the eighteenth century, when Englishmen in India reported on the work of the Hindu grammarians, that a drastic change in European ideas about language occurred. The Brahmin religion held sacred some ancient collections of hymns, and it became the task of a specially trained group of men to insure their correct pronunciation and interpretation. The oldest treatise of this sort that has come down to us is the grammar of Panini. This work records with the greatest detail every inflection, derivation, composition, and syntactic usage of its author's speech. For the first time Europeans saw a complete and accurate description of language based upon observation.

The descriptive linguist is not necessarily a polyglot; indeed, he may not even be fluent in a language which he is analyzing. His primary task is the complete description of each individual language of the world. To accomplish this he has developed a rigorous methodology that enables him to analyze and classify the facts of speech as they are uttered by native speakers.

In recent years there has been an intensification of research in the areas of verbal behavior, verbal learning and psycholinguistics. Workers in the various areas may or may not use a linguistic analysis of speech in their particular research, but they are all coming in contact with linguistic terminology and the results of linguistic analysis. Many participate with linguists in symposia and conferences, and some engage linguists as consultants on their own projects. Furthermore, since the descriptive linguist has developed a methodology for handling what is probably the most complex form of human behavior, the concepts underlying his methodology might prove useful to scientists studying other forms of human behavior. Having these two groups in mind, the social scientists, in general, and the students of language, in particular, the following is an attempt to elucidate, in as concise a manner as possible, the basic principles of descriptive linguistic analysis.

Phonology

PHONETICS

In listening to speech one hears a continuous stream of sounds separated into breath groups. Sounds in the stream are not separated from each other in any consistent manner. At this first level of analysis the linguist provides himself with a method of entering this continuum of behavior. If you say the word "maiden" and become very conscious of the movement of your lips and tongue, you will demonstrate to yourself a continuum of speech sounds. You will notice that there is continuous movement from the time you start the 'm' until the tip of your tongue reaches the upper teeth. Trying to describe "everything" that happened while you were producing just this one word would take a great deal of time. But, if you will repeat the word slowly you will notice that there are points of maximum closure and maximum openness of the lips and tongue. These crests and troughs are the centers of segments of sounds which have indefinite borders, and it is at these points that we enter the continuum of speech behavior. Schematically:

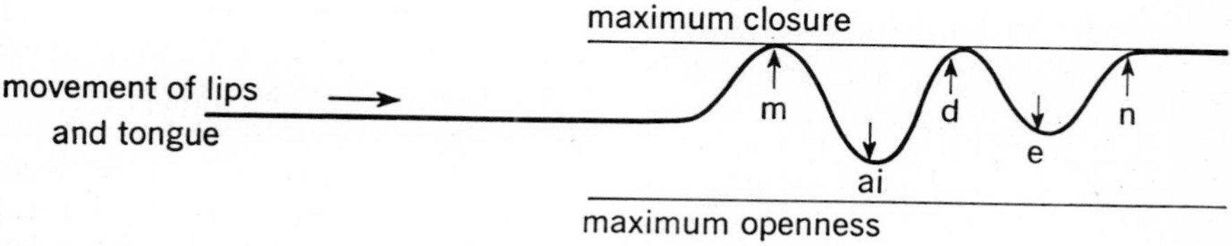

The arrows point to the centers of the segments.

The next task is to describe the sounds that occur at these centers. All of the sounds are physical events that have three main aspects: (1) *Physiological,* the movements of the organs involved in producing the sound; (2) *Acoustic,* the nature of the sound waves set in motion by the speech apparatus; and (3) *Auditory,* the transformation of the sound wave by the ear and the central nervous system into the perception of speech. Linguists have found the *physiological* aspect the most convenient of the three to describe sounds. The reasons are that the movements and positions of the vocal organs can be directly observed without previous training, that any sound can be unambiguously and simply described in terms of the movements which produce it, and that after some practice it is easy to convert a physiological description of a sound into the sound itself by simply making the movement specified.

The three mechanisms that are primarily involved in producing sounds are used to establish a three dimensional matrix which defines the cardinal value of any sound. These three dimensions are:

1. *The point of articulation*. This is the point of maximum constriction in the mouth or pharynx. For the 'd' in *maiden* it occurs when the apex of the tongue reaches the alveolar ridge.
2. *The degree of air-stream interruption*. If the air-stream is blocked completely during the articulation the sound is a *stop*. If the air-stream is only partially blocked, producing friction, the sound is *fricative*. If the constriction is not narrow enough to produce any degree of friction, and the only function of the mouth and nose is to modify a sound produced by the vocal cords, that sound is called *resonant*.
3. *The vocal cords*. If the vocal cords are active at the time of articulation, the sound is *voiced*. If the cords are not vibrating at the time of articulation, the sound is *voiceless*.

Having decided on a method for segmenting the sound continuum, and providing for the classification of the segments, the linguist now has a frame of reference with which he can describe the vocal products of any speaker. Furthermore, this method for providing *phonetic units* assures him, and any other interested observer, that different linguists working on the same continuum of speech sounds will arrive at the same conclusions regarding the phonetic units in that continuum.

PHONEMICS

The segmentation of the continuum of speech provides the linguist with his raw data. He next performs a series of operations on these raw data that will reduce their complexity and enable him to describe them parsimoniously. The first level of this analysis, the description of the sound system of a language, is called *phonemics*. The unit of description at this level of analysis is the *phoneme*, which is a class of speech sounds mutually exclusive of any other such class. The member sounds of each phoneme, the *allophones*, share some feature of articulation, or some combination of features, and show characteristic patterns of distribution.

A phonemic analysis can be demonstrated by examining the initial sounds in "keen" and "coat." On close examination the native speaker of English will find that the point of articulation of these sounds is different and distinct. For the 'k' in "keen" the back of the tongue moves forward on the palate. For the 'k' in "coat" the back of the tongue moves up and back to the velum. These two phonetic units are symbolized as [k̯] and [ḳ], respectively. The feature of articulation shared by both these units is the movement of the back of the tongue. The square brackets are always used when referring to phonetic units.

If all occurrences of the 'k' sound in English were examined we would find that [k̯] occurs only before vowels made with the front of the tongue, and [ḳ] occurs only before vowels made with the back of the tongue. These facts demonstrate *complementary distribution* (C.D.); each of the phonetic units occurs in a fixed context in which the other never occurs. On the basis of their phonetic similarity and C.D., [k̭] and [ḳ] are analyzed as being members of a class of sounds which are called the phoneme 'k', written /k/. The [k̭] and [ḳ] are allophones of /k/. The diagonal lines are used when referring to phonemic units.

There is another pattern of distribution of phonetic units that is created by repeated productions of one unit. If we were to measure everything that could possibly be measured about the [k̭] in repeated occurrences of "keen," we would discover that they are not exactly alike. A plot of the differences of each would result in a normal curve with the unit we call [k̭] as the mean. This type of distribution is called *non-distinctive variation*. The non-distinctive variation of the [k̭] forms a subclass of sounds of the allophone [k̭]. In general, the detection of such non-distinctive variation can only be accomplished by instrumentation or a highly skilled phonetician.

To establish each phoneme of a language as different and distinct from every other phoneme, the principle of *contrast* is invoked. To show contrast, varying phonetic units are substituted at one point in the word while all the other units are held constant. If another word is produced that is distinct and means something else to a native speaker, contrast has been shown and the existence of a distinct phoneme is proven. For example, there is the phoneme /k/ consisting of [k̭]∼[ḳ]. The ∼ means "in complementary distribution with." Similarly, there is a phoneme /g/ consisting of [g̭]∼[g̣]. If in the word "till" a [k̭] or a [g̭] is substituted for the 't', or if in the word "tore" a [ḳ] or a [g̣] is substituted for the 't', four new words are produced: "kill," "gill," "core" and "gore." To a native speaker of English each of these four words is distinct in the way it sounds and in what it means. This contrast justifies the existence of a /k/ and a /g/ in English.

In the preceding discussion we have been careful to use the qualification "native speaker of English." This was done to emphasize the fact that there is no general /k/ or /g/ for every language. The linguistically unsophisticated native speaker of English is rather hard put to find a difference between the initial sounds of "keen" and "coat," but to a linguistically unsophisticated speaker of Arabic this difference would be immediately apparent. The English speaker has a /k/ with [k̭]∼[ḳ], but for the Arabic speaker [ḳ] is part of a different phoneme, and the /k/ of English and the /k/ of Arabic are not identical.

Prosodic phonemes. The phonetic units of the language that proceed in one dimensional time succession are called *segmental phones*. The analysis of these units yields the *segmental phonemes*. These are what the layman recognizes as the vowels and consonants of the language. But there are also prosodic features of *length, loudness, tone,* and *manner of termination* that occur simultaneously with the segmental phones. The descriptive linguist records the discriminable variations of these prosodic features and subjects them to the same type of analysis as is used for segmental phones. The contrasting classes that result from this analysis are called the *prosodic* or *suprasegmental phonemes* of the language.

If the word "pin" is said a number of times to the speaker of English, each time increasing the amount of time spent on the 'i,' a word is never produced which he will say is different in meaning from any of the other words. As a matter of fact, it is not possible to find any word in English in which, by increasing the length of one of the segmental units, another word can be produced which has a different meaning. Since contrast does not exist, this feature of length is not phonemic in English. This is not true of all languages. In Finnish *peli* means "damper," but increasing the length of the '*l*' produces another utterance meaning "game," and length is phonemic in Finnish.

The loudness of the phonetic unit depends primarily on the force with which air is expelled from the lungs and secondarily on the energy with which the articulation is performed. The degree of loudness is approximately the same for all English monosyllabic utterances said in isolation. This degree of loudness is called "strong" and used as a standard of measurement for other degrees of loudness. If you say *permit,* once stressing the 'e' and once stressing the 'i,' you will produce two words different in sound and meaning, thereby showing that stress is phonemic in English. The degree of loudness on the stressed versions of the 'e' and 'i' is relatively close to that degree of loudness used with monosyllables in isolation. The degree of loudness in the unstressed 'e' and 'i' is much less than that of their stressed versions, or of any monosyllable said in isolation. The degree of loudness on the stressed 'e' and 'i,' and of monosyllables said in isolation, are conditioned variations of the standard "strong loudness," and are allophones of the phoneme *primary stress* (/′/). The weak loudness of the unstressed 'e' and 'i' are allophones comprising a weak loudness phoneme, /˘/.

The tone of our speech sounds is a function of the tension of the vocal cords and of their consequent rate of vibration. As with loudness, to demonstrate that tone is phonemic in English, multisyllabic words are used, since it is relative tone that is contrasted. The standard is the normal tone of a speaker. This normal tone varies from speaker to speaker and for the same speaker when he is speaking loudly and softly. But every speaker has a recognizable normal tone of voice. Examine, for example, the sentence "he's going home," said as a statement of fact, emphasizing *where* he's going and not the fact that he's going. Using lines to represent tone of voice, the sentence is said like this: he's going home. The line immediately below "he's going" represents the normal tone of voice. The line above the 'h' and part of the 'o' represents a tone of voice about two or three notes above the normal. The line under part of the 'o' and 'me' represents a tone of voice about two or three times below the normal. Humming the words of this sentence will demonstrate this clearly. The examination of many English sentences reveals four levels of tone that are in contrast with each other. These are symbolized as $/^1/$, $/^2/$, $/^3/$, and $/^4/$, and called low, mid, high, and extra-high pitch phonemes.

The phenomena relating to the way in which the sequence of phonetic units of the language are put together are called *junctural phenomena.* The word *nitrate* is an example of a sequence of segmental units with close transition between the members of the sequence. By changing the transition between the *t* and the *r* from close to more distant, another utterance is produced: *night-rate,* which has different sound and meaning. A comparison of such utterances as *I scream* vs. *ice cream, a name* vs. *an aim,* shows that the difference between a close transition and a more open one is phonemic in English. All the allophones of the open transition are classed into the phoneme called "plus juncture," symbolized as /+/.

There is another group of junctural phenomena that occur at places where /+/ would normally occur. These are used by the speaker to signal that he is terminating a sentence, or sequence of sentences. Say the following three sentences in the manner indicated by the conventional punctuation marks:

(1) He's going home.
(2) He's going home?
(3) He's going home for the week-end.

These sentences demonstrate three distinct ways of terminating *home.* In (1) there is a rapid fading away of the voice into silence. In (2) there is a rapid but short rise in pitch, and the voice seems to be sharply cut off. In (3) there is a sustention of pitch and a slight decrease in volume. This contrast shows that there are three terminal juncture phonemes in English: fading, /↘/; rising, /↗/; and sustained, /→/.

Phonemics and orthography. A frequent over-sight on the part of both laymen and scientists studying language behavior, is the fact that the sound system (phonemic structure) of a language is not necessarily isomorphic to the writing system (orthography) of that language. In English there are two major aspects to the discrepancy between sounds and letters of the alphabet. The first is that one sound (phoneme) may be pronounced in response to several different letters or combinations of letters. For example, the phoneme *k* (/k/) is the response to ten different letters or combinations of letters: *c*ar, a*cc*ount, ba*cch*anal, *ch*aracter, ba*ck*, a*cq*uaint, sa*que*, bis*cu*it, *k*ill, li*qu*or. The second is that one letter of the alphabet may represent several different phonemes. For example, the letter 's' can stand for four different phonemes as in: *s*ee, *s*ugar, ha*s*, mea*s*ure, which represent the phonemes /s, š, z, ž/, respectively.

A great deficiency in the orthography of English is the almost complete lack of symbols representing the prosodic phonemes. Except for the "marks of punctuation" (, , . , ?), which fairly well indicate the terminal juncture phonemes, there is no systematic method for indicating the stress, pitch, or plus-juncture phonemes.

Morphology

MORPHOPHONEMICS

The phonemic description of a language provides the basis from which the linguist analyzes the various "forms" in which the phonemes occur. The unit of description at this level of analysis is the *morpheme,* which is a class of one or more minimum sequences of phonemes that has a unique function in the *content structure* of the language.

The identification of morphemes proceeds in a manner similar to that used for the identification of phonemes. Words are compared and differences in phonemic form are matched with differences in meaning. Partial similarity both in phonemic form and meaning requires a *morphemic cut* in one or both of the forms compared. This procedure can be demonstrated by examining the words: *boy, boys, boyish; girl, girls, girlish; bear, bears, bearish*. The sequence of phonemes used in *boy, girl,* and *bear,* occur many times in the language. Furthermore, each has a unique meaning attached to it that differs from the other two, or, for that matter, from any other minimum sequence of phonemes in English. The fragments of the words left over from this classification, /-z/, and /-iš/ are also morphemes. They occur many times in the language, and a native speaker will attest to their having unique meaning. We have, then, discovered five morphemes: *boy, girl, bear,* /-z/, and /-iš/.

It is possible for a morpheme to contain within it a sequence of phonemes comprising another morpheme. If removing the contained sequence destroys or drastically alters its unique meaning and leaves a residue *that cannot be accounted for* (i.e., to which no meaning can be attached), then the large sequence retains its status as a morpheme. For example, *boil* contains the phoneme sequence of *boy,* and *bear* contains the phoneme sequence of *air,* but all four are morphemes, because removing *boy* from *boil,* and *air* from *bear* leaves the residue *-l* and *b-*, respectively, to which no meaning can be attached.

If two different minimum sequences of phonemes have the same meaning but can be shown to be in complementary distribution, they are allomorphs of one morpheme.

For example, the /-s/, /-z/, /-iz/ and /-in/, in *hats, boys, glasses,* and *oxen* are allomorphs of one morpheme. Their shared meaning is "plurality." The occurrence of /-s/, /-z/, or /-iz/ depends solely on the phonological characteristics of the *previous phoneme* that has occurred. Their distribution is, therefore, *phonologically conditioned*. The occurrence of /-in/ depends solely on the occurrence of the *previous morpheme* {ox-}, and its distribution is *morphologically conditioned*. Since they all share the same meaning and since they are in C.D., they are allomorphs of one morpheme which is labeled {-Z_1}. Braces are used to indicate morphemes.

Corresponding to the two types of phonemes are segmental and prosodic morphemes. *Segmental morphemes* are sequences of segmental phonemes in close transition. They are either *roots* like *boy, run, to,* or *affixes* like *-s, -ish, -ly, pre-, re-, con-*. The hyphens indicate the manner in which they are affixed. *Prosodic morphemes* are sequences of prosodic phonemes. They are either *superfixes* like {ˊ}, {ˊ ˗}, and {ˋ+ˊ} respectively; or they are *intonation patterns* like the {231↘} that occurs on "He's going home."

TACTICS

Tactics deals with the sequences of morphemes that are used to form the larger significant units of the language, and the classes of morphemes, or sequences of morphemes, that are identical in function. The concept of the *constituent* is important at this stage of analysis. A constituent is any morpheme, or sequence of morphemes, that can be replaced by some other morpheme or sequence of morphemes. For example, the constituents of *boys* are *boy* and *-s; girl* can be substituted for *boy,* and *-ish* can be substituted for *-s*. The constitutents of *the boys are from our school* are 1) *the boys: they* can be substituted; and 2) *are from our school:* the single morpheme *run* can be substituted for this entire sequence. The identification of the constituents of *are from our school* as *are* and *from our school* is facilitated by the fact that a single morpheme, *good,* can be substituted for *from our school.* In this manner the constituents of any sentence can be identified, and the rules for putting them together can be stated.

A *constituent class* is any group of constituents that has an identical function in the content structure of the language. The class is made up of all constituents that can fill the "gap" in an utterance left by the removal of one of its members. For example, in *the* ——— *saw our school,* all morphemes or sequences of morphemes that can fill the gap are of one class.

It is important in constituent analysis to keep in mind the fact that prosodic morphemes form an essential part of the environment of any constituent, and must be held constant when constituents are substituted at one point in that environment.

Paralanguage

There are identifiable vocal phenomena that accompany the stream of speech, which, because of a limited or unique distribution, cannot be analyzed as being part of the phonemic or morphological structure of language. The systematic observation of these phenomena has led to their classification into two categories: voice qualities and vocalizations.

Voice quality is the category that represents the speaker's control of the overall or background characteristics of the voice. These phenomena would include the speaker's control of articulation, tempo, intensity, quantity, pitch height, and pitch range. When any of these is used in amounts differing from normal, the listener is quite aware that something unusual has occurred. Analysis of the voice qualities has led to the conclusion that they occur in bipolar fashion, differing in a positive or negative way from a mid-point.

Vocalization is the category consisting of sounds which are identifiable segments of the sound continuum, or specifiable modifications of segments. The identifiable segments (e.g., the click in *tsk-tsk*) can be described in terms of the same three dimensions used for describing segmental phones, that is, point of articulation, manner of articulation, and activity in the larynx. These segments are called *vocal segregates,* to emphasize the point that they are segmental sounds, but are not analyzed as being part of the phonemic structure of the language. The specifiable prosodic modifications of segments (either segmental phones or vocal segregates) are intensity, pitch height, and length. These modifications, as a group, are called *vocal qualifiers.*[1]

[1] The formulations presented in this paper owe a debt to a number of sources. Among them, the following are certainly prominent: Block & Trager (1942); Bloomfield (1933); Fries (1952); Gleason (1961); McQuown (1954, 1957); Nida (1943); Pike (1943); Pittenger & Smith (1957); Trager (1958); Trager & Smith (1951).

23 The language of social control

S. I. HAYAKAWA

Making things happen

The most interesting and perhaps least understood relationship between words and the world is that between words and future events. When we say, for example, "Come here!" we are not describing the extensional world about us, nor are we merely expressing our feelings; we are trying to *make something happen*. What we call "commands," "pleas," "requests," and "orders" are the simplest ways we have of making things happen by means of words.

There are, however, more roundabout ways. When we say, for example, "Our candidate is a great American," we are of course making an enthusiastic purr about him, but we may also be influencing other people to vote for him. Again, when we say, "Our war against the enemy is God's war. God wills that we must triumph," we are saying something which, though unverifiable, may influence others to help in the prosecution of the war. Or if we merely state as a fact, "Milk contains vitamins," we may be influencing others to buy milk.

Consider, too, such a statement as "I'll meet you tomorrow at two o'clock in front of the Palace Theater." Such a statement about *future* events can only be made, it will be observed, in a system in which symbols are independent of things symbolized. The future, like the recorded past, is a specifically human dimension. To a dog, the expression "hamburger *tomorrow*" is meaningless —he will look at you expectantly, hoping for the extensional meaning of the word "hamburger" to be produced *now*. Squirrels, to be sure, store food for "next winter," but the fact that they store food regardless of whether or not their needs are adequately provided for demonstrates that such behavior (usually called "instinctive") is governed neither by symbols nor by other interpreted stimuli. Human beings are unique in their ability to react meaningfully to such expressions as "next Saturday," "on our next wedding anniversary," "twenty years after date I promise to pay," "some day, perhaps five hundred years from now." That is to say, maps can be made, even though the territories they stand for are not yet actualities. Guiding ourselves by means of such maps of territories-to-be, we can impose a certain predictability upon future events.

With words, therefore, we influence and to an enormous extent *control future events*. It is for this reason that writers write; preachers preach; employers, parents, and teachers scold; propagandists send out news releases; statesmen give addresses. All of them, for various reasons, are trying to influence our conduct—sometimes for our good, sometimes for their own. These attempts to control, direct, or influence the future actions of fellow human beings with words may be termed *directive uses of language*.

Now it is obvious that if directive language is going to direct, it cannot be dull or uninteresting. If it is to influence our conduct, it *must* make use of every affective element in language: dramatic variations in tone of voice, rhyme and rhythm, purring and snarling, words with strong affective connotations, endless repetition. If meaningless noises will move the audience, meaningless noises must be made; if facts move them, facts must be given; if noble ideals move them, we must make our proposals appear noble; if they will respond only to fear, we must scare them stiff.

The nature of the affective means used in directive language is limited, of course, by the nature of our aims. If we are trying to direct people to be more kindly toward each other, we obviously do not want to arouse feelings of cruelty or hate. If we are trying to direct people to think and act more intelligently, we obviously should not use subrational appeals. If we are trying to direct people to lead better lives, we use affective appeals that arouse their finest feelings. Included among directive utterances, therefore, are many of the greatest and most treasured works of literature: the Christian and Buddhist scriptures, the writings of Confucius, Milton's *Areopagitica*, and Lincoln's Gettysburg Address.

There are, however, occasions when it is felt that language is not sufficiently affective by itself to produce the results wanted. We supplement directive language, therefore, by *nonverbal affective appeals* of many kinds. We supplement the words "Come here" by gesturing with our hands. Advertisers are not content with saying in words how beautiful their products will make us; they supplement their words by the use of colored inks and by pictures. Newspapers are not content with saying that communism is a menace; they supply political cartoons depicting communists as criminally insane people placing sticks of dynamite under magnificent buildings labeled "American way of life." The affective appeal of sermons and religious exhortations may be supplemented by costumes, incense, processions, choir music, and church bells. A political candidate seeking office reinforces his speech-making with a considerable array of nonverbal affective appeals: brass bands, flags, parades, picnics, barbecues, and free cigars. Often a candidate's smile or, as in the case of President Kennedy, his wife's appearance and charm may be a powerful influence upon the voter.

Now, if we want people to do certain things and if we are indifferent as to *why they do them*, then no affective appeals need be excluded. Some political candidates want us to vote for them regardless of our reasons for doing so. Therefore, if we hate the rich, they will snarl at the rich for us; if we dislike strikers, they will snarl at the strikers; if we like clambakes, they will throw clambakes; if the majority of us like hillbilly music, they may say nothing about the problems of government, but travel among their constituencies with hillbilly bands. Again, many business firms want us to buy their products regardless of our reasons for doing so; therefore, if delusions and fantasies will lead us to buy their products, they will seek to produce delusions and fantasies; if we want to be popular with the other sex, they will promise us popularity; if we like pretty girls in bathing suits, they will associate pretty girls in bathing suits with their products, whether they are selling shaving cream, automobiles, summer resorts, ice-cream cones, house paint, or hardware. Only the law keeps them from presenting pretty girls without bathing suits. The records of the Federal Trade Commission, as well as the advertising pages of many magazines, show that some advertisers will stop at practically nothing.

The promises of directive language

Almost all directive utterances say something about the future. They are "maps," either explicitly or by implication, of *"territories" that are to be.* They direct us to do certain things with the stated or implied promise that if we do these things, certain consequences will follow: "If you adhere to the Bill of Rights, your civil rights too will be protected." "If you vote for me, I will have your taxes reduced." "Live according to these religious principles, and you will have peace in your soul." "Read this magazine, and you will keep up with important current events." "Take Lewis's Licorice Liver Pills and enjoy that glorious feeling that goes with regularity." Needless to say, some of these promises are kept, and some are not. Indeed, we encounter promises daily that are obviously incapable of being kept.

There is no sense in objecting as some people do to advertising and political propaganda—the only kind of directives they worry about—on the ground that they are based on "emotional appeals." Unless directive language has affective power of some kind, it is useless. We do not object to campaigns that tell us, "Give to the Community Chest and enable poor children to enjoy better care," although that is an "emotional appeal." Nor do we resent being reminded of our love of home, friends, and nation when people issue moral or patriotic directives at us. The important question to be asked of any directive utterance is, "Will things happen as promised if I do as I am directed to do? If I accept your philosophy, shall I achieve peace of mind? If I vote for you, will my taxes be reduced? If I use Lifeguard Soap, will my boy friend really come back to me?"

We rightly object to advertisers who make false or misleading claims and to politicians who ignore their promises, although it must be admitted that, in the case of politicians, they are sometimes compelled to make promises that later circumstances prevent them from keeping. Life being as uncertain and as unpredictable as it is, we are constantly trying to find out what is going to happen next, so that we may prepare ourselves. Directive utterances undertake to tell us how we can bring about certain desirable events and how we can avoid undesirable events. If we can rely upon what they tell us about the future, the uncertainties of life are reduced. When, however, directive utterances are of such a character that things do *not* happen as predicted—when, after we have done as we were told, the peace in the soul has not been found, the taxes have not been reduced, the boy friend has not returned, there is disappointment. Such disappointments may be trivial or grave; in any event, they are so common that we do not even bother to complain about some of them. They are, nevertheless, all serious in their implications. *Each of them serves, in greater or lesser degree, to break down that mutual trust that makes cooperation possible and knits people together into a society.*

Every one of us, therefore, who utters directive language, with its concomitant promises, stated or implied, is morally obliged to be as certain as he can, since there is no absolute certainty, that he is arousing no false expectations. Politicians promising the immediate abolition of poverty, national advertisers suggesting that tottering marriages can be restored to bliss by a change in the brand of laundry detergent used in the family, newspapers threatening the collapse of the nation if the party they favor is not elected—all such utterers of nonsense are, for the reasons stated, menaces to the social order. It does not matter much whether such misleading directives are uttered in ignorance and error or with conscious intent to deceive, because the disappointments they cause are all similarly destructive of mutual trust among human beings.

The foundations of society

But propaganda, no matter how persuasive, does not create society. We can, if we wish, ignore its directives. We come now to *directive utterances that we cannot ignore if we wish to remain organized in our social groups.*

What we call society is a vast network of mutual agreements. We agree to refrain from murdering our fellow citizens, and they in turn agree to refrain from murdering us; we agree to drive on the right-hand side of the road, and others agree to do the same; we agree to deliver specified goods, and others agree to pay us for them; we agree to observe the rules of an organization, and the organization agrees to let us enjoy its privileges. This complicated network of agreements, into which almost every detail of our lives is woven and upon which most of our expectations in life are based, consists essentially of *statements about future events which we are supposed, with our own efforts, to bring about.* Without such agreements, there would be no such thing as society. We would all be huddling in miserable and lonely caves, not daring to trust anyone. With such agreements, and a will on the part of the vast majority of people to live by them, behavior begins to fall into relatively predictable patterns; cooperation becomes possible; peace and freedom are established.

Therefore, in order that we shall continue to exist as human beings, we *must* impose patterns of behavior on each other. We must make citizens conform to social and civic customs; we must make husbands dutiful to their wives; we must make soldiers courageous, judges just, priests pious, and teachers solicitous for the welfare of their pupils. In early stages of culture the principal means of imposing patterns of behavior was, of course, physical coercion. But such control can also be exercised, as human beings must have discovered extremely early in history, by *words*—that is, by directive language. Therefore, directives about matters which society as a whole regards as essential to its own safety are made especially powerful, so that no individual in that society will fail to be impressed with a sense of his obligations. To make doubly sure, society further reinforces the directives by the assurance that punishment, possibly including imprisonment and death, may be visited upon those who fail to heed the words.

Directives with collective sanction

These directive utterances with collective sanction, which try to impose patterns of behavior upon the individual in the interests of the whole group, are among the most interesting of linguistic events. Not only are they usually accompanied by ritual; they are usually the central purpose of ritual. There is probably no kind of utterance that we take more seriously, that affects our lives more deeply, that we quarrel about more bitterly. Constitutions of nations and of organizations, legal contracts, and oaths of office are utterances of this kind; in marriage vows, confirmation exercises, induction ceremonies, and initiations, they are the essential constituent. Those terrifying verbal jungles called *laws* are simply such directives, accumulated, codified, and systematized through the centuries. In its laws, society makes its mightiest collective effort to impose predictability upon human behavior.

Directive utterances made under collective sanction may exhibit any or all of the following features:

1. Such language is almost always phrased in *words that have affective connotations*, so that people will be appropriately impressed and awed. Archaic and obsolete vocabulary or stilted phraseology quite unlike the language of everyday life is employed. For example: "Wilt thou, John, take this woman for thy lawful wedded wife?" "This lease, made this tenth day of July, A.D. One Thousand Nine Hundred and Sixty-three, between Samuel Smith, herein after called the Lessor, and Jeremiah Johnson, hereinafter called Lessee, WITNESSETH, that Lessor, in consideration of covenants and agreements hereinafter contained and made on the part of the Lessee, hereby leases to the Lessee for a private dwelling, the premises known and described as follows, to wit . . ."
2. Such directive utterances are often accompanied by *appeals to supernatural powers*, who are called upon to help us carry out the vows, or to punish us if we fail to carry them out. An oath, for example, ends with the words, "So help me God." Prayers, incantations, and invocations accompany the utterance of important vows in practically all cultures, from the most primitive to the most civilized. These further serve, of course, to impress our vows on our minds.
3. The *fear of direct punishment* is also invoked. If God does not punish us for failing to carry out our agreements, it is made clear either by statement or implication that our fellow men will. For example, we all realize that we can be imprisoned for desertion, nonsupport, or bigamy; sued for "breach of contract"; unfrocked" for activities contrary to priestly vows; "cashiered" for "conduct unbecoming an officer"; "impeached" for "betrayal of public trust"; hanged for "treason."
4. The formal and public utterance of the vows may be preceded by *preliminary disciplines* of various kinds: courses of training in the meaning of the vows one is undertaking; fasting and self-mortification, as before entering the priesthood; initiation ceremonies involving physical torture, as before induction into the warrior status among primitive peoples or membership in college fraternities.
5. The utterance of the directive language may be accompanied by other *activities or gestures calculated to impress the occasion on the mind.* For example, everybody in a courtroom stands up when a judge is about to open a court; huge processions and extraordinary costumes accompany coronation ceremonies; academic gowns are worn for commencement exercises; for many weddings, an organist and a soprano are procured and special clothes are worn.

6. The uttering of the vows may be immediately followed by *feasts, dancing, and other joyous manifestations.* Again the purpose seems to be to reinforce still further the effect of the vows. For example, there are wedding parties and receptions, graduation dances, banquets for the induction of officers and, even in the most modest social circles, some form of "celebration" when a member of the family enters into a compact with society. In primitive cultures, initiation ceremonies for chieftains may be followed by feasting and dancing that last for several days or weeks.
7. In cases where the first utterance of the vows is not made a special ceremonial occasion, the effect on the memory is usually achieved by *frequent repetition.* The flag ritual ("I pledge allegiance to the flag of the United States of America . . .") is repeated daily in most schools. Mottoes, which are briefly stated general directives, are repeated frequently; sometimes they are stamped on dishes, sometimes engraved on a warrior's sword, sometimes inscribed in prominent places such as on gates, walls, and doorways, where people can see them and be reminded of their duties.

The common feature of all these activities that accompany directive utterances, as well as of the affective elements in the language of directive utterances, is the deep effect they have on the memory. Every kind of sensory impression from the severe pain of initiation rites to the pleasures of banqueting, music, splendid clothing, and ornamental surroundings may be employed; every emotion from the fear of divine punishment to pride in being made the object of special public attention may be aroused. This is done in order that the individual who enters into his compact with society —that is, the individual who commits himself to the "map" of the not-yet-existent "territory"—shall never forget to try to bring that "territory" into existence.

For these reasons, such occasions as when a cadet receives his commission, when a Jewish boy has his *bar mitzvah,* when a priest takes his vows, when a policeman receives his badge, when a foreign-born citizen is sworn in as a citizen of the United States, or when a president takes his oath of office—these are events one never forgets. Even if, later on, a person realizes that he has not fulfilled his vows, he cannot shake off the feeling that he should have done so. All of us, of course, use and respond to these ritual directives. The phrases and speeches to which we respond reveal our deepest religious, patriotic, social, professional, and political allegiances more accurately than do the citizenship papers or membership cards that we may carry in our pockets or the badges that we may wear on our coats. A man who has changed his religion after reaching adulthood will, on hearing the ritual he was accustomed to hearing in childhood, often feel an urge to return to his earlier form of worship. In such ways, then, do human beings use words to reach out into the future and control each other's conduct.

It should be remarked that many of our social directives and many of the rituals with which they are accompanied are antiquated and somewhat insulting to adult minds. Rituals that originated in times when people had to be scared into good behavior are unnecessary to people who already have a sense of social responsibility. For example, a five-minute marriage ceremony performed at the city hall for a mature, responsible couple may "take" much better than a full-dress church ceremony performed for an infantile couple. In spite of the fact that the strength of social directives obviously lies in the willingness, the maturity, and the intelligence of the people to whom the directives are addressed, there is still a widespread tendency to rely upon the efficacy of ceremonies as such. This tendency is due, of course, to a lingering belief in word-magic, the notion that, by *saying* things repeatedly or in specified ceremonial ways, we can cast a spell over the future and force events to turn out the way we said they would. ("There'll always be an England!") An interesting manifestation of this superstitious attitude toward words and rituals is to be found among those members of patriotic societies who seem to believe that the way to educate school children in democracy is to stage bigger and better flag-saluting ceremonies and to treble the occasions for singing "God Bless America."

What are "rights"?

What, extensionally, is the meaning of the word "my" in such expressions as "my real estate," "my book," "my automobile"? Certainly the word "my" describes no characteristics of the objects named. A check changes hands and "your" automobile becomes "mine" but no change results in the automobile. What has changed?

The change is, of course, in *our social agreements covering our behavior* toward the automobile. Formerly, when it was "yours," you felt free to use it as you liked, while I did not. Now that it is "mine," I use it freely and you may not. The meaning of "yours" and "mine" lies not in the external world, but in *how we intend to act*. And when society as a whole recognizes my "right of ownership" (by issuing me, for example, a certificate of title), it agrees to protect me in my intentions to use the automobile and to frustrate, by police action if necessary, the intentions of those who may wish to use it without my permission. Society makes this agreement with me in return for my obeying its laws and paying my share of the expenses of government.

Are not, then, all assertions of ownership and statements about "rights" directives? Cannot, "This is *mine*," be translated, "I am going to use this object; you keep your hands off"? Cannot, "Every child has a *right* to an education," be translated, "*Give* every child an education"? And is not the difference between "moral rights" and "legal rights" the difference between agreements which people believe *ought* to be made, and those which, through collective, legislative sanction, *have been* made?

Directives and disillusionment

A few cautions may be added before we leave the subject of directive language. First, it should be remembered that, since words cannot "say all" about anything, the promises implied in directive language are never more than "outline maps" of "territories-to-be." The future will fill in those outlines, often in unexpected ways. Sometimes the future will bear no relation to our "maps" at all, in spite of all our endeavors to bring about the promised events. We swear always to be good citizens, always to do our duty, and so on, but we never quite succeed in being good citizens *every* day of our lives or in performing *all* our duties. A realization that directives cannot *fully* impose any pattern on the future saves us from having impossible expectations and therefore from suffering needless disappointments.

Secondly, one should distinguish between directive and informative utterances, which often look alike. Such statements as "A boy scout is clean and chivalrous and brave" or "Policemen are defenders of the weak" *set up goals* and do not necessarily describe the present situation. This is extremely important, because all too often people understand such definitions as descriptive and are then shocked and disillusioned when they encounter a boy scout who is not chivalrous or a policeman who is a bully. They decide that they are "through with the boy scouts" or "disgusted with all policemen," which, of course, is nonsense. They have, in effect, inferred an informative statement from what is to be taken only as a very general directive.

A third source of disappointment and disillusionment arising from the improper understanding of directives results from reading into directives promises that they do not make. A common instance is provided by advertisements of the antiseptics and patent medicines which people buy under the impression that the cure or prevention of colds was promised. Because of the ruling of the Federal Trade Commission, the writers of these advertisements carefully avoid saying that their preparations will prevent or cure anything. Instead, they say that they "help reduce the severity of the infection," "help relieve the symptoms of a cold," or "help guard against sniffling and other discomforts." If after reading these advertisements you feel that prevention or cure of colds has been promised, you are exactly the kind of sucker they are looking for. (Of course, if you buy the product knowing clearly what was promised and what was not, that is a different matter.)

Another way of reading into directives things that were not said is by believing promises to be more specific and concrete than they really are. When, for example, a candidate for political office promises to "help the farmer," and you vote for him, and then you discover that he helps the *cotton* farmer without helping the *potato* farmer (and you grow potatoes)—you cannot exactly accuse him of having broken his promise. Or, if another candidate promises to "protect union labor," and you vote for him, and he helps to pass legislation that infuriates the officials of your union (he calls it "legislation to protect union members from their own racketeering leadership")—again you cannot exactly accuse him of having broken his promise since his action may well have been sincerely in accord with his notion of "helping union labor." The ambiguities of campaign oratory are notorious.

Politicians are often accused of breaking their promises. No doubt many of them do. But it must be remarked that they often do not promise as much as their constituents think they do. The platforms of the major parties are almost always at high levels of abstraction ("they mean all things to all men," as the cynical say), but they are often understood by voters to be more specific and concrete (i.e., at lower levels of abstraction) than they are. If one is "disillusioned" by acts of a politician, sometimes the politician is to blame, but sometimes the voter is to blame for having had the illusion to start with—or, as we shall say, for having *confused different levels of abstraction.*

24 On the nature of meaning

CHARLES E. OSGOOD

The language process within an individual may be viewed as a more or less continuous interaction between two parallel systems of behavioral organization: sequences of central events ("ideas") and sequences of instrumental skills, vocalic, gestural, or orthographic, which constitute the communicative product. A communicator vocalizes, "It looks like rain today; I'd better not wash the car." This output is a sequence of skilled movements, complicated to be sure, but not different in kind from tying one's shoes. Even the smallest units of the product, phonetic elements like the initial "l"-sound of "looks," result from precisely patterned muscle movements. The organization of these movements into word-units represents skill sequences of relatively high predictability; certain longer period sequences involving syntactical order are also relatively predictable for a given language system. But execution of such sequences brings the communicator repeatedly to what may be called "choice-points"—points where the next skill sequence is not highly predictable from the objective communicative product itself. The dependence of "I'd better not wash the car" upon "looks like rain today," the *content* of the message, reflects determinants within the semantic system which effectively "load" the transitional probabilities at these choice-points.

It is the communicative product, the spoken or written words which follow one another in varying orders, that we typically observe. Since we are unable to specify the stimuli which evoke these communicating reactions—since it is "emitted" rather than "elicited" behavior in Skinner's terminology (1938) —measurements in terms of rates of occurrence and transitional probabilities (dependence of one event in the stream upon others) are particularly appropriate (cf., Miller, 1951). Interest may be restricted to the lawfulness of sequences in the observable communicative product itself, without regard to the semantic parallel. This is traditionally the field of the linguist, but even here it has proved necessary to make some assumptions about meaning (cf., Bloomfield, 1933). On the other hand, one may be specifically interested in the semantic or ideational level. Since he is presently unable to observe this level of behavior directly, he must use observable characteristics of the communicative product as a basis for making inferences about what is going on at the semantic level. He may use sequential orderliness in the product to draw conclusions as to semantic orderliness in the speaker's or writer's mediation processes (i.e., which "ideas" tend to go together in his thinking with greater than chance probabilities). Or he may wish to study the ways in which central, semantic processes vary from concept to concept, from person to person, and so on. It is the problem of measuring

Excerpted from "The nature and measurement of meaning," **Psychological Bulletin, 1952, 49,** 197–237, with permission of the author and the American Psychological Association.

meaning in this latter sense which will be discussed in the present paper.

Before inquiring into the measurement of the meaning of signs, for which there are no accepted, standardized techniques available, we may briefly mention certain fairly standard methods for measuring the comparative strength of verbal habits. Thorndike and his associates (1921, 1944) have made extensive *frequency-of-usage counts* of words in English; that this method gets at the comparative habit strengths of word skill sequences is shown by the fact that other measures of response strength, such as latency and probability within the individual (Thumb & Marbe, 1901; Cason & Cason, 1925), are correlated with frequency-of-usage. Zipf (1935, 1949, and elsewhere) has described innumerable instances of the lawfulness of such habit-strength measures. Whether samples be taken from Plautine Latin, newspaper English, or the English of James Joyce in his *Ulysses*, a fundamental regularity is found, such that frequency of occurrence of particular words bears a linear relation to their rank order in frequency, when plotted on double-log paper (Zipf's Law). Measurement of flexibility or diversity in communicative products is given by the *type-token ratio* (TTR): with each instance of any word counting as a token and each different word as a type, the greater the ratio of types to tokens the more varied is the content of a message. This measure can be applied comparatively to different forms of material, different kinds of individuals, and so forth (cf., Carroll 1938, 1944; Johnson 1944; Chotlos, 1944), provided the sizes of samples are constant. One may also count the ratios of adjectives to verbs (Boder, 1940), the frequencies of different pronouns, intensives, and so forth (cf., Johnson, 1944).

Although the above measures get at the comparative strengths of verbal skill sequences per se (i.e., without regard to meaning), this is not a necessary restriction. Frequency counts of this type can be applied to *semantic habit strengths* as well. Skinner (1937) has shown that a similar lawfulness applies to the frequencies of "free" associations in the Kent-Rosanoff tests. When frequencies of particular associates to given stimulus words for a group of subjects are plotted against their rank order in frequency, a straight-line function on double-log paper results (Zipf's Law). In other words, associations at the semantic level appear to be organized in such a way that few have very high probability of occurrence and many have low probabilities of occurrence. Bousfield and his collaborators (1944, 1950, 1937, 1944, 1950) have described a *sequential association method* for getting at comparative semantic habit strengths. When subjects associate successively from the same "pool," e.g., "names of four-legged animals," (*a*) the rate of successive associates shows a negatively accelerated curve, (*b*) varying in its constants with certain characteristics of materials and subjects, (*c*) the order of appearance of particular associates in individuals being predictable from the frequency of usage in the group, and (*d*) distortions in the function being related to particular transitional probabilities among associates, i.e., clustering. Useful though these measures are for many purposes, they do not get at meaning. The fact that "dog" has a higher probability of occurrence in sequential association than "otter" says nothing whatsoever about the differences in meaning of these two signs.

An extensive survey of the literature fails to uncover any generally accepted, standardized method for measuring meaning. Perhaps it is because of the philosophical haziness of this concept, perhaps because of the general belief that "meanings" are infinitely and uniquely variable, or perhaps because the word "meaning" as a construct in our language connotes mental stuff, more akin to "thought" and "soul" than to anything observable—for some combination of reasons there has been little attempt to devise methods here. Nevertheless, whether looked at from the viewpoints of philosophy or linguistics, from economic or sociological theory, or—interestingly enough—from within the core of psychological theories of individual behavior, the nature of meaning and change in meaning are found to be central issues. The proposals to be made in the latter portion of this paper are part of a program aimed at the development of objective methods of measuring meaning. Beyond obvious social implications, it is felt that this direction of research is a logical extension of scientific inquiry into an area generally considered immune to its attack.

Theories of meaning

Not all stimuli are signs. The shock which galvanizes a rat into vigorous escape movements usually does not stand for anything other than itself, nor does the pellet of food found at the end of a maze, nor a hammer in one's hand or a shoe on one's foot. The problem for any meaning theorist is to differentiate the conditions under which a pattern of stimulation is a sign of something else from those conditions where it is not. This certainly seems simple enough, yet it has troubled philosophers for centuries. By stating the problem somewhat formally, the chief differences between several conceptions of the sign-process can be made evident: let

$\dot{S}$ = object = any pattern of stimulation which evokes reactions on the part of an organism, and

$\boxed{s}$ = sign = any pattern of stimulation which is not this $\dot{S}$ but yet evokes reactions relevant to $\dot{S}$—conditions under which this holds being the problem for theory.

The definition of $\dot{S}$ is broad enough to include any pattern of stimulation which elicits any reaction from an organism. Although one usually thinks of "objects" as those things denoted by signs, actually any pattern of stimulation—a gust of northerly wind against the face, the sensations we call "bellyache," the sensations of being rained upon—is an "object" at this level of discourse. One sign may be the "object" represented by another sign, as when the picture of an apple is called "DAX" in certain experiments. The definition of $\boxed{s}$ is purposely left incomplete at this point, since it depends upon one's conception of the nature of the sign-process.

We may start a logical analysis of the problem with a self-evident fact: *the pattern of stimulation which is the sign is never identical with the pattern of stimulation which is the object.* The word "hammer" is not the same stimulus as is the object hammer. The former is a pattern of sound waves having characteristic oscillations in frequency and intensity; the latter, depending upon its mode of contact, may be a visual form having characteristic color and shape, a pattern of tactual and proprioceptive sensations, and so on. Similarly, the buzzer in a typical rat experiment is not identical as a form of stimulation with the shock which it comes to signify. Yet these signs—the word "hammer" and the buzzer—do elicit behaviors which are in some manner relevant to the objects they signify, a characteristic *not* shared with an infinite number of other stimulus patterns that are *not* signs of these objects. In simplest terms, therefore, the question is: *under what conditions does something which is not an object become a sign of that object?* According to the way in which this question is answered we may distinguish several theories of meaning.

MENTALISTIC VIEW

The classic interpretation derives directly from the natural philosophy of Western culture, in which the dualistic connotations of language dictate a correlation between two classes of events, material and nonmaterial. Since meanings are obviously "mental" events and the stimuli representing objects and signs are obviously "physical" events, any satisfying theory of meaning must specify interrelation between these levels of discourse. At the core of all mentalistic views, therefore, we find an "idea" as the essence of meaning; it is this mental event which links or relates the two different physical events, sign and object. The word "hammer" gives rise to the idea of that object in the mind; conversely, perception of the object hammer gives rise to the same idea, which can then be "expressed" in appropriate signs. In other words, *something which is not the object becomes a sign of that object when it gives rise to the idea associated with that object.* Probably the most sophisticated expression of this view is given by Ogden and Richards (1923) in their book, *The Meaning of Meaning*. Most readers will recall their triangular diagram of the sign-process: the relation between symbol and referent (the base of their triangle) is not direct but inferred, mediated through mental "thought" or "interpretation" (the third corner of their triangle).

SUBSTITUTION VIEW

Naïve application of Pavlovian conditioning principles by early behaviorists like Watson led to the theory that signs achieve their meanings simply by being conditioned to the same reactions originally made to objects. This, in essence, is the view one encounters in many introductory texts in general psychology. An object evokes certain behavior in an organism; if another pattern of stimulation is consistently paired with the original object, it becomes conditioned to the same responses and thus gets its meaning. The object is the unconditioned stimulus and the sign is the conditioned stimulus, the latter merely being substituted for the former. The definition of the sign-process here is that *whenever something which is not the object evokes in an organism the same reactions evoked by the object, it is a sign of that object*. The very simplicity of this theory highlights its inadequacy. Signs almost never evoke the *same* overt responses as do the objects they represent. The word FIRE has meaning to the reader without sending him into headlong flight. Nevertheless, this represents a first step toward a behavioral interpretation of the sign-process.

MEANING AS "SET" OR "DISPOSITION"

In a monograph entitled *Foundation of the Theory of Signs* (1938), Charles Morris, a semiotician working in the tradition established by Peirce and other American pragmatists, proposed a formula for the sign-process which avoids the pitfalls of substitution theory but seems to step backward toward the mentalistic view. In essence he states that signs achieve their meanings by eliciting reactions which "take account of" the objects signified. The sign "hammer" may evoke quite different responses from those evoked by the object signified, but these responses must have the character of being relevant to the object. The response made to the sign is called the "interpretant" which mediately takes account of the object signified. But it would seem that this process of "taking account of" is precisely what needs elucidation.

During the period intervening between this monograph and his recent book, *Signs, Language and Behavior* (1946), Morris studied with two prominent behavior theorists, Tolman and Hull. The effects of this immersion in learning theory are evident in his book, which is a pioneer attempt to reduce semiotic to an objective behavioral basis. He states that "if anything, A, is a preparatory stimulus which in the absence of stimulus-objects initiating response-sequences of a certain behavior-family causes a disposition in some organism to respond under certain conditions by response-sequences of this behavior-family, then A is a sign" (p. 10). Reduced to its essentials and translated into our terms, this becomes: *any pattern of stimulation which is not the object becomes a sign of that object if it produces in an organism a "disposition" to make any of the responses previously elicited by that object.* There is no requirement that the *overt* reactions originally elicited by the object also be made to the sign; the sign merely creates a disposition or set to make such reactions, actual occurrence depending upon the concurrence of supporting conditions.

Beyond the danger that "dispositions" may serve as mere surrogates for "ideas" in this theory, there are certain other difficulties with the view as stated. For one thing, Morris seems to have revived the substitution notion. The sign is said to dispose the organism to make overt response-sequences of the *same* behavior-family originally elicited by the object. But is this necessarily the case? Is my response to the word "apple" (e.g., free-associating the word "peach") any part of the behavior-family elicited by the object apple? For another thing, Morris' formulation fails to differentiate sign-behavior from many instinctive reactions and from ordinary conditioning. To appreciate this difficulty will require a brief digression.

When a breach is made in a termite nest, the workers set up a distinctive pounding upon the floor of the tunnel and the warriors come charging to the spot, where they take up defensive positions. Is this pounding sound a sign to the warrior-termites that there is a breach in the nest? It happens that this behavior is purely instinctive, and most students of sign-behavior believe that signs must achieve their signification through *learning*. But is learning a sufficient criterion? Are all stimuli that elicit learned reactions automatically signs? In developing any skill, such as tying the shoes, the proprioceptive stimuli produced by one response become conditioned to the succeeding response—but of what are these proprioceptive stimuli signs? With repeated experience on an electrified grill a rat will often learn to rear up on its hind legs and alternately lift them, this act apparently reducing the total intensity of pain—the painful stimulation is thus conditioned to a new response, but of what is the pain a sign?

If only some of the stimuli which elicit learned responses are signs, we must seek a reasonable distinction *within* the class of learned behaviors. We cannot draw a line between human and subhuman learning: the buzzer is operationally as much a sign of shock to the rat in avoidance-training experiments as are dark clouds a sign of rain to the professor—both stimuli elicit reactions appropriate, not to themselves, but to something other than themselves. Is voluntariness of response a criterion? Meaningful reactions may be just as involuntary as perceptions—try to observe a familiar word and avoid its meaning! Is it variability of response to the stimulus? Meaningful reactions may be just as stable and habitual as motor skills.

THE MEDIATION HYPOTHESIS

I shall try to show that the distinguishing condition of sign behavior is the presence or absence of *a representational mediation process* in association with the stimulus. This conception of sign behavior is based upon a general theory of learning rather than being concocted specifically to account for meaning as seen in human communication.[1] The essence of the viewpoint can be given as follows:

1. *Stimulus-objects* ($\dot{S}$) *elicit a complex pattern of reactions from the organism, these reactions varying in their dependence upon presence of the stimulus-object for their occurrence.* Electric shock galvanizes the rat into vigorous jumping, squeaking, and running activities, as well as autonomic "anxiety" reactions. Food objects elicit sequences of salivating, chewing, lip-smacking, and so forth. Components like salivating and "anxiety" are relatively independent of the food or shock stimulation respectively and hence can occur when such objects are not present.

2. *When stimuli other than the stimulus-object, but previously associated with it, are later presented without its support, they tend to elicit some reduced portion of the total behavior elicited by the stimulus-object.* This reduction process follows certain laws: (*a*) mediating reactions which interfere with goal-achievement tend to extinguish; (*b*) the more energy expenditure involved in making a particular reaction, the less likely it is to survive the reduction process; (*c*) there is evidence that certain reactions (e.g., autonomic) condition more readily than others (e.g., gross skeletal) and hence are more likely to become part of the mediation process—this may merely reflect factor (*b*) above.

3. *The fraction of the total object-elicited behavior which finally constitutes the stable mediation process elicited by a sign* ($\boxed{S}$) *will tend toward a minimum set by the discriminatory capacity of the organism.* This is because the sole function of such mediating reactions in behavior is to provide a distinctive pattern of self-stimulation (cf., Hull's conception of the "pure stimulus act").

4. *The self-stimulation produced by sign-elicited mediation processes becomes conditioned in varying strengths to the initial responses in hierarchies of instrumental skill sequences.* This mediated self-stimulation is assumed to pro-

[1] This hypothesis, as an elaboration from Hullian theory (1943), is described in my book, **Method and Theory in Experimental Psychology** (1953).

vide the "way of perceiving" signs or their "meaning," as well as mediating instrumental skill sequences—behaviors to signs which take account of the objects represented.

Whereas Morris linked sign and object through partial identity of object-produced and disposition-*produced* behaviors, we have linked sign and object through partial identity of the "disposition" *itself* with the behavior elicited by the object. Words represent things because they produce some replica of the actual behavior toward these things, as a mediation process. This is the crucial identification, the mechanism that ties particular signs to particular stimulus-objects and not to others. Stating the proposition formally: *a pattern of stimulation which is not the object is a sign of the object if it evokes in an organism a mediating reaction, this* (a) *being some fractional part of the total behavior elicited by the object and* (b) *producing distinctive self-stimulation that mediates responses which would not occur without the previous association of nonobject and object patterns of stimulation.* This definition may be cumbersome, but all the limiting conditions seem necessary. The mediation process must include some part of the same behavior made to the object if the sign is to have its particularistic representing property. What we have done here, in a sense, is to make explicit what may be implicit in Morris' term "disposition." The second stipulation (*b*) adds the learning requirement—the response of warrior-termites to pounding on the tunnel floor is ruled out since it does not depend upon prior association of pounding with discovery of a breach in the nest.

Paradigm A in Figure 1 gives an abbreviated symbolic account of the development of a *sign,* according to the mediation hypothesis. Take for illustration the connotative meaning of the word SPIDER. The stimulus-object ($\dot{S}$), the visual pattern of hairy-legged insect body often encountered in a threat context provided by other humans, elicits a complex pattern of behavior (R_T), which in this case includes a heavy loading of autonomic "fear" activity. Portions of this total behavior to the spider-object become conditioned to the heard word, SPIDER. With repetitions of the sign sequence, the mediation process becomes reduced to some minimally effortful and minimally interfering replica—but still includes those autonomic reactions which confer a threatening significance upon this sign. This mediating reaction (r_m) produces a distinctive pattern of self-stimulation (s_m) which may elicit a variety of overt behaviors (R_X)—shivering and saying "ugh," running out of a room where a spider is said to be lurking, and even refusing a job in the South, which is said to abound in spiders.

The vast majority of signs used in ordinary communication are what we may term *assigns*—their meanings are literally "assigned" to them via association with other signs rather than via direct association with the objects represented. The word ZEBRA is understood by most six-year-olds, yet few of them have ever encountered zebra-objects themselves. They have seen pictures of them, been told they have stripes, run like horses, and are usually found wild. As indicated in Figure 1 (*B*), this new stimulus pattern, ZEBRA, "picks up" by the mechanisms already described portions of the mediating reactions already elicited by the primary signs. In learning to read, for example, the "little black bugs" on the printed

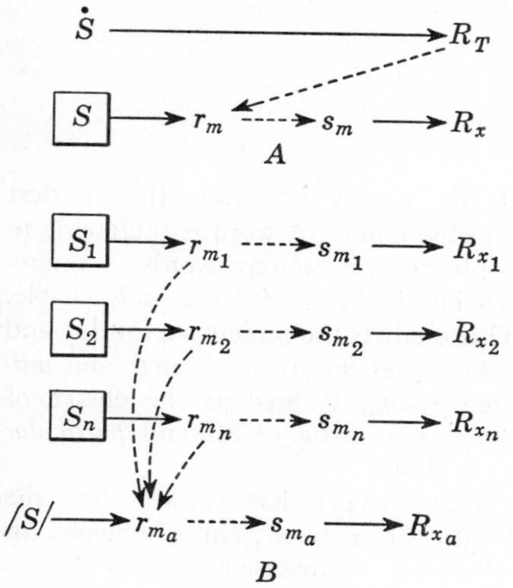

Figure 1. Symbolic account of the development of sign processes: A. development of a sign; B. development of an assign.

page are definitely assigns; these visual patterns are seldom directly associated with the objects signified, but rather with auditory signs (created by the child and teacher as they verbalize). Obviously, the more quickly the child can learn to make the right noises to these visual stimuli (the modern phonetic approach to reading), the more quickly these new, visual assigns will acquire significance. The child already has meanings for HOUSE, DOG, and even TYPEWRITER as *heard* stimulus patterns, but these mediation processes must be assigned to *seen* stimulus patterns.

It is apparent from the foregoing that the meanings which different individuals have for the same signs will vary with their behaviors toward the objects represented. This is because the composition of the mediation process, which *is* the meaning of a sign, is entirely dependent upon the composition of the total behavior occurring while the sign-process is being established. This indicates that to change the meaning of signs we must change behavior with respect to objects (keeping in mind that the "objects" for assigns are other signs). On the other hand, meanings are quite independent of the stimulus characteristics of the signs themselves, a point repeatedly stressed by linguists. According to the present theory, there is nothing sacred about the particular mouth-noises we use in communication any more than there is about the buzzer that becomes a sign of shock to the rat—a flash of light or a blast of air would serve as well. Of course, in human communication (in contrast to sign-behavior in the rat) it is necessary that the users of signs be able to produce as well as receive them.[2]

[2] The remainder of Prof. Osgood's original paper is a discussion of the measurement of meaning featuring a description of his semantic differential (see Osgood, Section VI). —Eds.

25 How shall a thing be called?

ROGER BROWN

The most deliberate part of first-language teaching is the business of telling a child what each thing is called. We ordinarily speak of *the* name of a thing as if there were just one, but in fact, of course, every referent has many names. The dime in my pocket is not only a *dime*. It is also *money*, a *metal object*, a *thing*, and, moving to subordinates, it is a *1952 dime*, in fact a *particular 1952 dime* with a unique pattern of scratches, discolorations, and smooth places. When such an object is named for a very young child how is it called? It may be named *money* or *dime* but probably not *metal object, thing, 1952 dime,* or *particular 1952 dime*. The dog out on the lawn is not only a *dog* but is also a *boxer*, a *quadruped*, an *animate being*; it is the *landlord's dog*, named *Prince*. How will it be identified for a child? Sometimes it will be called a *dog*, sometimes *Prince*, less often a *boxer*, and almost never a *quadruped*, or *animate being*. Listening to many adults name things for many children, I find that their choices are quite uniform and that I can anticipate them from my own inclinations. How are these choices determined and what are their consequences for the cognitive development of the child?

Adults have notions about the kind of language appropriate for use with children. Especially strong and universal is the belief that children have trouble pronouncing long names and so should always be given the shortest possible names. A word is preferable to a phrase and, among words, a monosyllable is better than a polysyllable. This predicts the preference for *dog* and *Prince* over *boxer, quadruped,* and *animate being*. It predicts the choice of *dime* over *metal object* and *particular 1952 dime*.

Zipf (1935) has shown that the length of a word (in phonemes or syllables) is inversely related to its frequency in the printed language. Consequently the shorter names for any thing will usually also be the most frequently used names for that thing, and so it would seem that the choice of a name is usually predictable from either frequency or brevity. The monosyllables *dog* and *Prince* have much higher frequencies according to the Thorndike-Lorge list (1944) than do the polysyllables *boxer, quadruped,* and *animate being*.

It sometimes happens, however, that the frequency-brevity principle makes the wrong prediction. The thing called a *pineapple* is also *fruit*. *Fruit* is the shorter and more frequent term, but adults will name the thing *pineapple*. Similarly they will say *apple, banana, orange,* and even *pomegranate*; all of them longer and less frequent words than the perfectly appropriate *fruit*. Brevity seems not to be the powerful determinant we had imagined. The frequency principle can survive this kind

Slightly abridged from the **Psychological Review**, 1958, 65, 14–22, with permission of the author and the American Psychological Association.

of example, but only if it is separated from counts like the Thorndike-Lorge of over-all frequency in the printed language. On the whole the word *fruit* appears more often than the word *pineapple* (and also is shorter), but we may confidently assume that, when pineapples are being named, the word *pineapple* is more frequent than the word *fruit*. This, of course, is a kind of frequency more directly relevant to our problem. Word counts of general usage are only very roughly applicable to the prediction of what will be said when something is named. What we need is referent-name counts. We don't have them, of course, but if we had them it is easy to see that they would improve our predictions. Bananas are called *banana*, apples *apple*, and oranges *orange* more often than any of them is called *fruit*. The broad frequency-brevity principle predicts that *money* and *dime* will be preferred to *metal object*, *1952 dime*, and *particular 1952 dime*, but it does not predict the neglect of the common monosyllable *thing*. For this purpose we must again appeal to imagined referent-name counts, according to which dimes would surely be called *dime* or *money* more often than *thing*.

While the conscious preference for a short name can be overcome by frequency, the preference nevertheless affects the naming act. I have heard parents designate the appropriate objects *pineapple*, *television*, *vinegar*, and *policeman*; all these to children who cannot reproduce polysyllabic words. Presumably they use these names because that is what the referents are usually called, but the adult's sense of the absurdity of giving such words to a child is often evident. He may smile as he says it or remark, "That's too hard for you to say, isn't it?"

Some things are named in the same way by all adults for all children. This is true of the apple and the orange. Other things have several common names, each of them used by a specifiable group of adults to specifiable children. The same dog is *dog* to most of the world and *Prince* in his own home and perhaps on his own block. The same man is a *man* to most children, *policeman* to some at some times, *Mr. Jones* to the neighborhood kids, and *papa* to his own. Referent-name counts from people in general will not predict these several usages. A still more particular name count must be imagined. The name given a thing by an adult for a child is determined by the frequency with which various names have been applied to such things in the experience of the particular adult. General referent-name counts taken from many people will predict much that the individual does, but, for a close prediction, counts specific to the individual would be needed.

The frequencies to which we are now appealing have not, of course, been recorded. We are explaining imagined preferences in names by imagined frequencies of names. It is conceivable, certainly, that some of these specific word counts might be made and a future naming performance independently predicted from a past frequency. Probably, however, such frequencies will never be known, and if we choose to explain particular naming performances by past frequencies we shall usually have to infer the frequency from the performance.

Beyond the frequency principle

A frequency explanation is not very satisfying even when the appeal is to known frequencies. The question will come to mind: "Why is one name more common than another?" Why is a dog called *dog* more often than *quadruped* and, by some people, called *Prince* more often than *dog?* Perhaps it just happened that way, like driving on the right side of the road in America and on the left in England. The convention is preserved but has no justification outside itself. As things have worked out, coins are usually named by species as *dime, nickel,* or *penny* while the people we know have individual names like *John, Mary,* and *Jim.* Could it just as easily be the other way around? Might we equally well give coins proper names and introduce people as types?

The referent for the word *dime* is a large class of coins. The name is equally appropriate to all members of this class. To name a coin *dime* is to establish its equivalence, for naming purposes, with all other coins of the same denomination. This equivalence for naming purposes corresponds to a more general equivalence for all purposes of economic exchange. In the grocery one dime is as good as another but quite different from any nickel or penny. For a child the name given an object anticipates the equivalences and differences that will need to be observed in most of his dealings with such an object. To make proper denotative use of the word *dime* he must be able to distinguish members of the referent category from everything else. When he learns that, he has solved more than a language problem. He has an essential bit of equipment for doing business. The most common names for coins could not move from the species level to the level of proper names without great alteration in our nonlinguistic culture. We should all be numismatists preparing our children to recognize a particular priceless 1910 dime.

Many things are reliably given the same name by the whole community. The spoon is seldom called anything but *spoon,* although it is also a piece of *silverware,* an *artifact,* and a *particular ill-washed restaurant spoon.* The community-wide preference for the word *spoon* corresponds to the community-wide practice of treating spoons as equivalent but different from knives and forks. There are no proper names for individual spoons because their individuality seldom signifies. It is the same way with pineapples, dimes, doors, and taxicabs. The most common name for each of these categorizes them as they need to be categorized for the community's nonlinguistic purposes. The most common name is at the level of usual utility.

People and pets have individual names as well as several kinds of generic name. The individual name is routinely coined by those who are disposed to treat the referent as unique, and is available afterwards to any others who will see the uniqueness. A man at home has his own name to go with the peculiar privileges and responsibilities binding him to wife and child. But the same man who is a one-of-a-kind *papa* to his own children is simply a *man* to children at large. He is, like the other members of this large category, someone with no time to play and little tolerance for noise. In some circumstances, this same man will be given the name of his occupation. He is a *policeman* equivalent to other policemen but different from *bus drivers* and *Good Humor men.* A policeman is someone to "behave in front of" and to go to when lost. To the kids in the neighborhood the man is *Mr. Jones,* unique in his way—a crank, bad tempered, likely to shout at you if you play out in front of his house. It is the same way with dogs as with people. He may be a unique *Prince* to his owners, who feed and house him, but he is just a *dog* to the rest of the world. A homeless dog reverts to namelessness, since there is none to single him out from his species. Dimes and nickels have much the same significance for an entire society, and their usual names are fixed at this level of significance. People and pets function uniquely for some and in various generic ways for others. They have a corresponding variety of designations, but each name is at the utility level for the group that uses it. Our naming practices for coins and people correspond to our nonlinguistic practices, and it is difficult to imagine changing the one without changing the other.

The names provided by parents for children anticipate the functional structure of the child's world. This is not, of course, something parents are aware of doing. When we name a thing there does not seem to be any process of choice. Each thing has its name, just one, and that is what we give to a child. The one name is, of course, simply the usual name for us. Naming each thing in accordance with local frequencies, parents unwittingly transmit their own cognitive structures. It is a world in which *Prince* is unique among dogs and *papa* among men, *spoons* are all alike but different from *forks*. It may be a world of *bugs* (to be stepped on), of *flowers* (not to be picked), and *birds* (not to be stoned). It may be a world in which *Niggers*, like *spoons* are all of a kind. A division of caste creates a vast categorical equivalence and a correspondingly generic name. *Mr. Jones* and *Mr. Smith* do not come out of racial anonymity until their uniqueness is appreciated.

Adults do not invariably provide a child with the name that is at the level of usual utility in the adult world. An effort is sometimes made to imagine the utilities of a child's life. Some parents will, at first, call every sort of coin *money*. This does not prepare a child to buy and sell, but then he may be too young for that. All coins are equivalent for the very young child in that they are objects not to be put into the mouth and not to be dropped down the register, and *money* anticipates that equivalence. A more differentiated terminology can wait upon the age of storegoing. Sometimes an adult is aware of a child's need for a distinction that is not coded in the English lexicon. A new chair comes into the house and is not going to be equivalent to the shabby chairs already there. A child is permitted to sit on the old chairs but will not be permitted on the new one. A distinctive name is created from the combinational resources of the language. *The new chair* or *the good chair* is not to be assimilated to *chairs* in general.

Eventually, of course, children learn many more names for each thing than the one that is most frequent and useful. Sometimes a name is supplied in order to bring forward an immediately important property of the referent. A child who starts bouncing the coffee pot needs to be told that it is *glass*. Sometimes a name is supplied to satisfy the child's curiosity as to the place of a referent in a hierarchy of categories. Chairs are *furniture* and so are tables; carrots are a *vegetable* but apples are not. Probably, however, both children and adults make some distinction among these various names. *The* name of a thing, the one that tells what it "really" is, is the name that constitutes the referent as it needs to be constituted for most purposes. The other names represent possible recategorizations useful for one or another purpose. We are even likely to feel that these recategorizations are acts of imagination, whereas the major categorization is a kind of passive recognition of the true character of the referent.

The child's concrete vocabulary

It is a commonplace saying that the mind of a child is relatively "concrete" and the mind of an adult "abstract." The words "concrete" and "abstract" are sometimes used in the sense of subordinate and superordinate. In this sense a relatively concrete mind would operate with subordinate categories and an abstract mind with superordinate categories. It is recorded in many studies of vocabulary acquisition (e.g., International Kindergarten Unit, 1928; Smith, 1926) that children ordinarily use the words *milk* and *water* before the word *liquid;* the words *apple* and *orange* before *fruit; table* and *chair* before *furniture; mamma* and *daddy* before *parent* or *person;* etc. Very high-level superordinate terms like *article, action, quality,* and *relation,* though they are common in adult speech (Thorndike-Lorge, 1944), are very seldom heard from preschool children (International Kindergarten Unit, 1928). Presumably this kind of vocabulary comparison is one of the sources of the notion that the child's mind is more concrete than the mind of the adult. However, the vocabulary of a child is not a very direct index of his cognitive preferences. The child's vocabulary is more immediately determined by the naming practices of adults.

The occasion for a name is ordinarily some particular thing. In the naming it is categorized. The preference among possible names seems to go to the one that is most commonly applied to the referent in question. That name will ordinarily categorize the referent so as to observe the equivalences and differences that figure in its usual utilization. There are not many purposes for which all liquids are equivalent or all fruits, furniture, or parents; and so the names of these categories are less commonly used for denotation than are the names of categories subordinate to them. It is true that words like *article, action, quality* and *relation* are rather common in adult written English, but we can be sure that these frequencies in running discourse are not equaled in naming situations. Whatever the purposes for which all articles are equivalent, or all actions or qualities, they are not among the pressing needs of children.

It is not invariably true that vocabulary builds from concrete to abstract. *Fish* is likely to be learned before *perch* and *bass; house* before *bungalow* and *mansion; car* before *Chevrolet* and *Plymouth* (Smith, 1926). The more concrete vocabulary waits for the child to reach an age where his purposes differentiate kinds of fish and makes of cars. There is much elaborately concrete vocabulary that is not introduced until one takes courses in biology, chemistry, and botany. No one has ever proved that vocabulary builds from the concrete to the abstract more often than it builds from the abstract to the concrete. The best generalization seems to be that each thing is first given its most common name. This name seems to categorize on the level of usual utility. That level sometimes falls on the most concrete categories in a hierarchy (proper names for significant people), and vocabulary then builds toward the more abstract categories (names for ethnic groups, personality types, social classes). Utility sometimes centers on a relatively abstract level of categorization (fish) and vocabulary then builds in both directions (perch and vertebrate). Probably utility never centers on the most abstract levels (thing, substance, etc.), and so probably there is no hierarchy within which vocabulary builds in an exclusively concrete direction.

In the literature describing first-language acquisition (McCarthy, 1946) there is much to indicate that children easily form large abstract categories. There are, to begin with, the numerous cases in which the child overgeneralizes the use of a conventional word. The word *dog* may, at first, be applied to every kind of four-legged animal. It sometimes happens that every man who comes into the house is called *daddy*. When children invent their own words, these often have an enormous semantic range. Wilhelm Stern's (1920) son Günther used *psee* for leaves, trees, and flowers. He used *bebau* for all animals. Lombroso (Werner, 1948) tells of a child who used *qua qua* for both duck and water and *afta* for drinking glass, the contents of a glass, and a pane of glass. Reports of this kind do not suggest that children are deficient in abstracting ability. It even looks as if they may favor large categories.

There are two extreme opinions about the direction of cognitive development. There are those who suppose that we begin by discriminating to the limits of our sensory acuity, seizing each thing in its uniqueness, noting every hair and flea of the particular dog. Cognitive development involves neglect of detail, abstracting from particulars so as to group similars into categories. By this view abstraction is a mature rather than a primitive process. The contrary opinion is that the primitive stage in cognition is one of a comparative lack of differentiation. Probably certain distinctions are inescapable; the difference between a loud noise and near silence, between a bright contour and a dark ground, etc. These inevitable discriminations divide the perceived world into a small number of very large (abstract) categories. Cognitive development is increasing differentiation. The more distinctions we make, the more categories we have and the smaller (more concrete) these are. I think the latter view is favored in psychology today. While there is good empirical and theoretical support (Gibson, *et al.*, 1955; Lashley, *et al.*, 1946; Lewin, 1935) for the view that development is differentiation, there is embarrassment for it in the fact that much vocabulary growth is from the concrete to the abstract. This embarrassment can be eliminated.

Suppose a very young child applies the word *dog* to every four-legged creature he sees. He may have abstracted a limited set of attributes and created a large category, but his abstraction will not show up in his vocabulary. Parents will not provide him with a conventional name for his category, e.g., *quadruped*, but instead will require him to narrow his use of *dog* to its proper range. Suppose a child calls all elderly ladies *aunt*. He will not be told that the usual name for his category is *elderly ladies* but, instead, will be taught to cut back *aunt* to accord with standard usage. In short, the sequence in which words are acquired is set by adults rather than children, and may ultimately be determined by the utility of the various categorizations. This will sometimes result in a movement of vocabulary toward higher abstraction and sometimes a movement toward greater concreteness. The cognitive development of the child may nevertheless always take the direction of increasing differentiation or concreteness.

The child who spontaneously hits on the category four-legged animals will be required to give it up in favor of dogs, cats, horses, cows, and the like. When the names of numerous subordinates have been mastered, he may be given the name *quadruped* for the superordinate. This abstraction is not the same as its primitive forerunner. The schoolboy who learns the word *quadruped* has abstracted from differentiated and named subordinates. The child he was abstracted through a failure to differentiate. Abstraction after differentiation may be the mature process, and abstraction from a failure to differentiate the primitive. Needless to say, the abstractions occurring on the two levels need not be coincident, as they are in our quadruped example.

26 The verbal community

B. F. SKINNER

The "languages" studied by the linguist are the reinforcing practices of verbal communities. When we say that *also* means *in addition* or *besides* "in English," we are not referring to the verbal behavior of any one speaker of English or the average performance of many speakers, but to the conditions under which a response is characteristically reinforced by a verbal community. (The lexical definition simply mentions other responses reinforced under the same circumstances; it does not describe the circumstances.) In studying the practices of the community rather than the behavior of the speaker, the linguist has not been concerned with verbal behavior in the present sense.

A functional analysis of the verbal community is not part of this book, but a few standard problems call for comment. One of them is the old question of the origin of language. Early man was probably not very different from his modern descendants with respect to behavioral processes. If brought into a current verbal community, he would probably develop elaborate verbal behavior. What was lacking was not any special capacity for speech but certain environmental circumstances. The origin of language is the origin of such circumstances. How could a verbal environment have arisen out of non-

Reprinted from the Appendix to **Verbal Behavior** (Copyright © 1957 by Appleton-Century-Crofts, Inc.), New York: Appleton-Century-Crofts, Division of Meredith Publishing Company, 1957, pp. 461–71, with permission of the author and the publisher.

verbal sources? Other classical problems have their parallels. How is a verbal community perpetuated, and why and how does it change? How do new forms of response and new controlling relations evolve, so that a language becomes more complex, more sensitive, more embracing, and more effective?

How the first verbal environment arose will probably always remain a matter for speculation. Theoretically it should be possible to rear a group of human infants in social isolation to discover whether verbal behavior would develop, and if so what it would be like, but there are obvious ethical problems. An experiment appears to have been tried by Frederick the Great in which children were reared in isolation with the object of discovering whether they would naturally speak Hebrew. The experiment failed when all the subjects died. Occasionally, through accidental circumstances, two or more children have grown up in partial isolation from established verbal communities and have developed fairly extensive idiosyncratic verbal systems, but the isolation has never been complete enough to prove that a verbal environment will arise spontaneously in the absence of prior verbal behavior.

Animal cries

A superficial resemblance between verbal behavior and the instinctive signal systems of animals (many of them vocal) has been the source of much confusion. The imitative vocal behavior of parrots, cat-birds, and so on, which duplicates the *forms* of human speech, has added to the confusion. It is true that vocal and other responses of animals constitute "systems of communication." The lost lamb bleats and in so doing "tells its mother where it is." The grazing animal "cries out in alarm" and "warns the rest of the flock of approaching danger." Mating calls bring male and female together. The mother drives predators away from her young with growls or cries of anger. Animal gestures have their place in this system of communication and have recently received special attention from the ethologists (Tinbergen, 1951). The language of bees has been analyzed by Von Frisch (1950).

Such responses appear to be elicited (or "released") by characteristic situations as part of the behavioral equipment of a given species. To say that they are instinctive is merely to say that each form of behavior is observed in most members of a given species, when there has been no opportunity for individual learning. In such cases we must fall back on an evolutionary explanation. Like other activities of the organism, such as digestion, respiration, or reproduction, some behavior with respect to the environment is acquired through natural selection because of its consequences in preserving the species.

There is a parallel between natural selection and operant conditioning. The selection of an instinctive response by its effect in promoting the survival of a species resembles, except for enormous differences in time scales, the selection of a response through reinforcement. The similarity is seen in the apparent purposiveness of both forms. Innate and acquired responses both appear to be emitted "in order to achieve effects"—in order to promote the welfare of the species or the individual. (In both cases it can be shown, of course, that only *prior* instances of such consequences are needed to explain the behavior.) When the instinctive response gains its advantage by affecting the behavior of another organism (when, for example, it is a cry), the parallel with verbal behavior is marked. The mother bird cries out in alarm "in order to" warn her young of approaching danger, as the human mother calls to her child in the street in order to save him from an approaching car. The young bird reacts to its mother's cry "in order to" escape danger, as the child responds to his mother's warning to avoid being hurt. But the interlocking systems in the two cases must be explained in quite different ways. The mother bird cries out not "in order to warn her young" but because the young of earlier members of the species who have cried out have survived to perpetuate the behavior. The young bird does not run for cover upon hearing the cry "in order to escape danger" but because earlier birds who have run under these circumstances have lived to bear their own young, possibly showing the same behavior. The behaviors of the human mother and child, on the other hand, are acquired during their life-times. De Laguna (1927) has ingeniously traced parallels between the two systems, identifying the circumstances under which a cry (or other vocal or nonvocal response) may be classed as a command, a proclamation, a declaration, and so on. As in the present analysis, the distinctions depend upon the situations of "speaker" and "listener" and upon the consequences for both. But the analogy remains an analogy.

It is unlikely, moreover, that verbal behavior in the present sense arose from instinctive cries. Well-defined emotional and other innate responses comprise reflex systems which are difficult, if not impossible, to modify by operant reinforcement. Vocal behavior below the human level is especially refractory. Although it is easy to condition a cat to assume various postures, move its limbs, and manipulate features of the environment through operant reinforcement, it appears to be impossible to get it to miaow or to purr exclusively through the same process. Apparent exceptions prove upon examination to be samples of a different process. The cat at the door, miaowing "to be let out," may actually be miaowing because it is *not* being let out. The miaow is an emotional response in a frustrating situation. It occurs at approximately the same time and with the same frequency as such an operant as scratching the door, but the two forms of behavior are under different forms of environmental control. Such refractory material does not seem propitious as a precursor of verbal behavior in the present sense. Whether innate *nonverbal* responses can be conditioned in the operant pattern is difficult to say, because the same musculature can be brought under operant control. The experimenter may succeed merely in producing an operant which imitates the innate response. (Since innate responses are commonly associated with emotional situations, the parallel with verbal behavior has been most compelling in explaining emotional "expression." Indeed, the doctrine of expression is sometimes reserved for verbal or nonverbal behavior under the control of emotional variables. Expressive theories of the origin of language build on this pattern.)

This is not to say that lower organisms are incapable of verbal behavior in the present sense. With sufficient exposure to relevant variables vocal verbal behavior could conceivably be set up. But the verbal behavior acquired by the individual under the reinforcing practices of a verbal community does not appear to be a modification of vocalizations acquired by the species because of specific consequences having survival value. The relatively undifferentiated babbling of the human infant from which vocal verbal behavior develops is undoubtedly an evolutionary product, but it is not the sort of behavior which is evoked (or "released") in specific forms on specific occasions. The same may be said of nonverbal behavior. In general, operant behavior emerges from undifferentiated, previously unorganized, and undirected movements.

We can account for the origin of a verbal response in the form of a mand [1] if any behavior associated with a state of deprivation is an important stimulus for a "listener" who is disposed to reinforce the "speaker" with respect to that state of deprivation. Consider, for example, a nursing mother and her baby. It is possible that there is an innate response of the human female to innate cries of the hungry human infant, similar to the systems of communication in other species, but we do not need to assume that this is the case. If a hungry infant behaves in some distinctive fashion—let us say, by crying or squirming in response to painful stimulation of the stomach—and if a mother is inclined to nurse her child, perhaps to escape from the aversive stimulation of a full breast, then the baby's cry (correlated, as it is, with a tendency to suck) will eventually control the mother's behavior of putting the baby to her breast. Once the mother has acquired this discrimination, her behavior of nursing her baby is contingent upon the baby's cry, and this may be reinforcing. Where the baby first cried as a reflex response to painful stimulation, it may now cry as an operant. It is probably not the reflex response which is reinforced but behavior resembling it. The form of the response is free to undergo a change provided the mother maintains the reinforcement. Eventually the response may not closely resemble the reflex pattern.

Such a response is reinforced with food, and its strength is a function of deprivation. The controlling relation which survives is characteristic of a full-fledged mand. Since we assumed a predisposition on the part of the mother to reinforce, it is the species of mand called a request. But eventually the mother may no longer be predisposed to reinforce with food, and the baby must compensate by creating an aversive condition from which the mother can escape only by supplying appropriate reinforcement. The baby's cry becomes "annoying," and the mother reinforces because the baby then stops crying. The response is no longer a request but a command.

A nonverbal environment may produce another kind of mand concerned with the "attention of the listener." Let us say that *A* is pouring drinks for a group, but has overlooked *B*. Any conspicuous movement by *B*, particularly if this produces a noise, will get the attention of *A* who may then reinforce *B* with a drink. Once this has happened, the behavior becomes verbal, similar to explicit mands of the form *Look here!* Verbal communities commonly rein-

[1] "A 'mand,' then, may be defined as a verbal operant in which the response is reinforced by a characteristic consequence and is therefore under the functional control of relevant conditions of deprivation or aversive stimulation. Adjectival and verbal uses of the term are self-explanatory. In particular, and in contrast with other types of verbal operants to be discussed later, the response has no specified relation to a prior stimulus" (Skinner, 1957).—Eds.

force mands which cannot have departed very far from the original nonverbal forms. Knocking at the door of a house is a conventional verbal response, which is easily traced to nonverbal origins, for it must have been originally close to the behavior of a dog scratching at the door "to be let in." It acquires a special style (the number, speed, and intensity of the knocks approach a standard) under appropriate reinforcement by the verbal environment. Rapping on an empty glass or table at a restaurant is comparable, as is the vocal *Har-rumph!*

Any behavior which has an effect upon another person as a mechanical object (pulling, pushing, striking, blocking, and so on) may acquire a behavioral effect if incipient stages of the behavior serve as stimuli. The contingent reinforcement is usually avoidance of, or escape from, the later stages of the behavior. For example, A stops the approach of B by holding out his arm and placing the palm of his hand against B's chest. At this stage the behavior of A would be roughly the same if B were an inanimate object (if B were swinging toward A, for example, at the end of a long rope). But if being stopped by A is aversive to B, or if A stops B only when likely to treat B aversively, B eventually responds to A's outstretched arm to avoid actual contact. When this change has occurred in B, A's response is reinforced not by its mechanical effect on B but by B's behavior. It becomes a "gesture" and is classified as verbal. Every listener and speaker need not pass through similar changes, for the gesture is eventually set up by the community. The traffic policeman's gestured "stop" is as culturally determined as a red light or the vocal response *Stop!*

Such gestures may gain current strength from similar nonverbal contingencies. The "speaker" may be readier to respond in a given way and achieve a more consistent effect upon the listener because of related mechanical effects. Even the railroad semaphore in its "stop" position probably borrows strength from the resemblance to an actual barring of the way. Familiar gestures having roughly the same effects as *Go away!*, *Come here!* (gestured with either the whole arm or the index finger), *Pass by!*, *Sit down!* (as to an audience), and *Stand up!* are subject to similar interpretations. These are all mands which specify behavior resembling the mechanical effect of the nonverbal responses from which they are derived. (Putting a finger on one's *own* lips shows something like the metaphorical extension of putting a finger on the lips of someone else. The latter may occur if the parties are close together.)

If, for purely physical reasons, A cups his hand behind his ear in order to hear B more clearly this becomes for B a stimulus in the presence of which louder behavior (vocal or nonvocal) is differentially reinforced. If B increases the intensity *because A cups his hand*, cupping the hand becomes a "gesture" and may be classed as verbal.

If B can avoid punishment at the hands of A by engaging in a particular form of activity, A may shape B's behavior by delivering or withholding aversive stimulation. For example, if A drives B away from a supply of food by beating him, A's raised fist eventually causes B to withdraw in order to *avoid* blows rather than to wait to *escape* from them. When this has happened, A may *gesture* rather than strike. If A sometimes allows B to eat, B eventually responds to A's fist as a stimulus upon which punishment for approach is contingent. A may eventually use a raised fist for finer shaping of behavior. For example, B may be kept active if A responds as soon as B stops. The contingencies are the same as in keeping a horse moving by *cracking* a whip. In addition to starting and stopping, B's behavior may also be *guided* in direction or intensity level.

If B is predisposed to reinforce A, A may shape B's behavior with any reaction indicating its reinforcing effect upon him. For example, conspicuous ingestive behavior on the part of A may reinforce B for cooking or serving a special kind of food. A's behavior in licking his chops may become a gesture equivalent to *Give me some more of that* as his vocal *m-m* may become the equivalent of the *Yum-yum* shaped by a particular verbal community. The unconditioned behavior of an audience which has been reinforced by an entertainer reinforces the entertainer in turn. Part of the reinforcing effect is the contrast between the intense quiet of the enthralled audience and the noisy release as the entertainer stops. If the audience can induce the entertainer to continue by heightening this contrast, the noise may become a gesture. Clapping, stamping, whistling, and other forms of applause are verbal responses equivalent to *Again!*, *Encore!*, or *Bis!* Eventually such a response may be used to shape up the behavior of a speaker —as in parliamentary debate.

Most of the mands we can account for without assuming a prior verbal environment are gestures. Paget (1930) has tried to derive vocal parallels by pointing to the fact that movements of the tongue are likely to accompany movements of the hand. A child, engrossed in some manual skill, may be observed to chew his tongue or move it about his lips. Paget has suggested that movements of the tongue accompanying manual gestures could modify breathing sounds or primitive vocalizations to supply vocal responses. But even such a process makes little progress in accounting for the diversity of vocal responses which specify kinds of reinforcement.

In explaining verbal behavior in the form of the tact,[2] we must look for different sources of nonverbal materials for the behavior of the "speaker" must be related to *stimulating circumstances* rather than to aversive stimulation or deprivation.

The behavior of a hunting dog may be said to "signal" the presence of game to the human hunter, as the barking of a watch dog "signals" the approach of an intruder. In so far as these are relatively invariable and unconditioned, the hunter and the householder respond to them as to any stimulus associated with a given event—say, the noise produced by the game or the intruder. It is only when the dog is trained as a "speaker" that new phenomena arise. As soon as the hunting dog is *reinforced* for pointing, or the watch dog for barking, the topography of the behavior may come to depend upon the contingencies of reinforcement rather than upon unconditioned reflex systems. In these examples the behavior is never greatly changed, but in others the form is eventually determined by

[2] "A tact may be defined as a verbal operant in which a response of given form is evoked (or at least strengthened) by a particular object or event or property of an object or event. We account for the strength by showing that in the presence of the object or event a response of that form is characteristically reinforced in a given verbal community" (Skinner, 1957).—Eds.

the community—that is, it becomes conventional. It has often been pointed out that the frequency of initial *m's* in words for *mother* may have some relation to the frequency of that sound as an unconditioned response in situations in which mothers frequently figure, where the rest of each word is presumably shaped by the particular community. The shortage of unconditioned vocal responses appropriate to specific situations is an obvious limitation in explaining an extensive repertoire in this way.

Another common explanation appeals to onomatopoeia. The old "bow-wow" theory of the origin of language emphasized formal similarities between stimulus and response which survive in onomatopoetic or "model-building" repertoires. We can "warn someone of the approach of a dog" by imitating its bark, as the tourist draws a picture of the article he wants to buy but cannot name, or as the Indian guide announces good fishing by moving his hand sinuously. The vocal, pictorial, or gestured response is effective because it is physically similar to "the situation described." But the "use of such signs" by either "speaker" or "listener" is not thereby accounted for. If we assume, however, that certain listeners-to-be run away when they hear a dog bark and that this is reinforcing to certain speakers-to-be, we have only to wait—a few thousand years if necessary—for someone to emit a vocal response similar enough to the bark of a dog to be reinforced by its effect on a listener. The result is at best an impure tact, scarcely to be distinguished from a mand. All onomatopoetic responses suffer from the fact that their distinguishing formal properties affect the listener in a way which is closely tied to a particular situation. But listeners may react to dogs in many ways and for many reasons, and some sort of generalized reinforcement could conceivably follow.

The origins of most forms of response will probably always remain obscure, but if we can explain the beginnings of even the most rudimentary verbal environment, the well-established processes of linguistic change will explain the multiplication of verbal forms and the creation of new controlling relationships. Fortunately changes in reinforcing contingencies can be traced historically and observed in current communities. On the side of form of response, we do not need to suppose that changes follow any particular pattern (such as that of Grimm's Law); indeed, to explain the creation of large numbers of forms, the more accidental changes there are the better. On the side of "meaning" modern historical linguistics has identified many sources of variation. Some are concerned with accidents or faults in transmission. Others arise from the structure of the verbal community. New controlling relations arise when a literal response is taken metaphorically or when a metaphorical response through subsequent restricted reinforcement becomes abstract. As an example of the latter process, if we assume that the standard response *orange* has been brought under the stimulus control of oranges, then we can imagine a first occasion upon which some other object of the same color evokes the response. If it is effective upon the listener, as it may be without special conditioning, it may be reinforced with respect to color alone. If this is sufficiently useful to the community, the relatively abstract color-term *orange* emerges.

More subtle abstractions seem to

emerge in the same way. The *fall* of a coin or die leads at last to the concept of *chance* when the defining properties are free of instances in which something falls. The method of John Horne Tooke is relevant here. A *Sequel to the Diversions of Purley* by John Barcley (London, 1826) examines the origins of terms concerning spirit and mind in an early anticipation of twentieth-century behaviorism, tracing them back etymologically to more robust concepts in human behavior.

It has often been pointed out, particularly in explaining the origin of myths, that this process works in reverse—that a metaphorical response may be taken literally. The metaphorical report that a man became *beastly* when drunk gives rise to the story of a man transformed into an animal upon drinking a magic potion. In the elaboration of such stories, new variables gain control of old responses.

The study of the verbal behavior of speaker and listener, as well as of the practices of the verbal environment which generates such behavior, may not contribute directly to historical or descriptive linguistics, but it is enough for our present purposes to be able to say that a verbal environment could have arisen from nonverbal sources and, in its transmission from generation to generation, would have been subject to influences which might account for the multiplication of forms and controlling relations and the increasing effectiveness of verbal behavior as a whole.

27 The psycholinguists: on the new scientists of language

GEORGE A. MILLER

Psychologists have long recognised that human minds feed on linguistic symbols. Linguists have always admitted that some kind of psycho-social motor must move the machinery of grammar and lexicon. Sooner or later they were certain to examine their intersection self-consciously. Perhaps it was also inevitable that the result would be called "psycholinguistics."

In fact, although the enterprise itself has slowly been gathering strength at least since the invention of the telephone, the name, in its unhyphenated form, is only about ten years old. Few seem pleased with the term, but the field has grown so rapidly and stirred so much interest in recent years that some way of referring to it is urgently needed. *Psycholinguistics* is as descriptive a term as any, and shorter than most.

Among psychologists it was principally the behaviourists who wished to take a closer look at language. Behaviourists generally try to replace anything subjective by its most tangible, physical manifestation, so they have had a long tradition of confusing thought with speech—or with "verbal behaviour," as many prefer to call it. Among linguists it was principally those with an anthropological sideline who were most willing to collaborate, perhaps because as anthropologists they were sensitive to all those social and psychological processes that support our linguistic practices. By working together they managed to call attention to an important field of scientific research and to integrate it, or at least to acquaint its various parts with one another, under this new rubric.[1]

The integration of psycholinguistic studies has occurred so recently that there is still some confusion concerning its scope and purpose; efforts to clarify it necessarily have something of the character of personal opinion.[2] In my own version, the central task of this new science is to describe the psychological processes that go on when people use sentences. The real crux of the psycholinguistic problem does not appear until one tries to deal with sentences, for only then does the importance of productivity become completely obvious. It is true that productivity can also appear with individual words, but there it is not overwhelming. With sentences, productivity is literally unlimited.

Before considering this somewhat technical problem, however, it might be

[1] A representative sample of research papers in this field can be found in **Psycholinguistics, a Book of Readings,** edited by S. Saporta (1962). R. Brown provides a readable survey from a psychologist's point of view in **Words and Things** (1957).

[2] My own opinions have been strongly influenced by Noam Chomsky. A rather technical exposition of this work can be found in Chapters 11–13 of the second volume of the **Handbook of Mathematical Psychology,** edited by R. D. Luce, R. R. Bush, and E. Galanter (1963), from which many of the ideas discussed here have been drawn.

Abridged from **Encounter,** 1964, 23, No. 1, 29–37, with permission of the author and the publisher.

well to illustrate the variety of processes that psycholinguists hope to explain. This can best be done if we ask what a listener can do about a spoken utterance, and consider his alternatives in order from the superficial to the inscrutable.

The simplest thing one can do in the presence of a spoken utterance is to listen. Even if the language is incomprehensible, one can still *hear* an utterance as an auditory stimulus and respond to it in terms of some discriminative set: how loud, how fast, how long, from which direction, etc.

Given that an utterance is heard, the next level involves *matching* it as a phonemic pattern in terms of phonological skills acquired as a user of the language. The ability to match an input can be tested in psychological experiments by asking listeners to echo what they hear; a wide variety of experimental situations —experiments on the perception of speech and on the rote memorisation of verbal materials—can be summarised as tests of a person's ability to repeat the speech he hears under various conditions of audibility or delay.

If a listener can hear and match an utterance, the next question to ask is whether he will *accept* it as a sentence in terms of his knowledge of grammar. At this level we encounter processes difficult to study experimentally, and one is forced to rely most heavily on linguistic analyses of the structure of sentences. Some experiments are possible, however, for we can measure how much a listener's ability to accept the utterance as a sentence facilitates his ability to hear and match it; grammatical sentences are much easier to hear, utter or remember than are ungrammatical strings of words, and even nonsense (*pirot, karol, elat,* etc.) is easier to deal with if it looks grammatical (*pirots karolise elatically,* etc.) (Epstein, 1961). Needless to say, the grammatical knowledge we wish to study does not concern those explicit rules drilled into us by teachers of traditional grammar, but rather the implicit generative knowledge that we all must acquire in order to use a language appropriately.

Beyond grammatical acceptance comes semantic interpretation: we can ask how listeners *interpret* an utterance as meaningful in terms of their semantic system. Interpretation is not merely a matter of assigning meanings to individual words; we must also consider how these component meanings combine in grammatical sentences. Compare the sentences: *Healthy young babies sleep soundly* and *Colourless green ideas sleep furiously.* Although they are syntactically similar, the second is far harder to perceive and remember correctly—because it cannot be interpreted by the usual semantic rules for combining the senses of adjacent English words (Miller & Isard, 1963; see also Katz & Fodor, 1963). The interpretation of each word is affected by the company it keeps; a central problem is to systematise the interactions of words and phrases with their linguistic contexts. The lexicographer makes his major contribution at this point, but psychological studies of our ability to paraphrase an utterance also have their place.

At the next level it seems essential to make some distinction between interpreting an utterance and understanding it, for understanding frequently goes well beyond the linguistic context provided by the utterance itself. A husband greeted at the door by "I bought some electric light bulbs to-day" must do more than interpret its literal reference; he must understand that he should go to the kitchen and replace that burned-out lamp. Such contextual information lies well outside any grammar or lexicon. The listener can *understand* the function of an utterance in terms of contextual knowledge of the most diverse sort.

Finally, at a level now almost invisible through the clouds, a listener may *believe* that an utterance is valid in terms of its relevance to his own conduct. The child who says "I saw five lions in the garden" may be heard, matched, accepted, interpreted, and understood, but in few parts of the world will he be believed.

The boundaries between successive levels are not sharp and distinct. One shades off gradually into the next. Still the hierarchy is real enough and important to keep in mind. Simpler types of psycholinguistic processes can be studied rather intensively; already we know much about hearing and matching. Accepting and interpreting are just now coming into scientific focus. Understanding is still over the horizon, and pragmatic questions involving belief systems are presently so vague as to be hardly worth asking. But the whole range of processes must be included in any adequate definition of psycholinguistics.

I phrased the description of these various psycholinguistic processes in terms of a listener; the question inevitably arises as to whether a different hierarchy is required to describe the speaker. One problem a psycholinguist faces is to decide whether speaking and listening are two separate abilities, coordinate but distinct, or whether they are merely different manifestations of a single linguistic faculty.

The mouth and ear are different organs; at the simplest levels we must distinguish hearing and matching from vocalising and speaking. At more complex levels it is less easy to decide whether the two abilities are distinct. At some point they must converge, if only to explain why it is so difficult to speak and listen simultaneously. The question is where.

It is easy to demonstrate how important to a speaker is the sound of his own voice. If his speech is delayed a fifth of a second, amplified, and fed back into his own ears, the voice-ear asynchrony can be devastating to the motor skills of articulate speech. It is more difficult, however, to demonstrate that the same linguistic competence required for speaking is also involved in processing the speech of others.

Recently Morris Halle and Kenneth Stevens (1962) of the Massachusetts Institute of Technology revived a suggestion made by Wilhelm von Humboldt over a century ago. Suppose we accept the notion that a listener recognises what he hears by comparing it with some internal representation. To the extent that a match can be obtained, the input is accepted and interpreted. One trouble with this hypothesis, however, is that a listener must be ready to recognise any one of an enormous number of different sentences. It is inconceivable that a separate internal representation for each of them could be stored in his memory in advance. Halle and Stevens suggest that these internal representations must be generated as they are needed by following the same generative rules that are normally used in producing speech. In this way the rules of the language are incorporated into the theory only once, in a generative form; they need not be learned once by the ear and again by the tongue. This is a theory of a language-user, not of a speaker or a listener alone.

The listener begins with a guess about the input. On that basis he generates an internal matching signal. The first attempt will probably be in error; if so, the mismatch is reported and used as a basis for a next guess, which should be closer. This cycle repeats (unconsciously, almost certainly) until a satisfactory (not necessarily a correct) match is obtained, at which point the next segment of speech is scanned and matched, etc. The output is not a transformed version of the input; it is the programme that was followed to generate the matching representation.

The perceptual categories available to such a system are defined by the generative rules at its disposal. It is also reasonably obvious that its efficiency is critically dependent on the quality of the initial guess. If this guess is close, an iterative process can converge rapidly; if not, the listener will be unable to keep pace with the rapid flow of conversational speech.

A listener's first guess probably derives in part from syntactic markers in the form of intonation, inflection, suffixes, etc., and in part from his general knowledge of the semantic and situational context. Syntactic cues indicate how the input is to be grouped and which words function together; semantic and contextual contributions are more difficult to characterise, but must somehow enable him to limit the range of possible words that he can expect to hear.

How he is able to do this is an utter mystery, but the fact that he can do it is easily demonstrated.

The English psychologist David Bruce (1956) recorded a set of ordinary sentences and played them in the presence of noise so intense that the voice was just audible, but not intelligible. He told his listeners that these were sentences on some general topic—sports, say—and asked them to repeat what they heard. He then told them they would hear more sentences on a different topic, which they were also to repeat. This was done several times. Each time the listeners repeated sentences appropriate to the topic announced in advance. When at the end of the experiment Bruce told them they had heard the same recording every time—all he had changed was the topic they were given—most listeners were unable to believe it.

With an advance hypothesis about what the message will be we can tune our perceptual system to favour certain interpretations and reject others. This fact is no proof of a generative process in speech perception, but it does emphasise the important role of context. For most theories of speech perception the facilitation provided by context is merely a fortunate though rather complicated fact. For a generative theory it is essential.

Note that generative theories do not assume that a listener must be able to articulate the sounds he recognises, but merely that he be able to generate some internal representation to match the input. In this respect a generative theory differs from a motor theory (such as that of Sir Richard Paget) which assumes that we can identify only those utterances we are capable of producing ourselves. There is some rather compelling evidence against a motor theory. The American psychologist Eric Lenneberg (1962) has described the case of an eight-year-old boy with congenital anarthria; despite his complete inability to speak, the boy acquired an excellent ability to understand language. Moreover, it is a common observation that utterances can be understood by young children before they are able to produce them. A motor theory of speech-perception draws too close a parallel between our two capacities as users of language. Even so, the two are more closely integrated than most people realise.

I have already offered the opinion that productivity sets the central problem for the psycholinguist and have even referred to it indirectly by arguing that we can produce too many different sentences to store them all in memory. The issue can be postponed no longer.

To make the problem plain, consider an example on the level of individual words. For several days I carried in my pocket a small white card on which was typed UNDERSTANDER. On suitable occasions I would hand it to someone. "How do you pronounce this?" I asked.

He pronounced it.

"Is it an English word?"

He hesitated. "I haven't seen it used very much. I'm not sure."

"Do you know what it means?"

"I suppose it means 'one who understands.' "

I thanked him and changed the subject.

Of course, understander *is* an English word, but to find it you must look in a large dictionary where you will probably read that it is "now rare." Rare enough, I think, for none of my respondents to have seen it before. Nevertheless, they all answered in the same way. Nobody seemed surprised. Nobody wondered how he could understand and pronounce a word without knowing whether it was a word. Everybody put the main stress on the third syllable and constructed a meaning from the verb "to understand" and the agentive suffix "*er.*" Familiar morphological rules of English were applied as a matter of course, even though the combination was completely novel.

Probably no one but a psycholinguist captured by the ingenuous behaviouristic theory that words are vocal responses conditioned to occur in the presence of appropriate stimuli would find anything exceptional in this. Since none of my friends had seen the word before, and so could not have been "conditioned" to give the responses they did, how would this theory account for their "verbal behaviour"? Advocates of a conditioning theory of meaning—and there are several distinguished scientists among them—would probably explain linguistic productivity in terms of "conditioned generalisations." [3] They could argue that my respondents had been conditioned to the word understand and to the suffix—*er*; responses to their union could conceivably be counted as instances of stimulus generalisation. In this way, novel responses could occur without special training.

Although a surprising amount of psychological ingenuity has been invested in this kind of argument, it is difficult to estimate its value. No one has carried the theory through for all the related combinations that must be explained simultaneously. One can speculate, however, that there would have to be many different kinds of generalisation, each with a carefully defined range of applicability. For example, it would be necessary to explain why ""understander" is acceptable, whereas "erunderstand" is not. Worked out in detail, such a theory would become a sort of Pavlovian paraphrase of a linguistic description. Of course, if one believes there is some essential difference between behaviour governed by conditioned habits and

[3] A dog conditioned to salivate at the sound of a tone will also salivate, though less copiously, at the sound of similar tones, the magnitude declining as the new tones become less similar to the original. This phenomenon is called "stimulus generalisation."

behaviour governed by rules, the paraphrase could never be more than a vast intellectual pun.

Original combinations of elements are the life blood of language. It is our ability to produce and comprehend such novelties that makes language so ubiquitously useful. As psychologists have become more seriously interested in the cognitive processes that language entails, they have been forced to recognise that the fundamental puzzle is not our ability to associate vocal noises with perceptual objects, but rather our combinatorial productivity—our ability to understand an unlimited diversity of utterances never heard before and to produce an equal variety of utterances similarly intelligible to other members of our speech community. Faced with this problem, concepts borrowed from conditioning theory seem not so much invalid as totally inadequate.

Some idea of the relative magnitudes of what we might call the productive as opposed to the reproductive components of any psycholinguistic theory is provided by statistical studies of language. A few numbers can reinforce the point. If you interrupt a speaker at some randomly chosen instant, there will be, on the average, about ten words that form grammatical and meaningful continuations. Often only one word is admissible and sometimes there are thousands, but on the average it works out to about ten. (If you think this estimate too low, I will not object; larger estimates strengthen the argument.) A simple English sentence can easily run to a length of twenty words, so elementary arithmetic tells us that there must be at least 10^{20} such sentences that a person who knows English must know how to deal with. Compare this productive potential with the 10^4 or 10^5 individual words we know—the reproductive component of our theory—and the discrepancy is dramatically illustrated. Putting it differently, it would take 100,000,000,000 centuries (one thousand times the estimated age of the earth) to utter all the admissible twenty-word sentences of English. Thus, the probability that you might have heard any particular twenty-word sentence before is negligible. Unless it is a cliché, every sentence must come to you as a novel combination of morphemes. Yet you can interpret it at once if you know the English language.

With these facts in mind it is impossible to argue that we learn to understand sentences from teachers who have pronounced each one and explained what it meant. What we have learned are not particular strings of words, but *rules* for generating admissible strings of words.

Consider what it means to follow a rule; this consideration shifts the discussion of psycholinguistics into very difficult territory. The nature of rules has been a central concern of modern philosophy and perhaps no analysis has been more influential than Ludwig Wittgenstein's. Wittgenstein remarked that the most characteristic thing we can say about "rule-governed behaviour" is that the person who knows the rules knows whether he is proceeding correctly or incorrectly. Although he may not be able to formulate the rules explicitly, he knows what it is to make a mistake. If this remark is accepted, we must ask ourselves whether an animal that has been conditioned is privy to any such knowledge about the correctness of what he is doing. Perhaps such a degree of insight could be achieved by the great apes, but surely not by all the various species that can acquire conditioned reflexes. On this basis alone it would seem necessary to preserve a distinction between conditioning and learning rules.

As psychologists have learned to appreciate the complexities of language, the prospect of reducing it to the laws of behaviour so carefully studied in lower animals has grown increasingly remote. We have been forced more and more into a position that non-psychologists probably take for granted, namely, that language is rule-governed behaviour characterised by enormous flexibility and freedom of choice.

The first thing we notice when we survey the languages of the world is how few we can understand and how diverse they all seem. Not until one looks for some time does an even more significant observation emerge concerning the pervasive similarities in the midst of all this diversity.

Every human group that anthropologists have studied has spoken a language. The language always has a lexicon and a grammar. The lexicon is not a haphazard collection of vocalisations, but is highly organised; it always has pronouns, means for dealing with time, space, and number, words to represent true and false, the basic concepts necessary for propositional logic. The grammar has distinguishable levels of structure, some phonological, some syntactic. The phonology always contains both vowels and consonants, and the phonemes can always be described in terms of distinctive features drawn from a limited set of possibilities. The syntax always specifies rules for grouping elements sequentially into phrases and sentences, rules governing normal intonation, rules for transforming some types of sentences into other types.

The nature and importance of these common properties, called "linguistic universals," are only beginning to emerge as our knowledge of the world's languages grows more systematic (Greenberg, 1963). These universals appear even in languages that developed with a minimum of interaction. One is forced to assume, therefore, either that (*a*) no other kind of linguistic practices are conceivable, or that (*b*) something in the biological makeup of human beings favours languages having these similarities. Only a moment's reflection is needed to reject (*a*). When one considers the variety of artificial languages developed in mathematics, in the communication sciences, in the use of computers, in symbolic logic, and elsewhere, it soon becomes apparent that the universal features of natural languages are not the only ones possible. Natural languages are, in fact, rather special and often seem unnecessarily complicated.

A popular belief regards human language as a more or less free creation of the human intellect, as if its elements were chosen arbitrarily and could be combined into meaningful utterances by any rules that strike our collective fancy. The assumption is implicit, for example, in Wittgenstein's well-known conception of "the language game." This metaphor, which casts valuable light on many aspects of language, can, if followed blindly, lead one to think that all linguistic rules are just as arbitrary as, say, the rules of chess or football. As Lenneberg (1960) has pointed out, however, it makes a great deal of sense to inquire into the biological basis for language, but very little to ask about the biological foundations of card games.

Man is the only animal to have a combinatorially productive language. In the jargon of biology, language is "a species-specific form of behaviour." Other animals have signalling systems of various kinds and for various purposes—but only man has evolved this particular and highly improbable form of communication. Those who think of language as a free and spontaneous intellectual invention are also likely to believe that any animal with a brain sufficiently large to support a high level of intelligence can acquire a language. This assumption is demonstrably false. The human brain is not just an ape brain enlarged; its extra size is less important than its different structure. Moreover, Lenneberg (1962) has pointed out that nanocephalic dwarfs, with brains half the normal size but grown on the human blueprint, can use language reasonably well, and even mongoloids, not intelligent enough to perform the simplest functions for themselves, can acquire the rudiments. Talking and understanding language do not depend on being intelligent or having a large brain. They depend on "being human."

Serious attempts have been made to teach animals to speak. If words were conditioned responses, animals as intelligent as chimpanzees or porpoises should be able to learn them. These attempts have uniformly failed in the past and, if the argument here is correct, they will always fail in the future—for just the same reason that attempts to teach fish to walk or dogs to fly would fail. Such efforts misconstrue the basis for our linguistic competence: they fly in the face of biological facts.

Human language must be such that a child can acquire it. He acquires it, moreover, from parents who have no idea how to explain it to him. No careful schedule of rewards for correct or punishments for incorrect utterances is necessary. It is sufficient that the child be allowed to grow up naturally in an environment where language is used.

The child's achievement seems all the more remarkable when we recall the speed with which he accomplishes it and the limitations of his intelligence in other respects. It is difficult to avoid an impression that infants are little machines specially designed by nature to perform this particular learning task.

I believe this analogy with machines is worth pursuing. If we could imagine what a language-learning automaton would have to do, it would dramatise—and perhaps even clarify—what a child can do. The linguist and logician Noam Chomsky (1962) has argued that the description of such an automaton would comprise our hypothesis about the child's innate ability to learn languages or (to borrow a term from Ferdinand de Saussure) his innate *faculté de langage*.

Consider what information a language-learning automaton would be given to work with. Inputs to the machine would include a finite set of sentences, a finite set of non-sentences accompanied by some signal that they were incorrect, some way to indicate that one item is a repetition or elaboration or transformation of another, and some access to a universe of perceptual objects and events associated with the sentences. Inside the machine there would be a computer so programmed as to extract from these inputs the nature of the language, i.e., the particular syntactic rules by which sentences are generated, and the rules that associate with each syntactic structure a particular phonetic representation and semantic interpretation. The important question, of course, is what programme of instructions would have to be given to the computer.

We could instruct the computer to discover any imaginable set of rules that might, in some formal sense of the term, constitute a grammar. This approach—the natural one if we believe that human languages can be infinitely diverse and various—is doomed from the start. The computer would have to evaluate an infinitude of possible grammars; with only a finite corpus of evidence it would be impossible, even if sufficient time were available for computation, to arrive at any unique solution.

A language-learning automaton could not possibly discover a suitable grammar unless some strong *a priori* assumptions were built into it from the start. These assumptions would limit the alternatives that the automaton considered—limit them presumably to the range defined by linguistic universals. The automaton would test various grammars of the appropriate form to see if they would generate all of the sentences and none of the non-sentences. Certain aspects would be tested before others; those found acceptable would be preserved for further evaluation. If we wished the automaton to replicate a child's performance, the order in which these aspects would be evaluated could only be decided after careful analysis of the successive stages of language acquisition in human children.

The actual construction of such an automaton is, of course, far beyond our reach at the present time. That is not the point. The lesson to learn from such speculations is that the whole project would be impossible unless the automaton—and so, presumably, a child—knew in advance to look for particular kinds of regularities and correspondences, to discover rules of a rather special kind uniquely characteristic of human language in general.

The features that human infants are prepared to notice sharply limit the structure of any human language. Even if one imagines creating by decree a Newspeak in which this generalisation were false, within one generation it would have become true again.

Psycholinguistics does not deal with social practices determined arbitrarily either by caprice or intelligent design, but with practices that grow organically out of the biological nature of man and the linguistic capacities of human infants. To that extent, at least, it is possible to define an area of empirical fact well within the reach of our scientific methods.

Another line of scientific investigation is opened up by the observation that we do not always follow our own rules. If this were not so, of course, we would not speak of rules, but of the laws of language. The fact that we make mistakes, and that we can know we made mistakes, is central to the psycholinguistic problem. Before we can see the empirical issue this entails, however, we should first draw a crucial distinction between theories of language and theories of the users of language.

There is nothing in the linguistic description of a language to indicate what mistakes will occur. Mistakes result from the psychological limitations of people who use the language, not from the language itself. It would be meaningless to state rules for making mistakes.

A formal characterisation of a natural language in terms of a set of elements and rules for combining those elements must inevitably generate an infinitude of possible sentences that will never occur in actual use. Most of these sentences are too complicated for us. There is nothing mysterious about this. It is very similar to the situation in arithmetic where a student may understand perfectly the rules for multiplication, yet find that some multiplication problems are too difficult for him to do "in his head," i.e., without extending his memory capacity by the use of pencil and paper.

There is no longest grammatical sentence. There is no limit to the number of different grammatical sentences. Moreover, since the number of elements and rules is finite, there must be some rules and elements that can recur any number of times in a grammatical sentence. Chomsky has even managed to pinpoint a kind of recursive operation in language that, in principle, lies beyond the power of any finite device to perform indefinitely often. Compare these sentences:

(*R*) *Remarkable is the rapidity of the motion of the wing of the hummingbird.*
(*L*) *The hummingbird's wing's motion's rapidity is remarkable.*
(*E*) *The rapidity that the motion that the wing that the hummingbird has has has is remarkable.*

When you parse these sentences you find that the phrase structure of (*R*) dangles off to the right; each prepositional phrase hangs to the noun in the prepositional phrase preceding it. In (*R*), therefore, we see a type of recurring construction that has been called right-branching. Sentence (*L*), on the other hand, is left-branching; each possessive modifies the possessive immediately following. Finally, (*E*) is an onion; it grows by embedding sentences within sentences. Inside "The rapidity is remarkable" we first insert "the motion is rapid" by a syntactic transformation that permits us to construct relative clauses, and so we obtain "The rapidity that the motion has is remarkable." Then we repeat the transformation, this time inserting "the wing has motion" to obtain "The rapidity that the motion that the wing has has is remarkable." Repeating the transformation once more gives (*E*).

It is intuitively obvious that, of these three types of recursive operations, self-embedding (*E*) is psychologically the most difficult. Although they seem grammatical by any reasonable standard of grammar, such sentences never occur in ordinary usage because they exceed our cognitive capacities. Chomsky's achievement was to prove rigorously that any language that does *not* restrict this kind of recursive embedding contains sentences that cannot be spoken or understood by devices, human or mechanical, with finite memories. Any device that uses these rules must remember each left portion until it can be related to its corresponding right portion; if the memory of the user is limited, but the number of admissible left portions is not, it is inevitable that some admissible sentences will exceed the capacity of the user to process them correctly (Chomsky, 1957).

It is necessary, therefore, to distinguish between a description of the language in terms of the rules that a person *knows* and uses and a description of that person's *performance* as a user of the rules. The distinction is sometimes criticised as "psycholatry" by strict adherents of behaviourism; "knowing" is considered too mentalistic and subjective, therefore unscientific. The objection cannot be taken seriously. Our conception of the rules that a language-user knows is indeed a hypothetical construct, not something observed directly in his behaviour. But if such hypotheses were to be forbidden, science in general would become an empty pursuit.

Given a reasonable hypothesis about the rules that a language-user knows, the exploration of his limitations in following those rules is proper work for an experimental psychologist. "Psychology should assist us," a great linguist once said, "in understanding what is going on in the mind of speakers, and more particularly how they are led to deviate from previously existing rules in consequence of conflicting tendencies." Otto Jespersen (1924, p. 344) made this request of psychology in 1924; now at last the work is beginning.

One example. Stephen Isard and I asked Harvard undergraduates to memorise several sentences that differed in degree of self-embedding. For instance, the twenty-two words in the right-branching sentence, "We cheered the football squad that played the team that brought the mascot that chased the girls that were in the park," can be rearranged to give one, two, three, or four self-embeddings; with four it becomes, "The girls (that the mascot (that the team (that the football squad (that we cheered) played) brought) chased) were in the park." One self-embedding caused no difficulty; it was almost as easy to memorise as the sentence with none. Three or four embeddings were most difficult. When the sentence had two self-embeddings—"The team (that the football squad (that we cheered) played) brought the mascot that chased the girls that were in the park"—some subjects found it as easy to memorise as sentences with zero or one embedding, others found it as difficult as sentences with three or four. That is to say, everybody can manage one embedding, some people can manage two, but everybody has trouble with three or more.

Records of eye movements while people are reading such sentences show that the trouble begins with the long string of verbs, "cheered played brought," at which point all grasp of the sentence structure crumbles and they are left with a random list of verbs. This is just what would be expected from a computer executing a programme that did not make provision for a sub-routine to refer to itself, i.e., that was not recursive. If our ability to handle this type of self-embedded recursion is really as limited as the experiment indicates, it places a strong limitation on the kinds of theories we can propose to explain our human capacities for processing information.

V PERSON PERCEPTION, INTERACTION, AND ROLE

Human interaction describes a nucleus around which most other matters encompassed by this book orbit. Psychological, sociological, and anthropological manifestations all coalesce about it producing its particular colorations. For most social psychologists, phenomena of social interchange are central points of reference in their scientific enterprise. Comprehension of the nature of social interaction is therefore a central task for social psychology.

It is generally agreed that interactions are a function both of factors external and internal to the person, though the immediate interests of a particular social analyst may understate one or the other. But, as the papers in this section make plain, no simple, categorical separation between the two can be maintained consistently. External and internal conditions sound a continual counterpoint to one another, with harmony the rule rather than the exception.

In looking at phenomena of interaction, psychological theorists have long tended to accord a pre-eminent explanatory position to processes of perception. How a person behaves in the course of interaction is widely held to be a consequence of constructions or perceptions of the situation, including other persons. It is virtually axiomatic that the person behaves according to what the situation "means" to him, or in W. I. Thomas's felicitous phrase, his "definition of the situation" (cf. Volkart, 1951, Introduction). Perception, in turn, depends upon the characteristics of the person himself and upon the information communicated to him, intentionally and unintentionally, in the situation. As Tagiuri has noted (1960, p. 569), a person's impressions of a situation including another person are a result of three major elements: the situation, the other person, and the perceiver. All of these are considered in the selections that follow, most of which view interaction from the standpoint of perception and contain elements anticipated particularly in the Bruner paper in Section I.

There are, of course, conditions of a less "perceptual" nature, in the sense of being less personalized, that can and do mold interaction. They reside in the fabric of the social system, its modal patterns of conduct, and in the general "life situation." Such factors have perhaps received somewhat less attention from social psychologists than have the kinds of perceptual conditions already mentioned, but psychological interest has been growing with reference to a complex of elements signaled by the coordinate concepts of *position* (or sometimes status) and *role*—concepts that R. G. Hunt considers at some length in this section.

In Hunt's account, positions may be roughly described as aggregations of functions standardized within a social system and "cued" by some set of conventionalized symbols. Roles are the behavioral expectancies usually associated with given positions and evoked by the appropriate symbols. Most analyses of roles, including Hunt's, emphasize the frequent complementary quality of positional differentiation in society and the resulting interlocking features of roles and their enactments. Consequently, roles contribute not only to the integration of individual behavior, they are fundamental to general social organization (see Miller, 1963).

The significance of position-role concepts was well described by Rommetveit (1954) when he characterized role as a sort of theoretical point of intersection between psychology and sociology. In his words, role is "the largest possible research unit within (psychology) and the smallest possible within (sociology)" (1954, p. 31). Therefore, it is easy to understand how, despite its "theoretical inelegance" and "lack of conceptual consistency" detected by Deutsch and Krauss (1965), role remains a primary reference point in analyses of social processes.

A more comprehensive and detailed review of role concepts may be found in Bredemeier and Stephenson's useful book (1962), but Hunt's discussion here is representative and captures the richness and complexity of the idea. Along with his differentiated definitions of position and role and his classification of varieties of role conflict, Hunt takes note of the relevance of role to questions of personal identity or self which we discussed in Section III and which are central to Cantril's paper later in the present section.

Contributions to the development of self and personality in terms of the parts one plays in society were recognized by William James (1892) in his distinction between the self as known ("Me") and the self as knower ("I") and by the sociologist C. H. Cooley (1902) in his notion of the "looking glass self." Both James and Cooley realized that one's conception of self derived, partly at least, from the ways others responded to him and that this in turn related to social expectancies or roles. But it remained, for George Herbert Mead (1934), with his emphases upon language, communication and "symbols," and, more recently, Robert Merton (1957) and Erving Goffman (1959, 1961), to articulate systematically the vital relation of role to personality. It is in this context that Hunt's paper should be seen. What then becomes clear is that major portions of interpersonal relations are regulated by "institutionalized" patterns of relation and the situational definitions they imply. Several of the other papers in the pages that follow, notably those by Steiner, Gouldner, and Goffman, also deal with this aspect of interactional influence.

Integrating the classes of interaction determinants mentioned in the preceding passages, social scientists have often spoken of different *levels* at which the same process may be analyzed; here, Goffman speaks of three —personality, interaction, and society—and suggests co-ordinations among them. Most popular, however, has been a distinction between *formal* and *informal* levels of analysis, though other terms with comparable meanings may be used. Formal analysis points most directly to an account of social behavior in terms of general patterns and widespread norms within a social system, with "society" and/or "culture" as the points of reference for analysis. Role theory, as one example, is often employed formalistically.

An analysis of social processes at an informal level lays stress upon aspects of the immediate interactional setting and participants, including their individual attributes, as determinants of events. Most phenomenological-perceptual-cognitive approaches to interaction concentrate upon analyses at informal levels.

These levels are not rigidly separable, they "interpenetrate" one another extensively, to borrow Parsons's (1959) term. As levels, they represent different selections of variables for study, variables having perhaps differing degrees of generality. Actual social behavior is a complex, multi-determined happening any instance of which involves processes that may be conceptualized at both levels. While psychological analyses correctly convey a preference for specifications at a more informal level, invoking processes operative "in" the individual (though not necessarily uniquely to a given person), it is nonetheless convenient and highly useful to consider variables at another level. Steiner's paper in this section is an excellent illustration of the utility in this practice.

Steiner reviews in his paper the conflicting evidence concerning relations between perceptual accuracy and the effectiveness of interaction. He proposes that accurate perception is not always essential and, in fact, may even be dysfunctional at times. Concluding that accuracy in perceiving the other person will materially affect social relations only when such accuracy is "relevant," Steiner suggests that, if structured role systems are present to regulate behavior, "veridical" social perception may not be important. He goes on to define roles and role systems and underscores their interlocking nature. Whenever well-structured role systems are operative in a situation, social behavior will tend to "run-off" in terms of their prescriptions, with "personal" attributes of the parties and their mutual apprehensions of those being of little moment.

Under such conditions, interaction can be formalistically conceptualized, as the so-called "symbolic interactionists" do (see Rose, 1962), as an interplay of positions and roles. Persons are only incidentally relevant as the "players of roles." But, when role systems are not clearly defined, informal influences will be stronger and the importance of perceptual accuracy increases proportionately. In a total interaction "episode" certain segments are likely to vary with respect to the weighting of formal-informal determinants. Which class or level is then more important depends upon the particular interaction segment looked at.

Steiner's paper makes evident that particular interpersonal relations are subject to influences "outside" the unique individualities of the actors. Gouldner's contribution here takes this matter a step further, proposing a norm of reciprocity as a cultural universal working to both stabilize and initiate relations in a social system. The norm of reciprocity is presumed to be of such generality that it will constitute a broad formal influence governing social systems even in the relative absence of clearly defined status-role stipulations.

Gouldner, in developing his thesis, systematically distinguishes between reciprocity and complementarity from a viewpoint of functional theory and a conception of interaction as exchange. He quite effectively details the implications of these constructs for power relations, conditions of unequal exchange, and for role systems as well. In doing so, he notes that the norm of reciprocity, as a modal cultural fact, becomes personally internalized as a moral sanction entailing sentiments of obligation and debt and otherwise functioning as a useful check upon "egoism." Gouldner also makes a point of the relative indeterminacy of the norm as a stabilizer, a factor which March also speaks of more generally in Section VII.

It is noteworthy that, while postulated as a cultural universal, Gouldner comments that the norm is not "unconditional." Psychologically, the internalization of reciprocity *sentiments* may vary across groups, such as social classes, and between individuals, and thereby lend markedly distinctive appearances to the interactions of given individuals. A generalized cultural norm of reciprocity may operate as an important source of dispositions relevant to interaction, but it is the individual representation of this norm that is directly relevant to immediate interaction. But, nonetheless, Gouldner sees interpersonal interaction as highly relative to circumstances characterizing the larger social world.

Thus, human interaction is subject to a number of broadly constraining social elements residing apart from the immediate relationship. From Steiner's offering, however, we can derive the idea that the actual implementation of interaction is directly dependent upon processes taking place within and between the actors. It may well be that not every interaction requires personalized perceptions of others as persons, but some minimal perceptual reference is required. Even if the particular behaviors that occur are strictly role-linked, it is still necessary for the interacting parties to "perceive" the positional cues signaling their performances. What is more, a de-emphasis upon perceptual *accuracy* does not contradict the axiom that *persons* behave chiefly in response to the *perceived* attributes of others and of the situations in which they are encountered.

From a transactional perspective Cantril makes this point well, asserting the dependence of behavior upon perception and then construing perception as "our own creation." In his need to order a "chaotic" world—to establish constancies—the person creates a "reality world" by classifying and categorizing events and persons. Perception, and subsequently performance, depends upon the character of these reality worlds. As Goffman also points out in a different context, once things are classified the situation becomes stabilized and behavior proceeds according to the significance (meanings) of the classes used. Consistent with Steiner's observations, Cantril implies that the other person's *real* features may be of only small moment, temporarily at least.

Cantril draws out the importance of "self" and its constancies as a key to social relations. The self serves first of all as an "anchor point" in perception. In addition, though related, the self is important because what one "brings to the situation" is a primary basis for determining the significance of "what is out there." What one perceives is very much related to prior dispositions or sets—a consideration as germane to the perception of persons as to things.

Phenomenally, then, things are literally what they seem. A question remains, though, concerning the "causation" of experience, and especially as this applies to impressions of others. The burden of Heider's distinguished book, *The Psychology of Interpersonal Relations* (1958), is to provide just such a causal analysis. The flavor of Heider's endeavor, along with his basic Gestalt-derived perspective and a number of key concepts, is well represented in the selection from that volume reprinted here. In it he features the dynamic interplay of processes in perception and focuses upon "coordination between stimulus conditions outside the person and his experience or phenomenal representation of them." He finds it analytically useful to break the total perceptual process into "stages" or cumulative sequences, as follows: distal stimulus—mediation—proximal stimulus—constructive processes of perception or, if one prefers, cognition.

Like Cantril, Heider also treats the import of constancy phenomena, with "meaning" occupying a central position integrating perception and controlling behavior. In distinguishing person perception from "thing" perception, he emphasizes the perception of psychological invariants in the other as guides to behavior. The discernment of dispositional characteristics (sentiments, motives, etc.) of the other serve as major factors structuring perception and interpersonal relations. Perception of the attributes of others controls the way the person behaves toward them and what he expects from them, and the specific behavior patterns by which these percepts are "cued" is psychologically of minor importance.

Thus Heider construes social perception in a "non-behavioristic" manner as a process between the center of one person and the center of another, all the while allowing due latitude to the contextual effects of the "stimulus field." Interpersonal relations are framed by mutual perceptions of the psychological attributes of others and interaction proceeds from these perceptual premises.

Examination of interpersonal sentiments, perceptions of the other, interpersonal attraction, and interaction processes, as might be expected, have become a prominent thread in social psychological research during recent years; for a representation of this focus, see Tagiuri and Petrullo (1958). Newcomb, in his paper here, reviews various notions about the *determinants* of attraction, touching upon all the nodal points mentioned, and offers a conceptual framework that emphasizes *attraction* as a feature of "reciprocal reward" associated with communicative behavior. He, like Gouldner in this section—and Homans, and Thibaut and Kelley in Section VII—looks upon social interaction as a form of exchange.

The core ideas in Newcomb's account of interpersonal attraction, represented more extensively in his text (Newcomb, 1950), in his paper on "Communicative Acts" (1953), and in the monumental survey of psychology edited by Koch (Newcomb, 1959), emphasize the importance of *attitudinal* similarity as an independent variable, where attitude is defined as sentiments toward an object. However, it is not the actual similarity of attitude that directly determines attraction, but the *perception* of similarity; since interaction will vary with attraction, it becomes plain then that interaction depends heavily upon interpersonal perceptions—notably of similarity of attitudes. The intertwining of these phenomena, however, is nicely elucidated by Newcomb in his comment that interaction enhances similarity, so that interaction and attraction are likely to be progressive phenomena, perceptually mediated. His book, *The Acquaintance Process* (1961), is a fuller account of his study covered in this paper.

This continued interplay of perceptions and the interactional accommodations to them, especially as relations extend through time, is much in evidence in Goffman's provocative book *The Presentation of Self in Everyday Life* (1959), excerpts from which provide the final selection in this section. He begins with the premise that what is perceived is important, then goes on to a penetrating focus upon the person as an agent purposefully influencing what is perceived. The "presentations" that persons make, whether deliberately or not, says Goffman, work to define and control the situation, thus contributing to orderly social processes; expectancies people develop vis-à-vis one another are determined by the mutual "impressions" they receive, and Goffman delineates ways in which information is presented, their varying effects upon behavior, and the motivations for their management.

He distinguishes between two kinds of sign-activity in which persons may engage, but concentrates mainly on those less "deliberate" varieties that tend to be "symptomatic" of what a person is like. His book engagingly shows the utility of viewing from a theatrical perspective general interpersonal performances and the settings in which they transpire. Interpersonal interactions are regulated and molded by mutual "stagings" and "readings" by the parties. These are influenced by numerous factors, as we have seen, but the course of their transactions depends upon the "script" upon which they collaborate.

28 Role and role conflict

RAYMOND G. HUNT

Conceptual framework

Any social system, and especially a formal organization, may be viewed structurally as an at least partially interlocking complex of *positions*. These positions represent the functional divisions of labor deemed useful to achievement of the system's goals and are populated by a collection of particular individuals each of whom occupies at least one but commonly more than one of them (cf. Gross, *et al.*, 1958, and in connection with much of what follows).

Organizationally the positional structure of social systems follows a general "principle" of complementarity. Positions tend to be grouped as dyadic units around a set of complementary rights and duties—complementary in that the "rights" of a given or *focal-position* are the "duties" of some other or *counter-position* and the "rights" of the latter are the "duties" of the former. Thus the focal-position "child" may be analyzed in relation to complementary counter-positions "mother" and/or "father." Each position in a system, therefore, is differentiated with reference to one or more other positions in relation to which it stands in complementary contrast.

This complementary contrast is, of course, a function basically of the complex patterns of behavior organized around these positions and embodying the relevant mutual expectations (the rights and duties) *vis à vis* one another held by occupants of positions. It is possible, therefore, to regard social process as an interaction of positions patterned in terms of these complementary expectations which are themselves called *roles.*

It will be seen that a role represents the content of a position or the behavioral implications of positional occupancy and that, for a given social system, the shape of social interaction will depend heavily upon the position-role differentiations and definitions current within it. Moreover, because roles entail expectations for attributes (i.e., personal characteristics) as well as for behavior, they also contribute to definitions of personal identity (self) and thereby further influence interaction indirectly (see Goffman, 1959, 1961).

It is important to remember that a role can be comprehensively described only with reference to other roles associated with positions complementary to that occupied by the "role player." In most instances a given focal-position or role (e.g., teacher) will stand in organizational relation to more than a single counter-position (e.g., pupil, colleague, principal, etc.). The totality of counter-positions that can be set in meaningful complementary contrast with a given focal-position is therefore said to describe that focal-position's *role-set* (cf. Kahn, *et al.*, 1964). Thus, the role-set

Abridged from Chapter 4 of H. J. Hartley & G. E. Holloway (Eds.), **Focus on Change and the School Administrator,** Buffalo, N.Y.: State University of New York, School of Education, 1965, pp. 37–46, with permission of the publisher.

of a "teacher" includes, among others, the counter-positions "pupil," "colleague," "principal," etc. Taking these counter-positions one at a time, the particular array of expectations associated with the relationship between a given focal-position (teacher) and a single counter-position (principal) is termed a *role-sector* (cf. Gross, *et al.*, 1958). The idea of the role-sector makes plain the fact that roles vary somewhat depending upon the particular counter-position comprising the other half of the dyad at a given time. In other words, the "teacher" role is different in relation to "principal" from what it is in relation to "pupil."

We might observe that some theorists (e.g., Sarbin, 1954) regard positions as the units of *society* (structure) and roles as the units of *culture* (content or function). It is also useful to point out that the term position is here used as some earlier theorists (Linton, 1945) used the term *status*.[1] We shall see later, however, that it is useful to reserve the term *status* for another purpose and so avoid much confusion.

The differentiation of roles

We may assume that through the complex processes of socialization individuals develop modes for representing the panoply of positional differentiations and role patternings defining the social system in which they operate. Some of these representations they will acquire as a result of direct experience and others will develop as a consequence of indirect influences. At all events these representations will be *individualized* matters and so will entail some variation between persons even within the same social system. Therefore, our conceptualization of roles must be sufficiently discriminated to accommodate the fact and ramifications of variation.

Hence it is helpful to consider the following role varieties:

1. *Role prescriptions:* These may be thought of as the "cultural requirements" within a social system. A description of a role prescription is an *abstraction* drawn from aggregating the behaviors of a number of occupants of comparable positions. Thus it represents some sort of behavioral central tendency among the several positional occupants distributed through space and time. Consequently, a role prescription, once stated, is extremely unlikely to be exemplified by any specific single individual. This is why, of course, the anthropologist commonly employs a number of informants before constructing a "model" of a society's role patterns.

2. *Role stereotypes:* While we can take role prescriptions to be abstractly defined cultural givens, we must recognize that individuals encounter concrete representations of them in a manifold of ways and contexts. These we can call variant manifestations. From these, we postulate, the individual synthesizes personalized representations of the cultural requirements which may exhibit considerable variation as between persons. These personal role constructions we call *role stereotypes*. It is important to bear in mind that the word stereotypes here implies no judgment of the adequacy of the construction. A given person's stereotype *may* be highly idiosyncratic or it may be largely shared. The point is that it is necessarily stereotypic psychologically for there is no determinate evidential base for its evalu-

[1] The term "office" has also been used to signify the same structural notion, but with some differences in connotation (see Gerth & Mills, 1946).

ation. It is a cognitive or mediational process built up from a "sample" from the universe of possible exposures.

3. *Role expectations:* We have already observed that any construction of a role includes specifications concerning the behavior both of the person himself and also of the behavior of the occupants of positions complementary to his own. It is common practice to refer to that aspect of a total role construction that refers to the behavior of another as a "role expectation." While we have talked of this matter in terms of complementarities of positions it would be perfectly legitimate to use the term "role expectation" to refer to any anticipation of particular behavior patterns contingent upon another's occupancy of any given position regardless of any relationship to one's own.

Persons holding expectations concerning the role performances of others commonly strive to communicate their expectations to the focal-person in hopes of influencing the latter to conform to them. Each of the counter-persons communicating such expectations can be thought of as a *role-sender* and his communicated expectations can be called a *sent-role* (cf. Kahn, *et al.*, 1964). A focal-person's perceptions of the totality of sent-roles respecting his position will weigh heavily in shaping his role stereotype—indeed, if we define any source of information (including mass media, films, etc.) concerning a role as a role-sender, then we could define role stereotypes as synthesized perceptions of sent-roles.

With these statements in mind, it can be seen that any social system constitutes a more or less complex mutual influence network. Organizationally, the system is describable and definable in terms of the temporally-relative functional relations or influence patterns among the positions into which the system has been structurally differentiated.

4. *Role enactments:* The constructs we have stated thus far have been cognitive or mediational in form.[2] We may posit that they will operate among the determinants of the actual behavior manifested by a given positional occupant. However, as these cognitive aspects of roles are abstract and/or stereotypic they function as schemas or behavior models and not as exclusive causal agents. In short, the actual role *behavior* exhibited by a person will be associated with a variety of antecedent conditions and variables among which the cognitive components of roles will be only one (though highly important ones). Thus we shall refer to a person's actual role behavior as a "role enactment." Now from what we have already said it is plain that role enactments can vary between individuals occupying similar positions either as a result of variations in their cognitive role constructions, or because of variations in the "stimulus" field in which they behave, or, of course, both. Furthermore, the role enactments of a single person can vary through time as a function of the same factors.

5. *Counter-role expectations:* While this label is unfortunately cumbersome, it refers to another highly important aspect of role phenomena that requires mention; from his perceptions of sent-roles, and also from more subtle sources (see Goffman, 1959), each person not only develops constructions pertaining to his own behavior and expectations of others' behavior, he likewise forms con-

[2] We have not and will not consider how roles are sent, but obviously they must be sent behaviorally. However, the role **expectation** communicated in the sent-role is itself cognitive.

structions of what others expect of him. Indeed, in practice these several conceptualizations mutually reinforce and modify one another and some theorists have even held that the latter one is a prime determiner of the former two (Mead, 1925). In any event, a person's conceptualization of others' expectations will be an important influence upon his behavior.

Salience and definiteness of role constructions

The *salience* of a role refers to its prominence and/or importance in a person's life situation. By implication, the more salient a role the greater will be a person's "investment" in it and its components, the more will he tend to organize his "view of things" around it, the more will he strive to augment its clarity, the more will he tend to resist change in it once cognitively organized, and, hence, the more will it tend to dominate his behavior. For present purposes we can view salience as a dimension of role that refers to the quantitative emotional involvement in it of the person. Anticipating subsequent discussion a bit, conflict among elements of salient roles will be more intense than any involving less salient roles.

Definiteness of a role refers to the clarity and/or articulation of elements in a differentiated role construction. The clearer and more articulated a role construction the more significant will it be as a behavior determinant. And the more a definite construction is articulated with other role constructions the more flexible will be the person's behavior. Finally, the more indefinite and inarticulate a role construction the greater will be the possibility for conflict involving it and the greater will be the person's anxiety in performing it.

Many factors influence the definiteness of a role construction, but we have need to mention only two: positional awareness and experience. Obviously the most basic requirement for a definite role construction is awareness of the positional differentiation defining the distal social system in which the person functions. As a corollary we may observe that it is also necessary that the person allocate position occupants with some precision. It should be clear that awareness of the positional structure of a system is, by itself, insufficient to effective social behavior without accompanying awareness of the distribution of particular others among these positions. Hence, without adequate and comprehensive positional awareness, a person's social behavior is likely to be less than apt—even inept.

The second factor of interest to us as a contributor to role definition is experience. It is highly credible that, in general, the more "practice" a person has in role playing the clearer and more differentiated will these roles become. Furthermore, their reciprocal features are likely to be sharpened with the result that greater consensus among role constructions is likely to be achieved. No less important is a growth in "sophistication" entailing a relaxation in the rigidity of role construction and enactment. This proceeds from greater awareness of and sensitivity to the variations in role construction and enactment common in the community and the functional interrelationships between these variations and other system components. Sophistication also implies a continued awareness of the fundamental invariance of the role as a positional attribute with observed variations being represented as variant forms of the same role structure.

Role conflict

In any complex social system involving a large number of interrelated positional differentiations and with individuals simultaneously occupying a variety of positions, some related and some not, there is obviously wide latitude for confusion and conflict. This will be especially true in any setting where normative guides are uncertain or inconsistent—a condition akin to what Durkheim and Merton have called *anomie*.

Actually there are a variety of conditions that can produce role conflict. None of these will be discussed in exhaustive detail, but we shall inventory certain prominent circumstances. Before doing so, however, we must be clear about the usage of the term "conflict" in this discussion. We shall use the term to denote one or both of two conditions, the second of which is not typical of psychological discussions of conflict.

In the first, and usual, sense conflict refers to a condition where an individual *experiences* the simultaneous arousal of two or more incompatible behavioral tendencies. In this case the person is likely to be "aware" of the conflict, though not necessarily able to resolve it or even to identify clearly its sources. In the second, atypical, sense "conflict" may refer to a situation in which the objective social *requirements* would be such as to demand simultaneous, incompatible responses from the person. In this case, the person himself might not be aware of the "conflict" owing to an inadequate definition of the situation or because of indefinite, inarticulate position-role differentiation. Thus the term conflict is used here to denote any condition wherein the person functions in a field the requirements of which are in conflict whether he perceives it so or not. The reason for this broad usage rather than the more usual "intrapersonal" formulation is that the focus of our interest in dealing with role concepts is *interpersonal* and conflict may exist if not, strictly speaking, within either of the participants, then *in the relationship* where the resulting "tension" may be expected to have behavioral consequences of great disruptive potential because its sources are unrecognized and therefore difficult to cope with adaptively.

With this preface we can turn to a survey of some prominent circumstances productive of conflict.

1. The most obvious of these is represented by a situation in which the person perceives himself to, or does in fact, occupy two or more positions, both of which are relevant to the situation and the role constructions of which are incompatible. An illustration of this variety of role conflict can be seen in the well-worn Hollywood plot theme in which a dedicated policeman is called upon to arrest his miscreant brother.
2. A second condition is one wherein an individual's role expectations are incompatible. In this case the conflict involves the projected performances of the occupants of counter-positions. Exemplification frequently can be found in the demands of parents that their adolescent offspring behave at once independently and subordinately.
3. A third condition is one wherein an individual's role stereotype is incom-

patible with his construction of the other's role expectations. This form of role conflict, involving perceptions of sent-roles, is authentically interpersonal whether the person's constructions are accurate or not for it refers explicitly to the matter of one's behavior in relation to others. In some ways this species of conflict is similar to the first type and, indeed, either or both kinds could be aroused by the same circumstances. What differentiates them is that in the first type the person perceives himself as occupying *multiple* and conflicting positions whereas in this third form he perceives himself as occupying a *single* position the counter-role expectations of which are inconsistent with his role stereotype. For instance, the policeman in our first example might regard the conflict as entirely one of his "duty" and his brother's expectations that he will subordinate duty to familial sentiment.

4. Another condition would be represented by a circumstance wherein an individual's role expectations are incompatible with the role enactments of the other or vice versa. This form of conflict hardly needs further elaboration; it simply refers to those frequent circumstances when another person's behavior is not what we think it should be.
5. A final circumstance, not typically included in these discussions, is one wherein some constraining element of a role is behaviorally inconsistent with some other non-role-related feature of the stimulus field. For example, a conscientious teacher concerned over his economic circumstances might be cast into conflict by perceiving his role-linked "professionalism" to be inconsistent with a seeming necessity to strike and picket as a means to produce change in an unsympathetic school board. This condition does not represent a role conflict *per se* perhaps, but one entailing conflict among behavior determinants. It is of great import, however, because of its relevance to problems of status to which we shall come presently.

Although we shall not discuss the matter, it is to be expected that different kinds of conflict will entail different implications for social process and it should be evident now that the varieties of role conflict and of role-linked conflict are many. What is important to keep in mind is that role-conflict can arise from actual requirements of the behavioral field whether veridically perceived or not, or from perceptual error, or from failure to achieve an adequately definite and articulated construction of position-role.

Status

Status in this discussion is not synonymous with position but is conceived as an attribute of positions. Without laboring the point, status can be thought of as referring to the "rank order" of a position within a system of positions. These rankings are a result of a number of factors a consideration of which would take us too far afield. Suffice it to say that any position may rank high or low relative to others and that this status connotes variations in the power and/or prestige-respect accruing to a position.

Now, there are a few complicating matters. In the first place, since status accrues to a position, any occupant of the position acquires or is *ascribed* that status. However, even within a given position, an individual's *achieved* status may vary upward or downward from this base, depending upon features of his performance in the position. To be brief, a person's role enactments serve to "validate" his status and so may modify it. Consequently, ineptness in role enactment will lead to a loss in status.

The second complicating factor is perhaps of even greater significance: There is a frequent tendency to think of status as a sort of unitary monolith. However, while it is true that we can grossly characterize a *person* as having a certain status, strictly speaking status is associated with positions, not persons. Since each person will occupy multiple positions, each of which accords him a status, we can with justice think of persons as being characterized by *statuses*. And Homans (1961), for one, has reasoned, there is an interpersonal tendency to maintain congruence among these statuses and any interaction involving incongruencies among statuses will be strained and conflictful, independently of any *specifics* of role behavior.

Conclusion

From the preceding remarks it can be seen that a large part of the variance in interpersonal relations and organizational functioning can be understood in terms of interactions among persons as occupants of positions and players of roles. In fact, many phenomena appearing in such relations and regularly ordered to personality traits and peculiarities of the individual parties involved are probably more properly viewed in terms of aspects and relations of positions and roles and their correlative status. In other words, it must of needs be recognized that large parts of individual social behavior are formally determined and have little to do with the specific intrapsychic aspects of the behaver.

29 Interpersonal behavior as influenced by accuracy of social perception

IVAN D. STEINER

This paper presents a critical examination of two propositions which link accurate social perception with competence in interpersonal behavior and with group efficiency. The first of these propositions maintains that the more knowledge an individual has concerning the intentions, preferences, and beliefs of other persons, the more effectively he can participate in group activity with those other persons. This proposition provides the rationale for much of the training we give to teachers, social workers, clinical psychologists, and others whose work involves continuing interaction with people.

Attempts to verify this proposition have ordinarily involved the use of high sociometric status or high sociometrically evaluated productivity as indexes of the individual's interpersonal competence. With these indexes as criteria, considerable empirical evidence has been produced in support of this proposition. Chowdhry and Newcomb (1952) found that persons who were sociometrically chosen, by various criteria, tended to make the most accurate estimates of group opinion on topics relevant to the group's aims and functions. Gage (1952) found that high school seniors who did the most accurate job of predicting the responses which others would make to the Kuder Preference Record also received a large percentage of their classmates' sociometric choices. Greer, Galanter, and Nordlie (1954) have reported that sociometrically popular members of infantry squads are more accurate than less popular members in predicting the sociometric positions of men in their squads. Norman (1953) analyzed data obtained by a Veterans Administration research project and found that graduate students who were most often rejected by their classmates had the least realistic perceptions of others. Other investigators (Bell, *et al.*, 1954; Cottrell, *et al.*, 1949; Gage, *et al.*, 1951; Wood, 1948) have also reported positive relationships between accuracy of social perception and interpersonal competence.

The second proposition to be examined here involves an extension of the first. It maintains that groups composed of individuals with accurate social perceptions will be more efficient than groups composed of members with less accurate social perceptions. Faith in this proposition guides much of our marriage counseling and has sometimes been a factor in the selection of work crews and play groups. Much of the empirical evidence in support of this proposition has been provided by studies which were not directly concerned with group efficiency. Thus, Festinger and his associates (1950) have frequently given group members erroneous impressions of one another and have found

Slightly abridged from the **Psychological Review**, 1955, 62, 268–74, with permission of the author and the American Psychological Association.

that such impressions can lead to restricted communication within the group, rejection of members, and to lowered group cohesiveness. Such findings strongly suggest that inaccurate social perception can reduce the efficiency with which groups achieve either individual or group goals. Similar indirect support for the proposition is provided in a study by Dymond (1953). She found that members of happily married couples (presumably groups which are efficient in achieving individual and group goals) made fewer errors than did members of unhappily married couples in predicting one another's responses to the Minnesota Multiphasic Personality Inventory. More direct support is provided by Cottrell and Dymond (1949), whose ratings of group efficiency were positively correlated with the average accuracy of group members in predicting one another's self-ratings. Greer, Galanter, and Nordlie (1954) have also provided direct support for the proposition. They found that infantry squads consisting of men who did a good job predicting one another's sociometric positions within the group were rated more highly than other squads on performance of field maneuvers.

Although the studies cited above provide some basis for confidence in each of the two propositions, other studies have failed to produce positive findings. Thus, the first proposition appears to be contradicted by Campbell's (Ohio State Univ., 1949) failure to obtain a positive relationship between the accuracy with which naval officers judged the attitudes of their men and the officers' popularity with the crew. Similarly, Sprunger (1949) failed to obtain a positive correlation between the accuracy with which office supervisors perceived their subordinates and the popularity of those supervisors with their workers. Perhaps the most notable failure to confirm the second proposition is contained in the work of Fiedler, who has studied the perceptual accuracy of members of efficient and inefficient basketball and surveying teams. His findings with respect to the effect of perceptual accuracy have been generally negative.[1] Indeed, there has sometimes appeared to be a slight association of perceptual accuracy with ineffective performance.

The existence of contradictory findings suggests that the two propositions are neither completely true nor completely false. It is probable that each is a true statement of a relationship which exists under certain limiting conditions, but a false statement when those limiting conditions do not prevail. If this is the case, it is desirable that the limiting conditions be identified and that the propositions be altered to take them into account.

Such limiting conditions might be identified by either of two methods. One method calls for a systematic and comprehensive analysis of the studies which have produced positive findings, and a comparison of those studies with others which have produced negative findings. Although in principle this method should be capable of identifying some of the conditions which determine the validity of the propositions, it is a procedure which involves all of the practical difficulties encountered in any ex post facto analysis. The other method seeks to identify the limiting conditions through an examination of the assumptions which are implicit in

[1] Fiedler, F. E. Personal communication, 1954. Fiedler (1954) has recently summarized other findings of these studies.

the two propositions. These implicit assumptions may themselves specify some of the conditions under which the two propositions are likely to be valid.

This paper will employ the second method in an attempt to identify certain of the conditions which must exist in order that accurate social perception can lead to increased interpersonal competence and group efficiency.

Assumptions concerning collective action

The term "collective action" will be used in this paper to designate the behaviors of two or more persons who are attempting to satisfy needs or attain goals through cooperative effort in a "face-to-face" situation. Certain assumptions concerning the nature of collective action are implicit in the propositions cited above. It is implied that efficient collective action is accomplished through a dyadic process in which each participant adjusts his own behavior in response to the intentions and preferences of others. This view of collective action has received wide support in the literature. Mead (1934) has contended that integrated collective action requires that each individual "take the role of the other," a process by which he gains insight into others' intentions and preferences. Asch (1952) has eloquently defended a theory of human interaction in which the existence of mutually shared psychological fields and the capacity for "taking into account the emotions and thoughts of others" provide the basis for coordinated group behavior. In a recent paper Newcomb (1953) has pictured the communication process as one in which two or more participating individuals seek "simultaneous orientation" to one another and to the events round about them. Such simultaneous orientation may be described as a relationship in which each individual takes cognizance of, and adjusts to, the attitudes of others. Newcomb says this relationship is essential to human life. Sears (1951a) has contended that "a dyadic unit can be derived from the combining of two or more monadic units" by taking into account the expectancies which one individual has of another's behavior. It is these expectancies which are "responsible for maintaining the stability of the dyadic unit." Hebb and Thompson (Lindzey, 1954) have proposed a similar explanation of collective action. Because of man's ability to anticipate not only his own next act and its effect, but also those of others, humans are capable of engaging in a kind of teamwork which is definitely lacking among other mammals.

It is easy to agree with these writers; efficient collective action often does require that each participant anticipate the behavior of others. If individuals engage in role taking, maintain simultaneous orientations, or have mutually shared fields, their collectively produced behavior sequences may constitute what Sears has called a "dyadic system." Group behavior can become "more than a fortuitously useful conjunction of individual actions" or a mere piling up of "parallel monadic sequences." It can be interlocking behavior which leads to the achievement of individual or group goals with a minimum of wasted effort or needless duplication of behavior. However, there are reasons for doubting that this conception of collective action is universally valid.

Basic to this conception of collective action is the assumption that individuals are relatively free agents who are permitted to alter their own behaviors in response to their perceptions of the intentions or preferences of others. Furthermore, it is assumed that the changes which such perceptions produce in the individual's behaviors will lead to a more thoroughly integrated dyadic system. Unless these assumptions are met, accurate social perception, whether it be achieved through role taking, simultaneous orientation, or shared psychological fields, can scarcely be expected to increase interpersonal competence or group efficiency. In the remainder of this paper it will be contended that much of our most efficient collective action occurs when neither of these assumptions is met, and under circumstances which make accurate social perception relatively unimportant.

Even when these two assumptions are met, accurate social perception may fail to permit or encourage efficient collective action. It should be expected to do so only when the attributes, preferences, or intentions which are accurately perceived are relevant to the task at hand. Accurate perception of irrelevant qualities in the other person may only prove to be distracting in its effect. In the remainder of this paper "accurate social perception" will refer to the perception of qualities, preferences, and intentions which are relevant to the activities of the group.

Role systems and social perception

Role systems often permit or compel individuals to produce efficient dyadic behavior sequences even though they know little about one another's intentions or preferences. This contention will be clarified by the construction of a model with which to represent some of the characteristics of a role system.

It will be helpful to imagine a matrix of columns and rows, creating a system of cells. Each of the columns will bear the name of a category of persons who are recognized as functionally distinct by the members of the collectivity. Such categories may fall along any of a number of dimensions like age, sex, material wealth, occupation, etc. It is not at all necessary that the categories be unidimensional, and in the case of most collectivities they will not be. It is only necessary that the members of the collectivity be capable of distinguishing between the people who belong in different categories. This requirement is easily met, for if people are not naturally distinguishable they may be made artificially distinguishable through the use of special clothing, insignia, spatial arrangements, and a variety of other means.

The rows in the matrix will each carry the name of a category of situations. Although groups may seldom categorize situations as explicitly as they categorize persons, the multiplicity of stimulus situations precludes the possibility that each can be responded to as something totally unique. As Merton (1940) has pointed out, groups tend to evolve standard ways of classifying the situations which are most frequently encountered in collective action. Similar situations tend to be classified into the same category and to be treated as though they were equivalent. Here, as in the case of categories of persons, there need be no apparent logic to the system. It is only necessary that participants be capable of assigning each situation to its proper niche. Standard assignment of situations to their appropriate categories can be achieved through a variety of socialization and indoctrination procedures.

Into the cells which are created by

the intersection of columns and rows will be placed the designation of the special behavior which is enforced by the collectivity. Thus, if the collectivity is a symphony orchestra, the cell created by the intersection of the column "first violinist" and the row "third bar, Brahms' Lullaby" might carry instructions to produce specific musical tones at a specific tempo. Not all cells will receive unique entries, and some cells may receive no entry at all because no special behavior is required of a category of persons in the situation represented by a row in the matrix.

In terms of this model, a role consists of all those behaviors which are in the cells of a single column of a complete matrix. In the case of a symphony orchestra, the role of each participant is ordinarily described in detail by the musical score and each musician will know his own role though he may have only a limited understanding of other persons' roles. The role system is represented by the entire matrix and includes the role of each participant. It constitutes a system because the various roles are interlocked in a way which produces highly integrated collective action. The behaviors expected of one person supplement those expected of others. Often, as in the case of a work group, the role of one participant cannot be enacted unless others are enacting their roles properly, and the inadequate performance of any one role may disrupt the entire system.

It is the advantage of role systems that behavior synthesis has been incorporated into the system itself, and that participants need not infer the strategies of their associates or improvise an effective synthesis as they engage in collective action. They need only to produce the behaviors which are situationally appropriate for members of their categories. To be sure, other people and their behaviors will often be important elements in the situations to which the individual must respond. But this ordinarily means only that each individual must take into account the overt behavior of other categories of persons; it does not mean that he must make inferences concerning the idiosyncratic intentions or preferences of *unique* individuals. Although participants may develop enduring expectations concerning the unique qualities of specific other individuals, these expectations are not part of the role system. Indeed, participants in a role system are often required to ignore unique qualities and to treat one another as though each were a standard representative of a whole category. The individual who accurately projects himself into the unique psychological fields of others is likely to find it difficult to perform as a standard person or to treat others as such. And as Merton (1940) has observed, any deviation from standard performance or standard treatment of others is likely to disrupt the whole role system. Consequently, those individuals who deviate from standard practice are likely to be ostracized. Given the existence of a role system, perceptual accuracy which goes beyond that required for correct categorization of others may decrease group efficiency and reduce interpersonal competence. In this connection it is instructive to recall that Hemphill (1950) found that members of large groups (30 or more persons) tended to prefer leaders who did not treat them as unique individuals.

A large proportion of all collective action must be presumed to occur within the framework of role systems where the intentions and preferences of other persons may be largely irrelevant and where the individual's freedom to adjust to such intentions and preferences is, in any case, highly restricted. Naval crews, office staffs, and surveying teams are probable examples of groups which do have elaborate role systems. It is to be noted that investigations of such groups have generally failed to obtain a positive relationship between accuracy of social perception and group efficiency or interpersonal competence. A possible contradiction of this trend is represented by the study of infantry squads (Greer, *et al.*, 1954) in which accuracy in predicting the sociometric status of squad members correlated with group efficiency. However, accuracy in perceiving a status hierarchy is a particular type of accuracy which may be a by-product of efficient use of a role system. If, as may be expected, the efficiency of a squad is a function of the degree to which its members adhere to a role system, then efficient squads will be those which demand that members enact specified roles, and deviation from standard role performance will serve as a major reason for rejection of members. Members of efficient squads would then tend to make accurate predictions of one another's positions in the status hierarchy because each will be aware of the major criterion which has guided the creation of that hierarchy. In squads where adherence to the role system is less highly stressed, efficiency should be lower and members should have more difficulty predicting the number of sociometric choices each man will receive. Until the correctness of this explanation is ascertained, it is probably unwise to regard this study as a clear contradiction of what appears to be a general trend.

Although the published reports of research in this area are not sufficiently detailed to permit categorical statements, the reported findings seem to support the contention that efficiency in groups which operate within the framework of a role system is not increased by accurate understanding of others' preferences and intentions. What are needed here are controlled studies in which groups with and without the benefit of a role system are confronted by situations requiring coordinated action. If role systems do, in fact, have the properties described above, accuracy of interpersonal understanding should have no relationship (or perhaps a negative relationship) to the efficiency of groups which have appropriate role systems. On the other hand, there should be a positive relationship between the perceptual accuracy and the efficiency of groups without role systems, assuming, of course, that members are motivated to cooperate.

30 The norm of reciprocity: a preliminary statement

ALVIN W. GOULDNER

The aims of this paper are: (1) to indicate the manner in which the concept of reciprocity is tacitly involved in but formally neglected by modern functional theory; (2) to clarify the concept and display some of its diverse intellectual contents, thus facilitating its theoretical employment and research utility; and (3) to suggest concretely ways in which the clarified concept provides new leverage for analysis of the central problems of sociological theory, namely, accounting for stability and instability in social systems.

Reciprocity and functional theory

My concern with reciprocity developed initially from a critical reexamination of current functional theory, especially the work of Robert Merton and Talcott Parsons. The fullest ramifications of what follows can best be seen in this theoretical context. Merton's familiar paradigm of functionalism stresses that analysis must begin with the identification of some problematic pattern of human behavior, some institution, role, or shared pattern of belief. Merton stipulates clearly the basic functionalist assumption, the way in which the problematic pattern is to be understood: he holds that the "central orientation of functionalism" is "expressed in the practice of interpreting data by establishing their consequences for larger structures in which they are implicated" (1957). The functionalist's emphasis upon studying the *existent* consequences, the ongoing functions or dysfunctions, of a social pattern may be better appreciated if it is remembered that this concern developed in a polemic against the earlier anthropological notion of a "survival." The survival, of course, was regarded as a custom held to be unexplainable in terms of its existent consequences or utility and which, therefore, had to be understood with reference to its consequences for social arrangements no longer present.

Functionalism, to repeat, explains the persistence of social patterns in terms of their ongoing consequences for existent social systems. If social survivals, which by definition have no such consequences, are conceded to exist or to be possible, then it would seem that functionalism is by its own admission incapable of explaining them. To suggest that survivals do not help us to understand other patterns of social behavior is beside the mark. The decisive issue is whether existent versions of functional theory can explain social survivals, not whether specific social survivals can explain other social patterns.

It would seem that functionalists have but one of two choices: either they must dogmatically deny the existence or possibility of functionless patterns (survivals), and assert that all social behavior is explainable parsimoniously on the basis of the same fundamental

Excerpted from the **American Sociological Review,** 1960, 25, 161–79, with permission of the author and the American Sociological Association.

functionalist assumption, that is, in terms of its consequences for surrounding social structures; or, more reasonably, they must concede that some social patterns are or may be survivals, admitting that existent functional theory fails to account for such instances. In the latter case, functionalists must develop further their basic assumptions on the generalized level required. I believe that one of the strategic ways in which such basic assumptions can be developed is by recognizing the manner in which the concept of *reciprocity* is tacitly involved in them, and by explicating the concept's implications for functional theory.

The tacit implication of the concept of reciprocity in functional theory can be illustrated in Merton's analysis of the latent functions of the political machine in the United States. Merton inquires how political machines continue to operate, despite the fact that they frequently run counter to both the mores and the law. The *general* form of his explanation is to identify the consequences of the machine for surrounding structures and to demonstrate that the machine performs "positive functions which are at the same time not adequately fulfilled by other existing patterns and structures" (1957, p. 73). It seems evident, however, that simply to establish its consequences for other social structures provides no answer to the question of the persistence of the political machine (cf. Gouldner, 1959b). The explanation miscarries because no explicit analysis is made of the feedback through which the social structures or groups, whose needs are satisfied by the political machine, in turn "reciprocate" and repay the machine for the services received from it. In this case, the patterns of reciprocity, implied in the notion of the "corruption" of the machine, are well known and fully documented.

To state the issue generally: the demonstration that A is functional for B can help to account for A's persistence only if the functional theorist tacitly assumes some principle of reciprocity. It is in this sense that some concept of reciprocity apparently has been smuggled into the basic but unstated postulates of functional analysis. The demonstration that A is functional for B helps to account for A's own persistence and stability only on two related assumptions: (1) that B *reciprocates* A's services, and (2) that B's service to A is *contingent* upon A's performance of positive functions for B. The second assumption, indeed, is one implication of the definition of reciprocity as a transaction. Unless B's services to A are contingent upon the services provided by A, it is pointless to examine the latter if one wishes to account for the persistence of A.

It may be assumed, as a first approximation, that a social unit or group is more likely to contribute to another which provides it with benefits than to one which does not; nonetheless, there are certain general conditions under which one pattern may provide benefits for the other despite a *lack* of reciprocity. An important case of this situation is where power arrangements constrain the continuance of services. If B is considerably more powerful than A, B may force A to benefit it with little or no reciprocity. This social arrangement, to be sure, is less stable than one in which B's reciprocity *motivates* A to continue performing services for B, but it is hardly for this reason sociologically unimportant.

The problem can also be approached

in terms of the functional autonomy (see Gouldner, 1959b) of two units relative to each other. For example, B may have many alternative sources for supplying the services that it normally receives from A. A, however, may be dependent upon B's services and have no, or comparatively few, alternatives. Consequently, the continued provision of benefits by one pattern, A, for another, B, depends not only upon (1) the benefits which A in turn receives from B, but also on (2) the power which B possesses relative to A, and (3) the alternative sources of services accessible to each, beyond those provided by the other. In short, an explanation of the stability of a pattern, or of the relationship between A and B, requires investigation of mutually contingent benefits rendered and of the manner in which this mutual contingency is sustained. The latter, in turn, requires utilization of two different theoretical traditions and general orientations, one stressing the significance of power differences and the other emphasizing the degree of mutual dependence of the patterns or parties involved.

Functional theory, then, requires some assumption concerning reciprocity. It must, however, avoid the "Pollyanna Fallacy" which optimistically assumes that structures securing "satisfactions" from others will invariably be "grateful" and will always reciprocate. Therefore it cannot be merely hypostatized that reciprocity will operate in every case; its occurrence must, instead, be documented empirically. Although reciprocal relations stabilize patterns, it need not follow that a lack of reciprocity is socially impossible or invariably disruptive of the patterns involved. Relations with little or no reciprocity may, for example, occur when power disparities allow one party to coerce the other. There may also be special mechanisms which compensate for or control the tensions which arise in the event of a breakdown in reciprocity. Among such compensatory mechanisms there may be culturally shared prescriptions of one-sided or unconditional generosity, such as the Christian notion of "turning the other cheek" or "walking the second mile," the feudal notion of "*noblesse oblige*," or the Roman notion of "clemency." There may also be cultural prohibitions banning the examination of certain interchanges from the standpoint of their concrete reciprocity, as expressed by the cliché, "It's not the gift but the sentiment that counts." The major point here is that if empirical analysis fails to detect the existence of functional reciprocity, or finds that it has been disrupted, it becomes necessary to search out and analyze the compensatory arrangements that may provide means of controlling the resultant tensions, thereby enabling the problematic pattern to remain stable.

The "exploitation" problem

It was not only the functionalist polemic against the concept of survivals that obscured the significance and inhibited the study of unequal exchanges. A similar result is also produced by the suspicion with which many modern sociologists understandably regard the concept of "exploitation." This concept of course is central to the traditional socialist critique of modern capitalism. In the now nearly-forgotten language of political economy, "exploitation" refers to a relationship in which unearned income results from certain kinds of unequal exchange.

The continued use of the concept of

exploitation in sociological analyses of sexual relations stems largely from the brilliant work of Willard Waller on the dynamics of courtship. Waller's ambivalent comments about the concept suggest why it has fallen into sociological disrepute. "The word exploitation is by no means a desirable one," explains Waller, "but we have not been able to find another which will do as well. The dictionary definition of exploitation as an 'unfair or unjust utilization of another' contains a value judgment, and this value judgment is really a part of the ordinary sociological meaning of the term" (1951, p. 163). In short, the concept of exploitation may have become disreputable because its value implications conflict with modern sociology's effort to place itself on a value-free basis, as well as because it is a concept commonly and correctly associated with the critique of modern society emphasized by the political left. But the concept *need* not be used in such an ideological manner; it can be employed simply to refer to certain transactions involving an exchange of things of unequal value. It is important to guarantee that the ordinary value implications of a term do not intrude upon its scientific use. It is also important, however, to prevent our distaste for the ideological implications of exploitation from inducing a compulsive and equally ideological neglect of its cognitive substance.

The unsavory implications of the concept of exploitation have *not* excluded it from studies of sexual relations, although almost all other specializations in sociology eschew it. Why this is so remains a tempting problem for the sociology of knowledge, but cannot be explored here. In the present context, the important implications are the following: If the possible sexual exploitation of daughters by fathers gives rise, as Davis (1949) suggests, to mechanisms that serve to prevent this, then it would seem that *other* types of exploitation may also be controlled by *other* kinds of mechanisms. These may be no less important and universal than the incest taboo. If the exploitation of women by men (or men by women) is worthy of sociological attention, then also worth studying is the exploitation of students by teachers, of workers by management or union leaders, of patients by doctors, and so on. If the notion of exploitation, in a value-free sense, is useful for the analysis of sexual relations then it can be of similar aid in analyzing many other kinds of social relations.

Doubtless "exploitation" is by now so heavily charged with misleading ideological resonance that the term itself can scarcely be salvaged for purely scientific purposes and will, quite properly, be resisted by most American sociologists. This is unimportant. Perhaps a less emotionally freighted—if infelicitous—term such as "reciprocity imbalance" will suffice to direct attention once again to the crucial question of unequal exchanges.

Complementarity and reciprocity

The question of the meaning of the concept of reciprocity should be reexamined. Consideration of some of the ways in which the reciprocity problem is treated by Parsons helps to distinguish reciprocity from other cognate concepts. "It is inherent in the nature of social interaction," writes Parsons, "that the gratification of ego's need-dispositions is contingent on alter's reaction and vice versa" (1951, p. 21). Presumably, therefore, if the gratification of either party's needs is not contingent upon the other's reactions, the stability of their relation is undermined. This, in turn, implies that if a social system is to be stable there must always be some "mutuality of gratification" (Parsons & Shils, 1951, p. 107). Social system stability, then, presumably depends in part on the mutually contingent exchange of gratifications, that is, on reciprocity as exchange.

This, however, remains an insight the implications of which are never systematically explored. For example, the implications of differences in the *degree* of mutuality or in the symmetry of reciprocity are neglected. Again, while the concept of "exploitation" assumes *central* importance in Parsons' commentary on the patient-doctor relation, it is never precisely defined, examined, and located in his *general* theory.

One reason for Parson's neglect of reciprocity is that he, like some other sociologists, does not distinguish it from the concept of complementarity. Parsons uses the two concepts as if they are synonymous and, for the most part, centers his analysis on complementarity to the systematic neglect of reciprocity rigorously construed. The term complementarity, however, is itself an ambiguous one and is not, in all of its meanings, synonymous with reciprocity. Complementarity has at least four distinct meanings:

Complementarity$_1$ may mean that a right (x) of Ego against Alter implies a duty ($-x$) of Alter to Ego. Given the often vague use of the term "right," it is quite possible that this proposition, in one aspect, is only an expansion of some definition of the concept "right." To that degree, of course, this is simply an analytic proposition. The interesting sociological questions, however, arise only when issues of empirical substance rather than logical implication are raised. For example, where a group shares a belief that some status occupant has a certain right, say the right of a wife to receive support from her husband, does the group in fact also share a belief that the husband has an obligation to support the wife? Furthermore, even though rights may logically or empirically imply duties, it need not follow that the reverse is true. In other words, it does not follow that rights and duties are always transitive. This can be seen in a second meaning of complementarity.

Complementarity$_2$ may mean that what is a duty (−x) of Alter to Ego implies a right (x) of Ego against Alter. On the *empirical* level, while this is often true, of course, it is also sometimes false. For example, what may be regarded as a duty of charity or forebearance, say a duty to "turn the other cheek," need not be *socially* defined as the *right* of the recipient. While a man may be regarded as having an unconditional obligation to tell the truth to everyone, even to a confirmed liar, people in his group might not claim that the liar has a *right* to have the truth told him.

The other two meanings of complementarity differ substantially. Complementarity$_3$ may mean that a right (x) of Alter against Ego implies a duty ($-y$) of Alter to Ego. Similarly, complementarity$_4$ may mean that a duty (−x) of Ego to Alter implies a right (y) of Ego against Alter.

In these four implications of complementarity—sometimes called reciprocal rights and obligations—there are two distinctive types of cases. Properly speaking, *complementarity* refers only to the first two meanings sketched above, where what is a right of Ego implies an obligation of Alter, or where a duty of Alter to Ego implies a right of Ego against Alter. Only the other two meanings, however, involve true instances of *reciprocity*, for only in these does what one party receives from the other require some return, so that giving and receiving are mutually contingent.

In short, complementarity connotes that one's rights are another's obligations, and *vice versa.* Reciprocity, however, connotes that *each* party has rights *and* duties. This is more than an analytic distinction: it is an *empirical* generalization concerning role systems the importance of which as a datum is so elemental that it is commonly neglected and rarely made problematic. The English philosopher MacBeath suggests that this empirical generalization may be accounted for by the principle of reciprocity (1952). This would seem possible in several senses, one of which is that, were there only rights on the one side and duties on the other, there need be no exchange whatsoever. Stated differently, it would seem that there can be stable patterns of reciprocity *qua* exchange only insofar as *each* party has both rights and duties. In effect, then, reciprocity has its significance for *role systems* in that it tends to structure *each* role so as to include both rights and duties. It is now clear, at any rate, that reciprocity is by no means identical with complementarity and that the two are confused only at theoretical peril.

The norm of reciprocity

Contrary to some cultural relativists, it can be hypothesized that a norm of reciprocity is universal. As Westermarck stated, "To requite a benefit, or to be grateful to him who bestows it, is probably everywhere, at least under certain circumstances, regarded as a duty" (1908, vol. 2, p. 154). A norm of reciprocity is, I suspect, no less universal and important an element of culture than the incest taboo, although, similarly, its concrete formulations may vary with time and place.

Specifically, I suggest that a norm of reciprocity, in its universal form, makes two interrelated, minimal demands: (1) people should help those who have helped them, and (2) people should not injure those who have helped them. Generically, the norm of reciprocity may be conceived of as a dimension to be found in all value systems and, in particular, as one among a *number* of "Principal Components" universally present in moral codes. (The task of the sociologist, in this regard, parallels that of the physicist who seeks to identify the basic particles of matter, the conditions under which they vary, and their relations to one another.)

To suggest that a norm of reciprocity is universal is not, of course, to assert that it is unconditional. Unconditionality would, indeed, be at variance with the basic character of the reciprocity norm which imposes obligations only contingently, that is, in response to the benefits conferred by others. Moreover, such obligations of repayment are contingent upon the imputed *value* of the benefit received. The value of the benefit and hence the debt is in proportion to and varies with—among other things—the intensity of the recipient's need at the time the benefit was bestowed ("a friend in need . . ."), the resources of the donor ("he gave although he could ill afford it"), the motives imputed to the donor ("without thought of gain"), and the nature of the constraints which are perceived to exist or to be absent ("he gave of his own free will . . ."). Thus the obligations imposed by the norm of reciprocity may vary with the *status* of the participants within a society.

Similarly, this norm functions differently in some degree in different *cultures*. In the Philippines, for example, the *compadre* system cuts across and pervades the political, economic, and other institutional spheres. *Compadres* are bound by a norm of reciprocity. If one man pays his *compadre's* doctor's bill in time of need, for example, the latter may be obligated to help the former's son to get a government job. Here the tendency to govern all relations by the norm of reciprocity, thereby undermining bureaucratic impersonality, is relatively legitimate, hence overt and powerful. In the United States, however, such tendencies are weaker, in part because friendship relations are less institutionalized. Nonetheless, even in bureaucracies in this country such tendencies are endemic, albeit less legitimate and overt. Except in friendship, kinship, and neighborly relations, a norm of reciprocity is not imposed on Americans by the "dominant cultural profile," although it is commonly found in the latent or "substitute" culture structure in all institutional sectors, even the most rationalized, in the United States.

In otherwise contrasting discussions of the norm of reciprocity one emphasis is notable. Some scholars, especially Homans (1958), Thurwald (1932), Simmel (1950), and Malinowski (1932), assert or imply that the reciprocity norm stipulates that the amount of the return to be made is "roughly equivalent" to what had been received. The problem of equivalence is a difficult but important one. Whether in fact there is a reciprocity norm specifically requiring that returns for benefits received be *equivalent* is an empirical question. So, too, is the problem of whether such a norm is part of or distinct from a more general norm which simply requires that one return some (unspecified) benefits to benefactors. Logically prior to such empirical problems, however, is the question of what the meaning of equivalence would be in the former norm of equivalent reciprocity.

Equivalence may have at least two forms, the sociological and psychodynamic significance of which are apt to be quite distinct. In the first case, heteromorphic reciprocity, equivalence may mean that the things exchanged may be concretely different but should be equal in *value*, as defined by the actors in the situation. In the second case, homeomorphic reciprocity, equivalence may mean that exchanges should be concretely alike, or identical in form, either with respect to the things exchanged or to the circumstances under which they are exchanged. In the former, equivalence calls for "tit for tat"; in the latter, equivalence calls for "tat for tat." Historically, the most important expression of homeomorphic reciprocity is found in the *negative* norms of reciprocity, that is, in sentiments of retaliation where the emphasis is placed not on the return of benefits but on the return of injuries, and is best exemplified by the *lex talionis*.

Finally, it should be stressed that equivalence in the above cases refers to a definition of the exchangeables made by actors in the situation. This differs of course, from holding that the things exchanged by people, in the long run, will be *objectively* equal in value, as measured by economists or other social scientists. Here, again, the adequacy of these conceptual distinctions will be determined ultimately by empirical test.

Reciprocity and social systems

As mentioned above, sociologists have sometimes confused the notion of complementarity with that of reciprocity and have recently tended to focus on the former. Presumably, the reason for this is because of the importance of complementarity in maintaining the stability of social systems. Clearly, if what one party deems his right is accepted by the other as his obligation, their relation will be more stable than if the latter fails to so define it. But if the group stabilizing consequences of complementarity are the basis of its theoretical significance, then the same consideration underwrites with equal potency the significance of reciprocity. For reciprocity has no less a role in maintaining the stability of social systems.

Note that there are at least two ways, not merely one, in which complementarity as such can break down. In the one case, Alter can refuse to acknowledge Ego's rights as his own duties. In the other case, however, Ego may not regard as rights that which Alter acknowledges as duties. The former is commonly viewed as the empirically more frequent and as the theoretically more significant case. That this often seems to be taken as a matter of course suggests the presence of certain tacit assumptions about basic human dispositions. It seems to assume, as Aristotle put it, that people are more ready to receive than to give benefits. In short, it premises a common tendency toward what used to be called "egoism," a salient (but not exclusive) concern with the satisfaction of one's own needs.

This or some cognate assumption appears to be eminently reasonable and empirically justified. There can be no adequate systematic sociological theory which boggles at the issue; indeed, it is one of the many virtues of Parsons' work that it confronts the egoism problem. His solution seems to be sidetracked, however, because his overwhelming focus on the problem of complementarity leads to the neglect of reciprocity. If assumptions about egoistic dispositions are valid, however, a complementarity of rights and obligations should be exposed to a persistent strain, in which each party is somewhat more actively concerned to defend or extend his own rights than those of others. There is nothing in complementarity as such which would seem able to control egoism.

One way out may be obtained by premising that socialization internalizes complementary rights and obligations in persons, before they fully assume responsible participation in a social system. Even if socialization were to work perfectly and so internalize such rights and obligations, there still remains the question as to what mechanism can sustain and reinforce these during full participation in the social system. The concept of complementarity takes mutually compatible expectations as given; it does not and cannot explain how they are maintained once established. For this we need to turn to the reciprocities processes because these, unlike pure complementarity, actually mobilize egoistic motivations and channel them into the maintenance of the social system. Benthamite utilitarianism has long understood that egoism can motivate one party to satisfy the expectations of the other, since by doing so he induces the latter to reciprocate and to satisfy his own. As Max Gluckman might put it with his penchant for Hegelian paradox, there is an altruism in egoism, made possible through reciprocity.

A full analysis of the ways in which the whole reciprocities complex is involved in the maintenance of social systems would require consideration of the linkages between each of its various elements, and their relation to other general properties of social systems. There is no space for such consideration here. Instead, I examine only one part of the complex, namely, the generalized *norm* of reciprocity, and suggest some of the ways in which it contributes to social system stability.

If, following Parsons, we suppose that social systems are stable to the extent that Ego and Alter conform with one another's expectations, we are confronted with the problem of why men *reciprocate* gratifications. Parsons holds that once a stable relation of mutual gratification has been established the system is self-perpetuating; presumably, no special mechanisms are necessary to maintain it. Insofar as this is not simply postulated in analogy with the principle of inertia in physics, apparently reciprocity is accounted for by Parsons, and also by Homans, as a result of the development of a beneficent cycle of mutual reinforcement. That is, Ego's conformity with Alter's expectations reinforces Alter's conformity with Ego's expectations, and so on.

This explanation of reciprocity *qua* transaction is particularly strange in Parsons' case since he often stresses, but here neglects, the significance of shared values as a source of stability in social systems. So far as the question here is not simply the general one of why men conform with the expectations of others but, rather, the more specific problem of why they *reciprocate* benefits, part of the answer would seem to be that they have commonly internalized some general *moral norm*. In short, the suggestion is that the motivation for reciprocity stems not only from the sheer gratification which Alter receives from Ego but also from Alter's internalization of a specific norm of reciprocity which morally obliges him to give benefits to those from whom he has received them. In this respect, the *norm* of reciprocity is a concrete and special mechanism involved in the maintenance of any stable social system.

Why should such a norm be necessary? Why is it that expedient considerations do not suffice to mobilize motivations to comply with other's expectations, thereby inducing them to provide reciprocal compliances? One major line of analysis here would certainly indicate the disruptive potentialities of power differences. Given significant power differences, egoistic motivations may seek to get benefits without returning them. The situation is then ripe for the breakdown of reciprocity and for the development of system-disrupting exploitation. The norm of reciprocity, however, engenders motives for returning benefits even when power differences might invite exploitation. The norm thus safeguards powerful people against the temptations of their own status; it motivates and regulates reciprocity as an exchange pattern, serving to inhibit the emergence of exploitative relations which would undermine the social system and the very power arrangements which had made exploitation possible (see Gouldner, 1959a).

As we have seen, Parsons stresses that

the stability of social systems largely derives from the *conformity* of role partners to each other's expectations, particularly when they do their duty to one another. This formulation induces a focus on conformity and deviance, and the degrees and types of each. Presumably, the more that people pay their social debts the more stable the social system. But much more than conformity and deviance are involved here.

Insofar as men live under such a rule of reciprocity, when one party benefits another, an obligation is generated. The recipient is now *indebted* to the donor, and he remains so until he repays. Once interaction is seen as taking place over time, we may note that the norm of reciprocity so structures social relations that, between the time of Ego's provision of a gratification and the time of Alter's repayment, falls the shadow of indebtedness. An adequate analysis of the dynamics of social interaction is thus required to go beyond the question of deviance from or conformity with the parties' obligations to one another. A second basic dimension needs to be examined systematically, namely, the time period when there is an obligation still to be performed, when commitments which have been made are yet to be fulfilled.

These outstanding obligations, no less than those already given compliance, contribute substantially to the stability of social systems. It is obviously inexpedient for creditors to break off relationships with those who have outstanding obligations to them. It may also be inexpedient for *debtors* to do so because their creditors may not again allow them to run up a bill of social indebtedness. In addition, it is *morally* improper, under the norm of reciprocity, to break off relations or to launch hostilities against those to whom you are still indebted.

If this conclusion is correct, then we should not only look for mechanisms which constrain or motivate men to do their duty and to pay off their debts. We should also expect to find mechanisms which induce people to *remain* socially indebted to each other and which *inhibit* their complete repayment. This suggests another function performed by the requirement of only *rough* equivalence of repayment that may be involved in one of the norms of reciprocity. For it induces a certain amount of ambiguity as to whether indebtedness has been repaid and, over time, generates uncertainty about who is in whose debt. This all hinges, however, on a shared conception of the moral propriety of repayment, engendered by the norm of reciprocity.

Still another way in which the general norm of reciprocity is implicated in the maintenance of social system stability is related to an important attribute of the norm, namely, its comparative indeterminancy. Unlike specific status duties and like other general norms, this norm does not require highly specific and uniform performances from people whose behavior it regulates. For example, unlike the status duties of American wives, it does not call upon them to cook and to take care of the children. Instead, the concrete demands it makes change substantially from situation to situation and vary with the benefits which one party receives from another.

This indeterminancy enables the norm of reciprocity to perform some of its most important system-stabilizing functions. Being indeterminate, the norm can be applied to countless *ad hoc* transactions, thus providing a flexible moral sanction for transactions which might not otherwise be regulated by specific status obligations. The norm, in this respect, is a kind of plastic filler, capable of being poured into the shifting crevices of social structures, and serving as a kind of all-purpose moral cement.

Not only does the norm of reciprocity play a stabilizing role in human relations in the *absence* of a well developed system of specific status duties, but it contributes to social stability even when these are *present* and well established. Status duties shape behavior because the status occupant believes them binding in their own right; they possess a kind of *prima facie* legitimacy for properly socialized group members. The general norm of reciprocity, however, is a second-order defense of stability; it provides a further source of motivation and an additional moral sanction for conforming with specific status obligations. For example, the employer may pay his workers not merely because he has contracted to do so; he may also feel that the workman has earned his wages. The housewife may take pains with her husband's meals not merely because cooking may be incumbent on her as a wife; she may also have a particularly considerate husband. In each case, the specific status duties are complied with not only because they are inherent in the status and are believed to be right in themselves, but also because each is further defined as a "*repayment*." In sum, the norm of reciprocity requires that if others have been fulfilling their status duties to you, you in turn have an additional or second-order obligation (repayment) to fulfill your status duties to them. In this manner, the sentiment of gratitude joins forces with the sentiment of rectitude and adds a safety-margin in the motivation to conformity.

Starting mechanisms

Two distinct points have been made about the social functions of the norm of reciprocity. One is that this norm serves a group *stabilizing* function and thus is quite familiar in functional theory. The second point, however, is the view that the norm is not only in some sense a defense or stabilizing mechanism but is also what may be called a "starting mechanism." That is, it helps to initiate social interaction and is functional in the early phases of certain groups before they have developed a differentiated and customary set of status duties.

In speaking of the norm of reciprocity as a "starting mechanism," indeed in conceiving of starting mechanisms, we find ourselves outside the usual perspective of functional theory. Functional theory commonly focuses on already-established, on-going systems, and on the mechanisms by means of which an established social system is enabled to maintain itself. Although functional theory is concerned with the problems of how individual actors are prepared by socialization to play a role in social systems, its general theoretical models rarely, if ever, include systematic treatment of the beginnings of a social system as such and, consequently, do not formally raise the question of the nature of the mechanisms needed to start such a system.

Every social system of course has a history, which means that it has had its beginnings even if these are shrouded in antiquity. Granted that the question of origins can readily bog down in a metaphysical morass, the fact is that many concrete social systems do have determinate beginnings. Marriages are not made in heaven, and whether they end in divorce or continue in bliss, they have some identifiable origins. Similarly, corporations, political parties, and all manner of groups have their beginnings. (Recent studies of friendship and other interpersonal relations in housing projects have begun to explore this problem.)

People are continually brought together in new juxtapositions and combinations, bringing with them the possibilities of new social systems. How are these possibilities realized? Is such realization entirely a random matter? These are the kinds of questions that were familiar to the earlier students of "collective behavior," who, in focusing on crowds, riots, and rumors, were often primarily concerned with investigating the development of groups in *statu nascendi*. Although this perspective may at first seem somewhat alien to the functionalist, once it is put to him, he may suspect that certain kinds of mechanisms, conducive to the crystallization of social systems out of ephemeral contacts, will in some measure be institutionalized or otherwise patterned in any society. At this point he would be considering "starting mechanisms." In this way, I suggest, the norm of reciprocity provides one among many starting mechanisms.

From the standpoint of a purely economic or utilitarian model (cf. Schelling, 1956), there are certain difficulties in accounting for the manner in which social interaction begins. Let us suppose two people or groups, Ego and Alter, each possesses valuables sought by the other. Suppose further that each feels that the only motive the other has to conduct an exchange is the anticipated gratification it will bring. Each may then feel that it would be advantageous to lay hold of the other's valuables without relinquishing his own. Furthermore, suppose that each party suspects the other of precisely such an intention, perhaps because of the operation of projective or empathic mechanisms. At least since Hobbes, it has been recognized that under such circumstances, each is likely to regard the impending exchange as dangerous and to view the other with some suspicion (cf. Deutsch, 1955). Each may then hesitate to part with his valuables before the other has first turned his over. Like participants in a disarmament conference, each may say to other, "You first!" Thus the exchange may be delayed or altogether flounder and the relationship may be prevented from developing.

The norm of reciprocity may serve as a starting mechanism in such circumstances by preventing or enabling the parties to break out of this impasse. When internalized in both parties, the norm *obliges* the one who has first received a benefit to repay it at some time; it thus provides some realistic grounds for confidence, in the one who first parts with his valuables, that he will be repaid. Consequently, there may be less hesitancy in being the first and a greater facility with which the exchange and the social relation can get underway.[1]

[1] Certain elaborations, illustrations (e.g., a discussion of Malinowski), and historical references in Prof. Gouldner's original article are omitted.—Eds.

31 Perception and interpersonal relations

HADLEY CANTRIL

Our perception depends in large part on the assumptions we bring to any particular occasion. It is, as Dewey and Bentley long ago pointed out, not a "reaction to" stimuli in the environment but may be more accurately described as a "transaction with" an environment.

This implies that the meanings and significances we assign to things, to symbols, to people, and to events are the meanings and significances we have built up through our past experience, and are not inherent or intrinsic in the "stimulus" itself.

Since our experience is concerned with purposive behavior, our perceptions are learned in terms of our purposes and in terms of what is important and useful to us.

Since the situations we are in seldom repeat themselves exactly and since change seems to be the rule of nature and of life, our perception is largely a matter of weighing probabilities, of guessing, of making hunches concerning the probable significance or meaning of "what is out there" and of what our reaction should be toward it, in order to protect or preserve ourselves and our satisfactions, or to enhance our satisfactions. This process of weighing the innumerable cues involved in nearly any perception is, of course, a process that we are generally not aware of.

Creating constancies

Since things in the world outside us—the physical world and more especially the social world—are by no means static, are not entirely determined and predictable, experience for most of us often carries at least some mild overtone of "concern" which we can label "curiosity," "doubt" or "anxiety" depending on the circumstances involved.

Thus we seldom can count on complete 100% surety in terms of a perfect correspondence between our assumptions concerning the exact experience we may have if we do a certain thing and the experience we actually do have as the consequence of the action we undertake.

In an attempt to try to minimize our potential lack of surety concerning any single occasion and thereby maximize our sense of surety concerning the effectiveness of our action in achieving our intent, we build up "constancies" and begin to count on them. While a great deal of experimental work has been done on "constancies" in the psychological laboratory, we still have much more to learn. And above all, we have a great deal to learn about constancy as we extend this concept into the field of our interpersonal relations.

Parenthetically, one of the most important things we have to learn is that the "constancy" we create and that we describe usually by means of some word, symbol, or abstract concept *is* man's creation, the validity of which can only be tested and the meaning of which can only be experienced in terms of some behavior which has consequences to us

Abridged from the **American Journal of Psychiatry,** 1957, 114, 119–27, with permission of the author and the American Psychiatric Association.

and signals to us what the concept refers to.

We create these constancies by attributing certain *consistent* and *repeatable* characteristics to what they refer to, so that we can guess with a fair degree of accuracy what the significances and meanings are of the various sensory cues that impinge upon us. We do this so that we will not have to make fresh guesses at every turn.

These significances we build up about objects, people, symbols, and events, or about ideas all orchestrate together to give us what we might call our own unique "*reality world*." This "reality world" as we experience it includes, of course, our own fears and hopes, frustrations and aspirations, our own anxiety and our own faith. For these psychological characteristics of life—as the psychiatrist knows better than anyone else—are just as real for us in determining our behavior as are chairs, stones or mountains or automobiles. It seems to me that anything that takes on significance for us in terms of our own personal behavioral center *is* "real" in the psychological sense.

Assigning significances

Let me illustrate with reference to a few recent experiments the way in which the significance we attach to others "out there" seems to be affected by what we bring to the situation. Incidentally but important: I do want to underscore that the experiments mentioned here are only exploratory; are only, I believe, opening up interesting vistas ahead. I am in no sense attempting to indicate what their full theoretical implications may be.

A whole series of most promising experiments now seems possible with the use of a modern adaptation of an old fashioned piece of psychological equipment, the stereoscope. Dr. Edward Engel who devised the apparatus has already published a description of it and reported some of his first findings (1956). The stereoscope in a psychological laboratory has been used to study binocular rivalry and fusion but the material viewed almost always consisted of dots and lines or geometrical patterns. Engel was curious to see what would happen if meaningful figures were used instead of the traditional material.

The results are really most exciting. In Engel's experiments he prepares what he calls "stereograms" consisting of photographs 2×2 inches, one of which is seen with the left eye, the other with the right. The photographs he used first were those of members of the Princeton football team just as they appeared in the football program. Although there were slight differences in the size and position of the heads and in the characteristics of light and shadow, still there was sufficient superimposition to get binocular fusion. And what happens? A person looks into the stereoscope and sees one face. He describes this face. And it almost invariably turns out that he is describing neither the face of the man seen with the left eye nor the face of the man seen with the right eye. He is describing a new and different face, a face that he has created out of the features of the two he is looking at. Generally the face seen in this particular case is made up of the dominant features of the two individuals. And generally the face created by the observer in this situation is more attractive and appealing than either of those seen separately. When the observer is shown the trick of the experiment by asking him to close first one eye and then the other and to compare the face he originally saw with the other two, he himself characterizes the face he created as more handsome, more pleasant, a fellow he'd like better, etc.

I hasten to add, however, that we should by no means jump to the conclusion that an individual picks out the "best" or "most attractive" features of figures presented to him in a situation of binocular fusion. For example, Professor Gordon Allport recently took one of Engel's stereoscopes with him to South Africa and initiated some experimental work there, using photographs of members of the different racial groups which make up that complex community.

While the experiments in South Africa have only just begun and no conclusion should be drawn, it is significant to note that in recent letters communicating the early results, Allport reported that when the stereograms consist of a European paired with an Indian, a colored person compared with an Indian, etc., the Zulus see an overwhelming preponderance of Indians. For the Zulu is most strongly prejudiced against the Indian who represents a real threat to him. Allport also reports that when Europeans in South Africa view the stereogram they tend to see more colored faces than white. It would seem, then, that a person sees what is "significant," with significance defined in terms of his relationship to what he is looking at.

One pair of slides we use in demonstrating this piece of equipment consists of two stereograms, each a photograph of a statue in the Louvre. One of the statues is that of a Madonna with Child, the other a lovely young female nude. While I am unable so far to predict what any given individual will "see," no doubt such a prediction might be made after some good psychiatric interviewing. But let me describe what happened in a typical viewing of these stereograms. The viewers happened to be two distinguished psychologists who were visiting me one morning, one from Harvard, the other from Yale. The first looked into the stereoscope and reported that he saw a Madonna with Child. A few seconds later he exclaimed, "But my God, she is undressing." What had happened so far was that somehow she had lost the baby she was holding and her robe had slipped down from her shoulders and stopped just above the breast line. Then in a few more seconds she lost her robe completely and became the young nude. For this particular professor, the nude never did get dressed again. Then my second friend took his turn. For a few seconds he could see nothing but the nude and then he exclaimed, "But now a robe is wrapping itself around her." And very soon he ended up with the Madonna with Child and as far as I know still remains with that vision. Some people will never see the nude; others will never see the Madonna if they keep the intensity of light the same on both stereograms.

In the situation described above, we do not have conditions for genuine fusion, but rather a condition which introduces conflict and choice in the possible meaning of the content represented. In order to learn whether or not there might be differences in choice that would be culturally determined, a cross cultural comparison was made by Dr. James Bagby (1957). He constructed pairs of stereograms that would create binocular rivalry: in one stereogram of each pair he had a picture of some individual, object or symbol that would be of particular interest to Mexicans; in the other stereogram he had a picture that would be of particular significance to Americans. For example, one pair of slides consisted of a picture of a bull fighter matched with a stereogram picturing a baseball player. When these pairs were shown to a sample of Mexican school teachers, an overwhelming proportion of them "saw" the Mexican symbol; when the same slides were presented to a group of American school teachers, the overwhelming proportion "saw" the American symbol.

Incidentally, the Engel stereoscope is so constructed that one can get some idea of the relative "strength" of each of the stereograms by adjusting the intensity of the lighting on each. Hence, if the lighting is equivalent on two stereograms in a rivalry situation, one can reduce the amount of lighting on the one that originally predominates, increase the amount of light on the one that was not "seen" and find the point where the first one disappears and the second one "comes in."

A modification of the stereoscope has just been completed by Mr. Adlerstein in the Princeton laboratory. Our thought was that it might be extremely useful both in the clinical and social areas, if instead of having to use photographs of objects or people, a person could view the real thing—that is, the faces of real, live individuals or pairs of actual objects. So by means of prisms and mirrors, this device was constructed and I have only very recently had the opportunity of experiencing the resulting phenomena. I must say it is strange and wonderful. For example, when I viewed Mr. Adlerstein and Mrs. Pauline Smith, Curator of our Demonstration Center, I seemed to be looking at a very effeminate Mr. Adlerstein who was wearing Mrs. Smith's glasses. Though weird, he was extremely "real." At one point while I was observing them Mrs. Smith began to talk yet it was Adlerstein's lips that were moving! Tingling with excitement and with a certain amount of anxiety, I drove home and asked my wife and daughter to come down to the laboratory so that I could take a look at them. I was, of course, fearful that I might see only one or the other. But fortunately, again I got an amazing fusion—a quite real and lovely head composed of a blending of my daughter's hair and chin and my wife's eyes and mouth—an harmonious composition that would do justice to any artist and which I created almost instantaneously and without any awareness of what was going on. These pieces of apparatus seem to me to have enormous potential usefulness for studying the way in which we create the world around us. I am hoping, for example, that before long someone in a position to do so may use this sort of equipment in a study of disturbed children. The child—having two eyes and two parents—might in some situations and in a very few seconds reveal a good bit about his inner life and his interpersonal family relations.

An interesting series of experiments on perception and interpersonal relations began systematically a few years ago after an observation I made one Sunday morning in our laboratory. An old friend of mine, who was a distinguished lawyer in New York and has since died, called me at home to say that he and his wife had been in town for the weekend and would I be willing to show them some of the Ames' demonstrations about which he had heard. It is important for this story to emphasize the fact that the gentleman in question was really a most unusual man in terms of his ability, charm, accomplishments, and his devotion to his family and friends.

Many of you are familiar, I am sure, with the "distorted room" designed by Adelbert Ames, Jr. which produces the same image on the retina as a regular square room if it is viewed monocularly from a certain point. Since the room is seen as square, persons or objects within the room or people looking through the windows become distorted. I had shown this room to hundreds of individuals and among other phenomena had demonstrated that when two people look through the back windows, the head of one individual appeared to be very large, the head of the other to be very small. When the individuals reversed the windows they were looking through, the size of their heads appeared to the observer to change. But on this Sunday morning when my friend's wife was observing him and me, she said, "Well, Louis, your head is the same size as ever, but Hadley your head is very small." Then we changed the windows we were looking through and she said, "Louis, you're still the same, but Hadley you've become awfully large." Needless to say this remark made a shiver go up my spine and I asked her how she saw the room. It turned out that for her—unlike any other observer until then—the room had become somewhat distorted. In other words, she was using her husband—to whom she was particularly devoted—as her standard. She would not let him go. His nickname for her was "Honi" and we have dubbed this the "Honi phenomenon."

This observation was followed systematically in a series of experiments on married couples by Dr. Warren Wittreich. He found that if couples had been married less than a year there was a very definite tendency not to let the new marital partner distort as quickly or as much as was allowed by people who had been married for a considerable time (1952). But, again, I hasten to add that it is not a simple matter of how long one has been married that determines how willing one is to distort the size or shape of one's marital partner! The original observation was made on a couple who were already grandparents. Preliminary investigation also seems to show that parents of young children will not allow their children to distort as readily as will parents of older children.

We could continue at some length reporting experiments which seem to show that what we "perceive" is, as already emphasized, in large part our own creation and depends on the assumptions we bring to the particular occasion. We seem to give meaning and order to sensory impingements in terms of our own needs and purposes and this process of selection is actively creative.

Social constancies and self-constancy

It is clear that when we look for constancies in other people either as individuals or as members of a group a variety of complications is introduced. For when people are involved, as contrasted to inorganic objects or most other forms of life, we are dealing with purposes, with motives, with intentions which we have to take into account in our perceptual process—the purposes, motives and intentions of other people often difficult to understand. The purposes and intentions of these other people will, of course, change as conditions change; and they will change as behavior progresses from one goal to another. Other people's purposes will be affected by our purposes, just as our purposes will be affected by theirs.

It is by no means a quick and easy process, then, to endow the people with whom we participate in our interpersonal relations with constancies and repeatabilities that we can always rely on. And yet we must, of course, continue the attempt to do so, so that our own purposeful action will have a greater chance of bringing about the satisfying consequences we intended. So we try to pigeonhole people according to some role, status, or position. We create constancies concerning people and social situations. These provide us with certain consistent characteristics that will ease our interpretation and make our actions more effective so long as there is some correspondence between the attribution we make and the consequence we experience from it in our own action.

The "social constancies" we learn obviously involve the relationships between ourselves and others. So if any social constancy is to be operational, there must also be a sense of "self-constancy." The two are interdependent. Since the human being necessarily derives so much of his value satisfaction from association with other human beings, his conception of his "self," his own "self-constancy" and "self-significance" is determined to a large extent by the significance he has to other people and the way they behave toward him. This point is, of course, a familiar one and has been eloquently illustrated in literature as, for example, in Shaw's *Pygmalion*.

But it seems to me of paramount importance in any discussion of perception and interpersonal relations that we should not slip into the error of positing an abstract "self" or "ego" that can somehow be isolated, pointed to, analyzed, or experienced apart from any social context. It is only through the life setting and the process of participation with others that meaning and continuity are given to the "self." If the constancy of "self" is upset, it becomes difficult for us to assess changes in our interpersonal relations and accommodate to them. We lose the compass that keeps us going in a direction. "We" are lost.

This does not mean in any sense that for self-constancy to be maintained there can be no development or growth. On the contrary, self-development and growth are themselves aspects of social constancy. But this development must flow from form if it is to be recognized, if there is to be continuity, and if there is to be a standard for comparison. Obviously, each of us surrounds himself with anchoring points of one kind or another which help to maintain this self-constancy in the process of ceaseless change around us. In this connection I think, for example, of Konrad Lorenz' interpretation of why people like dogs. In his book *King Solomon's Ring,* he writes that we should "not lie to ourselves that we need the dog as a protection for our house. We *do* need him, but not as a watch-dog. I, at least in dreary foreign towns, have certainly stood in need of my dog's company and I have derived, from the mere fact of his existence, a great sense of inward security, such as one finds in a childhood memory or in the prospect of the scenery of one's own home country, for me the Blue Danube, for you the White Cliffs of Dover. In the almost film-like flitting-by of modern life, a man needs something to tell him, from time to time, that he is still himself, and nothing can give him this assurance in so comforting a manner as the 'four feet trotting behind.' "

This interdependent problem of social constancy and self-constancy has been submitted to some preliminary investigation. For example, when a person is wearing a pair of aniseikonic spectacles, which greatly distort the shape of the environment when familiar monocular cues are ruled out, he will generally see another person as distorted if that person is standing in an environment which has itself already become distorted. With a certain pair of these spectacles, for example, an individual will be seen as leaning forward with the upper and lower half of his body distorted in length. Dr. Wittreich set up such a situation at the Naval Training Center at Bainbridge, Maryland, to see what might happen when the relationship of the person who was doing the viewing and the person being viewed was altered. His subjects were 24 white male Navy recruits. They first observed an authority figure dressed up as a first class petty officer and, second, a non-authority figure dressed up in a white enlisted uniform with the marks of a recruit. Wittreich found that the authority figure did not distort nearly as much as the non-authority figure. In other words, the disciplinary training imposed in an organization that depends for effective functioning on the rigid acceptance of roles had produced a "constancy" which overpowered physiological changes in the optical system.

Another finding using the aniseikonic spectacles may be of interest, namely, that a person tends to report much less distortion of his own image when he looks at himself in a full-length mirror while wearing aniseikonic spectacles than he reports when he is looking at a stranger. When one looks at one's self, the changes that appear seem to be minor and detailed—for example, slight distortions in the hands or feet; when one looks at a stranger, there is the more general bodily distortion plus the leaning one way or another, depending on the kind of spectacles used.

A subsequent study of Wittreich, and one which I emphasize is only suggestive, was made comparing 21 subjects obtained from the patient roster of the neuro-psychiatric unit at the Bethesda Naval Hospital. When these disturbed individuals were wearing aniseikonic spectacles and saw their own image in the mirror, they tended to see the gross distortions that the "normal" population attributed to others; and, conversely, when the disturbed clinic population looked at others, they tended to see the more detailed and minor distortions which the "normal" population had seen in themselves. All I should like to conclude about this particular experiment so far is that there seems to be some difference between the normal individual and the clinical patient in the functional importance assigned to his bodily image; the patient may conceivably be operating in terms of a relatively fixed and homogeneous image of himself which does not alter readily with the demands of the environment.

Perceptual change

Laboratory experimentation as well as research in the field of opinion and attitude change seems to demonstrate beyond a shadow of a doubt that the major condition for a change in our perception, our attitudes or opinions is a frustration experienced in carrying out our purposes effectively because we are acting on the basis of assumptions that prove "wrong." For example, Dr. Kilpatrick has demonstrated that apparently the only way in which we can "learn" to see our distorted room distorted is to become frustrated with the assumption that the room is "square" in the process of trying to carry out some action in the room (1954). It is clear that an "intellectual," "rational," or "logical" understanding of a situation is by no means sufficient to alter perception. The psychotherapist has taught us how successful reconditioning requires a therapy which simplifies goals so that their accomplishment can be assured through an individual's action as he experiences the successful consequences of his own behavior and thereby rebuilds his confidence in himself.

Parenthetically, while one of the outstanding characteristics of man is often said to be his amazing capacity to learn, it seems to me that an equally outstanding characteristic is man's amazing capacity to "unlearn" which is, I think, not the exact opposite. Because man is not entirely a creature of habit, he has the fortunate ability to slough off what is no longer of use to him.

The reality of abstractions and the commonness of purposes

In order to ease our interpersonal relations and to increase the commonness of the significances we may attribute to the happenings around us, man has created abstractions in his attempt to bring order into disorder and to find more universal guides for living no matter what the unique and individual purposes and circumstances of an individual may be. Such abstractions are represented by our scientific formulations, our ethical, political, legal and religious systems. The abstractions can be recalled and repeated at will. They can be communicated. They are repeatable because they are static and have fixed characteristics.

The value of these abstractions for us in our interpersonal relations seems to be that when the tangibles of our personal reality world break down, we can turn to the intangible—to the abstractions we have learned that have been created by others and have presumably proved useful to them. We can begin to check our own particular situation, possibly a frustrating one, against the abstraction and thereby, perhaps experience for ourselves what the abstraction is referring to. Only then will the abstraction become real for us. For when it does become functional for us in our own individual lives, it *is* real as a determinant of our experience and behavior.

32 The prediction of interpersonal attraction

THEODORE M. NEWCOMB

During the past 30 years, according to my estimate, 9,426 articles and books, plus or minus 2,712, have been published in English on the topic of "attitudes." A large proportion of them deal with attitudes toward people—most commonly toward family members, toward categories like ethnic, religious, or occupational groups, or toward prominent individuals like Franklin D. Roosevelt or Adolf Hitler. At the level of psychological generalization, such studies have probably taught us more about the organization of individual personality, and about group influences upon individual motivation and cognition, than about the nature of person-to-person relationships. At any rate it seems appropriate to pose the question whether persons, as objects of attitudes, have properties that distinguish them from other classes of objects. If so, it is possible that the determinants of attitudes toward persons are in some respects different from those of other attitudes. Since it is convenient to have a distinctive label for something that one wishes to keep distinct, I shall use the term "attraction" to refer to attitudes toward persons as a class of objects.

Perhaps the simplest—and, in many ways, still the most convincing—of the notions concerning determinants of positive attraction is that of *propinquity*. In its baldest form, the proposition of propinquity reads as follows: other things equal, people are most likely to be attracted toward those in closest contact with them. Everyday illustrations readily leap to mind. Adults generally have strongest attraction toward those children, and children toward those adults, with whom they are in most immediate contact—which is to say, their own children and their own parents. And this commonly occurs, let me remind you, in spite of the fact that neither parents nor children choose each other. Or, if we are willing to accept the fact of selection of marriage partners as an index of positive attraction, then the available data are strongly in support of a theory of propinquity. If we use an adequate range of distance—miles, or city blocks rather than yards, or within-block distances—there is a neat, monotonic relationship between residential propinquity and probability of marriage, other criteria of eligibility being held constant (e.g., Bossard, 1932; Campbell, 1939; Davie, *et al.*, 1939).

It is, of course, a truism that distance per se will have no consequences for attraction; what we are concerned with is something that is made possible, or more likely, with decreasing distance. I think we may also consider it a truism that that something is behavior. Further, it is behavior on the part of one person that is observed and responded to by another: it is interaction. So widespread and so compelling is the evidence for the relationship between frequency of

Abridged from the **American Psychologist**, 1956, 11, 575–87, with permission of the author and the American Psychological Association.

interaction and positive attraction that Homans (1950) has ventured to hypothesize that "If the frequency of interaction between two or more persons increases, the degree of their liking for one another will increase." Actuarially speaking, the evidence is altogether overwhelming that, *ignoring other variables,* the proposition is correct in a wide range of situations.

Why should this be so? Accepting the proposition only in an actuarial sense, and ignoring for the moment the other variables obviously involved, what theoretical considerations will enable us to make psychological sense out of it? The principle which comes first to mind is that of *reward and reinforcement*. Two simple assumptions will enable us to make direct use of this principle: first, that when persons interact, the reward-punishment ratio is more often such as to be reinforcing than extinguishing; and second, that the on-the-whole rewarding effects of interaction are most apt to be obtained from those with whom one interacts most frequently. These assumptions, together with the principles of reward and reinforcement and canalization, would account for the general association of frequency of interaction with positive attraction; they would not, of course, account for the many observed exceptions to the generalization.

To return to my earlier illustrations, this set of assumptions and principles would not apply in exactly the same way to the facts of attraction between parents and children and to the facts of marital selection. One difference, of course, is that selection is possible in the latter but not in the former case. As applied to the facts of parent-child attraction, the principle of propinquity asserts, in effect, that we are attracted to those whom "fate" has made rewarding. As applied to the facts of marital selection, the principle of propinquity says little more, in addition to this, than that the likelihood of being rewarded by interaction varies with opportunity for interaction. The problem of selection, among those with whom opportunity for interaction is the same, still remains.

The principle of *generalization* has often been called upon to account for selective attraction among those with whom opportunities for interaction are the same. Many Freudians, in particular, have assumed that in adolescence or adulthood attractions are largely determined by personal qualities resembling those of parents or siblings, initially determined by the Oedipus configuration—as illustrated by the old refrain, "I want a girl just like the girl that married dear old Dad." This principle, together with its variants, obviously cannot be omitted from a complete theory of interpersonal attraction, but neither can it be considered as a major contribution to it, since, in itself, it says nothing about the initial basis of attraction but only about extensions from one already attractive person to another, similar one. Perhaps the chief contribution of the principle of generalization lies in the enhanced probability that thresholds for interaction with persons resembling those toward whom one is already attracted are lower than for other persons; if so, then the likelihood of the rewards of interaction with such persons is greater than for other persons.

There is an interesting consequence of the proposition that attraction toward others varies with the frequency of being rewarded by them. Opportunities for being rewarded by others vary not only with propinquity, as determined by irrelevant considerations like birth and residence, but also with the motivations of the potentially rewarding persons. This suggests that the likelihood of being continually rewarded by a given person varies with the frequency with which that person is in turn rewarded, and thus we have a proposition of *reciprocal reward:* the likelihood of receiving rewards from a given person, over time, varies with the frequency of rewarding him. This proposition is significant for my problem in various ways, especially because it forces further consideration of the conditions under which continued interaction between the same persons is most likely, and under which, therefore, the possibilities of continued reciprocal reward are greatest.

The first of these may be most simply described as the possession by two or more persons of common interests, apart from themselves, that require interdependent behavior. If you like to play piano duets, or tennis, you are apt to be rewarded by those who make it possible for you to do so, and at the same time you are apt to reward your partner. Insofar as both partners are rewarded, another evening of duets or another set of tennis is likely to ensue, together with still further opportunities for reciprocal reward. Thus attraction breeds attraction.

The second condition favorable to continued reciprocal rewards has to do with complementary interests (rather than with similar ones) that require interdependent behavior. These are symbiotic relationships, like that in which cow and cowbird become attracted to each other: the cow provides sustenance for the bird in the form of parasitic insects, the removal of which is rewarding to both. Or, at the human level, consider the exchange of gratifications between a pair of lovers. Here, too, under conditions of complementary rather than of similar motivations, the general rule is that attraction breeds attraction.

There have also been interesting attempts, of late, to test the proposition that symbiotic personality needs tend to characterize marriage partners—who, it may be presumed, are reciprocally attracted to a greater than average degree. Professor E. L. Kelly's work, some of which was reported on this occasion one year ago (1955), has quite consistently revealed the existence of similar rather than complementary traits, both among spouses twenty-odd years married and among engaged couples. It is interesting, however, that his findings since last year suggest a curvilinear relationship between initial homogeneity and marriage durability; the best prognosis is provided by neither too much nor too little similarity. These findings, however, are not conclusive for my present problem—first, because there are many determinants of marriage durability other than personal attraction; and second, because comparatively few of the traits that he measured were such as could either confirm or disconfirm the hypothesis of personality symbiosis.

This problem has, however, been directly attacked by Professor Robert Winch, using measures derived from Murray's list of needs. My own perusal of his research reports (1955, 1956) suggests no conclusive findings for my problem, but if his personality ratings are free from contamination it seems clear that, within his sample of 25 middle-class couples, traits or needs can be found with regard to which spouses are more likely to be different than alike

—in particular a dimension labeled "assertive-receptive." It is not possible, from Winch's data (nor from any other data known to me), to estimate how much of the variance in marital selection can be accounted for in terms of symbiotic personality needs. But it is surely a plausible notion that an individual with strong needs for assertiveness is more likely to find himself rewarded in this area of his life by interaction with a person who is receptive to his assertiveness than with one who is not.

The most detailed of the analyses of sociometric structures, especially those of Jennings (1950), reveal analogous kinds of personality symbiosis; the over-chosen need the under-chosen, and vice versa. Many of the phenomena of choosing and accepting "leaders" (cf. Gibb, 1954) are also understandable from this point of view.

There is another common notion about interpersonal attraction, to the effect that it varies with similarity, as such: birds of a feather flock together. It is not a very useful notion, however, because it is indiscriminate. We have neither good reason nor good evidence for believing that persons of similar blood types, for example, or persons whose surnames have the same numbers of letters, are especially attracted to one another. The answer to the question, Similarity with respect to what?, is enormously complex—because similarities of many kinds are associated with sheer contiguity, for one thing. I shall therefore content myself with the guess (for which fairly good evidence exists) that the possession of similar characteristics predisposes individuals to be attracted to each other to the degree that those characteristics are both observable and valued by those who observe them—in short, insofar as they provide a basis for similarity of attitudes.

Up to this point I have noted that we acquire favorable or unfavorable attitudes toward persons as we are rewarded or punished by them, and that the principles of contiguity, of reciprocal reward, and of complementarity have to do with the conditions under which rewards are most probable. From now on I shall be primarily concerned with a special subclass of reciprocal rewards—those associated with communicative behavior.

The interaction processes through which reciprocal reward occurs have to do not with the exchange of energy but with the exchange of information, and are therefore communicative. I prefer the term "communicative behavior" to "social interaction" because it calls attention to certain consequences that are characteristic of information exchange, but not of energy exchange, among symbol-using humans. The use of symbols, needless to say, involves the expenditure of energy, but—even in so obvious an example as that of receiving a slap in the face—it is the consequences of the information exchange rather than the energy exchange which interest us, as psychologists.

I shall note two of these consequences, in the form of very general propositions—though each of them is in fact subject to very specific limitations. The first is this: Communicators tend to become more similar to each other, at least momentarily, in one or more respects, than they were before the communication. At the very least (assuming more or less accurate receipt of a message that has been intentionally sent), both sender and receiver now have the information that the sender wishes to call the attention of the receiver to the object of communication

—i.e., that which the symbols symbolize. If we stipulate still further conditions, the proposition will apply to a wider range of similarity. Suppose, for example, that a person has just expressed an opinion about something—say the United Nations; to the degree that he is sincere, and insofar as the receiver trusts his sincerity, the communication (if accurately received) will be followed by increased cognitive similarity, to the effect that the transmitter holds the stated opinion. Now suppose we add a further stipulation—that the receiver not only trusts the sender's sincerity but also respects his knowledgeability; under these conditions the opinions of sender and receiver are likely to be more similar than they were before.

It is this last kind of similarity—i.e., that of attitudes—that has a special importance for the problem of interpersonal attraction. In fact, the proposition, as applied to similarity of attitudes toward objects of communication, has already introduced, as independent variables, certain dimensions of attraction—namely, trust and respect. Change toward similarity in one kind of attitude following communication, I have asserted, varies with another kind of attitude—i.e., attraction.

My second proposition reverses this relationship: Attraction toward a co-communicator (actual or potential) varies with perceived similarity of attitudes toward the object of communication. Before specifying the limited conditions under which this proposition applies, let me briefly present its rationale.

While there are, of course, many exceptions, it is a highly dependable generalization that the life history of every human has made accurate communication rewarding far more often than punishing. Such is our dependence upon one another, from the very beginnings of communicative experience, and such is our indebtedness to culture, which is transmitted via communication, that success in the enterprise of becoming socialized depends upon success in transmitting and receiving messages. Insofar as accurate communication is in fact rewarding, reward value will attach to the co-communicator—which is to say that positive attraction toward him will increase (other things equal) with frequency of accurate communication with him. Please note the qualification: "insofar as accurate communication is in fact rewarding"; there are many messages—e.g., "I hate you"—the accurate receipt of which is not in fact rewarding.

If, as I have maintained, increased similarity in some degree and manner is the regular accompaniment of accurate communication, it would be no surprise to discover that increased similarity becomes a goal of communication, and that its achievement is rewarding. And if, as I have also maintained, the reward value of successful communication attaches to the co-communicator, then it follows that the two kinds of reward effects—perception of increased similarity as rewarding, and perception of the co-communicator as rewarding—should vary together. This, in brief, is the rationale of my second proposition.

It is, however, a very general statement, and its usefulness can be enhanced by a further specification of conditions. I shall mention only two of them. First, the discovery of increased similarity is rewarding to the degree that the object with regard to which there is similarity of attitudes is valued (either negatively or positively). The discovery of agreement between oneself and a new acquaintance regarding some matter of only casual interest will probably be less rewarding than the discovery of agreement concerning one's own pet prejudices. The reward value of increased similarity increases, secondly, with the common relevance of the attitude object to the communicators. The success of a certain presidential candidate, for example, is likely to be seen as having consequences for both, whereas matters regarded as belonging in the area of personal taste—like taking cream in one's coffee—are viewed as devoid of common consequences. The discovery of similarity of the latter kind is not very likely to have much reward value.

The thesis that interpersonal attraction varies with perceived similarity in regard to objects of importance and of common relevance is, from one point of view, opposed to the thesis of complementarity. In my own view, however, they are not in opposition; indeed, I regard the thesis of complementarity as a special case of similarity. Let me illustrate. Suppose, as Winch's data may indicate, that an assertive person is more likely to be attracted toward a receptive than toward another assertive person, as a marriage partner. It is my guess that this would most probably occur if they have similar attitudes to the effect that one of them should be assertive and the other receptive. In short, I am attempting to defend the thesis that interpersonal attraction always and necessarily varies with perceived similarity regarding important and relevant objects (including the persons themselves). While I regard similarity of attitudes as a necessary rather than a sufficient condition, I believe that it accounts for more of the variance in interpersonal attraction than does any other single variable.

As the foregoing implies, and as I have elsewhere suggested (1953), attraction and perceived similarity of attitude tend to maintain a constant relationship because each of them is sensitive to changes in the other. If newly received information about another person leads to increased or decreased attraction toward him, appropriate changes in perceived similarity readily ensue—often at the cost of accuracy. And if new information—either about the object or about another person's attitudes toward it—leads to perceptions of increased or decreased similarity with him, then the direction or the degree of attraction toward him easily accommodates itself to the situation as newly perceived. Change in attraction is one, but only one, of the devices by which some sort of tension state, associated with perceived discrepancy about important and relevant objects, is kept at a minimum.

At the outset, I raised the question whether persons, as objects of attitudes, have properties that distinguish them from other objects. I ought now to acknowledge that I have already assumed that they do. I have been assuming that persons, as *objects* of attitudes, also *have* attitudes of their own—and, in particular, that they have (or can have) attitudes toward the *same* objects as do persons who are sources of attitudes toward the object-persons. Further, I have been assuming that object-persons have the same capacities for being disturbed by perceived discrepancies as do those who are attracted toward them. In degree, if not *in toto*, these are distinctively human characteristics, as G. H. Mead long ago noted (1934), and any theory of interpersonal attraction that is at all distinctive from a general theory of attitudes must, I believe, pay homage to this fact.

The remainder of this paper is devoted to some tests of specific predictions derived from the two propositions already presented, which may be telescoped as follows: Insofar as communication results in the perception of increased similarity of attitude toward important and relevant objects, it will also be followed by an increase in positive attraction. I shall therefore consider perceived similarity of attitude as a predictor of attraction. I shall also, for obvious reasons, be interested in actual, or objective, similarity.[1]

I turn now to some specific predictions. First, if the basic generalization is correct, it should follow that, regardless of the content of communication, positive attraction will increase with opportunity for communication, other things equal. The only additional assumption involved in this prediction is that the likelihood of being rewarded by a co-communicator increases with opportunity for communication. I might add that there is nothing new about this prediction; it is, in fact, a restatement of our old friend, the principle of propinquity. Previous studies—e.g., by Festinger, Schachter, and Back (1950) and by Deutsch and Collins (1951)—have provided convincing support for it.

Our own data give partial, but not complete, support for the prediction. Perhaps the best illustration of our findings that I can offer stems from an experimental "failure." During our first project year, roommate assignments had, literally, been drawn from a hat. In planning for the second year, however, we decided to assign roommates by experimental criteria. Half of the roommate combinations were therefore assigned in such manner as to insure (as we thought) that *minimal* attraction between roommates would result, and *maximal* attraction in the other half of the combinations. (Our assignments were based upon data provided by mail, some weeks before the men arrived.) Our predictions received no support whatever; from the very beginning, and during each of the succeeding 15 weeks, the mean level of attraction between roommates—including those for whom we had predicted low attraction—was higher than for all non-roommate pairs. It is also worth reporting that, at the beginning but not at the end of the semester, mean attraction among all pairs living on each of the two floors of the house was higher than for all inter-floor pairs. During the final week, 90 per cent of all inter-roommate choices were in the upper three-eighths of all choices.

These findings, as I have said, were obtained during our second year. Now I must report that, during the first year, the relationship between attraction and room propinquity was nothing like so close. I shall not stop to give you the actual figures, but at the end of the semester inter-roommate attraction was only slightly higher than that between non-roommates. This inconsistency would be frustrating, indeed, if there were no other variables to which the differences could be related; after describing these other variables, I shall show that they account for much of

[1] At this point in the original paper, Prof. Newcomb describes his method and the subjects in his experiment: two groups, in separate, succeeding years of initially unacquainted male students living together under "natural" university conditions in a rooming house.—Eds.

this inconsistency with regard to proximity. Meanwhile, the proposition under consideration is that proximity, alone, cannot account for attraction, but only to the degree that it facilitates the development of perceived similarity of attitude does it contribute to attraction.

The remainder of my predictions, unlike the first, take into account the content of communication. They are of the following general form: If and when increased attraction between pairs of persons does occur with opportunity for communication, it will be associated with increased similarity of attitude toward important and relevant objects.

The first of these predictions is based upon the additional assumption that one's self is a valued object to oneself. If so, then attraction should vary closely with self-other agreement about oneself. More specifically, insofar as a person's presumably ambivalent self-orientations are predominantly positive, his attraction toward others will vary directly with their attraction toward him. In testing this proposition, reciprocal attraction may be treated either as "objective" (i.e., as actually expressed by others toward the individual being considered) or as "perceived" (i.e., as that individual estimates that others will express attraction toward himself). The latter prediction, however—that one's attraction toward others varies with their perceived attraction toward oneself—seems almost untestable except in circular fashion; there are few ways in which it can be demonstrated in a "natural" situation, that attraction toward others is the dependent variable and that perceived attraction toward oneself the independent variable.

Whatever the causal direction, our data show that an individual's distribution of General Liking among his associates is related to their liking for him. The relationship is almost as close on the fourth day as at the end of the fourth month, and as a general tendency is highly significant, though there are individual exceptions. One can predict an individual's liking for another individual with much better than chance accuracy if one knows the latter's liking for the former, at any time after the fourth day.

The prediction will be a good deal more accurate, however, if it is made from an individual's *estimate* of how well he is liked by the other. At any time from the second week on (when such estimates were first made), about three of every four estimates of another person's liking for oneself were in the same half of the distribution as own liking for that other person. Median rank-order correlations were .86 at the end, and .75 at the beginning, between each man's liking for each other man and his estimate of the reciprocals. As might be expected, this relationship was especially close at the extremes; 5 out of 6 predictions of liking for other persons would be in the correct quarter of the distribution, if based only upon subjects' estimates that they are in the highest or lowest quarter of reciprocated liking. Such findings correspond closely to those previously reported by Tagiuri (1952).

Apparently the close relationship between General Liking and its estimated reciprocal is but slightly influenced by communication. At any rate, the relationship does not increase significantly from the near-strangership to close acquaintance, nor is the relationship significantly closer for roommates, at the end of the four-month period, than for non-roommates. Neither, as a matter of fact, does accuracy in estimating reciprocal liking increase with further acquaintance, for most subjects. Estimates of others' liking for oneself are so closely correlated with own liking for those same persons (the relationship approaches the self-correlation of either measure, at any given time), that most of the variance of either can be accounted for by the other. Whatever influences either of them influences both in about the same way.

The proposition that perceived similarity in valuing the self contributes heavily to variance in attraction, together with the assumption that self-valuation tends to remain high at all times, is thus well supported. All persons, at all times, are liked according as they are judged to agree with oneself about oneself. These judgments become more accurate over time to the degree that one's actual changes in status make it possible to judge them accurately and at the same time continue to believe that one's own likings are reciprocated. For those who are discovering that their actual status is relatively low, the conflict—or, more specifically, the strain of perceived discrepancy—thus aroused is reduced at the cost of accuracy.

I have already implied that attraction is hypothetically predictable from cognitive as well as from cathectic similarity regarding objects of importance. I shall present findings concerning cognitive similarity regarding only one kind of object—persons. Each subject was asked to describe himself as well as the other house members by checking adjectives drawn from a list prepared by Professor Harrison Gough (1955). Each was also asked to describe his "ideal self," by using the same list, and to describe himself as he thought other house members would describe him. By comparing these responses with self-descriptions, we obtained measures of perceived similarity regarding the self. (This work closely parallels that by Fiedler (1954) concerning "assumed similarity.")

Attraction turns out to be closely related to perceived agreement (at considerably less than the .001 level). When the same data are analyzed individually, only two of 17 subjects fail to show the relationship in the predicted direction, and only one of these reverses it. This finding is more impressive than it would be if it resulted from attributing only favorable judgments of oneself to high-liked others, and only unfavorable judgments to low-liked others. Actually, eight of the ten subjects who accepted unfavorable adjectives as describing themselves, and who indicated that one or more others agreed with them, showed more agreement in these unfavorable descriptions with high-liked than with low-liked others. The relationship between attraction and perceived agreement on favorable items is, not surprisingly, a good deal closer. At any rate, the finding that attraction varies with perceived cognitive agreement about the self is not merely an artifactual result of the common-sense assumption that one is attracted toward those who are believed to think well of one.

My next prediction deals not with the self as object of attitudes but with other house members. Of all the objects about which we obtained responses, nothing compared in importance or in group relevance with the house members themselves. Very early they became differentiated in attraction status, so that it was easy to measure similarity, on the part of any pair of persons, in attraction toward the remaining members. Correlations were calculated between the attraction scores of each member and those of each other member (there were 136 such pairs, each year) toward all of the other 15 members; this was done for each of the 16 weeks that the group lived together. Thus the proposition could be tested that the greater the similarity between any two members in assigning General Liking scores to the other 15 members, the higher their attraction for each other. A related prediction is that this relationship will increase with communication—that is, with time.

Both propositions receive clear support, according to both criteria of attraction. On the fourth day the relationship between within-pair General Liking and within-pair correlation of General Liking for remaining members is barely significant, and only slightly higher a week later. It increases fairly steadily till, at the end of four months, two-thirds of all within-pair attractions would be correctly placed in the upper or lower half of the distribution, judging only from the fact of being in the upper or the lower half of the distribution of correlations. This finding emerges more clearly by comparing the mean within-pair correlations for various categories of within-pair attraction, as shown in Figure 1.

Individuals in high agreement with each other about the other 15 house members clearly tend to be attracted to each other. The opposite tendency is much less pronounced; none of the categories involving subjects in the lower eight ranks has a mean correlation much below the average of the total set of pairs. The lowest of all the mean correlations (shown by the "X" in Figure 1) is that of all pairs of which one member—and only one—is in the lowest quarter of attraction (ranks 13–16). For these 44 pairs the mean correlation is .35—not significantly different from zero.

Though it has, in general, proven easier to predict to high than to low attraction, those lowest in our house totem pole deserve a paragraph. The lowest three in our second-year group were truly rejected (according to objective criteria which I cannot stop to specify); they were literally disliked as none others were. (The next lowest two, on the other hand, were near-isolates, who were withdrawn and more or less ignored but not generally dis-

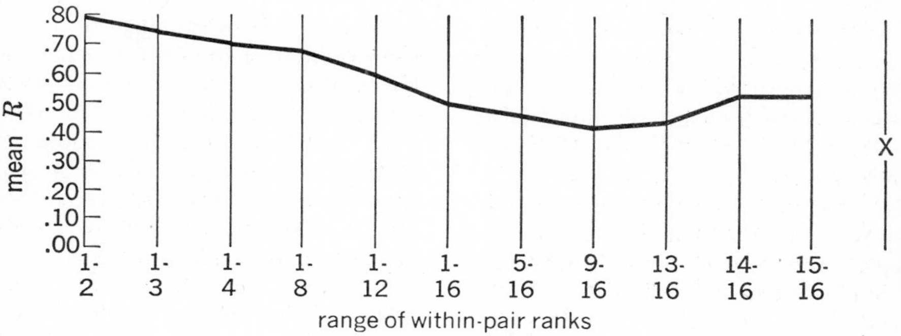

Figure 1. Mean within pair correlations of attraction toward other members.

liked.) All six of the attraction responses given and received within this set of three rejects were among the lowest possible three ranks, their average being exactly 15, when 15.5 is the lowest possible average; they were liked by each other even less than others liked them. At the same time, the three intra-pair correlations among these three rejects are slightly above the average for the entire group of subjects, and .7 sigmas above the mean correlation for the same individuals with all others except the rejects themselves (.52 as compared with .39). In short, they disliked each other but tended to agree with each other about the remaining individuals more than they agreed with the remaining individuals. This, of course, is very perverse of them, and it is tempting to conclude that such willful thwarting of my favorite hypothesis is all of a piece with their personalities, as rejected persons. I shall content myself, however, with suggesting that these three rejects developed a special set of standards: personal inoffensiveness in others was highly valued. If such standards did indeed exist, I believe they were developed by each of the three men in relative independence of the other two. They disliked each other too much to be very much influenced by each other. Such agreement as there was among them concerning the remaining men occurred, we know, without benefit of much communication, and it is well to be reminded that attitudinal similarity can occur on the part of individuals in the same predicament facing the same objective world, quite independently of one another's influence.

Since these two predictors (estimated reciprocation and within-pair agreement) are far from perfectly correlated (their relationship is indicated by a contingency coefficient of .60), one may ask about their comparative and their combined predictive power. The statistical breakdowns will eventually be published,[2] and so I shall not present them here. The fact is that if one merely wishes to pin-point the individual instances of high attraction, the estimated reciprocal, alone, is the most successful of all predictors; 97 per cent of the highest quarter of attractions are selected by the criterion of the upper half of the estimated reciprocals. But if one wishes to account for maximum variance, and at both ends of the distribution, the combined criteria are better than either alone. As indicated by a coefficient of contingency of .53 between the combined predictors and actual attraction scores, almost one-third of the variance in attraction is thus accounted for. High attraction is particularly well predicted by the joint criteria; virtually none of those predicted as high are in fact in the lower half of attraction scores.

At a theoretical level, I consider it highly significant that these two predictors, the combined effects of which are more successful than either alone, include one subjective index (estimates of reciprocal attraction) and one that is objective, in the sense of describing a relationship between a pair of persons and not referring to either person alone. Theoretically speaking, this is as it should be. Doubtless most forms of social behavior, like attraction, are jointly determined by individual characteristics and by relationships to others —relationships which pertain to the recipient of behavior quite as much as to the behaver himself.

Now let me return, briefly, to our

[2] See T. M. Newcomb, **The Acquaintance Process (1961).—Eds.**

finding that, in one year but not in the other, the mere fact of being a roommate accounted for much of the variance in the development of attraction. I have already implied that propinquity is a facilitator but not a sufficient condition for the development of positive attraction. It should follow, therefore, that attraction between roommates will be relatively high only insofar as their propinquity contributes to the development of one or more of the conditions favorable to high attraction. This is exactly what our data show: roommates scored much higher on both predictor variables during the second year than did non-roommates, but not during the first year.

The year-to-year differences in the relationship between attraction and room proximity are paralleled by comparable differences in the relationship between proximity and one of the predictor variables, namely, within-pair correlation of attraction toward the other members. Roommates differ from all others by one full standard deviation at the end of the second year, but by only one-fifth of a standard deviation at the end of the first year. According to the other predictor variable, perceived reciprocality of liking, the differences are of exactly the same order, and the curves are correspondingly parallel.

You are doubtless wondering about the generality of the proposition that attraction is predictable from similarity of attitude toward important and relevant objects, since the only objects that I have mentioned, so far, are persons. Although our analyses are far from complete, they indicate that the proposition also applies to objects other than persons, though at lower levels of confidence. But it is already clear that, in this research setting, there were no objects which compared in relevance, *for all members,* to house members themselves. We sampled a range of attitudes that extended virtually from cabbages to kings; there were several pairs of subjects for whom kings (or at least presidents) were highly relevant, and there may have been some whose within-pair attraction was influenced by attitudes toward cole slaw. There were, however, no *single* non-person objects of sufficient relevance for *all* members to account for very much variance in the attraction level among all pairs.

One way of describing this complication is to note that our subjects knew so much about so many of each others' attitudes that no single one was crucial for all pairs. This predicament is well illustrated by a series of experimental findings. On several occasions, outsiders were brought in to present a point of view on a controversial topic; our subjects' General Liking for these speakers, about whom they knew nothing apart from the one topic, was (as predicted) closely correlated with perceived agreement with them. Perhaps the moral to this story is that, if one wants uncomplicated findings, one should stick to brief, laboratory-like, rather than to long-term, "natural," situations.

There were two ways in which we were able, nevertheless, to show relationships between attraction and similarity in attitude toward non-person objects. The first of these was by regarding highly generalized values as objects. For example, agreement in Allport-Vernon scores was related to attraction, for the total population of 136 pairs; the significance levels ranged from .05 to .01, depending upon the exact measures of each variable. If Osgood's three-dimensional measure of meaning structure (1952) may be regarded as a highly generalized attitude, of both cognitive and cathectic nature, toward things-in-general, then the results of using this measure are also relevant. "Semantic harmony," derived from responses to a wide range of stimulus words (e.g., father, politics, sex, money), was significantly related to at least one of our measures of attraction, for all 136 pairs.

Our second approach was to take as an index of attitude similarity the *number* of non-person objects about which there was a given degree of similarity, rather than the *degree* of similarity regarding a single object. This index was related to attraction, for at least one of our two sets of subjects, though not, apparently, at significance levels below .05. This was one of the few measures, by the way, of pre-acquaintance similarity which successfully predicted, among all pairs, to later attraction. If, as appears to be the case, its predictive value tended to increase with time, this finding would be consistent with the assumption that, over time, our subjects tended to sort each other out as they gradually discovered one another's attitudes on a wide range of issues.

The fact seems to be that one can predict to interpersonal attraction, under specified conditions, from frequency of interaction, from the perception of reciprocated attraction, from certain combinations of personality characteristics, and from attitudinal agreement. There is no self-evident reason why such diverse variables, viewed common-sense-wise, should belong together; one might almost suspect that they had been drawn out of a hatful of miscellaneous variables. But predictive propositions about those variables all flow, as I have tried to show, from a very few psychological assumptions. I believe the confluence to be both theoretically required and empirically supported. These considerations seem to me to lend confidence to the point of view that a limited theory about a limited class of objects—namely, persons—can profit by taking account of the significant properties of those objects, and in particular those properties closely related to the fact of human dependence upon communication.

33 Perceiving the other person

FRITZ HEIDER

Through perception we come to cognize the world around us, a world made up of things and people and events. Obviously, the existence of the other person, *o*, as an object with not only physical and spatial particulars, but also with complex psychological properties, must be mediated in some way to the subject, that is perceived by *p*, if *o* is to feature in *p*'s thinking, feelings, and actions. Likewise, if *p* is to influence *o*, he must create changes that in some way can be perceived by *o*, barring, of course, internal reactions such as those instigated by drugs that affect *o*. The nature of this perception, in particular the principles that underly the coordination between the stimulus conditions outside the person and his experience or phenomenal representation of them, is the topic to which we shall address ourselves here.

Our orientation is directed toward explicating some of the naïve, implicit principles that underlie perception, principles that connect the stimulus configurations presented to the person with his apprehension of them. During the course of this explication, we shall leave the realm of naïve psychology and make use of knowledge gained from the scientific causal analysis of the perceptual process. Moreover, because many of the principles underlying social perception have parallels in the field of nonsocial or thing perception, and because in many instances their significance has first been recognized in this field, we shall frequently have recourse to knowledge about the perception of things. We shall speak of "thing perception" or "nonsocial perception" when we mean the perception of inanimate objects, and of "person perception" or "social perception" when we mean the perception of another person. The term "object perception" which has been traditionally used in discussions of the perception of things is avoided in this chapter, since the word "object" is also used in its more general sense—"the object of perception" or "the distal object"—which includes persons as well as things. Brunswik's (1934) conclusion, that the objects of social and nonsocial perception are similar in regard to their formal characteristics as well as in regard to the processes by which they are perceived, is in general a valid framework for discussion (p. 211).

This is not to say, of course, that there are no differences between the perception of things and people. It is a commonplace that inanimate objects differ from persons in important ways. In discussing thing perception, we assume that there are real, solid objects with properties of shape and color, things placed in particular positions in real space, having functional properties making them fit or interfere with our purposes, and in general defining their place in the space of means-end relations. There is a chair on which one

Excerpted from Chapter 2 of The Psychology of Interpersonal Relations, New York: Wiley, 1958, with permission of the author and the publisher.

can sit; there is an object with which one can cut paper, tie a package, or write a note.

In discussing person perception, we also assume that these "objects" have color and occupy certain positions in the environment. They are, however, rarely mere manipulanda; rather they are usually perceived as action centers and as such can do something to us. They can benefit or harm us intentionally, and we can benefit or harm them. Persons have abilities, wishes and sentiments; they can act purposefully, and can perceive or watch us. They are systems having an awareness of their surroundings and their conduct refers to this environment, an environment that sometimes includes ourselves. And yet, just as the contents of the nonsocial environment are interrelated by certain lawful connections, causal or otherwise, which define what can or will happen, we assume that there are connections of a similar character between the contents of the social environment.

Phenomenal and causal description in perception

By phenomenal description is meant the nature of the contact between the person and his environment as directly experienced by the person. By causal description is meant the analysis of the underlying conditions that give rise to perceptual experience. There is no a priori reason why the causal description should be the same as the phenomenal description, though, of course, the former should adequately account for the latter. We shall see, however, that though there are differences between the two, the parallels are marked.

It has often been stressed, especially by phenomenologists, that the person feels that he is in direct contact with things and persons in his environment. He sees objects directly, just by focusing his eyes upon them. He acts on objects directly by touching them and lifting them. The same is true of person perception. He not only perceives people as having certain spatial and physical properties, but also can grasp even such intangibles as their wishes, needs, and emotions by some form of immediate apprehension.

In contrast to phenomenal description is the causal analysis which, instead of revealing the person as being in direct contact with the objects of perception, distinguishes a number of steps. A somewhat technical vocabulary has been built up to describe these steps. According to causal analysis, the perceptual process may be conceived of as a perceptual arc (Brunswik, 1952) encompassing two end points—the object, i.e., the part of the environment toward which perception is directed; and the percept, i.e., the way the object appears to us. The former has been referred to by Brunswik (1952) as the *initial focus* inasmuch as it is the starting point of the perceptual arc. It has also been referred to as the *distal stimulus* since it pertains to something "outside the person's skin," at a distance from the person. It is the chair "out there" that is seen or the melody coming from the violin that is heard. Whatever its designation, it refers to the environmental reality, an objective stimulus defined by properties perceivable by everyone.

The distal stimulus, however, does not directly affect the person. Rather it is mediated, for example, by light or sound-wave patterns that excite his sensory organs. This stimulus pattern, impinging as it does directly upon the sense organs, has been designated the *proximal stimulus;* it is the stimulus that is physically in direct proximity to the person. With touch or taste the object must come in direct contact with the sensory receptors, and the starting point of the perceptual process is the proximal rather than the distal stimulus; nonetheless the distinction between the two is still meaningful inasmuch as the sensory quality is attributed to the distal object—the object as separate from the person.

The perceptual process thus far involves distal stimuli, and mediation ending in the proximal stimuli. Within the organism there is, then, the constructive process of perception which leads to some event corresponding to the awareness of the object, the reality as perceived. The terms, *representation* or *image* of the object have been used to describe this awareness. It has also been referred to as the percept, the phenomena, and the terminal focus, the latter pointing to the fact that it is the end point of the perceptual arc, completing its function of providing an awareness of the "environmental reality." The constructive part of the perceptual process within the person is sometimes spoken of as involving central or higher phenomena, processes, or layers, whereas the proximal stimuli entering the organism, the so-called raw material, involve more peripheral or lower layers. The proximal stimuli, being unorganized and uninterpreted are also described as being more superficial.

With person perception, causal analysis also divides the phenomenally given immediate presence of the other person into steps. The other person, with his psychological processes such as needs and intentions, functions as the distal stimulus. He is the "object" toward which *p*'s perception is directed. The mediation consists of the manifestations of the personality of the other, as they determine the proximal stimulus pattern. Often the manifestations of *o*'s inner psychological processes are behavioral though they may be data gained from other sources, such as verbal communication from a third person. Finally, there is the perceptual construction within the person that leads from this raw material to the awareness of the other.

However, the process does not proceed in a one-way fashion from peripheral to central excitation. There is an interaction between the central processes in the brain and the more peripheral data, the "raw material" from the outside, so that the former determine, in some cases more, in some cases less, how the raw material is organized. What is of primary importance is that the central processes provide the "terms" in which the lower layers are interpreted, making it possible, for instance, for a movement to be perceived as a personal action. Often only the contents of the higher levels are directly present, and the lower levels —the raw material of peripheral data —are either not given at all, or are already in terms of the higher levels.

Summarizing, we can say that in many cases of both thing and person perception the raw material remains phenomenally unidentifiable, the only fact that appears ready-made in our life space being the percept, the end product of the organizing process. In other cases the raw material is phenomenally given, or at least can become so as we concentrate on the "visual field" instead of the "visual world," to use Gibson's (1950) expression. It is then that the whole process of perception seems more visible, more spread out for our inspection. It is probably fair to say that the less one depends on direct visual properties such as size and shape, and the more on events or behavior, the more the mediation becomes accessible to awareness.

Coordination between distal object and percept

CONSTANCY PHENOMENA

In perception, the percepts (or impressions or representations) of the environment largely furnish an adequate picture of the surroundings. That is to say, there is a high degree of coordination between the percept and the distal object. According to a phenomenal description of naïve psychology this is to be expected, for if the person is in direct contact with his environment, a true correspondence is naturally expected.

But the causal analyst quickly realizes that the object as perceived is not equal to the stimuli that are actually in direct contact with the person, namely the proximal stimuli mediated, for example, by light waves. Thus, even though the light waves from the surface of a table form varying patterns on my retina depending on my position with respect to the table—sometimes a trapezoid, sometimes a parallelogram, sometimes a large retinal image, sometimes a tiny one—I still perceive the table as rectangular and do quite well at approximating its size. Or, even though the stimuli on the retina are affected by illumination, the color of an object appears surprisingly little influenced. In other words, perception of the object remains fairly constant in spite of the enormous variation in the proximal stimuli which mediate it through the excitation of sensory organs. This phenomenon is referred to as the problem of perceptual constancy. It should be noted, however, that constancy does not hold completely.

The term constancy phenomenon is usually applied to the perception of color, brightness, size, and shape, but it is also applicable in the social perception of such crucial distal stimuli as wishes, needs, beliefs, abilities, affects, and personality traits. If we assert that a "wish constancy" is possible just as there is a size, shape, or color constancy, that means we recognize a wish as being the same in spite of its being mediated by different cues. The same wish may be conveyed, for example, by an innumerable variety of word combinations, ranging from "I want that" to the lengthy and complicated reflections transmitted to the therapist in a psychonalytic session. Or, the same wish may be conveyed by a colorful array of actions, as when a child, wanting a red wagon above all else, goes up and takes it, pushes a competing child from it, and even angrily kicks it in a fit of frustration.

Thus, again we see that the interaction between the person and his environment, in this case between a person and someone he is observing, can best be described as going on between two foci separated by the mediation which can, to some extent, be neglected in the description. Later we shall examine the conditions that impede veridical perception, but in a first approach we will assume that the significant features of the other person (distal objects) are more or less invariantly connected with the perception of them, while neither object nor phenomenon show invariant relations to the mediation.

COORDINATION WITH DISPOSITIONAL PROPERTIES

A further point, closely related to the constancy phenomenon, also concerns the comparison between the way we experience the environment and the way a causal analysis presents it: The parts or characteristics of the environment that are directly given phenomenally and towards which perception (or action) is directed, are those parts that either themselves show an invariance (i.e., do not change very much in their properties), or which, when they change, change mostly in ways that follow macroscopically visible laws. Such properties have been referred to as *dispositional properties*. Here we should like to emphasize that the object as we perceive it is not coupled with just any arbitrarily selected part of the environment; rather it is coupled with such properties as shape, color, and size, properties that are relatively invariant features of the object and show consistent relations with other events. The shape of a solid object, for instance, is relatively enduring. It is something one can rely upon finding again. It is connected with important and lasting possibilities of the object. It allows us to predict to a certain degree how the object will behave when we handle it; for instance, if I see an object is spherical, I predict it can be rolled. This prediction is possible because shape is connected in an invariant way with a possible event, namely all spherical solid objects can be rolled. It is because these intrinsically invariant properties belong so often to distant objects, that is, objects separated in space from the person, that distal perception plays such an important role in interaction with the environment.

It is interesting that in social perception, also, the direct impressions we form of another person, even if they are not correct, refer to dispositional characteristics. At least, relative to the events that mediate these impressions, the characteristics show a high degree of intrinsic invariance. For instance, the impression that a person is friendly, which may be conveyed in any number of ways, points to a relatively enduring characteristic of the person. In fact, any personality trait refers to something that characterizes the person, that is, holds over time in spite of irregularities of circumstance and behavior. As a dispositional property, a personality characteristic enables one to grasp an unlimited variety of behavioral manifestations by a single concept, e.g., friendliness. A description of a manifold of interpersonal relations becomes far more systematically simple by reference to such enduring characteristics. Furthermore, insofar as personal dispositions are connected in lawful ways with other features, predictions about behavior of the other person become possible. Just as one can predict the rolling behavior of the ball because its spherical shape is a persisting property, so one can predict (albeit with less confidence) that *o* will help *p* because of his friendly nature, an enduring personality trait.

PSYCHOLOGICAL DISPOSITIONAL PROPERTIES IN SOCIAL PERCEPTION

The dispositional properties that are the important distal stimuli in social perception frequently refer to psychological or mental entities, to concepts that are not defined in a physical sense. The preceding example of friendliness is a case in point. Without the aid of such psychological, dispositional prop-

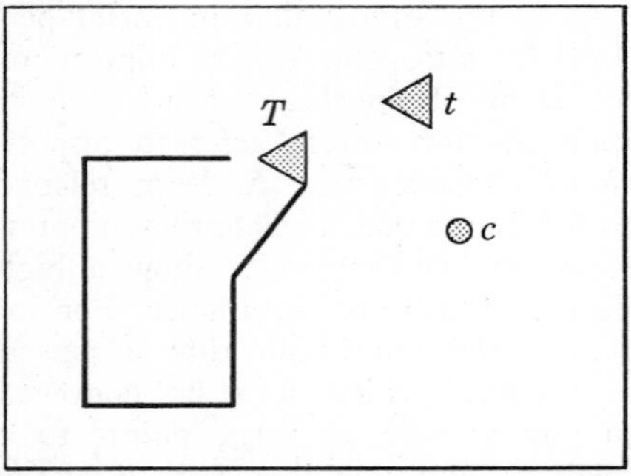

Figure 1. Geometrical figures in apparent behavior (Heider and Simmel, 1944, p. 244).

erties, the behavior of persons mediated by the proximal stimuli would remain largely unintelligible.

Experimentally, this has been demonstrated by the use of a film in which, physically speaking, only an enclosure with a movable part in the upper right-hand corner plus the movements of three geometrical figures are seen (Heider and Simmel, 1944). A still of this film is presented in Fig. 1. As long as the pattern of events shown in the film is perceived in terms of movements as such, it presents a chaos of juxtaposed items. When, however, the geometrical figures assume personal characteristics so that their movements are perceived in terms of motives and sentiments, a unified structure appears.

For social perception on the human level, the uses of "mental" dispositional concepts in the understanding and even description of interactions between persons are legion. Let us suppose that person *A* likes person *B* and that he wants to do him a favor. He takes into account *B*'s wishes, and also what *B* can do: perhaps there is something *B* desires very much but cannot get by himself. *A* also has to consider the possibility that the benefit might embarrass *B*, or that *B* might feel that it implies a lack of respect. Finally, A, deciding on a particular action, goes through with it. *B* is overjoyed. He concludes that A, about whose attitudes he had been in doubt, really likes him; he appreciates especially the tactful way in which A handled the matter.

Descriptions of this kind seem to capture the essential features of an interpersonal event. One might go even further and try to discover the reasons why *A* likes *B*, or why *B* was questioning *A*'s sentiments; or one might try to assess the personality characteristics that played a role in this event. Though the description as it stands does not go far back into the history of the relation between A and *B*, nor into deep psychological motivations, within its limits it is a meaningful episode.

If we examine the concepts that are used in making this episode intelligible, we find sentiments, wishes, abilities, and emotions. The particular behavioral data on which the judgments or perceptions of the other person's wishes, abilities, or traits are based are not mentioned. One may even feel that the description of the essential interpersonal process would not gain very much in exactitude if they were specified. Neither would a more detailed report of A's particular actions change very much our understanding of the main features of the event. The particular action by which A benefited *B* is of importance only insofar as it is judged by *B* and is related by him to his self-evaluation. To be sure, we might describe the event by concentrating on the surface, on the overt behavior, on what can be seen from the outside. But even then the reader would certainly translate the overt syndromes into concepts very much like the ones used in the description given above. These concepts provide the nodal points in terms of which the event can be described most economically, which allow for extrapolation to other possible events and which allow for prediction.

Social perception in general can best be described as a process between the center of one person and the center of another person, from life space to life space. When *A* observes *B*'s behavior, he "reads" it in terms of psychological entities (and his reactions, being guided by his own sentiments, expectations, and wishes, can again be understood only in terms of psychological concepts). *A*, through psychological processes in himself, perceives psychological processes in *B*.

One might say psychological processes such as motives, intentions, sentiments, etc., are the core processes which manifest themselves in overt behavior and expression in many variable ways. The manifestations are then directly grasped by *p*, the observer, in terms of these psychological core processes; they would otherwise remain undecipherable. By looking through the mediation, *p* perceives the distal object, the psychological entities that bring consistency and meaning to the behavior; *p*'s reaction is then to this meaning, not to the overt behavior directly, and this reaction is then carried back by the mediation to *o*, etc.

However, though the main process of social perception goes on between person and person spanning the mediation, and though often a first over-all description can catch the essentials without considering the mediation, we also want to know how the mediation carries the process. After all, the perceiving person gets information about the environment only through the proximal stimuli. This, then, poses the important problem of relating the proximal stimuli to two end points (the foci of the perceptual arc), namely the contents of the environment on the one hand and the phenomena, the way these contents appear to us, on the other. Only then will we also be able to explain cases in which one person misunderstands another, or in which an action (a primary medium for the transmission of psychological characteristics) does not correspond to the intention of the agent.

The mediation

ITS GRAMMATICAL STRUCTURE

The simplest model for the coordination of mediation to distal stimuli would be one in which a specific offshoot is coordinated to each content or property. The organism would then only have to learn the specific connections between offshoots and contents. He would, so to speak, have to memorize a vocabulary of mediation consisting only of nouns. If the organism perceived one of the offshoots, he would react to it as if he were perceiving the content, the offshoot being an unambiguous sign of the content. This would be the case, if, for example, a raised eyebrow were the necessary and sufficient indication that *o* was dubious.

However, the language of nature is more complicated. It offers its contents to us not merely through patterns comparable to univocal nouns but also through patterns that are in some way analogous to ambiguous words and synonyms, or to adjectives and verbs, and which even contain something of a grammatical structure. A parallel to ambiguous messages is seen when an offshoot is coordinated to two or more different contents. Then, of course, the manifestation taken by itself can be a sign of any one of these contents.

EMBEDDEDNESS

Carrying the analogy of grammatical structure further, we can say that, just as ambiguous words become more specifically defined when they are placed in sentences that give them a contextual setting the ambiguity of mediation events is reduced when the stimuli or manifestations referring to the distal stimulus are *embedded* in the total situation. In discussions of embeddedness, the term "local stimulus" is sometimes used to refer to a part of the stimulus pattern as distinct from the total stimulus which includes the surroundings as well.

Very often in social perception, what a person says and does provides important cues for such distal properties as motivations, intentions, abilities, etc. But this raw material is also not univocally coordinated to these important properties of the person. Corresponding to the surrounding in thing perception is the situation in social perception, with the consequence that the ambiguity of behavior as a local stimulus is reduced when it is seen in a situational context.

It is probably fair to say that the stimulus fields basic for person perception are usually *more extended in time* than those relevant to thing perception. Let us assume that we enter an unfamiliar room for the first time, and that in it we find a few people we have never met before. A glance around the room will suffice to get an approximately correct idea of the shape of the room and of the objects in it. We shall be much more insecure in our judgments of the people. We may get a global first impression of them but we do not perceive the relevant properties of the social situation as quickly. We do not know whether A likes or dislikes B, whether C intends to thwart D, and so on. Many more data, a much wider manifold of stimuli, are needed to give us this information. We have to get acquainted with these people. We have to interact with them and observe how they interact with each other. We might say that person perception will be like reduction screen vision (familiar in experiments on color constancy) if we exclude the perception of events and actions. Although we believe that we get to know something about a person from the shape of his face, or even the color of his hair, these physiognomic properties are far outweighed by his actions as cues to his personality. In most cases we cognize a person's traits, and especially his wishes, sentiments, or intentions from what he does and says, and we know considerably less when we are limited to what we can see of him as a static object.

STIMULUS CONFIGURATIONS

At first glance it seems difficult to arrive at scientific generalizations concerning the stimulus field mediating perception, for if we have to consider the total field in order to achieve good coordination between distal stimulus and percept, the task seems complex indeed.

But in social perception, the influence of additional data that resist geometrical definition is often essential, and it seems that the most fruitful way to treat the process of perception is to assume stages that intervene between the proximal stimulus and the percept. This would lead to the notion of a hierarchical process, in which the proximal stimulus gives rise to more peripheral meanings, which in turn play the role of data for the higher levels of construction.

Constructive processes within the observer

MEANINGS AS DATA

The proposition that meanings as "intervening variables" are necessary in order that stimulus patterns may be coordinated with phenomena is significant enough to warrant further explications. Let us suppose that *o* is perceived as being "courageous." This impression can be produced by many different concrete stimulus configurations. We can conceive of all these stimulus configurations as making up a manifold which is defined by the fact that each member of it produces the impression "*o* acts courageously." Then each configuration has the position of a synonym. Yet it is impossible to find a geometrical pattern, an ordinal stimulus definable by a figural feature, which would distinguish the members of this manifold from, let us say, stimulus patterns producing the impression "*o* acts in a cowardly way." It is even unlikely that one can point to a limited number of figurally identifiable subgroups of this manifold, as is possible to a certain extent, with the ordinal stimuli producing the impression "this surface is slanting." This, of course, does not preclude the possibility of finding a figural parameter coordinated to the impression "courageous" in a particular situation. Thus, if one presents different motion picture scenes in which an obviously dangerous animal is shown with different persons, the impression that person A is more courageous than *B* might be produced by simple motions of approachment or withdrawal. But one cannot say that motions of approachment or withdrawal defined in a temporal and spatial way, are *generally* coordinated with these impressions. Only when the level of meaning is included can a feature common to all the cases producing the impression "courageous" be found. The meaning might be something like: going ahead or not withdrawing in spite of danger ahead. Bear also in mind that in this case "going ahead" does not have to be defined spatially in the physical sense; it can be defined "hodologically," as doing something that is a condition for coming into contact. The actions can be in social space. Also "danger" cannot be defined figurally.

Perception through speech provides another area where the crucial data are meanings, and not simply stimulus patterns reduced to spatial coordinates. This is even clear in cases in which a person reports his thoughts and feelings literally, as when he says, "I am angry" or "I think thus and so." But it is even more sharply brought out when we infer his thoughts and feelings indirectly from what he says and how he says it. In either case we immediately are in the realm of meaning, but in the latter the direct or concrete meaning of the sentence is only one factor in understanding. Many other factors are taken into account, such as knowledge about the person uttering the sentence, to whom it is said, the relation between speaker and the one spoken to, the situation that provoked to utterance, etc. Again there is no simple coordination between a particular utterance and the impression produced by it: a particular utterance can have many different meanings in different situations and one and the same impression can be produced by many different utterances. Nevertheless, the hearer has the feeling of being directly in the presence of anger or other feelings of *o*, and it would be hard to find a difference between this feeling of presence and the feeling of being in the presence of directly, visually seen objects. There certainly does not have to intervene a "judgment" or an "inference" just because meanings are essential data in the perceptual process.

MEANINGS AS INTEGRATING FACTORS

The role of meanings in perception becomes even more central because the consistent representation of the world towards which perception tends depends upon meanings (or beliefs or interpretations or evaluations, to indicate a wider scope of connotations) as organizing factors. The integrative phenomenon may be expressed in general as follows: Let us assume that a certain stimulus, *x*, is ambiguous. It can be seen as *a* or *b*. Whether *a* or *b* is seen depends upon the *meaning* to which any additional stimuli give rise and how these meanings fit with *a* or *b*. We can even assume that the additional stimulus, *y*, is also ambiguous, that is, it can be seen as *c* or *d*. If meaning *b* fits with meaning *c*, while neither fits with *a* or *d*, nor *d* with *a* or *b*, then the first stimulus will be seen as *b*, the second as *c*. The world we perceive has to be consistent, and the equivocal stimuli, even ordinal stimuli, will give rise to percepts that fit together and produce an integrated picture.

That the valuations of different parts of the stimulus manifold are put together in such a way as to form an integrated impression leads to the assumption of a hierarchy of structures interposed between the stimulus manifold and the resulting impressions, of stages of intervening variables that help us to analyze in a fruitful manner the correlations between the total stimulus field and the total phenomenal field. The parts of the stimulus manifold are evaluated, and these evaluations combine to produce still more encompassing evaluations, and so on—though in considering this process we must never forget that its direction is not all one way, from stimuli to impressions, but that the evaluations or meanings of the higher levels in turn influence the meanings of the lower levels. We are aware of the fact that this description is still very inexact; however one can trust that it can be made more objective. A promising beginning in this direction has been made by Hayek (1952) with his ideas about a hierarchy of evaluations.

Within the hierarchy of required relations, conflicts arise when relations that hold between parts of the visual world are incompatible with relations required by other parts or by the total visual field. Such conflict is in evidence, for example, when I can see through an object which casts a shadow, or when Object A seems nearer than *B*, and *B* nearer than C, but also C nearer than A.

ECONOMY OF INTERPRETATION—REDUNDANCY

We have seen that a stimulus which is ambiguous as long as it is given singly, may become unequivocal with the addition of further data. It is important to stress that this specificity is established through the meaningfulness of the integrated perceptual field. But of two equally meaningful integrations, the one that is less complex, the one that requires fewer assumptions, fewer data in general, seems in general to be preferred. This is sometimes referred to as the principle of parsimony, a principle well known in the philosophy of science, and which may have its analogue in perception.

Social perception also has systems of implied facts, with the possibility that certain data may be superfluous for providing additional information. If, for example, one already knows that *A* is superior in power to *B*, then the fact that *A* is chasing *B* does not add much information about the power relation between *A* and *B*. Such behavior is "just what one expected." The motion of *A* moving behind *B* [as, for example, when *T* moves behind *t* in the Heider-Simmel film illustrated in Figure 1.—Eds.] will be seen as "chasing" and not "following" just because of the principle of economy of interpretation. If, however, the observer was told that *A*, though superior in power, is in fact following *B* (or that *B* is leading *A*) then additional information is presented, information that is not at all redundant and therefore sheds a new light on the relation between *A* and *B*. The integrative process then presses for a sensible explanation, one that brings order into the array of facts. One might conclude, for instance, that though *A* is more powerful than *B*, he is trying to teach *B* to assume qualities of leadership, or that he is engaged in a friendly game with *B*. But if the only fact at hand is the power superiority of *A*, such explanations are clearly more expensive than perceiving the notion of *A* and *B* as chasing. In these examples, the integration of only two data is required. The expense difference between the simplest and the most complicated hypothesis mounts very rapidly when examples with a greater manifold of data are considered.

In the first part of this chapter, it was pointed out that in person perception, the manifold of incoming messages (the proximal stimuli of perception) is encoded in terms of the motives, sentiments, beliefs, and personality traits of other persons. There we mentioned that these are dispositional properties, the relatively stable distal features that are relevant to us. We now should like to add that it is through the process of construction within the central layers of the observer that these dispositional features serve to integrate a bewildering mass of data in the most economical terms.

Misperception

The coordination between the percept and the distal stimulus in spite of ambiguities of the local proximal stimulus is, of course, of vital importance for an efficient interaction on the part of the person with his environment. To say that it would be confusing if the shape of objects were transformed with every positional shift, or if persons were perceived as changing character with every action, or if what I perceive as *o*'s desires might just as easily be his antipathies, is but a great understatement of how much more disturbing the world would be. We need to perceive things and people with their invariant properties more or less as they are, even though these properties are mediated to us in a complicated way and not simply by the local proximal stimulus.

As has already been stressed, the principle of embeddedness refers to a process essential to this coordination, namely the integration between the local stimulus and its surroundings. Moreover, the meaning of the local stimulus is often, if not always, a function of the integration of the perceptual field. As examples of this kind of constructive embeddedness, we have noted the perceptual constancies in which the surrounding helps determine the properties of the object by eliminating the ambiguity of the local stimulus. For social perception, it is the surrounding situation that makes it possible to determine the motivations and intentions that lie behind a specific overt behavior.

Unfortunately (or fortunately if distortion and pretense aid and abet one's intentions), though the surrounding influences the appearance of a subpart of the perceptual field, it does not always improve cognition. It may be so misleading as to interfere with the coordination between the distal object and the perception of it.

Many examples of the inadequate apprehension of the significant conditions surrounding behavior appear in Ichheiser's essay "Misunderstandings in human relations." He points out that a mother and teacher may have very different pictures of the personality of a child because they do not take into account the fact that the home situation is different from the school situation. Moreover, they tend to overestimate the unity of the child's personality because of a tendency to think that the child will behave in the same way in all situations.

Thus, the father always sees his son in the role of son, the employer sees the employee only as an employee behaving in front of the employer, etc. Varying somewhat an analogy of Ichheiser, we might say it is as if we always carried a flashlight with a filter of red color when examining an empty room; we would then ascribe the color to the room. We are reminded of discussions regarding the influence of the method of observation on what is observed in science.

Another case of misjudging the factor of situation occurs when the situation is perceived egocentrically, that is, if the situation of the other person is silently presupposed to be the same as the situation of the observer. Ichheiser (1949) quotes the example of Marie Antoinette who, upon being told that the people were hungry because they had no bread, asked why they did not eat cake instead.

Sometimes the raw materials of social perception are the things that belong to a person. We form an idea of a person when we see his room, his books, his pictures, etc. (Ichheiser, 1949, p. 5). If we are sure that the person himself selected the things because he likes them, then this idea may be more or less adequate. But again, in many cases other factors besides personal preference determined the ownership of the things, and we are misled by this raw material.

Misperceptions also occur when the properties of a person are mediated to us through what other people say or write about him, through gossip, newspapers, etc. Consequently, the interpretation of new behavioral data may also be in error because of its integration with false beliefs.

In all of the cases discussed, the reason for the misperceptions or differences in interpretations concerning another person lies in the lack of correlation between the raw material and the intended object of perception. We take the raw material too literally without taking into account additional factors that influence it.

Perceptual styles

The fact that there is a lack of correspondence between the raw material of perception and the intended object of perception allows idiosyncratic approaches to the world on the part of the observer a much freer reign in the organization and interpretation of incoming proximal stimuli. The issue here does not concern errors of perception as much as it does perceptual styles—what the person extracts from his world because of his manner of perceiving.

A striking case is the calculating prodigy who was so prone to perceive the world in terms of numerical combinations that, after seeing a play, he was entirely unaffected by the scene but instead "informed his hosts of the exact number of words uttered by the various actors, and of the number of steps taken by others in their dances" (Ball, 1956, p. 469).

Physiognomic perception, the mode of perception in which things appear animate, shows interesting individual differences. From Werner's (1948) writings, the proposition that physiognomic perception "plays a greater role in the primitive world than in our own" (p. 69) has become familiar. Children, for example, show more physiognomic perception than adults. Chronic schizophrenics, in a study by Ihrig (1953) produced fewer animistic responses to the Heider-Simmel film than the control groups. Even with normal adults there seem to be differences in the tendency to interpret stimulus configurations in terms of personal behavior.

Another case in point concerns depth of personal contact with one's environment. We know that the degree of intimacy of contact between two people depends on the situation, how long the persons have known each other, and on individual differences. Some people perceive the more superficial layers of personality in interpersonal relations and act accordingly, whereas the perceptions and actions of others are more concerned with central layers, the deeper and sometimes more covert psychological aspects of the person. Karl Buehler (1929), in his interesting analysis of interactions in a dyad, discusses examples of different degrees of depth of contact. Lewin (1948) has extended individual differences concerning this dimension to differences in national character, notably to differences between the United States and Germany (especially p. 24). Interesting differences in social perception between Russian displaced persons and Americans are described by Hanfmann (1957).

Phenomenologically oriented psychologists in particular have stressed that for one person to be in contact with another and to perceive and react to the other's sentiments and wishes, it is not enough that he is exposed to certain stimulus configurations. A general readiness to perceive psychologically is necessary; this receptivity makes possible the arousal of such percepts as "he is angry," or "he wants to tell me something." As we know, people vary widely in such social-psychological perceptivity.

The inclination of the observer to perceive his world according to individual perceptual styles could also be elaborated by reference to such concepts as "levelers" versus "sharpeners" (Klein, 1951), "authoritarians" versus "nonauthoritarians" (Titus and Hollander, 1957), the optimist who sees a rosy glow to everything versus the pessimist who extracts the negative values. All these are perceptual attitudes, general ways of "being in the world" which lead to the arousal of different percepts in spite of the fact that the stimulus configurations presented are the same.[1]

[1] Many comparative and documenting references in Prof. Heider's original chapter are omitted.—Eds.

34 The presentation of self in everyday life

ERVING GOFFMAN

When an individual enters the presence of others, they commonly seek to acquire information about him or to bring into play information about him already possessed. They will be interested in his general socio-economic status, his conception of self, his attitude toward them, his competence, his trustworthiness, etc. Although some of this information seems to be sought almost as an end in itself, there are usually quite practical reasons for acquiring it. Information about the individual helps to define the situation, enabling others to know in advance what he will expect of them and what they may expect of him. Informed in these ways, the others will know how best to act in order to call forth a desired response from him.

For those present, many sources of information become accessible and many carriers (or "sign-vehicles") become available for conveying this information. If unacquainted with the individual, observers can glean clues from his conduct and appearance which allow them to apply their previous experience with individuals roughly similar to the one before them or, more important, to apply untested stereotypes to him. They can also assume from past experience that only individuals of a particular kind are likely to be found in a given social setting. They can rely on what the individual says about himself or on documentary evidence he provides as to who and what he is. If they know, or know of, the individual by virtue of experience prior to the interaction, they can rely on assumptions as to the persistence and generality of psychological traits as a means of predicting his present and future behavior.

However, during the period in which the individual is in the immediate presence of the others, few events may occur which directly provide the others with the conclusive information they will need if they are to direct wisely their own activity. Many crucial facts lie beyond the time and place of interaction or lie concealed within it. For example, the "true" or "real" attitudes, beliefs, and emotions of the individual can be ascertained only indirectly, through his avowals or through what appears to be involuntary expressive behavior. Similarly, if the individual offers the others a product or service, they will often find that during the interaction there will be no time and place immediately available for eating the pudding that the proof can be found in. They will be forced to accept some events as conventional or natural signs of something not directly available to the senses. In Ichheiser's terms (1949, pp. 6–7), the individual will have to act so that he intentionally or unintentionally *expresses* himself, and the others will in turn have to be *impressed* in some way by him.

The expressiveness of the individual

Excerpted from **The Presentation of Self in Everyday Life,** New York: Doubleday-Anchor, 1959, with permission of the author and copyright owner, Erving Goffman.

(and therefore his capacity to give impressions) appears to involve two radically different kinds of sign activity: the expression that he *gives*, and the expression that he *gives off*. The first involves verbal symbols or their substitutes which he uses admittedly and solely to convey the information that he and the others are known to attach to these symbols. This is communication in the traditional and narrow sense. The second involves a wide range of action that others can treat as symptomatic of the actor, the expectation being that the action was performed for reasons other than the information conveyed in this way. As we shall have to see, this distinction has an only initial validity. The individual does of course intentionally convey misinformation by means of both of these types of communication, the first involving deceit, the second feigning.

Let us now turn from the others to the point of view of the individual who presents himself before them. He may wish them to think highly of him, or to think that he thinks highly of them, or to perceive how in fact he feels toward them, or to obtain no clear-cut impression; he may wish to ensure sufficient harmony so that the interaction can be sustained, or to defraud, get rid of, confuse, mislead, antagonize, or insult them. Regardless of the particular objective which the individual has in mind and of his motive for having this objective, it will be in his interests to control the conduct of the others, especially their responsive treatment of him. This control is achieved largely by influencing the definition of the situation which the others come to formulate, and he can influence this definition by expressing himself in such a way as to give them the kind of impression that will lead them to act voluntarily in accordance with his own plan. Thus, when an individual appears in the presence of others, there will usually be some reason for him to mobilize his activity so that it will convey an impression to others which it is in his interests to convey.

Of the two kinds of communication —expressions given and expressions given off—this report will be primarily concerned with the latter, with the more theatrical and contextual kind, the non-verbal, presumably unintentional kind, whether this communication be purposely engineered or not.

I have said that when an individual appears before others his actions will influence the definition of the situation which they come to have. Sometimes the individual will act in a thoroughly calculating manner, expressing himself in a given way solely in order to give the kind of impression to others that is likely to evoke from them a specific response he is concerned to obtain. Sometimes the individual will be calculating in his activitiy but be relatively unaware that this is the case. Sometimes he will intentionally and consciously express himself in a particular way, but chiefly because the tradition of his group or social status require this kind of expression and not because of any particular response (other than vague acceptance or approval) that is likely to be evoked from those impressed by the expression. Sometimes the traditions of an individual's role will lead him to give a well-designed impression of a particular kind and yet he may be neither consciously nor unconsciously disposed to create such an impression. The others, in their turn, may be suitably impressed by the individual's efforts to convey something, or may misunderstand the situation and come to conclusions that are warranted neither by the individual's intent nor by the facts. In any case, in so far as the others act *as if* the individual had conveyed a particular impression, we may take a functional or pragmatic view and say that the individual has "effectively" projected a given definition of the situation and "effectively" fostered the understanding that a given state of affairs obtains.

There is one aspect of the others' response that bears special comment here. Knowing that the individual is likely to present himself in a light that is favorable to him, the others may divide what they witness into two parts; a part that is relatively easy for the individual to manipulate at will, being chiefly his verbal assertions, and a part in regard to which he seems to have little concern or control, being chiefly derived from the expressions he gives off. The others may then use what are considered to be the ungovernable aspects of his expressive behavior as a check upon the validity of what is conveyed by the governable aspects. In this a fundamental asymmetry is demonstrated in the communication process, the individual presumably being aware of only one stream of his communication, the witnesses of this stream and one other. For example, in Shetland Isle one crofter's wife, in serving native dishes to a visitor from the mainland of Britain, would listen with a polite smile to his polite claims of liking what he was eating; at the same time she would take note of the rapidity with which the visitor lifted his fork or spoon to his mouth, the eagerness with which he passed food into his mouth, and the gusto expressed in chewing the food, using these signs as a check on the stated feelings of the eater.

Now given the fact that others are likely to check up on the more controllable aspects of behavior by means of the less controllable, one can expect that sometimes the individual will try to exploit this very possibility, guiding the impression he makes through behavior felt to be reliably informing.[1] For example, in gaining admission to a tight social circle, the participant observer may not only wear an accepting look while listening to an informant, but may also be careful to wear the same look when observing the informant talking to others; observers of the observer will then not as easily discover where he actually stands.

This kind of control upon the part of the individual reinstates the symmetry of the communication process, and sets the stage for a kind of information game—a potentially infinite cycle of concealment, discovery, false revelation, and rediscovery. It should be added that since the others are likely to be relatively unsuspicious of the presumably unguided aspect of the individual's conduct, he can gain much by controlling it. The others of course may sense that the individual is manipulating the presumably spontaneous aspects of his behavior, and seek in this very act of manipulation some shading of conduct that the individual has not managed to control. This again provides a check upon the individual's behavior, this time his presumably uncalculated behavior, thus re-establishing the asymmetry of the communication process.

When we allow that the individual projects a definition of the situation when he appears before others, we must

[1] The widely read and rather sound writings of Stephen Potter are concerned in part with signs that can be engineered to give a shrewd observer the apparently incidental cues he needs to discover concealed virtues the gamesman does not in fact possess.

also see that the others, however passive their role may seem to be, will themselves effectively project a definition of the situation by virtue of their response to the individual and by virtue of any lines of action they initiate to him. Ordinarily the definitions of the situation projected by the several different participants are sufficiently attuned to one another so that open contradiction will not occur. I do not mean that there will be the kind of consensus that arises when each individual present candidly expresses what he really feels and honestly agrees with the expressed feelings of the others present. This kind of harmony is an optimistic ideal and in any case not necessary for the smooth working of society. Rather, each participant is expected to suppress his immediate heartfelt feelings, conveying a view of the situation which he feels the others will be able to find at least temporarily acceptable. The maintenance of this surface of agreement, this veneer of consensus, is facilitated by each participant concealing his own wants behind statements which assert values to which everyone present feels obliged to give lip service. Further, there is usually a kind of division of definitional labor. Each participant is allowed to establish the tentative official ruling regarding matters which are vital to him but not immediately important to others, e.g., the rationalizations and justifications by which he accounts for his past activity. In exchange for this courtesy he remains silent or non-committal on matters important to others but not immediately important to him. We have then a kind of interactional *modus vivendi*. Together the participants contribute to a single over-all definition of the situation which involves not so much a real agreement as to what exists but rather a real agreement as to whose claims concerning what issues will be temporarily honored. Real agreement will also exist concerning the desirability of avoiding an open conflict of definitions of the situation. I will refer to this level of agreement as a "working consensus." It is to be understood that the working consensus established in one interaction setting will be quite different in content from the working consensus established in a different type of setting. Thus, between two friends at lunch, a reciprocal show of affection, respect, and concern for the other is maintained. In service occupations, on the other hand, the specialist often maintains an image of disinterested involvement in the problem of the client, while the client responds with a show of respect for the competence and integrity of the specialist. Regardless of such differences in content, however, the general form of these working arrangements is the same.

In noting the tendency for a participant to accept the definitional claims made by the others present, we can appreciate the crucial importance of the information that the individual *initially* possesses or acquires concerning his fellow participants, for it is on the basis of this initial information that the individual starts to define the situation and starts to build up lines of responsive action. The individual's initial projection commits him to what he is proposing to be and requires him to drop all pretenses of being other things. As the interaction among the participants progresses, additions and modifications in this initial informational state will of course occur, but it is essential that these later developments be related without contradiction to, and even built up from, the initial positions taken by the several participants. It would seem that an individual can more easily make a choice as to what line of treatment to demand from and extend to the others present at the beginning of an encounter than he can alter the line of treatment that is being pursued once the interaction is underway.

When the interaction that is initiated by "first impressions" (Whyte, 1946, pp. 132–3) is itself merely the initial interaction in an extended series of interactions involving the same participants, we speak of "getting off on the right foot" and feel that it is crucial that we do so.

Given the fact that the individual effectively projects a definition of the situation when he enters the presence of others, we can assume that events may occur within the interaction which contradict, discredit, or otherwise throw doubt upon this projection. When these disruptive events occur, the interaction itself may come to a confused and embarrassed halt. Some of the assumptions upon which the responses of the participants had been predicated become untenable, and the participants find themselves lodged in an interaction for which the situation has been wrongly defined and is now no longer defined. At such moments the individual whose presentation has been discredited may feel ashamed while the others present may feel hostile, and all the participants may come to feel ill at ease, nonplussed, out of countenance, embarrassed, experiencing the kind of anomy that is generated when the minute social system of face-to-face interaction breaks down.

In stressing the fact that the initial definition of the situation projected by an individual tends to provide a plan for the co-operative activity that follows —in stressing this action point of view —we must not overlook the crucial fact that any projected definition of the situation also has a distinctive moral character. It is this moral character of projections that will chiefly concern us in this report. Society is organized on the principle that any individual who possesses certain social characteristics has a moral right to expect that others will value and treat him in a correspondingly appropriate way. Connected with this principle is a second, namely that an individual who implicitly or explicitly signifies that he has certain social characteristics ought to have this claim honored by others and ought in fact to be what he claims he is. In consequence, when an individual projects a definition of the situation and thereby makes an implicit or explicit claim to be a person of a particular kind, he automatically exerts a moral demand upon the others, obliging them to value and treat him in the manner that persons of his kind have a right to expect. He also implicitly forgoes all claims to be things he does not appear to be and hence forgoes the treatment that would be appropriate for such individuals. The others find, then, that the individual has informed them as to what is and as to what they *ought* to see as the "is."

One cannot judge the importance of definitional disruptions by the frequency with which they occur, for apparently they would occur more frequently were not constant precautions taken. We find that preventive practices are constantly employed to avoid these embarrassments and that corrective practices are constantly employed to compensate for discrediting occurrences that have not been successfully avoided. When the individual employs these strategies and tactics to protect his own projections, we may refer to them as "defensive practices"; when a participant employs them to save the definition of the situation projected by another, we speak of "protective practices" or "tact." Together, defensive and protective practices comprise the techniques employed to safeguard the impression fostered by an individual during his presence before others. It should be added that while we may be ready to see that no fostered impression would survive if defensive practices were not employed, we are less ready perhaps to see that few impressions could survive if those who received the impression did not exert tact in their reception of it.

In addition to the fact that precautions are taken to prevent disruption of projected definitions, we may also note that an intense interest in these disruptions comes to play a significant role in the social life of the group. Practical jokes and social games are played in which embarrassments which are to be taken unseriously are purposely engineered. Fantasies are created in which devastating exposures occur. Anecdotes from the past—real, embroidered, or fictitious—are told and retold, detailing disruptions which occurred, almost occurred, or occurred and were admirably resolved. There seems to be no grouping which does not have a ready supply of these games, reveries, and cautionary tales, to be used as a source of humor, a catharsis for anxieties, and a sanction for inducing individuals to be modest in their claims and reasonable in their projected expectations.

To summarize, then, I assume that when an individual appears before others he will have many motives for trying to control the impression they receive of the situation. This report is concerned with some of the common techniques that persons employ to sustain such impressions and with some of the common contingencies associated with the employment of these techniques. The specific content of any activity presented by the individual participant, or the role it plays in the interdependent activities of an on-going social system, will not be at issue; I shall be concerned only with the participant's dramaturgical problems of presenting the activity before others.

For the purpose of this report, interaction (that is, face-to-face interaction) may be roughly defined as the reciprocal influence of individuals upon one another's actions when in one another's immediate physical presence. *An* interaction may be defined as all the interaction which occurs throughout any one occasion when a given set of individuals are in one another's continuous presence; the term "an encounter" would do as well. A "performance" may be defined as all the activity of a given participant on a given occasion which serves to influence in any way any of the other participants. Taking a particular participant and his performance as a basic point of reference, we may refer to those who contribute the other performances as the audience, observers, or co-participants. The pre-established pattern of action which is unfolded during a performance and which may be presented or played through on other occasions may be called a "part" or "routine." [2] These situational terms can easily be related to conventional structural ones. When an individual or performer plays the same part to the

[2] For comments on the importance of distinguishing between a routine of interaction and any particular instance when this routine is played through, see John von Neumann and Oskar Morgenstern, **The Theory of Games and Economic Behavior** (1947).

audience on different occasions, a social relationship is likely to arise. Defining social role as the enactment of rights and duties attached to a given status, we can say that a social role will involve one or more parts and that each of these different parts may be presented by the performer on a series of occasions to the same kinds of audience or to an audience of the same persons.

The framework

A social establishment is any place surrounded by fixed barriers to perception in which a particular kind of activity regularly takes place. I have suggested that any social establishment may be studied profitably from the point of view of impression management. Within the walls of a social establishment we find a team of performers who cooperate to present to an audience a given definition of the situation. This will include the conception of own team and of audience and assumptions concerning the ethos that is to be maintained by rules of politeness and decorum. We often find a division into back region, where the performance of a routine is prepared, and front region, where the performance is presented. Access to these regions is controlled in order to prevent the audience from seeing backstage and to prevent outsiders from coming into a performance that is not addressed to them. Among members of the team we find that familiarity prevails, solidarity is likely to develop, and that secrets that could give the show away are shared and kept. A tacit agreement is maintained between performers and audience to act as if a given degree of opposition and of accord existed between them. Typically, but not always, agreement is stressed and opposition is underplayed. The resulting work consensus tends to be contradicted by the attitude toward the audience which the performers express in the absence of the audience and by carefully controlled communication out of character conveyed by the performers while the audience is present. We find that discrepant roles develop: some of the individuals who are apparently teammates, or audience, or outsiders acquire information about the performance and relations to the team which are not apparent and which complicate the problem of putting on a show. Sometimes disruptions occur through unmeant gestures, *faux pas,* and scenes, thus discrediting or contradicting the definition of the situation that is being maintained. The mythology of the team will dwell upon these disruptive events. We find that performers, audience, and outsiders all utilize techniques for saving the show, whether by avoiding likely disruptions or by correcting for unavoided ones, or by making it possible for others to do so. To ensure that these techniques will be employed, the team will tend to select members who are loyal, disciplined, and circumspect, and to select an audience that is tactful.

These features and elements, then, comprise the framework I claim to be characteristic of much social interaction as it occurs in natural settings in our Anglo-American society. This framework is formal and abstract in the sense that it can be applied to any social establishment; it is not, however, merely a static classification. The framework bears upon dynamic issues created by the motivation to sustain a definition of the situation that has been projected before others.

An establishment may be viewed

"technically," in terms of its efficiency and inefficiency as an intentionally organized system of activity for the achievement of predefined objectives. An establishment may be viewed "politically," in terms of the actions which each participant (or class of participants) can demand of other participants, the kinds of deprivations and indulgences which can be meted out in order to enforce these demands, and the kinds of social controls which guide this exercise of command and use of sanctions. An establishment may be viewed "structurally," in terms of the horizontal and vertical status divisions and the kinds of social relations which relate these several groupings to one another. Finally, an establishment may be viewed "culturally," in terms of the moral values which influence activity in the establishment—values pertaining to fashions, customs, and matters of taste, to politeness and decorum, to ultimate ends and normative restrictions on means, etc. It is to be noted that all the facts that can be discovered about an establishment are relevant to each of the four perspectives but that each perspective gives its own priority and order to these facts.

It seems to me that the dramaturgical approach may constitute a fifth perspective, to be added to the technical, political, structural, and cultural perspectives. The dramaturgical perspective, like each of the other four, can be employed as the end-point of analysis, as a final way of ordering facts. This would lead us to describe the techniques of impression management employed in a given establishment, the principal problems of impression management in the establishment, and the identity and interrelationships of the several performance teams which operate in the establishment. But, as with the facts utilized in each of the other perspectives, the facts specifically pertaining to impression management also play a part in the matters that are a concern in all the other perspectives.

Personality-interaction-society

In recent years there have been elaborate attempts to bring into one framework the concepts and findings derived from three different areas of inquiry: the individual personality, social interaction, and society. I would like to suggest here a simple addition to these inter-disciplinary attempts.

When an individual appears before others, he knowingly and unwittingly projects a definition of the situation, of which a conception of himself is an important part. When an event occurs which is expressively incompatible with this fostered impression, significant consequences are simultaneously felt in three levels of social reality, each of which involves a different point of reference and a different order of fact.

First, the social interaction, treated here as a dialogue between two teams, may come to an embarrassed and confused halt; the situation may cease to be defined, previous positions may become no longer tenable, and participants may find themselves without a charted course of action. The participants typically sense a false note in the situation and come to feel awkward, flustered, and, literally, out of countenance. In other words, the minute social system created and sustained by orderly social interaction becomes disorganized. These are the consequences that the disruptions have from the point of view of social interaction.

Secondly, in addition to these disorganizing consequences for action at the moment, performance disruptions may have consequences of a more far-reaching kind. Audiences tend to accept the individual's particular performance as evidence of his capacity to perform the routine and even as evidence of his capacity to perform any routine. In a sense these larger social units—teams, establishments, etc.—become committed every time the individual performs his routine; with each performance the legitimacy of these units will tend to be tested anew and their permanent reputation put at stake. This kind of commitment is especially strong during some performances. Thus, when a surgeon and his nurse both turn from the operating table and the anesthetized patient accidentally rolls off the table to his death, not only is the operation disrupted in an embarrassing way, but the reputation of the doctor, as a doctor and as a man, and also the reputation of the hospital may be weakened. These are the consequences that disruptions may have from the point of view of social structure.

Finally, we often find that the individual may deeply involve his ego in his identification with a particular part, establishment, and group, and in his self-conception as someone who does not disrupt social interaction or let down the social units which depend upon that interaction. When a disruption occurs, then, we may find that the self-conceptions around which his personality has been built may become discredited. These are consequences that disruptions may have from the point of view of individual personality.

Performance disruptions, then, have consequences at three levels of abstraction: personality, interaction, and social structure. While the likelihood of disruption will vary widely from interaction to interaction, and while the social importance of likely disruptions will vary from interaction to interaction, still it seems that there is no interaction in which the participants do not take an appreciable chance of being slightly embarrassed or a slight chance of being deeply humiliated. Life may not be much of a gamble, but interaction *is*. Further, in so far as individuals make efforts to avoid disruptions or to correct for ones not avoided, these efforts, too, will have simultaneous consequences at the three levels. Here, then, we have one simple way of articulating three levels of abstraction and three perspectives from which social life has been studied.

Underlying all social interaction there seems to be a fundamental dialectic. When one individual enters the presence of others, he will want to discover the facts of the situation. Were he to possess this information, he could know, and make allowances for, what will come to happen and he could give the others present as much of their due as is consistent with his enlightened self-interest. To uncover fully the factual nature of the situation, it would be necessary for the individual to know all the relevant social data about the others. It would also be necessary for the individual to know the actual outcome or end product of the activity of the others during the interaction, as well as their innermost feelings concerning him. Full information of this order is rarely available; in its absence, the individual tends to employ substitutes—cues, tests, hints, expressive gestures, status symbols, etc.—as predictive devices. In short, since the reality that the individual is concerned with is unperceivable at the moment, appearances must be relied upon in its stead. And, paradoxically, the more the individual is concerned with the reality that is not available to perception, the more must he concentrate his attention on appearances.

We come now to the basic dialectic. In their capacity as performers, individuals will be concerned with maintaining the impression that they are living up to the many standards by which they and their products are judged. Because these standards are so numerous and so pervasive, the individuals who are performers dwell more than we might think in a moral world. But, *qua* performers, individuals are concerned not with the moral issue of realizing these standards, but with the amoral issue of engineering a convincing impression that these standards are being realized. Our activity, then, is largely concerned with moral matters, but as performers we do not have a moral concern with them. As performers we are merchants of morality. Our day is given over to intimate contact with the goods we display and our minds are filled with intimate understandings of them; but it may well be that the more attention we give to these goods, then the more distant we feel from them and from those who are believing enough to buy them. To use a different imagery, the very obligation and profitability of appearing always in a steady moral light, of being a socialized character, forces one to be the sort of person who is practiced in the ways of the stage.

Staging and the self

The general notion that we make a presentation of ourselves to others is hardly novel; what ought to be stressed in conclusion is that the very structure of the self can be seen in terms of how we arrange for such performances in our Anglo-American society.

In this report, the individual was divided by implication into two basic parts: he was viewed as a *performer*, a harried fabricator of impressions involved in the all-too-human task of staging a performance; he was viewed as a *character*, a figure, typically a fine one, whose spirit, strength, and other sterling qualities the performance was designed to evoke. The attributes of a performer and the attributes of a character are of a different order, quite basically so, yet both sets have their meaning in terms of the show that must go on.

In analyzing the self then we are drawn from its possessor, from the person who will profit or lose most by it, for he and his body merely provide the peg on which something of collaborative manufacture will be hung for a time. And the means for producing and maintaining selves do not reside inside the peg; in fact these means are often bolted down in social establishments. There will be a back region with its tools for shaping the body, and a front region with its fixed props. There will be a team of persons whose activity on stage in conjunction with available props will constitute the scene from which the performed character's self will emerge, and another team, the audience, whose interpretive activity will be necessary for this emergence. The self is a product of all of these arrangements, and in all of its parts bears the marks of this genesis.

Scaffolds are to build other things with, and should be erected with an eye to taking them down. This report is not concerned with aspects of theater that creep into everyday life. It is concerned with the structure of social encounters; the structure of those entities in social life that come into being whenever persons enter one another's immediate physical presence. The key factor in this structure is the maintenance of a single definition of the situation, this definition having to be expressed, and this expression sustained in the face of a multitude of potential disruptions.

VI ATTITUDES AND COGNITION

In Gordon Allport's widely cited coverage of the concept of attitude, in the earlier *Handbook of Social Psychology* (1935), he called it ". . . the most distinctive and indispensable concept in contemporary American social psychology" (p. 798). He also said there, "The nature of attitudes, however, is still in dispute . . . What is most urgently needed is a clarification of the doctrine of attitudes . . ." (p. 839). A re-reading of this review suggests that, while it still sustains contemporary interest, substantial reformulation of the central issues has taken place in the almost three decades passed. And, it is fair to add, that Allport's concerns are being met, even in unexpected ways.

Today, the nature of attitudes is generally agreed to lie in the direction of learned sets or dispositions to respond, often *evaluatively* (e.g., see Campbell, 1963). As Katz notes here, attitudes include affective (like-dislike) as well as cognitive (belief-disbelief) components. From this point of departure, there is a fair convergence of attention on three interrelated aspects of attitudes: source, in the sense of development; function, related to the way in which attitudes are integrated in personality; and change, having to do most expressly with the way in which new experience becomes incorporated into an already existing belief system.

The attractiveness of the attitude concept is readily understood. It serves, in the first place, as a simple, manageable representation of something quite complex: a brief summary of what has gone before in the individual's experience that may affect his present behavior. But, secondly, attitude is essentially a neutral concept which permits virtually any and all content to be contained within it; moreover, historically it provided a way of retaining, despite the climate of behaviorism prevailing over many years, some content of "mind" (see McClelland, 1955).

In terms of present-day thought, three lines in particular appear to be sources of attitudes; these are, direct experience with the object, explicit and implicit learning from others, and personality development. The latter source involves the effect of recurring interaction with others in establishing certain general sets to respond. Largely based in a psychoanalytic model, this position asserts that an individual, as a function of early experience, develops characteristic reactions as enduring orientations (see Fromm, 1941, 1947). The most notable research on this is no doubt *The Authoritarian Personality* (Adorno, *et al.*, 1950) and some associated endeavors, e.g., Rokeach (1960), as in Section III, among others. The work on "authoritarianism," especially, betrays the relationship between such predisposing personality factors and manifest attitudes of prejudice.

The two other categories of source are more obvious. One considers attitudes toward some "thing" in the outside world to be a function of *contact* with that thing. A dramatic experience, for example, might instigate an individual's attitudes and response patterns toward a category of similar things over a long time span. Secondly, people may learn attitudes quite apart from literal contact with the object of the attitude, by having contact with those holding the attitude. A substantial body of research supports the contention that children, without actually having experienced elements of the environment, take on prevailing attitudes toward them. Statements uttered by parents, encountered from the mass media, or conveyed in endless other ways, often serve to yield implicit learning of this sort. Subsequently, appropriate attitudes are bolstered by the person's attachment to groups.

Several other points of reference are useful in treating attitudes. They are both elements of perception ("cognitive structures" is a way of characterizing them in the aggregate), and they are elements of motivational force, insofar as they direct behavior. Put simply, they represent our outlooks and our inclinations toward action. However, not all attitudes are equally potent across time or situations, and indeed may be in conflict, as is considered at greater length in the papers by Festinger and Osgood. This leads to the conclusion that insofar as people "hold" attitudes, they are variously cued to "manifest" them, depending upon the social context and their relationship to it.

In his paper in this section, Katz speaks to the question of the function which attitudes fulfill for the individual. This so-called "functional approach" refers to the role of attitudes in personality, although the term "function" is sometimes used concerning the construct's service in social psychological thought. The reasons for holding or for changing attitudes, Katz suggests, are found in the part attitudes play in personality for such functions as adjustment, ego defense, value expression, and knowledge. By making these distinctions, broader implications for the mechanics of attitude change come into focus (cf. Katz & Stotland, 1959). It will be seen that Katz considers the learned nature of attitudes and the necessity in attitude change for relearning under appropriate motivational conditions.

Perhaps the most widely known theory of attitude change, or resistance, is the "dissonance" approach of Festinger. The essentials of his position are laid out here in an abridgement of Chapter 1 of his definitive work, *A Theory of Cognitive Dissonance* (1957). Festinger's major concern is with the cognitive elements that may have a "non-fitting" relationship with one another. He postulates in effect a motive for consonance, that is, the avoidance of dissonance. He is not concerned so much with the source of these as with their relationship in a process leading to dissonance reduction. His theory has encouraged a good deal of experimentation, based upon predictions which frequently are not of an obvious variety. And these have been affirmed by the findings obtained, as in papers by Festinger and Carlsmith (1959), Brehm (1956), and Brehm and Cohen (1959). One recent source for this work is the book *Explorations in Cognitive Dissonance* by Brehm and Cohen (1962).

Osgood presents a consideration here of several models of cognitive consistency, by way of speaking to the question of attitude change. He is known for his "mediation theory" (see Section IV) in which he accommodates cognitive processes in behavior. In his paper here, he includes a comparison of the Festinger dissonance theory, Heider's balance theory, and his own model, among others. Pointing out the similarities between these, insofar as they have to do with direction, or sign, he proceeds to a searching consideration of what it means to speak of congruity between elements which are so labeled. A particularly useful feature of the Osgood discussion is the application he draws from these processes to the world of everyday events. His formulation with Tannenbaum (1955), affording predictions about the degree of change which will occur as a function of exposure to incongruous elements, is especially noteworthy. The significant feature of this formulation is the lawful fashion in which the dynamics of interaction among cognitive elements are predicted, as a contribution to the understanding of attitude change phenomena.

Another approach to the organization of attitudes, or "beliefs" as he prefers to conceive them, is represented in Rokeach's paper here. His contribution is vitally based in the concept of cognitive organization, which synthesizes the affective and belief components treated separately in many viewpoints (e.g., Rosenberg, 1956).

Beliefs are *not* retained, says Rokeach, ". . . in an unorganized, chaotic state within our minds." Rather, they cohere in cognitive structures. Moreover, in Rokeach's view, beliefs vary in their importance to the individual along a dimension of centrality-peripherality. From this and several related concepts, he delineates implications for attitude change. His depiction of "primitive beliefs" as central to cognitive structures is especially important in terms of resistance to change. Thus, it may be relatively easy to alter a peripheral belief without affecting the broader structure in which it is imbedded. But changing—or even challenging—a primitive belief regarding, for instance, a person's identity, encounters considerable resistance coupled with negative feeling. This is in harmony with Katz's position regarding the functions in personality that central attitudes especially hold.

Since so many studies of attitude change have dealt with essentially trivial and peripheral beliefs, Rokeach's work raises some question about their generalizability to more central beliefs. It is also noteworthy that Rokeach's view suggests by implication that cognitive dissonance would be differentially produced depending upon the degree of centrality of the dissonant beliefs which were paired.

As we have already noted, an individual's attitudes are generally reinforced through some group to which he belongs, or to which he refers himself (see Sections I, II, and VII). To the extent that he is motivated to retain this affiliation, those attitudes are unlikely to change, whatever their initial source, as Cartwright discusses in Section VIII. Attitudes, then, are quite distinctively social psychological variables by virtue of their genesis in and linkage to social processes and groups.

This social linkage in the persistence of attitudes is nicely conveyed by Newcomb's report here. In it he presents the results of his follow-up study, after more than twenty years, of the women who were subjects in his now classic research in the 1930's at Bennington College. In that Bennington study he found that shifts toward the prevailing campus climate of liberal political attitudes, among these girls from mainly conservative homes, occurred from the freshman to senior years. Furthermore, these shifts were associated with social acceptance in terms of popularity and leadership. His follow-up study now supports the broader conclusion that such attitudes persist by the selection of a sustaining social environment. In particular, he finds that these women married men whose attitudes were more liberal than the conservative norm of the socio-economic stratum from which they came.

As Newcomb points out, his findings mesh well with the ideas of "balance" in Heider's work, discussed here by Osgood. Newcomb has dealt with this himself in terms of his "A-B-X Model" (1953). The essential point of this model is that a state of balance exists when persons *A* and *B* are mutually attracted to one another and share the same attitude toward object X. Imbalance can develop in various ways, including mutual liking with an opposite attitude toward the same object, or mutual disliking with the same attitude toward the object. Evidently, Newcomb's subjects achieved balance by finding spouses with attitudes similar to their own on political and social issues.

Carl Hovland was another major initiator of research on factors influencing attitude change. Together with his coworkers, he contributed materially to an understanding of this phenomenon through a rich array of concepts and experimental studies (e.g., Hovland, *et al.*, 1949, 1953, 1957). As a way of characterizing personality factors associated with attitude change, he had a particular interest in the variable of persuasibility (see especially Hovland & Janis, 1959). He saw this as a persisting individual disposition related psychodynamically to central attitudes regarding one's self, such as self-esteem. In Section VII Kelman, a one-time coworker of Hovland's, offers a conceptual scheme concerning social influence which is partly derivative of the persuasibility construct and also bears upon Katz's functional viewpoint discussed above.

In Hovland's more recent work with Muzafer Sherif, *Social Judgment* (Sherif & Hovland, 1961), they advanced their view that an attitude should be considered a range or latitude of acceptable positions, not as a single point on a continuum. As indicated in the selection from the first chapter of that book here, the "social judgment-involvement approach" considers that a person's own stand on an issue serves as an anchor point which influences the person's evaluation of alternative positions. The Sherif-Hovland view is associated with classical psychophysics and more recently with the work of Helson (1948) on "adaptation level." The essential feature of this newer approach to attitudes is its emphasis on the person's *own position* as a determinant of his latitudes of acceptance, rejection, and noncommitment on an issue. In this view, attitudes are cognitive structures, related to self perceptions and reference group affiliations of the individual, which determine his response to communications. This point is pursued further in the new work by Carolyn Sherif, Muzafer Sherif, and Roger Nebergall entitled *Attitude and Attitude Change: The Social Judgment-Involvement Approach* (1965).

For the most part, laboratory experimentation on attitude change has shown greater effects than have survey studies. In discussing this disparity, Hovland (1959) considered such factors as the selection of subjects and the focused intensity of the experimental situation to be potent determiners of this enhanced effect, as against the more diffuse context of the survey. He pointed to the major independent variables which yield communication effects, among them, the communicator, the nature and sequence of communication, and the position of the recipient of the communication. The paper here by Bauer is a departure from this traditional scheme.

Bauer's emphasis is upon social communication as a two-way influence process. He reviews the typical approach to communication, in terms of propaganda and attitude change through advertising, and concludes that it is inadequate to an understanding of what actually transpires. In referring to Hovland's (1959) comparison of laboratory and survey findings on attitude change, he says that it is quite clear that people receiving communications in their natural habitat are much less likely to attend to them and be influenced by them than they would be as subjects in a laboratory experiment. From a range of research findings, he proceeds to bolster the view that individuals are selective in what they attend to and seek a fair exchange when accepting influence assertions from a communicator. This approach is very much in keeping with the idea of social exchange considered in the work of Homans and Thibaut and Kelley in Section VII. Bauer also raises questions regarding the appropriateness of seeing persuasibility as a function of low self-esteem, since the importance of the issue for the person must also be taken into account. He thus implicitly deals with the centrality-peripherality dimension considered by Rokeach, and underscores its importance in understanding an individual's receptivity to attitude change.

Though attitudes have implications for varying levels of analysis, they continue to be especially important to social psychology in terms of behavioral manifestations. A persisting interest in the field has therefore centered about attitude measurement, through scales, surveys, the semantic differential, questionnaires, and other procedures. Since these methodological approaches are treated only indirectly in this section, the reader would do well to consult such primary sources as Edwards (1957), Hyman (1955), and Osgood, *et al.* (1957), among others, for a fuller detailing of the methodology of attitude study.

35 The functional approach to the study of attitudes

DANIEL KATZ

Early approaches to the study of attitude and opinion

There have been two main streams of thinking with respect to the determination of man's attitudes. The one tradition assumes an irrational model of man: specifically it holds that men have very limited powers of reason and reflection, weak capacity to discriminate, only the most primitive self-insight, and very short memories. Whatever mental capacities people do possess are easily overwhelmed by emotional forces and appeals to self-interest and vanity. The early books on the psychology of advertising, with their emphasis on the doctrine of suggestion, exemplify this approach. One expression of this philosophy is in the propagandist's concern with tricks and traps to manipulate the public. A modern form of it appears in *The Hidden Persuaders*, or the use of subliminal and marginal suggestion, or the devices supposedly employed by "the Madison Avenue boys." Experiments to support this line of thinking started with laboratory demonstrations of the power of hypnotic suggestion and were soon extended to show that people would change their attitudes in an uncritical manner under the influence of the prestige of authority and numbers. For example, individuals would accept or reject the same idea depending upon whether it came from a positive or negative prestige source (Sherif, 1936).

The second approach is that of the ideologist who invokes a rational model of man. It assumes that the human being has a cerebral cortex, that he seeks understanding, that he consistently attempts to make sense of the world about him, that he possesses discriminating and reasoning powers which will assert themselves over time, and that he is capable of self-criticism and self-insight. It relies heavily upon getting adequate information to people. Our educational system is based upon this rational model. The present emphasis upon the improvement of communication, upon developing more adequate channels of two-way communication, of conferences and institutes, upon bringing people together to interchange ideas, are all indications of the belief in the importance of intelligence and comprehension in the formation and change of men's opinions.

Now either school of thought can point to evidence which supports its assumptions, and can make fairly damaging criticisms of its opponent. Solomon Asch (1952) and his colleagues, in attacking the irrational model, have called attention to the biased character of the old experiments on prestige suggestion which gave the subject little opportunity to demonstrate critical

Excerpted from the **Public Opinion Quarterly**, 1960, 24, 163–77, with permission of the author and publisher.

thinking. And further exploration of subjects in these stupid situations does indicate that they try to make sense of a nonsensical matter as far as possible. Though the same statement is presented by the experimenter to two groups, the first time as coming from a positive source and the second time as coming from a negative source, it is given a different meaning dependent upon the context in which it appears. Thus the experimental subject does his best to give some rational meaning to the problem. On the other hand, a large body of experimental work indicates that there are many limitations in the rational approach in that people see their world in terms of their own needs, remember what they want to remember, and interpret information on the basis of wishful thinking. H. H. Hyman and and P. Sheatsley (1947) have demonstrated that these experimental results have direct relevance to information campaigns directed at influencing public opinion. These authors assembled facts about such campaigns and showed conclusively that increasing the flow of information to people does not necessarily increase the knowledge absorbed or produce the attitude changes desired.

The major difficulty with these conflicting approaches is their lack of specification of the conditions under which men do act as the theory would predict. For the facts are that people do act at times as if they had been decorticated and at times with intelligence and comprehension. And people themselves do recognize that on occasion they have behaved blindly, impulsively, and thoughtlessly. A second major difficulty is that the rationality-irrationality dimension is not clearly defined. At the extremes it is easy to point to examples, as in the case of the acceptance of stupid suggestions under emotional stress on the one hand, or brilliant problem solving on the other; but this does not provide adequate guidance for the many cases in the middle of the scale where one attempts to discriminate between rationalization and reason.

Reconciliation of the conflict in a functional approach

The conflict between the rationality and irrationality models was saved from becoming a worthless debate because of the experimentation and research suggested by these models. The findings of this research pointed toward the elements of truth in each approach and gave some indication of the conditions under which each model could make fairly accurate predictions. In general the irrational approach was at its best where the situation imposed heavy restrictions upon search behavior and response alternatives. Where individuals must give quick responses without adequate opportunities to explore the nature of the problem, where there are very few response alternatives available to them, where their own deep emotional needs are aroused, they will in general react much as does the unthinking subject under hypnosis. On the other hand, where the individual can have more adequate commerce with the relevant environmental setting, where he has time to obtain more feedback from his reality testing, and where he has a number of realistic choices, his behavior will reflect the use of his rational faculties (cf. Scott, 1958). The child will often respond to the directive of the parent not by implicit obedience but by testing out whether or not the parent really meant what he said.

The theory of psychological consonance, or cognitive balance, assumes that man attempts to reduce discrepancies in his beliefs, attitudes, and behavior by appropriate changes in these processes. While the emphasis here is upon consistency or logicality, the theory deals with all dissonances, no matter how produced. Thus they could result from irrational factors of distorted perception and wishful thinking as well as from rational factors of realistic appraisal of a problem and an accurate estimate of its consequences. Moreover, the theory would predict only that the individual will move to reduce dissonance, whether such movement is a good adjustment to the world or leads to the delusional systems of the paranoiac. In a sense, then, this theory would avoid the conflict between the old approaches of the rational and the irrational man by not dealing with the specific antecedent causes of behavior or with the particular ways in which the individual solves his problems.

In addition to the present preoccupation with the development of formal models concerned with cognitive balance and consonance, there is a growing interest in a more comprehensive framework for dealing with the complex variables and for bringing order within the field. The thoughtful system of Ulf Himmelstrand [presented in his 1960 paper], is one such attempt. Another point of departure is represented by two groups of workers who have organized their theories around the functions which attitudes perform for the personality. Sarnoff, Katz, and McClintock, in taking this functional approach, have given primary attention to the motivational bases of attitudes and the processes of attitude change (Sarnoff & Katz, 1954). The basic assumption of this group is that both attitude formation and attitude change must be understood in terms of the needs they serve and that, as these motivational processes differ, so too will the conditions and techniques for attitude change. Smith, Bruner, and White (1956) have also analyzed the different functions which attitudes perform for the personality. Both groups present essentially the same functions, but Smith, Bruner, and White give more attention to perceptual and cognitive processes and Sarnoff, Katz, and McClintock to the specific conditions of attitude change.

The importance of the functional approach is threefold. (1) Many previous studies of attitude change have dealt with factors which are not genuine psychological variables, for example, the effect on group prejudice of contact between two groups, or the exposure of a group of subjects to a communication in the mass media. Now contact serves different psychological functions for the individual and merely knowing that people have seen a movie or watched a television program tells us nothing about the personal values engaged or not engaged by such a presentation. If, however, we can gear our research to the functions attitudes perform, we can develop some generalizations about human behavior. Dealing with nonfunctional variables makes such generalization difficult, if not impossible.

(2) By concerning ourselves with the different functions attitudes can perform we can avoid the great error of oversimplification—the error of attributing a single cause to given types of attitude. It was once popular to ascribe radicalism in economic and political matters to the psychopathology of the insecure and to attribute conservatism to the rigidity of the mentally

aged. At the present time it is common practice to see in attitudes of group prejudice the repressed hostilities stemming from childhood frustrations, though Hyman and Sheatsley (1954) have pointed out that prejudiced attitudes can serve a normative function of gaining acceptance in one's own group as readily as releasing unconscious hatred. In short, not only are there a number of motivational forces to take into account in considering attitudes and behavior, but the same attitude can have a different motivational basis in different people.

(3) Finally, recognition of the complex motivational sources of behavior can help to remedy the neglect in general theories which lack specification of conditions under which given types of attitude will change. Gestalt theory tells us, for example, that attitudes will change to give better cognitive organization to the psychological field. This theoretical generalization is suggestive, but to carry out significant research we need some middle-level concepts to bridge the gap between a high level of abstraction and particularistic or phenotypical events. We need concepts that will point toward the types of motive and methods of motive satisfaction which are operative in bringing about cognitive reorganization.

Before we attempt a detailed analysis of the four major functions which attitudes can serve, it is appropriate to consider the nature of attitudes, their dimensions, and their relations to other psychological structures and processes.

Nature of attitudes: their dimensions

Attitude is the predisposition of the individual to evaluate some symbol or object or aspect of his world in a favorable or unfavorable manner. Opinion is the verbal expression of an attitude, but attitudes can also be expressed in nonverbal behavior. Attitudes include both the affective, or feeling core of liking or disliking, and the cognitive, or belief, elements which describe the object of the attitude, its characteristics, and its relations to other objects. All attitudes thus include beliefs, but not all beliefs are attitudes. When specific attitudes are organized into a hierarchical structure, they comprise *value systems*. Thus a person may not only hold specific attitudes against deficit spending and unbalanced budgets but may also have a systematic organization of such beliefs and attitudes in the form of a value system of economic conservatism.

The dimensions of attitudes can be stated more precisely if the above distinctions between beliefs and feelings and attitudes and value systems are kept in mind. The *intensity* of an attitude refers to the strength of the *affective* component. In fact, rating scales and even Thurstone scales deal primarily with the intensity of feeling of the individual for or against some social object. The cognitive, or belief, component suggests two additional dimensions, the *specificity* or *generality* of the attitude and the *degree of differentiation* of the beliefs. Differentiation refers to the number of beliefs or cognitive items contained in the attitude, and the general assumption is that the simpler the attitude in cognitive structure the easier it is to change (cf. Krech & Crutchfield, 1948, pp. 160–63). For simple structures there is no defense in depth, and once a single item of belief has been changed the attitude will change. A rather different dimension of attitude is the *number and strength of its linkages to a related value system.* If an attitude favoring budget balancing by the Federal government is tied in strongly with a value system of economic conservatism, it will be more difficult to change than if it were a fairly isolated attitude of the person. Finally, the relation of the value system to the personality is a consideration of first importance. If an attitude is tied to a value system which is closely related to, or which consists of, the individual's conception of himself, then the appropriate change procedures becomes more complex. The *centrality* of an attitude refers to its role as part of a value system which is closely related to the individual's self-concept.

An additional aspect of attitudes is not clearly described in most theories, namely, their relation to action or overt behavior. Though behavior related to the attitude has other determinants than the attitude itself, it is also true that some attitudes in themselves have more of what Cartwright (1949) calls an action structure than do others. Brewster Smith (1947) refers to this dimension as policy orientation and Katz and Stotland (1959) speak of it as the action component. For example, while many people have attitudes of approval toward one or the other of the two political parties, these attitudes will differ in their structure with respect to relevant action. One man may be prepared to vote on election day and will know where and when he should vote and will go to the polls no matter what the weather or how great the inconvenience. Another man will only vote if a party worker calls for him in a car. Himmelstrand's work is concerned with all aspects of the relationship between attitude and behavior, but he deals with the action structure of the attitude itself by distinguishing between attitudes where the affect is tied to verbal expression and attitudes where the affect is tied to behavior concerned with more objective referents of the attitude (cf. 1960). In the first case an individual derives satisfaction from talking about a problem; in the second case he derives satisfaction from taking some form of concrete action.

Attempts to change attitudes can be directed primarily at the belief component or at the feeling, or affective, component. Rosenberg theorizes that an effective change in one component will result in changes in the other component and presents experimental evidence to confirm this hypothesis (cf. 1960). For example, a political candidate will often attempt to win people by making them like him and dislike his opponent, and thus communicate affect rather than ideas. If he is successful, people will not only like him but entertain favorable beliefs about him. Another candidate may deal primarily with ideas and hope that, if he can change people's beliefs about an issue, their feelings will also change.

Four functions which attitudes perform for the individual

The major functions which attitudes perform for the personality can be grouped according to their motivational basis as follows:

1. *The instrumental, adjustive, or utilitarian function* upon which Jeremy Bentham and the utilitarians constructed their model of man. A modern expression of this approach can be found in behavioristic learning theory.

2. *The ego-defensive function* in which the person protects himself from acknowledging the basic truths about himself or the harsh realities in his external world. Freudian psychology and neo-Freudian thinking have been preoccupied with this type of motivation and its outcomes.

3. *The value-expressive function* in which the individual derives satisfactions from expressing attitudes appropriate to his personal values and to his concept of himself. This function is central to doctrines of ego psychology which stress the importance of self-expression, self-development, and self-realization.

4. *The knowledge function* based upon the individual's need to give adequate structure to his universe. The search for meaning, the need to understand, the trend toward better organization of perceptions and beliefs to provide clarity and consistency for the individual, are other descriptions of this function. The development of principles about perceptual and cognitive structure have been the contribution of Gestalt psychology.

Stated simply, the functional approach is the attempt to understand the reasons people hold the attitudes they do. The reasons, however, are at the level of psychological motivations and not of the accidents of external events and circumstances. Unless we know the psychological need which is met by the holding of an attitude we are in a poor position to predict when and how it will change. Moreover, the same attitude expressed toward a political candidate may not perform the same function for all the people who express it. And while many attitudes are predominantly in the service of a single type of motivational process, as described above, other attitudes may serve more than one purpose for the individual. A fuller discussion of how attitudes serve the above four functions is in order.

1. THE ADJUSTMENT FUNCTION

Essentially this function is a recognition of the fact that people strive to maximize the rewards in their external environment and to minimize the penalties. The child develops favorable attitudes toward the objects in his world which are associated with the satisfactions of his needs and unfavorable attitudes toward objects which thwart him or punish him. Attitudes acquired in the service of the adjustment function are either the means for reaching the desired goal or avoiding the undesirable one, or are affective associations based upon experiences in attaining motive satisfactions (Katz & Stotland, 1959). The attitudes of the worker favoring a political party which will advance his economic lot are an example of the first type of utilitarian attitude. The pleasant image one has of one's favorite food is an example of the second type of utilitarian attitude.

In general, then, the dynamics of attitude formation with respect to the adjustment function are dependent upon present or past perceptions of the utility of the attitudinal object for the individual. The clarity, consistency, and nearness of rewards and punishments, as they relate to the individual's activities and goals, are important factors in the acquisition of such attitudes. Both attitudes and habits are formed toward specific objects, people, and symbols as they satisfy specific needs. The closer these objects are to actual need satisfaction and the more they are clearly perceived as relevant to need satisfaction, the greater are the probabilities of positive attitude formation. These principles of attitude formation are often observed in the breach rather than the compliance. In industry, management frequently expects to create favorable attitudes toward job performance through programs for making the company more attractive to the worker, such as providing recreational facilities and fringe benefits. Such programs, however, are much more likely to produce favorable attitudes toward the company as a desirable place to work than toward performance on the job. The company benefits and advantages are applied across the board to all employees and are not specifically relevant to increased effort in task performance by the individual worker.

Consistency of reward and punishment also contributes to the clarity of the instrumental object for goal attainment. If a political party bestows recognition and favors on party workers in an unpredictable and inconsistent fashion, it will destroy the favorable evaluation of the importance of working hard for the party among those whose motivation is of the utilitarian sort. But, curiously, while consistency of reward needs to be observed, 100 per cent consistency is not as effective as a pattern which is usually consistent but in which there are some lapses. When animal or human subjects are invariably rewarded for a correct performance, they do not retain their learned responses as well as when the reward is sometimes skipped (Jenkins & Stanley, 1950).

2. THE EGO-DEFENSIVE FUNCTION

People not only seek to make the most of their external world and what it offers, but they also expend a great deal of their energy on living with themselves. The mechanisms by which the individual protects his ego from his own unacceptable impulses and from the knowledge of threatening forces from without, and the methods by which he reduces his anxieties created by such problems, are known as mechanisms of ego defense. A more complete account of their origin and nature will be found in Sarnoff (1960). They include the devices by which the individual avoids facing either the inner reality of the kind of person he is, or the outer reality of the dangers the world holds for him. They stem basically from internal conflict with its resulting insecurities. In one sense the mechanisms of defense are adaptive in temporarily removing the sharp edges of conflict and in saving the individual from complete disaster. In another sense they are not adaptive in that they handicap the individual in his social adjustments and in obtaining the maximum satisfactions available to him from the world in which he lives. The worker who persistently quarrels with his boss and with his fellow workers, because he is acting out some of his own internal conflicts, may in this manner relieve himself of some of the emotional tensions which beset him. He is not, however, solving his problem of adjusting to his work situation and thus may deprive himself of advancement or even of steady employment.

Defense mechanisms, Miller and Swanson (1960) point out, may be classified into two families on the basis of the more or less primitive nature of the devices employed. The first family, more primitive in nature, are more socially handicapping and consist of denial and complete avoidance. The individual in such cases obliterates through withdrawal and denial the realities which confront him. The exaggerated case of such primitive mechanisms is the fantasy world of the paranoiac. The second type of defense is less handicapping and makes for distortion rather than denial. It includes rationalization, projection, and displacement.

Many of our attitudes have the function of defending our self-image. When we cannot admit to ourselves that we have deep feelings of inferiority we may project those feelings onto some convenient minority group and bolster our egos by attitudes of superiority toward this underprivileged group. The formation of such defensive attitudes differs in essential ways from the formation of attitudes which serve the adjustment function. They proceed from within the person, and the objects and situation to which they are attached are merely convenient outlets for their expression. Not all targets are equally satisfactory for a given defense mechanism, but the point is that the attitude is not created by the target but by the individual's emotional conflicts. And when no convenient target exists the individual will create one. Utilitarian attitudes, on the other hand, are formed with specific reference to the nature of the attitudinal object. They are thus appropriate to the nature of the social world to which they are geared. The high school student who values high grades because he wants to be admitted to a good college has a utilitarian attitude appropriate to the situation to which it is related.

All people employ defense mechanisms, but they differ with respect to the extent that they use them and some of their attitudes may be more defensive in function than others. It follows that the techniques and conditions for attitude change will not be the same for ego-defensive as for utilitarian attitudes.

Moreover, though people are ordinarily unaware of their defense mechanisms, especially at the time of employing them, they differ with respect to the amount of insight they may show at some later time about their use of defenses. In some cases they recognize that they have been protecting their egos without knowing the reason why. In other cases they may not even be aware of the devices they have been using to delude themselves.

3. THE VALUE-EXPRESSIVE FUNCTION

While many attitudes have the function of preventing the individual from revealing to himself and others his true nature, other attitudes have the function of giving positive expression to his central values and to the type of person he conceives himself to be. A man may consider himself to be an enlightened conservative or an internationalist or a liberal, and will hold attitudes which are the appropriate indication of his central values. Thus we need to take account of the fact that not all behavior has the negative function of reducing the tensions of biological drives or of internal conflicts. Satisfactions also accrue to the person from the expression of attitudes which reflect his cherished beliefs and his self-image. The reward to the person in these instances is not so much a matter of gaining social recognition or monetary rewards as of establishing his self-identity and confirming his notion of the sort of person he sees himself to be. The gratifications obtained from value expression may go beyond the confirmation of self-identity. Just as we find satisfaction in the exercise of our talents and abilities, so we find reward in the expression of any attributes associated with our egos.

Value-expressive attitudes not only give clarity to the self-image but also mold that self-image closer to the heart's desire. The teenager who by dress and speech establishes his identity as similar to his own peer group may appear to the outsider a weakling and a craven conformer. To himself he is asserting his independence of the adult world to which he has rendered childlike subservience and conformity all his life. Very early in the development of the personality the need for clarity of self-image is important—the need to know "who I am." Later it may be even more important to know that in some measure I am the type of person I want to be. Even as adults, however, the clarity and stability of the self-image is of primary significance. Just as the kind, considerate person will cover over his acts of selfishness, so too will the ruthless individualist become confused and embarrassed by his acts of sympathetic compassion. One reason it is difficult to change the character of the adult is that he is not comfortable with the new "me." Group support for such personality change is almost a necessity, as in Alcoholics Anonymous, so that the individual is aware of approval of his new self by people who are like him.

The socialization process during the formative years sets the basic outlines for the individual's self-concept. Parents constantly hold up before the child the model of the good character they want him to be. A good boy eats his spinach, does not hit girls, etc. The candy and the stick are less in evidence in training the child than the constant appeal to his notion of his own character. It is small wonder, then, that children reflect the acceptance of this model by inquiring about the characters of the actors in every drama, whether it be a television play, a political contest, or a war, wanting to know who are the "good guys" and who are the "bad guys." Even as adults we persist in labeling others in the terms of such character images. Joe McCarthy and his cause collapsed in fantastic fashion when the telecast of the Army hearings showed him in the role of the villain attacking the gentle, good man represented by Joseph Welch.

A related but somewhat different process from childhood socialization takes place when individuals enter a new group or organization. The individual will often take over and internalize the values of the group. What accounts, however, for the fact that sometimes this occurs and sometimes it does not? Four factors are probably operative, and some combination of them may be necessary for internalization. (1) The values of the new group may be highly consistent with existing values central to the personality. The girl who enters the nursing profession finds it congenial to consider herself a good nurse because of previous values of the importance of contributing to the welfare of others. (2) The new group may in its ideology have a clear model of what the good group member should be like and may persistently indoctrinate group members in these terms. One of the reasons for the code of conduct for members of the armed forces, devised after the revelations about the conduct of American prisoners in the Korean War, was to attempt to establish a model for what a good soldier does and does not do. (3) The activities of the group in moving toward its goal permit the individual genuine opportunity for participation. To become ego-involved so that he can internalize group values, the new member must find one of two conditions. The group activity open to him must tap his talents and abilities so that his chance to show what he is worth can be tied into the group effort. Or else the activities of the group must give him an active voice in group decisions. His particular talents and abilities may not be tapped but he does have the opportunity to enter into group decisions, and thus his need for self-determination is satisfied. He then identifies with the group in which such opportunities for ego-involvement are available. It is not necessary that opportunities for self-expression and self-determination be of great magnitude in an objective sense, so long as they are important for the psychological economy of the individuals themselves. (4) Finally, the individual may come to see himself as a group member if he can share in the rewards of group activity which includes his own efforts. The worker may not play much of a part in building a ship or make any decisions in the process of building it. Nevertheless, if he and his fellow workers are given a share in every boat they build and a return on the proceeds from the earnings of the ship, they may soon come to identify with the ship-building company and see themselves as builders of ships.

4. THE KNOWLEDGE FUNCTION

Individuals not only acquire beliefs in the interest of satisfying various specific needs, they also seek knowledge to give meaning to what would otherwise be an unorganized chaotic universe. People need standards or frames of reference for understanding their world, and attitudes help to supply such standards. The problem of understanding, as John Dewey (1910) made clear years ago, is one "of introducing (1) *definiteness* and *distinction* and (2) *consistency* and *stability* of meaning into what is otherwise vague and wavering." The definiteness and stability are provided in good measure by the norms of our culture, which give the otherwise perplexed individual ready-made attitudes for comprehending his universe. Walter Lippmann's classical contribution to the study of opinions and attitudes was his description of stereotypes and the way they provided order and clarity for a bewildering set of complexities (1922). The most interesting finding in Herzog's familiar study of the gratifications obtained by housewives in listening to daytime serials was the unsuspected role of information and advice (1944). The stories were liked "because they explained things to the inarticulate listener."

The need to know does not of course imply that people are driven by a thirst for universal knowledge. The American public's appalling lack of political information has been documented many times. In 1956, for example, only 13 per cent of the people in Detroit could correctly name the two United States Senators from the state of Michigan and only 18 per cent knew the name of their own Congressman (Katz & Eldersveld, 1961). People are not avid seekers after knowledge as judged by what the educator or social reformer would desire. But they do want to understand the events which impinge directly on their own life. Moreover, many of the attitudes they have already acquired give them sufficient basis for interpreting much of what they perceive to be important for them. Our already existing stereotypes, in Lippmann's language, "are an ordered, more or less consistent picture of the world, to which our habits, our tastes, our capacities, our comforts and our hopes have adjusted themselves. They may not be a complete picture of the world, but they are a picture of a possible world to which we are adapted" (1922). It follows that new information will not modify old attitudes unless there is some inadequacy or incompleteness or inconsistency in the existing attitudinal structure as it relates to the perceptions of new situations.

Determinants of attitude arousal and attitude change

The problems of attitude arousal and of attitude change are separate problems. The first has to do with the fact that the individual has many predispositions to act and many influences playing upon him. Hence we need a more precise description of the appropriate conditions which will evoke a given attitude. The second problem is that of specifying the factors which will help to predict the modification of different types of attitude.

The most general statement that can be made concerning attitude arousal is that it is dependent upon the excitation of some need in the individual, or some relevant cue in the environment. When a man grows hungry, he talks of food. Even when not hungry he may express favorable attitudes toward a preferred food if an external stimulus cues him. The ego-defensive person who hates foreigners will express such attitudes under conditions of increased anxiety or threat or when a foreigner is perceived to be getting out of place.

The most general statement that can be made about the conditions conducive to attitude change is that the expression of the old attitude or its anticipated expression no longer gives satisfaction to its related need state. In other words, it no longer serves its function and the individual feels blocked or frustrated. Modifying an old attitude or replacing it with a new one is a process of learning, and learning always starts with a problem, or being thwarted in coping with a situation. Being blocked is a necessary, but not a sufficient, condition for attitude change. Other factors must be operative and will vary in effectiveness depending upon the function involved.[1]

[1] Prof. Katz's further elaboration of these latter points will be found in the original paper. —Eds.

36 An introduction to the theory of dissonance

LEON FESTINGER

It has frequently been implied, and sometimes even pointed out, that the individual strives toward consistency within himself. His opinions and attitudes, for example, tend to exist in clusters that are internally consistent. Certainly one may find exceptions. A person may think Negroes are just as good as whites but would not want any living in his neighborhood; or someone may think little children should be quiet and unobtrusive and yet may be quite proud when his child aggressively captures the attention of his adult guests. When such inconsistencies are found to exist, they may be quite dramatic, but they capture our interest primarily because they stand out in sharp contrast against a background of consistency. It is still overwhelmingly true that related opinions or attitudes are consistent with one another. Study after study reports such consistency among one person's political attitudes, social attitudes, and many others.

There is the same kind of consistency between what a person knows or believes and what he does. A person who believes a college education is a good thing will very likely encourage his children to go to college; a child who knows he will be severely punished for some misdemeanor will not commit it or at least will try not to be caught doing it. This is not surprising, of course; it is so much the rule that we take it for granted. Again what captures our attention are the exceptions to otherwise consistent behavior. A person may know that smoking is bad for him and yet continue to smoke; many persons commit crimes even though they know the high probability of being caught and the punishment that awaits them.

Granting that consistency is the usual thing, perhaps overwhelmingly so, what about these exceptions which come to mind so readily? Only rarely, if ever, are they accepted psychologically *as inconsistencies* by the person involved. Usually more or less successful attempts are made to rationalize them. Thus, the person who continues to smoke, knowing that it is bad for his health, may also feel (a) he enjoys smoking so much it is worth it; (b) the chances of his health suffering are not as serious as some would make out; (c) he can't always avoid every possible dangerous contingency and still live; and (d) perhaps even if he stopped smoking he would put on weight which is equally bad for his health. So, continuing to smoke is, after all, consistent with his ideas about smoking.

But persons are not always successful in explaining away or in rationalizing inconsistencies to themselves. For one reason or another, attempts to achieve consistency may fail. The inconsistency then simply continues to exist. Under such circumstances—that is, in the

Abridged and reprinted from **A Theory of Cognitive Dissonance** (Copyright © 1957 by Leon Festinger), Palo Alto, Calif.: Stanford University Press, 1957, Chapter 1, pp. 1–31, with the permission of the publishers and the author.

presence of an inconsistency—there is psychological discomfort.

First, I will replace the word "inconsistency" with a term which has less of a logical connotation, namely, *dissonance*. I will likewise replace the word "consistency" with a more neutral term, namely, *consonance*. A more formal definition of these terms will be given shortly; for the moment, let us try to get along with the implicit meaning they have acquired as a result of the preceding discussion.

The basic hypotheses I wish to state are as follows:

1. The existence of dissonance, being psychologically uncomfortable, will motivate the person to try to reduce the dissonance and achieve consonance.

2. When dissonance is present, in addition to trying to reduce it, the person will actively avoid situations and information which would likely increase the dissonance.

Before proceeding to develop this theory of dissonance and the pressures to reduce it, it would be well to clarify the nature of dissonance, what kind of concept it is, and where the theory concerning it will lead. The two hypotheses stated above provide a good starting point for this clarification. While they refer here specifically to dissonance, they are in fact very general hypotheses. In place of "dissonance" one can substitute other notions similar in nature, such as "hunger," "frustration," or "disequilibrium," and the hypotheses would still make perfectly good sense.

In short, I am proposing that dissonance, that is, the existence of nonfitting relations among cognitions, is a motivating factor in its own right. By the term *cognition*, I mean any knowledge, opinion, or belief about the environment, about oneself, or about one's behavior. Cognitive dissonance can be seen as an antecedent condition which leads to activity oriented toward dissonance reduction just as hunger leads to activity oriented toward hunger reduction. It is a very different motivation from what psychologists are used to dealing with but, as we shall see, nonetheless powerful.

The occurrence and persistence of dissonance

Why and how does dissonance ever arise? How does it happen that persons sometimes find themselves doing things that do not fit with what they know, or having opinions that do not fit with other opinions they hold? An answer to this question may be found in discussing two of the more common situations in which dissonance may occur.

1. New events may happen or new information may become known to a person, creating at least a momentary dissonance with existing knowledge, opinion, or cognition concerning behavior. Since a person does not have complete and perfect control over the information that reaches him and over events that can happen in his environment, such dissonances may easily arise. Thus, for example, a person may plan to go on a picnic with complete confidence that the weather will be warm and sunny. Nevertheless, just before he is due to start, it may begin to rain. The knowledge that it is now raining is dissonant with his confidence in a sunny day and with his planning to go to a picnic. Or, as another example, a person who is quite certain in his knowlege that automatic transmissions on automobiles are inefficient may accidentally come across an article praising

automatic transmissions. Again, at least a momentary dissonance is created.

2. Even in the absence of new, unforseen events or information, the existence of dissonance is undoubtedly an everyday condition. Very few things are all black or all white; very few situations are clear-cut enough so that opinions or behaviors are not to some extent a mixture of contradictions. Thus, a midwestern farmer who is a Republican may be opposed to his party's position on farm price supports; a person buying a new car may prefer the economy of one model but the design of another; a person deciding on how to invest his money may know that the outcome of his investment depends upon economic conditions beyond his control. Where an opinion must be formed or a decision taken, some dissonance is almost unavoidably created between the cognition of the action taken and those opinions or knowledges which tend to point to a different action.

There is, then, a fairly wide variety of situations in which dissonance is nearly unavoidable. But it remains for us to examine the circumstances under which dissonance, once arisen, persists. That is, under what conditions is dissonance not simply a momentary affair? If the hypotheses stated above are correct, then as soon as dissonance occurs there will be pressures to reduce it. To answer this question it is necessary first to have a brief look at the possible ways in which dissonance may be reduced.

Since there will be a more formal discussion of this point later on in this chapter, let us now examine how dissonance may be reduced, using as an illustration the example of the habitual cigarette smoker who has learned that smoking is bad for his health. He may have acquired this information from a newspaper or magazine, from friends, or even from some physician. This knowledge is certainly dissonant with cognition that he continues to smoke. If the hypothesis that there will be pressures to reduce this dissonance is correct, what would the person involved be expected to do?

1. He might simply change his cognition about his behavior by changing his actions; that is, he might stop smoking. If he no longer smokes, then his cognition of what he does will be consonant with the knowledge that smoking is bad for his health.

2. He might change his "knowledge" about the effects of smoking. This sounds like a peculiar way to put it, but it expresses well what must happen. He might simply end up believing that smoking does not have any deleterious effects, or he might acquire so much "knowledge" pointing to the good effects it has that the harmful aspects become negligible. If he can manage to change his knowledge in either of these ways, he will have reduced, or even eliminated, the dissonance between what he does and what he knows.

But in the above illustration it seems clear that the person may encounter difficulties in trying to change either his behavior or his knowledge. And this, of course, is precisely the reason that dissonance, once created, may persist. There is no guarantee that the person will be able to reduce or remove the dissonance. The hypothetical smoker may find that the process of giving up smoking is too painful for him to endure. He might try to find facts and opinions of others to support the view that smoking is not harmful, but these attempts might fail. He might then remain in the situation where he continues to smoke and continues to know that smoking is harmful. If this turns out to be the case, however, his efforts to reduce the dissonance will not cease.

The terms "dissonance" and "consonance" refer to relations which exist between pairs of "elements." It is consequently necessary, before proceeding to define these relations, to define the elements themselves as well as we can.

These elements refer to what has been called cognition, that is, the things a person knows about himself, about his behavior, and about his surroundings. These elements, then, are "knowledges," if I may coin the plural form of the word. Some of these elements represent knowledge about oneself: what one does, what one feels, what one wants or desires, what one is, and the like. Other elements of knowledge concern the world in which one lives: what is where, what leads to what, what things are satisfying or painful or inconsequential or important, etc.

It is clear that the term "knowledge" has been used to include things to which the word does not ordinarily refer—for example, opinions. A person does not hold an opinion unless he thinks it is correct, and so, psychologically, it is not different from a "knowledge." The same is true of beliefs, values, or attitudes, which function as "knowledges" for our purposes. This is not to imply that there are no important distinctions to be made among these various terms. Indeed, some such distinctions will be made later on. But for the definitions here, these are all "elements of cognition," and relations of consonance and dissonance can hold between pairs of these elements.

There are further questions of definition one would like to be able to answer. For example, when is an "element of cognition" *one* element, or a group of elements? Is the knowledge, "the winter in Minneapolis is very cold" an element, or should this be considered a cluster of elements made up of more specific knowledge? This is, at present, an unanswerable question. Indeed, it may be a question which does not need answering.

Another important question concerning these elements is, how are they formed and what determines their content? At this point we want to emphasize the single most important determinant of the content of these elements, namely, *reality*. These elements of cognition are responsive to reality. By and large they mirror, or map, reality. This reality may be physical or social or psychological, but in any case the cognition more or less maps it. This is, of course, not surprising. It would be unlikely that an organism could live and survive if the elements of cognition were not to a large extent a veridical map of reality. Indeed, when someone is "out of touch with reality," it becomes very noticeable.

In other words, elements of cognition correspond for the most part with what the person actually does or feels or with what actually exists in the environment. In the case of opinions, beliefs, and values, the reality may be what others think or do; in other instances the reality may be what is encountered experientially or what others have told him.

But let us here object and say that persons frequently have cognitive elements which deviate markedly from reality, at least as we see it. Consequently, the major point to be made is that *the reality which impinges on a person will exert pressures in the direction of bringing the appropriate cognitive elements into correspondence with that reality.* This does not mean that the existing cognitive elements will *always* correspond. Indeed, one of the important consequences of the theory of dissonance is that it will help us understand some circumstances where the cognitive elements do not correspond with reality. But it does mean that if the cognitive elements do not correspond with a certain reality which impinges, certain pressures must exist. We should therefore be able to observe some manifestations of these pressures. This hypothesized relation between the cognitive elements and reality is important in enabling measurement of dissonance, and we will refer to it again in considering data.

It is now possible to proceed to a discussion of the relations which may exist between pairs of elements. There are three such relations, namely, irrelevance, dissonance, and consonance. They will be discussed in that order.

Two elements may simply have nothing to do with one another. That is, under such circumstances where one cognitive element implies nothing at all concerning some other element, these two elements are irrelevant to one another.

Let us consider two elements which exist in a person's cognition and which are relevant to one another. The definition of dissonance will disregard the existence of all the other cognitive elements that are relevant to either or both of the two under consideration and simply deal with these two alone. *These two elements are in a dissonant relation if, considering these two alone, the obverse of one element would follow from the other.* To state it a bit more formally, x and y are dissonant if not-x follows from y. Thus, for example, if a person knew there were only friends in his vicinity and also felt afraid, there would be a dissonant relation between these two cognitive elements. Or, for another example, if a person were already in debt and also purchased a new car, the corresponding cognitive elements would be dissonant with one another. The dissonance might exist because of what the person has learned or come to expect, because of what is considered appropriate or usual, or for any of a number of other reasons.

It may be helpful to give a series of examples where dissonance between two cognitive elements stems from different sources, that is, where the two elements are dissonant because of different meanings of the phrase "follow from" in the definition of dissonance given above.

1. Dissonance could arise from logical inconsistency. If a person believed that man will reach the moon in the near future and also believed that man will not be able to build a device that can leave the atmosphere of the earth, these two cognitions are dissonant with one another. The obverse of one follows from the other on logical grounds in the person's own thinking processes.
2. Dissonance could arise because of cultural mores. If a person at a formal dinner uses his hands to pick up a recalcitrant chicken bone, the knowledge of what he is doing is dissonant with the knowledge of formal dinner etiquette. The dissonance exists simply because the culture defines what is consonant and what is not. In some other culture these two cognitions might not be dissonant at all.
3. Dissonance may arise because one specific opinion is sometimes included, by definition, in a more gen-

eral opinion. Thus, if a person is a Democrat but in a given election prefers the Republican candidate, the cognitive elements corresponding to these two sets of opinions are dissonant with each other because "being a Democrat" includes, as part of the concept, favoring Democratic candidates.

4. Dissonance may arise because of past experience. If a person were standing in the rain and yet could see no evidence that he was getting wet, these two cognitions would be dissonant with one another because he knows from experience that getting wet follows from being out in the rain. If one can imagine a person who had never had any experience with rain, these two cognitions would probably not be dissonant.

All dissonant relations, of course, are not of equal magnitude. It is necessary to distinguish degrees of dissonance and to specify what determines how strong a given dissonant relation is.

One obvious determinant of the magnitude of dissonance lies in the characteristics of the elements between which the relation of dissonance holds. *If two elements are dissonant with one another, the magnitude of the dissonance will be a function of the importance of the elements.* The more these elements are important to, or valued by, the person, the greater will be the magnitude of a dissonant relation between them. Thus, for example, if a person gives ten cents to a beggar, knowing full well that the beggar is not really in need, the dissonance which exists between these two elements is rather weak. Neither of the two cognitive elements involved is very important or very consequential to the person. A much greater dissonance is involved, for example, if a student does not study for a very important examination, knowing that his present fund of information is probably inadequate for the examination. In this case the elements that are dissonant with each other are more important to the person, and the magnitude of dissonance will be correspondingly greater.

Let us consider now the total context of dissonances and consonances in relation to one particular element. Assuming momentarily, for the sake of definition, that all the elements relevant to the one in question are equally important, *the total amount of dissonance between this element and the remainder of the person's cognition will depend on the proportion of relevant elements that are dissonant with the one in question.* Thus, if the overwhelming majority of relevant elements are consonant with, say, a behavioral element, then the dissonance with this behavioral element is slight. If in relation to the number of elements consonant with the behavioral element the number of dissonant elements is large, the total dissonance will be of appreciable magnitude. Of course, the magnitude of the total dissonance will also depend on the importance or value of those relevant elements which exist in consonant or dissonant relations with the one being considered.

The reduction of dissonance

The presence of dissonance gives rise to pressures to reduce or eliminate the dissonance. The strength of the pressures to reduce the dissonance is a function of the magnitude of the dissonance. In other words, dissonance acts in the same way as a state of drive or need or tension. The presence of dissonance leads to action to reduce it just as, for example, the presence of hunger leads to action to reduce the hunger. Also, similar to the action of a drive, the greater the dissonance, the greater will be the avoidance of situations that would increase the dissonance.

In order to be specific about how the pressure to reduce dissonance would manifest itself, it is necessary to examine the possible ways in which existing dissonance can be reduced or eliminated. In general, if dissonance exists between two elements, this dissonance can be eliminated by changing one of those elements. The important thing is how these changes may be brought about. There are various possible ways in which this can be accomplished, depending upon the type of cognitive elements involved and upon the total cognitive context.

CHANGING A BEHAVIORAL COGNITIVE ELEMENT

When the dissonance under consideration is between an element corresponding to some knowledge concerning environment (environmental element) and a behavioral element, the dissonance can, of course, be eliminated by changing the behavioral cognitive element in such a way that it is consonant with the environmental element. The simplest and easiest way in which this may be accomplished is to change the action or feeling which the behavioral element represents. Given that a cognition is responsive to "reality" (as we have seen), if the behavior of the organism changes, the cognitive element or elements corresponding to this behavior will likewise change. This method of reducing or eliminating dissonance is a very frequent occurrence. Our behavior and feelings are frequently modified in accordance with new information. If a person starts out on a picnic and notices that it has begun to rain, he may very well turn around and go home. There are many persons who do stop smoking if and when they discover it is bad for their health.

CHANGING AN ENVIRONMENTAL COGNITIVE ELEMENT

Just as it is possible to change a behavioral cognitive element by changing the behavior which this element mirrors, it is sometimes possible to change an *environmental* cognitive element by changing the situation to which that element corresponds. This, of course, is much more difficult than changing one's behavior, for one must have a sufficient degree of control over one's environment—a relatively rare occurrence.

Whenever there is sufficient control over the environment, this method of reducing dissonance may be employed. For example, a person who is habitually very hostile toward other people may surround himself with persons who provoke hostility. His cognitions about the persons with whom he associates are then consonant with the cognitions corresponding to his hostile behavior. The possibilities of manipulating the environment are limited, however, and most endeavors to change a cognitive element will follow other lines.

ADDING NEW COGNITIVE ELEMENTS

It is clear that in order to eliminate a dissonance completely, some cognitive element must be changed. It is also clear that this is not always possible. But even if it is impossible to eliminate a dissonance, it is possible to reduce the total magnitude of dissonance by adding new cognitive elements. Thus, for example, if dissonance existed between some cognitive elements concerning the effects of smoking and cognition concerning the behavior of continuing to smoke, the total dissonance could be reduced by adding new cognitive elements that are consonant with the fact of smoking. In the presence of such dissonance, then, a person might be expected to actively seek new information that would reduce the total dissonance and, at the same time, to avoid new information that might increase the existing dissonance. Thus, to pursue the example, the person might seek out and avidly read any material critical of the research which purported to show that smoking was bad for one's health. At the same time he would avoid reading material that praised this research. (If he unavoidably came in contact with the latter type of material, his reading would be critical indeed.)

Before moving on, it is worth while to emphasize again that the presence of pressures to reduce dissonance, or even activity directed toward such reduction, does not guarantee that the dissonance will be reduced. A person may not be able to find the social support needed to change a cognitive element, or he may not be able to find new elements which reduce the total dissonance. In fact, it is quite conceivable that in the process of trying to reduce dissonance, it might even be increased. This will depend upon what the person encounters while attempting to reduce the dissonance. The important point to be made so far is that in the presence of a dissonance, one will be able to observe the *attempts* to reduce it. If attempts to reduce dissonance fail, one should be able to observe symptoms of psychological discomfort, provided the dissonance is appreciable enough so that the discomfort is clearly and overtly manifested.

Resistance to reduction of dissonance

If dissonance is to be reduced or eliminated by changing one or more cognitive elements, it is necessary to consider how resistant these cognitive elements are to change. Whether or not any of them change, and if so, which ones, will certainly be determined in part by the magnitude of resistance to change which they possess. It is, of course, clear that if the various cognitive elements involved had no resistance to change whatsoever, there would never be any lasting dissonances. Momentary dissonance might occur, but if the cognitive elements involved had no resistance to change, the dissonance would immediately be eliminated. Let us, then, look at the major sources of resistance to change of a cognitive element.

RESISTANCE TO CHANGE OF BEHAVIORAL COGNITIVE ELEMENTS

The first and foremost source of resistance to change for *any* cognitive element is the responsiveness of such elements to reality. If one sees that the grass is green, it is very difficult to think it is not so.

Certainly much behavior has little or no resistance to change. We continually modify many of our actions and feelings in accordance with changes in the situation. If a street which we ordinarily use when we drive to work is being repaired, there is usually little difficulty in altering our behavior and using a different route. What, then, are the circumstances that make it difficult for the person to change his actions?

1. The change may be painful or involve loss. A person may, for example, have spent a lot of money to purchase a house. If for any reason he now wants to change, that is, live in a different house or differ-

ent neighborhood, he must endure the discomforts of moving and the possible financial loss involved in selling the house.

2. The present behavior may be otherwise satisfying. A person might continue to have lunch at a certain restaurant even though they served poor food if, for example, his friends always ate there.
3. Making the change may simply not be possible. It would be a mistake to imagine that a person could consummate any change in his behavior if he wanted to badly enough. It may not be possible to change for a variety of reasons. Some behavior, especially emotional reactions, may not be under the voluntary control of the person. For example, a person might have a strong reaction of fear which he can do nothing about. Also, it might not be possible to consummate a change simply because the new behavior may not be in the behavior repertory of the person. A father might not be able to change the way he behaves toward his children simply because he doesn't know any other way to behave. A third circumstance which could make it impossible to change is the irrevocable nature of certain actions.

RESISTANCE TO CHANGE OF ENVIRONMENTAL COGNITIVE ELEMENTS

Here again, as with behavioral cognitive elements, the major source of resistance to change lies in the responsiveness of these elements to reality. The result of this, as far as behavioral elements go, is to tie the resistance to change of the cognitive element to the resistance to change of the reality, namely, the behavior itself. The situation is somewhat different with regard to environmental elements. When there is a clear and unequivocal reality corresponding to some cognitive element, the possibilities of change are almost nil. If one desired, for example, to change one's cognition about the location of some building which one saw every day, this would indeed be difficult to accomplish.

In many instances, however, the reality corresponding to the cognitive element is by no means so clear and unambiguous. When the reality is basically a social one, that is, when it is established by agreement with other people, the resistance to change would be determined by the difficulty of finding persons to support the new cognition.

There is another source of resistance to change of both behavioral and environmental cognitive elements. We have postponed discussion of it until now, however, because it is a more important source of resistance to change for environmental elements than for others. This source of resistance to change lies in the fact that an element is in relationship with a number of other elements. To the extent that the element is consonant with a large number of other elements and to the extent that changing it would replace these consonances by dissonances, the element will be resistant to change.

Limits of the magnitude of dissonance

The maximum dissonance that can possibly exist between any two elements is equal to the total resistance to change of the less resistant element. The magnitude of dissonance cannot exceed this amount because, at this point of maximum possible dissonance, the less re-

sistant element would change, thus eliminating the dissonance.

This does not mean that the magnitude of dissonance will frequently even approach this maximum possible value. When there exists a strong dissonance that is less than the resistance to change of any of the elements involved, this dissonance can perhaps still be reduced for the total cognitive system by adding new cognitive elements. In this way, even in the presence of very strong resistances to change, the total dissonance in the system could be kept at rather low levels.

Let us consider an example of a person who spends what for him is a very large sum of money for a new car of an expensive type. Let us also imagine that after purchasing it he finds that some things go wrong with it and that repairs are very expensive. It is also more expensive to operate than other cars, and what is more, he finds that his friends think the car is ugly. If the dissonance becomes great enough, that is, equal to the resistance to change of the less resistant element, which in the situation would probably be the behavioral element, he might sell the car and suffer whatever inconvenience and financial loss is involved. Thus the dissonance could not exceed the resistance the person has to changing his behavior, that is, selling the car.

Now let us consider the situation where the dissonance for the person who bought a new car was appreciable but less than the maximum possible dissonance, that is, less than the resistance to change of the less resistant cognitive element. None of the existing cognitive elements would then be changed, but he could keep the total dissonance low by adding more and more cognitions that are consonant with his ownership of the car. He begins to feel that power and riding qualities are more important than economy and looks. He begins to drive faster than he used to and becomes quite convinced that it is important for a car to be able to travel at high speed. With these cognitions and others, he might succeed in rendering the dissonance negligible.

Avoidance of dissonance

The discussion thus far has focused on the tendencies to reduce or eliminate dissonance and the problems involved in achieving such reduction. Under certain circumstances there are also strong and important tendencies to avoid increases of dissonance or to avoid the occurrence of dissonance altogether. Let us now turn our attention to a consideration of these circumstances and the manifestations of the avoidance tendencies which we might expect to observe.

The avoidance of an increase in dissonance comes about, of course, as a result of the existence of dissonance. This avoidance is especially important where, in the process of attempting to reduce dissonance, support is sought for a new cognitive element to replace an existing one or where new cognitive elements are to be added. In both these circumstances, the seeking of support and the seeking of new information must be done in a highly selective manner. A person would initiate discussion with someone he thought would agree with the new cognitive element but would avoid discussion with someone who might agree with the element that he was trying to change. A person would expose himself to sources of information which he expected would add new elements which would increase consonance but would certainly avoid sources which would increase dissonance.

If there is little or no dissonance existing, we would not expect the same kind of selectivity in exposure to sources of support or sources of information. In fact, where no dissonance exists there should be a relative absence of motivation to seek support or new information at all. This will be true in general, but there are important exceptions. Past experience may lead a person to fear, and hence to avoid, the initial occurrence of dissonance. Where this is true, one might expect circumspect behavior with regard to new information even when little or no dissonance is present to start with.

The operation of a fear of dissonance may also lead to a reluctance to commit oneself behaviorally. There is a large class of actions that, once taken, are difficult to change. Hence, it is possible for dissonances to arise and to mount in intensity. A fear of dissonance would lead to a reluctance to take action—a reluctance to commit oneself. Where decision and action cannot be indefinitely delayed, the taking of action may be accompanied by a cognitive negation of the action. Thus, for example, a person who buys a new car and is very afraid of dissonance may, immediately following the purchase, announce his conviction that he did the wrong thing. Such strong fear of dissonance is probably relatively rare, but it does occur. Personality differences with respect to fear of dissonance and the effectiveness with which one is able to reduce dissonance are undoubtedly important in determining whether or not such avoidance of dissonance is likely to happen. The operational problem would be to independently identify situations and persons where this kind of a priori self-protective behavior occurs.

37 Cognitive dynamics in the conduct of human affairs

CHARLES E. OSGOOD

Over the past two decades a great deal of social-psychological research has been converging on a conclusion about human thinking that common sense had already isolated as the consistency which is the "hobgoblin of little minds." It appears, however, that "consistency" can plague big minds as well as little, in high places as well as low. Indeed, the difficulties we face today on both national and international levels can be traced, in part at least, to these dynamics of human thinking. Research that is relevant to our problem cuts a wide swathe through the social sciences—attitude formation and change; the effects of context upon the interpretation of both perceptual and linguistic signs; interpersonal perception and group dynamics; the interactions among beliefs, decisions, and social behavior; and even public affairs. The researchers have come from a diversity of theoretical molds. Accordingly, the purposes of this paper are to provide a brief purview of this research on cognitive dynamics, to indicate the essential similarities in the theoretical notions that have been proposed, and to point up the significance of such cognitive dynamics for contemporary human affairs. But first we need a few specimens of the phenomena we wish to study.

Specimen 1: International affairs. Before the delegates to the United Nations Khrushchev makes sweeping proposals for world disarmament. A large segment of the American press editorializes about the deceptive nature of these proposals, that, rather than sincere overtures toward peaceful solutions of problems, his proposals are carefully planned moves in the Cold War. It is cognitively inconsistent for us to think of people we dislike and distrust making honest, conciliatory moves, behaving as human beings ought to behave, and assuming noble postures.

Specimen 2: Internal affairs. A noted counterspy is invited to speak in the high school auditorium of a university town. In the course of his talk, he emphasizes the fact that the university hasn't invited any *anti*-Communists (including himself) to make public appearances in its halls. Although no allegations are directly made, many people in his audience are led to conclude (a) that the university has invited *pro*-Communists (which it hasn't), or at least (b) that the university must include some powerful Communist supporters.

Specimen 3: Individual behavior and belief. Some time after stories in the mass media about the relation between smoking and lung cancer had saturated the public, a survey in Minneapolis inquired about both the smoking habits of respondents and whether they thought the relationship between smoking and lung cancer had been proven or not proven. The results showed that 29 per

Reprinted with slight abridgment from the Public Opinion Quarterly, 1960, 24, 341–65, with permission of the author and publisher.

cent of nonsmokers, 20 per cent of light smokers, but only 7 per cent of heavy smokers believed it had been proven. It is cognitively inconsistent to believe one way and behave another; people who smoke heavily find it easier to *dis*-believe information that it is damaging to their health (Festinger, 1957).

Specimen 4: Interpersonal affairs. Fraternity men were asked to (a) name the men in their group they liked best and liked least, (b) rate themselves on a series of traits, and (c) rate the other men on the same series of traits. The results showed that these men *assumed* greater similarity in personality traits between people they liked and themselves than actually existed (Fiedler, Warrington, & Blaisdell, 1952). It has also been shown that husbands and wives attribute more similarity between them than actually exists, and this is more true for happily married than for unhappily married couples (Preston, *et al.*, 1952). It is "natural" to assume that people we like must think and feel as we do—at least, to the extent that we like ourselves.

Specimen 5: Making inferences about people. If we observe, or are told, that so-and-so is *intelligent* and *considerate,* and this is all the information we have, we are nevertheless able to generate many inferences about him—he is also likely to be *sensitive, socially adept, alert,* and so forth, we assume. The traits we infer are not haphazard: they are generated from the region of intersection of the meanings of the traits we know about, according to laws of cognitive interaction (Bruner & Tagiuri, 1954). Many of the predictions we make about people and the expectations we have of them are based on inferences of this type.

Specimen 6: Perceptual affairs. In his *Film Technique and Film Acting* Pudovkin (1954) describes a little experiment in film editing. A simple, passive close-up of the well-known Russian actor, Mosjukhin, was joined to three different strips of film. In one this close-up was followed by a shot of a bowl of soup on the table; in another it was followed by shots showing a dead woman in a coffin; in the third it was followed by shots of a little girl playing with a funny toy bear. The effects on an unsuspecting audience were terrific, according to Pudovkin. "The public raved about the acting of the artist. They pointed out the heavy pensiveness of his mood over the forgotten soup, were touched and moved by the deep sorrow with which he looked at the dead woman, and admired the light, happy smile with which he surveyed the girl at play. But we knew that in all three cases the face was exactly the same."

Specimen 7: A matter of naming. "A rose by any name would smell as sweet," we have been told—but would it? I do not know of any experiments on the influence of labels upon perception of odors, but this should be easily demonstrated, smells being the elusive, subjective business they are. But from the myth of suburbia we can gather many examples of the same sort—the cramped, standardized, insignificant little house with its postage-stamp yard in "Briarwood Valley," in "Larchmont Hills," or in "Sunnyvale Downs" somehow assumes a splendor and grace it could never have in "Southside Brighton Avenue, subdivision No. 7." The cheap panel-and-paste bedroom set, produced by the hundreds of thousands but garnished with the name "Beverley Charm by Rudet," acquires a distinction far beyond its cost and worth.

Specimen 8: Attitudinal affairs. Suppose that we are favorably disposed toward Eisenhower, both as a person and as the President of our country. In Uruguay, let us say, he is greeted with flowers and smiles, but in Paraguay an unruly mob of students boos him and has to be dispersed with tear gas. Having little information, and generally neutral attitudes, toward both Uruguay and Paraguay, we find ourselves considerably more favorable toward the former than toward the latter. Subsequent news that Uruguay lives under a harsh dictatorship will be discounted—it must really be "benevolent"—and the fact that Paraguay has a democratic form of government, much like our own, is somehow difficult to assimilate. As this hypothetical example shows, we strive to maintain internal consistency among our attitudes and beliefs, often at the price of doctoring reality.

So much for specimens of cognitive interaction in human affairs. Such examples could be elaborated *ad infinitum.* The important thing is that they are all cut from the same cloth; they are all instances of a basic dynamism according to which human judgment, belief, perception, and thought are transformed in midflight, so to speak.

Some theory of cognitive interaction

Insight into the dynamics of human thinking has been available in the writings of brilliant men of all periods. Certainly Aristotle was aware of these dynamics when he dealt with the principles of rhetoric; Shakespeare imposes the rules of psycho-logic (Abelson & Rosenberg, 1958) on the thought and behavior of his characters; and Machiavelli could not have had the understanding he did of politics without an intuitive grasp of the same rules. But intuitive grasp and common sense—essential though they may be to discovery in science—are not the same thing as explicit and testable principles of human behavior.

Among psychologists who have dealt with cognitive interaction in recent times, Fritz Heider undoubtedly has given the earliest and richest analysis, in his two papers in the middle forties (1944, 1946) and particularly as elaborated in his new book, *The Psychology of Interpersonal Relations* (1958), which is a much broader study of human perception and thinking than the title implies. Working in the area of human communication, particularly in small groups, Theodore Newcomb (1953) has utilized very similar theoretical notions to Heider's. In his *A Theory of Cognitive Dissonance,* Leon Festinger (1957) has probably given the clearest statement of this type of theory and, through his own ingenious experiments, has extended it into the whole area of relations between cognitions and overt behavior. Osgood and Tannenbaum (1955), working in the area of attitude change, have presented what they call "the congruity hypothesis"—which again has similar features to the Heider-Newcomb-Festinger approaches. The most explicit statement of this hypothesis appears in *The Measurement of Meaning* in the context of Osgood's mediation theory of meaning and the measurement procedures of the semantic differential (Osgood, Suci, & Tannenbaum, 1957). Rather than try to describe each of these theories in isolation, it will be more useful to describe them comparatively in terms of certain common and differential features.

1. *Cognitive modification results from*

the psychological stress produced by cognitive inconsistencies. We have here a kind of motivation, analogous to other drive states like hunger, sex, and anxiety, but purely cognitive in origin. It is necessary, of course, to define the states of cognitive "consistency" and "inconsistency" and in terms as close as possible to observables. Heider himself speaks in terms of *balance and imbalance* (from within a gestalt framework), but he does not provide us with a very clear statement, beyond the fact that "a balanced state is . . . a situation in which the relations among the entities fit together harmoniously; there is no stress toward change." In order to give meaning and order to the flux of distal stimuli (things, persons, events), the individual strives to maintain balance among the proximal signs (cognitions) of these external affairs.

Newcomb sees human communication as a means of achieving or maintaining *symmetry* in the orientations of individuals with respect to objects or events. Festinger's theory is expressed in terms of *consonance and dissonance.* These terms refer to the relations which may exist between pairs of cognitive elements (bits of knowledge about the world, other people, the self, one's own behavior).

Where Heider has not attempted a formal definition of balance in his system, Cartwright and Harary (1956) have done so in terms of the mathematical theory of linear graphs. To handle Heider's types of situation in graph theory requires, according to these authors, *signed, directed graphs of type 2*. We start with the cognitive elements (people, objects, etc.) defined as points. If these elements are involved in interactions (and they need not be, cf. section 2 below), then we connect them with a line; the line must be *directed* by means of an arrow in order to take into account Heider's distinction between agent and recipient. Since Heider talks about both sentiments (liking vs. disliking) and cognitive units (belonging vs. not belonging) as being two-valued, we also require a *signed* line—which Cartwright and Harary accomplish by means of solid vs. dashed lines. Finally, since Heider distinguishes the two types of relations, "liking" vs. "belonging," it is suggested that a type 2 graph, using two colors, for example, should be employed. However, Cartwright and Harary make little use of this last distinction and, in fact, criticize the ambiguity in Heider's "cognitive unit" conception (see section 2 below). In a more recent paper Harary (1959) has further elaborated this type of analysis, with special reference to the measurement of structural balance in small groups.

This brings up a source of confusion in this field that has hardly been recognized, as far as I am aware, but must be cleared up before we proceed. Cognitive interactions, obviously, transpire within the nervous systems of single individuals. The "maps" we draw to represent such interactions necessarily reflect person-person and person-object relations *as some individual perceives them.* Festinger is clearly aware of this; Heider also seems to be working on this basis—to the extent that his book might better have been titled "The Psychology of Interpersonal *Perceptions.*" But both Newcomb and Cartwright and Harary seem to shift too easily from the subjective (cognitive interactions in individuals) to the objective (group structure and dynamics) frame of reference. Now it may be that the laws which apply to the interactions, stresses, and resolutions among the cognitive processes of individuals can be directly transferred to interactions within groups of people—where persons are the elements rather than cognitions—but this remains to be proven. The bridge between the two levels presumably lies in the fact that the structuring of a group depends upon the cognitive "maps" individual members have of it.

Osgood *et al.* (1957) equate "cognitive elements" with the *meanings* of signs, and these are indexed in terms of *n* bipolar dimensions or factors. However, since interactions are assumed to occur on each dimension independently of the others, we may restrict our attention to the dominant evaluative factor of the meaning space—which is the one which has interested all other investigators. In the measurement system provided by the semantic differential, the evaluative factor runs from +3 (extremely good) through 0 (neutral) to −3 (extremely bad). The *evaluative meaning* of a concept (cognitive element) is its location along such a scale; the *polarization* of a concept is its distance from 0, regardless of sign. Now, it is assumed that evaluative meanings are mediated by a representational reaction system (perhaps here the autonomic nervous system and its connections with the central nervous system) which can only do one thing, assume one "posture," at one time. It must follow, therefore, that if two (or more) signs associated with different evaluative meanings occur near-simultaneously, only one cognitive reaction can occur in the system, and this must be a compromise. According to Osgood *et al.*, *congruity* exists when the evaluative meanings of interacting signs are equally polarized or intense—either in the same or opposite evaluative directions (see section 2 on types of *assertions*). To the extent that there are differences in polarization, some degree of *incongruity* must exist to be resolved in the process of cognizing these signs.

Although this theory will be shown to lead to similar conclusions about human thinking, it developed from a very different conceptual background than the others we have been considering, and certain critical differences should be noted at this point. First, *it attributes degrees of incongruity to single pairs of elements* rather than the all-or-nothing relations found in Heider and Festinger. Coupled with a measuring device like the semantic differential, this can lead to more refined predictions. Second, *it assigns affective or attitudinal values to the cognitive elements themselves,* and not to their relations, whereas Heider, at least, assigns both affective and connecting properties to the relations between cognitive elements. This double function of the relational variable is, to my mind, the major weakness in Heider's theory.

2. *If cognitive elements are to interact, they must be brought into some relation with one another.* Contiguity is a necessary, but not a sufficient, condition for interaction among cognitive elements. In "Tom is a thief; Paul will catch him," "Paul" is spatially and temporally closer to "thief" than is "Tom," but the *structure* of the sentence brings "Tom" and "thief" into interaction. We have varying attitudes toward myriad people, things, and events, many of them *potentially* incongruent, imbalanced, or dissonant as one's theory would have it, but these cognitions are not continuously interacting—only when they are brought together in some way.

Festinger's theory fails to give explicit

recognition to this variable. Implicit recognition of the need for linkage in some unit appears in the design of his experiments, however—dissonance only occurs when a person has been forced to make a choice between two gifts, when he has been exposed to information consistent or inconsistent with his beliefs, and so on. Analysis into "relevant" and "irrelevant" pairs of cognitive elements is not sufficient; cognitions of the attractiveness of an electric toaster and an electric clock are always potentially relevant, but only become effectively relevant when, by forced choice, the implied negative assertion that one is better than the other is made.

Heider, on the other hand, does give explicit recognition to this variable (1958, pp. 176ff) treating it in terms of gestalt perceptual factors. "Separate entities comprise a unit when they are perceived as belonging together. For example, members of a family are seen as a unit; a person and his deed belong together." Such factors as similarity, proximity, common fate, good continuation, set and past experience are cited as contributing to the formation of cognitive units, but it is evident in his examples that much more than perceptual organization in the traditional sense is involved. The difficulty with Heider's analysis, as Cartwright and Harary have implied, is that belonging in a unit (U or not U) is given the same status as liking (*L* vs. *DL*), both as relations between cognitive elements. Thus the triad, P *worships* O (P L O), O *told a lie* (O *U* X), and P *disapproves of lying* (P *DL* X), is said to be unbalanced because it has only one negative relation. One could also say that since O is + in evaluation and X is − in evaluation for P, the single assertion that O *told a lie* (i.e., +O + −X) is itself cognitively unbalanced or dissonant for P.

Osgood *et al.* (1957) make an absolute distinction between structure and content in the representation and analysis of cognitive interactions. In order for two cognitive elements to interact, they must be related in some kind of *assertion.* Assertions may be linguistic ("Eisenhower *favors* Big Business," as read in an editorial) or behavioral (a picture of Eleanor Roosevelt *patting the head of* a little colored boy), and they may be either associative (X *favors, likes, owns, is a member of,* etc., Y) or dissociative (X *attacks, dislikes, throws away, is excluded from,* etc., Y). But whether a particular cognitive pattern is congruent or not depends on both the structure *and* the content. Thus, in contradistinction to Heider, the assertion P *likes* O merely indicates an associative or positive structure; if both P and O have the same sign evaluatively, the assertion is congruent (e.g., "God is on our side" and "The Devil aids the enemy" are both congruent assertions), but if P is + and O −, or vice versa, then P *likes* O becomes incongruent (e.g., "God is with the enemy").

Although it is significant that Heider came to his theory via a very penetrating study of the ordinary *language* of human relations—which he calls a "naïve psychology"—it does not seem to me that he has fully explored the possibilities in rigorous linguistic (structural) analysis. Osgood, Saporta, and Nunnally (1956) have developed a technique for abstracting the affective content of messages, called *evaluative assertion analysis:* (1) Objects of attitude are isolated from common-meaning terms and then masked by substituting nonsense letter pairs like AZ, BY, and CW for them.

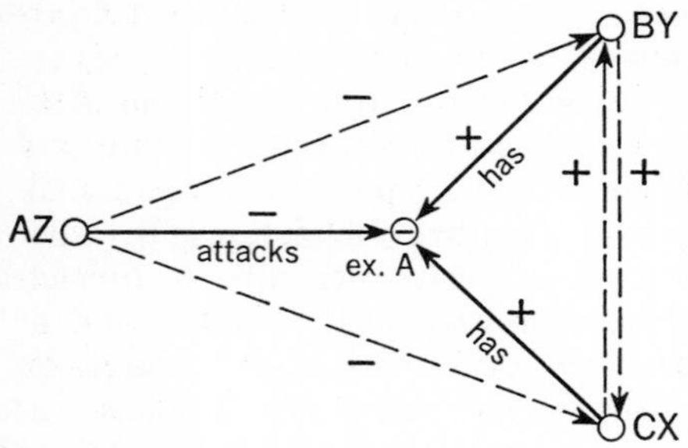

Figure 1

(2) Complex utterances in the masked message are broken down into component assertions of the actor-action-complement form. (3) Evaluative weights are given to the symbols for attitude objects in terms of their structural relations to evaluative common-meaning terms and other attitude objects. (4) The attitudinal consistency of the original utterances is checked by applying the congruity test (an even number of negative signs in each assertion).

Take, for example, the masked sentence, "AZ attacks *the expansionist ambitions* of both BY and CX." This breaks into three component assertions: /AZ/attacks/*expansionist ambitions*/, /BY/has/*expansionist ambitions*/, and /CX/has/*expansionist ambitions*/. The circles and solid lines in Figure 1 provide a signed di-graph of the structural relations actually given. However, if one is also given the valence of the common-meaning cognitive element, "expansionist ambitions," he can fill in by the rules of inference of psycho-logic what the valences of all of the attitude-object circles must be: AZ must be +, BY must be −, and CX must be −, otherwise we would have an assertion line with an odd number of negatives. But note that we still cannot decide whether or not this is a congruent or incongruent pattern until we know that, in fact and for some particular language user, AZ *is* + in evaluation, BY is −, and so forth. If AZ (e.g. Franco Spain) is in fact somewhat negative for a person, then it is incongruous psycho-logically for it to be "attacking" something (e.g. the "expansionist ambitions") belonging to two bad things (e.g. Russia and the Arab League), and he is under some pressure to modify his cognitive map.

The process of inference through psycho-logic—hence the possibility of predicting the effects of implicit assertions in linguistic and behavioral situations—is also illustrated in Figure 1 by the dashed lines. Given that AZ is +, BY is −, and CX is − (i.e. a balanced situation), even though nothing is *said* about other relations, we can predict (1) that AZ should be against BY and vice versa, (2) that AZ should be against CX and vice versa, and (3) that BY should be in favor of CX and vice versa. Much of what is communicated attitudinally by messages and by behavior is based on such inferences; this is, of course, the chief tool of the propagandist, the technique of "innuendo." The syntax of language and of behavior provides a structural framework within which meaningful contents are put; the structure indicates what is related to what, and how, but only when the meaningful values are added does the combination of structure and content determine psycho-logical congruence or incongruence.

It was Abelson and Rosenberg (1958) who introduced the term "psycho-logic" and contrasted it with "logic." They give a number of the rules of psycho-logic: rule 1—A *likes* B and B *likes* C implies that A likes C also; rule 2—A *likes* B and B *dislikes* C implies that

A dislikes C; rule 3—A *dislikes* B and B *dislikes* C implies that A likes C, and so forth. It is important to point out that the inferences from psycho-logic are not necessarily invalid; they are simply illogical. For example, if Krushchev were to indicate that he favors a particular American presidential hopeful —the so-called "kiss of death"—many people would, psycho-logically, become suspicious of this candidate. Now, Khrushchev's support might be valid grounds for suspicion, but the inference is not logically necessary.

Abelson and Rosenberg also make an assertional analysis of linguistic statements, very much as Osgood, Saporta, and Nunnally have done, and they extend this type of analysis to interlocking sets of statements on the same topic. If the connectives (positive, *p*, and negative, *n*) in the following assertions—"*I*'m for having *coeds* at Yale," "*I* want *good grades*," and "Having *coeds* would undoubtedly interfere with getting *good grades*"—are arranged in a matrix in this fashion,

	Ego	Coeds	Good Grades
Ego	*p*	*p*	*p*
Coeds	*p*	*p*	*n*
Good Grades	*p*	*n*	*p*

the degree and locus of incongruity can be clearly indicated. Since we cannot change the signs of any corresponding row and column in the matrix (always leaving the diagonal entries signed *p*) and thereby reduce the number of *n*'s in one half of the matrix, the minimum complexity or imbalance is 1. If the first statement were changed to "I am against having coeds at Yale," similar analysis shows that all entries could be changed to the same sign, and hence the matrix of statements would then be congruent. This approach is similar to that of Cartwright and Harary, but is based on matrix algebra rather than the mathematical theory of graphs.

3. *Magnitude of stress toward modification increases with the degree of cognitive inconsistency.* Most of the theories we have been considering express this relation, but it only becomes useful when a theory permits quantification. Heider's own statements remain essentially qualitative. Newcomb, on the other hand, states his principles in quantitative form, e.g., "the stronger the forces toward A's co-orientation in respect to B and X, . . . the greater A's strain toward symmetry with B in respect to X . . . ," (1953) but the units in which "forces toward co-orientation" and "strain toward symmetry" are to be measured remain obscure. Festinger specifies that the magnitude of dissonance increases (1) with the importance of the dissonant elements and (2) with the weighted proportion of all elements in a cognitive cluster that are dissonant. But again it is not clear how "importance" or "weighted proportion of elements that are dissonant" are to be quantified.

Association of the Osgood and Tannenbaum congruity hypothesis with the semantic differential provides quantification of cognitive inconsistency, but it also limits the types of situation that can be studied. Total *pressure toward congruity, P,* is stated to be equal to the difference between the initial scale position of a cognitive element (prior to interaction) and its location of perfect congruence (under the conditions of interaction). Perfect congruence between two elements was defined earlier as equal polarization (intensity), either in the same evaluative direction (for associative assertions) or in opposite evaluative directions (for dissociative assertions). Thus, for a hypothetical individual for whom Eisenhower is +3 and Uruguay is +1, the assertion "Eisenhower was greeted with flowers in Uruguay" *would* be congruent *if* Eisenhower were only +1 or Uruguay were +3. We therefore have 2 units of pressure toward congruity, *P*, in this situation—and it may be noted in passing that the *P's* associated with the various interacting elements are always equal according to this hypothesis.

Cartwright and Harary arrive at the *degree of balance* of an S-digraph by taking the ratio of the number of positive semicycles to the total number of semicycles (cf., above). They state that such an index makes it possible to deal with cognitive inconsistencies in probabilistic and statistical fashions; they do *not* state any relation between degree of balance and the total stress toward consistency, however. Abelson and Rosenberg define the *complexity of imbalance* as the minimum number of changes of relations necessary to achieve balance. In the example given earlier about having coeds at Yale, the sign of one of the three assertions would have to be changed to achieve psycho-logical consistency. Again, however, there is no statement to the effect that amount of stress toward consistency varies with the "complexity of imbalance." It is possible, of course, that total pressure toward cognitive modification does *not* vary in any simple way with degree of inconsistency. This may be the case particularly when only the structural relations and not the affective values of the contents are considered. Both Festinger and Osgood, who express the magnitude principle explicitly, deal with the properties of the cognitive elements themselves, not just their structural relation to each other.

4. *The dynamics of cognitive interaction are such that modifications under stress always reduce total cognitive inconsistency.* We have here a kind of "mental homeostasis" (Stagner, 1951) —cognitive inconsistencies set up pressures toward their own elimination. But we must say at the outset that modifications do not necessarily occur at all. People simply may not think about the matter or, as Festinger has shown, they may avoid exposing themselves to dissonance-arousing information. Furthermore, as Heider points out, some people seem to be able to "live with it" or even actively seek cognitively disturbing situations; they are more "tolerant of ambiguity," to borrow an older phrase. Such tolerance probably increases with intelligence and education, and it certainly decreases under states of heightened emotion. But even here there may be a larger consistency operating: it may be intrinsically disturbing for some people to follow the simple-minded dictates of psycho-logic, at least to the extent they are aware of them.

But let us assume that our subjects are exposed to inconsistency, that they are thinking about it, and that they are susceptible to psycho-logic—what are the alternative resolutions available and how can we decide which will occur? We will find that theories in this field have been better at stating alternatives than at deciding among them.

a. *The sign, or even existence, of a relationship may be changed.* For theories like Heider's that deal only with relations and not with the values of the included elements, this is the only type of resolution. However, since he deals with several types of relations, e.g. *L* vs. *DL* and *U* vs. *notU*, the situation is complicated. In the simplest diadic case, if P L O but also P *notU* O, either P may decide he doesn't like O or he may try to join O in some unit—what happens presumably depends upon the relative strengths of *L* vs. *notU*.

b. *The sign, or even existence, of a cognitive element may be changed.* Although Festinger does not attribute evaluations per se to cognitive elements, he does deal with changes of these elements in the direction of consonance. By making certain assumptions about the importance of different elements and other factors in particular experimental situations, Festinger is able to select among alternative resolutions.

Osgood and Tannenbaum have formulated a general law governing interactions among cognitive events: *Interacting elements are modified in inverse proportion to their intensity or polarization,* i.e. the congruity formula,

$$mc_1 = \frac{|p_2|}{|p_1| + |p_2|} P$$

$$mc_2 = \frac{|p_1|}{|p_1| + |p_2|} P$$

in which *mc* refers to *meaning change* on some dimension (e.g. attitude), *p* refers to *polarization* (deviation from neutrality regardless of sign), *P* refers to total *pressure toward congruity* (cf. section 3 above), and the subscripts 1 and 2 refer to the interacting cognitive elements. Given the assertion, "Eisenhower was greeted with flowers in Uruguay," and known values of +3 for Eisenhower and +1 for Uruguay, we can predict that three-fourths of the attitude change should be exerted on Uruguay and only one-fourth on Eisenhower. Similarly, in Heider's triadic P L O, P L X, O *DL* X, imbalance situation, if the attitude toward O were more intensely favorable than that toward X the formula would have to predict that most of the pressure in this dissociative assertion would be on making X much less favorable. The Eisenhower/Uruguay example illustrates another characteristic of the congruity hypothesis—it predicts changes on a quantitative basis even where relations are qualitatively balanced (here a + associated with a +).

However, some insufficiencies of the congruity hypothesis of Osgood and Tannenbaum appear when it is applied experimentally. First, although the associative or dissociative nature of assertions (relations) determines the direction of congruence (and hence the sign of *P*) in this model, the formula deals entirely with the changes in the meanings of the cognitive elements. Yet change in sign or even denial of the assertion itself is obviously one type of resolution. The assertion that Eisenhower is a card-carrying Communist produces incredulity and is denied. In order to generate accurate predictions in his attitude-change experiment, Tannenbaum had to apply a "correction for incredulity" that increased with the magnitude of *P* between values of 3 and 6, i.e. highly incongruous assertions. Second, the formula gives no weight to the direction of an assertion (cf. Heider's distinction between agent and recipient)—P *praises* O has the same effects upon the elements as O *praises* P, as far as the formula is concerned. Yet Tannenbaum's evidence, where Sources come out for or against Concepts, suggests that a greater share of the impact is exerted upon the recipient than the agent. The inverse proportionality formula underlying the congruity hypothesis may be valid in the "other things equal" sense, but there are certainly other factors to be considered.

In a recent paper titled "Modes of Resolution of Belief Dilemmas," Abelson (1958) presents a considerable variety of resolution types. He limits his consideration to the simplest diadic situations, in which A is either associated with or dissociated from B by assertions, but follows Osgood *et al.* (1957) in attributing positive or negative values to the cognitive elements A and B, themselves. His first type—which he unfortunately calls *denial*—includes both the major forms of resolution discussed above, (1) where the sign of the relation is changed and (2) where the sign of one or both of the cognitive elements is changed. The term "denial" implies an all-or-nothing quality and a consciousness of decision which certainly do not apply to many of the interactions we would like to handle, e.g. in perceptual modification or in semantic adjustments to word mixtures. But let us now look at some of these other resolution types.

c. *Other cognitive elements that are in balanced relation with one or the other of the dissonant elements may be adduced* (*bolstering*). As Abelson points out, this does not eliminate the imbalance but tends to "drown it out." This is a type of resolution stressed by Festinger, e.g. the heavy smoker who says that one is more likely to die in an automobile accident, that he has a large chest expansion, that he wouldn't be among the unlucky 15 per cent anyway, and so forth. Abelson also points out that it is usually the more strongly entrenched (attitudinally polarized?) element that receives bolstering: if one is a devout Catholic, yet intellectually agrees with the use of contraceptives, he is likely to react to the Church's condemnation of this practice by thinking of the Church's long history of being right, of God relying on him to exercise will power, and so on.

d. *Other cognitive elements that are in a relation of imbalance with one or the other of the dissonant elements may be adduced* (*undermining*). Abelson does not distinguish this type of resolution from "bolstering," perhaps because it is the converse. Here new cognitive elements that have a dissociative (imbalance) relation to the less firmly entrenched element are adduced—the familiar process of rationalization.

In most real-life situations we are dealing with complex clusters of cognitive elements, each with its valence and each connected with others by an interlocking set of assertions, explicit or implicit. Patterns of bolstering and undermining relations already exist, without need for adducing them. We may, following Abelson's analysis, suggest a general rule for resolution in complex cases: *those cognitive modifications* (changes in assertions or in element valences) *will occur which require the minimum restructuring of the entire cognitive map.*

e. *One or the other of the dissonant cognitive elements may be split into two parts, these parts being of opposed valence and dissociatively related* (*differentiation*). It may be interesting to note that what is involved in differentiation is a denotative reclassification of cognitive units forced by a connotative (affective) stress. Behaving the same way, having the same attitude, toward all members of a class (racial group, religious group, teachers, students, fried foods, sport-car owners, cats, etc.) often runs us into cognitive conflicts of an affective, psycho-logical sort, and intellectual redifferentiation provides one way out.

f. *Dissonant cognitive elements may be combined into a larger unit which, as a whole, is in balance with other cognitive elements (transcendence).* Abelson gives as an example of this the typical resolution of the dissonance between "rational man" (A) and "spiritual man" (B): joined together in a larger unit, "the whole man," they become congruent with positive concepts (C) like "the full life," "a balanced education," and so forth. Or another example: Cain and Abel are always squabbling with each other; their father manages to avoid choosing between them by saying, "You are both my sons, and I love my sons." In itself, transcendence does not resolve incongruities —it merely hides them. However, as Heider has pointed out, simply being included within a common unit implies a consonant relation among the dissonant elements, and this must weaken the total dissonance—the father is impelled toward believing that Cain and Abel really love one another, and our educator is impelled toward believing that religion can be rationalized.

Some evidence on cognitive interaction

Here some indication will be given of the diversity of phenomena which appear to follow the rules of cognitive interaction. These rules may be summarized as follows: When, in the course of human thinking, inconsistent cognitive elements are forced together by linguistic or behavioral assertions, stress is produced in proportion to the magnitude of the inconsistency, this stress producing cognitive modifications which —by changing the nature of the assertion, changing the connotative meanings of the elements, differentiating or integrating the denotations of the elements—serve to re-establish cognitive consistency. No attempt will be made to cover the experimental literature exhaustively; it has become quite extensive.

1. ATTITUDE CHANGE

Whenever a person reads a book or newspaper, listens to the belief statements of others, or even ruminates within his own storehouse of concepts, he is exposing himself to assertions which are likely to be incongruent to some degree with his existing frame of reference. In experiments we try to measure some part of his existing attitude structure, produce messages which are congruent or incongruent to some definable degree, predict what the effects on him should be, and then measure his attitude structure again to determine the correctness of these predictions (see Tannenbaum, 1953; Kerrick, 1959b).

2. COGNITION AND BEHAVIOR

Pressures toward consistency in what one believes and how one behaves have been studied most intensively by Festinger and his associates in a variety of ingeniously contrived, realistic experiments (1957). Two examples will have to suffice.

a. *Consequences of decisions.* The need for making a decision implies that there are dissonant elements in either course; therefore, to a degree dependent on the importance of the decision, the relative attractiveness of the unchosen course, and the degree of overlap of elements in the two courses, decisions will leave some dissonance to be reduced.

b. *Exposure to information.* Dissonance theory also leads to the prediction that people will avoid exposure to dissonance-increasing information and seek exposure to dissonance-decreasing information; if exposure to dissonant information is forced, they will defend against fully cognizing it.

3. INTERPERSONAL PERCEPTION

Although Heider himself has not contributed heavily on the experimental side, many other people have done research either inspired by or at least relevant to his theoretical notions. Jordan (1953) directly tested Heider's prediction that people prefer balanced to imbalanced situations. Sixty-four hypothetical (and, unfortunately, very abstract) triadic situations were given to subjects to rate for degree of pleasantness, half of them being cognitively balanced and half unbalanced. An example would be: "I dislike O; I have a sort of bond or relationship with X; O likes X." The ratings for balanced triads were significantly more "pleasant" than ratings for unbalanced triads, and Cartwright and Harary have shown that if the ambiguous *notU* situations are eliminated, the difference becomes even greater.

4. COMMUNICATION AND GROUP COHESIVENESS

Newcomb cites experiments by Festinger and Thibaut (1951), by Schachter (1951), and by Back (1951), which demonstrate (a) that attempts to influence others increase with the attractiveness of the others to Ego, (b) that communications in cohesive groups tend to be directed toward those perceived as most deviant (up to the point where the sign of the relation shifts and a deviate is ejected from the group), and (c) that communications within groups typically result in both increased uniformity (co-orientations toward relevant X's) and increased cohesiveness (co-attractions among members). There are many other experiments in which the role of interpersonal communication can legitimately be inferred even though it was not directly observed, e.g. in a study by Festinger, Schachter, and Back (1950) where a correlation of +.72 was found between a measure of interpersonal attractiveness and a measure of attitudinal conformity among people in a housing project.

5. SEMANTIC INTERACTIONS

Finally, we will look briefly at a series of experiments which—precisely because of their remoteness from familiar everyday matters like attitudes, beliefs, and interpersonal relations—may serve to indicate the generality of our principles. All these studies are alike in that *meaning* as measured with a form of semantic differential is the dependent variable. They are also alike in general design: subjects first judge the meanings of a set of component stimuli and then judge the meanings of various combinations of these stimuli; predicted meanings of the combinations, derived from applying the congruity formula to the component meanings, are checked against the actual meanings of the combinations derived from subject ratings.

a. *Word mixture.* All subjects first rated the meanings of eight adjectives ("sincere," "breezy," "listless," etc.) and eight nouns ("nurse," "husband," "prostitute," etc.). Then they rated eight of the sixty-four possible combinations ("sincere husband," "breezy prostitute," "listless nurse," etc.), eight groups being required to complete the design (Osgood, Suci, & Tannenbaum, 1957, pp. 275–84). Problem: Can the meanings of the combinations be predicted from the measured meanings of the components? Correlations between predicted and obtained meanings were high, .86, .86, and .90 for the evaluative, potency, and activity factors respectively. A constant error appeared for the evaluative factor, however—obtained evaluations of the mixtures were consistently less favorable than predicted evaluations. No obvious explanation for this error is at hand.

b. *Fusion of facial expressions.* The affective meanings of five facial expressions posed by the same person (intended to convey glee, rage, optimistic determination, complacency, and passive adoration) were obtained from thirty subjects in terms of two dominant factors, *pleasantness* and *activation* (Hastorf & Osgood, unpublished). Then the same subjects viewed all possible combinations of these expressions when fused in a steroscope under conditions designed to minimize eye dominance. The apparent meanings of these fused expressions proved to be predictable via the congruity formula to a high degree. The median intra-subject correlation (across the ten combinations) between predicted and obtained scores was .84 for pleasantness and .82 for activation. Furthermore, as must be predicted from the congruity hypothesis, the semantic profiles for combinations regularly correlated more highly with the more polarized component; that is, the more intensely meaningful expression dominated in the process of interaction.

c. *News photos and captions.* Kerrick (1959a) devised two unrelated captions ("A Quiet Minute Alone" and "Exiled Communist") to go with each of five pictures (e.g. a full profile shot of a well-dressed man on a park bench). Subjects judged the captions and pictures alone and then in combination (the design was such that subjects judging one set of captions alone would get the other set linked with the pictures). The results were strikingly different from those of (a) and (b) above: if picture and caption in isolation had opposed meaning, the meaning of their combination was predictable via congruity; but if picture and caption in isolation had similar meanings, their effects *summated* in combination, contrary to the congruity principle. In other words, combining a slightly "happy" picture with a slightly "happy" caption produced a very "happy" whole.

d. *Sound movies.* A similar summation effect was found by Gregory in an unpublished study on the combinations of words with sight in sound movies. Five short "takes" of an actor saying five phonetically similar things with different meanings, with appropriate facial expressions and gestures, were recorded on sound film (e.g., "I can't get over the death of my wife," or, "This is the happiest day of my life"). Subjects judged the heard words alone, the viewed movies alone, the original combinations, and crossed combinations produced by splicing the words of one "take" with the sight of another. The results of the crossed combinations were generally predictable from the components via congruity, but the meanings of the "natural" combinations were more polarized than either component alone. We can only guess at why meaningful summation occurs in experiments (c) and (d) but not in experiments (a) and (b); both situations (c) and (d) involve interactions *across modalities,* and it may be that in such situations something other than simple congruity is operating.

Cognitive dynamics in public affairs

In the absence of a science of public affairs, national and international, we can at least hypothesize that laws governing the thinking and behaving of individuals also govern the "thinking" and "behaving" of groups. The leap from individual cognitive maps to the structuring of relations within small groups has already been made—in some cases apparently without any self-consciousness of the shift in reference. However, application of the laws of cognitive dynamics to public affairs can be justified on several grounds: first, with nothing but communication to bind us together, it is clear that "decisions" and "behaviors" of nations must come down to myriad decisions in individual nervous systems and myriad behaviors of individual human organisms. Second, to the extent that government is popular, we can work on the basis of averaging over individuals, and to the extent that government is not, we are back to individuals anyhow. Finally, evidence abounds that we do "personalize" groups and issues—not so much by an error of oversimplification as by an intuitive grasp of the underlying laws.

The analogue of a cognitive element for an individual is what we may call a *cultural meaning* (stereotype, public image, etc.) for a group. Although individuals within groups may be expected to vary in their private meanings, it is characteristic of cohesive groups, as Newcomb has shown, for interpersonal communication to produce increased uniformity of opinion and attitude. Mass communications have this function for the larger groupings of individuals in modern society, such as nations. Many of the applications of the semantic differential—in the study of information about mental health and illness, of images of political personalities and issues, of commercial institutions and products, and so forth—have dealt with cultural meanings based on reasonably representative groups of people. The degree of conformity on issues is often striking, 90 to 100 per cent of subjects frequently choosing the same side, if not the same intensity. This happens both for common meanings (tornadoes are *active*) and for attitude objects (the Bible is *good*).

Now, to the extent that the cultural meanings of two socially significant referents have different evaluative locations, increasing proportions of individuals will necessarily experience pressures toward congruity when these items are forced into interaction by assertions in the mass media. If, under accusation by his rival or perhaps a mantle of honesty, a candidate for public office admits that he, John Jones, *does not believe in* God, we have for large numbers of people a somewhat unfamiliar and neutral source making a negative assertion about a deeply entrenched and favorably polarized concept. The result is inevitable—all the pressure toward consistency is on John Jones to move in a negative direction. Whenever political candidates, particularly unfamiliar ones, run into conflict with the mores—become associated with bad things, like gambling, call girls, and divorce, or become dissociated from good things, like Mother, God, and Country—they lose out. Conversely, political candidates themselves try to establish associative assertions with good things and dissociative assertions with bad, by their statements and by their behavior. Even if the private attitudes and beliefs of the elites in popular governments may be at variance with such a simple-minded organization of the universe, they rarely run counter to the tide. These are all very familiar facts about public affairs, but I think they illustrate the underlying laws.

Among our store of cultural meanings are a large number of "personalized" national stereotypes. Whether it is valid or not, populations in various countries do react to nations *as if* they were a collection of people, having certain "personality" traits and being organized into unstable group structures. The findings of Buchanan and Cantril (1953) in their book, *How Nations See Each Other,* are quite consistent with this idea. Following Heider, if P *likes* O (e.g. O *is an ally* of P) and P *dislikes* X (e.g. X *is an enemy* of P), then P should attribute favorable characteristics to O and unfavorable ones to X. We find that Americans most often attribute to the British the traits of being *intelligent, hard-working, brave,* and *peace-loving,* whereas they most often attribute to the Russians the traits of being *cruel, backward, hard-working,* and *domineering* (being "hard-working" is obviously independent of general evaluation). We would also expect people to view their own countrymen favorably, in the interest of cognitive balance; the four most frequent self-attributions (across the eight countries sampled) were *peace-loving, brave, intelligent,* and *hard-working.* Although Buchanan and Cantril did not get into this matter, Heider's notions of cognitive balance would lead us to expect that if P *likes* O and P *likes* Q, but P *dislikes* X, then P would infer that O *likes* Q and that O and Q *dislike* X, and vice versa. Americans expect the British to favor the French, and vice versa, but they expect both to be as antagonistic to the Russians as we are. If P *likes* O, he also must infer that O *likes* P reciprocally; but as studies like *The Ugly American* (Lederer & Burdick, 1958) show only too clearly, this doesn't necessarily follow.

The operation of psycho-logic in national and international affairs shows up quite generally once you start to look for it. All nations in time of conflict, for example, create "bogey men" on this basis. If we are *good, kind,* and *fair* and they are our enemy, then psycho-logic dictates that they must be *bad, cruel,* and *unfair.* However, when we are exposed to live Russians, as tourists in their country or as hosts to them in our homes and farms, and we find them in many ways *just like us,* cognitive disturbance is produced; it may be eliminated by the technique of differentiation—it is the Russian *leaders* who are bad, not the Russian *people.* And we confidently wait for the good *Russian people* to overthrow the bad *Russian leaders*—just as the Russians, no doubt, confidently wait for the good *American workers* to begin the revolution against their bad *capitalist leaders.* Abelson illustrates how differentiation works with a different example, the conflict over hydrogen bomb testing (+) being associated with poisonous fallout (−): if one can accept a distinction between using "clean bombs" and "dirty bombs," then a cognitively consistent resolution is achieved (Abelson, 1958).

Such examples could be adduced *ad infinitum,* but they would not further prove the thesis. The essential argument of this paper has been as follows: (1) there has been a considerable *confluence* (if not unanimity) *in theories* of cognitive interaction, sufficient at least to make it possible here to formulate several general principles; (2) there is a great deal of evidence for the operation of such principles *in the thinking and behaving of human individuals,* in areas as diverse as interpersonal relations and the semantics of word combination; and (3) we can at least hypothesize the operation of the same laws *at the level of groups, national and international,* and find illustrations which seem to support the hypothesis. How useful such a model would be for predicting in the area of public affairs remains to be seen.

38 The organization and modification of beliefs

MILTON ROKEACH

Most everyone would agree that the total number of beliefs which a grown person possesses is probably very large. By the time we have grown into adulthood we have formed tens, and possibly hundreds, of thousands of beliefs concerning what is, and what is not, true and beautiful and good about the physical and social world in which we live.

It is inconceivable that all these countless beliefs which we each possess would be retained in an unorganized, chaotic state within our minds. Rather, it must be assumed that man's beliefs—like the physicist's electrons and protons, like the astronomer's moons and planets and suns, like the geneticist's chromosomes and genes—become somehow organized into architectural systems having describable and measurable structural properties which, in turn, have observable behavioral consequences.

When I use the term belief I am not necessarily referring to a believer's verbal reports taken at face value; beliefs are inferences made by an observer about underlying states of expectancy. When a person says: "This I believe . . . ," he may or may not represent accurately to us what he truly believes because there are often compelling personal and social reasons, conscious and unconscious, why he will not or cannot tell us. For these reasons, beliefs—like motives, genes, and neutrons—cannot be directly observed but must be inferred as best one can, with whatever psychological devices available, from all the things the believer says or does.

A belief system may be defined as having represented within it, in some organized psychological—but not necessarily logical—form, each and every one of a person's countless beliefs about physical and social reality. By definition, we do not allow beliefs to exist outside

Abridged from the **Centennial Review,** 1963, 7, No. 4, 375–95, with permission of the author and the publisher.

the belief system for the same reason that the astronomer does not allow stars to remain outside the universe.

There are at least seven major kinds of interrelated questions which it is possible to ask about the nature of man's systems of belief. First, what are the structural properties which all belief systems have in common, regardless of content? Second, in what structural ways do belief systems differ from one another? Third, how are they developed and learned? Fourth, what motivational functions do belief systems serve? Fifth, what is the relation between belief and emotion or, in other terms, between cognition and affection? Sixth, how do belief systems guide perceiving, thinking, remembering, learning, and action? And, finally, what conditions facilitate and hinder the modification of belief systems?

It is not my intent to discuss all these questions here; they are mentioned only to point to the broader theoretical framework for the present concern, which is to focus particular attention on theory, method, and findings relevant to the first and last of the seven questions mentioned, namely, those mainly concerned with the organization and modification of systems of belief. In doing so, it is my hope that the discussion will serve to increase an understanding of a variety of situations in real life in which man's belief systems would seem to undergo change. For example, changes in systems of beliefs are often said to occur as a result of successful therapy, or as a result of political or religious conversion, or conversely, as a result of undergoing processes of ideological disillusionment and defection. Mention might be made also of various coercive attempts to alter belief systems, such as the "thought reform" procedures employed in Communist China and the so-called "brainwashing" techniques employed in North Korean prisoner-of-war camps and, somewhat earlier, by Khrushchev's own admission, in the great Soviet purge trials of the mid-thirties.

I

I will begin the analysis with three simple assumptions: first, not all beliefs are equally important to the individual; beliefs vary along a central-peripheral dimension; second, the more central—or, in our terminology, the more primitive—a belief, the more it will resist change; third, the more central the belief change, the more widespread the repercussions in the rest of the belief system. These assumptions are not unlike the assumptions made by the atomic physicist who conceives of a central nucleus within the atom wherein the particles within the nucleus are held together in a stable structure, and contain vast amounts of potential energy. Under some circumstances, for example, through processes of fission or fusion, the potential energy contained within the nucleus will be released, thus changing the structure of the nucleus and, thereby, the structure of the whole atom. Is it possible, in a roughly analogous fashion, to conceive also of belief systems as having "nuclear" beliefs which, if we only understand their nature and how to alter that nature, might lead us to better understand why it is that belief systems are typically in a relatively stable state highly resistant to change, and under what conditions they will change?

By what logical criteria can one decide which ones of a person's countless beliefs are central or primitive and which ones are not? To deal with this question, we have assumed that every one of a person's beliefs, whether conscious or unconscious, is at least in one sense a social belief. For every belief a person forms, he also forms some notion about how many others in a position to know believe it too. We define primitive beliefs as taken-for-granted, uncontroversial beliefs supported by a unanimous social consensus among those in a position to know. It is as if the believer says to himself: "I believe, and everyone else who could know believes it too."

Primitive beliefs can be thought of as being represented within the innermost core of the belief system. Such beliefs are called primitive because they are meant to be roughly analogous to the primitive terms of an axiomatic system in mathematics or science. A person's primitive beliefs represent his "basic truths" about physical reality, social reality, and the nature of the self; they represent a subsystem within the total system in which the person has the heaviest of commitments. In the ordinary course of life's events, they are so much taken for granted that they do not even come up as a subject for discussion or controversy. *I believe this is a table, I believe this is my mother, I believe my name is so-and-so* are examples, respectively, of primitive beliefs about the physical world, the social world, and the self supported by a unanimous consensus among those in a position to know.

Another way of describing primitive beliefs about physical reality, the social world, and the self is to talk about *object constancy, person constancy,* and *self-constancy.* Even though I see this rectangular table from many angles, I continue to believe (primitively) that it remains a table and that it remains rectangular. What many perception psychologists have overlooked thus far is that object constancy is also a social phenomenon, built up in childhood side-by-side with person constancy, both object and person constancy being necessary prerequisites for developing a sense of self-constancy. Not only does a child learn that objects maintain their constancy, but also that other people constantly experience physical objects as he does. Thus, two sets of primitive beliefs are built up together, one about the constancy of physical objects and the other about the constancy of people with respect to physical objects.

Object constancy and person constancy seem to serve an important function for the growing child. They build up within him a basic minimum of *trust* that the physical world will stay put and also that the world of people can at the very least be depended on to react constantly to physical objects as he does. It is as if nature and society had conspired to provide the child with a minimum guarantee of stability on the basis of which to build his own sense of self-constancy.

Actually, the child seems to need and to strive for far more person constancy than that provided by the physical contexts within which he learns object constancy. A child depends on his mother to remain his mother (with all that is meant by mother), and his family and social groups to remain his family and social groups, no less than on a table to remain a table.

It may be supposed that any inexplicable disruption of these taken-for-granted constancies, physical or social or self, would lead one to question the validity of one's own senses, one's competence as a person who can cope with reality, or even one's sanity. Put another way, violation of any primitive beliefs supported by unanimous consensus may lead to serious disruptions of beliefs about self-constancy or self-identity and from this other disturbances should follow.

In the beginning all beliefs are probably primitive ones, the young child not yet being capable of understanding that some beliefs are not shared by everybody. The young child's mental capacities and his experience are as yet too circumscribed for him to grasp the fact that he lives in a world in which there is controversy, or even armed conflict, over which authorities are positive and which negative, and which beliefs and ideologies associated with authority are the most valid. In the very beginning there is only one authority the infant looks to for information and nurturance—the mother; somewhat later, the father. These parental referents are the only referents which exist for the young child, and there does not yet exist for him either the conception that there are other positive referents, or that there exist negative referents.

As the infant develops toward maturity, one of three things can happen to his primitive beliefs:

1. Many of his primitive beliefs will continue to remain primitive throughout life, if they do not arise as subjects of controversy. As the child grows and broadens the range of his interactions with others outside the family, his authority base becomes gradually extended to include virtually everyone in a position to know. Thus, should any doubt arise about the validity of such a primitive belief—for example, is today Wednesday or Thursday?—he can check it by asking virtually any stranger who happens along.
2. But not all primitive beliefs owe their primitiveness to the universalization of social support. Through adverse experience, some primitive beliefs (about the self and about others) may become transformed into a second kind of primitive belief, in which support from external authority is abandoned altogether. A primitive belief originally supported by 100 per cent consensus may become transformed through adverse or traumatic learning experiences into a primitive belief supported by zero consensus. For example, a child may come to believe through intense experience or through an accretion of less intense experiences that he lives in a totally hostile world, or that he is unlovable or, phobically, that certain heretofore benign objects or places are now dangerous. In this second kind of primitive belief, it is as if the believer says: "I believe, but nobody else could know. It, therefore, does not matter what others believe." Or, to quote from a more popular refrain: "Nobody knows the troubles I've seen."
3. Finally, as the child interacts with others, his expanding repertoire of primitive beliefs is continually brought into play and he thus stands to discover at any moment that a particular belief he had heretofore believed everyone else believed, such as the belief in God or Country or Santa Claus, is not shared by everyone. At this point the child is forced to work through a more selective conception of positive and negative authority, and this point marks the beginning of the development of the non-primitive parts of the child's ever-expanding belief system.

Non-primitive beliefs are conceived

to develop out of the primitive beliefs and to be in a functional relationship with them. They seem to serve the purpose of helping the person to round out his picture of the world, realistically and rationally to the extent possible, defensively and irrationally to the extent necessary. In using the concept of non-primitive beliefs, I am trying to point to a class of beliefs which do not seem to have the same taken-for-granted character as primitive beliefs. We learn to expect differences of opinion and controversy concerning them, however much we might cherish them. Such beliefs, while important and generally resistant to change, are nevertheless conjectured to be less important and easier to change than those I have called primitive beliefs.

Most important of these non-primitive beliefs would seem to be those concerning positive and negative authority—what the sociologists call reference persons or reference groups. Such beliefs concern not only which authorities are those who *could* know but also which authorities *would* know. Which authorities, positive and negative, are we to trust and distrust, to look to and not look to, as we go about our daily lives seeking information about the world? The particular authorities relied on for information, in order to have a basis for action, differ from one person to the next and would depend upon learning experiences within the context of the person's social structure—family, class, peer group, ethnic group, religious and political group, country, *et cetera.*

If we know about a person only that he believes in a particular authority, we should be able to deduce a great number of his other beliefs, those which emanate or derive from the authorities he happens to identify with. Because they are derived from other beliefs, I have called them peripheral beliefs. They are less important, dynamically, than beliefs about authority, and therefore a change of belief with respect to authority, or a direct communication from one's authority, should lead to many other changes in beliefs deriving from authority. It is these peripheral beliefs which form what is ordinarily referred to as an ideology and, along with the identifications with reference persons and groups on which such ideologies are based, provide one with a sense of group identity.

In summary, a person's total belief system includes peripheral beliefs, pre-ideological beliefs about specific authority, and pre-ideological primitive beliefs about the nature of the physical world, society, and the self. All such beliefs are assumed to be formed and to develop very early in the life of a child. They are undoubtedly first learned in the context of interactions with parents. As the child grows older, he somehow learns that there are certain beliefs which virtually all others believe, other beliefs which are true for him even though no one else were to believe them, and still other beliefs about which men differ. Taken together, the total belief system may be seen as an organization of beliefs varying in depth, formed as a result of living in nature and in society, designed to help a person maintain, insofar as possible, a sense of ego and group identity, stable and continuous over time, an identity which experiences itself to be a part of, and simultaneously apart from, a stable physical and social environment.

II

To be discussed next is a series of investigations designed to test various hypotheses stemming from our theoretical formulations. The full details of these investigations are too complex to present here; they will be reported in separate publications. Instead, I will have to content myself here with a relatively brief discussion of the different types of phenomena studied, the methods employed, as well as some of the major findings and their implications for everyday life.

In one study, done in collaboration with Albert Zavala, we tried to ascertain whether primitive beliefs, as defined, are indeed more resistant to change than other beliefs, as would be expected by our theory. Table 1 shows nine statements which were presented to about 70 subjects representing the three kinds of beliefs designated as primitive, authority, and peripheral beliefs. They were asked to rank these nine statements in terms of which one they would be most reluctant to relinquish under any circumstance, which one they would be next most reluctant to relinquish, and so on. The subjects were also asked to indicate how strongly they agreed with each of the nine beliefs and to estimate how many others believed as they did with respect to each of the nine beliefs.

The first column of Table 1 shows the rank order of resistance to change of the nine beliefs, as judged by our subjects. It is seen that the three primitive ones are ranked highest in resistance to change. These are followed by the three authority beliefs and, finally, by the three peripheral beliefs. The rankings of all nine beliefs conform to theoretical expectations without exception. Moreover, as shown in the second column of Table 1, the vast majority of our subjects adhere to primitive beliefs with absolute intensity while considerably fewer sub-

TABLE 1

DEGREE OF RESISTANCE TO CHANGE, INTENSITY OF AGREEMENT, AND PERCEIVED CONSENSUS OF PRIMITIVE, AUTHORITY, AND PERIPHERAL BELIEFS

	Mean rank	% who absolutely accept or reject belief	% reporting unanimous social consensus
Primitive beliefs			
1. Death is inevitable	2.47	92	72
2. We cannot live unless we have oxygen	2.67	91	74
3. My name is ________	2.86	98	83
		93.7	76.3
Authority beliefs			
4. There is only one true Bible	4.17	50	4
5. The U. S. Constitution is the best constitution ever framed	5.30	21	7
6. The Pope is infallible in matters of faith and morals	5.97	55	2
		42.0	4.3
Peripheral beliefs			
7. I favor birth control	6.37	48	2
8. Adam had a navel	7.22	28	9
9. It is wrong to smoke	7.89	34	0
		36.7	3.7

jects do so with respect to authority and peripheral beliefs. Finally, as shown in the last column of Table 1, about three-fourths of our subjects report that all others unanimously believe as they do with respect to primitive beliefs while only a scattered few claim unanimous social consensus for authority and peripheral beliefs. Thus, the theoretical distinctions drawn among central, authority, and peripheral beliefs are operationally demonstrated. Naive subjects who know nothing of our theory seem to behave as if they, too, can tell the difference among the three kinds of beliefs.

These results suggest that beliefs about such things as the Bible, the fallibility or infallibility of the Pope, or the United States Constitution are not among the most deeply held of man's beliefs. More deeply held and possibly more resistant to change are those beliefs which all men would share with one another, which rarely come up for discussion or controversy, namely, primitive beliefs. These results would further suggest that in the event there is a conflict between two beliefs varying in centrality, that the more central belief would win out. Such a conflict is neatly exemplified in a slogan we are all familiar with, a political slogan first made famous by Bertrand Russell: *Better red than dead* and the counter-slogan *Better dead than red.* These slogans become theoretically interesting precisely because they seem to pit two beliefs against each other, one a primitive belief which is shared by everybody, *It is better to be alive than dead,* and the other an ideological belief, in our terms, a peripheral belief, *It is better to be anti-Communist than Communist.* In line with our theory, we would have to predict, contrary to what many Americans would undoubtedly predict, that most people, even anti-Communist Americans, would prefer the state of redness to the state of deadness, simply because of the greater potency of primitive beliefs over peripheral beliefs.

To find out if this is indeed so, a study was recently conducted at Michigan State University in collaboration with Irwin Horowitz in which subjects were simply asked to agree or disagree with the statement: "Death is preferable to living under a Communist regime." Only 40% reported that they would rather be dead than red, while 60% reported they would rather be red than dead. But even the finding of 40% who prefer being dead seems questionable in the light of some additional data which were available for the subjects.

We found further that a majority of the better-dead-than-red group believes that no one would be mad enough to start a nuclear holocaust and a majority of them does not believe that war is probable in the next decade. The subjects are college students, as I have already indicated, and it may be assumed that a decade represents for such subjects a very long time. In other words, the subjects who say they prefer death to life under Communism do not seem to conceive of their own death as a realistic or immediate possibility: they would rather be dead than red, but no one would be mad enough to start a nuclear war; and, besides, it won't come within the next decade. In contrast, a sizable majority of the better-red-than-dead group admits to the fear that a madman can start an atomic war at any moment. On the basis of these additional data, it may be doubted that even 40% of our sample really prefer death to life under Communism.

Following a similar line of reasoning, it may be suggested that whenever people have been given a choice between such alternatives as death and life under Fascism, between death and religious conversion, as was the case during the Spanish Inquisition, their belief systems and psyches have been so constituted that, by and large, they have preferred life to death. Thus on psychological grounds, I would not be inclined to accept seriously an invitation to die for this or that cause because it is doubtful that those who advocate dying for causes would, when the chips are down, themselves die for that cause. The deliberate choice of death over life under an alien ideology is probably an extremely rare event in human history, and martyrdom is probably better understood as a state conferred *a posteriori* rather than freely chosen *a priori*.

All the preceding is not to deny, of course, that most of us possess primitive beliefs regarding conditions under which we would prefer death to life, which would serve as genuine guides to action. For example, most mothers primitively believe that they would prefer to sacrifice their own lives to save the life of a loved child. Most of us primitively believe that we would prefer to die rather than betray a comrade to death at the hands of an enemy. But such instances are altogether different from those previously discussed. What seems to be involved in the examples just cited is not a primitive belief pitted against a peripheral belief but primitive beliefs supported by unanimous social consensus, or one altogether independent of social consensus, about the value of the life of one's own child as compared with one's own, or about the utter worthlessness of one's own life when bought at the expense of a comrade's.

In addition to the three kinds of beliefs already discussed—primitive beliefs, authority beliefs, and peripheral beliefs—we have recently found it necessary to posit a fourth kind of belief not previously discussed, called inconsequential beliefs. The latter refers to beliefs involving matters of taste which, if changed, are not expected to lead to any important consequences in the rest of the belief system.

Some examples of peripheral beliefs, that is, ideological beliefs derivable from authority, are: "The Russians were justified in putting down the Hungarian revolt in 1956." "The Gettysburg Address does not really say anything important," and "I think this country would have been better off if the South had won the Civil War."

Finally, let me give some examples of inconsequential beliefs, beliefs which if changed, are not expected to produce any significant changes in other beliefs: "There is no doubt in my mind that Elizabeth Taylor is more beautiful than Dinah Shore," and "I think summertime is a much more enjoyable time of the year than winter."

Consider next several instances in which there is a violation of primitive beliefs about physical reality. The television program *Candid Camera* often achieves its "entertaining" effects precisely because the audience is observing the reactions of persons whose primitive beliefs are being violated. Another example comes from the well-known Asch experiments, in which a subject overhears five other subjects in a group experiment report that two lines are of equal length when in fact they are clearly of unequal length. The subject does not know that these other five subjects are really confederates of the experimenter, instructed in advance to give the same wrong answer when comparing lines of varying length. This experiment is typically emotionally upsetting to the subject because all the other subjects are clearly in a position to know, yet they all disagree with him. There has been a violation of primitive belief which is relieved only when, at the end, the subject is let in on the nature of the experiment.

Ethical considerations clearly forbid social scientists from conducting "thought control" experiments or tampering with a normal child's or adult's primitive beliefs for prolonged periods. It was because of such considerations that it was necessary to turn away from further investigations with normal persons to focus instead on psychotic persons holding delusional belief systems. It is the object of psychotherapy and social policy to alter the psychotic's delusional beliefs and to readjust him to reality insofar as possible. Thus, experimental attempts over prolonged periods to change beliefs become ethically more justifiable when they serve therapeutic rather than destructive or "thought control" or "brainwashing" ends.

Such considerations culminated in our bringing together for study over a two-year period three chronic paranoid schizophrenic patients, each believing he was the re-incarnation of Jesus Christ. Leon, in his mid-thirties, had been hospitalized five years before. Joseph was in his late fifties and Clyde was about seventy years of age. Both had been institutionalized almost two decades before. The three delusional Christs were assigned to adjacent beds in one ward, ate at one table in the dining room, worked together on the same job, and met daily for group discussions. Each one was thus confronted with two others laying claim to the same identity within a controlled environment for a prolonged period. In addition, other experimental procedures were employed with Leon and Joseph. They received written suggestions to change their beliefs and behavior from authority figures they looked up to, figures who existed only in their imagination. Actually these communications were written and sent by me. All such procedures were designed to test the following hypotheses: first, having to live with others claiming the same identity over a prolonged period is as dissonance-producing a situation as is humanly conceivable and, consequently, changes in delusional beliefs and in behavior designed to reduce this dissonance should result; second, a persuasive communication emanating with one's positive authority figure can only be responded to in one of two ways: either the suggestion to change is accepted from the positive authority or, if it is unacceptable, the attitude toward the positive authority figure will undergo change. In either event, changes in delusions should result.

The full story of what happened as a result of these experimental procedures is reported in *The Three Christs of Ypsilanti* (Rokeach, 1964). At the risk of over-simplification let me here try to summarize briefly the main findings. First, the effect of confrontations over identity produced changes in the identity and in the delusional beliefs of the youngest of the three delusional Christs, the changes involving the destruction of existing delusions and the formation of new delusions concerning identity, bolstered by additional delusions emerging for the first time. Second, the effect of the persuasive communications from delusional authority figures was that it produced many changes in the delusions and in the behavior of Leon and Joseph, including eventually the destruction of both Leon's and Joseph's delusional authority figures. In general, it may be said that Leon, the youngest of the three, changed most as a result of our experimental procedures and Clyde, the oldest, changed the least.

It should perhaps be most emphasized in closing, that although each of our investigations has served to increase our understanding of the internal architecture of belief systems and of the conditions for their modification, we have not yet learned how to control experimentally induced modifications in belief systems in order to achieve socially desirable, therapeutic effects. In the last experiment referred to, we were indeed able to produce changes but we were not able to control the direction the changes took. It would thus seem that the nuclear physicists are way ahead of us in this respect; they have not only learned how to produce a schizophrenic shattering of the atom which destroys everything in its path but also how to slow down and control its nuclear reaction in order to achieve socially desirable ends. The task for psychology is a roughly similar one: to learn enough about the structure of belief systems in order to know how to form them in the first place and how to modify them in the second place so that they will best serve to increase the happiness and freedom of the individual and his society.

39 Persistence and regression of changed attitudes: long-range studies

THEODORE M. NEWCOMB

I

One's attitude toward something is not only a resultant of one's previous traffic with one's environment but also a determinant of selective response to present and future environments. Viewed in the latter way, existing attitudes may determine one's selection among alternative environmental settings, and these in turn may serve to preserve or undermine the very attitudes that had been initially responsible for one's selection among the alternatives. Insofar as attitudes are self-preserving, such tendencies to select a supportive environment would, if empirically supported, provide an important explanation of their persistence. In its most general form, the hypothesis would run somewhat as follows: Existing attitudes are most likely to persist, other things equal, when one's environment provides most rewards for their behavioral expression. But this platitudinous proposition ("things persist when conditions are favorable to their persistence") is not very interesting, and is probably not even testable. A more interesting and more testable form of the proposition would take account of both change and persistence, both of attitudes and of environmental supportiveness. In particular, it would say something about a changed selection of environments following attitude change, about the ways in which the recently formed attitude is or is not reinforced by the new environment, and about the persistence of the attitude in both supportive and hostile environments. Such a proposition, in its simplest form, would run somewhat as follows: A recently changed attitude is likely to persist insofar as it leads to the selection of subsequent environments that provide reinforcements for the behavioral expression of the changed attitude.

Among the many possible forms of environmental reinforcements of behavioral expressions of attitudes, I shall consider a single class: behavior on the part of other people that one perceives as supportive of one's own attitudes. With few exceptions, such support comes from persons or groups toward whom one is positively attracted, according to the principles of what is perhaps most frequently known as balance theory (cf. Heider, 1958; Brown, 1962; Newcomb, 1963). I am, in short, about to defend the limited proposition that a recently changed attitude is most likely to persist if one of its behavioral expressions is the selection of a social environment which one finds supportive of the changed attitude. This proposition differs from the one about autistic hostility primarily in that persistence of

Reprinted with slight abridgment from the **Journal of Social Issues,** 1963, 19, 3–14, with permission of the author and the Society for the Psychological Study of Social Issues.

a recently acquired attitude depends upon continuing rather than cutting off sources of information about the attitude-object.

II

There are various ways in which such a proposition might be tested in the laboratory. But insofar as one is interested, as I have been, in long-range effects, one will make use of "natural" settings. I shall therefore cite a few findings from two of my own studies, mentioning only briefly the less immediately relevant one (1961), which involved the daily observation of two populations of 17 male students, all initial strangers to one another, who lived intimately together for four-month periods. The only attitudes of these subjects that showed much change, from first to last, were their attractions toward each other—attitudes which had not even existed, of course, before their initial encounters in this research setting. Expressions of interpersonal attraction during the first week or two were highly unstable, but after about the fifth week they showed only slow and slight changes (cf. Newcomb, 1963).

Under the conditions of this research, imposed environments (in the form of arbitrarily assigned rooms, roommates, and floors) had no consistent effects beyond the first week or two in interpersonal preferences. That is, one could predict little or nothing about interpersonal attraction from the fact of being roommates or floormates. Self-selected interpersonal environment, however, was closely associated with interpersonal attraction. At all times later than the first week or two, pairs of subjects who were reported by others to belong to the same voluntary subgroups were almost invariably pairs whose members chose each other at very high levels of attraction. If this seems to be a commonplace observation (as indeed it is), let me remind you of my reason for reporting it; interpersonal environments are not only consequences of existing attraction but also sources of future attraction. It is an everyday phenomenon that, having developed differential attitudes toward one's several acquaintances, one manipulates one's interpersonal environment, insofar as one can, to correspond with one's interpersonal preferences. And insofar as one is successful, chances are that the preferences will be further reinforced. My data, showing stability both of preferences and of voluntarily associating subgroups following the first month or so, indicate that exactly this was occurring. The fact that it is an everyday occurrence enhances rather than negates the importance of the principle involved, namely, that a recently acquired attitude will persist insofar as it results in the selection of an environment that is supportive of that attitude.

III

I now turn to a totally different set of data, or rather to two sets of data from the same subjects, obtained over an interval of more than 20 years. The earlier responses were obtained between 1935 and 1939 at Bennington College (Newcomb, 1943); the later ones, obtained in 1960 and 1961, were from almost all of the subjects who had been studied for three or more consecutive years during the 1930's. To be specific, out of 141 former students in this category who in 1960 were alive, resident in continental United States, and not hopelessly invalided, 130 (scattered in 28 states) were interviewed, and 9 of the remaining 11 completed more or less parallel questionnaires. The interview dealt primarily with their present attitudes toward a wide range of public-affairs issues, with attitudes of their husbands and other contemporary associates, and with their histories and careers since leaving the College.

Before telling you some of the follow-up findings, I ought to report a few of the original ones. During each of four consecutive years (1935–36 through 1938–39), juniors and seniors were on the average markedly less conservative than freshmen in attitude toward many public issues of the day. Studies of the same individuals over three- and four-year intervals showed the same trend, which was not attributable to selective withdrawal from the College. Comparisons with other colleges showed almost no intercollege differences in freshmen attitudes, but much less conservatism at Bennington than at the other institutions on the part of seniors. Individual studies showed that at Bennington nonconservatism was rather closely associated with being respected by other students, with participation in college activities, and with personal involvement in the College as an institution. The relatively few malcontents were, with surprisingly few exceptions, those who held conservative attitudes toward public issues.

Given these initial findings, one of my concerns in planning the follow-up study was the following: Under what conditions would individuals who had become less conservative during their college years remain relatively nonconservative 20-odd years later, and under what conditions would they "regress" to relatively conservative positions? (As to the problem of comparing attitudes toward one set of issues in the 1930's with those toward quite different issues in the 1960's, I shall for present purposes note only that at both times we used indices of relative, not absolute standing: each subject is compared with the same set of peers.)

By way of noting the general pattern of persistence vs. regression on the part of the total population, I shall first compare one early with one later datum. In the 1940 presidential election, 51% of our interview sample who reported a preference for either major candidate chose the Democrat, F. D. Roosevelt, and 49% the Republican, W. Willkie. Twenty years later, the comparable figures were 60% for J. F. Kennedy and 40% for R. M. Nixon. No single election, of course, provides a very good test of what might be termed "general conservatism concerning public affairs," but at any rate this particular comparison does not suggest any conspicuous regression toward freshman conservatism. This conclusion is also supported by the following finding: In six consecutive presidential elections (1940 through 1960), an outright majority of our interviewees (51%) reported that they had preferred the Republican candidate either once or never, whereas only 27% of them had preferred that candidate as many as five times out of the six times.

The problem of regressive effects can also be approached by comparing relative conservatism on the part of the same individuals over the interval of 20-odd years. In terms of party or candidate preference in 1960, the degree of individual stability is startling. As shown in Table 1, individuals who were in the least conservative quartile of the total population, on graduating, preferred Kennedy by frequencies of 30 to 3, and those in the next quartile by 25 to 8; 83% of this half of the population preferred Kennedy 20 years

TABLE 1

PRESIDENTIAL PREFERENCES IN 1960, ACCORDING TO QUARTILES OF PEP * SCORES ON LEAVING COLLEGE IN THE LATE 1930'S

PEP quartile	Nixon preferred	Kennedy preferred	Total
1 (least conservative)	3	30	33
2	8	25	33
3	18	13	31
4 (most conservative)	22	11	33
TOTAL	51	79	130

* Political and Economic Progressivism—Eds.

later, while 37% of the initially more conservative half preferred Kennedy after 20 years. Political party preferences, and also an index of general political conservatism, showed about the same relationship to political conservatism more than two decades earlier. These data provide no support for a prediction of general regression—either toward previous conservatism or in the statistical sense of regression toward the mean.

Other evidence concerning the general nonconservatism in this population in the early 1960's includes the following:

77% of them considered themselves "liberal" or "somewhat liberal," as compared with 17% who were "conservative" or "somewhat conservative";

76% "approved" or "strongly approved" of "Medicare" for the aged under Social Security;

61% "approved" or "strongly approved" of admitting Red China into the United Nations.

These and other data suggest that the population as a whole is now far less conservative than is to be expected in view of its demographic characteristics. Its socio-economic level may be judged from these facts: (1) 77% of the 117 respondents who were or had been married were judged by the interviewer to be at least "fairly well-to-do," with annual incomes of not less than $20,000; and (2) of 113 mothers in the population, 65% had sent at least one of their children to a private school. In religious background, about three-quarters of them were Protestants (more than half of whom were Episcopalian), and less than 10% were either Catholic or Jewish. According to information assembled for me by the Survey Research Center of the University of Michigan,* the proportion of Protestant women college graduates at the income level of this population who in 1960 expressed a preference for Kennedy over Nixon was less than 25—as compared with 60% of this alumnae population.

I shall now revert to my earlier theme: If this population is now less conservative than one might expect, to what extent is this explainable in terms of its members' selection of post-college environments that were supportive of nonconservative attitudes? It proves to be very difficult to categorize total environments from this point of view, and so for the present I shall limit myself to a single aspect of post-college environments: husbands. I am making no assumptions here except that (1)

* By my colleague Philip Converse, to whom I am most grateful.

husbands were indeed a part of their wives' environments; (2) wives had had something to do with selecting this part of their environments; and (3) husbands, as environmental objects, were capable of being either supportive or nonsupportive of their wives' attitudes.

Nearly 80% of our respondents both had a husband and were able to report on his attitudes toward most of the issues with which we were concerned, during all or most of the past 20 years; one reason for placing a good deal of confidence in their reports is that they seem highly discriminating, as indicated by such responses as these: "I don't think I know how he'd feel on that particular issue," or "Now on *that* one he doesn't agree with me at all." Here are some summaries concerning all husbands whose wives were willing to attribute attitudes toward them (nearly all wives on most issues):

54% of the husbands in 1960 favored Kennedy over Nixon;
64% of them either "approved" or "strongly approved" of "Medicare" for the aged under Social Security;
57% of them either "approved" or "strongly approved" of admitting Red China into the United Nations.

And so it is almost as true of husbands as of wives that they are less conservative than is to be expected in view of their demographic characteristics: husbands' and wives' demographic characteristics are taken to be identical except for a very few couples differing in religious background, and their present attitudes are highly similar (90% of 1960 presidential preferences by pairs of spouses, for example, being reported as the same in 1960). It would hardly seem to be a matter of sheer chance that a set of men who are less conservative than is to be expected are married to a set of women of whom just the same thing is true. It seems necessary, therefore, to assume that attitudes toward public affairs had something to do with husbands' and wives' reciprocal selection of one another, or with postmarital influence upon one another, or with both. Here is one statistical support for this assumption: the correlation between wives' scores on an instrument labeled Political and Economic Progressivism, as of their graduating from college in the late 1930's, with the number of Republican candidates that their subsequent husbands voted for between 1940 and 1960 was .32; this does not account for much of the variance, but its p value is $< .0005$.

Another interesting finding has to do with the number of women in our interview sample whose husbands had attended Ivy League colleges; one would expect this proportion to be high, since so many of the women's fathers and brothers had attended these colleges. The actual frequency turned out to be just 50%. These Ivy League husbands' voting preferences in 1960, however, turned out to be much more like their wives' preferences than like their classmates' preferences: 52% of husbands whose wives were able to state a preference were for Kennedy—which is to say that they did not differ at all in voting preferences from all non-Ivy League husbands. This total set of facts can best be interpreted as follows: Our Bennington graduates of the late 1930's found their husbands in the kinds of places where their families expected them to be found, but they selected somewhat atypical members of these "proper" populations of eligibles; they tended not to have conservative attitudes that were then typical of these populations.

One evidence of this atypical selection is to be seen in the occupational distribution of these women's husbands. Only 38% of all husbands are classifiable as "in management or business," the remaining 62% representing for the most part a wide range of professions (especially college teaching, entertainment, and the arts) and public employment (especially in government). Husbands in these two general categories (management and business vs. all others) differed sharply in their voting preferences in 1960; of the 113 husbands whose wives attributed preferences to them, 26% of those in management and business preferred Kennedy, and 68% of all other husbands preferred Kennedy. In sum, these women's husbands had typically come from "the right" places but a majority of them did not have "the right" attitudes or occupational interests.

If, therefore, I were to select a single factor that contributed most to these women's maintenance of nonconservative attitudes between the late 1930's and early 1960's, I think it would be the fact of selecting husbands of generally nonconservative stripe who helped to maintain for them an environment that was supportive of their existing attributes.

IV

Now I shall turn from the total population of interviewees to some comparisons of subpopulations. The most crucial of these, from the point of view of my proposition about supportive environments, are to be found within the population of nonconservatives on leaving college in the late 1930's: What seems to be the differences between those who do and those who do not remain nonconservative in the early 1960's? Such comparisons will have to be impressionistic, since numbers of cases are small.

Among 22 individuals previously labeled as clearly nonconservative in their third or fourth year of attendance at the College, just half belong in the same category now. Only three of them are clearly conservative today, the remaining eight being classified as intermediate. Here are these wives' descriptions of their husbands' political positions over the years:

3 presently conservative wives: 3 Republican husbands (100%)
7 presently intermediate wives: 3 Republican husbands (42%)
8 presently nonconservative wives: 2 Republican husbands (25%)

Of the three presently conservative women, none mentions having engaged in activities related to political or other public issues; of the eight who are intermediate, six mention some activity of this kind, but they identify their activity only in such general terms as "liberal" or "Democratic Party"; of the 11 still nonconservative women, eight mention such activities, more than half of them specifying such "causes" or organizations as labor unions, civil liberties, the ADA, or the NAACP.

Each interviewee was also asked about the general orientation of "most of your friends" toward political and other public affairs. More than half (12) of the 22 women originally labeled as clearly nonconservative described their environment of friends as "liberal," in spite of the fact that most of them lived in suburbs or other geographical areas not generally renowned for liberalism. Interestingly enough, those who are now relatively conservative answered this question in just about the same way as did those who are still relatively nonconservative. The 16 women originally labeled as clearly conservative, on leaving college, answered this question somewhat differently; more than half of them (9) described their environment of friends as predominantly "conservative," but answers differed with the present attitudes of the respondents. That is, those who are now, in fact, relatively conservative with near-unanimity describe their friends as conservative, whereas those who are now relatively nonconservative consider a substantial proportion or even most of their friends to be "liberal." Thus only those who were quite conservative in the late 1930's and who still remain so see themselves surrounded by friends who are primarily conservative.

In sum, nearly all of the still nonconservative women mention either husbands or public activities (most commonly both) that have served to support and maintain previously nonconservative attitudes, while none of the three formerly nonconservative but presently conservative women mentions either husband or public activities which have served to maintain earlier attitudes.

What about attitude persistence on the part of those who, after three or four years in college, were still relatively conservative? Sixteen of those who were then labeled conservative were interviewed in the early 1960's, ten of them being categorized as still conservative and three as now nonconservative. Only one of the nonchangers reported having a husband who was a Democrat, and in this lone case he turned out to have voted for Nixon in 1960. Two of the three changers, on the other hand, report husbands who were Democrats and Kennedy voters in 1960. Only two of the persistent conservatives mentioned public activities presumably supportive of their attitudes (in behalf of the Republican Party, in both cases); eight of the ten described most of their friends either as conservative or as Republicans. The conditions that favor the persistence of conservatism over the 20-odd years are thus about the same as those that favor the persistence of nonconservatism: supportive environments in the form of husbands, local friends, and (for the nonconservatives but not the conservatives) in the form of associates in activities related to public issues.

There is a special subpopulation of students who, as of graduating in the late 1930's, were candidates for regression; that is, they became much less conservative during their college years. Of these, about one-third (9 of 28) were among the most conservative half of the same population in the early 1960's, and may be regarded as regressors, in some degree at least. Eight of these potential regressors were, for various reasons, unable to report on husbands' preferences. Among the remaining 19 respondents, five were actual regressors, four of whom reported their husbands to be Republicans or "conservative Republicans." Among 14 actual non-regressors reporting, ten described their husbands as Democrats or "liberal Democrats," two referred to them as "Republicans who have been voting Democratic," and only two call their husbands Republicans. These are highly significant differences: the actual regressors can pretty well be differentiated from the nonregressors merely by knowing their husbands' present attitudes. By this procedure only 3 of 19, or 16% of all predictions would not have been correct.

This total set of data suggests that either regression and persistence of attitudes as of leaving college are, over the years, influenced by husbands' attitudes, or early post-college attitudes had something to do with the selection of husbands, or both. In either case, both regression and persistence are facilitated by the supportiveness of husbands.

V

If there is any very general principle that helps to account for this whole range of phenomena (both my 1946 and my 1963 versions), I believe that it is to be found in an extended version of "balance theory," as originally outlined by Heider (1946, 1958). Heider's formulations are formulated in individual and phenomenological terms; a balanced state is a strictly intrapersonal, psychological state. But it is also possible to conceptualize an objective, multi-person state of balance, referring to the actual relationships among different persons' attitudes, regardless of the person's awareness of each other. Such a concept is psychologically useful not only because it describes an actual, existing situation—an environment of which each person is himself a part, as suggested by Asch (1952)—but also because it describes a relationship which, given reasonably full and accurate communication, comes to be accurately perceived. My own recent work on the acquaintance process has been interesting to me primarily because it inquires into the processes by which and the conditions under which *intra*personal states of balance come to correspond with *inter*personal ones. As outlined by Heider, and subsequently by many others (cf. Brown, *et al.*, 1962), the processes by which imbalanced states serve as goals toward the attainment of balanced ones include both internal, psychological changes and external modifications of the environment. Thus, one may achieve a balanced state with the important figures in one's social environment—whether by selecting those figures, by modifying one's own attitudes, or by influencing others' attitudes—and at the same time continue to perceive that environment accurately.

According to such an extended, *inter*personal concept of balance, an imbalanced state under conditions of continued interaction is likely to be an unstable one, simply because when it is discovered it arouses *intra*personal imbalance on the part of one or more of the interactors, and this state arouses forces toward change. Given marked attitude change on the part of one but not the other member of a dyad actually in balance with respect to that attitude, imbalance results. This was what typically happened to students at Bennington College vis-à-vis their parents, in the 1930's. A common way in which they attempted to reduce imbalance was by avoidance—not necessarily of parents but of the divisive issues as related to parents. As Heider might say, unit formation between issue and parents was broken up, and psychological imbalance thus reduced. Such a "solution" resembles autistic hostility in that it involves a marked restriction of communication.

But this solution, as many of my subjects testified, was not a particularly comfortable one. Hence, it would hardly be surprising if many of them, during early post-college years, were in search of environments that would provide less uncomfortable solutions—or, better yet, more positively rewarding ones. An ideal one, of course, would be a husband who was rewarding as a supporter of one's own attitudes as well as in other ways.

And so, vis-à-vis parents and fellow-students at first, and later vis-à-vis husbands (or perhaps working associates), forces toward balance were at work. Specifically, support from important people concerning important issues came to be the rule, and its absence the exception. Support sometimes came about by changing one's own attitudes toward those of needed supporters, or, more commonly, by selecting supporters for existing attitudes. The latter stratagem represented not merely an automatic tendency for attitudes to perpetuate themselves. More significantly, I believe, it represents an adaptation to a world that includes *both* persons and issues. Such a dual adaptation can be made, of course, by sacrificing one's stand on the issues (regression). But if the dual adaptation is to be made without this sacrifice, then an interpersonal world must be selected (or created) that is supportive—in which case we can say that the attitude has been expressed by finding a supportive environment.

An existing attitude may be maintained by creating environments in which *either* new information can be avoided *or* in which other persons support one's own information. In either case, the fate of an attitude is mediated by the social environment in which the individual attempts to maintain or to restore balance regarding that same attitude. Insofar as that environment excludes disturbing information or provides reinforcing information, the attitude persists. And insofar as the selection or the acceptance of that environment is a consequence of holding the attitude, we have a steady-state, self-maintaining system.

40 Judgmental processes and problems of attitude

MUZAFER SHERIF and CARL I. HOVLAND

Traditional approaches to attitude and attitude change

Studies of attitude conducted during the twenties and thirties were mainly of the "survey" type in which individuals were asked to check prepared categories on an issue. The primary concern was with the extent to which different groups held particular attitudes, for example the difference between attitudes toward war of student and nonstudent populations. Relatively little concern was manifested in regard to the psychological processes underlying the individual's expression of his attitudes or to the pattern of stimulus conditions under which the responses were obtained. Thurstone (1929) and his associates made a major contribution in providing more systematic means for scaling attitudinal responses. But their underlying assumption, that the intervals between various positions on an attitude scale are independent of the position of the individual who is making the judgments, has been called into question by the research of the writers (Hovland & Sherif, 1952; Sherif & Hovland, 1953). It now appears that distances between different points on an attitude scale derived by the method of equal appearing intervals are affected by the position of the individual making the evaluation.

During the same span of years interest in the effect of communications on attitudes was largely in showing that changes in questionnaire or "attitude scale" checkings occur as a consequence of exposure to communication. There was much less concern with the psychological processes underlying the changes. Considerable divergence in results was obtained, some showing change in the direction of the communication and others showing shifts in the opposite direction. Thus while a number of studies showed that lecturers, pamphlets, and motion pictures could produce changes in attitude, few studies were made until the forties to show how specific content transmitted by specific communicators affects particular audiences (cf. e.g., Hovland, Lumsdaine, & Sheffield, 1949).

The change which has taken place in the analysis of attitudes is well illustrated by the studies presented in the recent special issue of the *Public Opinion Quarterly* (Katz, ed., 1960). It will be seen that in the fifties there has been an increased concern with fundamental factors underlying attitudes and their modification. Illustrative of recent approaches to these problems are the studies of Heider (1958) and Festinger (1957). It is the writers' belief, however, that attitude research should be more solidly based on previous work in basic psychological processes, particu-

Abridged from Chapter 1 of **Social Judgment**, New Haven, Conn.: Yale University Press, 1961, pp. 2–14, with permission of the first author and the publisher.

larly of judgment. What appears to be seriously needed is more extensive exploration of the underlying principles governing attitudinal evaluations by the individual and the factors by which such evaluations are modified. It is to this type of analysis that the present volume is addressed.

Relevance of judgment processes to attitude problems

Our underlying assumption is that the processes of judgment are critical for understanding research findings in the area of attitude and attitude change. A few illustrations may serve to give substance to our assumption.

During the baseball season, one may observe judgments from thousands of spectators relative to the decisions of the umpire. When he declares the verdict "You're out" against their favored team, the boos from the partisans are resounding expressions of their own judgment of the event. Of course, the fans are capable of making objectively correct judgments if they have the opportunity to examine all the details of the episode through slow-motion pictures. However, in complex stimulus situations such as that in a crowded stadium, "committed" individuals with a strong attitude on an issue do not wait: they readily *pass judgments* and *act* in terms of them.

As the above example implies, a person's attitude on an issue may well influence the way he appraises relevant behavior and events. Thus individuals who straddle the fence in public life are frequently judged differently by people holding one extreme position than by people taking an extreme stand on the opposite side. For example, the vacillating labor lead, Samuel Gompers, was judged as rather radical by the conservatives of his day, but he was dubbed a conservative by left-wingers in the labor movement. Supreme Court justices Charles Evans Hughes and (probably to a lesser extent) Owen J. Roberts balanced between the "conservatives" and "liberals" of the "Roosevelt court" in the thirties. Evaluations rendered by various authors of these two justices are strongly colored by the attitudes of the writer passing judgment. Liberal writers tend to place these justices on the conservative side, but this is not the judgment of writers who are not liberals.

As discussed in earlier volumes of this series, an attitude toward an object, person, group, or social issue is not directly observable but is inferred from a persistent and *characteristic* mode of reaction to that stimulus or stimulus class. This characteristic mode of reaction signifies differential treatment of the object of attitude. It is inferred that the object of attitude is placed in a category or class favorable or unfavorable in some degree, high or low in some degree, acceptable or unacceptable in some degree in the individual's scheme of things. In short, one essential aspect of the attitudinal reaction is a categorization process, whether or not the individual is aware that he is passing a judgment.

Categorization as an essential aspect of attitudinal response

When one solicits an expression of an individual's attitude toward some social issue, person, or group, one typically finds that the process involves placement of the issue in a framework and assignment to a category. Thus if a person (who is a practicing member of one of the religious groups that use some kind of baptism as part of the initiation of new members) is asked to express his attitude toward baptism, he is likely to place baptismal ceremonies into differentiated rankings, the preferred practice of his own group probably being at the top and serving as the standard. Likewise, if one asks an individual for his opinion as to acceptability of various groups, he is likely to place them in a certain number of categories ranging from encouragement of close personal association, through the category of tolerating residence in his own neighborhood, all the way to the category of desiring their exclusion from the country. We typically find that the individual has internalized categories designating relative positions or "social distance" for placement of the individual in a group, and that each category is endowed with certain qualities. A person's attitude is revealed in his favorable or derogatory reactions regulated by the category in question and by the attributes attached to that category. If the X group is "endowed" by the Y group with qualities a, b, and c (favorable or unfavorable) the representative members of the Y group will tend to see these qualities in the collective or individual behavior of the X group and react accordingly in a characteristic way.

Differentiation of judgment processes: discrimination, placement, and acceptance-rejection

From the point of view of conceptual analysis and experimental specification, it is feasible to differentiate the judgment process in various ways. A conceptual differentiation can be made in terms of item discrimination, placement of items, and acceptance-rejection of items. A great deal of experimental work has accumulated along each of these three lines.

Discrimination refers to the task of identifying a stimulus item (a weight, a tone, a statement) as different from another item. The tremendous amount of work dealing with just noticeable differences (j.n.d.s) between two stimuli differing along the same dimension is representative.

It is convenient to refer to that kind of discrimination which locates a given stimulus relative to more than two other discriminable items as *placement* or *categorization* of the item. Studies dealing with scaling of neutral items, like weights or tones, are representative of this approach. Our concern in this [account] is primarily with reactions to motivationally relevant items, as exemplified by statements evaluating a social issue or a group of people. However, even in placement of motivationally neutral items, variations occur as a function of the stimulus arrangements and procedures of the experimental conditions. Therefore, if the effects of attitudes upon placement of items are to be assessed adequately, it is necessary first to consider judgmental variations attributable to such stimulus arrangements and procedures. In particular, such consideration will yield methodological guides for evaluating the conditions in which attitudinal factors are maximally or minimally effective in producing judgmental variations, such as displacements, over- and under-estimations. The general problem was illustrated earlier with reference to judgments concerning an umpire's verdict at the baseball stadium or on the basis of slow-motion pictures after the game.

The judgment task carried out under *acceptance-rejection* instructions also requires placement or categorization of items (statements, objects, human groups) in terms of the preferences of the individuals. Scales of judgment instructing the subjects to place the most acceptable items at one end, the most objectionable ones at the other extreme, and other items in appropriate places between the extremes, are representative of this line of analysis. Placement of groups along a social-distance scale and rank-order scales based on preference (such as ranking of composers or painters) are representative of placement in terms of affectively charged attitudes.

Motivational and learning factors relevant to placement of items

A judgment always involves a comparison between two or more stimuli. For purposes of conceptual analysis, psychologists devise laboratory experiments in which judgment consists of the comparison of only two objects or items. One of the objects is just noticeably heavier, brighter, louder, or longer than the comparison object. Or one stimulus item is noticeably more pleasant or more favorable than another item. The items may be compared simultaneously or successively with a very short interval between presentations. In such experiments, the task is discrimination and the main psychological problem is the keenness of discrimination. When keenness of discrimination (keenness of tactual, visual, auditory, or kinesthetic sense, or keenness in discriminating the dictionary meaning of words) is the principal problem, experimental procedures requiring the subject to make this kind of comparison are suitable.

However, if the primary problem of research concerns the judgmental activity ordinarily involved when a person judges stimuli related to an attitude, the above procedures and analysis may not be appropriate. Procedures suitable for the study of simple discrimination circumscribe the stimulus pattern drastically and thereby constrict the operation of attitudinal factors in the judgment process.

Learning factors. Judgment of a stimulus item relevant to an individual's attitude is necessarily related to other similar items to which the individual has been exposed. The individual forms an attitude as a consequence of repeated encounters with objects, persons, or communications. Comparison of an item related to an attitude is made against a whole background of similar objects which constitutes the range of such objects perceived and categorized on the basis of the individual's prior encounters with them. Therefore, the process of comparison in judgment of a relevant stimulus is not represented by having the individual compare two objects presented simultaneously or in close succession.

We shall refer to the background for a particular comparison as the *reference scale* of the individual in that respect. Placement of stimulus items is made relative to a reference scale formed by the individual. The formation of reference scales by the individual whether in relation to objects, human groups, or social norms is clearly a problem of *learning.*

Motivational factors. As stated above, the judgment of an item relevant to an attitude involves comparison with an appropriate reference scale, rather than a simple comparison between two items as in a typical laboratory experiment on discrimination. It follows that attitudinal judgments are typically of the *placement* type, and this has definite implications for fruitful research practice in this area.

In the study of judgment processes underlying attitudinal reactions, the identification of judgment categories in an individual's reference scale and placement of items within it are crucial problems. For example, in a study of attitudes toward the segregation-desegregation issue, it is necessary to learn what kind and how many categories individuals actually use in judging behavior or verbal statements ranging from the most extreme segregationist position to the most extreme desegregationist position. In assessing an individual's attitude on this issue, it is necessary to know that a person with a desegregationist stand on the issue places statements advocating segregation on the bus or on the train in the unfavorable category. From the outset, research in this area involves the problem of *placement*.

Research on the problem of scaling items relevant to social attitudes has frequently been facilitated by circumscribing the stimuli to be compared in the manner of discrimination experiments. As useful as this procedure may be for test construction, it cannot be regarded as appropriate for studying judgment of items related to attitudes as this activity typically occurs in actual life. The inadequacy of such procedures can be illustrated. Faced with the task of discrimination between the relative favorableness of segregation applied on the train and on the bus, a desegregationist can render a judgment. The fact remains that both examples are in an objectionable category for him. In the discrimination task which requires the individual with a strong attitude on an issue to choose one of two objectionable statements as more favorable than the other, the subject's reactions to such a task and toward the experimenter subjecting him to it may be more significant psychologically than the choice itself.

When the problems of research pertain to the judgmental process underlying specific attitudinal reactions, it is appropriate to use procedures which allow motivational factors to be manifested. If keenness of discrimination is the primary research problem, it is possible, as we have seen, to minimize the effect of attitude or past experience (learning) by circumscribing the judgment situation to the comparison of two clearly defined items and requiring a choice. However, the latter procedure does not represent typical conditions in which the individual judges an attitude-related item. A stimulus related to an attitude is necessarily judged against the reference scale which the individual has formed relative to the particular class of stimulus items in question.

On a scale of positions on a social issue ranging from one extreme to the opposite extreme, for example, one of the positions is appropriated to represent the individual's own stand or commitment. This stand on the issue is a major factor in regulating his relationships with other individuals involving that issue. His acceptances and rejections in that regard are regulated accordingly. As experiments show, placement of items related to the issue is significantly affected by their relative proximity or distance from the individual's own stand. In short, the judgment of items related to an attitude involves placement in terms of the individual's reference scale, but it becomes placement in which the degree of acceptance or rejection is significant.

Psychological reference scales and the stimulus conditions during their formation

Laboratory findings on judgment have shown that placement of a particular stimulus in a series is not made solely in terms of the discrete physical properties of that stimulus. A judgment is rendered in terms of the psychological reference scale which the individual has formed on the basis of his previous encounters with similar stimuli.

In other words, judgment of a particular stimulus in a series involves placement in categories, and it is influenced by the whole background of similar stimuli which constitutes the basis for an appropriate reference scale. Analysis of the stimulus conditions on the basis of which the individual forms a psychological reference scale has far-reaching implications for the study of judgment of social issues and communication concerning them.

In laboratory studies of judgment, psychological scales are usually formed during repeated presentations of a well-graded series of stimuli (weights, tones, statements). The reference scale consists of categories whose labels are ordinarily provided through instructions. In the traditional experiments, each stimulus to be judged is presented with a *standard* stimulus, which serves as a salient reference point or anchorage in the formation of a psychological scale. However, it was found that the use of a formal standard is not necessary for the formation of a reference scale. If each stimulus is presented singly throughout several presentations of a definite series of stimuli, the individual still forms a scale of judgment consisting of a number of categories. In the latter case, the stimuli at the ends of the particular series are utilized by the individual as anchorages in the formation of a psychological scale.

Once a psychological scale is formed, subsequent judgment of a similar stimulus is greatly affected by the position of that stimulus relative to the prevailing reference scale. When stimuli are presented with values greater than or less than any in the series which was the basis of the reference scale, the categories of the scale are subject to alterations. These phenomena constitute the area of research investigating reciprocal relationships between psychological scales and anchorages.

When psychological scales are based on encounters with a well-graded stimulus series such as a definite range of discriminable physical stimuli, there is a close relationship between the stimulus series and the psychological scale. The psychological scale is readily susceptible to adjustments with the addition of new stimuli to the series or with shifts of the total range of the objective stimulus series. This may be one reason why psychological scales related to technological developments in various societies change somewhat more readily than scales related to socio-political and religious values.

Let us go a step further. It is not necessary to have a definitely graded series of stimuli for the formation of psychological scales. Even when the stimulus series is not well-graded, individuals still form psychological scales. In these instances, the range of the scale and the number of categories within it are significantly influenced by the judgments of other people. As a result, the stimulus conditions affecting the formation of a reference scale have to include the social setting: established norms, the properties of the interaction among the individuals involved, the general setting of their interaction, the prevailing pattern of relationships among them, and so on.

Once established, psychological scales initially based on *psycho-social actualities* serve a function similar to those based on series of physical gradations. Namely, they serve as a basis for comparison and appraisal of relevant stimulus items on subsequent encounters. Social reference scales that individuals in human groups use in judging political, religious, ethical, and aesthetic matters cannot be gauged against an objectively graded stimulus series. They are psycho-social in origin and can be gauged against social realities. They define and regulate one's relationship to other individuals, groups, social objects, and institutions. A certain category in such a reference scale becomes the individual's preferred category. This position within the scale represents his own stand on the issue and serves as a major anchor in judgment. If the issue is a significant one to him, he is willing to tolerate only slight deviation from this category and finds further deviation obnoxious.

On a social reference scale, we may refer to the range of positions that includes an individual's stand and other positions that he will tolerate as his *latitude of acceptance*. Beyond this, other positions on the issue are rejected, and that range of positions is his *latitude of rejection*.

The individual's reactions to a communication and the effect of that communication on his attitude can be studied relative to his established categorizations of the issue, that is, his reference scale for judgment of the issue. Investigation of these problems must determine the location of his latitudes of acceptance and rejection relative to the stand advocated in communication. The resulting information about the individual's placement of the communication and his evaluation of it may clarify problems of attitude change.

41 The obstinate audience: the influence process from the point of view of social communication

RAYMOND A. BAUER

The model held by the general public, and by social scientists when they talk about advertising, and somebody else's propaganda, is one of the exploitation of man by man. It is a model of one-way influence: The communicator *does* something to the audience, while to the communicator is generally attributed considerable latitude and power to do what he pleases to the audience. This model is reflected—at its worst—in such popular phrases as "brainwashing," "hidden persuasion," and "subliminal advertising."

The second model—which *ought* to be inferred from the data of research—is of communication as a transactional process in which two parties each expect to give and take from the deal approximately equitable values. This, although it *ought* to be the scientific model, is far from generally accepted as such, a state of affairs on which W. Philips Davison (1959) makes the comment:

> the communicator's audience is not a passive recipient—it cannot be regarded as a lump of clay to be molded by the master propagandist. Rather, the audience is made up of individuals who demand something from the communications to which they are exposed, and who select those that are likely to be useful to them. In other words, they must get something from the manipulator if he is to get something from them. A bargain is involved. Sometimes, it is true, the manipulator is able to lead his audience into a bad bargain by emphasizing one need at the expense of another or by representing a change in the significant environment as greater than it actually has been. But audiences, too, can drive a hard bargain. Many communicators who have been widely disregarded or misunderstood know that to their cost (p. 360).

Davison does not contend that all the exchanges are equitable, but that the inequities may be on either side. He only implies that neither the audience nor the communicator would enter into this exchange unless each party expected to "get his money's worth," at least most of the time. After all, Davison is not speaking as a social philosopher nor as an apologist for the industry, but as an experienced researcher trying to make sense out of the accumulated evidence.

Whether fortunately or unfortunately, social criticism has long been associated with the study of communication. The latter was largely stimulated by the succession of exposés of propaganda following World War I, particularly of the munitions-makers' lobby and of the extensive propaganda of the public utilities. There was also social concern over the new media, the movies and radio, and the increasingly monopolistic control of newspapers. Propaganda analysis, which is what research communication was called in those days, was occupied with three inquiries: the structure of the media (who owns and controls them, and what affects what

Abridged from the **American Psychologist,** 1964, 19, 319–28, with permission of the author and the American Psychological Association.

gets into them); content analysis (what was said and printed); and propaganda techniques (which are the devil's devices to influence people). In this period, *effects* for the most part were not studied: They were taken for granted. Out of this tradition evolved Laswell's (Smith, Laswell, & Casey, 1946) formulation of the process of communication that is the most familiar one to this day: "Who says what, through what channels [media] of communication, to whom [with] what . . . results [p. 121]." This apparently self-evident formulation has one monumental built-in assumption: that the initiative is exclusively with the communicator, the effects being exclusively on the audience.

While the stimulus and the model of research on communication were developing out of the analysis of propaganda, survey research, relatively independently, was evolving its technology in the commercial world of market research and audience and leadership measurement. As is well known, Crossley, Gallup, and Roper each tried their hands at predicting the 1936 presidential election and whipped the defending champion, the *Literary Digest*. By 1940, Lazarsfeld was ready to try out the new technology on the old model with a full-scale panel study of the effects of the mass media on voting in a national election, having tested his strategy in the New Jersey gubernatorial race in 1938.

The results of this study, again, are well known. Virtually nobody in the panel changed his intention, and most of the few who did so attributed it to personal influence (Lazarsfeld, Berelson, & Gaudet, 1948). The mass media had had their big chance—and struck out. Negative results had been reached before but none which had been demonstrated by such solid research. A number of equally dramatic failures to detect effects of campaigns carried on in the mass media followed, and by the end of the decade Hyman and Sheatsley (1947) were attempting to explain why. No one could take the effects of communication for granted.

As a matter of fact a considerable number of the sociologists studying communication grew discouraged with inquiring into the immediate effects of the mass media, and went looking for "opinion leaders," "influentials," the "web of influence," and so on. At the same time, a few here and there began doing something we now call "functional studies." They were curious to know how the audience was behaving.

In the meantime, at just about the time that the students of the effect of communication in a natural setting were beginning to wonder if communication ever had effects, experimental studies were burgeoning under essentially laboratory conditions. Experiments had been conducted before, but the tradition of experimenting on the effects of communication was vastly enhanced by the War Department's Information and Education Division, and after the war by Hovland and his associates at Yale (Hovland, Lumsdaine, & Sheffield, 1949). The Yale group's output, and that of colleagues and students of Kurt Lewin, account for a very high proportion of the experimental work on the subject in the past two decades.

The experimenters generally had no trouble conveying information or changing attitudes. Of course nobody stopped to record very explicitly the main finding of all the experiments: that communication, given a reasonably large audience, varies in its impact. It affects some one way, some in the opposite way, and some not at all. But nevertheless the experimenters got results.

By the end of the fifties it was quite clear that the two streams of investigation needed reconciling, and Carl Hovland (1959) did so. More recently, pursuing the same theme, I stated Hovland's major point as being that the audience exercises much more initiative outside the laboratory than it does in the experimental situation (Bauer, 1962). The audience selects what it will attend to. Since people generally listen to and read things they are interested in, these usually are topics on which they have a good deal of information and fixed opinions. Hence the very people most likely to attend to a message are those most difficult to change; those who can be converted do not look or listen. A variety of studies attribute to this circumstance alone the fact that actual campaigns have often produced no measurable results, while quite marked effects could be produced in a laboratory.

Two favorite problems of the laboratory experimenters take on quite a different aspect when considered in a natural setting. One is the question of the order of presentation of arguments. Is it an advantage to have your argument stated first (the so-called law of primacy) or stated last (the so-called law of recency)? In a laboratory the answer is complex but it may be quite simple in a natural situation: He who presents his argument first may convert the audience and they in turn may exercise their oft-exercised prerogative of not listening to the opposing case. Hence to have the first word rather than the last could be decisive in the real world, but for a reason which may seem irrelevant to the relative merits of primacy versus recency.

Of course, another important variable is the credibility of the source. By creating an impression of the credibility of the stooge or experimenter in the laboratory, it is often possible to convert a person to a position far removed from his original one. But in real life, the audience usually does its own evaluation of sources, and at a certain point sometimes arrives at a result quite the opposite of that reached experimentally. If the audience is confronted with a communicator trying to convert it to a position opposed to its own it is likely to see him as "biased," and the like, and come away further strengthened in its own convictions.

It was quite clear from Hovland's piece, and should have been even earlier, that the characteristic behavior of the audience in its natural habitat is such as to bring about crucial modifications of the results seen in the laboratory. In general, these modifications are strongly in the direction of suppressing effect.

In a sense, Joseph Klapper's 1960 book, *The Effects of Mass Communication,* marks the end of an era. Twenty years earlier, a social scientist would have taken effects for granted and specified the devices the propagandist employed to achieve them. But Klapper (1960) makes statements like these: "[my position] is in essence a shift *away* from the tendency to regard mass communication as a necessary and sufficient cause of audience effects, toward a view of the media as influences, working amid other influences, in a total situation [p. 5]." He sees communications as operating through mediating factors—group membership, selective exposure, defense mechanisms—"such that they typically render mass communication a contributory agent, but not the sole cause in a process of reinforcing the existing conditions. (Regardless of the condition in question . . . the media are more likely to reinforce [it] than to change) [p. 8]." Change takes place, according to Klapper, in those rare circumstances when mediating forces are inoperative, when they are occasionally mobilized to facilitate change, or in certain residual situations. He reviews the literature on the effect of variation in content, mode of presentation, media, and so on, but rather than taking effects for granted, he searches for the exceptional case in which the mass media change rather than fortify and entrench.

Klapper recommends what he calls the "phenomenalistic" and others have called the functional approach. The study of communication has traditionally (although not exclusively) been conducted from the point of view of the *effects intended by the communicator*. From this perspective, the disparity between actual and intended results has often been puzzling. The answer has come increasingly to be seen in entering the phenomenal world of the audience and studying the functions which communication serves. The failure in research to this point has been that the audience has not been given full status in the exchange: The intentions of its members have not been given the same attention as those of the communicator.

Some will argue that these generalizations do not hold true of advertising. They do. But until now no one has undertaken to match the effects of communication in various areas according to comparable criteria and against realistic expectation.

Actually much more is expected of the campaigns with which academic psychologists are associated than is expected of commercial promotion. For example, a paper on governmental informational campaigns concluded with these words (Seidenfeld, 1961): "while people are willing to walk into a drugstore and buy low calorie preparations and contraceptives, they are not very anxious to take shots for protection against polio or attend a clinic dealing with sexual hygiene." By the author's own figures, 60% of the public had had one or more polio shots and 25% had had the full course of four. According to his expectations, and probably ours, these were hardly satisfactory accomplishments.

Yet, what about the highly advertised product, low in calories, with which he was comparing polio inoculations? Presumably he had heard that it was a smashing commercial success, or had seen some dollar volume figure on gross sales. Actually, it was being bought by 4% of the market—and 60% and even 25% are larger figures than 4%. Our unacknowledged expectations must be reckoned with.

These differences in expectation and criteria produce much confusion, usually on the side of convincing people that commercial campaigns are more successful than others. Yet, consistently successful commercial promotions convert only a very small percentage of people to action. No one cigarette now commands more than 14% of the cigarette market, but an increase of 1% is worth $60,000,000 in sales. This means influencing possibly .5% of all adults, and 1% of cigarette smokers. This also means that a successful commercial campaign can alienate many more than it wins, and still be highly profitable.

Equally misleading is the frequent

reference to percentage increase on some small base. This device has been a particular favorite of both the promoters and the critics of motivation research: One party does it to sell its services, the other purportedly to warn the public; both exaggerate the effect. Thus, for example, the boast, "a 300% increase in market share," means that the product increased; but it may easily be from 1% of the market to 3%. Or we may have a 500% gain in preference for "the new package" over the old one. That there is that much consensus in the esthetic judgment of the American public is a matter of interest, but it tells nothing about the magnitude of consequences on any criterion in which we are interested. I have made some computations on the famous Kate Smith war-bond marathon, which elicited $39 million in pledges. Kate Smith moved apparently a maximum of 4% of her audience to pledge to buy bonds; the more realistic figure may be 2%! In the commercial world this is a rather small effect as judged by some expectations, but yet an effect which often adds up to millions of dollars.

But commercial promotions often do not pay their way. The word is currently being circulated that a mammoth corporation and a mammoth advertising agency have completed a well-designed experiment that proves the corporation has apparently wasted millions of dollars on promoting its corporate image. Some studies have shown that an increase in expenditures for advertising has, under controlled experimental conditions, produced a decrease in sales.

The truth is now out: that our social model of the process of communication is morally asymmetrical; it is concerned almost exclusively with inequities to the advantage of the initiators, the manipulators. From the social point of view this may be all to the good. The answer to the question whether our social and scientific models should be identical is that there is no reason why we should be equally concerned with inequities in either direction; most of us consider it more important to protect the weak from the powerful, than vice versa. However, no matter how firmly committed to a morally asymmetrical social model, investigators should note that inequities fall in either direction and in unknown proportions.

The combination of this asymmetry and the varying expectations and criteria mentioned earlier fortifies the model of a one-way exploitative process of communication. And it is probably further reinforced by the experimental design in which the subject is seen as *re*acting to conditions established by the experimenter.

Traditionally, the name "functional studies" has been applied to any work concerned with a range of consequences wider than or different from those intended by the communicator. Two early classics, both done in the forties, are studies of listening to daytime radio serials: one by Herta Herzog (1944), and the other by Warner and Henry (1948). They established that women used the radio serials as models for their behavior in real life. In the late forties, Berelson (1949) studied how people reacted to not having newspapers during a strike, work which Kimball (1959) replicated in the newspaper strike of 1948. The variety of functions the newspapers proved to serve is amazing, including the furnishing of raw material for conversation. "The radio is no substitute for the newspaper. I like to make intelligent conversation [Kimball, 1959, p. 395]." There was also research on the adult following of comics (Bogart, 1955), children's use of TV (Maccoby, 1954), and the reading of *Mad* magazine (Winick, 1962).

Meanwhile, new trends have been developing in psychological research on communication. Until about a decade ago, the failure of experimental subjects to change their opinions was regarded as a residual phenomenon. Little systematic or sympathetic attention was paid to the persistence of opinion. The considerable volume of recent research using what the Maccobys (Maccoby & Maccoby, 1961) call a homeostatic model is dominated by theories based on the psychology of cognition, Heider's balance theory, Festinger's dissonance theory, Osgood and Tannenbaum's congruity theory, and Newcomb's strain for symmetry. While the proponents of each theory insist on adequate grounds on their distinctiveness, all agree that man acts so as to restore equilibrium in his system of belief. In any event, homeostatic studies do finally accord some initiative to the audience. Specifically, they reveal individuals as deliberately seeking out information on persons either to reinforce shaken convictions or consolidate those recently acquired. Festinger, for example, is interested in the reduction of dissonance following upon decisions—which means he views people as reacting to their own actions as well as to the actions of others. This influx of new ideas and new research is a valuable and welcome addition to both the theory and practice of social communication.

Restoring cognitive equilibrium is, however, only one of the tasks for which man seeks and uses information. Furthermore, the homeostatic theories, while according initiative to the audience, make it peculiarly defensive. They do little to counteract the notion of a one-way flow of influence—although it must be conceded that a scientific model is under no moral obligation to correct the defects, if any, of the social model.

Much is gained by looking upon the behavior of the audience as full-blown problem solving. Such a viewpoint requires the assumption that people have more problems to solve than simply relating to other people and reducing their psychic tension, among them being the allocation and conservation of resources.

The necessity for taking explicit cognizance of the audience's intention was forced on us when we were studying Soviet refugees. We knew that virtually every Soviet citizen was regularly exposed to meetings at which were conveyed a certain amount of news, the party line on various issues, and general political agitation and indoctrination. In free discussion our respondents complained endlessly of the meetings so we knew they were there. But when we asked them, "From what sources did you draw most of your information about what was happening?" only 19% specified them, in contrast to 87% citing newspapers, 50% citing radio, and another 50% word of mouth (Inkeles & Bauer, 1959, p. 163). Gradually the obvious dawned on us; our respondents were telling us where they learned what *they* wanted to know, not where they learned what the regime wanted them to know.

A similar perplexity arose with respect to the use of word-of-mouth sources of information. It was the least anti-Soviet of our respondents who claimed to make most use of this unofficial fountain of information. Re-

reading the interviews, and further analysis, unraveled the puzzle. It was the people most involved in the regime, at least in the upper social groups, who were using word-of-mouth sources the better to understand the official media, and the better to do their jobs (Inkeles & Bauer, 1959, p. 161)! As a result we had to conduct analysis on two levels, one where we took into account the intentions of the regime, the other, the intentions of the citizen. Thus, viewed from the vantage point of the regime's intention, the widespread dependence upon word of mouth was a failure in communication. From the point of view of the citizen and what he wanted, his own behavior made eminent sense.

At the next stage, we benefited from the looseness of our methods, the importance of the people we were studying, and from highly imaginative colleagues from other disciplines. We were studying the processes of decision, communication, and the like, in the business and political community. As we studied "influence" by wandering around and getting acquainted with the parties of both camps, and kept track of what was going on, the notion of a one-way flow became preposterous. It became clear that men in influential positions did a great deal to determine what sort of communication was directed toward them (Bauer, Pool, & Dexter, 1963). At this juncture, Ithiel de Sola Pool crystallized the proposition that the audience in effect influences the communicator by the role it forces on him. This idea became the organizing hypothesis behind the Zimmerman and Bauer demonstration (1956) that individuals process new information as a function of their perceived relationship to future audiences. Specifically, they are less likely to remember information that would conflict with the audience's views than they are to remember information to which the audience would be hospitable.

The final crystallization of my present views began several years ago when a decision theorist and I together reviewed the studies by motivation researchers of the marketing of ethical drugs to doctors. Surprisingly, I found the level of motivation discussed in these reports quite trivial, but the reports provided perceptive cognitive maps of the physician's world and the way he went about handling risk. The now well-known studies of the adoption of drugs by Coleman, Menzel, and Katz (1959) contributed data consistent with the following point: Physicians become increasingly selective in their choice of information as risk increases either because of the newness of the drug or difficulty in assessing its effects. Thereupon, a group of Harvard Business School students (in an unpublished manuscript) established by a questionnaire survey that as the seriousness of the disease increased, physicians were increasingly likely to prefer professional to commercial sources of information.

Why doesn't the physician always prefer professional to commercial sources of information? The physician is a busy man whose scarcest resources are time and energy, two things which commercial sources of information, on the whole, seem to help him conserve. Even so, he is selective. Let us assume two components in the choice of source of information: social compliance and the reduction of risk. Consider, then, that the doctor may be influenced by his liking either for the drug company's salesman who visits his office, or for the company itself. We may assume that, of these two components of influence, social compliance will be more associated with his sentiments toward the salesman and risk reduction with the company's reputation.

In a study conducted with the Schering Corporation (Bauer, 1961), I found that in the case of relatively riskless drugs, the correlation of preference for drugs with preference for salesman and for company was about equal. However, with more hazardous drugs—and with large numbers of subjects—preference for the company carried twice the weight of preference for the salesmen: The physicians selected the source closest associated with reduction of risk.

In the latest and fullest development of this point of view, Cox (1962) asked approximately 300 middle-class housewives to evaluate the relative merits of "two brands" of nylon stockings (Brand N & Brand R) as to over-all merits and as to each of 18 attributes. After each rating the subject was asked to indicate how confident she was in making it. The subjects then listened to a tape-recorded interview with a supposed salesgirl who stated that Brand R was better as to six attributes, whereupon they were asked to judge the stockings again and to evaluate the salesgirl and their confidence in rating her. Finally, they completed a questionnaire which included three batteries of questions on personality, one of which was a measure of self-confidence.

The findings of interest here bear upon personality and persuasibility. Male subjects low in generalized self-confidence are generally the more persuasible. Females are more persuasible in general but on the whole this is not correlated with self-confidence or self-esteem.

The reigning hypotheses on the relationship of self-confidence to persuasibility have been based either on the concept of ego defense (Cohen, 1959) or social approval (Janis, 1954), and Cox chose to add *perceived self-confidence in accomplishing a task*. He was dealing, then, with two measures of self-confidence: generalized self-confidence, presumably an attribute of "personality"; and specific self-confidence, that is, perceived confidence in judging stockings.

It has been suggested that the reason that in women personality has not been found correlated with persuasibility is that the issues used in experiments have not been important to them. And importance may account for the strong relationship Cox found when he gave them the task of rating stockings.

The virtue of Cox's data is that they enable us to relate the problem-solving dimensions of behavior to social relationships and ego defensive. It is interesting that—in this study—the more "psychological" processes come into play only at the point at which felt self-confidence in accomplishing the task falls below a critical point. Thus, tendency to accept the suggestions of the alleged salesgirl in Cox's experiment must be seen as a function of both ability to deal with the task and personality.

The difficulty of the task may either fortify or suppress the more "social-psychological" processes, depending on the specific circumstances. Thus, study of drug preference shows that as the task gets easier, the individual can indulge in the luxury of concurring with someone whom he likes, whereas when risk is great he has to concentrate on the risk-reducing potentialities of the source of information.

Thus the full-blown, problem-solving interpretation of the behavior of an audience in no sense rules out the problems with which students of communication have recently concerned themselves: ego defense and social adjustment. As a matter of fact, such problems seem explorable in a more profitable fashion if, simultaneously, attention is paid to the more overt tasks for which people use information. Yet, while there has been a consistent drift toward granting the audience more initiative, it cannot be said that the general literature on communication yet accords it a full range of intentions.

Of course, the audience is not wholly a free agent: It must select from what is offered. But even here, the audience has influence, since it is generally offered an array of communications to which it is believed it will be receptive. The process of social communication and of the flow of influence in general must be regarded as a transaction. "Transactionism," which has had a variety of meanings in psychology, is used here in the sense of an exchange of values between two or more parties; each gives in order to get.

The argument for using the transactional model for *scientific* purposes is that it opens the door more fully to exploring the intention and behavior of members of the audience and encourages inquiry into the influence of the audience on the communicator by specifically treating the process as a two-way passage. In addition to the influence of the audience on the communicator, there seems little doubt that influence also operates in the "reverse" direction. But the persistence of the one-way model of influence discourages the investigation of both directions of relationship. With amusing adroitness some writers have assimilated the original experiment of Zimmerman and Bauer (1956) to establish concepts such as reference groups, thereby ignoring what we thought was the clear implication of a two-way flow of influence.

At our present state of knowledge there is much to be said for the transactional model's pragmatic effect on research, but at the same time it is the most plausible description of the process of communication as we know it. Yet there seems to be a tendency to assume that words such as "transaction," "reciprocity," and the like imply exact equality in each exchange, measured out precisely according to the value system and judgment of the observer. This is nonsense. Obviously there are inequities, and they will persist, whether we use our own value systems as observers or if we have perfect knowledge of the people we observe.

The rough balance of exchange is sufficiently equitable in the long run to keep *most* individuals in our society engaged in the transactional relations of communication and influence. But some "alienated" people absent themselves from the network of communication as do, also, many businessmen who have doubts about the money they spend on advertising. The alienation is by no means peculiar to one end of the chain of communication or influence.

This point of view may be taken as a defense of certain social institutions such as advertising and the mass media. There is a limited range of charges against which *impotence* may indeed be considered a defense. Once more, ironically, both the communicator and the critic have a vested interest in the exploitative model. From the point of view of the communicator, it is reassuring that he will receive *at least* a fair return for his efforts; to the critic, the exploitative model gratifies the sense of moral indignation.

VII NORMATIVE BEHAVIOR, CONFORMITY, AND INTRA-GROUP PROCESSES

Social psychology has increasingly been concerned with the inter-related processes of conformity and influence. While these are sometimes stated in differing terms, it is essential nonetheless to deal with both in order to expose mechanisms that produce adherence to expected standards. One locus of such attention is the functional group where, by definition, members have some common goal and an associated "structure" for achieving it. Structure includes some division of labor and status differentiation, a pattern of communication, a sense of identity, and expectations for conformity to normative demands. Though our focus here is upon processes leading to conformity within such groups, the leadership of a group serves a significant influence function which is a counterpart to this and remains to be considered in the next section.

Social interaction within any social framework implies demands for regularized behaviors in the form of patterned actions or attitudinal expressions, as has been pointed out in previous sections. Gouldner in his paper in Section V illustrates one such persisting demand, "the norm of reciprocity," but apart from that kind of broad societal expectation, norms frequently originate and reside in the functional group. The question of why individuals conform to the expectations of these groups is at the heart of social psychological concern, and a range of emphases, some at times more dominant than others, has been suggested by way of answer. One thing is, however, certain: groups could not effectively achieve their goals without conforming behavior, nor could societies be sustained. A word is in order then on the motivational basis for conformity and some misconceptions that prevail about it, before we examine some of these emphases.

Affiliation with functional groups is frequently based upon a voluntary desire by the individual to take part in the group's activity; it is also true, though, that the individual thereby gains a number of social rewards which sustain his participation, i.e., recognition, a shared pride in achievement, a sense of belonging and approval; and, in addition, groups may provide individuals with a frame of reference for perceiving their world which they might lack alone, what Festinger calls "social reality." Conformity thus affords various inducements to the individual as a consequence of his continued acceptance as a member in good standing. If membership in a group is not forced, then a person who loses interest, or becomes attracted to other sources of reward, or finds the membership composition of the group no longer to his taste, may move away from it and not be concerned, all other things being equal, about the rejection he engenders.

Individuals therefore gain quite directly from conforming, despite the view that they give up some precious individuality in the process, and the related commonplace that conformity is inimical to individuality (see Cantril in Section I; Gardner in Section II). A way of clarifying this point is to think of true individuality not as slavish nonconformity (or *anti*-conformity), but rather as a range of choices *not* relying at either extreme upon a norm as the determinant of conduct, whether *pro* or *anti*. Therefore, as Willis points out here, what is called nonconformity is probably two quite distinct patterns: *anticonformity*, which is fixed to a norm as much as is its opposite, and *independence*, which is a freer expression of individual choice, whether or not it coincides with the norm. Gardner, in Section II, speaks to this more productive conception of individuality.

Social psychology studies conforming behavior without invoking any judgments about the nature of the norm as such. Though conformity is usually observed and considered as a behavioral outcome, there is also a covert level involved, as Kelman indicates in his paper here about processes of social influence.

Returning now to the emphases noted earlier, there are mainly four elements associated with conformity. They may be summarized as: (1) the individual, with his own characteristics, exemplified by personality; (2) the qualities of the group and its setting; (3) the nature of the norm itself; and (4) the past and present interchange between the individual and the others within the situation.

A great deal of attention has been directed along the lines of the first two emphases, the person and the situation. Several kinds of issues are at work in this debate. In the first place, there is a contention that individuals bring to numerous situations a differential inclination to conform and that, at the extreme, some people are "conformists" and others "nonconformists." Yet, at another level, it is recognized that persons may react differently to different situations as a function of how they perceive them. The differing properties of situations, filtered through the perception of individuals, have some effect even if persons bring different dispositions with them to many social settings. And this suggests a range within which people are variously sensitized to the demands for conformity across situations.

A further feature of this dialogue is represented in the concern with the psychological meaning of a "group" (see F. Allport, 1962). Here the essential question is whether indeed people in a group share common expectations for behavior, that is, whether they define a norm in some consistently similar fashion. If they do, then pressure for adherence is uniform; otherwise it is likely to be fragmented. Newcomb, in Section V, represents a latter-day position that groups have a quality of "shared expectations," and that it arises from interaction and serves to facilitate uniformity. This view has support in a substantial array of research findings and suggests at the very least that there are some observable behaviors which group members commonly see as appropriate, other things being equal. But differences probably do intrude depending upon the nature of the "norm." Of special interest in this regard is Floyd Allport's early work, not strictly speaking within functional groups, which established the "J-curve," with its relatively fixed point for full conformity to the norm and its deviations of decreasing frequency from that point. In some form or other, this continues to be a fashionable representation of conformity, though it obscures what is probably more true of group norms, i.e., that they stand as "normative perceptions" of what is expected and that they are neither fixed nor general. In this sense, norms may apply to group members on an individually varying basis, so that not everyone must conform in the same way;

relatedly, roles may be thought of as highly differentiated expectations which are person-specific, as Hollander notes in this section in considering the properties of status.

The personality line of emphasis is represented by Crutchfield's (1955) study of the individual differences in conforming behavior produced by "group pressure" induced in the manner of the original studies by Sherif (1935) and Asch (1952). Another line of work on personality dispositions toward conformity is seen in the studies of "persuasibility" reported by Hovland and Janis (1959). One problem with such results is that the "groups" studied in these various experiments are low on functionality, and normative expectations often are set by the experimenter. Furthermore, little or no interaction occurs between subjects.

Festinger's paper here is a classic formulation of the variables within the group situation which affect the communication between group members and lead to "uniformity" of opinion. His work represents an outgrowth of Lewin's group dynamics movement which highlights the play of forces within the social context. As is traditional, Festinger views the norm as a point where some consensus rests. However, he also provides for the processes which may alter the consensus, in contrast to the "personality disposition" approach which conceives the process of conformity as dependent upon a relatively fixed standard to which compliance is demanded, without reference to change. Another significant feature of Festinger's approach is the importance which he attaches to individual requirements for "social reality," something mentioned above as an inducement the group offers by way of what one might call a shared outlook. This conception relates in various ways to his later theory of "cognitive dissonance," covered in the preceding section.

The norm as an essentially fixed point has been challenged along several lines, some touched on here. March's paper in this section gives expression to dissatisfaction on the grounds that this traditional formulation is inadequate for an understanding of observed phenomena. A norm, he asserts, need *not* be confined to a modal point or central tendency. Indeed, it may follow several forms and be multi-dimensional. He deals with norms less in terms of behavior than as descriptive characteristics of his respondents. However, his essential point remains quite valid, i.e., that there is *more than one way* of characterizing norms. This prospect raises some intriguing conceptual, as well as practical, questions. What happens to a group whose normative expectations become increasingly complex and variegated? Does compliance decrease? Are new members frustrated in their attempt to "do right" by virtue of this multi-dimensionality? Is it more difficult, as one would suppose, for a member to "know where he stands"?

The Willis paper here represents a much more up-to-date description of the differential responses associated with conformity and nonconform-it. His major distinction between two modes of nonconformity, i.e., anti-conformity and independence, is an essential departure from the traditional single-dimensional representation of conformity and nonconformity at opposite ends of a single line. The "diamond" model which Willis presents affords a better indication of the various options available to the individual in terms of behavior in a given influence situation. It should also be clearly recognized that he is not referring to "types" of people, in the sense of a disposition toward anticonformity, for example, but to possible modes of response by an individual.

In a related way, Kelman treats the relationship between manifest and underlying aspects of conformity in his paper here. He distinguishes influence processes leading to compliance, identification, and internalization. An individual may not be motivated to conform but be unable to do as he wishes. Accordingly, he may behave in one way but actually have different underlying tendencies. Kelman draws distinctions between these three processes of influence with specific regard to the psychodynamics of their motivational underpinnings.

The four papers which follow in this section are illustrative of the consideration of norms and conformity to them as part of an evolving process of interaction in time. All of them give some place of importance to an implicit interchange of reciprocated response. Homans has for some years devoted attention to conformity, and his book, *Social Behavior: Its Elementary Forms* (1961), extends his ideas on social exchange presented in his paper in this section. His conception of rewards and costs is based in a set of reinforcement mechanisms and resembles the rewards-costs matrix model set forth by Thibaut and Kelley. Homans uses not only reinforcement theory, but employs his construct "distributive justice" as another component in social interaction. This has a certain resonance with the ideas of Heider on "balance" and Festinger on "dissonance," emphasizing as they do a degree of symmetry or aptness between actions and counter-actions, as well as actions and perceptions.

Thibaut and Kelley are represented in this section by a discussion from their provocative book *The Social Psychology of Groups* (1957), which serves in particular to underscore the utility of norms for the maintenance of influence independent of the repetitive exercise of personal power. While they use here the diadic relationship as a referent, a range of implications is provided in their book for intra-group processes. An important psychological construct which they employ is "comparison level for alternatives," which has to do with other available rewards and is suggestive of adaptation level phenomena (see Helson, 1948).

There are other similarities in the key concepts of Homans and of Thibaut and Kelley, and some elements of distinction. Both views imply an interchange in the responses of individuals one to another in a diadic relationship, but with implications to larger groups. While the concept of an exchange is implied as well in the theory of "idiosyncrasy credit" presented in the Hollander paper, the emphasis there is more upon the interpersonal perceptions which individuals hold of *each other* and the latitude that this comes to provide as one gains "credit" in the eyes of others through impacts of positive impressions. An important distinction here is the fact that normative demands become associated with individuals as a feature of ongoing interaction. Acceptable behavior from one person, within a stable group context, would therefore not be necessarily acceptable behavior for another. Thus, the notion of credit is tied to the latitude an individual may have for behaving in various ways depending upon his status, in these credit terms. The prospect for change, considered in the next section, is afforded largely through the potential for innovation available by using credits. Thus, conformity at one time may allow nonconformity, in the sense of greater independence, at another.

In his paper here, Jones is also concerned with manifest conformity as it affects others' perceptions. In his new book, *Ingratiation* (1964), he sees manifest conformity as one tactic of "ingratiation," especially where a person of relatively lower status seeks to gain more favorable outcomes from a person of relatively higher status. This viewpoint meshes well with the Hollander concept of "idiosyncrasy credit" in that they both stress the gains the individual may achieve through observable conformity in social interaction.

The question associated with the motivational basis for conformity is handled differently in these papers. Festinger conceives of two essential ingredients as determining this process—"social reality" and "group locomotion." Thibaut and Kelley tend to give greater weight to the rewards an individual might secure as against what it costs him, as would Homans in his exchange conception. Hollander treats motivation as being a necessary basis for conformity but not in itself a sufficient one, since an individual might wish to conform but be unable accurately to perceive what is expected of him. This gives rise to the consideration that conformity to any kind of normative expectation implies a degree of veridicality of perception (cf. Steiner, Section V). At the extreme, an individual might wish to conform but would lack the basis for doing so. Hence, what might appear to be nonconformity might be in fact the consequence of a faulty perception. Given a basis for knowing what is expected, Jones considers conformity to be motivated by a practical desire to secure benefits from another person in a more powerful position.

Still another issue is the identification which an individual might develop with a group and its effect upon him, independent of *actual* participation in the group. This is where the utility of the concept of the "reference group" is of special importance. In Section II, Shibutani conveys the sense that a group may provide a perspective quite apart from literal membership in that group. Viewed in these terms, the *psychological* effect of group membership is not established by the mere fact of membership but by a process of matching inducements against individual motives, summarized under several headings, e.g., acceptance by the group and social approval; incorporation of a structure for one's world, especially under conditions of ambiguity; satisfaction from the task; prestige from others for being thought to be associated with the group. Thus, multiple motivations may be at work in determining the basis for conformity; these are crucially dependent upon the way in which the individual perceives others within his situation, and various rewards must be entertained as possible motive sources whatever conception of conformity is employed.

42 Informal social communication

LEON FESTINGER

The importance of strict theory in developing and guiding programs of research is becoming more and more recognized today. Yet there is considerable disagreement about exactly how strict and precise a theoretical formulation must be at various stages in the development of a body of knowledge. Certainly there are many who feel that some "theorizing" is too vague and indefinite to be of much use. It is also argued that such vague and broad "theorizing" may actually hinder the empirical development of an area of knowledge.

On the other hand there are many who express dissatisfaction with instances of very precise theories which do exist here and there, for somehow or other a precise and specific theory seems to them to leave out the "real" psychological problem. These persons seem to be more concerned with those aspects of the problem which the precise theory has not yet touched. From this point of view it is argued that too precise and too strict theorizing may also hinder the empirical development of an area of knowledge.

It is probably correct that if a theory becomes too precise too early it can have tendencies to become sterile. It is also probably correct that if a theory stays too vague and ambiguous for too long it can be harmful in that nothing can be done to disprove or change it. This probably means that theories, when vague, should at least be stated in a form which makes the adding of precision possible as knowledge increases. It also probably means that theory should run ahead, but not too far ahead, of the data so that the trap of premature precision can be avoided. It certainly means that theories, whether vague or precise, must be in such a form that empirical data can influence them.

This article is a statement of the theoretical formulations which have been developed in the process of conducting a program of empirical and experimental research in informal social communication. It has grown out of our findings thus far and is in turn guiding the future course of the research program. This program of research concerns itself with finding and explaining the facts concerning informal, spontaneous communication among persons and the consequences of the process of communication. It would seem that a better understanding of the dynamics of such communication would in turn lead to a better understanding of various kinds of group functioning. The theories and hypotheses presented below vary considerably in precision, specificity and the degree to which corroborating data exist. Whatever the state of precision, however, the theories are empirically oriented and capable of being tested.

Since we are concerned with the spontaneous process of communication which goes on during the functioning of groups we must first differentiate the variety of types of communication which occur

Reprinted from the Psychological Review, 1950, 57, 271–82, with permission of the author and the American Psychological Association.

according to the theoretical conditions which give rise to tendencies to communicate. It is plausible to assume that separating the sources or origins of pressures to communicate that may act on a member of a group will give us fruitful areas to study. This type of differentiation or classification is, of course, adequate only if it leads to the separation of conceptually clear areas of investigation within which communication can be organized into statable theoretical and empirical laws.

We shall here deal with those few of the many possible sources of pressures to communicate in which we have thus far been able to make theoretical and empirical progress. We shall elaborate on the theory for regarding them as giving rise to pressures to communicate and on specific hypotheses concerning the laws of communication which stem from these sources.

I. Pressures toward uniformity in a group

One major source of forces to communicate is the pressure toward uniformity which may exist within a group. These are pressures which, for one reason or another, act toward making members of a group agree concerning some issue or conform with respect to some behavior pattern. It is stating the obvious, of course, to say that these pressures must be exerted by means of a process of communication among the members of the group. One must also specify the conditions under which such pressures toward uniformity arise, both on a conceptual and an operational level so that in any specific situation it is possible to say whether or not such pressures exist. We shall, in the following discussion, elaborate on two major sources of pressures toward uniformity among people, namely, social reality and group locomotion.

1. *Social reality:* Opinions, attitudes, and beliefs which people hold must have some basis upon which they rest for their validity. Let us as a start abstract from the many kinds of bases for the subjective validity of such opinions, attitudes, and beliefs one continuum along which they may be said to lie. This continuum we may call a scale of degree of physical reality. At one end of this continuum, namely, complete dependence upon physical reality, we might have an example such as this: A person looking at a surface might think that the surface is fragile or he might think that the surface is unbreakable. He can very easily take a hammer, hit the surface, and quickly be convinced as to whether the opinion he holds is correct or incorrect. After he has broken the surface with a hammer it will probably make little dent upon his opinion if another person should tell him that the surface is unbreakable. It would thus seem that where there is a high degree of dependence upon physical reality for the subjective validity of one's beliefs or opinions the dependence upon other people for the confidence one has in these opinions or beliefs is very low.

At the other end of the continuum where the dependence upon physical reality is low or zero, we might have an example such as this: A person looking at the results of a national election feels that if the loser had won, things would be in some ways much better than they are. Upon what does the subjective validity of this belief depend? It depends to a large degree on whether or not other people share his opinion and feel the same way he does. If there are other people around him who believe the same thing, then his opinion is, to him, valid. If there are not others who believe the same thing, then his opinion is, in the same sense, not valid. Thus where the dependence upon physical reality is low the dependence upon social reality is correspondingly high. An opinion, a belief, an attitude is "correct," "valid," and "proper" to the extent that it is anchored in a group of people with similar beliefs, opinions, and attitudes.

This statement, however, cannot be generalized completely. It is clearly not necessary for the validity of someone's opinion that everyone else in the world think the way he does. It is only necessary that the members of that group to which he refers this opinion or attitude think the way he does. It is not necessary for a Ku Klux Klanner that some northern liberal agree with him in his attitude toward Negroes, but it is eminently necessary that there be other people who also are Ku Klux Klanners and who do agree with him. The person who does not agree with him is seen as different from him and not an adequate referent for his opinion. The problem of independently defining which groups are and which groups are not appropriate reference groups for a particular individual and for a particular opinion or attitude is a difficult one. It is to some extent inherently circular since an appropriate reference group tends to be a group which does share a person's opinions and attitudes, and people tend to locomote *into* such groups and *out of* groups which do not agree with them.

From the preceding discussion it would seem that if a discrepancy in opinion, attitude, or belief exists among persons who are members of an appropriate reference group, forces to communicate will arise. It also follows that the less "physical reality" there is to validate the opinion or belief, the greater will be the importance of the social referent, the group, and the greater will be the forces to communicate.

2. *Group locomotion:* Pressures toward uniformity among members of a group may arise because such uniformity is desirable or necessary in order for the group to move toward some goal. Under such circumstances there are a number of things one can say about the magnitude of pressures toward uniformity.

(a) They will be greater to the extent that the members perceive that group movement would be facilitated by uniformity.

(b) The pressures toward uniformity will also be greater, the more dependent the various members are on the group in order to reach their goals. The degree to which other groups are substitutable as a means toward individual or group goals would be one of the determinants of the dependence of the member on the group.

We have elaborated on two sources of pressure toward uniformity among members of groups. The same empirical laws should apply to communications which result from pressures toward uniformity irrespective of the particular reasons for the existence of the pressures. We shall now proceed to enumerate a set of hypotheses concerning communication which results from pressures toward uniformity.

II. Hypotheses about communication resulting from pressures toward uniformity

Communications which arise from pressures toward uniformity in a group may be seen as "instrumental" communications. That is, the communication is not an end in itself but rather is a means by which the communicator hopes to influence the person he addresses in such a way as to reduce the discrepancy that exists between them. Thus we should examine the determinants of: (1) when a member communicates, (2) to whom he communicates and (3) the reactions of the recipient of the communication.

(1) Determinants of the magnitude of pressure to communicate:

Hypothesis 1a: *The pressure on members to communicate to others in the group concerning "item x" increases monotonically with increase in the perceived discrepancy in opinion concerning "item x" among members of the group.*

Remembering that we are considering only communication that results from pressures toward uniformity, it is clear that if there are no discrepancies in opinion, that is, uniformity already exists in the group, there will be no forces to communicate. It would be plausible to expect the force to communicate to increase rapidly from zero as the state of affairs departs from uniformity.

Hypothesis 1b: *The pressure on a member to communicate to others in the group concerning "item x" increases monotonically with increase in the degree of relevance of "item x" to the functioning of the group.*

If "item x" is unimportant to the group in the sense of not being associated with any of the values or activities which are the basis for the existence of the group, or if it is more or less inconsequential for group locomotion, then there should be few or no forces to communicate even when there are perceived discrepancies in opinion. As "item x" becomes more important for the group (more relevant), the forces to communicate when any given magnitude of perceived discrepancy exists, should increase.

Corroborative evidence for this hypothesis is found in an experiment by Schachter (1951) where discussion of the same issue was experimentally made relevant for some groups and largely irrelevant for others. It is clear from the data that where the discussion was relevant to the functioning of the group there existed stronger forces to communicate and to influence the other members. Where the issue is a relevant one the members make longer individual contributions to the discussion and there are many fewer prolonged pauses in the discussion.

Hypothesis 1c: *The pressure on members to communicate to others in the group concerning "item x" increases monotonically with increase in the cohesiveness of the group.*

Cohesiveness of a group is here defined as the resultant of all the forces acting on the members to remain in the group. These forces may depend on the attractiveness or unattractiveness of either the prestige of the group, members in the group, or the activities in which the group engages. If the total attraction toward the group is zero, no forces to communicate should arise; the members may as easily leave the group as stay in it. As the forces to remain in the group increase (given perceived discrepancies in opinion and given a certain relevance of the item to the functioning of the group) the pressures to communicate will increase.

Data from an experiment by Back (1951) support this hypothesis. In this experiment groups of high and low cohesiveness were experimentally created using three different sources of attraction to the group, namely, liking the members, prestige attached to belonging, and possibility of getting a reward for performance in the group activity. For each of the three types of attraction to the group the more cohesive groups were rated as proceeding at a more intense rate in the discussion than the corresponding less cohesive groups. In addition, except for the groups where the attraction was the possibility of reward (perhaps due to wanting to finish and get the reward) there was more total amount of attempted exertion of influence in the highly cohesive groups than in the less cohesive groups. In short, highly cohesive groups, having stronger pressures to communicate, discussed the issue at a more rapid pace and attempted to exert more influence.

(2) Determinants of choice of recipient for communications:

Hypothesis 2a: *The force to communicate about "item x" to* A PARTICULAR MEMBER *of the group will increase as the discrepancy in opinion between that member and the communicator increases.*

We have already stated in Hypothesis 1a that the pressure to communicate in general will increase as the perceived non-uniformity in the group increases. In addition the force to communicate will be strongest toward those whose opinions are most different from one's own and will, of course, be zero towards those in the group who at the time hold the same opinion as the communicator. In other words, people will tend to communicate to those within the group whose opinions are most different from their own.

There is a clear corroboration of this hypothesis from a number of studies. In the previously mentioned experiment by Schachter (1951) the distribution of opinions expressed in the group was always as follows: Most of the members' opinions clustered within a narrow range of each other while one member, the deviate, held and maintained an extremely divergent point of view. About five times as many communications were addressed to the holder of the divergent point of view as were addressed to the others.

In an experiment by Festinger and Thibaut (1951) the discussion situation was set up so that members' opinions on the issue spread over a considerable range. Invariably 70 to 90 per cent of the communications were addressed to those who held opinions at the extremes of the distribution. The curve of number of communications received falls off very rapidly as the opinion of the recipient moves away from the extreme of the distribution. The hypothesis would seem to be well substantiated.

Hypothesis 2b: *The force to communicate about "item x" to* A PARTICULAR PERSON *will decrease to the extent that he is perceived as not a member of the group or to the extent that he is not wanted as a member of the group.*

From the previous hypothesis it follows that communications will tend to be addressed mainly toward those with extreme opinions within the group. This does not hold, however, for any arbitrarily defined group. The present hypothesis, in effect, states that such relationships will apply only within *psychological* groups, that is, collections of people that exist as groups psychologically for the members. Communications will tend not to be addressed towards those who are not members of the group.

The study by Schachter (1951) and the study by Festinger and Thibaut (1951) both substantiate this hypothesis. In Schachter's experiment those group members who do not want the person holding the extremely divergent point of view to remain in the group tend to stop communicating to him towards the end of the discussion. In the experiment by Festinger and Thibaut, when the subjects have the perception that the persons present include different kinds of people with a great variety of interests, there tends to be less communication toward the extremes in the last half of the discussion after the rejection process has had time to develop. In short, communication towards those with different opinions decreases if they are seen as not members of the *psychological* group.

Hypothesis 2c: *The force to communicate "item x" to a particular member will increase the more it is perceived that the communication will change that member's opinion in the desired direction.*

A communication which arises because of the existence of pressures toward uniformity is made in order to exert a force on the recipient in a particular direction, that is, to push him to change his opinion so that he will agree more closely with the communicator. If a member is perceived as very resistant to changing his opinion, the force to communicate to him decreases. If it seems that a particular member will be changed as the result of a communication so as to increase the discrepancy between him and the communicator, there will exist a force not to communicate to him. Thus under such conditions there will be tendencies *not* to communicate this particular item to that member.

There is some corroboration for this hypothesis. In a face to face verbal discussion where a range of opinion exists, the factors which this hypothesis points to would be particularly important for those members whose opinions were near the middle of the range. A communication which might influence the member at one extreme to come closer to the middle might at the same time influence the member at the other extreme to move farther away from the middle. We might then expect from this hypothesis that those holding opinions in the middle of the existing range would communicate less (because of the conflict) and would address fewer communications to the whole group (attempting to influence only one person at a time).

A number of observations were conducted to check these derivations. Existing groups of clinical psychologists who were engaging in discussions to reconcile their differences in ratings of applicants were observed. Altogether, 147 such discussions were observed in which at least one member's opinion was in the middle of the existing range. While those with extreme opinions made an average of 3.16 units of communication (number of communications weighted by length of the communication), those with middle opinions made an average of only 2.6 units of communication. While those with extreme opinions addressed 38 per cent of their communications to the whole group, those with middle opinions addressed only 29 per cent of their communications to everyone.

(3) Determinants of change in the recipient of a communication:

Hypothesis 3a: *The amount of change in opinion resulting from receiving a communication will increase as the pres-*

sure towards uniformity in the group increases.

There are two separate factors which contribute to the effect stated in the hypothesis. The greater the pressure towards uniformity, the greater will be the amount of influence exerted by the communications, and consequently, the greater the magnitude of change that may be expected. But the existence of pressures toward uniformity will not only show itself in increased attempts to change the opinions of others. Pressures toward uniformity will also produce greater readiness to change in the members of the group. In other words, uniformity may be achieved by changing the opinions of others and/or by changing one's own opinions. Thus we may expect that with increasing pressure towards uniformity there will be less resistance to change on the part of the members. Both of these factors will contribute to produce greater change in opinion when the pressure toward uniformity is greater.

There is evidence corroborating this hypothesis from the experiment by Festinger and Thibaut (1951). In this experiment three degrees of pressure towards uniformity were experimentally induced in different groups. Irrespective of which of two problems were discussed by the group and irrespective of whether they perceived the group to be homogeneously or heterogeneously composed, the results consistently show that high pressure groups change most, medium pressure groups change next most, and low pressure groups change least in the direction of uniformity. While the two factors which contribute to this effect cannot be separated in the data, their joint effect is clear and unmistakable.

Hypothesis 3b: *The amount of change in opinion resulting from receiving a communication will increase as the strength of the resultant force to remain in the group increases for the recipient.*

To the extent that a member wishes to remain in the group, the group has power over that member. By power we mean here the ability to produce real change in opinions and attitudes and not simply change in overt behavior which can also be produced by means of overt threat. If a person is unable to leave a group because of restraints from the outside, the group can then use threats to change overt behavior. Covert changes in opinions and attitudes, however, can only be produced by a group by virtue of forces acting on the member to remain in the group. Clearly the maximum force which the group can successfully induce on a member counter to his own forces can not be greater than the sum of the forces acting on that member to remain in the group. The greater the resultant force to remain in the group, the more effective will be the attempts to influence the member.

This hypothesis is corroborated by two separate studies. Festinger, Schachter and Back (1950) investigated the relationship between the cohesiveness of social groups in a housing project (how attractive the group was for its members) and how effectively a group standard relevant to the functioning of the group was maintained. A correlation of .72 was obtained between these two variables. In other words, the greater the attractiveness of the group for the members, the greater was the amount of influence which the group could successfully exert on its members with the result that there existed greater conformity in attitudes and behavior in the more cohesive groups.

Back (1951) did a laboratory experiment specifically designed to test this hypothesis. By means of plausible instructions to the subjects he experimentally created groups of high and low cohesiveness, that is, conditions in which the members were strongly attracted to the group and those in which the attraction to the group was relatively weak. The subjects, starting with different interpretations of the same material, were given an opportunity to discuss the matter. Irrespective of the source of the attraction to the group (Back used three different types of attraction in both high and low cohesive conditions) the subjects in the high cohesive groups influenced each other's opinions more than the subjects in the low cohesive groups. In short, the greater the degree of attraction to the group, the greater the amount of influence actually accomplished.

Hypothesis 3c: *The amount of change in opinion resulting from receiving a communication concerning "item x" will decrease with increase in the degree to which the opinions and attitudes involved are anchored in other group memberships or serve important need satisfying functions for the person.*

If the opinion that a person has formed on some issue is supported in some other group than the one which is at present attempting to influence him, he will be more resistant to the attempted influence. Other sources of resistance to being influenced undoubtedly come from personality factors, ego needs and the like.

Specific evidence supporting this hypothesis is rather fragmentary. In the study of social groups in a housing project by Festinger, Schachter and Back (1950), the residents were asked whether their social life was mainly outside the project or not. Of those who conformed to the standards of their social groups within the project about 85 per cent reported that their social life was centered mainly within the project. Less than 50 per cent of those who did not conform to the standards of the project social group, however, reported that their social life was centered mainly in the project. It is likely that they were able to resist the influences from within the project when their opinions and attitudes were supported in outside groups.

The experiments by Schachter (1951) and by Festinger and Thibaut (1951) used the same discussion problem in slightly different situations. In the former experiment subjects identified themselves and verbally supported their opinions in face-to-face discussion. In the latter experiment the subjects were anonymous, communicating only by written messages on which the sender of the message was not identified. Under these latter conditions many more changes in opinion were observed than under the open verbal discussion situation even though less time was spent in discussion when they wrote notes. This difference in amount of change in opinion is probably due to the ego defensive reactions aroused by openly committing oneself and supporting one's opinions in a face-to-face group.

(4) Determinants of change in relationship among members:

Hypothesis 4a: *The tendency to change the composition of the psychological group (pushing members out of the group) increases as the perceived discrepancy in opinion increases.*

We have already discussed two of the responses which members of groups make to pressures toward uniformity, namely, attempting to influence others and being more ready to be influenced. There is still a third response which serves to move toward uniformity. By rejecting those whose opinions diverge from the group and thus redefining who is and who is not in the psychological group, uniformity can be accomplished. The greater the discrepancy between a person's opinion and the opinion of another, the stronger are the tendencies to exclude the other person from the psychological group.

There is evidence that members of groups do tend to reject those whose opinions are divergent. In the study of social groups within a housing project Festinger, Schachter and Back (1950) found that those who did not conform to the standards of their social group were underchosen on a sociometric test, that is, they mentioned more persons as friends of theirs than they received in return. Schachter (1951) did an experiment specifically to test whether or not members of groups would be rejected simply for disagreeing on an issue. Paid participants in the groups voiced divergent or agreeing opinions as instructed. In all groups the paid participant who voiced divergent opinion on an issue was rejected on a postmeeting questionnaire concerning whom they wanted to have remain in the group. The same paid participants, when voicing conforming opinions in other groups, were not rejected.

Hypothesis 4b: *When non-conformity exists, the tendency to change the composition of the psychological group increases as the cohesiveness of the group increases and as the relevance of the issue to the group increases.*

We have previously discussed the increase in forces to communicate with increase in cohesiveness and relevance of issue. Similarly, these two variables affect the tendency to reject persons from the group for non-conformity. Theoretically we should expect any variable which affected the force to communicate (which stems from pressures toward uniformity) to affect also the tendency to reject non-conformers in a similar manner. In other words, increases in the force to communicate concerning an item will go along with increased tendency to reject persons who disagree concerning that item.

The previously mentioned experiment by Schachter (1951) was designed to test this hypothesis by experimentally varying cohesiveness and relevance in club groups. In this experiment the more cohesive groups do reject the non-conformer more than the less cohesive groups and the groups where the issue is relevant reject the non-conformer more than groups where the issue is not very relevant to the group functioning. Those groups where cohesiveness was low and the issue was not very relevant show little, if any, tendency to reject the deviate.

III. Forces to change one's position in a group

Another important source of forces to communicate are the forces which act on members of groups to locomote (change their position) in the group, or to move from one group to another. Such forces to locomote may stem from the attractiveness of activities associated with a different position in the group or from the status of that position or the like. Thus a new member of a group may wish to become more central in the group, a member of an organization may wish to rise in the status hierarchy, a member of a business firm may want to be promoted or a member of a minority group may desire acceptance by the majority group. These are all instances of forces to locomote in a social structure.

It is plausible that the existence of a force acting on a person in a specific direction produces behavior in that direction. Where locomotion in the desired direction is not possible, at least temporarily, there will exist a force to communicate in that direction. The existence of a force in a specific direction will produce behavior in that direction. One such kind of behavior is communication. This hypothesis is not very different from the hypothesis advanced by Lewin (1940) to account for the superior recall of interrupted activities.

An experiment by Thibaut (1950) tends to corroborate this theoretical analysis. In his experiment he created two groups, one of high status and privileged, the other of low status and under-privileged. These two groups, equated in other respects, functioned together so that the members of the high status group could play an attractive game. The low status group functioned merely as servants. It was clear that forces were acting on the members of the low status group to move into the other group. As the privilege position of the high status group became clearer and clearer the amount of communication from the low status team to the high status group increased. The number of communications from members of the high status group to the low status group correspondingly decreased. When, in some groups, the status and privilege relationship between the two teams was reversed toward the end of the experimental session, thus reducing the forces to locomote into the other group, the number of communications to that other group correspondingly decreased.

Further corroboration is found in a preliminary experiment, mainly methodologically oriented, conducted by Back *et al.* (1950). In this experiment new items of information were planted with persons at various levels in the hierarchy of a functioning organization. Data on transmission of each of the items of information were obtained through cooperators within the organization who were chosen so as to give adequate coverage of all levels and all sections within it. These cooperators recorded all instances of communication that came to their attention. Of seventeen acts of communication recorded in this manner, eleven were directed upwards in the hierarchy, four toward someone on the same level and only two were directed downwards. The existence of forces to move upward in such a hierarchical organization may be taken for granted. The great bulk of the communications recorded went in the same direction as these forces to locomote.

In considering communication among members of differentiated social structures it is important also to take into account restraints against communication.

Infrequent contact in the ordinary course of events tends to erect restraints against communication. It is undoubtedly easier to communicate a given item to a person whom one sees frequently or to a person to whom one has communicated similar items in the past. The structuring of groups into hierarchies, social clusters, or the like, undoubtedly tends to restrict the amount and type of contact between members of certain different parts or levels of the group and also undoubtedly restricts the content of the communication that goes on between such levels in the ordinary course of events. These restrictions erect restraints against certain types of communication.

There are some data which tend to specify some of the restraints against communication which exist. In the study of the communication of a spontaneous rumor in a community by Festinger, Cartwright *et al.* (1948) it was found that intimacy of friendship tended to increase ease of communication. Persons with more friends in the project heard the rumor more often than those with only acquaintances. Those who had few friends or acquaintances heard the rumor least often. At the same time this factor of intimacy of friendship was not related to how frequently they relayed the rumor to others. In other words, it was not related to forces to communicate but seemed to function only as a restraint against communicating where friendship did not exist.

There is also some evidence that the mere perception of the existence of a hierarchy sets up restraints against communication between levels. Kelley (1951) experimentally created a two-level hierarchy engaging in a problem-solving task during which they could and did communicate within levels and between levels. Control groups were also run with the same task situation but with no status differential involved between the two subgroups. There was more communication between subgroups under these control conditions than where there was a status differential involved.

It seems that, in a hierarchy, there are also restraints against communicating hostility upwards when the hostility is about those on upper levels. In the same experiment by Kelley there was much criticism of the *other group* expressed by both high status and low status members. The proportion of these critical expressions which are directed upward by the low status group is much less, however, than the proportion directed downward by the high status groups.

IV. Emotional expression

An important variety of communications undoubtedly results from the existence of an emotional state in the communicator. The existence of joy, anger, hostility and the like seems to produce forces to communicate. It seems that communications resulting from the existence of an emotional state are consummatory rather than instrumental.

By an instrumental communication we mean one in which the reduction of the force to communicate depends upon the effect of the communication on the recipient. Thus in communication resulting from pressures toward uniformity in a group, the mere fact that a communication is made does not affect the force to communicate. If the effect has been to change the recipient so that he now agrees more closely with the communicator, the force to communicate will be reduced. If the recipient changes in the opposite direction, the force to communicate to him will be increased.

By a consummatory communication we mean one in which the reduction of the force to communicate occurs as a result of the expression and does not depend upon the effect it has on the recipient. Certainly in the case of such communications the reaction of the recipient may introduce new elements into the situation which will affect the force to communicate, but the essence of a consummatory communication is that the simple expression does reduce the force.

Specifically with regard to the communication of hostility and aggression, much has been said regarding its consummatory nature. The psychoanalytic theories of catharsis, in particular, develop the notion that the expression of hostility reduces the emotional state of the person. There has, however, been very little experimental work done on the problem. The previously mentioned experiment by Thibaut in which he created a "privileged-underprivileged" relationship between two equated groups has some data on the point. There is evidence that those members of the "underprivileged" groups who expressed their hostility toward the "privileged" groups showed less residual hostility toward them in post-experimental questionnaires. There is, however, no control over the reactions of the recipients of the hostile communications nor over the perceptions of the communicators of what these reactions were. An experiment is now in progress which will attempt to clarify some of these relationships with both negative and positive emotional states.

V. Summary

A series of interrelated hypotheses has been presented to account for data on informal social communication collected in the course of a number of studies. The data come from field studies and from laboratory experiments specifically designed to test the hypotheses.

Three sources of pressures to communicate have been considered:

1. Communication arising from pressures toward uniformity in a group. Here we considered determinants of magnitude of the force to communicate, choice of recipient for the communication, magnitude of change in recipient and magnitude of tendencies to reject nonconformers.

2. Communications arising from forces to locomote in a social structure. Here we considered communications in the direction of a blocked locomotion and restraints against communication arising in differentiated social structures.

3. Communications arising from the existence of emotional states. In this area data are almost completely lacking. Some theoretical distinctions were made and an experiment which is now in progress in this area was outlined.

43 Group norms and the active minority

JAMES G. MARCH

The analysis reported in this paper has two goals: (1) To test a basic hypothesis concerning the relationship between group norms and the active minority by using data from a local League of Women Voters organization. (2) To utilize the same data to suggest a beginning to a theory of group-approval functions.

A recurrent proposition in the literature of group research identifies a tendency toward fulfillment of group norms as a differentiating characteristic of the active minority. In their classic study of the Bank Wiring Room at Western Electric, Roethlisberger and Dickson (1939, pp. 412–23) assembled information on (among other things) the work norms of the group, the actual production and activities of the individual members of the group, and the structure of leadership and friendship within the group. Among the workers, 6,000 connections was considered to represent a reasonable work load for a single day. Individual production varied substantially around that norm, but the individuals who consistently came closest to satisfying this (and other) norms were found to rank high in the group (according to sociometric indices).

Homans (1950, p. 141) formulated these observations into the hypothesis that "the higher the rank of a person within a group, the more nearly his activities conform to the norms of the group." He found further support for the hypothesis in the research of Whyte (1943) and Newcomb (1943). Whyte, in his study of a street gang, frequently noted that the leader of the gang and his lieutenants fulfilled their obligations with much greater regularity than did the persons of lesser status within the group. In a group that valued skill at bowling and *Realpolitik*, the leaders were the best bowlers and the toughest politicians (p. 259). Newcomb's study of attitudes and leadership in a college community indicated that in a group distinguished by, and cognizant of, its radical reputation, leadership was closely related to the degree of radicalism (pp. 65–73).

More recently, Matthews (1953) has shown how relatively slight differences between the attitudes of party representatives in the United States Senate in 1949 were accentuated by the choice of leaders. Senate Democratic leaders were found to be more "Democratic" that the Democrats in the Senate as a whole, and Senate Republican leaders more "Republican" that the Republicans in the Senate as a whole.

Discussion

It was predicted that the active members of this organization [the League of Women Voters] would (as a group) be better educated, have higher incomes, be less Republican, and feel more independent of their husbands than would the in-

Excerpted from the **American Sociological Review,** 1954, 19, 733–41, with permission of the author and the American Sociological Association.

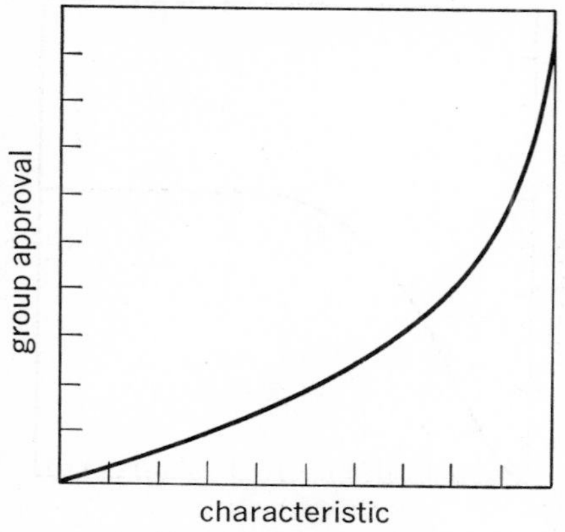

Figure 1. An unattainable-ideal norm.

active members (as a group). These predictions were based upon the observation that all of these characteristics distinguished the organization as a whole from the remainder of the community from which it was drawn and, consequently, could be considered to be norms of the organization.

The data presented [1] indicate support for the hypothesis with regard to the political attitudes (party affiliation and political independence) of the group, but do not appear to support the specific hypotheses with regard to education and income. In the case of income, there appears to be no difference either of central value or in the form of the distribution of family incomes among the active members and the inactive members. The data on education, on the other hand, indicate that although there is no difference in the median amount of education in the two subgroups, there is a significant difference in dispersion.

[1] These data, from a questionnaire completed by 32 members of a local League of Women Voters organization in an Eastern suburban town, have been omitted here.—Eds.

These results suggests that we should examine our conception of the characteristics of a group norm and the form of the function relating group approval to a variable valued by the group. The hypotheses that were originally outlined appear to have been based upon a conception of a norm as an *unattainable-ideal.* In such a norm, group approval is pictured as a monotonically-increasing continuous function of an individual characteristic. Figure 1 indicates roughly the type of function underlying such a prediction.

Although it is difficult to classify with certainty a norm as one of this type, we can recognize certain varieties of individual characteristics that in some groups approximate this model of a norm. Thus, the faster a man can run, the more acceptance and approval he is likely to secure from a group of track enthusiasts; the more saintly a man is, the greater will be the approval of a priestly group; the more brilliant a man is, the more approval he will gain in an academic group. The data in each of these cases are limited and (at least in the latter example) we may have some reservations about so describing the group norms involved, but at least in some circumstances this is a valid model. In the case of the League of Women Voters group studied, the data on political attitudes are consistent with the unattainable-ideal model; although, as is suggested below, it may also be described—and perhaps more correctly—in terms of a special case of another model.

A second model of a group-approval function seems to be indicated by the data presented above on educational level and activity within the League of Women Voters organization. Instead of thinking of a norm as an unattain-

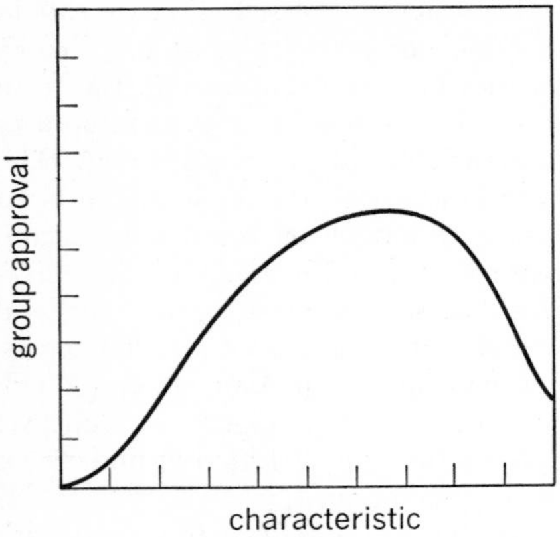

Figure 2. A preferred-value norm.

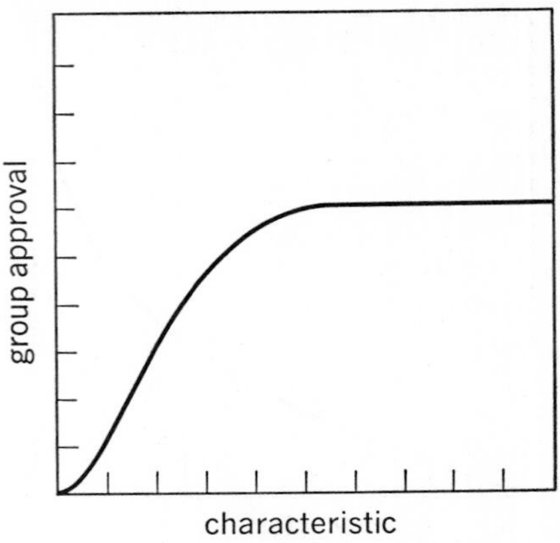

Figure 3. An attainable-ideal norm.

able-ideal, we can conceive it to be a *preferred-value*. In this case, deviations from the norm are measured in both directions rather than in just one as in the previous model. Group approval can be represented as a continuous function, monotonically-increasing up to the preferred-value and thereafter monotonically decreasing. Figure 2 indicates the form of this type of norm.

In the organization studied here, the average deviation from the median number of years of formal education was more than twice as large among the inactive members than it was among the active members; and the frequency of deviations of more than two years from the median of 16 was significantly greater among the actives than among the inactives. Similarly, the Roethlisberger and Dickson studies indicated that deviations on both sides of the work norms were disvalued. Both findings would fit the preferred-value model.

In addition, some norms that are manifestly of the unattainable-ideal type may be basically a segmentation of the preferred-value norm in which the range of values that have been achieved are all less than the preferred-value. Thus in the League organization, there is some evidence from personal conversations with members that there may be a limit to the extent of "un-Republicanism" to be positively valued. And in Newcomb's Bennington study, it is not clear whether there was some limit beyond which one lost favor by becoming more radical.

A third type of norm that seems important enough to be mentioned is one that can be called an *attainable-ideal*. Here the group-approval function is defined to be continuous and monotonically-increasing up to a point and constant thereafter, such as in Figure 3.

Consider a football team in possession of the ball on the opponents' twenty-yard line. A halfback at this point will gain approval as a function of the distance he can carry the ball before being tackled. In general, the farther he runs, the more approval he will gain; but after twenty yards, the approval function is a constant. The halfback is no greater a hero if he runs twenty-five yards than he is if he runs twenty-one. None of the norms examined above in the case of the League of Women Voters group appear to fit this model, but *a priori* it is of sufficient importance for inclusion as a major type of norm function.

All three of the above models have been defined by continuous functions; but there is no reason to assume that all group-approval functions will, in fact, be continuous. The most striking discontinuities are those associated with membership criteria. In the local League studied here, although age is apparently not related to activity within the group, no one under the age of twenty-one is a member. In effect, we have a two-step attainable-ideal function with a discontinuity at age twenty-one.

The three basic norm types constitute a beginning to a theory of norms. It is possible, for example, to describe the education norm of the League of Women Voters group in these terms.[2] The data indicated that the inactive members were more likely to deviate more than two years from the median number of years of formal education than were the active members. In Table 1 more complete information on deviations is provided. It can be seen that the differences between the two subgroups are concentrated in the "more than 2" category. This suggests that there is a range of tolerance around the education norm and that the group-approval function would basically be of the preferred-value type with considerable flattening around the norm. In addition, no one in the sample had less than 12 years of formal education. This suggests that the function should show

TABLE 1

DEVIATION FROM MEDIAN NUMBER OF YEARS OF EDUCATION BY ACTIVE AND INACTIVE MEMBERS

	Number of years of deviation				
	0	1	2	more than 2	
Active members	5	5	3	0	13
Inactive members	5	5	2	6	18*
	10	10	5	6	31*

* There is no information on one inactive member.

a constant low value up to the 12 year mark and a discontinuity at that point.

Since the information on political attitudes is dichotomized into attribute data, it is not feasible to propose a picture of the relevant norms involved. It has already been suggested that they may be best represented as a segment of a preferred-value norm, but the values that are assumed by the independent variable are thus far defined only in terms of attribute possession and group percentages. Further analysis is not practicable with the present data.

Summary and conclusions

The hypothesis that the more active members of an organization will tend to exhibit a higher degree of conformity to group norms than will the less active members has been tested in a local League of Women Voters organization. General support for the hypothesis has been revealed, but the failure of specific hypotheses has motivated a consideration of the theory of norms. Three models of group-approval functions have been presented and discussed representing an unattainable-ideal norm, a pre-

[2] From this point, the writer is assuming what was originally to be proved (i.e., that the active members fulfill group norms to a greater extent than do inactive members). Nonetheless, the exercise has some merit.

ferred-value norm, and an attainable-ideal norm.

In the judgment of the present writer, this type of theoretical formulation in the examination of group norms has considerable advantage over the attempt to deal with the concept of a norm without a conception of the characteristics of the group-approval function. For example, it can be used fruitfully in the study of role conflict. Consider the probable outcome of a conflict of roles involving sharply peaked preferred-value group norms as contrasted with the probable outcome where the function is relatively flat (cf. Stouffer, 1949, pp. 707–17).

In addition, it should be observed that when attention is focused upon the desirability of defining group-approval functions, there is a simultaneous suggestion of the need for developing techniques for doing so. How do we measure group approval? To what extent can group-approval functions be defined in such a way as to exhibit stability over time? Do group norms exist that cannot be portrayed in the two-dimensional space utilized in the models suggested here? If such norms exist, what type of conceptual model can fruitfully be applied in their analysis? These are some of the unanswered questions that have high priority in the possible further development of a theory of group-approval functions.

44 The basic response modes of conformity, independence, and anticonformity

RICHARD H. WILLIS

Definition of conformity

Conformity always means conformity to something. Because it is possible for more than one norm or standard to be salient in a given situation, it is possible for a particular act to constitute both conformity and nonconformity at the same time. As the term conformity is most frequently used, the behavior prescription derives either from a group norm or from a role requirement. In either case, the social pressure originates from normative expectations held by members of the group.

The following is proposed as a general conceptual definition of conformity, from which a number of operational definitions can be derived in various research settings:

Conformity is behavior intended to fulfill normative group expectations as these expectations are perceived by the individual.

A number of points deserve brief

Abridged from **Human Relations**, 1965, 18, 373–88 with permission of the author and the publisher.

discussion in connection with this definition. First, the individual need not be a member of the group, and, if not, the group can consist of a single other person.

The expectations are normative rather than predictive. That is, they are expectations about the kind of behavior the individual should execute, as opposed to expectations about the probable occurrence of events. These normative expectations include both role and norm expectations.

The expectations must be shared by the group to some extent, although complete consensus is not necessary. The greater the extent of dissensus among group members, the less the degree of *overt* conformity that can be exhibited. Dissensus places no limit on the individual's motivation to fulfill expectations, however.

It is necessary to distinguish between achieved and attempted conformity. The above definition specifically refers to the latter. Since conformity is here conceptualized as being first and foremost a motivational concept, attempted conformity is taken as the more basic, as important as achieved conformity may be. Because the motivational aspect of conformity is taken as fundamental, the definition specifies that the expectations are as perceived by the individual.

Not infrequently *conflict* is included as one of the defining characteristics of conformity. No conflict, no conformity —according to this view. However, even if the individual holds no opinion whatsoever on a particular issue, he may still be motivated to appear to go along with the group. Although the individual experiences no conflict in advocating the majority position, such behavior would be counted as conformity by the definition above.

Definition of nonconformity

One way of defining nonconformity is to equate it with behavior which fails to meet the conditions outlined above. Such a definition-by-exclusion is of so broad a scope, however, as to be of precious little use. It becomes necessary to inquire into the various ways in which behavior can fail to meet the conditions of conformity.

At this point it is appropriate to provide a broad formal definition of nonconformity:

> *Nonconformity is behavior which is intended to facilitate the attainment of some goal other than that of fulfilling perceived normative group expectations.*

If the individual pursues this other goal, whatever it may be, through actions which incidentally happen to fulfill the normative expectations of the group, it will appear as if he is conforming. In one sense he is, of course, but not in the sense that conformity was formally defined in the preceding section.

Customary usage of such terms as conformity, typicality, and normality fails to distinguish between conditions arising from various sources. Beloff (1958) has attempted to ameliorate the situation by introducing a distinction between two kinds of conformity which she labels *conventionality* and *acquiescence*. The former refers to the extent of agreement between an individual's responses and the mean responses of other individuals coming from similar backgrounds. The latter refers to the degree to which the individual yields to pressures arising from the immediate social situation. Measures of the two were found to be correlated, but imperfectly. By analogy, one can differentiate between *unconventionality* and *nonacquiescence*.

A further necessary distinction is that between nonconformity and *deviant behavior*. Deviant behavior customarily denotes patterns of behavior engendering social disapproval and negative sanctions (Clinard, 1963, p. 22), whereas nonconformity generally neither denotes nor connotes such disapproval.

Basic response modes

Assuming maximal relevance—that is, assuming that the normative expectations provide sufficient cues to allow the individual to select a single alternative from the set—four basic response modes can be identified. They are conformity, independence, anticonformity, and variability.

1. *Conformity*. It follows directly from the definition of conformity that, in its pure form, it consists of a *completely consistent* attempt to behave in accordance with normative expectations as perceived.

2. *Independence*. Pure independence behavior occurs whenever the individual perceives relevant normative expectations, but gives *zero weight* to these perceived expectations in formulating his decisions. This does not mean that he does not "weigh" the expectations in the sense of evaluating their importance and appropriateness, but rather that the outcome of this process of evaluation leads him to reject them as guides to his behavior. The independent person is one capable of *resisting* social pressures, rather than one who is unaware of them or who merely ignores them. He "sticks to his guns," so to speak.

It is important not to confuse dependent behavior with determined behavior. If the doctrine of determinism is accepted, it follows that all behavior is fully dependent in the sense of depending entirely upon some combination of antecedent factors. In this context, independent behavior has no meaning except that of undetermined or indeterminate behavior.

The terms dependence and independence are intended here in quite a different sense. The behavior of an independent person is affected less by the immediate and immediately preceding stimulus conditions than is the behavior of the dependent person. To draw a physical analogy, the independent person has greater "mass" than the dependent one; the greater the mass of an object, the less its course is deflected by an impinging force of given magnitude.

3. *Anticonformity*. In pure anticonformity behavior, the response is directly antithetical to the norm prescription. Pure anticonformity, like pure conformity, is pure dependence behavior. Assume that the individual is faced with a decision between two alternatives, one of which has been socially defined as right, the other as wrong. If the two alternatives can be considered to be diametrically opposed, then choosing the one defined as wrong would exemplify pure anticonformity. Anticonformity rarely, if ever, occurs in undiluted form, but as a limiting case it is of considerable theoretical importance.

4. *Variability*. Variability in pure form, like anticonformity, occurs only with two diametrically opposed response alternatives. The individual invariably changes his response if given an opportunity, without regard for the fact that

one of the responses is defined as correct and the other as wrong. Variability reflects complete indecision. As soon as the individual has responded in one way, he changes his mind.

Because the completely variable person changes his mind incessantly without giving any consideration to the norm, variability represents a second kind of independence from the social environment. It is the direct opposite of the "sticking to one's guns" variety of independence described above, but it does represent, nevertheless, the assignment of zero weight to the normative expectations of the group. The relation between conformity, independence, anticonformity, and variability can be diagrammed as shown in Figure 1. For obvious reasons, this scheme has been designated the *diamond model.* Points *C* and *A* represent pure conformity and anticonformity, respectively. Point *I* represents pure independence of the "sticking to one's guns" variety;

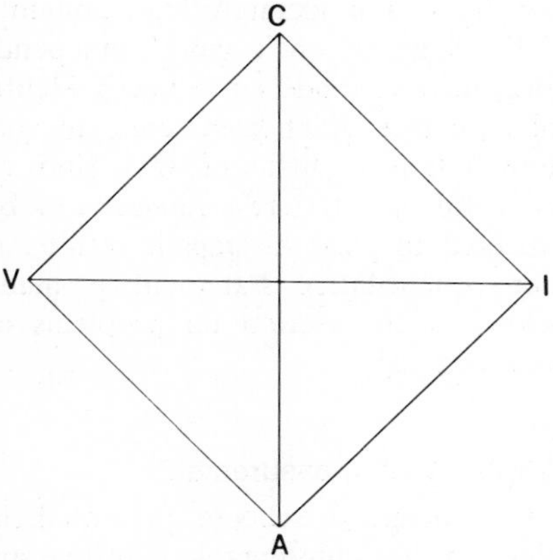

Figure 1. The diamond model interrelating conformity, independence, anticonformity, and variability. Variability is also a form of independence of the external source of social pressure.

Point *V* represents that second, more bizarre, lack of dependence upon the social environment termed variability.

If the name were not so clumsy, the horizontal axis could well be named the *independence-dependence-independence* axis, for each end corresponds to one kind of independence and the midpoint corresponds to complete dependence upon the norm. Pure dependence behavior, in fact, can fall anywhere along Line *CA*. Line *CI* represents the Asch/Jahoda model [see especially Asch, 1956; Jahoda, 1959], for positions along this line correspond to various combinations of conformity and independence, with no trace of anticonformity or variability. Figure 1 reveals very clearly the fact that the Asch/Jahoda conformity-independence model is a special case of the two-dimensional diamond model used here. Points located along the perimeter of the diamond represent combinations of two modes of response, while points within the diamond represent various combinations of all four basic modes of response.

The fact that the two dimensions of response in Figure 1 are drawn orthogonally does not imply that scores on the two dimensions are uncorrelated. The magnitude of such a correlation is an empirical matter, and it can be expected to vary from sample to sample and from one set of circumstances to another.

Why is the response space in Figure 1 diamond-shaped, rather than filling out the full square? The answer is that the conceptual framework does not permit all possible combinations; in fact, it does not allow just those combinations which lie outside the diamond. Consider for the moment just the right half of the diamond. The figure converges to the right, terminating at Point *I* because, to the extent that the individual acts independently, he cannot indulge in either conformity or anticonformity. This is so because conformity and anticonformity have been defined in terms of *intended* congruence rather than *incidental* congruence.

If the vertical axis represented degrees of congruence *per se*, whether motivated or not, the right half of the figure would be a rectangle rather than a triangle, for it is possible for the perfectly independent person to exhibit any degree of incidental congruence with the group norms. It is theoretically possible, for example, for the perfectly independent individual to behave exactly as the group norms prescribe, even though these group norms play no role in determining his behavior. An analogous argument can be developed for the left half of the diamond.

Another perspective on the interrelationships among the four modes of response can be gained by noting that the ends of the horizontal axis correspond to two kinds of independence, while the ends of the vertical axis correspond to two kinds of dependence. Yet another way of interpreting the diamond model is to think of independence as *self*-conformity and variability as *self*-anticonformity, thus yielding altogether two kinds of "conformity" and two kinds of "anticonformity."

The recognition of alternatives to conformity additional to independence has been noted by others. Pauline Pepinsky (1961) has used the term *negative conformity*, and Krech, Crutchfield, and Ballachey (1962, pp. 506–7) speak of *counterformity*. These latter authors consider conformity, independence, and counterformity to be interrelated as the vertices of a triangle, but do not identify the actual dimensions of response.

At an earlier time the author (Willis, 1963) also subscribed to a triangular model of social response. This model was similar to that of Krech, Crutchfield, and Ballachey, but the two dimensions of independence and net conformity were used to specify the interrelations between the three modes of response.

In many cases the diamond model and the author's earlier triangular model lead to identical conclusions. In those cases in which a difference arises, the picture given by the diamond model is to be preferred. One can say that the triangular model is like a map of North America that omits northern Canada. Most of the time such a map suffices, but not always. Likewise, one can usually make do without the variability vertex or even the entire left half of the diamond, but occasionally some individuals must be located to the left of center. As a general rule, if subjects display high or moderately high amounts of "sticking to one's guns" independence, the two models give nearly identical outcomes. If at least some subjects show relatively little of this kind of independence, the two models can be expected to yield discrepant results. A more quantitative statement is made below, in the section on problems of measurement.

Problems of measurement

The conceptual scheme presented in Figure 1 has considerable intuitive appeal, but in order for it to have scientific utility it is necessary to specify operations whereby individuals are located along each of the dimensions of response.

Consider the simplest social situation, the dyad. Assume that both individuals are required to make binary judgments about a series of stimuli. One frequently employed procedure in a social influence experiment is to require one of the subjects, *S*, to follow the other on each trial. Call this other, going first on each trial, the model, *M*. It would be customary in such a situation to define operationally the extent of conformity of *S* as the frequency with which *S* agrees with *M* over that expected by chance. Almost exactly this procedure was employed by Croner and Willis (1961), and literally hundreds of studies have been conducted which equate extent of conformity with level of congruence between the behavior of *S* and one or more others.

This "conformity as congruence" approach can be criticized for failing to differentiate between intended and incidental agreement, as required by the diamond model. Leverage on the problem can be gained by collecting more data on each trial. Let *S* make the first judgment, *M* the second, and finally give *S* an opportunity to change or reaffirm his initial response.

With three binary responses per trial, there are eight possible outcomes, and considerations of symmetry allow these to be grouped into four basic *response patterns:*

C: + − − or − + +
I: + − + or − + −
A: + + − or − − +
U: + + + or − − −

C, I, and A stand for conformity, independence, and anticonformity, respectively, for reasons which should be fairly apparent. Thus, for the trial outcome + − −, *M* disagrees with the initial judgment of *S*, and on his second response *S* changes his judgment so as to agree with that of *M*. This is clearly describable as conformity behavior. Response pattern *U* cannot be given such a clear-cut interpretation, and it is accordingly assigned the noncommittal label of *U* for uniformity.

The sum of the frequencies of *C* and *I* will be a constant, and the same is true for the sum of A and *U* frequencies. This is so because those trials on which *M agrees* with *S*'s initial response yield A and *U* patterns, whereas those trials on which *M disagrees* with *S*'s initial response yield *C* and *I* patterns. Using these relations, frequencies are converted to proportions of the maximum frequencies; designate these proportions *c, i, a,* and *u*. For example, if there are 50 disagreement trials in the series, and if the *C* pattern appears 20 times and the *I* pattern appears 30 times, the corresponding proportions are .40 and .60.

An *independence* score, *x*, and a *net conformity* score, *y*, are defined in the following way:

$$x = i + u - 1$$
$$y = c - a$$

These scores can be interpreted as the horizontal and vertical coördinates of *S*'s position in the diamond of Figure 1. Both scores can range between plus and minus one. A positive *x*-score indicates some degree of independence of the "sticking to one's guns" variety, while a negative *x*-score indicates some degree of variability. A positive *y*-score reflects a tendency to conform and a negative *y*-score indicates that the tendencies to anticonform outweigh those to conform. All obtainable score combinations correspond to locations on or within the diamond of Figure 1.

By having *S* respond both before and after exposure to the response of *M*, and by employing scoring formulas which yield precisely the possible combinations required by the conceptual model, a resolution of intended and incidental congruence is obtained. This conclusion, of course, involves certain assumptions, probably the most important being that *S*'s second response is a function only of his initial response and the response of *M*. A detailed explication of the logic underlying the *x* and *y* scoring equations has been presented elsewhere (Willis, 1963), although the argument was developed with reference to the triangular model and certain modifications (which will not be gone into here) would be necessary to adapt the argument to the diamond model.

45 Three processes of social influence

HERBERT C. KELMAN

The study of social influence

Social influence has been a central area of concern for experimental social psychology almost since its beginnings. Three general research traditions in this area can be distinguished: (1) the study of social influences on judgments, stemming from the earlier work on prestige suggestion (e.g. see Asch, 1952); (2) the study of social influences arising from small-group interaction (e.g. see Cartwright & Zander, 1953); and (3) the study of social influences arising from persuasive communications (e.g. see Hovland, *et al.*, 1953). In recent years, there has been a considerable convergence between these three traditions, going hand in hand with an increased interest in developing general principles of social influence and socially induced behavior change.

One result of these developments has been that many investigators found it necessary to make qualitative distinctions between different types of influence. In some cases, these distinctions arose primarily out of the observation that social influence may have qualitatively different effects, that it may produce different kinds of change. For example, under some conditions it may result in mere public conformity—in superficial changes on a verbal or overt level without accompanying changes in belief; in other situations it may result in private acceptance—in a change that is more general, more durable, more integrated with the person's own values (Festinger, 1953; Kelman, 1953; French & Raven, 1959; Jahoda, 1959). Other investigators found it necessary to make distinctions because they observed

Excerpted from "Processes of Opinion Change," **Public Opinion Quarterly**, 1961, 25, 57–78, with permission of the author and publisher.

that influence may occur for different reasons, that it may arise out of different motivations and orientations. For example, under some conditions influence may be primarily informational—the subject may conform to the influencing person or group because he views him as a source of valid information; in other situations influence may be primarily normative—the subject may conform in order to meet the positive expectations of the influencing person or group (Deutsch & Gerard, 1955; Thibaut & Strickland, 1956; Jackson & Saltzstein, 1958).

My own work can be viewed in the general context that I have outlined here. I started out with the distinction between public conformity and private acceptance, and tried to establish some of the distinct determinants of each. I became dissatisfied with this dichotomy as I began to look at important examples of social influence that could not be encompassed by it. I was especially impressed with the accounts of ideological conversion of the "true believer" variety, and with the recent accounts of "brainwashing," particularly the Chinese Communist methods of "thought reform" (Lifton, 1956). It is apparent that these experiences do not simply involve public conformity, but that indeed they produce a change in underlying beliefs. But it is equally apparent that they do not produce what we would usually consider private acceptance—changes that are in some sense integrated with the person's own value system and that have become independent of the external source. Rather, they seem to produce new beliefs that are isolated from the rest of the person's values and that are highly dependent on external support.

These considerations eventually led me to distinguish three processes of social influence, each characterized by a distinct set of antecedent and a distinct set of consequent conditions. I have called these processes *compliance, identification,* and *internalization.*

Three processes of social influence

Compliance can be said to occur when an individual accepts influence from another person or from a group because he hopes to achieve a favorable reaction from the other. He may be interested in attaining certain specific rewards or in avoiding certain specific punishments that the influencing agent controls. For example, an individual may make a special effort to express only "correct" opinions in order to gain admission into a particular group or social set, or in order to avoid being fired from his government job. Or, the individual may be concerned with gaining approval or avoiding disapproval from the influencing agent in a more general way. For example, some individuals may compulsively try to say the expected thing in all situations and please everyone with whom they come in contact, out of a disproportionate need for favorable responses from others of a direct and immediate kind. In any event, when the individual complies, he does what the agent wants him to do—or what he thinks the agent wants him to do—because he sees this as a way of achieving a desired response from him. He does not adopt the the induced behavior—for example, a particular opinion response—because he believes in its content, but because it is instrumental in the production of a satisfying social effect. What the individual learns, essentially, is to say or do the expected thing in special situations, regardless of what his private beliefs may be. Opinions adopted through compliance should be expressed only when the person's behavior is observable by the influencing agent.

Identification can be said to occur when an individual adopts behavior derived from another person or a group because this behavior is associated with a satisfying self-defining relationship to this person or group. By a self-defining relationship I mean a role relationship that forms a part of the person's self-image. Accepting influence through identification, then, is a way of establishing or maintaining the desired relationship to the other, and the self-definition that is anchored in this relationship.

The relationship that an individual tries to establish or maintain through identification may take different forms. It may take the form of classical identification, that is, of a relationship in which the individual takes over all or part of the role of the influencing agent. To the extent to which such a relationship exists, the individual defines his own role in terms of the role of the other. He attempts to be like or actually to *be* the other person. By saying what the other says, doing what he does, believing what he believes, the individual maintains this relationship and the satisfying self-definition that it provides him. An influencing agent who is likely to be an attractive object for such a relationship is one who occupies a role desired by the individual—who possesses those characteristics that the individual himself lacks—such as control in a situation in which the individual is helpless, direction in a situation in which he is disoriented, or belongingness in a situation in which he is isolated.

The behavior of the brainwashed prisoner in Communist China provides one example of this type of identification. By adopting the attitudes and beliefs of the prison authorities—including *their* evaluation of *him*—he attempts to regain his identity, which has been subjected to severe threats. But this kind of identification does not occur only in such severe crisis situations. It can also be observed, for example, in the context of socialization of children, where the taking over of parental attitudes and actions is a normal, and probably essential, part of personality development. The more or less conscious efforts involved when an individual learns to play a desired occupational role and imitates an appropriate role model would also exemplify this process. Here, of course, the individual is much more selective in the attitudes and actions he takes over from the other person. What is at stake is not his basic sense of identity or the stability of his self-concept, but rather his more limited "professional identity."

The self-defining relationship that an individual tries to establish or maintain through identification may also take the form of a reciprocal role relationship—that is, of a relationship in which the roles of the two parties are defined with reference to one another. An individual may be involved in a reciprocal relationship with another specific individual, as in a friendship relationship between two people. Or he may enact a social role which is defined with reference to another (reciprocal) role, as in the relationship between patient and doctor. A reciprocal-role relationship can be maintained only if the participants have mutually shared expectations of one another's behavior. Thus, if an individual finds a particular relationship satisfying, he will tend to behave in such a way as to meet the expectations of the other. In other words, he will tend to behave in line with the requirements of this particular relationship. This should be true regardless of whether the other is watching or not: quite apart from the reactions of the other, it is important to the individual's own self-concept to meet the expectations of his friendship role, for example, or those of his occupational role.

Thus, the acceptance of influence through identification should take place when the person sees the induced behavior as relevant to and required by a reciprocal-role relationship in which he is a participant. Acceptance of influence based on a reciprocal-role relationship is similar to that involved in classical identification in that it is a way of establishing or maintaining a satisfying self-defining relationship to another. The nature of the relationship differs, of course. In one case it is a relationship of identity; in the other, one of reciprocity. In the case of reciprocal-role relationships, the individual is not identifying with the other in the sense of taking over *his* identity, but in the sense of empathically reacting in terms of the other person's expectations, feelings, or needs.

Identification may also serve to maintain an individual's relationship to a group in which his self-definition is anchored. Such a relationship may have elements of classical identification as well as of reciprocal roles: to maintain his self-definition as a group member an individual, typically, has to model his behavior along particular lines and has to meet the expectations of his fellow members. An example of identification with a group would be the member of the Communist Party who derives strength and a sense of identity from his self-definition as part of the vanguard of the proletarian revolution and as an agent of historical destiny. A similar process, but at a low degree of intensity, is probably involved in many of the conventions that people acquire as part of their socialization into a particular group.

Identification is similar to compliance in that the individual does not adopt the induced behavior because its content per se is intrinsically satisfying. Identification differs from compliance, however, in that the individual actually believes in the opinions and actions that he adopts. The behavior is accepted both publicly and privately, and its manifestation does not depend on observability by the influencing agent. It does depend, however, on the role that an individual takes at any given moment in time. Only when the appropriate role is activated—only when the individual is acting within the relationship upon which the identification is based—will the induced opinions be expressed. The individual is not primarily concerned with pleasing the other, with giving him what he wants (as in compliance), but he is concerned with meeting the other's expectations for his own role performance. Thus, opinions adopted through identification do remain tied to the external source and dependent on social support. They are not integrated with the individual's value system, but rather tend to be isolated from the rest of his values—to remain encapsulated.

Finally, *internalization* can be said to occur when an individual accepts influence because the induced behavior is congruent with his value system. It is the content of the induced behavior that is intrinsically rewarding here. The individual adopts it because he finds it useful for the solution of a problem, or because it is congenial to his own orientation, or because it is demanded by his own values—in short, because he perceives it as inherently conducive to the maximization of his values. The characteristics of the influencing agent do play an important role in internalization, but the crucial dimension here—as we shall see below—is the agent's credibility, that is, his relation to the content.

The most obvious examples of internalization are those that involve the evaluation and acceptance of induced behavior on rational grounds. A person may adopt the recommendations of an expert, for example, because he finds them relevant to his own problems and congruent with his own values. Typically, when internalization is involved, he will not accept these recommendations *in toto* but modify them to some degree so that they will fit his own unique situation. Or a visitor to a foreign country may be challenged by the different patterns of behavior to which he is exposed, and he may decide to adopt them (again, selectively and in modified form) because he finds them more in keeping with his own values than the patterns in his home country. I am not implying, of course, that internalization is always involved in the situations mentioned. One would speak of internalization only if acceptance of influence took the particular form that I described.

Internalization, however, does not necessarily involve the adoption of induced behavior on rational grounds. I would not want to equate internalization with rationality, even though the description of the process has decidedly rationalist overtones. For example, I would characterize as internalization the adoption of beliefs because of their congruence with a value system that is basically *irrational.* Thus, an authoritarian individual may adopt certain racist attitudes because they fit into his paranoid, irrational view of the world. Presumably, what is involved here is internalization, since it is the content of the induced behavior and its relation to the person's value system that is satisfying. Similarly, it should be noted that congruence with a person's value system does not necessarily imply logical consistency. Behavior would be congruent if, in some way or other, it fit into the person's value system, if it seemed to belong there and be demanded by it.

It follows from this conception that behavior adopted through internalization is in some way—rational or otherwise—integrated with the individual's existing values. It becomes part of a personal system, as distinguished from a system of social-role expectations. Such behavior gradually becomes independent of the external source. Its manifestation depends neither on observability by the influencing agent nor on the activation of the relevant role, but on the extent to which the underlying values have been made relevant by the issues under consideration. This does not mean that the individual will invariably express internalized opinions, regardless of the social situation. In any specific situation, he has to choose among competing values in the face of a variety of situational requirements. It does mean, however, that these opinions will at least enter into competition with other alternatives whenever they are relevant in content.

It should be stressed that the three

processes are not mutually exclusive. While they have been defined in terms of pure cases, they do not generally occur in pure form in real-life situations. The examples that have been given are, at best, situations in which a particular process predominates and determines the central features of the interaction.

Antecedents and consequents of the three processes

For each of the three processes, a distinct set of antecedents and a distinct set of consequents have been proposed. These are summarized in the table below. First, with respect to the antecedents of the three processes, it should be noted that no systematic quantitative differences between them are hypothesized. The probability of each process is presented as a function of the same three determinants: the importance of the induction for the individual's goal achievement, the power of the influencing agent, and the prepotency of the induced response. For each process, the magnitude of these determinants may vary over the entire range: each may be based on an induction with varying degrees of importance, on an influencing agent with varying degrees of power, and so on. The processes differ only in terms of the *qualitative* form that these determinants take. They differ, as can be seen in the table, in terms of the *basis* for the importance of the induction, the *source* of the influencing agent's power, and the *manner* of achieving prepotency of the induced response.

SUMMARY OF THE DISTINCTIONS BETWEEN THE THREE PROCESSES

	COMPLIANCE	IDENTIFICATION	INTERNALIZATION
ANTECEDENTS:			
1. Basis for the *importance of the induction*	Concern with social effect of behavior	Concern with social anchorage of behavior	Concern with value congruence of behavior
2. Source of *power of the influencing agent*	Means control	Attractiveness	Credibility
3. Manner of achieving *prepotency of the induced response*	Limitation of choice behavior	Delineation of role requirements	Reorganization of means-ends framework
CONSEQUENTS:			
1. Conditions of performance of induced response	Surveillance by influencing agent	Salience of relationship to agent	Relevance of values to issue
2. Conditions of change and extinction of induced response	Changed perception of conditions for social rewards	Changed perception of conditions for satisfying self-defining relationships	Changed perception of conditions for value maximization
3. Type of behavior system in which induced response is embedded	External demands of a specific setting	Expectations defining a specific role	Person's value system

1. The processes can be distinguished in terms of the basis for the importance of the induction, that is, in terms of the nature of the motivational system that is activated in the influence situation. What is it about the influence situation that makes it important, that makes it relevant to the individual's goals? What are the primary concerns that the individual brings to the situation or that are aroused by it? The differences between the three processes in this respect are implicit in the descriptions of the processes given above: (a) To the extent that the individual is concerned—for whatever reason—with the *social effect* of his behavior, influence will tend to take the form of compliance. (b) To the extent that he is concerned with the *social anchorage* of his behavior, influence will tend to take the form of identification. (c) To the extent that he is concerned with the *value congruence* of his behavior (rational or otherwise), influence will tend to take the form of internalization.

2. A difference between the three processes in terms of the source of the influencing agent's power is hypothesized. (a) To the extent that the agent's power is based on his *means control*, influence will tend to take the form of compliance. An agent possesses means control if he is in a position to supply or withhold means needed by the individual for the achievement of his goals. The perception of means control may depend on the agent's *actual* control over specific rewards and punishments, or on his *potential* control, which would be related to his position in the social structure (his status, authority, or general prestige). (b) To the extent that the agent's power is based on his *attractiveness*, influence will tend to take the form of identification. An agent is attractive if he occupies a role which the individual himself desires (see Whiting, 1959) or if he occupies a role reciprocal to one the individual wants to establish or maintain. The term "attractiveness," as used here, does not refer to the possession of qualities that make a person likable, but rather to the possession of qualities on the part of the agent that make a continued relationship to him particularly desirable. In other words, an agent is attractive when the individual is able to derive satisfaction from a self-definition with reference to him. (c) To the extent that the agent's power is based on his *credibility*, influence will tend to take the form of internalization. An agent possesses credibility if his statements are considered truthful and valid, and hence worthy of serious consideration. Hovland, Janis, and Kelley (1953, p. 21) distinguish two bases for credibility: expertness and trustworthiness. In other words, an agent may be perceived as possessing credibility because he is likely to *know* the truth, or because he is likely to *tell* the truth. Trustworthiness, in turn, may be related to over-all respect, likemindedness, and lack of vested interest.

3. It is proposed that the three processes differ in terms of the way in which prepotency is achieved. (a) To the extent that the induced response becomes prepotent—that is, becomes a "distinguished path" relative to alternative response possibilities—because the individual's choice behavior is limited, influence will tend to take the form of compliance. This may happen if the individual is pressured into the induced response, or if alternative responses are blocked. The induced response thus becomes prepotent because it is, es-

sentially, the only response permitted: the individual sees himself as having no choice and as being restricted to this particular alternative. (b) To the extent that the induced response becomes prepotent because the requirements of a particular role are delineated, influence will tend to take the form of identification. This may happen if the situation is defined in terms of a particular role relationship and the demands of that role are more or less clearly specified; for instance, if this role is made especially salient and the expectations deriving from it dominate the field. Or it may happen if alternative roles are made ineffective because the situation is ambiguous and consensual validation is lacking. The induced response thus becomes prepotent because it is one of the few alternatives available to the individual: his choice behavior may be unrestricted, but his opportunity for selecting alternative responses is limited by the fact that he is operating exclusively from the point of view of a particular role system. (c) Finally, to the extent that the induced response becomes prepotent because there has been a reorganization in the individual's conception of means-ends relationships, influence will tend to take the form of internalization. This may happen if the implications of the induced response for certain important values—implications of which the individual had been unaware heretofore—are brought out, or if the advantages of the induced response as a path to the individual's goals, compared to the various alternatives that are available, are made apparent. The induced response thus becomes prepotent because it has taken on a new meaning: as the relationships between various means and ends become restructured, it emerges as the preferred course of action in terms of the person's own values.

Depending, then, on the nature of these three antecedents, the influence process will take the form of compliance, identification, or internalization. Each of these corresponds to a characteristic pattern of internal responses—thoughts and feelings—in which the individual engages as he accepts influence. The resulting changes will, in turn, be different for the three processes, as indicated in the second half of the table. Here, again, it is assumed that there are no systematic quantitative differences between the processes, but rather qualitative variations in the subsequent histories of behavior adopted through each process.

1. It is proposed that the processes differ in terms of the subsequent conditions under which the induced response will be performed or expressed. (a) When an individual adopts an induced response through compliance, he tends to perform it only under conditions of *surveillance* by the influencing agent. These conditions are met if the agent is physically present, or if he is likely to find out about the individual's actions. (b) When an individual adopts an induced response through identification, he tends to perform it only under conditions of *salience* of his relationship to the agent. That is, the occurrence of the behavior will depend on the extent to which the person's relationship to the agent has been engaged in the situation. Somehow this relationship has to be brought into focus and the individual has to be acting within the particular role that is involved in the identification. This does not necessarily mean, however, that he is consciously aware of the relationship; the role can be activated without such awareness. (c)

When an individual adopts an induced response through internalization, he tends to perform it under conditions of *relevance of the values* that were initially involved in the influence situation. The behavior will tend to occur whenever these values are activated by the issues under consideration in a given situation, quite regardless of surveillance or salience of the influencing agent. This does not mean, of course, that the behavior will occur every time it becomes relevant. It may be out-competed by other responses in certain situations. The probability of occurrence with a given degree of issue relevance will depend on the strength of the internalized behavior.

2. It is hypothesized that responses adoped through the three processes will differ in terms of the conditions under which they will subsequently be abandoned or changed. (a) A response adopted through compliance will be abandoned if it is no longer perceived as the best path toward the attainment of social rewards. (b) A response adopted through identification will be abandoned if it is no longer perceived as the best path toward the maintenance or establishment of satisfying self-defining relationships. (c) A response adopted through internalization will be abandoned if it is no longer perceived as the best path toward the maximization of the individual's values.

3. Finally, it is hypothesized that responses adopted through the three processes will differ from each other along certain qualitative dimensions. These can best be summarized, perhaps, by referring to the type of behavior system in which the induced response is embedded. (a) Behavior adopted through compliance is part of a system of external demands that characterize a specific setting. In other words, it is part of the rules of conduct that an individual learns in order to get along in a particular situation or series of situations. The behavior tends to be related to the person's values only in an instrumental rather than an intrinsic way. As long as opinions, for example, remain at that level, the individual will tend to regard them as not really representative of his true beliefs. (b) Behavior adopted through identification is part of a system of expectations defining a particular role—whether this is the role of the other which he is taking over, or a role reciprocal to the other's. This behavior will be regarded by the person as representing himself, and may in fact form an important aspect of himself. It will tend to be isolated, however, from the rest of the person's values—to have little interplay with them. In extreme cases, the system in which the induced response is embedded may be encapsulated and function almost like a foreign body within the person. The induced responses here will be relatively inflexible and stereotyped. (c) Behavior adopted through internalization is part of an internal system. It is fitted into the person's basic framework of values and is congruent with it. This does not imply complete consistency: the degree of consistency can vary for different individuals and different areas of behavior. It does mean, however, that there is some interplay between the new beliefs and the rest of the person's values. The new behavior can serve to modify existing beliefs and can in turn be modified by them. As a result of this interaction, behavior adopted through internalization will tend to be relatively idiosyncratic, flexible, complex, and differentiated.

46 Social behavior as exchange

GEORGE C. HOMANS

The problems of small-group research

This essay will hope to honor the memory of Georg Simmel in two different ways. So far as it pretends to be suggestive rather than conclusive, its tone will be Simmel's; and its subject, too, will be one of his. Because Simmel, in essays such as those on sociability, games, coquetry, and conversation, was an analyst of elementary social behavior, we call him an ancestor of what is known today as small-group research. For what we are really studying in small groups is elementary social behavior: what happens when two or three persons are in a position to influence one another, the sort of thing of which those massive structures called "classes," "firms," "communities," and "societies" must ultimately be composed.

As I survey small-group research today, I feel that, apart from just keeping on with it, three sorts of things need to be done. The first is to show the relation between the results of experimental work done under laboratory conditions and the results of *quasi*-anthropological field research on what those of us who do it are pleased to call "real-life" groups in industry and elsewhere. If the experimental work has anything to do with real life—and I am persuaded that it has everything to do—its propositions cannot be inconsistent with those discovered through the field work. But the consistency has not yet been demonstrated in any systematic way.

The second job is to pull together in some set of general propositions the actual results, from the laboratory and from the field, of work on small groups—propositions that at least sum up, to an approximation, what happens in elementary social behavior, even though we may not be able to explain why the propositions should take the form they do. A great amount of work has been done, and more appears every day, but what it all amounts to in the shape of a set of propositions from which, under specified conditions, many of the observational results might be derived, is not at all clear—and yet to state such a set is the first aim of science.

The third job is to begin to show how the propositions that empirically hold good in small groups may be derived from some set of still more general propositions. "Still more general" means only that empirical propositions other than ours may also be derived from the set. This derivation would constitute the explanatory stage in the science of elementary social behavior, for explanation *is* derivation (see Braithwaite, 1953). (I myself suspect that the more general set will turn out to contain the propositions of behavioral psychology. I hold myself to be an "ultimate psychological reductionist," but I cannot know that I am right so long as the reduction has not been carried out.)

I have come to think that all three of

Reprinted from the **American Journal of Sociology**, 1958, 63, 597–606, with permission of the author and the University of Chicago Press.

these jobs would be furthered by our adopting the view that interaction between persons is an exchange of goods, material and non-material. This is one of the oldest theories of social behavior, and one that we still use every day to interpret our own behavior, as when we say, "I found so-and-so rewarding"; or "I got a great deal out of him"; or, even, "Talking with him took a great deal out of me." But, perhaps just because it is so obvious, this view has been much neglected by social scientists. So far as I know, the only theoretical work that makes explicit use of it is Marcel Mauss's *Essai sur le don*, published in 1925, which is ancient as social science goes (see Cunnison, 1954). It may be that the tradition of neglect is now changing and that, for instance, the psychologists who interpret behavior in terms of transactions may be coming back to something of the sort I have in mind (see Newcomb, 1956).

An incidental advantage of an exchange theory is that it might bring sociology closer to economics—that science of man most advanced, most capable of application, and, intellectually, most isolated. Economics studies exchange carried out under special circumstances and with a most useful built-in numerical measure of value. What are the laws of the general phenomenon of which economic behavior is one class?

In what follows I shall suggest some reasons for the usefulness of a theory of social behavior as exchange and suggest the nature of the propositions such a theory might contain.

An exchange paradigm

I start with the link to behavioral psychology and the kind of statement it makes about the behavior of an experimental animal such as the pigeon (Skinner, 1953). As a pigeon explores its cage in the laboratory, it happens to peck a target, whereupon the psychologist feeds it corn. The evidence is that it will peck the target again; it has learned the behavior, or, as my friend Skinner says, the behavior has been reinforced, and the pigeon has undergone *operant conditioning*. This kind of psychologist is not interested in how the behavior was learned: "learning theory" is a poor name for his field. Instead, he is interested in what determines changes in the rate of emission of learned behavior, whether pecks at a target or something else.

The more hungry the pigeon, the less corn or other food it has gotten in the recent past, the more often it will peck. By the same token, if the behavior is often reinforced, if the pigeon is given much corn every time it pecks, the rate of emission will fall off as the pigeon gets *satiated*. If, on the other hand, the behavior is not reinforced at all, then, too, its rate of emission will tend to fall off, though a long time may pass before it stops altogether, before it is *extinguished*. In the emission of many kinds of behavior the pigeon incurs *aversive stimulation*, or what I shall call "cost" for short, and this, too, will lead in time to a decrease in the emission rate. Fatigue is an example of a "cost." Extinction, satiation, and cost, by decreasing the rate of emission of a particular kind of behavior, render more probable the emission of some other kind of behavior, including doing nothing. I shall only add that even a hard-boiled psychologist puts "emotional" behavior, as well as such things as pecking, among the unconditioned responses that may be reinforced in operant conditioning. As a statement of the propositions of behavioral psychology, the foregoing is, of course, inadequate for any purpose except my present one.

We may look on the pigeon as engaged in an exchange—pecks for corn—with the psychologist, but let us not dwell upon that, for the behavior of the pigeon hardly determines the behavior of the psychologist at all. Let us turn to a situation where the exchange is real, that is, where the determination is mutual. Suppose we are dealing with two men. Each is emitting behavior reinforced to some degree by the behavior of the other. How it was in the past that each learned the behavior he emits and how he learned to find the other's behavior reinforcing we are not concerned with. It is enough that each does find the other's behavior reinforcing, and I shall call the reinforcers—the equivalent of the pigeon's corn—*values*, for this, I think, is what we mean by this term. As he emits behavior, each man may incur costs, and each man has more than one course of behavior open to him.

This seems to me the paradigm of elementary social behavior, and the problem of the elementary sociologist is to state propositions relating the variations in the values and costs of each man to his frequency distribution of behavior among alternatives, where the values (in the mathematical sense) taken by these variables for one man determine in part their values for the other (Skinner, 1953, pp. 297–329; Parsons & Shils, 1951, pp. 14–16).

I see no reason to believe that the propositions of behavioral psychology do not apply to this situation, though the complexity of their implications in the concrete case may be great indeed. In particular, we must suppose that, with men as with pigeons, an increase in extinction, satiation, or aversive stimulation of any one kind of behavior will increase the probability of emission of some other kind. The problem is not, as it is often stated, merely, what a man's values are, what he has learned in the past to find reinforcing, but how much of any one value his behavior is getting him now. The more he gets, the less valuable any further unit of that value is to him, and the less often he will emit behavior reinforced by it.

The influence process

We do not, I think, possess the kind of studies of two-person interaction that would either bear out these propositions or fail to do so. But we do have studies of larger numbers of persons that suggest that they may apply, notably the studies by Festinger, Schachter, Back, and their associates on the dynamics of influence. One of the variables they work with they call *cohesiveness*, defined as anything that attracts people to take part in a group. Cohesiveness is a value variable; it refers to the degree of reinforcement people find in the activities of the group. Festinger and his colleagues consider two kinds of reinforcing activity: the symbolic behavior we call "social approval" (sentiment) and activity valuable in other ways, such as doing something interesting.

The other variable they work with they call *communication* and others call *interaction*. This is a frequency variable; it is a measure of the frequency of emission of valuable and costly verbal behavior. We must bear in mind that, in general, the one kind of variable is a function of the other.

Festinger and his co-workers show

that the more cohesive a group is, that is, the more valuable the sentiment or activity the members exchange with one another, the greater the average frequency of interaction of the members (Back, 1950). With men, as with pigeons, the greater the reinforcement, the more often is the reinforced behavior emitted. The more cohesive a group, too, the greater the change that members can produce in the behavior of other members in the direction of rendering these activities more valuable (Schachter, *et al.*, 1951). That is, the more valuable the activities that members get, the more valuable those that they must give. For if a person is emitting behavior of a certain kind, and other people do not find it particularly rewarding, these others will suffer their own production of sentiment and activity, in time, to fall off. But perhaps the first person has found their sentiment and activity rewarding, and, if he is to keep on getting them, he must make his own behavior more valuable to the others. In short, the propositions of behavioral psychology imply a tendency toward a certain proportionality between the value to others of the behavior a man gives them and the value to him of the behavior they give him (Skinner, 1953, p. 100).

Schachter also studied the behavior of members of a group toward two kinds of other members, "conformers" and "deviates" (1951). I assume that conformers are people whose activity the other members find valuable. For conformity is behavior that coincides to a degree with some group standard or norm, and the only meaning I can assign to *norm* is "a verbal description of behavior that many members find it valuable for the actual behavior of themselves and others to conform to." By the same token, a deviate is a member whose behavior is not particularly valuable. Now Schachter shows that, as the members of a group come to see another member as a deviate, their interaction with him—communication addressed to getting him to change his behavior—goes up, the faster the more cohesive the group. The members need not talk to the other conformers so much; they are relatively satiated by the conformers' behavior: they have gotten what they want out of them. But if the deviate, by failing to change his behavior, fails to reinforce the members, they start to withhold social approval from him: the deviate gets low sociometric choice at the end of the experiment. And in the most cohesive groups—those Schachter calls "high cohesive-relevant"—interaction with the deviate also falls off in the end and is lowest among those members that rejected him most strongly, as if they had given him up as a bad job. But how plonking can we get? These findings are utterly in line with everyday experience.

Practical equilibrium

At the beginning of this paper I suggested that one of the tasks of small-group research was to show the relation between the results of experimental work done under laboratory conditions and the results of field research on real-life small groups. Now the latter often appear to be in practical equilibrium, and by this I mean nothing fancy. I do not mean that all real-life groups are in equilibrium. I certainly do not mean that all groups must tend to equilibrium. I do not mean that groups have built-in antidotes to change: There is no homeostasis here. I do not mean that we assume equilibrium. I mean only that we sometimes *observe* it, that for the time we are with a group—and it is often short—there is no great change in the values of the variables we choose to measure. If, for instance, person A is interacting with B more than with C both at the beginning and at the end of the study, then at least by this crude measure the group is in equilibrium.

Many of the Festinger-Schachter studies are experimental, and their propositions about the process of influence seem to me to imply the kind of proposition that empirically holds good of real-life groups in practical equilibrium. For instance, Festinger *et al.* find that, the more cohesive a group is, the greater the change that members can produce in the behavior of others members. If the influence is exerted in the direction of conformity to group norms, then, when the process of influence has accomplished all the change of which it is capable, the proposition should hold good that, the more cohesive a group is, the larger the number of members that conform to its norms. And it does hold good (Festinger, *et al.*, 1950).

Again, Schachter found, in the experiment I summarized above, that in the most cohesive groups and at the end, when the effort to influence the deviate had failed, members interacted little with the deviate and gave him little in the way of sociometric choice. Now two of the propositions that hold good most often of real-life groups in practical equilibrium are precisely that the more closely a member's activity conforms to the norms the more interaction he receives from other members and the more liking choices he gets from them too. From these main propositions a number of others may be derived that also hold good (Homans, 1950; Riecken & Homans, 1954).

Yet we must ever remember that the truth of the proposition linking conformity to liking may on occasion be masked by the truth of other propositions. If, for instance, the man that conforms to the norms most closely also exerts some authority over the group, this may render liking for him somewhat less than it might otherwise have been (see Homans, 1950, pp. 244–8; Hare, Borgatta, & Bales, 1953).

Be that as it may, I suggest that the laboratory experiments on influence imply propositions about the behavior of members of small groups, when the process of influence has worked itself out, that are identical with propositions that hold good of real-life groups in equilibrium. This is hardly surprising if all we mean by equilibrium is that all the change of which the system is, under present conditions, capable has been effected, so that no further change occurs. Nor would this be the first time that statics has turned out to be a special case of dynamics.

Profit and social control

Though I have treated equilibrium as an observed fact, it is a fact that cries for explanation. I shall not, as structural functional sociologists do, use an assumed equilibrium as a means of explaining, or trying to explain, why the other features of a social system should be what they are. Rather, I shall take practical equilibrium as something that is itself to be explained by the other features of the system.

If every member of a group emits at the end of, and during, a period of time much the same kinds of behavior and in much the same frequencies as he did at the beginning, the group is for that period in equilibrium. Let us then ask why any one member's behavior should persist. Suppose he is emitting behavior of value A_1. Why does he not let his behavior get worse (less valuable or reinforcing to the others) until it stands at $A_1 - \Delta A$? True, the sentiments expressed by others toward him are apt to decline in value (become less reinforcing to him), so that what he gets from them may be $S_1 - \Delta S$. But it is conceivable that, since most activity carries cost, a decline in the value of what he emits will mean a reduction in cost to him that more than offsets his losses in sentiment. Where, then, does he stabilize his behavior? This is the problem of social control (Homans, 1950, pp. 281–301).

Mankind has always assumed that a person stabilizes his behavior, at least in the short run, at the point where he is doing the best he can for himself under the circumstances, though his best may not be a "rational" best, and what he can do may not be at all easy to specify, except that he is not apt to think like one of the theoretical antagonists in the *Theory of Games*. Before a sociologist rejects this answer out of hand for its horrid profit-seeking implications, he will do well to ask himself if he can offer any other answer to the question posed. I think he will find that he cannot. Yet experiments designed to test the truth of the answer are extraordinarily rare.

I shall review one that seems to me to provide a little support for the theory, though it was not meant to do so. The experiment is reported by H. B. Gerard, a member of the Festinger-Schachter team, under the title "The Anchorage of Opinions in Face-to-Face Groups" (1954). The experimenter formed artificial groups whose members met to discuss a case in industrial relations and to express their opinions about its probable outcome. The groups were of two kinds: high-attraction groups, whose members were told that they would like one another very much, and low-attraction groups, whose members were told that they would not find one another particularly likable.

At a later time the experimenter called the members in separately, asked them again to express their opinions on the outcome of the case, and counted the number that had changed their opinions to bring them into accord with those of other members of their groups. At the same time, a paid participant entered into a further discussion of the case with each member, always taking, on the probable outcome of the case, a position opposed to that taken by the bulk of the other members of the group to which the person belonged. The experimenter counted the number of persons shifting toward the opinion of the paid participant.

The experiment had many interesting results, from which I choose only those summed up in Tables 1 and 2. The

TABLE 1

PERCENTAGE OF SUBJECTS CHANGING TOWARD SOMEONE IN THE GROUP

	Agreement	Mild disagreement	Strong disagreement
High attraction	0	12	44
Low attraction	0	15	9

TABLE 2

PERCENTAGE OF SUBJECTS CHANGING TOWARD THE PAID PARTICIPANT

	Agreement	Mild disagreement	Strong disagreement
High attraction	7	13	25
Low attraction	20	38	8

three different agreement classes are made up of people who, at the original sessions, expressed different degrees of agreement with the opinions of other members of their groups. And the figure 44, for instance, means that, of all members of high-attraction groups whose initial opinions were strongly in disagreement with those of other members, 44 per cent shifted their opinion later toward that of others.

In these results the experimenter seems to have been interested only in the differences in the sums of the rows, which show that there is more shifting toward the group, and less shifting toward the paid participant, in the high-attraction than in the low-attraction condition. This is in line with a proposition suggested earlier. If you think that the members of a group can give you much—in this case, liking—you are apt to give them much—in this case, a change to an opinion in accordance with their views—or you will not get the liking. And, by the same token, if the group can give you little of value, you will not be ready to give it much of value. Indeed, you may change your opinion so as to depart from agreement even further, to move, that is, toward the view held by the paid participant.

So far so good, but, when I first scanned these tables, I was less struck by the difference between them than by their similarity. The same classes of people in both tables showed much the same relative propensities to change their opinions, no matter whether the change was toward the group or toward the paid participant. We see, for instance, that those who change least are the high-attraction, agreement people and the low-attraction, strong-disagreement ones. And those who change most are the high-attraction, strong-disagreement people and the low-attraction, mild-disagreement ones.

How am I to interpret these particular results? Since the experimenter did not discuss them, I am free to offer my own explanation. The behavior emitted by the subjects is opinion and changes in opinion. For this behavior they have learned to expect two possible kinds of reinforcement. Agreement with the group gets the subject favorable sentiment (acceptance) from it, and the experiment was designed to give this reinforcement a higher value in the high-attraction condition than in the low-attraction one. The second kind of possible reinforcement is what I shall call the "maintenance of one's personal integrity," which a subject gets by sticking to his own opinion in the face of disagreement with the group. The experimenter does not mention this reward, but I cannot make sense of the results without something much like it. In different degrees for different subjects, depending on their initial positions, these rewards are in competition with one another: they are alternatives. They are not absolutely scarce goods, but some persons cannot get both at once.

Since the rewards are alternatives, let me introduce a familiar assumption from economics—that the cost of a particular course of action is the equivalent of the foregone value of an alternative (Stigler, 1952, p. 99)—and then add the definition: Profit = Reward − Cost.

Now consider the persons in the corresponding cells of the two tables. The behavior of the high-attraction, agreement people gets them much in the way of acceptance by the group, and for it they must give up little in the way of personal integrity, for their views are from the start in accord with those of the group. Their profit is high, and they are not prone to change their behavior. The low-attraction, strong-disagreement people are getting much in integrity, and they are not giving up for it much in valuable acceptance, for they are members of low-attraction groups. Reward less cost is high for them, too, and they change little. The high-attraction, strong-disagreement people are getting much in the way of integrity, but their costs in doing so are high, too, for they are in high-attraction groups and thus foregoing much valuable acceptance by the group. Their profit is low, and they are very apt to change, either toward the group or toward the paid participant, from whom they think, perhaps, they will get some acceptance while maintaining some integrity. The low-attraction, mild-disagreement people do not get much in the way of integrity, for they are only in mild disagreement with the group, but neither are they giving up much in acceptance, for they are members of low-attraction groups. Their rewards are low; their costs are low too, and their profit—the difference between the two—is also low. In their low profit they resemble the high-attraction, strong-disagreement people, and, like them, they are prone to change their opinions, in this case, more toward the paid participant. The subjects in the other two cells, who have medium profits, display medium propensities to change.

If we define profit as reward less cost, and if cost is value foregone, I suggest that we have here some evidence for the proposition that change in behavior is greatest when perceived profit is least. This constitutes no direct demonstration that change in behavior is least when profit is greatest, but if, whenever a man's behavior brought him a balance of reward and cost, he changed his behavior away from what got him, under the circumstances, the less profit, there might well come a time when his behavior would not change further. That is, his behavior would be stabilized, at least for the time being. And, so far as this were true for every member of a group, the group would have a social organization in equilibrium.

I do not say that a member would stabilize his behavior at the point of greatest conceivable profit to himself, because his profit is partly at the mercy of the behavior of others. It is a commonplace that the short-run pursuit of profit by several persons often lands them in positions where all are worse off than they might conceivably be. I do not say that the paths of behavioral change in which a member pursues his profit under the condition that others are pursuing theirs too are easy to describe or predict; and we can readily conceive that in jockeying for position they might never arrive at any equilibrium at all.

Distributive justice

Yet practical equilibrium is often observed, and thus some further condition may make its attainment, under some circumstance, more probable than would the individual pursuit of profit left to itself. I can offer evidence for this further condition only in the behavior of subgroups and not in that of individuals. Suppose that there are two subgroups, working close together in a factory, the job of one being somewhat different from that of the other. And suppose that the members of the first complain and say: "We are getting the same pay as they are. We ought to get just a couple of dollars a week more to show that our work is more responsible." When you ask them what they mean by "more responsible," they say that, if they do their work wrong, more damage can result, and so they are under more pressure to take care (Homans, 1953). Something like this is a common feature of industrial behavior. It is at the heart of disputes not over absolute wages but over wage differentials—indeed, at the heart of disputes over rewards other than wages.

In what kind of proposition may we express observations like these? We may say that wages and responsibility give status in the group, in the sense that a man who takes high responsibility and gets high wages is admired, other things equal. Then, if the members of one group score higher on responsibility than do the members of another, there is a felt need on the part of the first to score higher on pay too. There is a pressure, which shows itself in complaints, to bring the *status factors,* as I have called them, into line with one another. If they are in line, a condition of *status congruence* is said to exist. In this condition the workers may find their jobs dull or irksome, but they will not complain about the relative position of groups.

But there may be a more illuminating way of looking at the matter. In my example I have considered only responsibility and pay, but these may be enough, for they represent the two kinds of thing that come into the problem. Pay is clearly a reward; responsibility may be looked on, less clearly, as a cost. It means constraint and worry—or peace of mind foregone. Then the proposition about status congruence becomes this: If the costs of the members of one group are higher than those of another, distributive justice requires that their rewards should be higher too. But the thing works both ways: If the rewards are higher, the costs should be higher too. This last is the theory of *noblesse oblige,* which we all subscribe to, though we all laugh at it, perhaps because the *noblesse* often fails to *oblige.* To put the matter in terms of profit: though the rewards and costs of two persons or the members of two groups may be different, yet the profits of the two—the excess of reward over cost—should tend to equality. And more than "should." The less-advantaged group will at least try to attain greater equality, as, in the example I have used, the first group tried to increase its profit by increasing its pay.

I have talked of distributive justice. Clearly, this is not the only condition determining the actual distribution of rewards and costs. At the same time, never tell me that notions of justice are not a strong influence on behavior, though we sociologists often neglect them. Distributive justice may be one of the conditions of group equilibrium.

Exchange and social structure

I shall end by reviewing almost the only study I am aware of that begins to show in detail how a stable and differentiated social structure in a real-life group might arise out of a process of exchange between members. This is Peter Blau's description of the behavior of sixteen agents in a federal law-enforcement agency (1955, pp. 99–116).

The agents had the duty of investigating firms and preparing reports on the firms' compliance with the law. Since the reports might lead to legal action against the firms, the agents had to prepare them carefully, in the proper form, and take strict account of the many regulations that might apply. The agents were often in doubt what they should do, and then they were supposed to take the question to their supervisor. This they were reluctant to do, for they naturally believed that thus confessing to him their inability to solve a problem would reflect on their competence, affect the official ratings he made of their work, and so hurt their chances for promotion. So agents often asked other agents for help and advice, and, though this was nominally forbidden, the supervisor usually let it pass.

Blau ascertained the ratings the supervisor made of the agents, and he also asked the agents to rate one another. The two opinions agreed closely. Fewer agents were regarded as highly competent than were regarded as of middle or low competence; competence, or the ability to solve technical problems, was a fairly scarce good. One or two of the more competent agents would not give help and advice when asked, and so received few interactions and little liking. A man that will not exchange, that will not give you what he has when you need it, will not get from you the only thing you are, in this case, able to give him in return, your regard.

But most of the more competent agents were willing to give help, and of them Blau says:

> A consultation can be considered an exchange of values: both participants gain something, and both have to pay a price. The questioning agent is enabled to perform better than he could otherwise have done, without exposing his difficulties to his supervisor. By asking for advice, he implicitly pays his respect to the superior proficiency of his colleague. This acknowledgment of inferiority is the cost of receiving assistance. The consultant gains prestige, in return for which he is willing to devote some time to the consultation and permit it to disrupt his own work. The following remark of an agent illustrates this: "I like giving advice. It's flattering, I suppose, if you feel that others come to you for advice" (1955, p. 108).

Blau goes on to say: "All agents liked being consulted, but the value of any one of very many consultations became deflated for experts, and the price they paid in frequent interruptions became inflated" (1955, p. 108). This implies that, the more prestige an agent received, the less was the increment of value of that prestige; the more advice an agent gave, the greater was the increment of cost of that advice, the cost lying precisely in the foregone value of time to do his own work. Blau suggests that something of the same sort was true of an agent who went to a more competent colleague for advice: the more often he went, the more costly to him, in feelings of inferiority, became any further requests. "The repeated admission of his inability to solve his own problems . . . undermined the self-confidence of the worker and his standing in the group" (1955, p. 109).

The result was that the less competent agents went to the more competent ones for help less often than they might have done if the costs of repeated admissions of inferiority had been less high and that, while many agents sought out the few highly competent ones, no single agent sought out the latter much. Had they done so (to look at the exchange from the other side), the costs to the highly competent in interruptions to their own work would have become exorbitant. Yet the need of the less competent for help was still not fully satisfied. Under these circumstances they tended to turn for help to agents more nearly like themselves in competence. Though the help they got was not the most valuable, it was of a kind they could themselves return on occasion. With such agents they could exchange help and liking, without the exchange becoming on either side too great a confession of inferiority.

The highly competent agents tended to enter into exchanges, that is, to interact with many others. But, in the more equal exchanges I have just spoken of, less competent agents tended to pair off as partners. That is, they interacted with a smaller number of people, but interacted often with these few. I think I could show why pair relations in these more equal exchanges would be more economical for an agent than a wider distribution of favors. But perhaps I have gone far enough. The final pattern of this social structure was one in which a small number of highly competent agents exchanged advice for prestige with a large number of others less competent and in which the less competent agents exchanged, in pairs and in trios, both help and liking on more nearly equal terms.

Blau shows, then, that a social structure in equilibrium might be the result of a process of exchanging behavior rewarding and costly in different degrees, in which the increment of reward and cost varied with the frequency of the behavior, that is, with the frequency of interaction. Note that the behavior of the agents seems also to have satisfied my second condition of equilibrium: the more competent agents took more responsibility for the work, either their own or others', than did the less competent ones, but they also got more for it in the way of prestige. I suspect that the same kind of explanation could be given for the structure of many "informal" groups.

Summary

The current job of theory in small-group research is to make the connection between experimental and real-life studies, to consolidate the propositions that empirically hold good in the two fields, and to show how these propositions might be derived from a still more general set. One way of doing this job would be to revive and make more rigorous the oldest of theories of social behavior—social behavior as exchange.

Some of the statements of such a theory might be the following. Social behavior is an exchange of goods, material goods but also non-material ones, such as the symbols of approval or prestige. Persons that give much to others try to get much from them, and persons that get much from others are under pressure to give much to them. This process of influence tends to work out at equilibrium to a balance in the exchanges. For a person engaged in exchange, what he gives may be a cost to him, just as what he gets may be a reward, and his behavior changes less as profit, that is, reward less cost, tends to a maximum. Not only does he seek a maximum for himself, but he tries to see to it that no one in his group makes more profit than he does. The cost and the value of what he gives and of what he gets vary with the quantity of what he gives and gets. It is surprising how familiar these propositions are; it is surprising, too, how propositions about the dynamics of exchange can begin to generate the static thing we call "group structure" and, in so doing, generate also some of the propositions about group structure that students of real-life groups have stated.

In our unguarded moments we sociologists find words like "reward" and "cost" slipping into what we say. Human nature will break in upon even our most elaborate theories. But we seldom let it have its way with us and follow up systematically what these words imply. Of all our many "approaches" to social behavior, the one that sees it as an economy is the most neglected, and yet it is the one we use every moment of our lives—except when we write sociology.

47 On norms

JOHN W. THIBAUT and HAROLD H. KELLEY

Conceptualization of norms

Consider two people in a dyadic relationship and assume that the pattern of their outcomes is such that they cannot achieve their best outcomes at the same time. For example, this might be a husband and wife whose problem is that the wife likes to go dancing in the evening and the husband prefers that they go to the movies. The outcomes are illustrated in Figure 1. It is apparent that trading is necessary if both are to obtain good outcomes even occasionally.

Trading can be established through exercise of the power that each possesses, if this power is adequate. For example, the husband can use his control over the wife's outcomes by promising to go dancing if she will go with him to the movies. Or he can threaten to go to the movies anyway if she fails to cooperate, in which case she will have poor outcomes. Similar influence opportunities exist for the wife.

The moment-to-moment use of personal power can be obviated if the two can agree upon some rule for trading. For example, they might agree that they will alternate between dancing and attending the movies, making the shift upon some mutually acceptable signal; for example, a word from the momentarily favored person to the effect that he or she is satiated with the present activity. Once agreement is reached on a rule of this sort, shifts are likely to proceed smoothly and predictably and, in view of the limitations inherent to

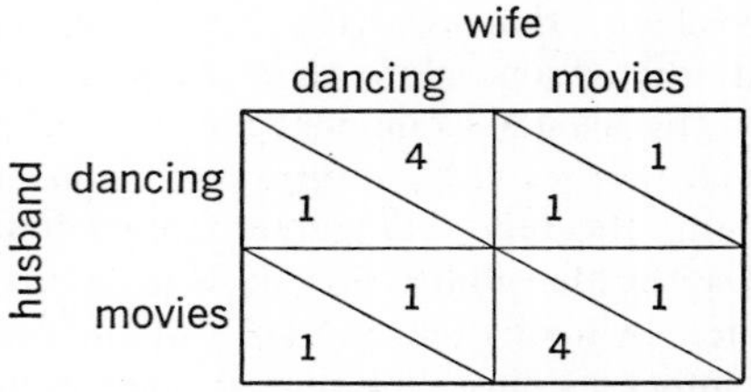

Figure 1. Illustration of relationship requiring trading.

Excerpted from Chapter 8 of **The Social Psychology of Groups,** New York: John Wiley and Sons, Inc., 1959, pp. 127–35, with permission of the authors and the publisher.

the relationship (noncorrespondence of high outcomes), each person is likely to feel that his own outcomes are satisfactory.

Agreements of this sort may be matters of mere convenience, repeated for their immediate value in reducing the costs involved in face-to-face influence and in smoothing out the course of the interaction. However, as Waller and Hill (1951) so aptly put it, "The *usual* quickly becomes the *right* . . ." (p. 49). The rule is likely to take on the characteristics of a moral obligation (or even to have them from the start). This means, in brief, that conformity to agreements becomes rewarding in and of itself.

Just how this transformation occurs is a complex matter. It probably has some basis in the fact that conformity to rules and agreements has proven rewarding in past relationships in which some external agent has delivered extrinsic rewards for conformity. For example, two brothers disagree about what to play because they prefer different games. Their mother steps in and says, "Play what Jimmy wants for awhile, and, after you've done that, give Johnny a chance," and rewards them if they follow her rule. Agreement to rules is also reinforced by the value they have for the relationship in cutting costs and enhancing rewards. We shall elaborate this shortly.

These reinforcing conditions make it likely that the two boys will learn to value "fair play." They will *accept* the rule in the sense that their equitable turn-taking behavior will no longer occur simply as a result of their compliance to external sanctions but also because they have *internalized* the rule [see Kelman, 1961].

Thus a predisposition to value and abide by a trading rule may exist at the outset of the husband and wife relationship. Norms need not be invented anew for each relationship but may often be transferred from other ones. These learning conditions also make it likely that a general value for agreements and rules of this sort will be acquired.

When an agreement about a matter such as trading exists between the members of a dyad and when it is accepted to some degree by both, we would say that a norm exists. This would manifest itself to an outside observer in several ways:

(1) There would be regularity in behavior (in our example, a routinized sequence of shifts in activities of the pair).

(2) In the event of disruption of this regularity, the "injured" person would attempt to restore it by appealing, at least initially, to the rule and he would exercise his personal power as an enforcer of the rule.

(3) The person disrupting the regularity would be likely to feel some obligation to adhere to the agreement and might even exhibit some conflict or guilt about deviating from it, as if he were punishing himself for his nonconformity.

Once a norm exists, it appears to the pair almost as if a third agent had entered the relationship, a feeling which undoubtedly is reinforced by the fact that in earlier relationships the enforcers of rules often actually were third persons (e.g., the mother in the case of the two brothers). The third agent exercises power over each member in the usual sense of making it desirable for him to act in certain ways at certain times and does so in an impartial way without regard to the special interests of either one. This normative power, when the rule has been accepted or internalized, seems to be exclusively behavior control, except in the case we discuss later in which the person is unable to make the necessary discriminations or perform the specified behavior. In one sense this power accrues to the norm because the two persons give up some of their individual power to it. This is evidenced by their exercising personal power in the name of the norm rather than to advance their personal interests. In another sense, the norm may have power over them independently of their enforcement of it: to the degree that the norm is accepted by individuals to whom it applies, conformity is more rewarding, other things being equal, than nonconformity.

From the preceding discussion the reader can deduce our definition of norm. A norm is a behavioral rule that is accepted, at least to some degree, by both members of the dyad. (A rule which one person advances and tries to enforce but which the other person does not accept cannot be called a norm, at least in a dyad. In large groups, on the other hand, acceptance by all members is not an essential part of the concept, although acceptance by a sizable number is.) Thus both members feel some obligation to adhere to it. Nonadherence is met with the use of power to attempt to produce conformity, but the influence appeal is to a supra-individual value ("Do it for the group" or "Do it because it's good") rather than to personal interests ("Do it for me" or "Do it and I'll do something for you").

The reader may wish to compare the present treatment of norm with similar conceptualizations advanced by other social scientists. Most similar is Homans' (1950) definition:

> A norm, then, is an idea in the minds of the members of a group, an idea that can be put in the form of a statement specifying what the members or other men should do, ought to do, are expected to do, under given circumstances. . . . A statement of the kind described is a norm only if any departure of real behavior from the norm is followed by some punishment (p. 123).

In the Lewinian tradition, Festinger, Schachter and Back (1950) give a definition in terms of forces: ". . . a uniform set of directions which the group induces on the forces which act on the members of the group" (p. 166). Rommetveit (1954) distinguishes carefully between the individual acting as enforcer of a norm, on the one hand, and the individual subject to it, on the other: "A social norm is a pressure existing between a norm-sender and a norm-receiver's behaviour in a category of recurrent situations" (p. 45). The last phrase excludes accidental and temporary interpersonal pressures. Pressure is said to be manifested in the norm sender's expectations that the norm receiver will behave in a specific way, or in his wish for this behavior, and in overt sanctions applied by the norm sender in response to the norm receiver's actions (pp. 45 ff.).

Norms as substitutes for informal influence

The foregoing discussion illustrates the characteristics of normative processes and also implies what we take to be the major broad functional value of norms —that they serve as substitutes for the exercise of personal influence and produce more economically and efficiently certain consequences otherwise dependent upon personal influence processes. Let us now consider this point in detail by examining the various problems created by the use of informal, interpersonal power and the ways in which norms may avoid or solve them.

In the first place norms may function to prevent or delay the development of any of the dependencies on which interpersonal power is based. Particularly in the very early stages of the relationship, when it is not yet clear whether the relationship will be formed, norms may assist in preventing premature commitments. As Hiller (1947) says ". . . norms supply a means for evading an implication of affectional relations. This is accomplished by treating with strict politeness or rigid etiquette a person who wishes to occupy a position which is too intimate. . . . Formality indicates a categorical rather than a unique personal footing; and unwanted approaches are repelled by confronting the other with decorous conduct. . . ." (pp. 105–106).

Let us go on though to consider a relationship that has formed. Assume first that A has greater power than B, at least within some limited segment of the matrix. From B's point of view a number of problems exist. If A has behavior control [1] over him, the unbridled use of this power tends to reduce the quality of B's outcomes. If A has fate control [2] and converts it in order to control B's behavior, the unstandardized use of this converted control places B in an uncomfortable situation. A's conversion of his fate control is more or less arbitrary; that is to say, he has several alternative ways in which he can use it. If he shifts among these in an unpredictable way, B may on any given occasion act upon the wrong assumption about what A intends and thereby suffer reduced payoffs. Even without actually making incorrect behavioral choices, B may worry about the possibility of doing so, and this tends to raise his costs for all the activities involved. The uncertainty is most extreme, of course, when A uses his fate control willy-nilly. If A converts and uses his control in one standardized manner, B's situation becomes that of having control over his *own* outcomes.

From the point of view of A, the more powerful individual, there are also problems, but of a different sort. If he is not careful in the use of whatever behavior control he may have, it will be reduced or even lost entirely. Because of the effects of interruptions in reducing B's outcomes, A must use his behavior control sparingly if he is to conserve it. If, on the other hand, A uses converted fate power to induce B to respond differentially, A must often monitor B's action, and such monitoring or surveillance is usually costly.

Given the above problems, both the weaker and the more powerful members of a dyad are likely to be somewhat dissatisfied with the informal exercise of personal power. However, many occasions arise in the course of their interaction in which some sort of control over behavior is necessary. Behavioral norms provide a means of meeting this dilemma: they control behavior but do not entail the difficulties created by the unrestrained use of interpersonal power. For example, they may include a definite

[1] "If, by varying his behavior, A can make it desirable for B to vary his behavior too, then A has behavior control over B" (Thibaut & Kelley, 1957, p. 103).—Eds.

[2] "If, by varying his behavior, A can affect B's outcomes, **regardless of what B does**, A has **fate control** over B" (Thibaut & Kelley, 1957, p. 102).—Eds.

and unchanging statement that behavior *x* is expected from person B, the weaker of the two. Knowing this, B need not worry about a change in the rules; he can always be confident about what to do in order to attain good outcomes or avoid poor ones. Furthermore, if he accepts the norm, B will perform the required behavior even in the absence of surveillance, thus relieving A of the necessity of monitoring him. (In larger groups wide acceptance of a norm has the further consequence that there can be sharing of the task of maintaining whatever surveillance is necessary, thereby reducing the cost to each individual.) The general point is that both weaker and stronger persons stand to gain from the introduction of mutually acceptable rules which introduce regularity and control into the relationship without recourse to the direct interpersonal application of power.

Consistent with this view is evidence obtained by Wispe and Lloyd (1955) that structured normative procedures are preferred to more informal and spontaneous ones by low-power members. Forty-three life insurance agents were interviewed about their preferences for various types of interactions between agents and managers. The main result of the study was that, as compared with highly productive agents, the less productive ones preferred their interaction with managers to be structured and normative rather than informal and spontaneous. Since the productivity of the agents fluctuated over time rather erratically, nearly all of the agents performed poorly from time to time. The authors interpret their findings to mean that those who are currently producing poorly, hence are very vulnerable, experience less anxiety about their vulnerability if there are structured procedures to protect them from managerial power.

The general contention advanced above can be argued from a slightly different point of view. Consider a dyad in which one member, A, performs a certain special behavior that is highly rewarding to B. As long as A continues to perform this sequence, there will be no problem; B will come to *expect* it in the sense of predicting that A is likely to repeat it in the future. However, if A is somewhat undependable or even merely exhibits covert tendencies not to perform his special function, B's dependency upon him is dramatized and becomes somewhat difficult to tolerate. This might be explained by assuming the existence of a need for autonomy (Murray, 1938) that motivates people to avoid interpersonal situations in which they are dependent upon others. Perhaps it is simpler merely to suggest that dependency upon an unreliable person is cost increasing. In interaction with such a person one often begins behavioral sequences without being able to consummate them, and one frequently does things for him without getting anything in return. On the other hand, dependency is no problem with a perfectly reliable deliverer of rewards, for example, a bountiful environment or the corner grocer with his stable prices.

So B's problem is to strengthen A's tendency to perform the desired sequence without making too apparent his dependency upon A, that is, without suffering power loss. This is done by an appeal to a supra-individual value connected with the welfare of some third agent, set of persons, or organization rather than with B's own welfare. Such appeals as "Do it because it's good," "People expect it of you," or "Do it for the group" are essentially power-maintenance strategies. They play down the value of the behavior to the person making the appeal or request but at the same time insure that the performance will continue. Allport (1954) summarizes an extremely cynical version of this point, advanced by Le Dantec. Moral standards such as those expressed in the Ten Commandments are described as being promulgated merely for the convenience of those who have some interest to protect, as, for example, property owners—"Thou shalt not steal"—and persons who have sexual partners—"Thou shalt not commit adultery." Thus B attempts to change the basis for A's performing the behavior from that of doing B a personal favor to that of satisfying social or moral obligations.

This process of transforming the value basis for compliance is probably supported and reinforced by conflict reduction on the part of A, the performer. If he has impulses not to help his partner, he has a recurring conflict between incompatible activities, those rewarding to B versus those which are not. This conflict is costly and can be reduced by mobilizing powerful instigations to only one kind of behavior. These are provided by the moralistic or social value appeals used by B which give A a justification for overvaluing the desirability of the behavior. Thus acceptance of supra-individual, depersonalized values as the basis for behavior has functional value both for the actor and the one dependent upon his actions.

Norms have similar functional values in many dyads in which power is evenly distributed. In highly cohesive groups the great power the two members have over each other not only gives them ability to carry out strong influence measures but also to resist each other's influence. This situation potentially leads to interpersonal conflicts and unresolved "stand-offs" in which neither one is able to get the other to engage in desired acitivities. This type of conflict can be avoided by procedural rules in which power is transferred, so to speak, from personal agents to the norms. Then, when A tries to induce B to do something, B is expected to perceive the locus of causality for the influence attempt not as internal to a whimsical or self-aggrandizing A but as existing in the depersonalized norm on behalf of which A is acting. We might expect that the counterpower (or resistance) that B might mobilize against A's suggestion would not exist for an impersonal set of rules. Alternatively stated, in a highly cohesive dyad B's counterpower derives from his ability to affect A's fate; this source of resistance is eliminated when power is depersonalized by transfer to a set of procedures or rules. (Note the implication that norms will develop more rapidly and more surely in highly cohesive groups, assuming that the majority of the members have about the same degree of dependence on the group, than in less cohesive groups.) Frank (1944) provides evidence that an appeal to an impersonal value encounters less resistance than does the direct exercise of personal power.

Even if equal power does not lead to interpersonal impasses, the interaction process is likely to be characterized by a good deal of argument and informal litigation. Unless argument and uncertainty happen to be rewarding in themselves, they merely represent unnecessary costs. These costs can be substantially reduced by agreements that enable the individuals to run off their most frequent interaction sequences according to automatic routines, without moment-by-moment decision making. Green (1956) comments on this point, "What an utter chaos human life would be—it could not long endure—if every day we had to settle by family debate or authoritarian decision how many meals we would eat *this* day, at what hour of the day or night" (p. 75). In a similar vein, MacIver and Page (1949) write of norms, "Without them the burden of decision would be intolerable and the vagaries of conduct utterly distracting" (p. 207). It may also be noted that for both members of a dyad the necessity of invoking power on the one hand and the necessity of complying with it on the other tend to bring to mind and dramatize the dependence of each upon the other. As we have stated above, the feeling of dependence is probably something most people would rather avoid. To the extent that there is depersonalization of influence, the source of power and control being external to both individuals, the basic fact of their interdependence goes unstated and probably unnoticed.

In short, we may view norms as social inventions that accomplish more effectively what otherwise would require informal social influence. We do not intend to imply that norms are deliberately developed for this purpose. The contention is merely that there exists a basis for unconscious collusion between weaker and stronger persons, between controllers and the controlled, between persons highly dependent upon each other—a collusion that has the effect of bringing regularity and control into the relationship without the informal exercise of personal power.

Some implications

This point of view has several important implications. *First,* if the central assertion is correct, that norms are means of influence and control which minimize the problems created by informal influence, then from a close examination of informal influence and its problems we should be able to infer the general *properties of norms.* This requires little explanation beyond that contained in the preceding pages. Norms are, in the first place, *rules about behavior.* They tell each person what is expected of him in certain situations, and in so doing they indirectly indicate requests that others may not properly make of him. In this way, he is protected from subjugation to another's whimsically exercised power. Norms are also *stable* so that the individual knows not only what is expected of him today but what will be expected of him tomorrow. Furthermore, norms are based upon *agreement or consensus* which reduces the necessity for thorough surveillance and, in large groups, distributes the responsibility for surveillance rather widely. The enforcement of norms often involves *appeals to impersonal values or suprapersonal agents,* which reduce the extent to which compliance is viewed as a matter of giving in to a more powerful person and thereby reduces resistance. Also these values are often *widely held* among the group members, so that once they have been associated with compliance it becomes directly rewarding and the need for exercise of external control is greatly reduced. Simmel (1902) puts the last point this way:

> In the morality of the individual, society creates for itself an organ which is not only more fundamentally operative than law and

custom, but which also spares society the different sorts of costs involved in these institutions. Hence the tendency of society to satisfy its demands as cheaply as possible results in appeals to "good conscience," through which the individual pays to himself the wages for his righteousness, which otherwise would probably have to be assured to him in some way through law or custom (p. 19*n*).

The *second* implication is this: If norms are to control or replace interpersonal influence, then they should have some relevance to the things about which this influence is exercised. What norms are about, that which is commonly called the *content of norms,* should be inferable from a consideration of the things about which group members find it necessary to influence each other.

48 Conformity, status, and idiosyncrasy credit

E. P. HOLLANDER

Something of a paradox exists in the prevailing treatments of conformity and status. Students of social psychology are likely to be left with the pat impression that the freely chosen leader conforms to, and perhaps tenaciously upholds, the norms of his group. Yet this kind of leadership is also presented as a status sufficient to provide latitude for directing and altering group norms (Homans, 1950, p. 416). From their recent experimental work in this area, Dittes and Kelley have voiced a doubt that the relationship between conformity and status is ever a simple one (1956, p. 106). The evidence favors their assertion.

Although these phenomena may be treated as discrete entities, they both arise from interaction between an individual and a set of relevant other individuals constituting a group. To say that an individual conforms, or that he has status, is not to say that these are independently determined states nor that they are terminal; they have some common origin in a phenomenal relationship which persists over time. Conformity and status may be thought of therefore as mutually dependent, and transitionally effective upon subsequent interactions. With this as a framework, several general conceptions will be expressed here regarding mechanisms which produce these phenomena and govern their relationship to one another.

In a gross way, three classes of variables, or elements, are necessary to this conceptual scheme: characteristics of the individual himself; characteristics of the group with which he interacts; and outcomes of interaction represent-

Reprinted from the **Psychological Review,** 1958, 65, 117–27, with permission of the American Psychological Association.

ing a past history which may alter the relationship of the former elements.

Of particular importance as a mediating process is the changing perception brought about in the individual and the group by their interaction; the third element is, in effect, this process. A distinction is required, therefore, between the phenomenal and perceptual features of behavior. An individual's behavior is not only phenomenally present in interaction but is also subject to view and appraisal by the other members of the group. If there are to be consequences involving these others, it is essential that there be a perceptual intake on their part. And so too must the individual perceive a group norm; the fact that it is manifestly there is not enough.

It is worth emphasizing that the focus here is upon how the individual fares in the group rather than upon more global consequences to the group. Two kinds of interlocking mechanisms are of concern: those giving rise to behavior in conformity with group demands, and those giving rise to status. The issues at stake may be put simply as follows: What produces conformity? And what allows for nonconformity?

Some questions on conformity

Fundamental to these issues is the matter of determining *when* an individual may be said to be conforming. One may note that a twofold assumption underpins the usual view of conformity, i.e., that the individual is aware of the existence of a given group norm, and that his behavior in accordance with this norm is evidence of conformity. It is doubtful that both features of this assumption necessarily hold simultaneously. This being so, difficulties of interpretation will arise. If the individual were to be insensitive to the norm he could hardly be said to be conforming to it, whatever his behavior seemed to betray; correspondingly, a kind of "conformity" might prevail in terms of adherence to an incorrectly perceived norm; and thus, an evident failure to conform might or might not be "nonconformity" depending upon the accuracy of the individual's perception of the norm in the first place.

A related question concerns the individual's motivation. Is there a motive for nonconformity identifiable? Insofar as they are distinguishable, is it necessarily so, after all, that a conflict obtains between the individual's dispositions and the group's demands? Since behavior is taken to be more than a random event, the motivation for instances of conformity or nonconformity should be accountable, once the presence of an adequate recognition of the norm is established.

There remains too the question of who perceives a given behavior to be conforming, i.e., an external observer, a group member, or the actor himself. Employing a fixed-norm baseline for observation, as is often done, serves to obscure differential expectations which render conforming behavior for one individual nonconforming for another —with regard, that is, to others' perceptions *in situ*. Thus, the degree of familiarity with the unique properties of the group context is critical in verifying and understanding conformity.

Norms, roles, and group expectancies

The usual conception of conformity examined here requires some group referent and a standard of behavior abstracted therefrom and defined as a norm. Probably because many studies of groups have involved highly manifest behaviors, norms are conceived to be quite literally evident. On the other hand, in the related concept of role a recognition exists that the behavioral standard may not be manifest, but rather may be an *expectancy*.[1]

Though persisting, the distinction between norms and roles is neither essential nor easy to maintain (cf. Newcomb, 1950; Bates, 1956). Roles are normative in that they involve some implicit shared expectancy among group members; and norms themselves, lacking visibility, may nonetheless dwell in expectancies. It is these expectancies, then, which may be normative, in the sense of typicality. Norms and roles are only distinguishable insofar as norms usually imply expectancies applicable to many persons, while roles are expectancies restrictive to one or a very few individuals in a group.

Objective observers might delimit common expectancies appropriate to group members in general from differential expectancies having reference to particular individuals as such. For the individual in the setting, however, manifest conformity probably comes about without regard to a separate awareness of norms as distinct from roles, but more likely in terms of behaviors which he perceives to be expected of him by relevant others, i.e., "doing the *right* thing."

In the world of daily interaction, the perception an individual holds of what relevant others expect of him is a singularly important determinant of his social behavior; and the degree to which an individual perceives the group to be rewarding serves to enhance or elaborate the effect produced by his motivation to belong. An alternative sequence may be seen to occur as well: motivation having reference to some fulfillment through the group serves to heighten the individual's perception of its expectancies.[2]

Individual variables

Granted that conformity derives from certain features of individual perception and motivation, it still remains necessary to identify these features more pointedly. In this formulation, there are four such to be noted: perceptual ability (P_a), representing a general alertness to the social stimulus field; perceptual error (P_e), with particular reference to group expectancies; motivation to gain or sustain social approval (M_a); and, motivation to take part in the focal activities of the group (M_g). Taken together, the latter two variables may be considered as the individual's motivation to belong to the group (M).

The perceptual variables can readily be related to personality typologies. Many of these, e.g., authoritarianism, rigidity, or empathy, appear to lend themselves to a reduction to perceptual function as a core element (cf. Rokeach, 1948; Adorno, *et al.*, 1950; Bender & Hastorf, 1953). Terms like "perceptual rigidity," "perceptual defense," and "social imperceptiveness," often appear as concomitants of these

[1] The term "expectancy" refers to another's perception of some object person (cf. Steiner, 1955). What the object person then perceives to be the expectancy is quite important, but its locus is first of all in the "other." Reference is not made, therefore, to the term in Tolman's sense.

[2] The work on selective perception (e.g., Postman, Bruner, and McGinnies, 1948) sustains some such formulation, in general. But the linkage between motivation and perception has considerably greater complexity, as Bruner (1957) has more recently pointed out.

broader characterizations; evidently, this element accounts for certain diversities in behavior which distinguish individuals from one another.

It is useful here, however, to recognize a differential between that which is given and that which is emergent, i.e., perceptual ability and perceptual error, though the interaction of the two is not challenged. The distinction basically is that the former serves as a parameter setting the lower limit on the latter. Thus, the minimum level of an individual's P_e is set by his basic capacity, P_a. This should not be taken as neglect of the potentials of learning, however. The concept of capacity introduced here may be understood to be similar to that of cognitive structures (cf. Krech, 1951). No assumptions are made about the source of the "capacity"; it is only significant as a feature of the individual which bears upon interaction. It seems reasonable to believe that some individuals have an initial advantage over others as regards accuracy in perceiving group expectancies.

Concerning motivation to belong, mention has already been made that it involves two continua: motivation specific to the activity—or instrumental features—of the group, M_g; and motivation rooted in a generalized need for social approval, M_a. This view cuts across a number of other motivational schema suggested elsewhere (cf. Festinger, 1950; Bovard, 1953; Deutsch & Gerard, 1955; Jackson & Saltzstein, 1956; Thibaut & Strickland, 1956), and is intended more as a resolution than a departure. Briefly, these other distinctions appear to involve an "activity focus" and an "other people focus." Activity involves others, of course, but not necessarily to gain their approval. What really seems to matter is the nature of the reward sought.

The approval variable might be viewed as a parameter of personality, but not one so static as to be unaffected by interaction, within certain limits. Since those members having interests which can only be satisfied through participation in group activity do not of necessity have a high need for social approval, and since those cast into groups of little positive activity valence to them may still require approval, it is possible that these variables may be related negatively or positively, depending upon the circumstances considered.

Status emergence

The foregoing points have concentrated on individual characteristics that absorb and deal with features of the social context. Ultimately, these have consequences in behavior, which in its turn has an impact upon the group. It is appropriate now to consider the implications of this process to the emergence of status.

At bottom, status may be taken to be an outcome of the group's differentiated perception of the individual, leading to a set of particularized expectancies regarding his behavior. This occurs as a function of certain of the behaviors or characteristics evidenced by the individual in interaction, which then yield a reconstruction of the group's perception of him. Cast in these terms, status has special value as a kind of middle ground in relating the individual to the group. It exists in the first place as a feature in someone's perceptual field, for without reference to a perceiver status has no intrinsic value or meaning in itself. And, similarly, role cannot be divorced from its perceptual locus; behavior is only appropriate to status insofar as someone perceives it to be so. Perceptual differentiation by the group has consequences, then, in terms of the behaviors it expects the individual to display.

Though not necessarily the case, it is desirable to conceive of status within this framework as having hierarchical properties on some sort of group-acceptance continuum (cf. Dittes & Kelley, 1956). This is by no means critical as a feature, but is of heuristic value. Still further, it is convenient to represent status as permitting greater latitude in the manifestation of behaviors which would be seen to be nonconformist for the other members of the group; we refer here to common expectancies, a term introduced earlier. The implications of this aspect of status are of especial relevance to what follows.

Idiosyncrasy credit

Status will hereafter be considered to be an outcome of interaction referred to as "idiosyncrasy credit" (C). This represents an accumulation of positively-disposed impressions residing in the perceptions of relevant others; it is defined operationally in terms of the degree to which an individual may deviate from the common expectancies of the group. In this view, each individual within a group—disregarding size and function, for the moment—may be thought of as having a degree of group-awarded credits such as to permit idiosyncratic behavior in certain dimensions *before* group sanctions are applied. By definition, affiliation with the group—as perceived by the group—ceases when the individual's credit balance reaches zero.

It is noteworthy that this concept is applicable to the limited, artificially produced laboratory group, as well as to the total society. And, since the individual may have simultaneous membership in many groups, he may be considered to have a distinct credit balance in all groups with which he is in some sense involved; in each case he has achieved some level of status. Affixed to this concept of "credit" is the further consideration that "debits" of varying magnitudes may be charged against the credit balance, depending upon the gravity and frequency of the idiosyncrasy manifested, and the credit level which the individual holds.[3]

Taking our society today as an illustration, one's credit balance very likely will be rapidly exhausted by publicly espousing Communist doctrine. In a different sphere, a fraternity man may experience comparable rejection by his peers for growing a beard, though other factors would come into play, so that for some individuals the consequences—in terms of group sanctions—would be disastrous and for others hardly disturbing. This requires some consideration of factors which determine the awarding of credit.

Among other determinants, the credit balance that a group member achieves depends upon the group, its function, and other properties to be considered below. It is useful for our purposes here to conceive of an "open system," i.e., an autonomous group providing focal activities, as well as free face-to-face interaction yielding expectancies; this would permit the simultaneous observation of an individual's behavior by all group members and the generation of impressions representing credit.

There are three general variables which can be delineated as determinants

[3] Alterations upward or downward in credit may be conceived as a negative, monotonic function of credit balance. Thus, for the same idiosyncratic behavior or negative weight attached to value, the individual with high status loses less credit than the marginal individual of low status (cf. Schachter, 1951).

of these impressions. The first of these is alpha value (V_α), referring to the individual's task competence or performance in regard to focal group activities; the second is beta value (V_β), referring to characteristics of the individual not specific to these activities, e.g., status in a broader group, *bonhomie*, and the like; the third is immediate past idiosyncratic behavior (*B*), constituting a drain on credits.[4] It is not contended that credit is necessarily related linearly to these variables, nor is their very likely interrelationship ignored. They are doubtless intercorrelated, though of varying degrees of significance in generating or dissipating credits. As a generalization, value (*V*) tends to increase credit while idiosyncratic behavior (*B*) acts to decrease credit—though the potential for negative value exists, e.g., in the case of prejudice.

Group variables

From the foregoing it should be apparent that an individual can only be accurate in perceiving expectancies insofar as they are normative, in some modal sense, and are communicated. Two interrelated group variables which have importance in this regard are group attraction (*A*) and the communicality of any given expectancy (*Y*).

The former variable may be thought of as "cohesiveness," a term more usually applied. But since this term may have at least several operational meanings, it is preferable to specify two kinds of literal attraction, or an aggregation of these: attraction to group members, and attraction to focal group activities. This duality follows the M_a and M_g distinction made earlier in connection with motivation to belong. Although one may deal with a nondiscriminate aggregation of these, it is quite true that the sum of individual attractions in the group may be based predominately in M_a needs or M_g needs, and that differences in the emergent characteristics of groups thus constituted will be evident. Thus, where group attraction derives mainly from M_a one might predict it would be more stable than where its source is mainly M_g, since the latter variable is more temporally based.

Communicality is conceived to be directly related to group attraction in a mutual dependency; it refers to the degree to which an expectancy is literally communicated, i.e., made evident, and bears a relationship to both relevance and communication variables, as they have been introduced in other formulations (cf. Chowdhry & Newcomb, 1952; Talland, 1954), though this is by no means a complete statement. Studies of leaders' ability to estimate group attitudes, for example, have yielded highly conflicting results (cf. Steiner, 1955, p. 268). Where attitudes are "relevant," leaders *may or may not* be superior to nonleaders in their respective estimates; where leaders *are* found to be superior to nonleaders in estimating relevant attitudes, this has been ascribed to the heightened social sensitivity of leaders or alternatively to the proposition that leaders are instrumental in the shaping of group attitudes and hence tend to know them better.

Whatever the explanation chosen, there is reason to contend that the

4 Still another variable related to credit balance, probably curvilinearly, would be the duration of the individual's affiliation with the group over time. This has been disregarded, since it is useful to deal with individuals as though they have been in the group for an equal period of time, more particularly from its inception. It is also likely that the degree to which the individual is "visible" may alter the effects produced by his value and idiosyncratic behavior.

variable of relevance may not be the most fruitful one for purposes of study. If one were disposed to test the tenability of the hypothesis that leaders have this greater social sensitivity, it would seem desirable not only to raise the question of whether leaders, and others, tend to use their own personal attitudes as an anchorage for estimating group attitudes, but to ask in addition whether this exists independently of the degree to which given attitudes actually are foci of communication within real groups. Another approach, accordingly, might be to utilize some index of the degree to which a specific attitude—or an expectancy—actually evidences itself in a given group. There is utility, then, in introducing the operationalizable property "communicality."

Though a level of communicality may characterize a group, the particular center of interest here resides in a given expectancy. One may venture in this vein that the communicality of an expectancy will be at a lower relative level than that of other expectancies, if it is less applicable to the group as a whole; common expectancies ought to have higher communicality than the differential expectancies associated with increased status. Since communicality rests on behavior, it may be seen to follow, too, that interpersonal interaction results in higher communicality. Through a related mechanism, interpersonal interaction may contribute to group attraction (cf. Homans, 1950; Newcomb, 1956).

Summary of variables

For convenience, the variables described may now be set forth definitionally.

B—*Idiosyncratic behavior,* i.e., any group member's behavior which may be perceived by the group to deviate from a given group expectancy.

C—*Idiosyncrasy credit,* i.e., the extent to which a given group member's idiosyncratic behavior (*B*) is allowable, in terms of gravity and frequency, before group sanctions are applied.

V_α—*Alpha value,* i.e., the weight assigned the current performance of a given individual, which may be perceived by the group as bearing upon its focal activities, e.g., task competence.

V_β—*Beta value,* i.e., the weight assigned the characteristics of a given individual which may be perceived by the group, but are not specific to its current focal activities, e.g., status external to the group.

P_a—The *perceptual ability* of a given individual, in the sense of a capacity to perceive events and relationships in the social field.

P_e—The *perceptual error* of a given individual in perceiving events or relationships in a particular social field, e.g., group expectancies.

M_a—The *motivation* of a given individual to affiliate with a given group, in terms of gaining or sustaining *social approval.*

M_g—The *motivation* of a given individual to affiliate with a group, in terms of interest in focal *group activity.*

M—*Individual motivation to gain or sustain membership,* i.e., some composite of a given individual's motivation of both the M_a and M_g variety.

A—In general, *attraction of the group to its members,* i.e., some aggregate of all group members' *M.*

Y—The *communicality of a given group expectancy,* in terms of the degree to which a given expectancy is evident.

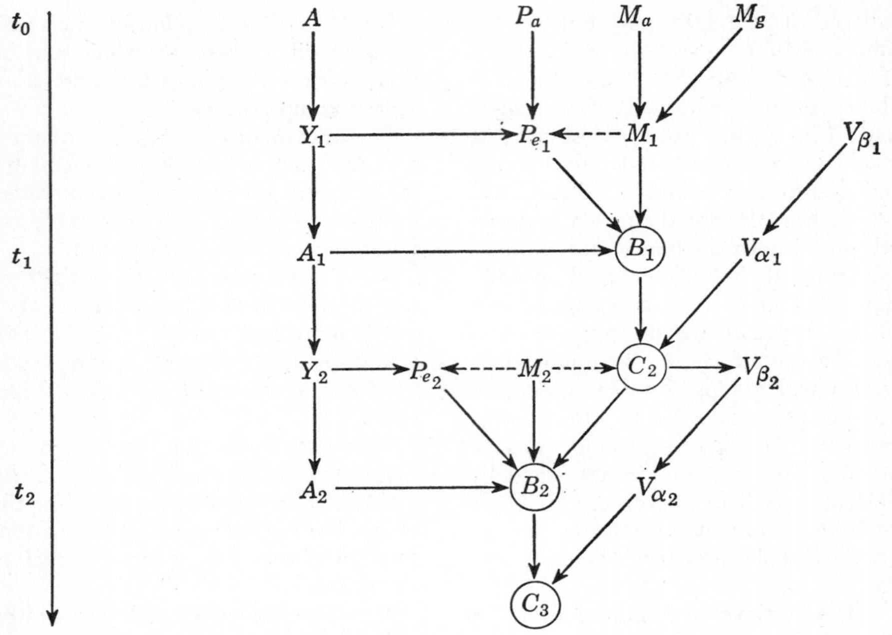

Figure 1. Schematic representation of mechanisms demonstrating relationships over time.

Schematic representation

In Fig. 1 our symbolic notation has been employed to represent relationships schematically. Since a sequential pattern is of particular importance, a time dimension is involved throughout; thus, subscripts are introduced to indicate the time interval to which reference is made; e.g., t_1 is read as the first time interval; or, P_{e_2} as perceptual error in the second time interval.

The system originates at the top with group attraction as a motivational context, and three individual variables, perceptual ability, motivation to gain or sustain social approval, and motivation with reference to the group's activity. At the next level, group attraction has given rise to the communicality of certain expectancies which are then perceived by the individual, thus yielding a perceptual error; and motivation to belong has been aggregated at this level, as well. Beta value is also introduced to signify the group's perception of the individual's characteristics, e.g., pleasant appearance.[5]

Moving down in time, the individual's idiosyncratic behavior during the period just elapsed has been generated by his error in perceiving expectancies together with his motivation—within the constraints imposed by the level of

[5] The term "group perception" refers to an abstraction; it is unlikely that all members of a group will perceive a given feature of an individual identically; the intent therefore is only to suggest a modal tendency. However, some very recent research has illuminated just this point and given credence to the general conception of differentially-determined value (cf. Jones & deCharms, 1957).

group attraction. The group's perception of the individual's contribution to its focal activities, alpha value, is influenced by the immediately prior perception of his characteristics, beta value.

In the next stage, status is generated —in the form of group-awarded credits —by the effects of behavior relative to expectancies and the sequence of beta value to alpha value to credits. At this point the full set of interactions are in play, with credits affecting beta value; the latter serving as a repository of group perceptions of the individual's characteristics; perceptual error and motivation are reintroduced for this new phase, with the former affected by communicality of expectancies. Idiosyncratic behavior is subsequently determined by available credits, as this is checked by motivation, in particular, and perceptual error.

Discussion and implications

Early in interaction, conformity to group expectancies serves to maintain or increase status, particularly as it is seen to be combined with manifest contributions to the group; at a later phase, however, the status thus generated permits greater latitude for idiosyncratic behavior. Thus, if an individual conforms to expectancies early in his exposure to the group and if he shows characteristics of competence, he accrues credits. For evident deviations from expectancies, or poor performance, he loses credits. If he exhausts his credit balance completely, pressures are applied to remove him from the group, or, at the very least, he is no longer perceived to be a member. At the other pole, if he continues to amass credits he attains a threshold permitting deviations from common expectancies, but with constraints imposed by newly differentiated expectancies.

The apparent paradox—that leaders both conform to group norms and yet may act to alter them by an exercise of influence—may be explained by reference to this sequential process. In this regard, it should not be supposed that an abundance of credits must lead perforce to influence. While an individual thus endowed has the potential to display more idiosyncratic behavior than others, he might not do so, nor would he of necessity become a leader thereby. Some further points of clarification are in order.

It is easy enough for the individual to continue to do habitually that which is rewarded by relevant others, so long as expectancies remain relatively stable. Consider the state of affairs which holds, however, in the case of the person who has marked status mobility in the group. He cannot simply continue to redisplay behaviors which were appropriate to the group's earlier expectancies, because the expectancies applicable to him are now altered in keeping with his rising status. Other things being equal, this suggests two features appropriate to the attainment of status in an open system: (*a*) accuracy of social perception; and (*b*) modifiability of behavior. Insofar as the incipient status person is attuned to the altering group expectancies and is capable of reacting appropriately to them, his status will very likely move upward. The relationship of these points to research on leadership is noteworthy; for example, the proposition that leaders have a heightened sensitivity to certain properties of the social context is in consonance with the foregoing. Note, too, that whether or not the leader has actually created a feature of the context with which he is then familiar, he may well have evidenced perceptual accuracy in an earlier phase, as he rose to leadership. Accordingly, the finding of Talland (1954) that leaders are only better in judging norms where they have had a part in their evolution is not inconsistent with a finding like that of Chowdhry and Newcomb (1952) to the effect that leaders have superior social perception; it would appear that the time phase under study is critical in yielding one process or the other.

Previously the point was made that the high-status person could effect changes in the common expectancies of the group because he has latitude for the manifestation of what would be seen to be nonconforming behavior for others. But, in contrast, the expectancies regarding the role itself are less amenable to alteration by the incumbent. Hence, the leader could readily lose credits and find his influence diminished if he were to show idiosyncratic behavior in terms of expectancies associated with his role. Regarding such deviation, we may conceive of one requirement which is quite likely significant, i.e., perception by the members of the group that the leader's motivation to belong be both high and sincere. Should this condition not be fulfilled, status may be threatened. To take another illustration, innovation by the leader may be of high valence to the group. It is conceivable that this could yield the seeming anomaly of a leader who, in the face of this expectancy, adopts a passive and ostensibly safe course, but loses status.

Leadership status, therefore, assuredly demands conformity to the group's expectancies regarding the role, but still leaves the leader with sway in the sphere of common expectancies associated with members at large. The leader may deviate from these, or bring about their reconstruction, if his prior activities have generated an appropriately high level of credit.

The motivational aspects of this process require consideration in terms of the individual set against the background of the group's activity. The restraining effect of M on the expenditure of C has been accounted for in the foregoing. What is more to the point, however, is the fact that a person with M_g will more likely achieve status in a largely M_g group than will a person with M_a; the status achieved, therefore, is a part function of the congruence of the individual's motivation with the generalized character of the motivation extant in the group. Since motivation is related, as well, to performance and other characteristics represented by alpha value and beta value, it is to be regarded as a key element.

If the group has a primary focal activity, then presumably M_g becomes more highly valued, particularly in combination with alpha value. At the other extreme, i.e., where the group activities are quite diffuse, M_a becomes important in combination with beta value. We may conceptualize groups of the M_a variety as being essentially "socially minded." With a minimum group-centered function requiring broad participation, the person having beta value is more likely to achieve status through being well liked; in the M_g group, to the contrary, alpha value becomes critical and task competence has greater weight in determining status. The relationship of this to the current situational view of leadership is evident.[6]

[6] For example, the finding of Jennings (1950) that leadership and popularity are highly related in her groups can be considered in this framework.

Whether group members do distinguish between value of one kind or another can be inferred from the literature of sociometry. Evidence will be found there indicating that individuals can give scaled evaluations of their peers with quite adequate discriminations between those they like, those they consider competent, and so forth. Though these sociometrically based status continua are likely to be related, as we have previously noted, they are by no means in universal, one-to-one correspondence (cf. Hollander & Webb, 1955). Viewing status in the aggregative, credit-amassing sense still allows for the integrity of the roots which feed it. Recent experimental evidence on the basis for shifts in the group's perception of a member also accords with this conception (cf. Jones & deCharms, 1957).

Certain of the assumptions made here—e.g., that an individual will have a level of credit reposing unitarily in others' perceptions of him, and that he may know and make use of the credits at his disposal—are only approximations of reality. Their literal tenability is not crucial to the mechanisms postulated, however. One could argue that the individual operates *as if* these assumptions were in fact true: the "they" commonly invoked to denote the upholders of some social pattern are never quite as homogeneous as the term suggests; but, to the individual, the use of "they" to represent a supposed uniformity is a necessary convenience as a basis for behavior. Furthermore, in accordance with this position, the individual apparently does react differentially to what he believes to be the view of him held by the "they," as Dittes and Kelley (1956) have demonstrated by manipulating the level of group "acceptance" which an individual is permitted to sense. In general, then, it appears that the individual seeks to know where he stands and does the best he can with the information available to him. These conceptions therefore do no violence to the reality with which the individual deals, but rather describe this reality in terms congruent with his concern.

49 Conformity as a tactic of ingratiation

EDWARD E. JONES

There seems to be much promise in looking at social interaction with an eye to the unfolding of strategies designed to gain or maintain personal power. There is nothing novel in the suggestion that there is a strategic side to social behavior—that people try to calculate ways to make the most of a particular relationship—but the attempt to study such strategies by laboratory experimentation is a recent development (see Jones, 1964).[1]

All interpersonal relationships involve mutual dependence; this is the equivalent of saying that each party to a social interchange has potential influence over certain rewards available to and costs incurred by the other. If the dependences of one on the other are not only mutual but approximately equal, then there is a balance of power in which each can enforce a certain minimal receipt of rewards through his capacity to enact or fail to enact the responses sought by the other. When the power in a two-person relationship is asymmetrical, however, the more dependent person is somewhat at the mercy of the more powerful one. In any event, we can well understand why the more dependent person is concerned about his poor position and, under most circumstances, tries in various ways to improve it.

[1] Ingratiation is "strategic behaviors . . . designed to influence a particular other person concerning the attractiveness of one's personal qualities" (p. 11).—Eds.

When we look at the strategic alternatives available to the more dependent person, it appears that some of these strategies guarantee him at least a certain minimum of rewards but do so at the expense of confirming or strengthening the power asymmetry which defines his dependence. Other strategies, however, may be effective in modifying the asymmetry itself so that the dependent person's power is, in the long run, increased. Compliance is an example of one kind of dependence-confirming tactic. The dependent person may, through overt obedience, avoid punishment and secure the rewards available to him, but such compliance tends to perpetuate the power differential to which it is a response. For example, the more reliable the worker becomes in meeting the supervisor's demands, the more confident the supervisor will be that these demands are reasonable, and that the worker is happy with the "bargain" symbolized by the difference in their power. In contrast to compliance, we may view ingratiation as power-enhancing or dependence-reducing. By making himself attractive to the more powerful person, the more dependent person increases the value of his own sanctioning responses at the same time that he makes it more difficult for the powerful person to apply the full range of sanctions that were initially part of his repertory. In other words, as the dependent person becomes more attrac-

Excerpted from **Science**, 1965, 149, No. 3680. 144–50, with permission of the author and publisher.

tive, the powerful person cannot punish him without greater cost to himself. This, in effect, means that his power has been reduced.

By what specific tactical means may the dependent person increase his attractiveness? Such tactics are undoubtedly as various as social behavior itself—there is an appealing and an unappealing way of doing almost everything. But I have found it particularly useful to consider three main classes of tactics available to the "ingratiator:" compliments, agreement, and presentation of oneself in a favorable light. We may support and flatter others, convince them that we share their views, or present our characteristics in terms that they can appreciate. In this article, I single out agreement, or conformity of opinion, as the dependent variable of particular interest. The experiments reviewed all show how persons modify their publicly expressed opinions as a way of coping with a condition of social dependence.

First, however, it is appropriate to comment on some of the moral issues involved in the behavior we are studying. *Ingratiation*, like its sister term, *flattery*, is at least mildly pejorative in everyday usage. The word has connotations of dissimulation and deceit in social communication. Am I suggesting, then, that most of us are so concerned with the effects of our behavior on others that we deliberately engage in manipulative and deceitful tactics in order to gain their esteem? I do not know how one could ever obtain actuarial figures on this point, but I would argue—without great alarm—that all of us under appropriate circumstances do shape our social responses to increase our attractiveness to particular people. The scientific student of such response-shaping is unlikely to make much progress by interviews or naturalistic observation. In this particular area, I have learned through research experience that people are extremely likely to deceive themselves. Not only do they want to avoid publicizing the extent to which their responses to others are conditioned by approval-seeking motives, they work busily to protect themselves from awareness of the link between wanting to be liked and modifying one's behavior to this end. It is my current belief that only by comparing appropriate experimental and control treatments can we begin to explore the conditions favorable to the tactics of ingratiation and thus begin to specify the variables essential to construction of a theory concerning it. Questions of the frequency of occurrence and the extent of such behavior in the natural environment, and questions concerning individual differences, are not considered here.

The ingratiator's dilemma

Much of the fascination in studying ingratiation comes from the fact that the same situational factors that increase one person's desire to be found attractive by another alert the other (the "target" person) to the likelihood of tactical behavior. Thus, the dependent person will be strongly motivated to be ingratiating, but the fact that his dependence stands revealed reduces the likelihood that his overtures will be effective. His dilemma is magnified further by his natural reluctance to see himself as deceitful or manipulative. Thus, the more dependent he is on another, the more he will be forced to justify to himself any actions conceivably designed to curry favor with the other. These two factors—the target person's alertness to overtures from a dependent person and the dependent person's reluctance to see himself as one who uses manipulative social tactics—would seem almost to rule out ingratiating tactics in those very situations where it is important to be liked. Indeed, there is fairly good evidence that such tactics can boomerang; especially when the "actor" is highly dependent on the target person, the latter is apt to be more attracted to him if he shows some restraint in his praise or in the degree of his agreement. The results of three studies (see Jones, 1965) show that, in the ambiguous area of social responses that may or may not make one seem attractive to another person, the role relation between the ingratiator and the target person is a critical factor which affects the latter's judgments of manipulative intentions or ulterior motivation.

To some extent, however, the ingratiator is protected by the vanity of the target person from having such judgments go against him. Each of us likes to believe the best about himself, and many of us must be exposed to the most blatant praise before we begin to suspect that we are the targets of manipulative intentions. Often, no doubt, the ingratiator joins his target in what might be called an autistic conspiracy, since, for understandable psychological reasons, both the ingratiator and the target person are anxious to believe that the latter is better than he is.

I now feel that this autistic conspiracy may be maintained by the most intricate interpersonal tactics—tactics designed to conceal from both the "tactician" and the target person the former's underlying intentions. Since I believe that not many of us deliberately and consciously calculate such tactical maneuvers, I am suggesting that, from well-learned orientations toward those more powerful than ourselves, we develop patterns of social behavior unwittingly designed to attract, while avoiding the extremes of sycophancy. Such extremes would reveal to both parties the true nature of the autistic conspiracy.

Issue relevance and agreement

My central thesis thus far has been that dependence increases the motivation to make oneself seem attractive, but public knowledge of this dependence makes it more difficult to gain esteem through such simple stratagems as slavish agreement or effusive compliments. In order to be successful, the ingratiator must complicate his tactics and inject some subtlety. One obvious way to increase subtlety is to convey the impression of agreeing in a discerning way. The ingratiator must steer between the Scylla of errant disagreement and the Charybdis of blatant conformity, conveying minor disagreement within the context of a general similarity of position. Beyond this, if we know something about the social context in which opinions are being exchanged, it may be possible to specify the issues on which agreement is most likely and the issues on which moderate disagreement may be expected.

One important aspect of the social context is the relative difference in status between the two persons involved in the interchange. Status differences usually imply asymmetrical power, which is one of the preconditions for ingratiation tactics.[2]

[2] Several research studies (e.g., Jones, Gergen, & Jones, 1963) which are considered at this point in Professor Jones's paper have been omitted in this abridgment.—Eds.

VIII LEADERSHIP, POWER, AND INNOVATION

Leadership is a phenomenon of enduring interest in social psychology. It was initially studied in terms of the leader's attributes, and more recently as an outgrowth of the effects induced by the demands of the situation. While evidences of these "trait" and "situational" viewpoints persist in some approaches to leadership, it is being seen increasingly as a process of interaction involving an influence person and those who are influenced. Furthermore, refined empirical procedures have been applied to its study, and a number of newer concepts have been stimulated through this effort. One of these distinguishes between the leader who gains his authority by consent of followers, the so-called "emergent leader," and the leader whose authority is imposed by an external source, the "appointed leader" found in most organizations.

The greatest focus of research on leadership has been in experiments in "small groups," i.e., goal-oriented, functional groups. Several good sources for this literature are Katz and Lazarsfeld (1955), Olmsted (1959), Cartwright and Zander (1960), Hare (1962), Hare, Borgatta, and Bales (1965), and McGrath and Altman (1966). Two themes running through this research effort are the "how" of leadership emergence and the effectiveness of leadership in terms of productivity and member satisfaction. Related questions of concern are those directed at the maintenance of leader status and the processes defining successful leadership and the exercise of power. There are also implications in such research for innovation and change.

The paper by Hollander which begins this section is drawn from his book, *Leaders, Groups, and Influence* (1964), and serves as an introduction to modern developments. It distinguishes the two classic approaches to leadership and notes the waning of earlier attention to the "mystique" of the leader's personality. Relatedly, Hollander emphasizes the extension of interest into the interactive characteristics of leadership as these bear upon both the emergence of leadership as well as its maintenance. Of particular importance is the present impetus toward a view of leader-follower relations in terms of interpersonal perception. Thus, Hollander sees the leader's influence to be affected by the perceptions followers hold of his actions as well as the motives which underlie them. This process appears to be a relevant feature of leader-follower interaction, whether the leader emerges by group consent or is imposed from above.

In looking at imposed leadership within organizations, there are, however, some distinguishing features that require attention, as is more fully explicated in Section IX. In his paper here, Bavelas considers a number of these. His analysis updates the "man vs. situation" issue by stressing that the *function* to be fulfilled is an essential element in the organizational situation in which the leader operates. Thus, the leader's individual characteristics must mesh with these functional demands. It is therefore no longer sensible, he says, to ask merely who the leader is but rather to ask how leadership functions are distributed. The book *Organizations* by March and Simon (1958) provides a worthwhile expansion of this issue.

While Bavelas recognizes that differences exist between organizational requirements and, indeed, in their unique "personalities," he feels that the functions of leadership have a core of similarity calling forth characteristics of a distinctive sort. It is the nature of these functions that stamps organizations uniquely. Within the broader demands made by these functions, however, the leader provides for what Bavelas considers "uncertainty reduction." This definition is suggestive of Hemphill's (1958) concept of the leader as one who "initiates structure," discussed in the Hollander paper. Both the Bavelas and Hemphill conceptions lend themselves to a study of the maintenance of leadership in terms of some criteria of individual performance, which is by way of saying that "effective leadership" is assessed both from below and from above within the organizational constraints.

Fiedler is concerned with the interaction of leaders and followers as it is affected by several situational variables. The extensive empirical work with which Fiedler has been identified gives a special place to the leader's social perception, in the special sense of a measure of perceptual discrimination. This measure is based on a simple scale indicating the degree to which the rater describes favorably or unfavorably his least preferred coworker, hence the designation LPC. Fiedler's research, over a considerable range of subjects and contexts, indicates ". . . . that a person who describes his least preferred coworker in a relatively favorable manner tends to be permissive, human relations oriented, and considerate of the feelings of his men. But a person who describes his least preferred coworker in an unfavorable manner—who has what we have come to call a low LPC rating—tends to be managing, task-controlling, and less concerned with the human relations aspects of the job" (p. 116).

In discussing styles of leadership here, Fiedler finds support for his conception that LPC is a leader characteristic which interacts with various situational factors in determining his effectiveness. The research he reports represents a significant melding of leader attributes and situational circumstances, as represented in the latter instance by quality of leader-member relations, the degree of task structure, and the leader's power. Depending upon the combination of these elements and the leader's permissiveness as measured by the LPC, Fiedler finds striking differences in the leader's ability to achieve productive outcomes. Thus the leader's style is a function of his construction of his relationship with followers (see G. A. Kelly, 1963), and its appropriateness to such situational factors as those Fiedler has studied.

A suggestion from Fiedler's work is that power varies as a consequence of other factors. Bavelas too suggests that the span of control of the organizational leader may be increasingly delimited in the face of other demands made upon him, such as decision-making. Therefore, though such terms as power, authority, and control are often used interchangeably with leadership, they are not necessarily the same.

Elsewhere in their book, an excerpt from which is presented in the preceding section, Thibaut and Kelley present a useful conception concerning power by distinguishing between "behavior control" and "fate control." By fate control they mean that "A can affect B's outcomes *regardless of what B does . . .*" while in behavior control, "by varying his behavior, A can make it desirable for B to vary his behavior too. . . ." They point out that power of the behavior control variety may be thought of in the sense of a statistical interaction, i.e., B's outcomes are determined not as a function either of A's behavior nor his own, but as a result of the joint effects of these. Note, however, that in the case of fate control, A can provide high rewards to B at low cost to himself, though he need not. The choice is his; but, as Thibaut and Kelley suggest, in most functional groups the fact that the members are to a degree dependent upon one another for satisfactions tends to place limits upon each person's "usable power" even under conditions where fate control prevails. Untrammeled exploitation of less powerful by more powerful group members may occur, though a more likely pattern is the fostering of various kinds of mutually profitable bargaining relations—especially when these are supported by the kind of reciprocity orientations discussed by Gouldner in Section V.

French and Raven present an analysis here of the differential bases for power. They make a distinction parallel to the one by Thibaut and Kelley just noted, but also extend their concern with reward power and coercive power to a consideration of legitimate power, referent power, and expert power. All of these have characteristics which are distinctive, though they may occur together. In any case, power need not be translated directly into leadership, in the more interactive sense of that term.

Reward power and coercive power are counterparts of one another. The first represents gains, the other potential losses, for compliance and noncompliance, respectively. Referent power is an extension of reward power through a process of identification which does not require continuous surveillance for its effectiveness. The less powerful person incorporates as his own the demands of the more powerful one. Expert power arises from conditions of specialized knowledge that is valued. Legitimate power is based upon the assimilation of norms which require the acceptance of influence by one person from another, as in employer-employee relations viewed broadly.

In connection with the fate control conception, there is the significant central question of the means at the disposal of a person to reject the demand for compliance, which casts the problem of power in terms of the "resisting force" accessible to a person. A clear relationship is evident between this and the considerations of conformity touched on in the previous section and in French and Raven's discussion.

It is, of course, always artificial to speak of dimensions of leadership as if they had independent identity—such things as power, innovation potential, or effectiveness traits. These are intermingled and serve only as guidelines for hypothesis testing, just as conceptions of "emergent leaders" and "imposed leaders" represent a form of typology which deals in abstractions that may in the real world have considerably greater congruence. It seems clear that what is found to typify the effective "imposed leader" might parallel qualities found in those who emerge as leaders under prevailing situational conditions.

A view of leadership from a different perspective is provided by Elihu Katz in his paper here. His book with Lazarsfeld, *Personal Influence* (1955), is among other things a report of the "Decatur Study" of opinion leadership. Here he gives an overview of "the two-step flow of communication" conception from *The People's Choice* (Lazarsfeld, *et al.*, 1948), a study of the 1940 election, elaborated in the study just noted. Katz provides information on subsequent research approaches to the effects of interpersonal influence as channels of communication, sources of social pressure, and sources of social support. These apply in diverse ranges such as politics, fashions, professional practice, and other aspects of society. A point which bears especially on the interrelated consideration of emergent leadership is the finding that the opinion leader is very much like his followers, not a distinct, definably different kind of person.

Most relevant in the Katz discussion is the role of the opinion leader as an agent of innovation or social change. Indeed, one consequential result of leadership is its function in facilitating change. All societies and the groups within them face the need for some alteration of past practices to meet new demands, and this appears to be an elementary fact of survival. Yet changes are resisted, however beneficial, for a host of reasons including the security of the familiar, particularly the maintenance of congenial social practices. In Festinger's term, "dissonance" is created by a challenge to prevailing structures and belief systems; a useful source in this vein is Lippitt, Watson, and Westley, *The Dynamics of Planned Change* (1958).

Resistance to change takes many forms, including expressions of fears as well as their rationalization. For social forces to overcome these and for change to occur, it is essential that there be leadership events to create an appropriate atmosphere. As Cartwright points out in his paper in this section, change requires these preconditions in the social context. This underscores the importance of situational requirements as ingredients of the leadership process associated with meeting the challenge for change.

In this particularly incisive coverage of principles from group dynamics, Cartwright presents material which ties in well with the substance of the preceding sections. Drawing together the research findings on group dynamics, he discusses their implications for change. He emphasizes the substantive foundation which sustains these principles, and gives impetus to a view of group dynamics as larger in scope than a set of devices. A clear convergence is discernible between the principles that he presents in connection with rendering change and the earlier consideration here of effective leadership.

In practical terms, leadership plays its most pervasive part in organizational settings. What we learn from studies of emergent leadership often has considerable relevance to the functioning of organizations. It is appropriate therefore that in the next section we extend our view of leadership to organizational processes.

50 Leadership, innovation, and influence: an overview

EDWIN P. HOLLANDER

As a current focal point for studying influence effects from social interaction, leadership has ramifications to many other concerns relevant to group process, including conformity, morale, and social change. The study of leadership accordingly contributes to knowledge about the dynamics of influence processes because, in a strict sense, leadership is neither a unique personal attribute, nor is it separable from social influence more generally. Speaking to this point, Thibaut and Kelley have said, "In virtually all cases, leadership seems to be analyzable in terms of other, simpler concepts . . . [every] member of the group can be considered as exhibiting leadership insofar as he exercises power effectively, promotes organization along functional lines, or has symbolic value" (1959, p. 289).

The trait approach to leadership

In the most traditional study of leadership, unique characteristics of "leaders" were sought. The emphasis was placed upon what "made" a leader. But this obscured some important distinctions including the source of authority and the nature of the function to be fulfilled in diverse situations. Leadership had been interwoven for so long with notions of the "man on horseback" and associated images that the more common and pedestrian, work-a-day exercise of leadership was left aside as a process unworthy of attention under the same heading.

Why an emphasis on traits should have prevailed is easy to understand. The literary, prescientific conception of the leader as a special person, a "great man," called attention to inherent qualities that one either possesses or does not, in short, "leadership traits" in the traditional usage. Illustrations of this viewpoint abound, especially in popular literature. Emerson has said, "He is great who is what he is from Nature. . . ." And Thomas Heggen, in introducing the hero of his novel about naval leadership, *Mister Roberts,* says of him: "He was a born leader; there is no other kind."

In psychology, furthermore, the trait approach found a congenial reception because of the psychologist's essential interest in individual characteristics. To measure and assess the personality of "leaders" seemed eminently appropriate to the psychologically-oriented investigator. What was overlooked, however, in the view that leaders are uniquely endowed, was the actual fact of daily life, that is, that persons function as leaders in a particular time and place, and that these are both varying and delimiting conditions; that there are several pathways to leadership, sometimes

Reprinted with slight abridgment from Chapter 1 of **Leaders, Groups, and Influence.** New York: Oxford University Press. 1964, pp. 3–15, with permission of the publisher.

from higher authority, other times from group consent, and at times from both; and that a good many leadership events transpire routinely between individuals in reciprocal relationships, as illustrated by husband and wife, work partners, and playmates. To speak therefore of "the leader" or of leadership as if those terms conveyed an immutable "state of being" from genetics or social tradition, was to leave out a great deal of real-life social process. Indeed, if any point stands forth in the modern day view of leadership it is that leaders are made by circumstance even though some come to those circumstances better equipped than others. It is this line of development which led ultimately to the so-called "situational approach" to the study of leadership.

The situational approach to leadership

The distinctive asset in the situational view lies in the way it frames leadership events in the life context in which they occur. If a leader—let us take the fictional Mr. Roberts, for example—is effective, this is a relevant datum only insofar as it speaks of his setting, a ship's crew, and its associated conditions, as a time-space-person complex. His responsiveness to those men, in their circumstances, at that time, is what helps us to know and understand his effectiveness; and characteristics which make him effective there in securing a willing, responsive group support might not carry through to other situations with different demands.

It is in the nature of situational requirements that they call forth certain expectations for leadership, and these may be fulfilled by various individuals in the situation. Cartwright and Zander (1960) have put it this way: ". . . while certain minimal abilities are required of all leaders, these are widely distributed among nonleaders as well. Furthermore, the traits of the leader which are necessary and effective in one group or situation may be quite different from those of another leader in a different setting" (p. 492). Thus, the situational approach conceives of leadership in terms of function performed, rather than in terms of persisting traits of the leader. Closely related to this is the importance attached to the source of authority as a leader, a matter which is often discussed in terms of so-called "emergent" as contrasted with "imposed" leadership.

Emergent and imposed leadership

The distinction made in contemporary social psychology between emergent and imposed leadership has a broad significance for the nature of groups and their internal dynamics. The acceptance of influence, which is conditional upon the consent of followers, produces "emergent" leadership. "Imposed" leadership tends to be determined by superior authority; it is also possible to have an interlocking state of affairs where these reside in the same person, as in many institutions whose imposed leaders have characteristics which would make them acceptable as emergent leaders as well. In addition, much that has been learned about emergent leaders has applicability to the maintenance of status by those who are imposed leaders (see Hollander, 1961a).

"INFORMAL" AND "FORMAL" LEADERSHIP

Another way this emergent-imposed differentiation is made is in terms of "informal" as against "formal" leadership.

The former suggests emergence and the latter imposition; but using them as if they sharply defined different functions is unrealistic in light of what Homans (1961) calls "elementary social behavior," which he considers to have rules of social interaction applicable all the time. However, the terms formal and informal do have utility *not* with reference to definable modes of interaction as much as to the source of the "structure" which determines the pattern of authority of influence persons. These terms represent, in brief, situational forces rather than categories of mutually exclusive behavior.

WHAT FUNCTIONS ARE TO BE FULFILLED?

Clearly much leadership in the world is of an institutional or "imposed" variety such that task requirements are frequently set by an organization and the structure which it establishes. This means that "leaders" may be people who have highly confined, programmed functions, e.g., decision-making, within the determination of organizational constraints and expectations. This carries operational implications quite different from the usual conception of those interpersonal qualities we think of in the leader-follower relation involving freer personal interaction and "social exchange." This kind of imposed leader makes choices within tightly-limited organizational guidelines, entirely apart from being the traditional "supervisor." On this point Alex Bavelas says that the *function* of the organizational leader may be definably different from his personal characteristics (1960). He suggests that in the aggregate such "leaders" are those who perform certain categories of task rather than share characteristic attributes of personality. The question in organizational leadership, says Bavelas, is not "Who is the leader?" but "What functions are to be fulfilled?" This viewpoint of common functional requirements in institutional situations reveals the expectation of an interchangeability of managerial personnel.

Interactive characteristics of leadership

Granting the demands of the situation, the question nonetheless persists whether there are characteristics of leadership which *do* cut across and pervade many situations in our society. And there appear to be some, although they must be understood in finer detail. Gibb (1954), for example, has said that where situations are limited in certain ways leaders do exhibit various "outstanding qualifications." What these may be, and whether they refer to the task or interpersonal demands, is another matter. In either event, if these existed, that would not in and of itself contradict the potency of situational factors since their content may in fact be determined by those features of the social context which have high priority or thrust. As a case in point, competence in providing for some group function is one kind of requirement for group acceptance; but *what* that competence should be is necessarily linked to the social forces at work in that time and place. Because many groups operate in terms of verbal communication, it is hardly surprising that many studies should point up verbal effectiveness as an attribute of those who are leaders. Consequently, strangers brought together in a common plight may be expected to coalesce about the one among them who speaks out suggesting a course of action; on that same probability basis he also has a high likelihood of becoming influential in the sense of taking on a leadership role (cf. Riecken, 1958).

A further point to consider is that leaders must be aware of the circumstances which prevail in order to affect group activity. Where the leader is out of touch with the group's situation and its inclinations about it, he is ill-equipped to meet the expectations for action. Clearly then leaders must be attuned to what is expected of them, recognizing that they can and do initiate changes, including those in the social expectations themselves. It follows therefore that social perceptiveness is a feature that is demanded of leaders in many circumstances, but this need not be a "trait" since it has been found to be moderated by other elements. The leader's motivation and the nature of the group are among them. Also, where a person is *more* motivated to be aware of the happenings in a social context, he is more likely to perceive what is occurring. This holds true whenever persons have a desire to be accepted in a group, to use it as a model for action, or to identify with it even at a distance, as with some "reference groups." Therefore, if leaders are said to be more socially perceptive, this should be understood to involve not just a capacity for perceptiveness alone but quite likely some impelling motivation as well.

Status emergence and status maintenance

The relationships producing leadership can be further distinguished by studying the interrelated processes of status emergence, concerning factors at work in the *achievement* of influence, and status maintenance, covering those which allow the *retention* of influence. A failure to make this distinction has led to findings which appear contradictory on the face of it. These processes not only differ from one another but they also differ from the informal-formal distinction. Imposing authority and forcing compliance by followers to the formal structure does not eliminate the need for influence to be retained. Even with a mandate from above, as in most organizations, imposed leadership must also rest on the responsiveness of followers, and their willingness to comply. This is a lesson that organizationally imposed leaders learn at times with regret. The retention of leadership necessarily depends somewhat upon others' perceptions of competence and effectiveness.

STRUCTURE AND FUNCTION: PROCESS AND EFFECT

Since the idea of "structure" is central to what has been said and what follows, it is useful here to place it in the broader picture of the dynamics of groups. Toward that end, two pairs of distinctions are required: (1) *structure* and *function;* and (2) *process* and *effect.* While these terms are often used arbitrarily, more usually a group's "structure" refers to its organization including distribution of labor, status differentiation, patterns of communication, and such normative expectations as procedures, roles, and the like. On the other hand, a group's "function" refers to the activities or behaviors carried on mutually for the achievement of some common goal, reflecting the purpose or *raison d'être* of the group. Thus, structure by definition includes influence patterns, which optimally are supposed to be harmonious with the function to be fulfilled and, in turn, the goal to be commonly attained.

In the case of emergent leadership, the structure arises from the group's perception of its function, and if that function should change grossly then the structure must also be altered for the group to act effectively. Effective leadership therefore is a structural feature of the functional or task requirements presented to the group (see Hollander, 1964, Ch. 20). However, structures have a self-sustaining quality which, as will be noted, supports the maintenance of present leadership. This tendency is all the more marked in institutional settings where the structure is imposed from above, and where leadership is anchored in the prevailing structure. But in either case, whether structures are informal or formal, leaders are beneficiaries of the present structure, even though a change in situational conditions may instigate alterations in the structure. The basis for the leader's hold on the structure lies significantly in his role in molding it to his design, or to his exemplification of its associated function by his competence in a focal group task.

In the other distinction noted, group "process" may be thought of as the ongoing nature of intra-group activities, including for example goal-seeking behavior and related patterns of interaction. In an important sense, process encompasses the inter-relationship over time between function and structure. Group "effects" refer to the *products* of process, including member attitudes seen in such things as cohesiveness, or shifts in leadership expectations, or in broad social change.

INITIATING STRUCTURE

Structure is vital in, for example, Hemphill's (1958, 1961) view that leadership involves the "initiation of structure" in the group. He sees leadership not simply as a part of structure, but rather as an instrumental agent determining the shape it should take. In his terms, *attempted* leadership is based on such initiations of new structure; however, the leadership act is incomplete unless that initiation is *accepted*. A completed sequence in Hemphill's phrase is "successful leadership"; and "effective leadership" occurs when a contribution is made to the solution of the group's mutual problem. Hemphill and his co-workers, Pepinsky and Shevitz (1958), have reported at least one study where the degree of initiation of structure by a subject is significantly raised or lowered by the acceptance that person is led to believe he has, through a form of social reinforcement. This serves as a demonstration of the situational constraints or enhancements which shape leadership acts. And most importantly, it speaks to processes which determine an individual's *attempts* at influence assertion.

On the other side of this process there is the broader issue of conditions which determine the *acceptance* of influence. Several kinds of approaches may be fruitful in highlighting one or more variables which have potency in this respect. High in contemporary interest are the interaction characteristics of leader-follower relationships. Here the focus rests upon what conditions permit acceptable assertions of influence. Several clusters of elements are bound up in this interest. One of these is the nature of the group context, suggesting variables in the group's function and structure, its cohesiveness, communication, and the like.

PERCEPTION OF THE LEADER

Also of key importance is the perception "relevant others" hold of the potential leader, the influence-person, in that setting. Considering leadership as an interpersonal encounter necessarily involving person perception, three categories of qualities appear to be in the nature of distinctions made. Though variously labeled, these are: (1) the perceived competence of the individual, broadly conceived in terms of the specific task of the group at the time; (2) the adherence of the individual to agreed upon procedures, that is, what he does to demonstrate his identification with the group; and (3) those of his personal characteristics or attributes perceived as valued for their own sake, though they may contribute less specifically to the function of the group. The first two factors appear to have prime significance in the attainment of a position of influence where emergence is possible. This suggests that the individual must be in a group sufficiently long to develop in others a degree of trust or esteem for him, and for them to note his part in helping to fulfill group goals.

While this process of status attainment goes on, the group's prevailing social forms must be adhered to, unless the potential influence person is extremely competent, or is in the category of an expert, which presents special circumstances. Generally speaking, it is unlikely that just any member of a group could achieve leadership by a suggestion for innovation very early in his exposure to a group. The context is simply not yet favorable. And this is the common observation made in connection with the newcomer to a group: he is considerably more restricted in behavior than the person who has established himself there over a longer time and has gained "idiosyncrasy credit" by proving himself.

Once attained, the maintenance of leadership requires innovation and change as acceptable, indeed often expected, functions on the part of the leader. Having accorded high acceptance to this individual, the group may receive his suggested innovations more favorably. This is related to a number of formulations, including Homans's (1961) concept of "status congruence," that is, the appropriateness of behaviors and functions in relation to hierarchical status.

Power and influence

A frequently made assumption is that influence necessarily involves the exercise of power. This would suggest that any act of influence would represent power over the person actually influenced; however, in this sense, the terms influence and power are not synonymous. Another questionable assumption is that imposed leadership, with authority vested from above, must operate in terms of the assertion of power.

There are several factors which should be borne in mind to qualify these beliefs. In the first place, power may be both influence potential as well as resistance potential as Cartwright (1959, Ch. 1) has pointed out. Second, the absence of influence acceptance in the face of an assertion of influence does not necessarily mean that the influence agent is powerless but could mean that he does not fully assert the influence potential at his command. This matter of restraint in the use of power available in imposed organizational structures is a necessarily vital condition for smooth relationships. Where the person in authority consistently uses the full power of his position this undercuts his long-term effectiveness because of the resistance built up over time, as well as other disadvantages. Unfettered use of power obviously does occur, but a greater likelihood exists that bargaining relationships of a jointly rewarding nature will develop to offset resistance, as Thibaut and Kelley (1959) have contended in their model of social exchange.

Another consideration then is that power may be employed by degrees. It is not an all-or-nothing matter. Even in the most authoritatively oriented structures, it is not identical to exercising "effective leadership." Indeed, imposed leaders must reckon with the structure of the emergent group which serves as a base of security for the individual and provides power in the form of a mutual resistance potential to the dictatorial use of power. This is by way of saying that power to avoid untrammeled exploitation rests with the work group and that this must be recognized as a counterforce by the supervisor. Even in extreme conditions, where power is founded on physical force which overdetermines the outcome, power is *not* an instrument of successful leadership in its own right.

The key consideration to be emphasized is that the influence assertions of the imposed leader are evaluated by the group in the context of the perceived motivation involved and the consequences for some common good represented in a group goal. It is in this sense that the maintenance of leadership, even by an imposed leader, requires a regard for the working relationships which are affected by assertions of power.

Social change

An expansion of these points leads to the consequential issue of social change. All societies, and the groups comprising them, must continually undergo some change as an elemental fact of nature. There are, however, forces resisting change, whatever the desirability of the new course offered. Very often these arise because of the essential security provided by the familiar. Accordingly, a central question in considering social change is how groups come to recognize that some well-entrenched social form ought to be altered. It is especially useful to employ terms associated with status emergence in pursuing this further.

For social change to be instigated there must be a comparison between things as they are and things as they might be. This suggests a flow of information through some channel of communication, and calls attention to the work on diffusion and innovation by Katz and Lazarsfeld (1955) and Menzel and Katz (1955) in which the leader is found to be a person who provides an interpretation of the world outside the immediate group. It is he who conveys a structure in terms of "social reality," and the acceptance of innovation. Partly because of this, social change no longer can be cast in the tidy terms of the venerable historical controversy of "the man *or* the times." More accurately, in contemporary social psychology, this problem seems a matter of studying the combined impact of the leader and the social context upon the view that followers will hold of their world. This is significant to their associated willingness to undertake change. In short, neither man nor the situation exists independently of the other since, in the *emergence* aspect of leadership, group members operate from the base of a situation and the particular demands it makes for "task requirements."

In a related vein, it is also true that suggestions offered are variously reacted to depending upon the status of the person from whom they come, a point already noted here (see Hollander, 1961b). This offers a tie with balance or congruity theories of attitude change which suggest the cognitive aptness of similarly "signed" terms, i.e., leader positively signed, his recommended course of action positively signed, then "balanced." The work of Osgood and Tannenbaum (1955) and of Heider (1958), among others, is suggestive of this line of analysis. If we take the relatively simple case of the leader as a positively signed term, his neutral idea or negatively signed idea may carry the day: it is cognitively consistent for him to be identified with positive things, and so balancing occurs. Still, equally possible, a negatively signed person, or a neutral person, may gain status by espousing a potent "positive" idea with which he becomes associated and from which he then draws residual benefits.

An expansion of these considerations would lead to a somewhat richer, more nuance-laden conception of social influence involving the leader as the emitter of complex multi-signed stimuli which become relevant to the follower, as recipient, in terms of the motivational and reference group contexts of which he partakes at a given time.

The leader's emergence or waning of status is thus inextricably linked to the prevailing situation, both as group members understand it from the information at hand and as they hold attachments to persons or orientations, present but also past. A change of the influence structure must necessarily overcome the resistance which these factors erect and encourage. It is not so much, then, the "man or the times" as it appears to be the perception of the man and what he represents himself to be and to stand for in the context of the already enveloping situation. Yet, once having achieved status of high influence, what he does may not and indeed need not fit past expectations for, in the maintenance of his position, he is obliged to fulfill new expectations which arise as the situation inevitably is altered.

51 Leadership: man and function

ALEX BAVELAS

There is a useful distinction to be made between the idea of leadership as a personal quality and the idea of leadership as an organizational function. The first refers to a special combination of personal characteristics; the second refers to the distribution throughout an organization of decision-making powers. The first leads us to look at the qualities and abilities of individuals; the second leads us to look at the patterns of power and authority in organizations. Both of these ideas or definitions of leadership are useful, but it is important to know which one is being talked about, and to know under what conditions the two must be considered together in order to understand a specific organizational situation.

Early notions about leadership dealt with it almost entirely in terms of personal abilities. Leadership was explicitly associated with special powers. An outstanding leader was credited not only with extensions of the normal abilities possessed by most men but with extraordinary powers such as the ability to read men's minds, to tell the future, to compel obedience hypnotically. These powers were often thought of as gifts from a god, as conditional loans from a devil, or as the result of some accidental supernatural circumstance attending conception, birth, or early childhood. Today, claims of supernatural powers are made more rarely, but they are not entirely unknown. Of course, milder claims—tirelessness, infallibility of intuition, lightning-quick powers of decision—are made in one form or another by many outstandingly successful men. And when they do not make them for themselves, such claims are made for them by others who, for their own reasons, prefer such explanations of success to other more homely ones.

Outright supernatural explanations of leadership have, in recent times, given way to more rational explanations. Leadership is still generally thought of in terms of personal abilities, but now the assumption is made that the abilities in question are the same as those possessed by all normal persons: individuals who become leaders are merely presumed to have them to a greater degree.

For many years, attempts to define these abilities and to measure them failed. This was not only because the early techniques of measurement were primitive and unreliable but for a more important reason. The traits that were defined as important for leadership were often nothing more than purely verbal expressions of what the researcher felt leaders *ought* to be like. Few of the many lists of traits that were developed had very much in common. Typical of the items that frequently appeared on such lists were piety, honesty, courage, perseverance, intelligence, reliability, imagination, industriousness. This way of thinking about leadership is still very common. It persists, not because it is helpful in analyzing and understanding the phenomenon of leadership, but be-

Reprinted from the Administrative Science Quarterly, 1960, 4, 491–98, with permission of the author and publisher.

cause it expresses a deep and popular wish about what leaders *should* be like.

Modern trait research proceeds in a very different way. Leadership traits are no longer selected arbitrarily. They are, instead, largely derived from the results of tests that are carefully designed, administered, and interpreted. And the techniques of measurement and analysis which are applied to the data that are gathered have been extensively developed and refined. Numerous trait studies have been made of the physical, intellectual, and social characteristics of leaders. On various tests, persons who are leaders tend to be brighter, tend to be better adjusted psychologically, and tend to display better judgment. Studies that have concentrated on the social behavior of leaders show that they "interact" more than nonleaders. They tend to give more information, ask for more information, and to take the lead in summing up or interpreting a situation.

Despite these accomplishments, the trait approach has in recent years been subjected to increasing criticism. A common objection is that the results are obtained by a method that requires an initial separation of people into "leaders" and "nonleaders" or "good leaders" and "not-so-good leaders." The validity of the distinguishing traits that come out of such work, the argument goes, can only be as good as the validity of the preliminary grouping of the persons being studied. All of this leads to the question, "On what basis is the initial separation of subjects made, and how is it justified?"

At first glance, this may appear a trivial and carping question. In fact, however, it is one of the most serious obstacles in the way of all leadership research. It is obviously impossible to define "good leaders" without reference to a system of values. To say that a man is a "good leader" means that his behavior and its consequences are held to be of greater worth than other behaviors and results.

What system of values shall the researcher adopt that is both scientifically acceptable and socially useful in distinguishing good or successful leaders from others? Many attempts have been made to find a suitable criterion, but the results have been generally unsatisfactory —not that it is difficult to find standards which are desirable and inspiring, but that such standards tend to be based, just as the early lists of traits were, on qualities that are difficult or impossible to measure. And often they just do not seem to "work." For example, there have been attempts to distinguish leaders from nonleaders in terms that rest essentially on moral and ethical considerations. It may be a significant commentary on our society that there appears to be no particular correlation between a man's ethics and morals and his power to attract followers.

It has been suggested that many of the philosophical difficulties that attend the definition of "good leader" can be avoided if one accepts the more limited task of defining "good executive." In business and industry, one would like to think, there should be practical, quantitative ways of making the distinction. Many attempts have been made in this direction. Reputation, financial success, hierarchical position, influence, and many other criteria have been tried without much satisfaction. The inadequacies of such standards are obvious to any experienced executive.

There is a second and more interesting objection that has been made to the trait approach. It is based not on the question of the accuracy or the validity of the assumptions that are made but upon the nature of the "traits" themselves. Traits are, after all, statements about personal characteristics. The objection to this is that the degree to which an individual exhibits leadership depends not only on *his characteristics*, but, also, on the *characteristics of the situation* in which he finds himself. For example, a man who shows all the signs of leadership when he acts as the officer of a well-structured authoritarian organization may give no indication of leadership ability in a less-structured, democratic situation. A man may become influential in a situation requiring deliberation and planning but show little evidence of leadership if the situation demands immediate action with no opportunity for weighing alternatives or thinking things out. Or, to take still another instance, a man may function effectively and comfortably in a group whose climate is friendly and co-operative but retreat and become ineffective if he perceives the atmosphere as hostile.

The case for the situational approach to leadership derives its strength from this fact: while organizations in general may exhibit broad similarities of structure and function, they also, in particular, show strong elements of uniqueness.

It is a matter of common observation that within any normal industrial organization, providing there has been a sufficient past, there will be found patterns of relationships and interaction that are highly predictable and highly repetitive. Some of these reoccurring situations will be unique to that organization. It is this uniqueness that is referred to when one speaks of the "personality" of a company. This is what a management has in mind when it selects a new member with an eye to how he will "fit in." The argument of the researcher who stresses the situational aspects of leadership is that these unique characteristics of an organization are often crucial in determining which of two equally competent and gifted men will become a "leader," and further that in the very same organization these unique patterns may change significantly at different levels of the hierarchy. The very same "leadership abilities" that helped a man rise to the top may, once he is there, prove a positive detriment.

The status of trait and situational leadership research can be summed up in this way: (1) the broad similarities which hold for a great number of organizations make it possible to say useful things about the kind of person who is likely to become a leader in any of those organizations, and (2) the unique characteristics of a particular organization make it necessary to analyze the situational factors that determine who is likely to become a leader *in one particular organization*. To put it another way, when specific situational patterns are different from organization to organization, one cannot say what personal traits will lead to acknowledged leadership. Instead, one must try to define the leadership functions that must be performed in those situations and regard as leadership those acts which perform them. This point of view suggests that almost any member of a group may become its leader under circumstances that enable him to perform the required functions of leadership and that different persons may contribute in different ways to the leadership of the group.

In these terms we come close to the notion of leadership, not as a personal quality, but as an *organizational func-*

tion. Under this concept it is not sensible to ask of an organization "who is the leader?" Rather we ask "how are the leadership functions distributed in this organization?" The distribution may be wide or narrow. It may be so narrow—so many of the leadership functions may be vested in a single person—that he is the leader in the popular sense. But in modern organizations this is becoming more and more rare.

What are these "leadership functions?" Many have been proposed: planning, giving information, evaluating, arbitrating, controlling, rewarding, punishing, and the like. All of these stem from the underlying idea that leadership acts are those which help the group achieve its objectives, or, as it is also put, to satisfy its "needs." In most face-to-face groups, the emergence of a leader can well be accounted for on this basis. That person who can assist or facilitate the group most in reaching a satisfactory state is most likely to be regarded as the leader. If one looks closely at what constitutes assistance or facilitation in this sense, it turns out to be the making of choices or the helping of the group to make choices—"better" choices, of course.

But can the function of leadership be reduced simply to decision making or the facilitation of decision making? The objection can be raised that such a definition is much too wide to be useful. Every action, even every physical movement one makes, is after all "chosen" out of a number of possible alternatives. If when I am at my workbench I pick up a screwdriver in preference to a hammer, I am clearly making a choice; am I, by virtue of that choice, displaying leadership? Something is obviously wrong with a definition of leadership which imputes it to any act that can be shown to have involved a choice. Common sense would argue that customary, habitual, and "unconscious" actions, although they may logically contain elements of choice, should be separated from actions that are subjectively viewed by the person taking them as requiring a decision. Common sense would also argue that questions of choice that can be settled on the basis of complete information should be considered differently from questions of choice in which decisions must be taken in the face of uncertainty. And common sense would argue that some distinction should be made between decisions that, although made on equally uncertain grounds, involve very different orders of risk.

This is, of course, the implicit view of the practicing manager, and although it may contain very knotty problems of logic it is the view that will be taken here. Stated in general terms, the position that will be taken is that organizational leadership consists of *uncertainty reduction*. The actual behavior through which this reduction is accomplished is the making of choices.

We saw above that not all choices are equally difficult or equally important. Some choices are considered unimportant or irrelevant and are ignored, and of course whole areas may be seen as so peripheral to the interests of the organization that they are not perceived as areas of choice at all. Other choices that *must* be made are so well understood that they become habitual and automatic. Some of these are grouped into more or less coherent bundles and given a job name. The employee learns to make them correctly as he becomes skilled in the job. In most job evaluation plans, additional credit is given if the job requires judgment. This is a way of saying that there are choices remaining in the job that cannot be completely taken care of by instructions but must be made by the employee as they come along.

There are other choices which, although they are equally clear and habitual, are of a more general nature and do not apply just to a specific job but apply to all. These are customarily embodied in rules and procedures. Rules and procedures are, in this sense, decisions made in advance of the events to which they are to be applied. Obviously, this is possible and practical only to the extent that the events to which the rules and procedures apply can be foreseen, and the practical limit of their completeness and specificity depends on how these future events can be predicted.

Following this line of analysis, it is theoretically possible to arrange all the logically inherent choices that must be made in operating an industrial organization along scales of increasing uncertainty and importance. At some level in this hierarchy of choices, it is customary for management to draw a line, reserving for itself from that point on the duty and the privilege of making the required decisions.

Precisely where a management draws this line defines its scope. The way in which a management distributes the responsibility for making the set of choices it has thus claimed to itself defines its structure. What organizational leadership *is* and what kinds of acts constitute it are questions that can be answered only within this framework of scope and structure. In these terms leadership consists of the continuous choice-making process that permits the organization as a whole to proceed toward its objectives despite all sorts of internal and external perturbations.

But as every practicing manager knows, problems occasionally arise that are not amenable to the available and customary methods of analysis and solution. Although uncertain about which choice to make, a management may nevertheless have to make a decision. It is in situations of this kind that many of the popular traits attributed to leaders find their justification: quickness of decision, the courage to take risks, coolness under stress, intuition, and, even, luck. There is no doubt that quick, effective, and daring decisions are a highly prized commodity in a crisis, but just as precious a commodity is the art of planning and organizing so that such crises do not occur. The trend of management has been to remove as many of its decisions as possible from the area of hunch and intuition to that of rational calculation. More and more, organizations are choosing to depend less on the peculiar abilities of rare individuals and to depend instead on the orderly processes of research and analysis. The occasions and opportunities for personal leadership in the old sense still exist, but they are becoming increasingly rare and circumscribed.

This new emphasis has not eliminated the role of personal leadership, but it has significantly redefined it. Under normal conditions of operation, leadership in the modern organization consists not so much in the making of decisions personally as it does of maintaining the operational effectiveness of the decision-making systems which comprise the management of the organization. The picture of the leader who keeps his own counsel and in the nick of time pulls the rabbit out of the hat is out of date. The popular stereotype now is the thoughtful executive discussing in committee the information supplied by a staff of experts. In fact it may be that the brilliant innovator, in the role of manager, is rapidly becoming as much an organizational embarrassment as he is an asset.

This trend, reasonable though it may appear on the surface, conceals two serious dangers. First, we may be systematically giving up the opportunity of utilizing the highest expressions of personal leadership in favor of managerial arrangements which, although safer and more reliable, can yield at best only a high level of mediocrity. And second, having committed ourselves to a system that thrives on the ordinary, we may, in the interests of maintaining and improving its efficiency, tend to shun the extraordinary.

It is no accident that daring and innovation wane as an organization grows large and successful. On different levels this appears to have been the history of men, of industries, of nations, and even of societies and cultures. Success leads to "obligations"—not the least of which is the obligation to hold what has been won. Therefore, the energies of a man or administration may be absorbed in simply maintaining vested interests. Similarly, great size requires "system," and system, once established, may easily become an end in itself.

This is a gloomy picture, because it is a picture of decay. It has been claimed, usually with appeals to biological analogies, that this is an inevitable cycle, but this view is, very probably, incorrect. Human organizations are not biological organisms; they are social inventions.

52 Styles of leadership

FRED E. FIEDLER

Leadership is a personal relationship in which one person directs, coordinates, and supervises others in the performance of a common task. This is especially so in "interacting groups," where men must work together cooperatively in achieving organizational goals.

In oversimplified terms, it can be said that the leader manages the group in either of two ways. He can:

Tell people what to do and how to do it.

Or share his leadership responsibilities with his group members and involve them in the planning and execution of the task.

There are, of course, all shades of leadership styles in between these two polar positions, but the basic issue is this: the work of motivating and coordinating group members has to be done either by brandishing the proverbial stick or by dangling the equally proverbial carrot. The former is the more

Abridged from "Engineer the Job To Fit the Manager," **Harvard Business Review**, 1965, 43, 115–22, with permission of the author and the publisher.

orthodox job-centered, autocratic style. The latter is the more nondirective, group-centered procedure.

Research evidence exists to support both approaches to leadership. Which, then, should be judged more appropriate? On the face of it, the first style of leadership is best under some conditions, while the second works better under others. Accepting this proposition immediately opens two avenues of approach. Management can:

Determine the specific situation in which the directive or the nondirective leadership style works best, and then select or train men so that their leadership style fits the particular job.

Or determine the type of leadership style which is most natural for the man in the executive position, and then change the job to fit the man.

The first alternative has been discussed many times before; the second has not. We have never seriously considered whether it would be easier to fit the executive's job to the man.

Needed style?

How might this be done? Some answers have been suggested by a research program on leadership effectiveness that I have directed under Office of Naval Research auspices since 1951. This program has dealt with a wide variety of different groups, including basketball teams, surveying parties, various military combat crews, and men in open-hearth steel shops, as well as members of management and boards of directors. When possible, performance was measured in terms of objective criteria—for instance, percentage of games won by high school basketball teams; tap-to-tap time of open-hearth shops (roughly equivalent to the tonnage of steel output per unit of time); and company net income over a three-year period. Our measure of leadership style was based on a simple scale indicating the degree to which a man described, favorably or unfavorably, his least-preferred co-worker (LPC). This co-worker did not need to be someone he actually worked with at the time, but could be someone the respondent had known in the past. Whenever possible, the score was obtained before the leader was assigned to his group.

The study indicates that a person who describes his least-preferred co-worker in a relatively favorable manner tends to be permissive, human relations-oriented, and considerate of the feelings of his men. But a person who describes his least-preferred co-worker in an unfavorable manner—who has what we have come to call a low LPC rating—tends to be managing, task-controlling, and less concerned with the human relations aspects of the job. It also appears that the directive, managing, and controlling leaders tend to perform best in basketball and surveying teams, in open-hearth shops, and (provided the leader is accepted by his group) in military combat crews and company managements. On the other hand, the nondirective, permissive, and human relations-oriented leaders tend to perform best in decision-making and policy-making teams and in groups that have a creative task—provided that the group likes the leader or the leader feels that the group is pleasant and free of tension.

Critical dimensions

But in order to tell which style fits which situation, we need to categorize groups. Our research has shown that "it all depends" on the situation. After reviewing the results of all our work and the findings of other investigators, we have been able to isolate three major dimensions that seem to determine, to a large part, the kind of leadership style called for by different situations.

It is obviously a mistake to think that groups and teams are all alike and that each requires the same kind of leadership. We need some way of categorizing the group-task situation, or the job environment within which the leader has to operate. If leadership is indeed a process of influencing other people to work together effectively in a common task, then it surely matters how easy or difficult it is for the leader to exert his influence in a particular situation.

Leader-member relations. The factor that would seem most important in determining a man's leadership influence is the degree to which his group members trust and like him, and are willing to follow his guidance. The trusted and well-liked leader obviously does not require special rank or power in order to get things done. We can measure the leader-member relationship by the so-called sociometric nomination techniques that ask group members to name in their group the most influential person, or the man they would most like to have as a leader. It can also be measured by a group-atmosphere scale indicating the degree to which the leader feels accepted and comfortable in the group.

The task structure. The second important factor is the "task structure." By this term I mean the degree to which the task (a) is spelled out step by step for the group and, if so, the extent to which it can be done "by the numbers" or according to a detailed set of standard operating instructions, or (b) must be left nebulous and undefined. Vague and ambiguous or unstructured tasks make it difficult to exert leadership influence, because neither the leader nor his members know exactly what has to be done or how it is to be accomplished.

Why single out this aspect of the task rather than the innumerable other possible ways of describing it? Task groups are almost invariably components of a larger organization that assigns the task and has, therefore, a big stake in seeing it performed properly. However, the organization can control the quality of a group's performance only if the task is clearly spelled out and programmed or structured. When the task can be programmed or performed "by the numbers," the organization is able to back up the authority of the leader to the fullest; the man who fails to perform each step can be disciplined or fired. But in the case of ill-defined, vague, or unstructured tasks, the organization and the leader have very little control and direct power. By close supervision one can ensure, let us say, that a man will correctly operate a machine, but one cannot ensure that he will be creative.

It is therefore easier to be a leader in a structured task situation in which the work is spelled out than in an unstructured one which presents the leader and his group with a nebulous, poorly defined problem.

Position power. Thirdly, there is the power of the leadership position, as distinct from any personal power the leader might have. Can he hire or fire and promote or demote? Is his appointment for life, or will it terminate at the pleasure of his group? It is obviously easier to be a leader when the position power is strong than when it is weak.

Model for analysis

When we now classify groups on the basis of these three dimensions, we get a classification system that can be represented as a cube; see Exhibit 1. As each group is high or low in each of the three dimensions, it will fall into one of the eight cells.

From examination of the cube, it seems clear that exerting leadership influence will be easier in a group in which the members like a powerful leader with a clearly defined job and where the job to be done is clearly laid out (Cell 1); it will be difficult in a group where a leader is disliked, has little power, and has a highly ambiguous job (Cell 8).

In other words, it is easier to be the well-esteemed foreman of a construction crew working from a blueprint than it is to be the disliked chairman of a volunteer committee preparing a new policy.

I consider the leader-member relations the most important dimension,

Exhibit 1. A model for classifying group-task situations.

and the position-power dimension the least important, of the three. It is, for instance, quite possible for a man of low rank to lead a group of higher-ranking men in a structured task—as is done when enlisted men or junior officers conduct some standardized parts of the training programs for medical officers who enter the Army. But it is not so easy for a disrespected manager to lead a creative, policy-formulating session well, even if he is the senior executive present.

Varying requirements

By first sorting the eight cells according to leader-member relations, then task structure, and finally leader position power, we can now arrange them in order according to the favorableness of the environment for the leader. This sorting leads to an eight-step scale, as in Exhibit 2. This exhibit portrays the results of a series of studies of groups performing well but (a) in different situations and conditions, and (b) with leaders using different leadership styles. In explanation:

The *horizontal* axis shows the range of situations that the groups worked in, as described by the classification scheme used in Exhibit 1.

The *vertical* axis indicates the leadership style which was best in a certain

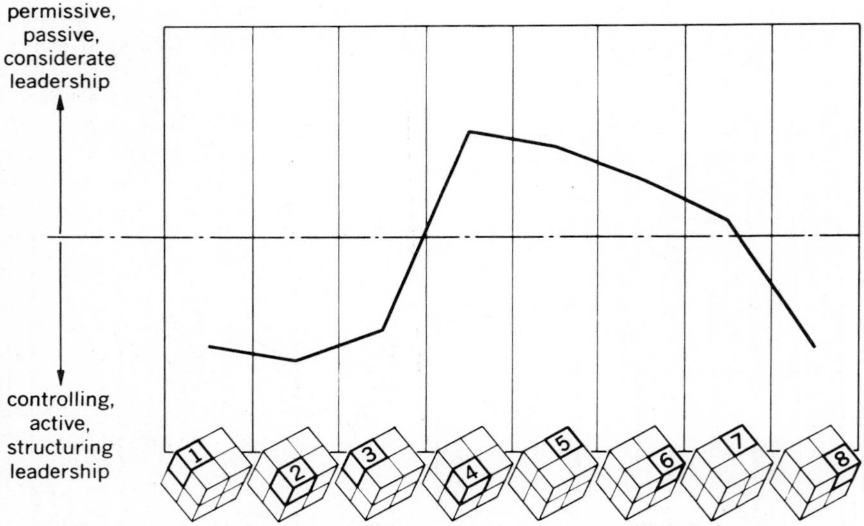

leader-member relations	good	good	good	good	poor	poor	poor	poor
task structure	structured		unstructured		structured		unstructured	
leader position power	strong	weak	strong	weak	strong	weak	strong	weak

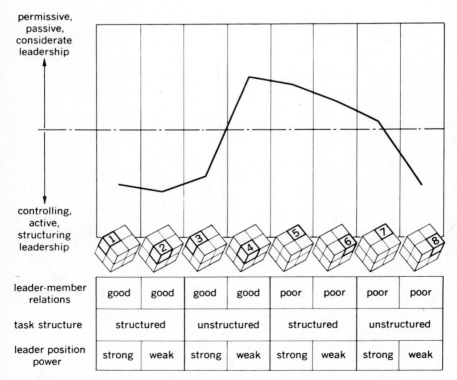

Exhibit 2. How the style of effective leadership varies with the situation.

situation, as shown by the correlation coefficient between the leader's LPC and his group's performance.

A positive correlation (falling above the midline) shows that the permissive, nondirective, and human relations-oriented leaders performed best; a negative correlation (below the midline) shows that the task-controlling, managing leader performed best. For instance, leaders of effective groups in situation categories 1 and 2 had LPC-group performance correlations of — .40 to — .80, with the average between — .50 and — .60; whereas leaders of effective groups in situation categories 4 and 5 had LPC-group performance correlations of .20 to .80, with the average between .40 and .50.

Exhibit 2 shows that both the directive, managing, task-oriented leaders and the non-directive, human relations-oriented leaders are successful under some conditions. Which leadership style is the best depends on the favorableness of the particular situation for the leader. In very favorable or in very unfavorable situations for getting a task accomplished by group effort, the autocratic, task-controlling, managing leadership works best. In situations intermediate in difficulty, the nondirective, permissive leader is more successful.

This corresponds well with our everyday experience. For instance:

Where the situation is very favorable, the group expects and wants the leader to give directions. We neither expect nor want the trusted airline pilot to turn to his crew and ask, "What do you think we ought to check before takeoff?"

If the disliked chairman of a volunteer committee asks his group what to do, he may be told that everybody ought to go home.

The well-liked chairman of a planning group or research team must be nondirective and permissive in order to get full participation from his members. The directive, managing leader will tend to be more critical and to cut discussion short; hence he will not get the full benefit of the potential contributions by his group members.

The varying requirements of leadership styles are readily apparent in organizations experiencing dramatic changes in operating procedures. For example:

The manager or supervisor of a routinely operating organization is expected to provide direction and supervision that the subordinates should follow. However, in a crisis the routine is no longer adequate, and the task becomes ambiguous and unstructured. The typical manager tends to respond in such instances by calling his principal assistants together for a conference. In other words, the effective leader changes his behavior from a directive to a permissive, nondirective style until the operation again reverts to routine conditions.

In the case of a research planning group, the human relations-oriented and permissive leader provides a climate in which everybody is free to speak up, to suggest, and to criticize. Osborn's brainstorming method (1953) in fact institutionalizes these procedures. However, after the research plan has been completed, the situation becomes highly structured. The director now prescribes the task in detail, and he specifies the means of accomplishing it. Woe betide the assistant who decides to be creative by changing the research instructions!

Practical tests

Remember that the ideas I have been describing emanate from studies of real-life situations; accordingly, as might be expected, they can be validated by organizational experience. Take, for instance, the dimension of leader-member relations described earlier. We have made three studies of situations in which the leader's position power was strong and the task relatively structured with clear-cut goals and standard operating procedures. In such groups as these the situation will be very favorable for the leader if he is accepted; it will be progressively unfavorable in proportion to how much a leader is disliked. What leadership styles succeed in these varying conditions? The studies confirm what our theory would lead us to expect. In all three studies, the highly accepted and strongly rejected leaders perform best if they are controlling and managing, while the leaders in the intermediate acceptance range, who are neither rejected nor accepted, perform best if they are permissive and nondirective.

53 The bases of power

JOHN R. P. FRENCH, JR. and BERTRAM H. RAVEN

By the basis of power we mean the relationship between O and P which is the source of that power.[1] It is rare that we can say with certainty that a given empirical case of power is limited to one source. Normally, the relation between O and P will be characterized by several qualitatively different variables which are bases of power (Lippitt, *et al.*, 1952, Ch. 11). Although there are undoubtedly many possible bases of power which may be distinguished, we shall here define five which seem especially common and important. These five bases of O's power are: (1) reward power, based on P's perception that O has the ability to mediate rewards for him; (2) coercive power, based on P's perception that O has the ability to mediate punishments for him; (3) legitimate power, based on the perception by P that O has a legitimate right to

[1] "Our theory of social influence and power is limited to influence on the person, P, produced by an agent, O, where O can be either another person, a role, a norm, a group, or a part of a group" (French & Raven, 1959, p. 151).—Eds.

Excerpted from "The Bases of Social Power," Chapter 9 of D. Cartwright (Ed.) **Studies in Social Power,** Ann Arbor: University of Michigan, Institute for Social Research, 1959, pp. 150–67, with permission of the authors and the publisher.

prescribe behavior for him; (4) referent power, based on P's identification with O; (5) expert power, based on the perception that O has some special knowledge or expertness.

Our first concern is to define the bases which give rise to a given type of power. Next, we describe each type of power according to its strength, range, and the degree of dependence of the new state of the system which is most likely to occur with each type of power. We shall also examine the other effects which the exercise of a given type of power may have upon P and his relationship to O. Finally, we shall point out the interrelationships between different types of power, and the effects of use of one type of power by O upon other bases of power which he might have over P. Thus we shall both define a set of concepts and propose a series of hypotheses. Most of these hypotheses have not been systematically tested, although there is a good deal of evidence in favor of several. No attempt will be made to summarize that evidence here.

Reward power

Reward power is defined as power whose basis is the ability to reward. The strength of the reward power of O/P increases with the magnitude of the rewards which P perceives that O can mediate for him. Reward power depends on O's ability to administer positive valences and to remove or decrease negative valences. The strength of reward power also depends upon the probability that O can mediate the reward, as perceived by P. A common example of reward power is the addition of a piece-work rate in the factory as an incentive to increase production.

The new state of the system induced by a promise of reward (for example the factory worker's increased level of production) will be highly dependent on O. Since O mediates the reward, he controls the probability that P will receive it. Thus P's new rate of production will be dependent on his subjective probability that O will reward him for conformity minus his subjective probability that O will reward him even if he returns to his old level. Both probabilities will be greatly affected by the level of observability of P's behavior. Incidentally, a piece rate often seems to have more effect on production than a merit rating system because it yields a higher probability of reward for conformity and a much lower probability of reward for nonconformity.

The utilization of actual rewards (instead of promises) by O will tend over time to increase the attraction of P toward O and therefore the referent power of O over P. As we shall note later, such referent power will permit O to induce changes which are relatively independent. Neither rewards nor promises will arouse resistance in P, provided P considers it legitimate for O to offer rewards.

The range of reward power is specific to those regions within which O can reward P for conforming. The use of rewards to change systems within the range of reward power tends to increase reward power by increasing the probability attached to future promises. However, unsuccessful attempts to exert reward power outside the range of power would tend to decrease the power; for example if O offers to reward P for performing an impossible act, this will reduce for P the probability of receiving future rewards promised by O.

Coercive power

Coercive power is similar to reward power in that it also involves O's ability to manipulate the attainment of valences. Coercive power of O/P stems from the expectation on the part of P that he will be punished by O if he fails to conform to the influence attempt. Thus negative valences will exist in given regions of P's life space, corresponding to the threatened punishment by O. The strength of coercive power depends on the magnitude of the negative valence of the threatened punishment multiplied by the perceived probability that P can avoid the punishment by conformity, i.e., the probability of punishment for nonconformity minus the probability of punishment for conformity (French, *et al.*, 1960). Just as an offer of a piece-rate bonus in a factory can serve as a basis for reward power, so the ability to fire a worker if he falls below a given level of production will result in coercive power.

Coercive power leads to dependent change also; and the degree of dependence varies with the level of observability of P's conformity. An excellent illustration of coercive power leading to dependent change is provided by a clothes presser in a factory observed by Coch and French (1948). As her efficiency rating climbed above average for the group the other workers began to "scapegoat" her. That the resulting plateau in her production was not independent of the group was evident once she was removed from the presence of the other workers. Her production immediately climbed to new heights.

At times, there is some difficulty in distinguishing between reward power and coercive power. Is the withholding of a reward really equivalent to a punishment? Is the withdrawal of punishment equivalent to a reward? The answer must be a psychological one—it depends upon the situation as it exists for P. But ordinarily we would answer these questions in the affirmative; for P, receiving a reward is a positive valence as is the relief of suffering. There is some evidence that conformity to group norms in order to gain acceptance (reward power) should be distinguished from conformity as a means of forestalling rejection (coercive power) (Dittes & Kelley, 1956).

The distinction between these two types of power is important because the dynamics are different. The concept of "sanctions" sometimes lumps the two together despite their opposite effects. While reward power may eventually result in an independent system, the effects of coercive power will continue to be dependent. Reward power will tend to increase the attraction of P toward O; coercive power will decrease this attraction (French, *et al.*, 1960; Raven & French, 1958b). The valence of the region of behavior will become more negative, acquiring some negative valence from the threatened punishment. The negative valence of punishment would also spread to other regions of the life space. Lewin (1935, pp. 114–70) has pointed out this distinction between the effects of rewards and punishment. In the case of threatened punishment, there will be a resultant force on P to leave the field entirely. Thus, to achieve conformity, O must not only place a strong negative valence in certain regions through threat of punishment, but O must also introduce restraining forces, or other strong valences, so as to prevent P from withdrawing completely from O's range of coercive power. Otherwise the probability of receiving the punishment, if P does not conform, will be too low to be effective.

Legitimate power

Legitimate power is probably the most complex of those treated here, embodying notions from the structural sociologist, the group-norm and role oriented social psychologist, and the clinical psychologist.

There has been considerable investigation and speculation about socially prescribed behavior, particularly that which is specific to a given role or position. Linton (1945) distinguishes group norms according to whether they are universals for everyone in the culture, alternatives (the individual having a choice as to whether or not to accept them), or specialties (specific to given positions). Whether we speak of internalized norms, role prescriptions and expectations, or internalized pressures (Herbst, 1953), the fact remains that each individual sees certain regions toward which he should locomote, some regions toward which he should not locomote, and some regions toward which he may locomote if they are generally attractive for him. This applies to specific behaviors in which he may, should, or should not engage; it applies to certain attitudes or beliefs which he may, should, or should not hold. The feeling of "oughtness" may be an internalization from his parents, from his teachers, from his religion, or may have been logically developed from some idiosyncratic system of ethics. He will speak of such behaviors with expressions like "should," "ought to," or "has a right to." In many cases, the original source of the requirement is not recalled.

Though we have oversimplified such evaluations of behavior with a positive-neutral-negative trichotomy, the evaluation of behaviors by the person is really more one of degree. This dimension of evaluation, we shall call "legitimacy." Conceptually, we may think of legitimacy as a valence in a region which is induced by some internalized norm or value. This value has the same conceptual property as power, namely an ability to induce force fields (Lewin, 1951, pp. 40–41). It may or may not be correct that values (or the superego) are internalized parents, but at least they can set up force fields which have a phenomenal "oughtness" similar to a parent's prescription. Like a value, a need can also induce valences (i.e., force fields) in P's psychological environment, but these valences have more the phenomenal character of noxious or attractive properties of the object or activity. When a need induces a valence in P, for example, when a need makes an object attractive to P, this attraction applies to P but not to other persons. When a value induces a valence, on the other hand, it not only sets up forces on P to engage in the activity, but P may feel that all others ought to behave in the same way. Among other things, this evaluation applies to the legitimate right of some other individual or group to prescribe behavior or beliefs for a person even though the other cannot apply sanctions.

Legitimate power of O/P is here defined as that power which stems from internalized values in P which dictate that O has a legitimate right to influence P and that P has an obligation to accept this influence. We note that legitimate power is very similar to the notion of legitimacy of authority which has long been explored by sociologists, particularly by Weber (1947), and more recently by Goldhammer and Shils (1939). However, legitimate power is not always a role relation: P may accept an induction from O simply because he had previously promised to help O and he values his word too much to break the promise. In all cases, the notion of legitimacy involves some sort of code or standard, accepted by the individual, by virtue of which the external agent can assert his power. We shall attempt to describe a few of these values here.

Bases for legitimate power. Cultural values constitute one common basis for the legitimate power of one individual over another. O has characteristics which are specified by the culture as giving him the right to prescribe behavior for P, who may not have these characteristics. These bases, which Weber (1947) has called the authority of the "eternal yesterday," include such things as age, intelligence, caste, and physical characteristics. In some cultures, the aged are granted the right to prescribe behavior for others in practically all behavior areas. In most cultures, there are certain areas of behavior in which a person of one sex is granted the right to prescribe behavior for the other sex.

Acceptance of the social structure is another basis for legitimate power. If P accepts as right the social structure of his group, organization, or society, especially the social structure involving a hierarchy of authority, P will accept the legitimate authority of O who occupies a superior office in the hierarchy. Thus legitimate power in a formal organization is largely a relationship between offices rather than between persons. And the acceptance of an office as *right* is a basis for legitimate power—a judge has a right to levy fines, a foreman should assign work, a priest is justified in prescribing religious beliefs, and it is the management's prerogative to make certain decisions (French, et al., 1957). However, legitimate power also involves the perceived right of the person to hold the office.

Designation by a legitimizing agent is a third basis for legitimate power. An influencer O may be seen as legitimate in prescribing behavior for P because he has been granted such power by a legitimizing agent whom P accepts. Thus a department head may accept the authority of his vice-president in a certain area because that authority has been specifically delegated by the president. An election is perhaps the most common example of a group's serving to legitimize the authority of one individual or office for other individuals in the group. The success of such legitimizing depends upon the acceptance of the legitimizing agent and procedure. In this case it depends ultimately on certain democratic values concerning election procedures. The election process is one of legitimizing a person's right to an office which already has a legitimate range of power associated with it.

Range of legitimate power of O/P. The areas in which legitimate power may be exercised are generally specified along with the designation of that power. A job description, for example, usually specifies supervisory activities and also designates the person to whom the job-holder is responsible for the duties described. Some bases for legitimate authority carry with them a very broad range. Culturally derived bases for legitimate power are often especially broad. It is not uncommon to find cultures in which a member of a given caste can legitimately prescribe behavior for all members of lower castes in practically all regions. More common, however, are instances of legitimate power where the range is specifically and narrowly prescribed. A sergeant in the army is given a specific set of regions within which he can legitimately prescribe behavior for his men.

The attempted use of legitimate power which is outside of the range of legitimate power will decrease the legitimate power of the authority figure. Such use of power which is not legitimate will also decrease the attractiveness of O (French, *et al.*, 1960; Raven & French, 1958a, 1958b).

Legitimate power and influence. The new state of the system which results from legitimate power usually has high dependence on O though it may become independent. Here, however, the degree of dependence is not related to the level of observability. Since legitimate power is based on P's values, the source of the forces induced by O include both these internal values and O. O's induction serves to activate the values and to relate them to the system which is influenced, but thereafter the new state of the system may become directly dependent on the values with no mediation by O. Accordingly this new state will be relatively stable and consistent across varying environmental situations since P's values are more stable than his psychological environment.

We have used the term legitimate not only as a basis for the power of an agent, but also to describe the general behaviors of a person. Thus, the individual P may also consider the legitimacy of the attempts to use other types of power by O. In certain cases, P will consider that O has a legitimate right to threaten punishment for nonconformity; in other cases, such use of coercion would not be seen as legitimate. P might change in response to coercive power of O, but it will make a considerable difference in his attitude and conformity if O is not seen as having a legitimate right to use such coercion. In such cases, the attraction of P for O will be particularly diminished, and the influence attempt will arouse more resistance (French, *et al.*, 1960). Similarly the utilization of reward power may vary in legitimacy; the word "bribe," for example, denotes an illegitimate reward.

Referent power

The referent power of O/P has its basis in the identification of P with O. By identification, we mean a feeling of oneness of P with O, or a desire for such an identity. If O is a person toward whom P is highly attracted, P will have a desire to become closely associated with O. If O is an attractive group, P will have a feeling of membership or a desire to join. If P is already closely associated with O he will want to maintain this relationship. P's identification with O can be established or maintained if P behaves, believes, and perceives as O does. Accordingly O has the ability to influence P, even though P may be unaware of this referent power. A verbalization of such power by P might be, "I am like O, and therefore I shall behave or believe as O does," or "'I want to be like O, and I will be more like O if I behave or believe as O does." The stronger the identification of P with O the greater the referent power of O/P.

Similar types of power have already been investigated under a number of different formulations. Festinger (1950) points out that in an ambiguous situation, the individual seeks some sort of "social reality" and may adopt the cognitive structure of the individual or group with which he identifies. In such a case, the lack of clear structure may be threatening to the individual and the agreement of his beliefs with those of a reference group will both satisfy his need for structure and give him added security through increased identification with his group (Hochbaum, 1954; Jackson & Saltzstein, 1958).

We must try to distinguish between referent power and other types of power which might be operative at the same time. If a member is attracted to a group and he conforms to its norms only because he fears ridicule or expulsion from the group for nonconformity, we would call this coercive power. On the other hand if he conforms in order to obtain praise for conformity, it is a case of reward power. The basic criterion for distinguishing referent power from both coercive and reward power is the mediation of the punishment and the reward by O: to the extent that O mediates the sanctions (i.e., has means control over P) we are dealing with coercive and reward power; but to the extent that P avoids discomfort or gains satisfaction by conformity based on identification, regardless of O's responses, we are dealing with referent power. Conformity with majority opinion is sometimes based on a respect for the collective wisdom of the group, in which case it is expert power. It is important to distinguish these phenomena, all grouped together elsewhere as "pressures toward uniformity," since the type of change which occurs will be different for different bases of power.

The concepts of "reference group" (Kelley, 1952) and "'prestige suggestion" may be treated as instances of referent power. In this case, O, the prestigeful person or group, is valued by P; because P desires to be associated or identified with O, he will assume attitudes or beliefs held by O. Similarly a negative reference group which O dislikes and evaluates negatively may exert negative influence on P as a result of negative referent power.

It has been demonstrated that the power which we designate as referent power is especially great when P is attracted to O (Back, 1951; Festinger, 1950; Festinger, *et al.*, 1952; Festinger, *et al.*, 1953; Gerard, 1954; Kelman, 1961; Lippitt, *et al.*, 1952). In our terms, this would mean that the greater the attraction, the greater the identification, and consequently the greater the referent power. In some cases, attraction or prestige may have a specific basis, and the range of referent power will be limited accordingly: a group of campers may have great referent power over a member regarding campcraft, but considerably less effect on other regions (Lippitt, *et al.*, 1952). However, we hypothesize that the greater the attraction of P toward O, the broader the range of referent power of O/P.

The new state of a system produced by referent power may be dependent on or independent of O; but the degree of dependence is not affected by the level of observability to O (Festinger, 1953; Kelman, 1961). In fact, P is often not consciously aware of the referent power which O exerts over him. There is probably a tendency for some of these dependent changes to become independent of O quite rapidly.

Expert power

The strength of the expert power of O/P varies with the extent of the knowledge or perception which P attributes to O within a given area. Probably P evaluates O's expertness in relation to his own knowledge as well as against an absolute standard. In any case expert power results in primary social influence on P's cognitive structure and probably not on other types of systems. Of course changes in the cognitive structure can change the direction of forces and hence of locomotion, but such a change of behavior is secondary social influence. Expert power has been demonstrated experimentally (Festinger, *et al.*, 1952; Moore, 1921). Accepting an attorney's advice in legal matters is a common example of expert influence; but there are many instances based on much less knowledge, such as the acceptance by a stranger of directions given by a native villager.

Expert power, where O need not be a member of P's group, is called "informational power" by Deutsch and Gerard (1955). This type of expert power must be distinguished from influence based on the content of communication as described by Hovland, *et al.* (Hovland, *et al.*, 1949; Hovland & Weiss, 1951; Kelman, 1961; Kelman & Hovland, 1953). The influence of the content of a communication upon an opinion is presumably a secondary influence produced after the *primary* influence (i.e., the acceptance of the information). Since power is here defined in terms of the primary changes, the influence of the content on a related opinion is not a case of expert power as we have defined it, but the initial acceptance of the validity of the content does seem to be based on expert power or referent power. In other cases, however, so-called facts may be accepted as self-evident because they fit into P's cognitive structure; if this impersonal acceptance of the truth of the fact is independent of the more or less enduring relationship between O and P, then P's acceptance of the fact is not an actualization of expert power. Thus we distinguish between expert power based on the credibility of O and informational influence which is based on characteristics of the stimulus such as the logic of the argument or the "self-evident facts."

Wherever expert influence occurs it seems to be necessary both for P to think that O knows and for P to trust that O is telling the truth (rather than trying to deceive him).

Expert power will produce a new cognitive structure which is initially relatively dependent on O, but informational influence will produce a more independent structure. The former is likely to become more independent with the passage of time. In both cases the degree of dependence on O is not affected by the level of observability.

The "sleeper effect" (Hovland & Weiss, 1951; Kelman & Hovland, 1953) is an interesting case of a change in the degree of dependence of an opinion on O. An unreliable O (who probably had negative referent power but some positive expert power) presented "facts" which were accepted by the subjects and which would normally produce secondary influence on their opinions and beliefs. However, the negative referent power aroused resistance and resulted in negative social influence on their beliefs (i.e., set up a force in the direction opposite to the influence attempt), so that there was little change in the subjects' opinions. With the passage of time, however, the subjects tended to forget the identity of the negative communicator faster than they forgot the contents of his communication, so there was a weakening of the negative referent influence and a consequent delayed positive change in the subject's beliefs in the direction of the influence attempt ("sleeper efect"). Later, when the identity of the negative communicator was experimentally reinstated, these resisting forces were reinstated, and there was another negative change in belief in a direction opposite to the influence attempt (Kelman & Hovland, 1953).

The range of expert power, we assume, is more delimited than that of referent power. Not only is it restricted to cognitive systems but the expert is seen as having superior knowledge or ability in very specific areas, and his power will be limited to these areas, though some "halo effect" might occur. Recently, some of our renowned physical scientists have found quite painfully that their expert power in physical sciences does not extend to regions involving international politics. Indeed, there is some evidence that the attempted exertion of expert power outside of the range of expert power will reduce that expert power. An undermining of confidence seems to take place.

54 The two-step flow of communication: an up-to-date report on an hypothesis

ELIHU KATZ

Analysis of the process of decision-making during the course of an election campaign led the authors of *The People's Choice* (Lazarsfeld, Berelson, Gaudet, 1948) to suggest that the flow of mass communications may be less direct than was commonly supposed. It may be, they proposed, that influences stemming from the mass media first reach "opinion leaders" who, in turn, pass on what they read and hear to those of their every-day associates for whom they are influential. This hypothesis was called "the two-step flow of communication."

The hypothesis aroused considerable interest. The authors themselves were intrigued by its implications for democratic society. It was a healthy sign, they felt, that people were still most successfully persuaded by give-and-take with other people and that the influence of the mass media was less automatic and less potent than had been assumed. For social theory, and for the design of communications research, the hypothesis suggested that the image of modern urban society needed revision. The image of the audience as a mass of disconnected individuals hooked up to the media but not to each other could not be reconciled with the idea of a two-step flow of communication implying, as it did, networks of interconnected individuals through which mass communications are channeled.

Findings of "The People's Choice"

The starting point for this review must be an examination of the evidence in the 1940 voting study which led to the original formulation of the hypothesis. Essentially, three distinct sets of findings seem to have been involved. The first had to with with *the impact of personal influence*. It is reported that people who made up their minds late in the campaign, and those who changed their minds during the course of the campaign, were more likely than other people to mention personal influence as having figured in their decisions. The political pressure brought to bear by everyday groups such as family and friends is illustrated by reference to the political homogeneity which characterizes such groups. What's more, on an average day, a greater number of people reported participating in discussion of the election than hearing a campaign speech or reading a newspaper editorial. From all of this, the authors conclude that personal contacts appear to have been both more frequent and more effective than the mass media in influencing voting decisions (Lazarsfeld, *et al.*, 1948, pp. 135–52).

The second ingredient that went into the formulation of the hypothesis concerned *the flow of personal influence*. Given the apparent importance of interpersonal influence, the obvious next step

Excerpted from the **Public Opinion Quarterly**, 1957, 21, 61–78, with permission of the author and the publisher.

was to ask whether some people were more important than others in the transmission of influence. The study sought to single out the "opinion leaders" by two questions: "Have you recently tried to convince anyone of your political ideas?", and "Has anyone recently asked you for your advice on a political question?" Comparing the opinion leaders with others, they found the opinion leaders more interested in the election. And from the almost even distribution of opinion leaders throughout every class and occupation, as well as the frequent mention by decision-makers of the influence of friends, co-workers and relatives, it was concluded that opinion leaders are to be found on every level of society and presumably, therefore, are very much like the people whom they influence (Lazarsfeld, *et al.*, 1948, pp. 50–51).

A further comparison of leaders and others with respect to mass media habits provides the third ingredient: *the opinion leaders and the mass media.* Compared with the rest of the population, opinion leaders were found to be considerably more exposed to the radio, to the newspapers and to magazines, that is, to the formal media of communication (Lazarsfeld, *et al.*, 1948, p. 51).

Now the argument is clear: If word-of-mouth is so important, and if word-of-mouth specialists are widely dispersed, and if these specialists are more exposed to the media than the people whom they influence, then perhaps "ideas often flow from radio and print to opinion leaders and from these to the less active sections of the population" (Lazarsfeld, *et al.*, 1948, p. 151).

It will be useful to return to the three categories singled out in discussing *The People's Choice:* (1) the impact of personal influence; (2) the flow of personal influence; and (3) opinion leaders and the mass media. Evidence from three studies, as well as from the 1948 Elmira study (Berelson, Lazarsfeld, McPhee, 1954), and from others, will be brought together here; but in every case the characteristics of each study's design must be borne in mind in evaluating the evidence presented.

A. THE IMPACT OF PERSONAL INFLUENCE

1. *Personal and the mass media influence.* The 1940 study indicated that personal influence affected voting decisions more than the mass media did, particularly in the case of those who changed their minds during the course of the campaign. The Decatur study went on to explore the relative impact of personal influences and the mass media in three other realms: marketing, fashions and movie-going. Basing its conclusions on the testimony of the decision-makers themselves, and using an instrument for evaluating the relative effectiveness of the various media which entered into the decisions, the Decatur study again found that personal influence figured both more frequently and more effectively than any of the mass media (Katz & Lazarsfeld, 1955, pp. 169–86).

In the analysis to date, the drug study (Coleman, Katz, and Menzel, 1957) has not approached the problem of the relative effectiveness of the various media from the point of view of the doctor's own reconstruction of what went into the making of his decision. Comparing mere frequency of mention of different media, it is clear that colleagues are by no means the most frequently mentioned source. Nevertheless, exploration of the factors related to whether the doctor's decision to adopt the drug came early or late indicates that the factor most strongly associated with the time of adoption of the new drug is the extent of the doctor's integration in the medical community. That is, the more frequently a doctor is named by his colleagues as a friend or a discussion partner, the more likely he is to be an innovator with respect to the new drug. Extent of integration proves to be a more important factor than any background factor (such as age, medical school, or income of patients), or any other source of influence (such as readership of medical journals) that was examined.

Investigation of why integration is related to innovation suggests two central factors: (1) interpersonal communication—doctors who are integrated are more in touch and more up-to-date; and (2) social support—doctors who are integrated feel more secure when facing the risks of innovation in medicine. Thus the drug study, too, provides evidence of the strong impact of personal relations—even in the making of scientific decisions.

2. *Homogeneity of opinion in primary groups.* The effectiveness of interpersonal influence, as it is revealed in the studies under review, is reflected in the homogeneity of opinions and actions in primary groups. The medium of primary group communication is, by definition, person-to-person. Both of the voting studies indicate the high degree of homogeneity of political opinion among members of the same families, and among co-workers and friends. The effectiveness of such primary groups in pulling potential deviates back into line is demonstrated by the fact that those who changed their vote intentions were largely people who, early in the campaign, had reported that they intended to vote differently from their family or friends.

The drug study, too, was able to examine the extent of homogeneity in the behavior of sociometrically related doctors, and was able to demonstrate that there were situations where similar behavior could be observed. For example, it was found that, when called upon to treat the more puzzling diseases, doctors were likely to prescribe the same drug as their sociometric colleagues. The study also showed that, very early in the history of a new drug, innovating doctors who were sociometrically connected tended to adopt the new drug at virtually the same time. This phenomenon of homogeneity of opinion or behavior among interacting individuals confronting an unclear or uncertain situation which calls for action has often been studied by sociologists and social psychologists.

3. *The various roles of the media.* The 1940 voting study explored some of the reasons why personal influence might be expected to be more influential in changing opinions than the mass media: It is often non-purposive; it is flexible; it is trustworthy. It was suggested that the mass media more often play a reinforcing role in the strengthening of predispositions and of decisions already taken. Nevertheless, it was assumed that the various media and personal influence are essentially competitive, in the sense that a given decision is influenced by one *or* the other. The Decatur study tended toward this assumption too, but at one point the study does attempt to show that different media play different parts in the decision-making process and take patterned positions in a sequence of several influences. The drug study elaborates on the roles of the media even further, distinguishing be-

tween media that "inform" and media that "legitimate" decisions. Thus in doctors' decisions, professional media (including colleagues) seem to play a legitimating role, while commercial media play an informing role.

B. THE FLOW OF PERSONAL INFLUENCE

The 1940 voting study found that opinion leaders were not concentrated in the upper brackets of the population but were located in almost equal proportions in every social group and stratum. This finding led to efforts in subsequent studies to establish the extent to which this was true in areas other than election campaigns and also to ascertain what it is that *does* distinguish opinion leaders from those whom they influence.

The first thing that is clear from the series of studies under review is that the subject matter concerning which influence is transmitted has a lot to do with determining who will lead and who follow. Thus, the Rovere study suggests that within the broad sphere of public affairs one set of influentials is occupied with "local" affairs and another with "cosmopolitan" affairs (Merton, 1948, pp. 187–8). The Decatur study suggests that in marketing, for example, there is a concentration of opinion leadership among older women with larger families, while in fashions and movie-going it is the young, unmarried girl who has a disproportionate chance of being turned to for advice. There is very little overlap of leadership: a leader in one sphere is not likely to be influential in another unrelated sphere as well (Katz & Lazarsfeld, 1955, pp. 327–34).

Yet, even when leadership in one or another sphere is heavily concentrated among the members of a particular group—as was the case with marketing leadership in Decatur—the evidence suggests that people still talk, most of all, to others like themselves. Thus, while the marketing leaders among the older "large-family wives" also influenced other kinds of women, most of their influence was directed to women of their own age with equally large families. In marketing, fashions, and movie-going, furthermore, there was no appreciable concentration of influentials in any of the three socio-economic levels. Only in public affairs was there a concentration of leadership in the highest status, and there was some slight evidence that influence flows from this group to individuals of lower status. The Elmira study also found opinion-leaders in similar proportions on every socio-economic and occupational level and found that conversations concerning the campaign went on, typically, between people of similar age, occupation, and political opinion.

What makes for the concentration of certain kinds of opinion leadership within certain groups? And when influential and influencee are outwardly alike—as they so often seem to be—what, if anything, distinguishes one from the other? Broadly, it appears that influence is related (1) to the *personification of certain values* (who one is); (2) to *competence* (what one knows); and (3) to *strategic social location* (whom one knows). Social location, in turn, divides into whom one knows within a group; and "outside."

Influence is often successfully transmitted because the influencee wants to be as much like the influential as possible. That the young, unmarried girls are fashion leaders can be understood easily in a culture where youth and youthfulness are supreme values. This is an example where "who one is" counts very heavily.

But "what one knows" is no less important (cf. Merton, 1948, p. 197). The fact is that older women, by virtue of their greater experience, are looked to as marketing advisers and that specialists in internal medicine—the most "scientific" of the practicing physicians—are the most frequently mentioned opinion leaders among the doctors. The influence of young people in the realm of movie-going can also be understood best in terms of their familiarity with the motion picture world. The Elmira study found slightly greater concentrations of opinion leadership among the more educated people on each socioeconomic level, again implying the importance of competence. Finally, the influence of the "cosmopolitans" in Rovere rested on the presumption that they had large amounts of information.

It is, however, not enough to be a person whom others want to emulate, or to be competent. One must also be accessible. Thus, the Decatur study finds gregariousness—"whom one knows"—related to every kind of leadership. The Rovere study reports that the leadership of the "local" influentials is based on their central location in the web of interpersonal contacts. Similarly, studies of rumor transmission have singled out those who are "socially active" as agents of rumor (Allport & Postman, 1943, p. 183).

Of course, the importance of whom one knows is not simply a matter of the number of people with whom an opinion leader is in contact. It is also a question of whether the people with whom he is in touch happen to be interested in the area in which his leadership is likely to be sought. For this reason, it is quite clear that the greater interest of opinion leaders in the subjects over which they exert influence is not a sufficient explanation of their influence. While the voting studies as well as the Decatur study show leaders to be more interested, the Decatur study goes on to show that interest alone is not the determining factor (Katz & Lazarsfeld, 1955, pp. 249–52). In fashion, for example, a young unmarried girl is considerably more likely to be influential than a matron with an equally great interest in clothes. The reason, it is suggested, is that a girl who is interested in fashion is much more likely than a matron with an equally high interest to know other people who share her preoccupation, and thus is more likely than the matron to have followers who are interested enough to ask for her advice. In other words, it takes two to be a leader—a leader and a follower.

Finally, there is the second aspect of "whom one knows." An individual may be influential not only because people within his group look to him for advice but also because of whom he knows outside his group. Both the Elmira and Decatur studies found that men are more likely than women to be opinion leaders in the realm of public affairs and this, it is suggested, is because they have more of a chance to get outside the home to meet people and talk politics. Similarly, the Elmira study indicated that opinion leaders belonged to more organizations, more often knew workers for the political parties, and so on, than did others. The drug study found that influential doctors could be characterized in terms of such things as their more frequent attendance at out-of-town meetings and the diversity of places with which they maintained contact, particularly far-away places. It is interesting that a study of the farmer-innovators responsible for the diffusion of hybrid seed-corn in Iowa concluded that these leaders also could be characterized in terms of the relative frequency of their trips out of town (cf. Ryan & Gross, 1942, pp. 15–24).

C. THE OPINION LEADERS AND THE MASS MEDIA

The third aspect of the hypothesis of the two-step flow of communication states that opinion leaders are more exposed to the mass media than are those whom they influence. In *The People's Choice* this is supported by reference to the media behavior of leaders and non-leaders.

The Decatur study corroborated this finding, and went on to explore two additional aspects of the same idea. First of all, it was shown that leaders in a given sphere (fashions, public affairs, etc.) were particularly likely to be exposed to the media appropriate to that sphere. This is essentially a corroboration of the Rovere finding that those who proved influential with regard to "cosmopolitan" matters were more likely to be readers of national news magazines, but that this was not at all the case for those influential with regard to "local" matters. Secondly, the Decatur study shows that at least in the realm of fashions, the leaders are not only more exposed to the mass media, but are also more affected by them in their own decisions. This did not appear to be the case in other realms, where opinion leaders, though more exposed to the media than non-leaders, nevertheless reported personal influence as the major factor in their decisions. This suggests that in some spheres considerably longer chains of person-to-person influence than the dyad may have to be traced back before one encounters any decisive influence by the mass media, even though their contributory influence may be perceived at many points. This was suggested by the Elmira study too. It found that the leaders, though more exposed to the media, also more often reported that they sought information and advice from other persons (Berelson, *et al.*, 1954, p. 110).

Similarly, the drug study showed that the influential doctors were more likely to be readers of a large number of professional journals and valued them more highly than did doctors of lesser influence. But at the same time, they were as likely as other doctors to say that local colleagues were an important source of information and advice in their reaching particular decisions.

Finally, the drug study demonstrated that the more influential doctors could be characterized by their greater attention not only to medical journals, but to out-of-town meetings and contacts as well. This finding has already been discussed in the previous section treating the *strategic location* of the opinion leader with respect to "the world outside" his group. Considering it again under the present heading suggests that the greater exposure of the opinion leader to the mass media may only be a special case of the more general proposition that opinion leaders serve to relate their groups to relevant parts of the environment through whatever media happen to be appropriate. This more general statement makes clear the similar functions of big city newspapers for the Decatur fashion leader; of national news magazines for the "cosmopolitan" influentials of Rovere; of out-of-town medical meetings for the influential doctor; and of contact with the city for the farmer-innovator in Iowa as well as for the newly-risen, young opinion leaders in underdeveloped areas throughout the world.

Conclusions

Despite the diversity of subject matter with which they are concerned, the studies reviewed here constitute an example of continuity and cumulation both in research designs and theoretical commitment. Piecing together the findings of the latter-day studies in the light of the original statement of the two-step flow hypothesis suggests the following picture.

Opinion leaders and the people whom they influence are very much alike and typically belong to the same primary groups of family, friends and co-workers. While the opinion leader may be more interested in the particular sphere in which he is influential, it is highly unlikely that the persons influenced will be very far behind the leader in their level of interest. Influentials and influencees may exchange roles in different spheres of influence. Most spheres focus the group's attention on some related part of the world outside the group, and it is the opinion leader's function to bring the group into touch with this relevant part of its environment through whatever media are appropriate. In every case, influentials have been found to be more exposed to these points of contact with the outside world. Nevertheless, it is also true that, despite their greater exposure to the media, most opinion leaders are primarily affected not by the communication media but by still other people.

The main emphasis of the two-step flow hypothesis appears to be on only one aspect of interpersonal relations—interpersonal relations as channels of communication. But from the several studies reviewed, it is clear that these very same interpersonal relations influence the making of decisions in at least two additional ways. In addition to serving as networks of communication, interpersonal relations are also sources of pressure to conform to the group's way of thinking and acting, as well as sources of social support. The workings of group pressure are clearly evident in the homogeneity of opinion and action observed among voters and among doctors in situations of unclarity or uncertainty. The social support that comes from being integrated in the medical community may give a doctor the confidence required to carry out a resolution to adopt a new drug. Thus, interpersonal relations are (1) channels of information, (2) sources of social pressure, and (3) sources of social support, and each relates interpersonal relations to decision-making in a somewhat different way.

55 Achieving change in people: some applications of group dynamics theory

DORWIN CARTWRIGHT

I

We hear all around us today the assertion that the problems of the twentieth century are problems of human relations. The survival of civilization, it is said, will depend upon man's ability to create social inventions capable of harnessing, for society's constructive use, the vast physical energies now at man's disposal. Or, to put the matter more simply, we must learn how to change the way in which people behave toward one another. In broad outline, the specifications for a good society are clear, but a serious technical problem remains: How can we change people so that they neither restrict the freedom nor limit the potentialities for growth of others; so that they accept and respect people of different religion, nationality, color, or political opinion; so that nations can exist in a world without war, and so that the fruits of our technological advances can bring economic well-being and freedom from disease to all the people of the world? Although few people would disagree with these objectives when stated abstractly, when we become more specific, differences of opinion quickly arise. How is change to be produced? Who is to do it? Who is to be changed? These questions permit no ready answers.

Before we consider in detail these questions of social technology, let us clear away some semantic obstacles. The word "change" produces emotional reactions. It is not a neutral word. To many people it is threatening. It conjures up visions of a revolutionary, a dissatisfied idealist, a trouble-maker, a malcontent. Nicer words referring to the process of changing people are education, training, orientation, guidance, indoctrination, therapy. We are more ready to have others "educate" us than to have them "change" us. We, ourselves, feel less guilty in "training" others than in "changing" them. Why this emotional response? What makes the two kinds of words have such different meanings? I believe that a large part of the difference lies in the fact that the safer words (like education or therapy) carry the implicit assurance that the only changes produced will be good ones, acceptable within a currently held value system. The cold, unmodified word "change," on the contrary, promises no respect for values; it might even tamper with values themselves. Perhaps for this very reason it will foster straight thinking if we use the word "change" and thus force ourselves to struggle directly and self-consciously with the problems of value that are involved. Words like education, training, or therapy, by the very fact that they are not so disturbing, may close our eyes to the fact that they too inevitably involve values.

Another advantage of using the word "change" rather than other related words is that it does not restrict our

Reprinted from **Human Relations**, 1951, 4, 381–93, with permission of the author and publisher.

thinking to a limited set of aspects of people that are legitimate targets of change. Anyone familiar with the history of education knows that there has been endless controversy over what it is about people that "education" properly attempts to modify. Some educators have viewed education simply as imparting knowledge, others mainly as providing skills for doing things, still others as producing healthy "attitudes," and some have aspired to instill a way of life. Or if we choose to use a word like "therapy," we can hardly claim that we refer to a more clearly defined realm of change. Furthermore, one can become inextricably entangled in distinctions and vested interests by attempting to distinguish sharply between, let us say, the domain of education and that of therapy. If we are to try to take a broader view and to develop some basic principles that promise to apply to all types of modifications in people, we had better use a world like "change" to keep our thinking general enough.

The proposal that social technology may be employed to solve the problems of society suggests that social science may be applied in ways not different from those used in the physical sciences. Does social science, in fact, have any practically useful knowledge which may be brought to bear significantly on society's most urgent problems? What scientifically based principles are there for guiding programs of social change: In this paper we shall restrict our considerations to certain parts of a relatively new branch of social science known as "group dynamics." We shall examine some of the implications for social action which stem from research in this field of scientific investigation.

What is "group dynamics"? Perhaps it will be most useful to start by looking at the derivation of the word "dynamics." It comes from a Greek word meaning force. In careful usage of the phrase, "group dynamics," refers to the forces operating in groups. The investigation of group dynamics, then, consists of a study of these forces: what gives rise to them, what conditions modify them, what consequences they have, etc. The practical application of group dynamics (or the technology of group dynamics) consists of the utilization of knowledge about these forces for the achievement of some purpose. In keeping with this definition, then, it is clear that group dynamics, as a realm of investigation, is not particularly novel, nor is it the exclusive property of any person or institution. It goes back at least to the outstanding work of men like Simmel, Freud, and Cooley.

Although interest in groups has a long and respectable history, the past fifteen years have witnessed a new flowering of activity in this field. Today, research centers in several countries are carrying out substantial programs of research designed to reveal the nature of groups and of their functioning. The phrase "group dynamics" has come into common usage during this time and intense efforts have been devoted to the development of the field, both as a branch of social science and as a form of social technology.

In this development the name of Kurt Lewin has been outstanding. As a consequence of his work in the field of individual psychology and from his analysis of the nature of the pressing problems of the contemporary world, Lewin became convinced of society's urgent need for a *scientific approach* to the understanding of the dynamics of groups. In 1945 he established the Research Center for Group Dynamics to meet this need. Since that date the Center has been devoting its efforts to improving our scientific understanding of groups through laboratory experimentation, field studies, and the use of techniques of action research. It has also attempted in various ways to help get the findings of social science more widely used by social management. Much of what I have to say in this paper is drawn from the experiences of this Center in its brief existence of a little more than five years (Cartwright, 1950).

II

For various reasons we have found that much of our work has been devoted to an attempt to gain a better understanding of the ways in which people change their behavior or resist efforts by others to have them do so. Whether we set for ourselves the practical goal of improving behavior or whether we take on the intellectual task of understanding why people do what they do, we have to investigate processes of communication, influence, social pressure—in short, problems of change.

In this work we have encountered great frustration. The problems have been most difficult to solve. Looking back over our experience, I have become convinced that no small part of the trouble has resulted from an irresistible tendency to conceive of our problems in terms of the individual. We live in an individualistic culture. We value the individual highly, and rightly so. But I am inclined to believe that our political and social concern for the individual has narrowed our thinking as social scientists so much that we have not been able to state our research problems properly. Perhaps we have taken the individual as the unit of observation and study when some larger unit would have been more appropriate. Let us look at a few examples.

Consider first some matters having to do with the mental health of an individual. We can all agree, I believe, that an important mark of a healthy personality is that the individual's self-esteem has not been undermined. But on what does self-esteem depend? From research on this problem we have discovered that, among other things, repeated experiences of failure or traumatic failures on matters of central importance serve to undermine one's self-esteem. We also know that whether a person experiences success or failure as a result of some undertaking depends upon the level of aspiration which he has set for himself. Now, if we try to discover how the level of aspiration gets set, we are immediately involved in the person's relationships to groups. The groups to which he belongs set standards for his behavior which he must accept if he is to remain in the group. If his capacities do not allow him to reach these standards, he experiences failure, he withdraws or is rejected by the group and his self-esteem suffers a shock.

Suppose, then, that we accept a task of therapy, of rebuilding his self-esteem. It would appear plausible from our analysis of the problem that we should attempt to work with variables of the same sort that produced the difficulty, that is to work with him either in the groups to which he now belongs or to introduce him into new groups which are selected for the purpose and to work upon his relationships to groups as such. From the point of view of preventive mental health, we might even attempt to train the groups in our communities—classes in schools, work groups in business, families, unions, religious and cultural groups—to make use of practices better designed to protect the self-esteem of their members.

Consider a second example. A teacher finds that in her class she has a number of trouble-makers, full of aggression. She wants to know why these children are so aggressive and what can be done about it. A foreman in a factory has the same kind of problem with some of his workers. He wants the same kind of help. The solution most tempting to both the teacher and the foreman often is to transfer the worst trouble-makers to someone else, or if facilities are available, to refer them for counselling. But is the problem really of such a nature that it can be solved by removing the trouble-maker from the situation or by working on his individual motivations and emotional life? What leads does research give us? The evidence indicates, of course, that there are many causes of aggressiveness in people, but one aspect of the problem has become increasingly clear in recent years. If we observe carefully the amount of aggressive behavior and the number of trouble-makers to be found in a large collection of groups, we find that these characteristics can vary tremendously from group to group even when the different groups are composed essentially of the same kinds of people. In the now classic experiments of Lewin, Lippitt, and White (1939) on the effects of different styles of leadership, it was found that the same group of children displayed markedly different levels of aggressive behavior when under different styles of leadership. Moreover, when individual children were transferred from one group to another, their levels of aggressiveness shifted to conform to the atmosphere of the new group. Efforts to account for one child's aggressiveness under one style of leadership merely in terms of his personality traits could hardly succeed under these conditions. This is not to say that a person's behavior is entirely to be accounted for by the atmosphere and structure of the immediate group, but it is remarkable to what an extent a strong, cohesive group can control aspects of a member's behavior traditionally thought to be expressive of enduring personality traits. Recognition of this fact rephrases the problem of how to change such behavior. It directs us to a study of the sources of the influence of the group on its members.

Let us take an example from a different field. What can we learn from efforts to change people by mass media and mass persuasion? In those rare instances when educators, propagandists, advertisers, and others who want to influence large numbers of people, have bothered to make an objective evaluation of the enduring changes produced by their efforts, they have been able to demonstrate only the most negligible effects (Cartwright, 1949). The inefficiency of attempts to influence the public by mass media would be scandalous if there were agreement that it was important or even desirable to have such influences strongly exerted. In fact, it is no exaggeration to say that all of the research and experience of generations has not improved the efficiency of lectures or other means of mass influence to any noticeable degree. Something must be wrong with our theories of learning, motivation, and social psychology.

Within very recent years some research data have been accumulating which may give us a clue to the solution of our problem. In one series of experiments directed by Lewin, it was found that a method of group decision, in which the group as a whole made a decision to have its members change their behavior, was from two to ten times as effective in producing actual change as was a lecture presenting exhortation to change (Lewin, 1951). We have yet to learn precisely what produces these differences of effectiveness, but it is clear that by introducing group forces into the situation a whole new level of influence has been achieved.

The experience has been essentially the same when people have attempted to increase the productivity of individuals in work settings. Traditional conceptions of how to increase the output of workers have stressed the individual: select the right man for the job; simplify the job for him; train him in the skills required; motivate him by economic incentives; make it clear to whom he reports; keep the lines of authority and responsibility simple and straight. But even when all these conditions are fully met we are finding that productivity is far below full potential. There is even good reason to conclude that this individualistic conception of the determinants of productivity actually fosters negative consequences. The individual, now isolated and subjected to the demands of the organization through the commands of his boss, finds that he must create with his fellow employees informal groups, not shown on any table of organization, in order to protect himself from arbitrary control of his life, from the boredom produced by the endless repetition of mechanically sanitary and routine operations, and from the impoverishment of his emotional and social life brought about by the frustration of his basic needs for social interaction, participation, and acceptance in a stable group. Recent experiments have demonstrated clearly that the productivity of work groups can be greatly increased by methods of work organization and supervision which give more responsibility to work groups, which allow for fuller participation in important decisions, and which make stable groups the firm basis for support of the individual's social needs (Coch & French, 1948). I am convinced that future research will also demonstrate that people working under such conditions become more mature and creative individuals in their homes, in community life, and as citizens.

As a final example, let us examine the experience of efforts to train people in workshops, institutes, and special training courses. Such efforts are common in various areas of social welfare, intergroup relations, political affairs, industry, and adult education generally. It is an unfortunate fact that objective evaluation of the effects of such training efforts has only rarely been undertaken, but there is evidence for those who will look that the actual change in behavior produced is most disappointing. A workshop not infrequently develops keen interest among the participants, high morale and enthusiasm, and a firm resolve on the part of many to apply all the wonderful insights back home. But what happens back home? The trainee discovers that his colleagues don't share his enthusiasm. He learns that the task of changing others' expectations and ways of doing things is discouragingly difficult. He senses, perhaps not very clearly, that it would make all the difference in the world if only there were a few other people sharing his enthusiasm and insights with whom he could plan activities, evaluate consequences of efforts, and from whom he could gain emotional and motivational support. The approach to training which conceives of its task as being merely that of changing the individual probably produces frustration, demoralization, and disillusionment in as large a measure as it accomplishes more positive results.

A few years ago the Research Center for Group Dynamics undertook to shed light on this problem by investigating the operation of a workshop for training leaders in intercultural relations (Lippitt, 1949). In a project, directed by Lippitt, we set out to compare systematically the different effects of the workshop upon trainees who came as isolated individuals in contrast to those who came as teams. Since one of the problems in the field of intercultural relations is that of getting people of good will to be more active in community efforts to improve intergroup relations, one goal of the training workshop was to increase the activity of the trainees in such community affairs. We found that before the workshop there was no difference in the activity level of the people who were to be trained as isolates and of those who were to be trained as teams. Six months after the workshop, however, those who had been trained as isolates were only slightly more active than before the workshop whereas those who had been members of strong training teams were now much more active. We do not have clear evidence on the point, but we would be quite certain that the maintenance of heightened activity over a long period of time would also be much better for members of teams. For the isolates the effect of the workshop had the characteristic of a "shot in the arm" while for the team member it produced a more enduring change because the team provided continuous support and reinforcement for its members.

III

What conclusions may we draw from these examples? What principles of achieving change in people can we see emerging? To begin with the most general proposition, we may state that the behavior, attitudes, beliefs, and values of the individual are all firmly grounded in the groups to which he belongs. How aggressive or cooperative a person is, how much self-respect and self-confidence he has, how energetic and productive his work is, what he aspires to, what he believes to be true and good, whom he loves or hates, and what beliefs and prejudices he holds—all these characteristics are highly determined by the individual's group memberships. In a real sense, they are properties of groups and of the relationships between people. Whether they change or resist change will, therefore, be greatly influenced by the nature of these groups. Attempts to change them must be concerned with the dynamics of groups.

In examining more specifically how groups enter into the process of change, we find it useful to view groups in at least three different ways. In the first view, the group is seen as a source of influence over its members. Efforts to change behavior can be supported or blocked by pressures on members stemming from the group. To make constructive use of these pressures the group must be used *as a medium of change*. In the second view, the group itself becomes the *target of change*. To change the behavior of individuals it may be necessary to change the standards of the group, its style of leadership, its emotional atmosphere, or its stratification into cliques and hierarchies. Even though the goal may be to change the behavior of *individuals,* the target of change becomes the group. In the third view, it is recognized that many changes of behavior can be brought about only by the organized efforts of groups *as agents of change.* A committee to combat intolerance, a labor union, an employers association, a citizens group to increase the pay of teachers—any action group will be more or less effective depending upon the way it is organized, the satisfactions it provides to its members, the degree to which its goals are clear, and a host of other properties of the group.

An adequate social technology of change, then, requires at the very least a scientific understanding of groups viewed in each of these ways. We shall consider here only the first two aspects of the problem: the group as a medium of change and as a target of change.

THE GROUP AS A MEDIUM OF CHANGE

Principle No. 1. If the group is to be used effectively as a medium of change, those people who are to be changed and those who are to exert influence for change must have a strong sense of belonging to the same group.

Kurt Lewin described this principle well: "The normal gap between teacher and student, doctor and patient, social worker and public, can . . . be a real obstacle to acceptance of the advocated conduct." In other words, in spite of whatever status differences there might be between them, the teacher and the student have to feel as members of one group in matters involving their sense of values. The chances for re-education seem to be increased whenever a strong we-feeling is created (Lewin, 1948). Recent experiments by Preston and Heintz have demonstrated greater changes of opinions among members of discussion groups operating with participatory leadership than among those with supervisory leadership (1949). The implications of this principle for classroom teaching are far-reaching. The same may be said of supervision in the factory, army, or hospital.

Principle No. 2. The more attractive the group is to its members the greater is the influence that the group can exert on its members.

This principle has been extensively documented by Festinger and his co-workers (1950). They have been able to show in a variety of settings that in more cohesive groups there is a greater readiness of members to attempt to influence others, a greater readiness to be influenced by others, and stronger pressures toward conformity when conformity is a relevant matter for the group. Important for the practitioner wanting to make use of this principle is, of course, the question of how to increase the attractiveness of groups. This is a question with many answers. Suffice it to say that a group is more attractive the more it satisfies the needs of its members. We have been able to demonstrate experimentally an increase in group cohesiveness by increasing the liking of members for each other as persons, by increasing the perceived importance of the group goal, and by increasing the prestige of the group among other groups. Experienced group workers could add many other ways to this list.

Principle No. 3. In attempts to change attitudes, values, or behavior, the more relevant they are to the basis of attraction to the group, the greater will be the influence that the group can exert upon them.

I believe this principle gives a clue to some otherwise puzzling phenomena. How does it happen that a group, like a labor union, seems to be able to exert such strong discipline over its members in some matters (let us say in dealings with management), while it seems unable to exert nearly the same influence in other matters (let us say in political action)? If we examine why it is that members are attracted to the group, I believe we will find that a particular reason for belonging seems more related to some of the group's activities than to others. If a man joins a union mainly to keep his job and to improve his working conditions, he may be largely uninfluenced by the union's attempt to modify his attitudes toward national and international affairs. Groups differ tremendously in the range of matters that are relevant to them and hence over which they have influence. Much of the inefficiency of adult education could be reduced if more attention were paid to the need that influence attempts be appropriate to the groups in which they are made.

Principle No. 4. The greater the prestige of a group member in the eyes of the other members, the greater the influence he can exert.

Polansky, Lippitt, and Redl (1950) have demonstrated this principle with great care and methodological ingenuity in a series of studies in children's summer camps. From a practical point of view it must be emphasized that the things giving prestige to a member may not be those characteristics most prized by the official management of the group. The most prestige-carrying member of a Sunday School class may not possess the characteristics most similar to the minister of the church. The teacher's pet may be a poor source of influence within a class. This principle is the basis for the common observation that the official leader and the actual leader of a group are often not the same individual.

Principle No. 5. Efforts to change individuals or subparts of a group which, if successful, would have the result of making them deviate from the norms of the group will encounter strong resistance.

During the past few years a great deal of evidence has been accumulated showing the tremendous pressures which groups can exert upon members to conform to the group's norms. The price of deviation in most groups is rejection or even expulsion. If the member really wants to belong and be accepted, he cannot withstand this type of pressure. It is for this reason that efforts to change people by taking them from the group and giving them special training so often have disappointing results. This principle also accounts for the finding that people thus trained sometimes display increased tension, aggressiveness toward the group, or a tendency to form cults or cliques with others who have shared their training.

These five principles concerning the group as a medium of change would appear to have readiest application to groups created for the purpose of producing changes in people. They provide certain specifications for building effective training or therapy groups. They also point, however, to a difficulty in producing change in people in that they show how resistant an individual is to changing in any way contrary to group pressures and expectations. In order to achieve many kinds of changes in people, therefore, it is necessary to deal with the group as a target of change.

THE GROUP AS A TARGET OF CHANGE

Principle No. 6. Strong pressure for changes in the group can be established by creating a shared perception by members of the need for change, thus making the source of pressure for change lie within the group.

Marrow and French (1945) report a dramatic case-study which illustrates this principle quite well. A manufacturing concern had a policy against hiring women over thirty because it was believed that they were slower, more difficult to train, and more likely to be absent. The staff psychologist was able to present to management evidence that this belief was clearly unwarranted at least within their own company. The psychologist's facts, however, were rejected and ignored as a basis for action because they violated accepted beliefs. It was claimed that they went against the direct experience of the foremen. Then the psychologist hit upon a plan for achieving change which differed drastically from the usual one of argument, persuasion, and pressure. He proposed that management conduct its own analysis of the situation. With his help management collected all the facts which they believed were relevant to the problem. When the results were in they were now their own facts rather than those of some "outside" expert. Policy was immediately changed without further resistance. The important point here is that facts are not enough. The facts must be the accepted property of the group if they are to become an effective basis for change. There seems to be all the difference in the world in changes actually carried out between those cases in which a consulting firm is hired to do a study and present a report and those in which technical experts are asked to collaborate with the group in doing its own study.

Principle No. 7. Information relating to the need for change, plans for change, and consequences of change must be shared by all relevant people in the group.

Another way of stating this principle is to say that change of a group ordinarily requires the opening of communication channels. Newcomb (1947) has shown how one of the first consequences of mistrust and hostility is the avoidance of communicating openly and freely about the things producing the tension. If you look closely at a pathological group (that is, one that has trouble making decisions or effecting coordinated efforts of its members), you will certainly find strong restraints in that group against communicating vital information among its members. Until these restraints are removed there can be little hope for any real and lasting changes in the group's functioning. In passing it should be pointed out that the removal of barriers to communication will ordinarily be accompanied by a sudden increase in the communication of hostility. The group may appear to be falling apart, and it will certainly be a painful experience to many of the members. This pain and the fear that things are getting out of hand often stop the process of change once begun.

Principle No. 8. Changes in one part of a group produce strain in other related parts which can be reduced only by eliminating the change or by bringing about readjustments in the related parts.

It is a common practice to undertake

improvements in group functioning by providing training programs for certain classes of people in the organization. A training program for foremen, for nurses, for teachers, or for group workers is established. If the content of the training is relevant for organizational change, it must of necessity deal with the relationships these people have with other subgroups. If nurses in a hospital change their behavior significantly, it will affect their relations both with the patients and with the doctors. It is unrealistic to assume that both these groups will remain indifferent to any significant changes in this respect. In hierarchical structures this process is most clear. Lippitt has proposed on the basis of research and experience that in such organizations attempts at change should always involve three levels, one being the major target of change and the other two being the one above and the one below.

IV

These eight principles represent a few of the basic propositions emerging from research in group dynamics. Since research is constantly going on and since it is the very nature of research to revise and reformulate our conceptions, we may be sure that these principles will have to be modified and improved as time goes by. In the meantime they may serve as guides in our endeavors to develop a scientifically based technology of social management.

In social technology, just as in physical technology, invention plays a crucial role. In both fields progress consists of the creation of new mechanisms for the accomplishment of certain goals. In both fields inventions arise in response to practical needs and are to be evaluated by how effectively they satisfy these needs. The relation of invention to scientific development is indirect but important. Inventions cannot proceed too far ahead of basic scientific development, nor should they be allowed to fall too far behind. They will be more effective the more they make good use of known principles of science, and they often make new developments in science possible. On the other hand, they are in no sense logical derivations from scientific principles.

I have taken this brief excursion into the theory of invention in order to make a final point. To many people "group dynamics" is known only for the social inventions which have developed in recent years in work with groups. Group dynamics is often thought of as certain techniques to be used with groups. Role playing, buzz groups, process observers, post-meeting reaction sheets, and feedback of group observations are devices popularly associated with the phrase "group dynamics." I trust that I have been able to show that group dynamics is more than a collection of gadgets. It certainly aspires to be a science as well as a technology.

This is not to underplay the importance of these inventions nor of the function of inventing. As inventions they are all mechanisms designed to help accomplish important goals. How effective they are will depend upon how skillfully they are used and how appropriate they are to the purposes to which they are put. Careful evaluative research must be the ultimate judge of their usefulness in comparison with alternative inventions. I believe that the principles enumerated in this paper indicate some of the specifications that social inventions in this field must meet.

IX ORGANIZATIONAL PROCESSES

By all accounts much of the life of Western man has increasingly come under the domination of large, formal organizations. Bureaucratic structures and organizations of all sorts—business, governmental, educational, social—have proliferated in our modern era to the point where much of our daily life, one way or another, is spent in organizational activity. So complete has this organizational immersion become that social commentators like William H. Whyte (1956), and scholars like those discussed by Bronfenbrenner in Section II, discern a fundamental shift of American values from traditional entrepreneurial outlooks toward a more managerial-administrative orientation. Whyte considers this a shift from the traditional "Protestant ethic" to a newer "social ethic." It has led, he contends, to a conversion of Western character and the appearance of the "organization man." According to social critics like Whyte, the values of the organization in essence have become the values of society.

Whatever may be the specific merits of arguments such as Whyte's, the same concerns have also motivated others toward searching appraisals of relations between the individual and the group, epitomized perhaps by Gardner's discussion in Section II. Moreover, there has emerged a new interest in close scrutiny of organizational values to measure the degree to which these values contribute to the "good life," as well as to organizational efficiency. Max Weber's warning of the social alienation of modern man caught in the remote, impersonal toils of giant and fractionated organizations has taken on a renewed vigor in an America of computers and automated factories (see, e.g., Etzioni, 1964). And, in one way or another, the papers in this section all reflect the efforts of contemporary organization theorists not just to understand organizations as abstract social systems, but to come to grips with these normative managerial issues so that organizations may be fit places for people to live.

Actually "organization" is probably a poor choice of terms, for it mixes a label for a social phenomenon with a term referring to a social process. By definition, organization is a basic property of groups. All groups, large or small, are organized in some fashion; hence all groups are organizations. However, the noun organization is rarely used so broadly. More usually, the term is used to specify special cases of groups which are often, although not always, large in size, and in which the *fact* of organization is somehow especially striking or salient. In the study of organizations, description of their particular structure is therefore generally of more immediate interest than it is in analyses of other social aggregations.

More specifically, the phenomenon of the organization has been variously defined in the literature; the reader interested in more extended and technical discussion of definitional matters can find exemplary treatments in March's new *Handbook of Organizations* (1964), in W. R. Scott's chapter in the *Handbook of Modern Sociology* (1964), and in Katz and Kahn's recent textbook (1966). In general, however, an organization may be characterized as a generally orderly arrangement of particular social means geared to the accomplishment of certain more or less specific goals or ends. Put differently, organizations are "species of social systems in which an attempt has been made to formulate rationally a position-role pattern productive of some predetermined end" (R. G. Hunt, 1965, p. 37). Etzioni (1964), too, has emphasized the "deliberate" or self-conscious quality of organizations, but the inference must not therefore be drawn that *all* organizational events are either rational or planned. Indeed, more than a little organizational analysis has been concerned to show the operation of non-rational, unplanned and even capricious happenings in organizations (see, e.g., March & Simon, 1958, especially Ch. 6). Furthermore, the fact is familiar that organizations tend to have a life of their own that makes them as much the masters as the servants of men.

Organizations may be populated with and worked by people, but their structures tend to be elaborated independently of any particular individuals or groups of individuals. They reflect primarily the demands imposed by impersonal goals as these may be defined at some point in time. When we speak of *formal* organizations, then, it is these abstract, impersonal features we have in mind.

Co-extensive with the formal organization, however, is an *informal* one consisting of a unique system of particular interpersonal relations. Informal organizations necessarily arise as soon as the formal structure is fleshed-out with persons some of whose needs differ from those of the organization, yet who operate within it.

Groups or organizations differ in the comparative degree to which formal and informal processes predominate and, really, formality-informality is best thought of as a continuous organizational dimension rather than as a typology. Organizations might range from highly formal bureaucracies to very informal temporary social aggregations, but none would be regarded either as purely formal or informal.

The significance of informal interpersonal aspects of organization was first clearly recognized in the wake of the now famous studies at the Hawthorne plant of the Western Electric Company. They provided the impetus for a drastic change in the perspectives of organizational analysis from a preoccupation with work as such to an interest in human relations. Leading off this section, Scott, in the course of his excellent review of the major schools of thought about organizations, takes note of this point. After some comments on the functions of organization, he presents a delineation of, in his terminology, classical theory, neo-classical theory, and modern theory.

The first of these is intimately tied to Taylor's so-called "scientific management" and has been aptly called "physiological organization theory" by March and Simon because of its preoccupation with relations between components of work routines and the physical capacities of workers. As Scott makes evident, machine-oriented classical theory devoted the major share of its attention to the *forms* of organization. Time and methods study is its major tool and the legendary "efficiency expert" its symbol.

Neo-classical theory, or the human relations approach, most clearly associated initially with the name of Elton Mayo and the work during the late twenties and early thirties at the Hawthorne plant, signalled a shift of emphasis from the formal to the informal organization—from the forms to the functions of organization. Although the human relations approach has had its vocal critics, Scott indicates that its broad conceptual contributions are beyond basic dispute. He points out, furthermore, that the neo-classical emphasis on organizations as "social systems" forms a direct bridge to modern system theories of organization.

The burden of modern theory has been to reintegrate the formal and informal organization, via the concept of the system, so as to portray the mutual structural-functional patterns of influence that lie at its core. In addition to the works by March and Simon and by Haire, mentioned by Scott as representative of this outlook, a most provocative discussion of organizational models can be found in Gouldner's chapter in *Sociology Today* (1959); an excellent excursion into the difficult system concept is to be found in the Katz and Kahn text already cited and, closer at hand, in Allport's paper in Section III. What modern system theorists have in mind is the idea that the distinction between formal and informal organization is much more conceptual than actual. In reality a functional organization is a complex synthesized resultant of dynamic structural and interpersonal processes rather than an uncertain marriage of expedient convenience between separate, and competing, formal and informal systems.

The kinds of questions about organizations occasioned by this point of view are delineated well in Katz's examination here of the vital motivational processes by which persons become attached to organizations and, once they are attached, are prompted to perform in them. Katz identifies three behavioral requirements fundamental to organizational functioning: recruitment and retention of personnel; dependable performance of assigned roles; non-routine innovative problem solving. He then proceeds to show that different inducements and organizational circumstances are relevant to each of these requirements and then presents a systematic analysis of the conditions conducive to motivating their fulfillment.

Katz's references to innovative requirements, of course, re-direct attention to problems of leadership as reviewed in Section VIII. The papers there by Bavelas and by Fiedler are of special relevance to organizational interests. It might be mentioned that Fiedler's emphasis upon relations between leader styles and properties of the situation as determinants of leadership outcomes is most pertinent to the kinds of questions raised by Katz. Moreover, Fiedler's view, and Bavelas's as well, fit neatly into the system ethos.

There is also an obvious connection between leadership and power in organizational functioning. In addition to ways of dividing and relating work, organizations include control systems with rules for allocating and using power. However, the topics discussed in Sections V and VII are no less vital to an understanding of organizational processes; questions of normative behavior, conformity, roles, and other group processes are fully cogent to them as social systems—all of which illustrates the fact that, whatever they are in particular, organizations in general are groups and no social process is wholly irrelevant to them.

We have already taken notice of a contemporary concern with relations between the individual and the organization. Such concerns were central to the neo-classical preoccupation with the informal organization and are implicit in Katz's interest in motivation. At the forefront of those students of organization who have fastened their interests on person-organization relations is Chris Argyris, whose books, *Personality and Organization* (1957) and *Integrating the Individual and the Organization* (1964), are basic references in this area. His paper in this section relates nicely to Katz's comments on the relations between individual needs and organizational participation and, from a sharply evaluative stance, it highlights some important difficulties besetting attempts to achieve satisfactory integration of the individual with the traditional organization. Argyris demonstrates the essential incompatibility of human needs with the requirements of such organizations, but his is not a bleakly fatalistic view; as he says, the problem is one of redesigning organizations to improve their human fit. The fact that such reformation can be seen to be in the organization's interest as well as in society's supports an optimistic appraisal of its prospects.

Bennis, too, in his incisive paper here, exposes the deficiencies of bureaucratic forms of organization and, unwinding further the thread untied in Katz's article, directs attention to motivational issues and to organizational requirements. One of these latter in particular, the requirement of adaptability to a changing environment, he considers crucial as a lever to loose organizational modification in more person-centered directions.

Bennis also offers some engaging forecasts of futuristic organizational designs in which special purpose, non-hierarchic structures figure prominently. In common with his late colleague at M.I.T., Douglas McGregor, who was a principal protagonist of participative management (see 1960),

Bennis places confidence in group methods for organizational administration rather than in authority *per se* (see also Gross, 1965). He views organizational response to changing needs and issues in terms of special-purpose "task-forces," group decision-making, and executives as "coordinators" of problem-solving activities throughout the organization. The manager thus becomes a kind of "linking-pin" tieing together into a coherent system the individual functional units that are the organization's elements.

The idea of the linking-pin is the key concept in Rensis Likert's up-to-date group-based view of organizational conduct. The selection we have included here from his influential book, *New Patterns of Management* (1961), provides an excellent summary of his basic thought. Likert not only clarifies the essential meaning of participative management, he provides an empirically based structure, albeit not a universally accepted one, for its implementation.

In his book he presents detailed summaries of the research, much of it conducted under his direction at the University of Michigan's Institute for Social Research, justifying his assertions that, in practice, the most productive managers are employee-centered rather than work-centered, in their orientations toward their jobs. In effect, Likert reasons that if it is even a part of one's purpose effectively to redesign organizational formats, one might sensibly take as guidelines the kinds of things already happening in the most successful organizations. It is reasonable, after all, to assume that these organizations will have developed generally suitable means for the satisfaction of the organizational requirements identified by Katz, Argyris, and Bennis. In fact, of course, that would presumably be the reason for their success. Moreover, comparative analyses of different kinds of organizations (see, for example, Etzioni, 1961, 1964), and of "good" and "bad" ones, can serve as a means for directly testing the validity of the general premises undergirding modern theories of organization.

Looked at whole, this section affords a quite comprehensive view of contemporary thinking about organizations. It is, however, a view more of the forest than of the trees. But bearing in mind that organizations are social systems, it will be realized that much of the material in this book provides the means for understanding the inner workings of organizational processes.

56 Organization theory: an overview and an appraisal

WILLIAM G. SCOTT

Man is intent on drawing himself into a web of collectivized patterns. "Modern man has learned to accommodate himself to a world increasingly organized. The trend toward ever more explicit and consciously drawn relationships is profound and sweeping; it is marked by depth no less than by extension" (Seidenberg, 1951, p. 1). This comment by Seidenberg nicely summarizes the pervasive influence of organization in many forms of human activity.

Some of the reasons for intense organizational activity are found in the fundamental transitions which revolutionized our society, changing it from a rural culture, to a culture based on technology, industry, and the city. From these changes, a way of life emerged characterized by the *proximity* and *dependency* of people on each other. Proximity and dependency, as conditions of social life, harbor the threats of human conflict, capricious antisocial behavior, instability of human relationships, and uncertainty about the nature of the social structure with its concomitant roles.

Traditionally, organization is viewed as a vehicle for accomplishing goals and objectives. While this approach is useful, it tends to obscure the inner workings and internal purposes of organization itself. Another fruitful way of treating organization is as a mechanism having the ultimate purpose of offsetting those forces which undermine human collaboration. In this sense, organization tends to minimize conflict, and to lessen the significance of individual behavior which deviates from values that the organization has established as worthwhile. Further, organization increases stability in human relationships by reducing uncertainty regarding the nature of the system's structure and the human roles which are inherent to it. Corollary to this point, organization enhances the predictability of human action, because it limits the number of behavioral alternatives available to an individual.

In addition to all of this, organization has built-in safeguards. Besides prescribing acceptable forms of behavior for those who elect to submit to it, organization is also able to counterbalance the influence of human action which transcends its established patterns.[1]

[1] Regulation and predictability of human behavior are matters of degree varying with different organizations on something of a continuum. At one extreme are bureaucratic type organizations with tight bonds of regulation. At the other extreme are voluntary associations, and informal organizations with relatively loose bonds of regulation.

This point has an interesting sidelight. A bureaucracy with tight controls and a high degree of predictability of human action appears to be unable to distinguish between destructive and creative deviations from established values. Thus the only thing which is safeguarded is the **status quo.**

Abridged from the **Journal of the Academy of Management,** 1961, 4, 7–27, with permission of the author and the publisher.

Organization theory, however, is not a homogeneous science based on generally accepted principles. Various theories of organization have been, and are being evolved. For example, something called "modern organization theory" has recently emerged, raising the wrath of some traditionalists, but also capturing the imagination of a rather elite *avant-garde*.

In any event, three theories of organization are having considerable influence on management thought and practice. They are arbitrarily labeled in this paper as the classical, the neo-classical, and the modern. Each of these is fairly distinct; but they are not unrelated. Also, these theories are on-going, being actively supported by several schools of management thought.

The classical doctrine

For lack of a better method of identification, it will be said that the classical doctrine deals almost exclusively with the *anatomy of formal organization*. This doctrine can be traced back to Frederick W. Taylor's interest in functional foremanship and planning staffs. But most students of management thought would agree that in the United States, the first systematic approach to organization, and the first comprehensive attempt to find organizational universals, is dated 1931 when Mooney and Reiley published *Onward Industry* (1931). Subsequently, numerous books, following the classical vein, have appeared. Two of the more recent are Brech's, *Organization* (1957) and Allen's, *Management and Organization* (1958).

Classical organization theory is built around four key pillars. They are the division of labor, the scalar and functional processes, structure, and span of control. Given these major elements just about all of classical organization theory can be derived.

(1) *The division of labor* is without doubt the cornerstone among the four elements (e.g., Koontz & O'Donnell, 1959, Ch. 7). From it the other elements flow as corollaries. For example, *scalar* and *functional* growth requires specialization and departmentalization of functions. Organization *structure* is naturally dependent upon the direction which specialization of activities travels in company development. Finally, *span of control* problems result from the number of specialized functions under the jurisdiction of a manager.

(2) *The scalar and functional processes* deal with the vertical and horizontal growth of the organization, respectively (see Davis, 1951, Ch. 7). The scalar process refers to the growth of the chain of command, the delegation of authority and responsibility, unity of command, and the obligation to report.

The division of the organization into specialized parts and the regrouping of the parts into compatible units are matters pertaining to the functional process. This process focuses on the horizontal evolution of the line and staff in a formal organization.

(3) *Structure* is the logical relationships of functions in an organization, arranged to accomplish the objectives of the company efficiently. Structure implies system and pattern. Classical organization theory usually works with two basic structures, the line and the staff. However, such activities as committee and liaison functions fall quite readily into the purview of structural considerations. Again, structure is the vehicle for introducing logical and con-

sistent relationships among the diverse functions which comprise the organization (see Newman, 1951, Ch. 16).

(4) *The span of control* concept relates to the number of subordinates a manager can effectively supervise. Graicunas (1937) has been credited with first elaborating the point that there are numerical limitations to the subordinates one man can control. In a recent statement on the subject, Brech points out, "span" refers to ". . . the number of persons, themselves carrying managerial and supervisory responsibilities, for whom the senior manager retains his over-embracing responsibility of direction and planning, co-ordination, motivation, and control" (1957, p. 78). Regardless of interpretation, span of control has significance, in part, for the shape of the organization which evolves through growth. Wide span yields a flat structure; short span results in a tall structure. Further, the span concept directs attention to the complexity of human and functional interrelationships in an organization.

It would not be fair to say that the classical school is unaware of the day-to-day administrative problems of the organization. Paramount among these problems are those stemming from human interactions. But the interplay of individual personality, informal groups, intraorganizational conflict, and the decision-making processes in the formal structure appears largely to be neglected by classical organization theory. Additionally, the classical theory overlooks the contributions of the behavioral sciences by failing to incorporate them in its doctrine in any systematic way. In summary, classical organization theory has relevant insights into the nature of organization, but the value of this theory is limited by its narrow concentration on the formal anatomy of organization.

Neoclassical theory of organization

The neoclassical theory of organization embarked on the task of compensating for some of the deficiencies in classical doctrine. The neoclassical school is commonly identified with the human relations movement. Generally, the neoclassical approach takes the postulates of the classical school, regarding the pillars of organization as givens. But these postulates are regarded as modified by people, acting independently or within the context of the informal organization.

One of the main contributions of the neoclassical school is the introduction of behavioral sciences in an integrated fashion into the theory of organization. Through the use of these sciences, the human relationists demonstrate how the pillars of the classical doctrine are affected by the impact of human actions. Further, the neoclassical approach includes a systematic treatment of the informal organization, showing its influence on the formal structure.

Thus, the neoclassical approach to organization theory gives evidence of accepting classical doctrine, but superimposing on it modifications resulting from individual behavior, and the influence of the informal group. The inspiration of the neoclassical school were the Hawthorne studies (see Roethlisberger & Dickson, 1939). Current examples of the neoclassical approach are found in human relations books like Gardner and Moore, *Human Relations in Industry* (1955), and Davis, *Human Relations in Business* (1957). To a more limited extent, work in industrial sociology also reflects a neoclassical point of view (see, e.g., Miller & Form, 1951).

It would be useful to look briefly at some of the contributions made to organization theory by the neoclassicists. First to be considered are modifications of the pillars of classical doctrine; second is the informal organization.

EXAMPLES OF THE NEOCLASSICAL APPROACH TO THE PILLARS OF FORMAL ORGANIZATION THEORY

(1) The *division of labor* has been a long standing subject of comment in the field of human relations. Very early in the history of industrial psychology study was made of industrial fatigue and monotony caused by the specialization of the work (see Munsterberg, 1913). Later, attention shifted to the isolation of the worker, and his feeling of anonymity resulting from insignificant jobs which contributed negligibly to the final product.[2]

Also, specialization influences the work of management. As an organization expands, the need concomitantly arises for managerial motivation and coordination of the activities of others. Both motivation and coordination in turn relate to executive leadership. Thus, in part, stemming from the growth of industrial specialization, the neoclassical school has developed a large body of theory relating to motivation, coordination, and leadership. Much of this theory is derived from the social sciences.

(2) Two aspects of the *scalar and functional* processes which have been treated with some degree of intensity by the neoclassical school are the delegation of authority and responsibility, and gaps in or overlapping of functional jurisdictions. The classical theory assumes something of perfection in the delegation and functionalization processes. The neoclassical school points out that human problems are caused by imperfections in the way these processes are handled.

For example, too much or insufficient delegation may render an executive incapable of action. The failure to delegate authority and responsibility equally may result in frustration for the delegatee. Overlapping of authorities often causes clashes in personality. Gaps in authority cause failures in getting jobs done, with one party blaming the other for shortcomings in performance (see Davis, 1957, pp. 60–66).

The neoclassical school says that the scalar and functional processes are theoretically valid, but tend to deteriorate in practice. The ways in which they break down are described, and some of the human causes are pointed out. In addition the neoclassicists make recommendations, suggesting various "human tools" which will facilitate the operation of these processes.

(3) *Structure* provides endless avenues of analysis for the neoclassical theory of organization. The theme is that human behavior disrupts the best laid organizational plans, and thwarts the cleanness of the logical relationships founded in the structure. The neoclassical critique of structure centers on frictions which appear internally among people performing different functions.

Line and staff relations is a problem area, much discussed, in this respect. Many companies seem to have difficulty keeping the line and staff working together harmoniously. Both Dalton (1950) and Juran (1956) have engaged in research to discover the causes of friction, and to suggest remedies.

[2] Probably the classic work is: Elton Mayo, **The Human Problems of an Industrial Civilization** (1946), first printed in 1933.

Of course, line-staff relations represent only one of the many problems of structural frictions described by the neoclassicists. As often as not, the neoclassicists will offer prescriptions for the elimination of conflict in structure. Among the more important harmony-rendering formulae are participation, junior boards, bottom-up management, joint committees, recognition of human dignity, and "better" communication.

(4) An executive's *span of control* is a function of human determinants, and the reduction of span to a precise, universally applicable ratio is silly, according to the neoclassicists. Some of the determinants of span are individual differences in managerial abilities, the type of people and functions supervised, and the extent of communication effectiveness.

Coupled with the span of control question are the human implications of the type of structure which emerges. That is, is a tall structure with a short span or a flat structure with a wide span more conducive to good human relations and high morale? The answer is situational. Short span results in tight supervision; wide span requires a good deal of delegation with looser controls. Because of individual and organizational differences, sometimes one is better than the other. There is a tendency to favor the looser form of organization, however, for the reason that tall structures breed autocratic leadership, which is often pointed out as a cause of low morale (Gardner & Moore, 1955).

THE NEOCLASSICAL VIEW OF THE INFORMAL ORGANIZATION

Nothing more than the barest mention of the informal organization is given even in the most recent classical treatises on organization theory (see, e.g., Brech, 1957; Allen, 1958). Systematic discussion of this form of organization has been left to the neoclassicists. The informal organization refers to people in group associations at work, but these associations are not specified in the "blueprint" of the formal organization. The informal organization means natural groupings of people in the work situation.

In a general way, the informal organization appears in response to the social need—the need of people to associate with others. However, for analytical purposes, this explanation is not particularly satisfying. Research has produced the following, more specific determinants underlying the appearance of informal organizations.

(1) The *location* determinant simply states that in order to form into groups of any lasting nature, people have to have frequent face-to-face contact. Thus, the geography of physical location in a plant or office is an important factor in predicting who will be in what group (see Festinger, *et al.*, 1950).

(2) *Occupation* is a key factor determining the rise and composition of informal groups. There is a tendency for people performing similar jobs to group together (see, e.g., Cottrell, 1940, Ch. 3).

(3) *Interests* are another determinant for informal group formation. Even though people might be in the same location, performing similar jobs, differences of interest among them explain why several small, instead of one large, informal organizations emerge.

(4) *Special issues* often result in the formation of informal groups, but this determinant is set apart from the three previously mentioned. In this case, people who do not necessarily have similar

interests, occupations, or locations may join together for a common cause. Once the issue is resolved, then the tendency is to revert to the more "natural" group forms.[3] Thus, special issues give rise to a rather impermanent informal association; groups based on the other three determinants tend to be more lasting.

When informal organizations come into being they assume certain characteristics. Since understanding these characteristics is important for management practice, they are noted below:

(1) Informal organizations act as agencies of *social control*. They generate a culture based on certain norms of conduct which, in turn, demands conformity from group members. These standards may be at odds with the values set by the formal organization. So an individual may very well find himself in a situation of conflicting demands.

(2) The form of human interrelationships in the informal organization requires *techniques of analysis* different from those used to plot the relationships of people in a formal organization. The method used for determining the structure of the informal group is called sociometric analysis. Sociometry reveals the complex structure of interpersonal relations which is based on premises fundamentally unlike the logic of the formal organization.

(3) Informal organizations have *status and communication* systems peculiar to themselves, not necessarily derived from the formal systems. For example, the grapevine is the subject of much neoclassical study.

(4) Survival of the informal organization requires stable continuing relationships among the people in them. Thus, it has been observed that the informal organization *resists change* (see e.g., Coch & French, 1948). Considerable attention is given by the neoclassicists to overcoming informal resistance to change.

(5) The last aspect of analysis which appears to be central to the neoclassical view of the informal organization is the study of the *informal leader*. Discussion revolves around who the informal leader is, how he assumes this role, what characteristics are peculiar to him, and how he can help the manager accomplish his objectives in the formal organization (see e.g., Saltonstall, 1959; Davis, 1957).

This brief sketch of some of the major facets of informal organization theory has neglected, so far, one important topic treated by the neoclassical school. It is the way in which the formal and informal organizations interact.

Some neoclassical writing in organization theory, especially that coming from the management-oriented segment of this school, gives the impression that the formal and informal organizations are distinct, and at times, quite irreconcilable factors in a company. The interaction which takes place between the two is something akin to the interaction between the company and a labor union, or a government agency, or another company.

The concept of the social system is another approach to the interactional climate. While this concept can be properly classified as neoclassical, it borders on the modern theories of organization. The phrase "social system" means that an organization is a complex of mutually interdependent, but variable, factors.

[3] Except in cases where the existence of an organization is necessary for the continued maintenance of employee interest. Under these conditions the previously informal association may emerge as a formal group, such as a union.

These factors include individuals and their attitudes and motives, jobs, the physical work setting, the formal organization, and the informal organizations. These factors, and many others, are woven into an overall pattern of interdependency. From this point of view, the formal and informal organizations lose their distinctiveness, but find real meaning, in terms of human behavior, in the operation of the system as a whole. Thus, the study of organization turns away from descriptions of its component parts, and is refocused on the system of interrelationships among the parts.

The neoclassical school of organization theory has been called bankrupt. Criticisms range from, "human relations is a tool for cynical puppeteering of people," to "human relations is nothing more than a trifling body of empirical and descriptive information." There is a good deal of truth in both criticisms, but another appraisal of the neoclassical school of organization theory is offered here. The neoclassical approach has provided valuable contributions to lore of organization. But, like the classical theory, the neoclassical doctrine suffers from incompleteness, a shortsighted perspective, and lack of integration among the many facets of human behavior studied by it. Modern organization theory has made a move to cover the shortcomings of the current body of theoretical knowledge.

Modern organization theory

The distinctive qualities of modern organization theory are its conceptual-analytical base, its reliance on empirical research data and, above all, its integrating nature. These qualities are framed in a philosophy which accepts the premise that the only meaningful way to study organization is to study it as a system. As Henderson put it, the study of a system must rely on a method of analysis, ". . . involving the simultaneous variations of mutually dependent variables" (1935, p. 13). Human systems, of course, contain a huge number of dependent variables which defy the most complex simultaneous equations to solve.

Nevertheless, system analysis has its own peculiar point of view which aims to study organization in the way Henderson suggests. It treats organization as a system of mutually dependent variables. As a result, modern organization theory, which accepts system analysis, shifts the conceptual level of organization study above the classical and neoclassical theories. Modern organization theory asks a range of interrelated questions which are not seriously considered by the two other theories.

Key among these questions are: (1) What are the strategic parts of the system? (2) What is the nature of their mutual dependency? (3) What are the main processes in the system which link the parts together, and facilitate their adjustment to each other? (4) What are the goals sought by systems?

Modern organization theory is in no way a unified body of thought. Each writer and researcher has his special emphasis when he considers the system. Perhaps the most evident unifying thread in the study of systems is the effort to look at the organization in its totality. Representative books in this field are March and Simon, *Organizations* (1958), and Haire's anthology, *Modern Organization Theory* (1959a).

Instead of attempting a review of different writers' contributions to modern organization theory, it will be more useful to discuss the various ingredients involved in system analysis. They are the parts, the interactions, the processes, and the goals of systems.

THE PARTS OF THE SYSTEM AND THEIR INTERDEPENDENCY

The first basic part of the system is the *individual*, and the personality structure he brings to the organization. Elementary to an individual's personality are motives and attitudes which condition the range of expectancies he hopes to satisfy by participating in the system.

The second part of the system is the formal arrangement of functions, usually called the *formal organization*. The formal organization is the interrelated pattern of jobs which make up the structure of a system. Certain writers, like Argyris (see 1957, esp. Chs. 2, 3, 7), see a fundamental conflict resulting from the demands made by the system, and the structure of the mature, normal personality. In any event, the individual has expectancies regarding the job he is to perform; and, conversely, the job makes demands on, or has expectancies relating to, the performance of the individual. Considerable attention has been given by writers in modern organization theory to incongruencies resulting from the interaction of organizational and individual demands.

The third part in the organization system is the *informal organization*. Enough has been said already about the nature of this organization. But it must be noted that an interactional pattern exists between the individual and the informal group. This interactional arrangement can be conveniently discussed as the mutual modification of expectancies. The informal organization has demands which it makes on members in terms of anticipated forms of behavior, and the individual has expectancies of satisfaction he hopes to derive from association with people on the job. Both these sets of expectancies interact, resulting in the individual modifying his behavior to accord with the demands of the group, and the group, perhaps, modifying what it expects from an individual because of the impact of his personality on group norms (see Homans, 1950, Ch. 5).

Much of what has been said about the various expectancy systems in an organization can also be treated using status and role concepts. Part of modern organization theory rests on research findings in social psychology relative to reciprocal patterns of behavior stemming from role demands generated by both the formal and informal organizations, and role perceptions peculiar to the individual. Bakke's *fusion process* (1959) is largely concerned with the modification of role expectancies. The fusion process is a force, according to Bakke, which acts to weld divergent elements together for the preservation of organizational integrity.

The fifth part of system analysis is the *physical setting* in which the job is performed. Although this element of the system may be implicit in what has been said already about the formal organization and its functions, it is well to separate it. In the physical surroundings of work, interactions are present in complex man-machine systems. The human "engineer" cannot approach the problems posed by such interrelationships in a purely technical, engineering fashion. As Haire says, these problems lie in the domain of the social theorist (1959b). Attention must be centered on responses demanded from a logically ordered production function, often with the view of minimizing the error in the system. From this standpoint, work cannot be effectively organized unless the psychological, social, and physiological characteristics of people participating in the work environment are considered. Machines and processes should be designed to fit certain generally observed psychological and physiological properties of men, rather than hiring men to fit machines.

In summary, the parts of the system which appear to be of strategic importance are the individual, the formal structure, the informal organization, status and role patterns, and the physical environment of work. Again, these parts are woven into a configuration called the organizational system. The processes which link the parts are taken up next.

THE LINKING PROCESSES

One can say, with a good deal of glibness, that all the parts mentioned above are interrelated. Although this observation is quite correct, it does not mean too much in terms of system theory unless some attempt is made to analyze the processes by which the interaction is achieved. Role theory is devoted to certain types of interactional processes. In addition, modern organization theorists point to three other linking activities which appear to be universal to human systems of organized behavior. These processes are communication, balance, and decision making.

(1) Communication is mentioned often in neoclassical theory, but the emphasis is on description of forms of communication activity, i.e., formal-informal, vertical-horizontal, line-staff. Communication, as a mechanism which links the segments of the system together, is overlooked by way of much considered analysis.

One aspect of modern organization theory is study of the communication network in the system. Communication is viewed as the method by which action is evoked from the parts of the system. Communication acts not only as stimuli resulting in action, but also as a control and coordination mechanism linking the decision centers in the system into a synchronized pattern. Deutsch points out that organizations are composed of parts which communicate with each other, receive messages from the outside world, and store information. Taken together, these communication functions of the parts comprise a configuration representing the total system (Deutsch, 1952). More is to be said about communication later in the discussion of the cybernetic model.

(2) The concept of *balance* as a linking process involves a series of some rather complex ideas. Balance refers to an equilibrating mechanism whereby the various parts of the system are maintained in a harmoniously structured relationship to each other.

The necessity for the balance concept logically flows from the nature of systems themselves. It is impossible to conceive of an ordered relationship among the parts of a system without also introducing the idea of a stabilizing or an adapting mechanism.

Balance appears in two varieties—quasi-automatic and innovative. Both forms of balance act to insure system integrity in face of changing conditions, either internal or external to the system. The first form of balance, quasi-automatic, refers to what some think are "homeostatic" properties of systems. That is, systems seem to exhibit built-in propensities to maintain steady states.

If human organizations are open,

self-maintaining systems, then control and regulatory processes are necessary. The issue hinges on the degree to which stabilizing processes in systems, when adapting to change, are automatic. March and Simon (1958) have an interesting answer to this problem, which in part is based on the type of change and the adjustment necessary to adapt to the change. Systems have programs of action which are put into effect when a change is perceived. If the change is relatively minor, and if the change comes within the purview of established programs of action, then it might be fairly confidently predicted that the adaptation made by the system will be quasi-automatic.

The role of innovative, creative balancing efforts now needs to be examined. The need for innovation arises when adaptation to a change is outside the scope of existing programs designed for the purpose of keeping the system in balance. New programs have to be evolved in order for the system to maintain internal harmony.

New programs are created by trial and error search for feasible action alternatives to cope with a given change. But innovation is subject to the limitations and possibilities inherent in the quantity and variety of information present in a system at a particular time. New combinations of alternatives for innovative purposes depend on:

(a) the possible range of output of the system, or the capacity of the system to supply information.

(b) the range of available information in the memory of the system.

(c) the operating rules (program) governing the analysis and flow of information within the system.

(d) the ability of the system to "forget" previously learned solutions to change problems (Cadwallader, 1959, p. 156). A system with too good a memory might narrow its behavioral choices to such an extent as to stifle innovation. In simpler language, old learned programs might be used to adapt to change, when newly innovated programs are necessary.

Much of what has been said about communication and balance brings to mind a cybernetic model in which both these processes have vital roles. Cybernetics has to do with feedback and control in all kinds of systems. Its purpose is to maintain system stability in the face of change. Cybernetics cannot be studied without considering communication networks, information flow, and some kind of balancing process aimed at preserving the integrity of the system.

Cybernetics directs attention to key questions regarding the system. These questions are: How are communication centers connected, and how are they maintained? Corollary to this question: what is the structure of the feedback system? Next, what information is stored in the organization, and at what points? And as a corollary: how accessible is this information to decision-making centers? Third, how conscious is the organization of the operation of its own parts? That is, to what extent do the policy centers receive control information with sufficient frequency and relevancy to create a real awareness of the operation of the segments of the system? Finally, what are the learning (innovating) capabilities of the system? (These are questions adapted from Deutsch, 1952.)

Answers to the questions posed by cybernetics are crucial to understanding both the balancing and communication processes in systems (see Beer, 1959).

Although cybernetics has been applied largely to technical-engineering problems of automation, the model of feedback, control, and regulation in all systems has a good deal of generality. Cybernetics is a fruitful area which can be used to synthesize the processes of communication and balance.

(3) A wide spectrum of topics dealing with types of decisions in human systems makes up the core of analysis of another important process in organizations. Decision analysis is one of the major contributions of March and Simon in their book *Organizations* (1958, Chs. 3 & 4). The two major classes of decisions they discuss are decisions to produce and decisions to participate in the system.

Decisions to produce are largely a result of an interaction between individual attitudes and the demands of organization. Motivation analysis becomes central to studying the nature and results of the interaction. Individual decisions to participate in the organization reflect on such issues as the relationship between organizational rewards versus the demands made by the organization. Participation decisions also focus attention on the reasons why individuals remain in or leave organizations.

March and Simon treat decisions as internal variables in an organization which depend on jobs, individual expectations and motivations, and organizational structure. Marschak (1959) looks on the decision process as an independent variable upon which the survival of the organization is based. In this case, the organization is viewed as having, inherent to its structure, the ability to maximize survival requisites through its established decision processes.

THE GOALS OF ORGANIZATION

Organization has three goals which may be either intermeshed or independent ends in themselves. They are growth, stability, and interaction. The last goal refers to organizations which exist primarily to provide a medium for association of its members with others. Interestingly enough these goals seem to apply to different forms of organization at varying levels of complexity, ranging from simple clockwork mechanisms to social systems.

These similarities in organizational purposes have been observed by a number of people, and a field of thought and research called general system theory has developed, dedicated to the task of discovering organizational universals. The dream of general system theory is to create a science of organizational universals, or if you will, a universal science using common organizational elements found in all systems as a starting point.

Modern organization theory is on the periphery of general system theory. Both general system theory and modern organization theory studies:

(1) the parts (individuals) in aggregates, and the movement of individuals into and out of the system.

(2) the interaction of individuals with the environment found in the system.

(3) the interactions among individuals in the system.

(4) general growth and stability problems of systems (see Boulding, 1956).

Modern organization theory and general system theory are similar in that they look at organization as an integrated whole. They differ, however, in terms of their generality. General system theory is concerned with every level of system, whereas modern organizational theory focuses primarily on human organization.

Modern organization theory leads, as it has been shown, almost inevitably into a discussion of general system theory. A science of organization universals has some strong advocates, particularly among biologists (see, e.g., von Bertalanffy, 1952). Organization theorists in administrative science cannot afford to overlook the contributions of general system theory. Indeed, modern organization concepts could offer a great deal to those working with general system theory. But the ideas dealt with in the general theory are exceedingly elusive.

Speaking of the concept of equilibrium as a unifying element in all systems, Easton says, "It [equilibrium] leaves the impression that we have a useful general theory when in fact, lacking measurability, it is a mere pretence for knowledge" (1953, p. 39). The inability to quantify and measure universal organization elements undermines the success of pragmatic tests to which general system theory might be put.

57 The motivational basis of organizational behavior

DANIEL KATZ

The basic problem to which I shall address myself is how people are tied into social and organizational structures so that they become effective functioning units of social systems. What is the nature of their involvement in a system or their commitment to it?

The major input into social organizations consists of people. The economist or the culturologist may concentrate on inputs of resources, raw materials, technology. To the extent that human factors are recognized, they are assumed to be constants in the total equation and are neglected. At the practical level, however, as well as for a more precise theoretical accounting, we need to cope with such organizational realities as the attracting of people into organizations, holding them within the system, insuring reliable role performance, and in addition stimulating actions which are generally facilitative of organizational accomplishment. The material and psychic returns to organizational members thus constitute major determinants, not only of the level of effectiveness of organizational functioning, but of the very existence of the organization.

The complexities of motivational

Reprinted with slight abridgment from **Behavioral Science**, 1964, 9, 131–46, with permission of the author and the publisher.

problems in organizations can be understood if we develop an analytic framework which will be comprehensive enough to identify the major sources of variance and detailed enough to contain sufficient specification for predictive purposes. The framework we propose calls for three steps in an analysis process, namely, the formulation of answers to these types of questions: (1) What are the types of behavior required for effective organizational functioning? Any organization will require not one, but several patterns of behavior from most of its members. And the motivational bases of these various behavioral requirements may differ. (2) What are the motivational patterns which are used and which can be used in organizational settings? How do they differ in their logic and psycho-logic? What are the differential consequences of the various types of motivational patterns for the behavioral requirements essential for organizational functioning? One motivational pattern may be very effective in bringing about one type of necessary behavior and completely ineffective in leading to another. (3) What are the conditions for eliciting a given motivational pattern in an organizational setting? We may be able to identify the type of motivation we think most appropriate for producing a given behavioral outcome but we still need to know how this motive can be aroused or produced in the organization (Katz, 1962).

Behavioral requirements

Our major dependent variables are the behavioral requirements of the organization. Three basic types of behavior are essential for a functioning organization: (1) People must be induced to enter and remain within the system. (2) They must carry out their role assignments in a dependable fashion. (3) There must be innovative and spontaneous activity in achieving organizational objectives which go beyond the role specifications.

ATTRACTING AND HOLDING PEOPLE IN A SYSTEM

First of all, sufficient personnel must be kept within the system to man its essential functions. People thus must be induced to enter the system at a sufficiently rapid rate to counteract the amount of defection. High turnover is costly. Moreover, there is some optimum period for their staying within the system. And while they are members of the system they must validate their membership by constant attendance. Turnover and absenteeism are both measures of organizational effectiveness and productivity, though they are partial measures. People may, of course, be within the system physically but may be psychological absentees. The child may be regular and punctual in his school attendance and yet daydream in his classes. It is not enough, then, to hold people within a system.

DEPENDABLE ROLE PERFORMANCE

The great range of variable human behavior must be reduced to a limited number of predictable patterns. In other words, the assigned roles must be carried out and must meet some minimal level of quantity and quality of performance. A common measure of productivity is the amount of work turned out by the individual or by the group carrying out their assigned tasks. Quality of performance is not as easily measured and the problem is met by quality controls which set minimal standards for the pieces of work sampled. In general, the major role of the member is clearly set forth by organizational protocol and leadership. The man on the assembly line, the nurse in the hospital, the teacher in the elementary school all know what their major job is. To do a lot of it and to do it well are, then, the most conspicuous behavioral requirements of the organization. It may be, of course, that given role requirements are not functionally related to organizational accomplishment. This is a different type of problem and we are recognizing here only the fact that some major role requirements are necessary.

INNOVATIVE AND SPONTANEOUS BEHAVIOR

A neglected set of requirements consists of those actions not specified by role prescriptions which nevertheless facilitate the accomplishment of organizational goals. The great paradox of a social organization is that it must not only reduce human variability to insure reliable role performance but that it must also allow room for some variability and in fact encourage it.

There must always be a supportive number of actions of an innovative or relatively spontaneous sort. No organizational planning can foresee all contingencies within its operations, or can anticipate with perfect accuracy all environmental changes, or can control perfectly all human variability. The resources of people in innovation, in spontaneous co-operation, in protective and creative behavior are thus vital to organizational survival and effectiveness. An organization which depends solely upon its blueprints of prescribed behavior is a very fragile social system.

CO-OPERATION

The patterned activity which makes up an organization is so intrinsically a co-operative set of interrelationships, that we are not aware of the co-operative nexus any more than we are of any habitual behavior like walking. Within every work group in a factory, within any division in a government bureau, or within any department of a university are countless acts of co-operation without which the system would break down. We take these everyday acts for granted, and few, if any, of them form the role prescriptions for any job. One man will call the attention of his companion on the next machine to some indication that his machine is getting jammed, or will pass along some tool that his companion needs, or will borrow some bit of material he is short of. Or men will come to the aid of a fellow who is behind on his quota. In a study of clerical workers in an insurance company one of the two factors differentiating high-producing from low-producing sections was the greater co-operative activity of the girls in the high-producing sections coming to one another's help in meeting production quotas (Katz, Maccoby, & Morse, 1950). In most factories specialization develops around informal types of help. One man will be expert in first aid, another will be expert in machine diagnosis, etc. We recognize the need for co-operative relationships by raising this specific question when a man is considered for a job. How well does he relate to his fellows, is he a good team man, will he fit in?

PROTECTION

Another subcategory of behavior facilitative of organizational functioning is the action which protects the organization against disaster. There is nothing in the role prescriptions of the worker which specifies that he be on the alert to save life and property in the organization. Yet the worker who goes out of his way to remove the boulder accidentally lodged in the path of a freight car on the railway spur, or to secure a rampant piece of machinery, or even to disobey orders when they obviously are wrong and dangerous, is an invaluable man for the organization.

CONSTRUCTIVE IDEAS

Another subcategory of acts beyond the line of duty consists of creative suggestions for the improvement of methods of production or of maintenance. Some organizations encourage their members to feed constructive suggestions into the system, but coming up with good ideas for the organization and formulating them to management is not the typical role of the worker. An organization that can stimulate its members to contribute ideas for organizational improvement is a more effective organization in that people who are close to operating problems can often furnish informative suggestions about such operations. The system which does not have this stream of contributions from its members is not utilizing its potential resources effectively.

SELF-TRAINING

Still another subcategory under the heading of behavior beyond the call of duty concerns the self-training of members for doing their own jobs better and self-education for assuming more responsible positions in the organization. There may be no requirement that men prepare themselves for better positions. But the organization which has men spending their own time to master knowledge and skills for more responsible jobs in the system has an additional resource for effective functioning.

FAVORABLE ATTITUDE

Finally, members of a group can contribute to its operations by helping to create a favorable climate for it in the community, or communities, which surround the organization. Employees may talk to friends, relatives, and acquaintances about the excellent or the poor qualities of the company for which they work. A favorable climate may help in problems of recruitment, and sometimes product disposal.

In short, for effective organizational functioning many members must be willing on occasion to do more than their job prescriptions specify. If the system were to follow the letter of the law according to job descriptions and protocol, it would soon grind to a halt. There have to be many actions of mutual co-operation and many anticipations of organizational objectives to make the system viable.

Now these three major types of behavior, and even the subcategories, though related, are not necessarily motivated by the same drives and needs. The motivational pattern that will attract and hold people to an organization is not necessarily the same as that which will lead to higher productivity. Nor are the motives which make for higher productivity invariably the same as those which sustain co-operative interrelationships in the interests of organizational accomplishment. Hence, when we speak about organizational practices and procedures which will further the attainment of its mission, we need to specify the type of behavioral requirement involved.

Types of motivational patterns

It is profitable to consider the possible motivational patterns in organizations under six major headings. Before considering their specific modes of operation and their effects, let me briefly describe the six motivational patterns which seem most relevant. These patterns are: (1) conformity to legal norms or rule compliance; (2) instrumental system rewards; (3) instrumental individual rewards; (4) intrinsic satisfaction from role performance; (5) internalization of organizational goals and values; and (6) involvement in primary-group relationships.

Rule compliance or conformity to system norms. Conformity constitutes a significant motivational basis for certain types of organizational behavior. Though people may conform for different reasons I am concerned here with one common type of reason, namely a generalized acceptance of the rules of the game. Once people enter a system they accept the fact that membership in the system means complying with its legitimate rules. In our culture we build up during the course of the socialization process a generalized expectation of conforming to the recognized rules of the game if we want to remain in the game. We develop a role readiness, i.e., a readiness to play almost any given role according to the established norms in those systems in which we become involved.

Instrumental system rewards. These are the benefits which accrue to individuals by virtue of their membership in the system. They are the across-the-board rewards which apply to all people in a given classification in an organization. Examples would be the fringe benefits, the recreational facilities, and the working conditions which are available to all members of the system or subsystem. These rewards are instrumental in that they provide incentives for entering and remaining in the system and thus are instrumental for the need satisfaction of people.

Instrumental reward geared to individual effort or performance. System rewards apply in blanket fashion to all members of a subsystem. Individual rewards of an instrumental character are attained by differential performance. For example, the piece rate in industry or the singling out of individuals for honors for their specific contributions would fall into this category of instrumental individual rewards.

Intrinsic satisfactions accruing from specific role performance. Here the gratification comes not because the activity leads to or is instrumental to other satisfactions such as earning more money but because the activity is gratifying in itself. The individual may find his work so interesting or so much the type of thing he really wants to do that it would take a heavy financial inducement to shift to a job less congenial to his interests. It is difficult to get professors in many universities to take administrative posts such as departmental chairmanships or deanships because so many of them prefer teaching and research. This motivational pattern has to do with the opportunities which the organizational role provides for the expressions of the skills and talents of the individual.

Internalized values of the individual which embrace the goals of the organization. Here the individual again finds his organizational behavior rewarding in itself, not so much because his job gives him a chance to express his skill, but because he has taken over the goals of the organization as his own. The person who derives his gratifications from being a good teacher could be equally happy in teaching in many institutions but unhappy as an administrator in any one. The person who has identified himself with the goals of his own particular university and its specific problems, potentialities, and progress wants to stay on at his university and, moreover, is willing to accept other assignments than a teaching assignment.

Social satisfactions derived from primary-group relationships. This is an important source of gratification for organizational members. One of the things people miss most when they have to withdraw from organizations is the sharing of experiences with like-minded colleagues, the belonging to a group with which they have become identified. Whether or not these social satisfactions become channelled for organizational objectives leads us to a consideration of the two basic questions with which we started: (1) What are the consequences of these motivational patterns for the various organizational requirements of holding people in the system, maximizing their role performances, and stimulating innovative behavior? and (2) What are the conditions under which these patterns will lead to a given organizational outcome?

Motivational patterns: consequences and conditions

COMPLIANCE WITH LEGITIMIZED RULES

In discussing bureaucratic functioning Max Weber pointed out that the acceptance of legal rules was the basis for much of organizational behavior (Weber, 1947). Compliance is to some extent a function of sanctions but to a greater extent a function of generalized habits and attitudes toward symbols of authority. In other words, for the citizen of modern society the observance of legitimized rules has become a generalized value. A great deal of behavior can be predicted once we know what the rules of the game are. It is not necessary to take representative samplings of the behavior of many people to know how people will conduct themselves in structured situations. All we need is a single informant who can tell us the legitimate norms and appropriate symbols of authority for given types of behavioral settings. Individuals often assume that they can control their participation with respect to organizational requirements when they enter an organization. Before they are aware of it, however, they are acting like other organizational members and complying with the rules and the authorized decisions.

The major impact of compliance with the legitimate rules of the organization primarily concerns only one type of organizational requirement, namely reliable role performance. The way in which any given role occupant is to perform in carrying out his job can be determined by the rules of the organization. But individuals cannot be held in the system by rule enforcement save for exceptions like the armed services. Nor can innovative behavior and actions beyond the call of duty be prescribed.

Though compliance with legitimate rules is effective for insuring reliable role performance it operates to insure minimal observance of role requirements. In other words, the minimal standards for quantity and quality of work soon become the maximum standards. The logic of meeting legal norms is to avoid infractions of the rules and not to go beyond their requirements, for as Allport has pointed out (1934), it is difficult, if not impossible, to be more proper than proper. Why, however, cannot the legal norms be set to require high standards with respect to both quantity and quality of production? Why cannot higher production be legislated? It can, but there is an important force working against such raising of standards by changing rules. The rule which sets a performance standard in a large organization is also setting a uniform standard for large numbers of people. Hence it must be geared to what the great majority are prepared to do. If not, there will be so many defections that the rule itself will break down. Timing of jobs in industry illustrates this principle. Management does not want a loose standard, but if the standards are set so that many workers can meet them only with difficulty, management is in for trouble.

In the third area of behavior necessary for effective organizational functioning, namely innovative and spontaneous acts which go beyond the call of duty, rule compliance is useless by definition. There can be exceptions, in that rules can be devised to reward unusual behavior under specified conditions. The army, for example, will move the man who has pulled off a brilliant military exploit from a court martial to a court of honors. Though such exceptions may occur, organizations cannot stimulate innovative actions by decreeing them. In general the greater the emphasis upon compliance with rules the less the motivation will be for individuals to do more than is specified by their role prescriptions. The great weakness of a system run according to rules is the lack of the corrective factor of human enterprise and spontaneity when something goes wrong. Two years ago in a hospital in New York State several infants died because salt rather than sugar was put into the formula. The large container for sugar had been erroneously filled with salt. The tragic fact was that day after day for about a week the nurses fed the babies milk saturated with salt in spite of the fact that the infants reacted violently to the food, crying and vomiting after each feeding session. But the hospital continued poisoning the children until many of them died. Not a single nurse, attendant, supervisor, or person connected with the nursery tasted the milk to see what was wrong. The error was discovered only when a hospital employee broke a rule and used some of the substance in the sugar container in her own coffee.

CONDITIONS CONDUCIVE TO THE ACTIVATION OF RULE ACCEPTANCE

Though compliance with rules can bring about reliable role performance, the use of rules must take account of the following three conditions for maximum effectiveness: (1) the appropriateness of the symbols of authority and the relevance of rules to the social system involved; (2) the clarity of the legal norms and rule structure; and (3) the reinforcing character of sanctions.

Appropriateness and relevance. The acceptance of communications and directives on the basis of legitimacy requires the use of symbols and procedures recognized as the proper and appropriate sources of authority in the system under consideration. The worker may grumble at the foreman's order but he recognizes the right of the foreman to give such an order. The particular directives which are accepted as legitimate will depend upon their matching the type of authority structure of the system. The civilian in the army with officer status, uniform, and unassimilated rank is not accepted by the enlisted man as the proper giver of orders. In a representative democracy a policy decision of an administrator may be rejected since it lacks the legal stamp of the accepted procedures of the system. An industrial company may have a contract with a union that changes in the speed of the assembly line have to be agreed to by both organizations. The workers accordingly will accept a speedup in the line if it is sanctioned by the union-management agreement, but not if it is the work of a foreman attempting to impress his superiors.

The acceptance of legal rules is also restricted to the relevant sphere of activity. Union policy as formulated in its authority structure is binding upon its members only as it relates to relations with the company. The edicts of union officials on matters of desegregation or of support of political parties are not necessarily seen as legal compulsions by union members. In similar fashion, employees do not regard the jurisdiction of the company as applying to their private lives outside the plant. And areas of private behavior and personal taste are regarded in our democratic society as outside the realm of coercive laws. The most spectacular instance of the violation of a national law occurred in the case of the Volstead Act. While people were willing to accept laws about the social consequences resulting from drinking, such as reckless driving, many of them were not willing to accept the notion that their private lives were subject to federal regulation.

Another prerequisite to the use of rules as the appropriate norms of the system is their impersonal character. They are the rules of the system and are not the arbitrary, capricious decisions of a superior aimed at particular individuals. The equivalents of bills of attainder in an organization undermine rule compliance. We speak of the officiousness of given individuals in positions of authority when they use their rank in an arbitrary and personal fashion.

Clarity. A related condition for the acceptance of legal norms is the clarity of authority symbols, of proper procedures, and the content of the legitimized decisions. Lack of clarity can be due to the vagueness of the stimulus situation or to the conflict between opposed stimulus cues. In some organizations, symbols of authority are sharply enough defined, but the relationship between competing symbols may lack such clarity of definition. One difficulty of using group decision in limited areas in an otherwise authoritarian structure is that group members may not perceive the democratic procedure as legitimized by the structure. They will question the compelling effect of any decisions they reach. And often they may be right. Moreover, the procedure for the exercise of power may not be consistent with the type of authority structure. The classic case is that *of ordering* a people to be democratic.

Specific laws can be ambiguous in their substance. They can be so complex, so technical, or so obscure that people will not know what the law is. The multiplication of technical rulings and the patchwork of legislation with respect to tax structure means that while people may feel some internal compulsion to pay taxes, they also feel they should pay as little as they can without risking legal prosecution. A counter dynamic will arise to the tendency to comply with legal requirements, namely, the use of legal loopholes to defy the spirit of the law. Any complex maze of rules in an organization will be utilized by the guardhouse lawyers in the system to their own advantage.

Though our argument has been that legal compliance makes for role performance rather than for holding people in a system, the clarity of a situation with well-defined rules is often urged as a condition making for system attractiveness. People know what is expected of them and what they should expect in turn from others, and they much prefer this clarity to a state of uncertainty and ambiguity. There is merit in this contention, but it does not take into account all the relevant variables. The armed services were not able to hold personnel after World War II, and recruitment into systems characterized by rules and regulations is traditionally difficult in the United States. The mere multiplication of rules does not produce clarity. Even when certainty and clarity prevail they are not relished if it means that individuals are certain only of non-advancement and restrictions on their behavior.

In brief, the essence of legal compliance rests upon the psychological belief that there are specific imperatives or laws which all good citizens obey. If there is doubt about what the imperative is, if there are many varying interpretations, then the law is not seen as having a character of its own but as the means for obtaining individual advantage. To this extent, the legitimacy basis of compliance is undermined.

Reinforcement. To maintain the internalized acceptance of legitimate authority there has to be some reinforcement in the form of penalties for violation of the rules. If there is no policing of laws governing speeding, speed limits will lose their force over time for many people. Sometimes the penalties can come from the social disapproval of the group as well as from legal penalties. But the very concept of law as an imperative binding upon everyone in the system requires penalties for violation either from above or below. Where there is no enforcement by authorities and no sanctions for infractions from the group itself, the rule in question becomes a dead letter.

INSTRUMENTAL SYSTEM REWARDS

It is important to distinguish between rewards which are administered in relation to individual effort and performance and the system rewards which accrue to people by virtue of their membership in the system. In the former category would belong piece-rate incentives, promotion for outstanding performance, or any special recognition bestowed in acknowledgment of differential contributions to organizational functioning. In the category of system rewards would go fringe benefits, recreational facilities, cost of living raises, across-the-board upgrading, job security save for those guilty of moral turpitude, pleasant working conditions. System rewards differ, then, from individual rewards in that they are not allocated on the basis of differential effort and performance but on the basis of membership in the system. The major differentiation for system rewards is seniority in the system—a higher pension for thirty years of service than for twenty years of service. Management will often overlook the distinction between individual and system rewards and will operate as if rewards administered across the board were the same in their effects as individual rewards.

System rewards are more effective for holding members within the organization than for maximizing other organizational behaviors. Since the rewards are distributed on the basis of length of tenure in the system, people will want to stay with an attractive setup which becomes increasingly attractive over time. Again the limiting factor is the competition with the relative attraction of other systems. As the system increases its attractions, other things being equal, it should reduce its problems of turnover. In fact, it may sometimes have the problem of too low turnover with too many poorly motivated people staying on until retirement.

System rewards will not, however, lead to higher quality of work or greater quantity than the minimum required to stay in the organization. Since rewards are given across-the-board to all members or differentially to them in terms of their seniority, they are not motivated to do more than meet the standards for remaining in the system. It is sometimes assumed that the liking for the organization created by system rewards will generalize to greater productive effort within the system. Such generalization of motivation may occur to a very limited extent, but it is not a reliable basis for the expectation of higher productivity. Management may expect gratitude from workers because it has added some special fringe benefit or some new recreational facility. The more likely outcome is that employees will feel more desirous of staying in an enterprise with such advantages than of working harder for the company for the next twelve months.

System rewards will do little, moreover, to motivate performance beyond the line of duty, with two possible exceptions. Since people may develop a liking for the attractions of the organization they may be in a more favorable mood to reciprocate in co-operative relations with their fellows toward organizational goals, provided that the initiation of task-oriented co-operation comes from some other source. Otherwise, they may just be co-operative with respect to taking advantage of the system's attractions, such as the new bowling alley. Another possible consequence of system rewards for activity supportive of organizational goals is the favorable climate of opinion for the system in the external environment to which the members contribute. It may be easier for a company to recruit personnel in a community in which their employees have talked about what a good place it is to work.

Though the effects of system rewards are to maintain the level of productivity not much above the minimum required to stay in the system, there still may be large differences between systems with respect to the quantity and quality of production as a function of system rewards. An organization with substantially better wage rates and fringe benefits than its competitors may be able to set a higher level of performance as a minimal requirement for its workers than the other firms and still hold its employees. In other words, system rewards can be related to the differential productivity of organizations as a whole, though they are not effective in maximizing the potential contributions of the majority of individuals within the organization. They may account for differences in motivation between systems rather than for differences in motivation between individuals in the same system. They operate through their effects upon the minimal standards for all people in the system. They act indirectly in that their effect is to make people want to stay in the organization; to do so people must be willing to accept the legitimately derived standards of role performance in that system. Hence, the direct mechanism for insuring performance is compliance with legitimacy, but the legal requirements of the organization will not hold members if their demands are too great with respect to the demands of other organizations. The mediating variable in accounting for organizational differences based upon system rewards is the relative attractiveness of the system for the individual compared to other available systems in relation to the effort requirements of the system. If the individual has the choice of a job with another company in the same community which requires a little more effort but offers much greater system rewards in the way of wages and other benefits, he will in all probability take it. If, however, the higher requirements of the competing system are accompanied by very modest increases in system rewards, he will probably stay where he is.

CONDITIONS CONDUCIVE TO EFFECTIVE SYSTEM REWARDS

We have just described one of the essential conditions for making system rewards effective in calling attention to the need to make the system as attractive as competing systems which are realistic alternatives for the individual. In this context seniority becomes an important organizational principle in that the member can acquire more of the rewards of the system the longer he stays in it. The present trends to permit the transfer of fringe benefits of all types across systems undercuts the advantages to any one system of length of membership in it, though of course there are other advantages to permitting people to retain their investment in seniority when they move across systems.

Another condition which is important for the effective use of system rewards is their uniform application for all members of the system or for major groupings within the system. People will perceive as inequitable distinctions in amounts of rewards which go to members by virtue of their membership in the system where such differences favor some groups over other groups. Management is frequently surprised by resentment of differential system rewards when there has been no corresponding resentment of differential individual rewards. One public utility, for example, inaugurated an attractive retirement system for its employees before fringe benefits were the acceptable pattern. Its employees were objectively much better off because of the new benefits and yet the most hated feature about the whole company was the retirement system. Employee complaints centered on two issues: years of employment in the company before the age of thirty did not count toward retirement pensions, and company officials could retire on livable incomes because of their higher salaries. The employees felt intensely that if they were being rewarded for service to the company it was unfair to rule out years of service before age thirty. This provision gave no recognition for the man who started for the company at age twenty compared to the one who started at age thirty. Moreover, the workers felt a lifetime of service to the company should enable them to retire on a livable income just as it made this possible for company officials. The company house organ directed considerable space over a few years to showing how much the worker actually benefited from the plan, as in fact was the case. On the occasion of a companywide survey, this campaign was found to have had little effect. The most common complaint still focused about the patent unfairness of the retirement system.

The critical point, then, is that system rewards have a logic of their own. Since they accrue to people by virtue of their membership or length of service in an organization, they will be perceived as inequitable if they are not uniformly administered. The perception of the organization member is that all members are equal in their access to organizational benefits. Office employees will not be upset by differences in individual reward for differences in responsibility. If, however, their organization gives them free meals in a cafeteria and sets aside a special dining room for their bosses, many of them will be upset. In our culture we accept individual differences in income but we do not accept differences in classes of citizenship. To be a member of an organization is to be a citizen in that community, and all citizens are equal in their membership rights. A university which does not extend the same tenure rights and the same fringe benefits accorded its teaching staff to its research workers may have a morale problem on its hands.

INSTRUMENTAL INDIVIDUAL REWARDS

The traditional philosophy of the free-enterprise system gives priority to an individual reward system based upon the quality and quantity of the individual effort and contribution. This type of motivation may operate effectively for the entrepreneur or even for the small organization with considerable independence of its supporting environment. It encounters great difficulties, however, in its application to large organizations which are in nature highly interdependent co-operative structures. We shall examine these difficulties in analyzing the conditions under which individual rewards of an instrumental character are effective.

Basically the monetary and recognition rewards to the individual for his organizational performance are directed at a high level of quality and quantity of work. In other words, they can be applied most readily to obtain optimal role performance rather than to innovative and nonspecific organizational needs. They may also help to hold the individual in the organization, if he feels that his differential efforts are properly recognized. Nonetheless there is less generalization, or rubbing off, of an instrumental individual reward to love for the organization than might be anticipated. If another organization offers higher individual rewards to a person, his own institution may have to match the offer to hold him.

Individual rewards are difficult to apply to contributions to organizational functioning which are not part of the role requirements. Spectacular instances of innovative behavior can be singled out for recognition and awards. In the armed services, heroism beyond the call of duty is the basis for medals and decorations, but the everyday co-operative activities which keep an organization from falling apart are more difficult to recognize and reward. Creative suggestions for organizational improvement are sometimes encouraged through substantial financial rewards for employees' suggestions. The experience with suggestion systems of this sort has not been uniformly positive though under special conditions they have proved of value.

CONDITIONS CONDUCIVE TO EFFECTIVE INDIVIDUAL INSTRUMENTAL REWARDS

If rewards such as pay incentives are to work as they are intended they must meet three primary conditions. (1) They must be clearly perceived as large enough in amount to justify the additional effort required to obtain them. (2) They must be perceived as directly related to the required performance and follow directly on its accomplishment. (3) They must be perceived as equitable by the majority of system members many of whom will not receive them. These conditions suggest some of the reasons why individual rewards can work so well in some situations and yet be so difficult of application in large organizations. The facts are that most enterprises have not been able to use incentive pay, or piece rates, as reliable methods for raising the quality and quantity of production (McGregor, 1960).

In terms of the first criterion many companies have attempted incentive pay without making the differential between increased effort and increased reward proportional from the point of view of the worker. If he can double his pay by working at a considerably increased tempo, that is one thing. But if such increased expenditure means a possible 10 per cent increase, that is another. Moreover, there is the tradition among workers, and it is not without some factual basis, that management cannot be relied upon to maintain a high rate of pay for those making considerably more than the standard and that their increased efforts will only result in their "being sweated." There is, then, the temporal dimension of whether the piece rates which seem attractive today will be maintained tomorrow.

More significant, however, is the fact that a large-scale organization consists of many people engaging in similar and interdependent tasks. The work of any one man is highly dependent upon what his colleagues are doing. Hence individual piece rates are difficult to apply on any equitable basis. Group incentives are more logical, but as the size of the interdependent group grows, we move toward system rather than toward individual rewards. Moreover, in large-scale production enterprises the role performance is controlled by the tempo of the machines and their co-ordination. The speed of the worker on the assembly line is not determined by his decision but by the speed of the assembly line. An individual piece rate just does not accord with the systemic nature of the co-ordinated collectivity. Motivational factors about the amount of effort to be expended on the job enter the picture not on the floor of the factory but during the negotiations of the union and management about the manning of a particular assembly line. Heads of corporations may believe in the philosophy of individual enterprise, but when they deal with reward systems in their own organizations they become realists and accept the pragmatic notion of collective rewards.

Since there is such a high degree of collective interdependence among rank-and-file workers the attempts to use individual rewards are often perceived as inequitable. Informal norms develop to protect the group against efforts which are seen as divisive or exploitive. Differential rates for subsystems within the organization will be accepted much more than invidious distinctions within the same subgrouping. Hence promotion or upgrading may be the most potent type of individual reward. The employee is rewarded by being moved to a different category of workers on a better pay schedule. Some of the same problems apply, of course, to this type of reward. Since differential performance is difficult to assess in assembly-type operations, promotion is often based upon such criteria as conformity to company requirements with respect to attendance and absenteeism, observance of rules, and seniority. None of these criteria are related to individual performance on the job. Moreover, promotion is greatly limited by the technical and professional education of the worker.

It is true, of course, that many organizations are not assembly-line operations, and even for those which are, the conditions described here do not apply to the upper echelons. Thus General Motors can follow a policy of high individual rewards to division managers based upon the profits achieved by a given division. A university can increase the amount of research productivity of its staff by making publication the essential criterion for promotion. In general, where assessment of individual performance is feasible and where the basis of the reward system is clear, instrumental individual rewards can play an important part in raising productivity.

INTRINSIC JOB SATISFACTION

The motivational pathway to high productivity and to high-quality production can be reached through the development of intrinsic job satisfaction. The man who finds the type of work he delights in doing is the man who will not worry about the fact that the role requires a given amount of production of a certain quality. His gratifications accrue from accomplishment, from the expression of his own abilities, from the exercise of his own decisions. Craftsmanship was the old term to refer to the skilled performer who was high in intrinsic job satisfaction. This type of performer is not the clock watcher, nor the shoddy performer. On the other hand, such a person is not necessarily tied to a given organization. As a good carpenter or a good mechanic, it may matter little to him where he does work, provided that he is given ample opportunity to do the kind of job he is interested in doing. He may, moreover, contribute little to organizational goals beyond his specific role.

CONDITIONS CONDUCIVE TO AROUSAL OF INTRINSIC JOB SATISFACTION

If intrinsic job satisfaction or identification with the work is to be aroused and maximized, then the job itself must provide sufficient variety, sufficient complexity, sufficient challenge, and sufficient skill to engage the abilities of the worker. If there is one confirmed finding in all the studies of worker morale and satisfaction, it is the correlation between the variety and challenge of the job and the gratifications which accrue to workers (Morse, 1953). There are, of course, people who do not want more responsibility and people who become demoralized by being placed in jobs which are too difficult for them. These are, however, the exceptions. By and large people seek more responsibility, more skill-demanding jobs than they hold, and as they are able to attain these more demanding jobs, they become happier and better adjusted. Obviously, the condition for securing higher motivation to produce, and to produce quality work, necessitates changes in organizational structure—specifically job enlargement rather than job fractionation. And yet the tendency in large-scale organizations is toward increasing specialization and routinization of jobs. Workers would be better motivated toward higher individual production and toward better quality work if we discarded the assembly line and moved toward the craftsmanlike operations of the old Rolls Royce type of production. Industry has demonstrated, however, that it is more efficient to produce via assembly-line methods with lowered motivation and job satisfaction than with highly motivated craftsmen with a large area of responsibility in turning out their part of the total product. The preferred path to the attainment of production goals in turning out cars or other mass physical products is, then, the path of organizational controls and not the path of internalized motivation. The quality of production may suffer somewhat, but it is still cheaper to buy several mass-produced cars, allowing for programming for obsolescence, than it is to buy a single quality product like the Rolls Royce.

In the production of physical objects intended for mass consumption, the assembly line may furnish the best model. This may also apply to service operations in which the process can be sufficiently simplified to provide service to masses of consumers. When, however, we move to organizations which have the modifications of human beings as their product, as in educational institutions, or when we deal with treating basic problems of human beings, as in hospital, clinics, and remedial institutions, we do not want to rely solely upon an organizational control to guarantee minimum effort of employees. We want employees with high motivation and high identification with their jobs. Jobs cannot profitably be fractionated very far and standardized and co-ordinated to a rigorous time schedule in a research laboratory, in a medical clinic, in an educational institution, or in a hospital.

In addition to the recognition of the inapplicability of organizational devices of the factory and the army to all organizations, it is also true that not all factory operations can be left to institutional controls without regard to the motivations of employees. It frequently happens that job fractionation can be pushed to the point of diminishing returns even in industry. The success of the Tavistock workers in raising productivity in the British coal mines through job enlargement was due to the fact that the specialization of American long-wall methods of coal mining did not yield adequate returns when applied to the difficult and variable conditions under which British miners had to operate (Trist & Bamforth, 1951). The question of whether to move toward greater specialization and standardization in an industrial operation or whether to move in the opposite direction is generally an empirical one to be answered by research. One rule of thumb can be applied, however. If the job can be so simplified and standardized that it is readily convertible to automated machines, then the direction to take is that of further institutionalization until automation is possible. If, however, the over-all performance requires complex judgment, the differential weighing of factors which are not markedly identifiable, or creativity, then the human mind is a far superior instrument to the computer.

The paradox is that where automation is feasible, it can actually increase the motivational potential among the employees who are left on the job after the change-over. Mann and Hoffman (1960) conclude from their study of automation in an electric power plant that the remaining jobs for workers can be more interesting, that there can be freer association among colleagues, and that the elimination of supervisory levels brings the top and bottom of the organization closer together.

INTERNALIZATION OF ORGANIZATIONAL GOALS AND VALUES

The pattern of motivation associated with value expression and self-identification has great potentialities for the internalization of the goals of subsystems and of the total system, and thus for the activation of behavior not prescribed by specific roles. Where this pattern prevails individuals take over organizational objectives as part of their own personal goals. They identify not with the organization as a safe and secure haven but with its major purposes. The internalization of organizational objectives is generally confined to the upper echelons or to the officer personnel. In voluntary organizations it extends into some of the rank-and-file, and in fact most voluntary organizations need a core of dedicated people—who are generally referred to as the dedicated damn fools.

Now the internalization of organizational goals is not as common as two types of more partial internalization. The first has to do with some general organizational purposes which are not unique to the organization. A scientist may have internalized some of the research values of his profession but not necessarily of the specific institution to which he is attached. As long as he stays in that institution, he may be a well-motivated worker. But he may find it just as easy to work for the things he believes in in another institution. There is not the same set of alternative organizations open to liberals who are political activists and who are part of the core of dedicated damn fools in the Democratic party. They have no other place to go, so they find some way of rationalizing the party's deviation from their liberal ideals.

A second type of partial internalization concerns the values and goals of a subsystem of the organization. It is often easier for the person to take over the values of his own unit. We may be attached to our own department in a university more than to the goals of the university as a whole.

CONDITIONS CONDUCIVE TO INTERNALIZATION OF SYSTEM GOALS

Internalization of organization objectives can come about through the utilization of the socialization process in childhood or through the adult socialization which takes place in the organization itself. In the first instance, the selective process, either by the person or the organization, matches the personality with the system. A youngster growing up in the tradition of one of the military services may have always thought of himself as an Air Force officer. Similarly, the crusader for civil liberties and the American Civil Liberties Union find one another.

The adult socialization process in the organization can build upon the personal values of its members and integrate them about an attractive model of its ideals. People can thus identify with the organizational mission. If the task of an organization has emotional significance, the organization enjoys an advantage in the creation of an attractive image. If the task is attended by hazard, as in the tracking down of criminals by the FBI, or of high adventure, as in the early days of flying, or of high service to humanity, as in a cancer research unit, it is not difficult to develop a convincing model of the organization's mission.

The imaginative leader can also help in the development of an attractive picture of the organization by some new conceptualization of its mission. The police force entrusted with the routine and dirty business of law enforcement carried out by dumb cops and "flatfeet" can be energized by seeing themselves as a corps of professional officers devoted to the highest form of public service. Reality factors limit the innovative use of symbols for the glorification of organizations. Occupational groups, however, constantly strive to achieve a more attractive picture of themselves, as in the instances of press agents who have become public relations specialists or undertakers who have become morticians.

Internalization of subgroup norms can come about through identification with fellow group members who share the same common fate. People take over the values of their group because they identify with their own kind and see themselves as good group members, and as good group members they model their actions and aspirations in terms of group norms. This subgroup identification can work for organizational objectives only if there is agreement between the group norms and the organizational objectives. Often in industry the norms of the work group are much closer to union objectives than to company objectives.

This suggests three additional factors which contribute to internalization of group objectives: (1) participating in important decisions about group objectives; (2) contributing to group performance in a significant way: and (3) sharing in the rewards of group accomplishment. When these three conditions are met, the individual can regard the group as his, for he in fact has helped to make it.

SOCIAL SATISFACTIONS FROM PRIMARY-GROUP RELATIONSHIPS

Human beings are social animals and cannot exist in physical or psychological isolation. The stimulation, the approval, and the support they derive from interacting with one another comprise one of the most potent forms of motivation. Strictly speaking, such affiliative motivation is another form of instrumental-reward-seeking, but some of its qualitative aspects are sufficiently different from the instrumental system and individual rewards previously described to warrant separate discussion.

The desire to be part of a group in itself will do no more than hold people in the system. The studies of Elton Mayo and his colleagues during World War II showed that work groups which provided their members social satisfactions had less absenteeism than less cohesive work groups (Mayo & Lombard, 1944). Mann and Baumgartel (1953) corroborated these findings in a study of the Detroit Edison Company. With respect to role performance, moreover, Seashore (1954) has demonstrated that identification with one's work group can make for either above-average or below-average productivity depending upon the norms of the particular group. In the Seashore study the highly-cohesive groups, compared to the low-cohesive groups, moved to either extreme in being above or below the production standards for the company.

Other studies have demonstrated that though the group can provide important socioemotional satisfactions for the members it can also detract from task orientation (Bass, 1960). Members can have such a pleasant time interacting with one another that they neglect their work. Again the critical mediating variable is the character of the values and norms of the group. The affiliative motive can lead to innovative and co-operative behavior, but often this assumes the form of protecting the group rather than maximizing organizational objectives. So the major question in dealing with the affiliative motive is how this motive can be harnessed to organizational goals.

58 Beyond bureaucracy

WARREN G. BENNIS

Most of us spend all of our working day and a great deal of our non-working day in a unique and extremely durable social arrangement called "bureaucracy." I use the term "bureaucracy" descriptively, not as an epithet about those "guys in Washington" or as a metaphor *à la* Kafka's *Castle* which conjures up an image of red tape, or faceless and despairing masses standing in endless lines. Bureaucracy, as I shall use the term here, is a social invention, perfected during the industrial revolution to organize and direct the activities of the business firm.

It is my premise that the bureaucratic form of organization is becoming less and less effective; that it is hopelessly out of joint with contemporary realities; that new shapes, patterns, and models are emerging which promise drastic changes in the conduct of the corporation and of managerial practices in general. In the next 25 to 50 years we should witness, and participate in, the end of bureaucracy and the rise of new social systems better suited to twentieth-century demands of industrialization. (Sociological evolutionists substantially agree that 25 to 50 years from now most people in the world will live in industrialized societies.)

Corsica, according to Gibbon, is much easier to deplore than to describe. The same holds true for bureaucracy. Basically, bureaucracy is a social invention which relies exclusively on the power to influence through rules, reason, and law. Max Weber, the German sociologist who developed the theory of bureaucracy around the turn of the century, once described bureaucracy as a social machine:

> Bureaucracy is like a modern judge who is a vending machine into which the pleadings are inserted together with the fee and which

Reprinted from **Trans-action**, 1965, 2, 31–5, with permission of the author and the publisher.

then disgorges the judgment together with its reasons mechanically derived from the code. [Cited in Bendix, 1960, p. 421.]

The bureaucratic "machine model" Weber outlined was developed as a reaction against the personal subjugation, nepotism, cruelty, emotional vicissitudes, and capricious judgment which passed for managerial practices in the early days of the industrial revolution. The true hope for man, it was thought, lay in his ability to rationalize, calculate, to use his head as well as his hands and heart. Thus, in the bureaucratic system social roles were institutionalized and reinforced by legal tradition rather than by the "cult of personality"; rationality and predictability were sought for in order to eliminate chaos and unanticipated consequences; emphasis was placed on technical competence rather than arbitrary or "iron whims." These are oversimplifications, to be sure, but contemporary analysts of organizations would tend to agree with them. In fact, there is a general consensus that the anatomy of bureaucracy consists of the following "organs":

a division of labor based on functional specialization;

a well-defined hierarchy of authority;

a system of rules covering the rights and duties of employees;

a system of procedures for dealing with work situations;

impersonality of interpersonal relations;

promotion and selection based on technical competence.

It does not take great critical imagination to detect the flaws and problems in the bureaucratic model. We have all *experienced* them:

bosses without (and underlings with) technical competence;

arbitrary and zany rules;

an underworld (or informal) organization which subverts or even replaces the formal apparatus;

confusion and conflict among roles;

cruel treatment of subordinates based not on rational or legal grounds but upon inhumanity.

The tremendous range of unanticipated consequences provides a gold mine of material for comics like Charlie Chaplin and Jacques Tati who capture with a smile or a shrug the absurdity of authority systems based on pseudo-logic and inappropriate rules.

Almost everybody, including many observers of organizational behavior, approaches bureaucracy with a chip on his shoulder. It has been attacked for many reasons: for theoretical confusion and contradictions; for moral and ethical reasons; on practical grounds such as its inefficiency; for methodological weaknesses; for containing too many implicit values and for containing too few. I have recently catalogued the criticisms of bureaucracy and they outnumber and outdo the ninety-five theses tacked on the church door at Wittenberg in attacking another bureaucracy. A small sample of these:

(1) Bureaucracy does not adequately allow for personal growth and the development of mature personalities.

(2) It develops conformity and "groupthink."

(3) It does not take into account the "informal organization" and the emergent and unanticipated problems.

(4) Its systems of control and authority are hopelessly outdated.

(5) It has no adequate juridical process.

(6) It does not possess adequate means for resolving differences and conflicts between ranks, and most particularly, between functional groups.

(7) Communication (and innovative ideas) are thwarted or distorted due to hierarchical divisions.
(8) The full human resources of bureaucracy are not being utilized due to mistrust, fear of reprisals, etc.
(9) It cannot assimilate the influx of new technology or scientists entering the organization.
(10) It modifies personality structure so that people become and reflect the dull, gray, conditioned "organization man."

Max Weber, the developer of the theory of bureaucracy, came around to condemn the apparatus he helped immortalize. While he felt that bureaucracy was inescapable, he also thought it might strangle the spirit of capitalism or the entrepreneurial attitude, a theme which Schumpeter later developed. And in a debate on bureaucracy Weber once said, more in sorrow than in anger:

> It is horrible to think that the world could one day be filled with nothing but those little cogs, little men clinging to little jobs and striving towards bigger ones—a state of affairs which is to be seen once more, as in the Egyptian records, playing an ever-increasing part in the spirit of our present administrative system, and especially of its offspring, the students. This passion for bureaucracy . . . is enough to drive one to despair. It is as if in politics . . . we were deliberately to become men who need "order" and nothing but order, who become nervous and cowardly if for one moment this order wavers, and helpless if they are torn away from their total incorporation in it. That the world should know no men but these: it is such an evolution that we are already caught up in, and the great question is therefore not how we can promote and hasten it, but what can we oppose to this machinery in order to keep a portion of mankind free from this parcelling-out of the soul, from this supreme mastery of the bureaucratic way of life. [See Hall, 1963, p. 33.]

In what ways has bureaucracy been modified over the years in order to cope more successfully with the problems that beset it? Before answering that, we have to say something about the nature of organizations, *all* organizations, from mass production leviathans all the way to service industries such as the university or hospital. Organizations are primarily complex, goal-seeking units. In order to survive they must also accomplish the secondary tasks of (1) maintaining their internal system and co-ordinating the "human side of enterprise"—a process of mutual compliance here called *reciprocity*—and (2) adapting to and shaping the external environment—here called *adaptability*. These two organizational dilemmas can help us to organize the pivotal ways in which the bureaucratic mechanism has been altered—and found wanting.

Reciprocity primarily covers the processes which can mediate conflict between the goals of management and the individual goals of the workers. Over the past several decades a number of interesting theoretical and practical resolutions have been made which truly allow for conflict and mediation of interest. They revise, if not transform, the very nature of the bureaucratic mechanism by explicit recognition of the inescapable tension between individual and organizational goals. These theories can be called, variously, *exchange, group, value, structural, situational*—depending on what variable of the situation one wishes to modify (see Bennis, 1966; March & Simon, 1958).

The *exchange* theories postulate that wages, incomes, and services are given to the individual for an equal contribution to the organization in work. If the inducements are not adequate, men may withdraw and work elsewhere. This may be elaborated upon by regarding "payments" to individuals as including motivational units. That is to say, the organization provides a psychological anchor in times of rapid social change and a hedge against personal loss, as well as position, growth and mastery, success experience, and so forth—in exchange for energy, work, commitment.

Management tends to interpret motivation in economic terms. Man is logical; man acts in the manner which serves his self-interest; man is competitive. Elton Mayo (1945) and his associates were among the first to see human *affiliation* as a motivating force, to view industrial organization as a *social* system as well as an economic-technical system. A manager, they stated, should be judged in terms of his ability to sustain co-operation. In fact, once a cohesive, primary work group is seen as a motivating force, a managerial elite may become obsolete, and the work group itself becomes the decision maker. This allows decisions to be made at the most relevant point of the organization, where the data are most available.

Before this becomes possible, however, some theorists believe that the impersonal *value* system of bureaucracy must be modified. In this case the manager plays an important role as the instrument of change in interpersonal relations. He must instill values which permit and reinforce the expression of feeling, experimentalism, and norms of individuality, trust, and concern. Management, according to R. R. Blake (1964), is successful insofar as it maximizes a "concern for people"—with "concern for production."

Others believe that a new conception of the *structure* of bureaucracy will create more relevant attitudes towards the function of management than formal role specifications now do. If the organization is seen as organic rather than mechanistic, as adapting spontaneously to its needs, then decisions will be made at the critical point and roles and jobs will devolve on the "natural" organizational incumbent. The shift would probably be from the individual level to co-operative group effort, from delegated to shared responsibility, from centralized to decentralized authority, from obedience to confidence, from antagonistic arbitration to problem-solving. Management centered upon problem-solving, that assumes or relaxes authority according to task demands, has most concerned some theorists who are as much interested in an organization's success and productivity as in its social system.

However, on all sides we find a growing belief that the effectiveness of bureaucracy should be evaluated by human *situation* as well as economic criteria. Social satisfaction and personal growth of employees must be considered as well as the productivity and profit of the organization. The criticism and revisions of the bureaucratic organization tend to concentrate on the internal system and its human components. But although it appears on the surface that the case against bureaucracy has to do with its ethical-moral posture and the social fabric, the real *coup de grace* has come from the environment.

Bureaucracy thrives in a highly competitive, undifferentiated and stable environment, such as the climate of its youth, the Industrial Revolution. A pyramidal structure of authority, with power concentrated in the hands of a few with the knowledge and resources to control an entire enterprise was, and is, an eminently suitable social arrangement for routinized tasks.

However, the environment has changed in just those ways which make the mechanism most problematic. Stability has vanished. As Ellis Johnson said, ". . . the once-reliable constants have now become galloping variables" (1954, xii).

The factors accelerating change include:

the growth of science, research and development activities, and intellectual technology;

the increase of transactions with social institutions (and their importance in conducting the enterprise)—including government, distributors and consumers, shareholders, competitors, raw material and power suppliers, sources of employees (particularly managers), trade unions, and groups within the firms. There is also more interdependence between the economic and other facets of society, leading to greater complications of legislation and public regulation;

competition between firms diminishing as their fates intertwine and become positively correlated.

My argument so far, to summarize quickly, is that the first assault on bureaucracy arose from its incapacity to manage the tension between individual and management goals. However, this conflict is somewhat mediated by the growth of a new ethic of productivity which includes personal growth and/or satisfaction. The second and more major shock to bureaucracy is caused by the scientific and technological revolution. It is the requirement of *adaptability* to the environment which leads to the predicted demise of bureaucracy and to the collapse of management as we know it now.

A forecast falls somewhere between a prediction and a prophecy. It lacks the divine guidance of the latter and the empirical foundation of the former. On thin empirical ice, I want to set forth some of the conditions that will dictate organizational life in the next 25 to 50 years.

The environment. Those factors already mentioned will continue in force and increase. Rapid technological change and diversification will lead to interpenetration of the government—its legal and economic policies—with business. Partnerships between industry and government (like Telstar) will be typical. And because of the immensity and expense of the projects, there will be fewer identical units competing for the same buyers and sellers. Or, in reverse, imperfect competition leads to an oligopolistic and government-business controlled economy. The three main features of the environment will be (1) interdependence rather than competition, (2) turbulence rather than steadiness, and (3) large scale rather than small enterprises.

Population characteristics. We are living in what Peter Drucker calls the "educated society," and I think this is the most distinctive characteristic of our times. Within fifteen years, two-thirds of our population living in metropolitan areas will have attended college. Adult education programs, especially the management development courses of such universities as M.I.T., Harvard, and Stanford, are expanding and adding intellectual breadth. All this, of course, is not just "nice," but necessary. For as Secretary of Labor Wirtz has pointed out, computers can do the work of most high school graduates—cheaper and more effectively. Fifty years ago education used to be regarded as "nonwork" and intellectuals on the payroll (and many of the staff) were considered "overhead." Today, the survival of the firm depends, more than ever before, on the proper exploitation of brain power.

One other characteristic of the population which will aid our understanding of organizations of the future is increasing job mobility. The lowered expense and ease of transportation, coupled with the real needs of a dynamic environment, will change drastically the idea of "owning" a job—or "having roots," for that matter. Participants will be shifted from job to job and even employer to employer with much less fuss than we are accustomed to.

Work values. The increased level of education and mobility will change the values we hold about work. People will be more intellectually committed to their jobs and will probably require more involvement, participation, and autonomy in their work. (This turn of events is due to a composite of the following factors: (1) positive correlation between a person's education and his need for autonomy; (2) job mobility places the educated in a position of greater influence in the system; (3) job requirements call for more responsibility and discretion.)

Also, people will tend to be more "other-directed" in their dealings with others. David McClelland's studies (1961) suggest that as industrialization increases, "other-directedness" increases; so we will tend to rely more heavily on temporary social arrangements, on our immediate and constantly-changing colleagues.

Tasks and goals. The tasks of the firm will be more technical, complicated, and unprogrammed. They will rely more on the intellect than muscle. And they will be too complicated for one person to handle or for individual supervision. Essentially, they will call for the collaboration of specialists in a project or team form of organization.

Similarly there will be a complication of goals. "Increased profits" and "raised productivity" will sound like over-simplifications and cliches. Business will concern itself increasingly with its adaptive or innovative-creative capacity. In addition, *meta*-goals will have to be articulated and developed; that is, supra-goals which shape and provide the foundation for the goal structure. For example, one meta-goal might be a system for detecting new and changing goals; another could be a system for deciding priorities among goals.

Finally, there will be more conflict and contradiction among diverse standards of organizational effectiveness, just as in hospitals and universities today there is conflict between teaching and research. The reason for this is the increased number of professionals involved, who tend to identify as much with the supra-goals of their profession as with those of their immediate employer. University professors can be used as a case in point. More and more of their income comes from outside sources, such as private or public foundations and consultant work. They tend not to make good "company men" because they are divided in their loyalty to professional values and organizational demands.

Organization. The social structure of organizations of the future will have some unique characteristics. The key word will be "temporary"; there will be adaptive, rapidly changing *temporary systems* (see Miles, 1964). These will be "task forces" organized around problems-to-be-solved. The problems will be solved by groups of relative strangers who represent a set of diverse professional skills. The groups will be arranged on organic rather than mechanical models; they will evolve in response to a problem rather than to programmed role expectations. The "executive" thus becomes a co-ordinator or "linking pin" between various task forces. He must be a man who can speak the diverse languages of research, with skills to relay information and to mediate between groups. *People will be differentiated not vertically, according to rank and role, but flexibly and functionally according to skill and professional training.*

Adaptive, problem-solving, temporary systems of diverse specialists, linked together by co-ordinating and task evaluating specialists in an organic flux—this is the organizational form that will gradually replace bureaucracy as we know it. As no catchy phrase comes to mind, let us call this an *organic-adaptive* structure.

As an aside—what will happen to the rest of society, to the manual laborers, to the less educated, to those who desire to work under conditions of high authority, and so forth? Many such jobs will disappear; other jobs will be automated. However, there will be a corresponding growth in the service-type occupations, such as those in the "war on poverty" and the Peace Corps programs. In times of change, where there is a discrepancy between cultures, when industrialization and especially urbanization proceeds rapidly, the market for men with training and skill in human interaction increases. We might guess that approximately 40 percent of the population would be involved in jobs of this nature, 40 percent in technological jobs, with a 20 percent bureaucratic minority.

Motivation. Our above discussion of "reciprocity" indicated the shortcomings of bureaucracy in maximizing employee effectiveness. The "organic-adaptive" structure should increase motivation, and thereby effectiveness, because it enhances satisfactions intrinsic to the task. There is a harmony between the educated individual's need for meaningful, satisfactory, and creative tasks and a flexible organizational structure.

Of course, where the reciprocity problem is ameliorated, there are corresponding tensions between the individual's involvement in his professional community and his involvement in his employing organization. Professionals are notoriously "disloyal" to organizational demands.

There will, however, also be reduced commitment to work groups, for these groups, as I have already mentioned, will be transient and changing. While skills in human interaction will become more important, due to the growing needs for collaboration in complex tasks, there will be a concomitant reduction in group cohesiveness. I would predict that in the organic-adaptive system people will have to learn to develop quick and intense relationships on the job, and learn to bear the loss of more enduring work relationships.

In general I do not agree with Clark Kerr (1960), Harold Leavitt (1964), and others in their emphasis on a "New Bohemianism" in which leisure—not work—becomes the emotional-creative sphere of life. They assume a technological slow-down and leveling-off, and a stabilizing of social mobility. This may happen in a society of the distant future. But long before then we will face the challenge of creating the new service-type organizations with an organic-adaptive structure.

Jobs in the next century should become more rather than less involving; man is a problem-solving animal and the tasks of the future guarantee a full agenda of problems. In addition, the adaptive process itself may become captivating to many. At the same time, I think that the future I described is not necessarily a "happy" one. Coping with rapid change, living in the temporary work systems, setting up (in quick-step time) meaningful relations—and then breaking them—all augur social strains and psychological tensions. Learning how to live with ambiguity and to be self-directing will be the task of education and the goal of maturity.

In these new organizations, participants will be called on to use their minds more than at any other time in history. Fantasy, imagination, and creativity will be legitimate in ways that today seem strange. Social structures will no longer be instruments of psychic repression but will increasingly promote play and freedom on behalf of curiosity and thought. I agree with Herbert Marcuse's thesis in *Eros and Civilization* (1955) that the necessity of repression and the suffering derived from it, decreases with the maturity of the civilization.

Not only will the problem of adaptability be overcome through the organic-adaptive structure, but the problem we started with, reciprocity, will be resolved. Bureaucracy, with its "surplus repression," was a monumental discovery for harnessing muscle power *via* guilt and instinctual renunciation. In today's world, it is a lifeless crutch that is no longer useful. For we now require structures of freedom to permit the expression of play and imagination and to exploit the new pleasure of work.

59 Being human and being organized

CHRIS ARGYRIS

It is hard to imagine being "civilized" without being "organized." Yet too much organization, or the wrong kind, can injure the individuals involved and through them can spoil an organization or a civilization. How can we design or "grow" organizations that maintain the right balance between individual needs on the one hand, and organizational requirements on the other?

The classical design for a formal organization has some very serious flaws. The nature of these flaws appears when we set side by side two pictures: first, a view of how human beings need to behave in our society in order to be healthy, productive, growing individuals; and second, how a formal organization (a factory, business, or hospital) requires them to behave. Comparing these pictures, we see that the organization's requirements, as presented by "classical" descriptions, are sharply opposed to the individual's needs. We can, however, suggest some lines along which action and study might improve the "fit" between the human being and the non-human organization.

Picture of health

There are certain lines along which the child becoming a man develops, in our culture. We can discuss, as being most important, seven of these "developmental dimensions":

From being passive as infants, humans grow toward activeness as adults.

From being dependent on others, an individual grows toward being relatively independent of others. He develops the ability to "stand on his own two feet" while at the same time acknowledging a healthy dependency. He does not react to others (his boss, for instance) in terms of patterns learned during childhood; thus, such independence is partly a matter of accurate perception of himself and those around him.

From only a few types of reaction or behavior, he develops many.

He moves from the shallow, brief, and erratic interests of his infancy to the intense, long-term, and coherent commitments of adulthood. He requires increasingly varied challenges; he wants his tasks to be not easy but hard, not simple but complex, not a collection of separate things but a variety of parts he can put together.

He begins to want long-term challenges that link his past and future, in place of the old brief and unconnected jobs which typically were engaged in by him as a child.

He begins wanting to go up the totem pole, instead of staying in the low place a child has.

He develops from being not very self-aware and impulsive to being both self-aware and self-controlled, and this lets him develop a sense of integrity and self-worth.

No one, of course, finishes his development along these seven lines. For one thing, if everyone became totally inde-

Reprinted from Trans-action, 1964, 1, 3–6, with permission of the author and the publisher.

pendent, incessantly active, and completely equal if not superior, society would be in a pretty difficult situation —sort of all fleas and no dog. One function of culture is to hold back, by our manners and morals, the self-expression of some individualists, so that others may also have a chance at self-development. Then too, people simply differ in needs and skills; not everybody wants to go into orbit, and some are too frail, too fat, or too stupid to be given the chance.

Admitting, then, that no one is ever through developing along these dimensions, we can still say that his self-actualization is the overall "profile" of how far he has developed along them. At this point we must add that in drawing this profile, not the surface appearance but the underlying meanings of a man's behavior are what have to be considered. For instance, an employee might seem to be always going against what management wants, so that people call him "independent," yet his contrariness may be due to his great need to be dependent on management, a need he dislikes to admit. The truly independent person is the one whose behavior is not mainly a reaction against the influence others have over him (though, of course, no person is totally independent). The best test of such independence is how fully the person will let other people be independent and active. Autocratic leaders may claim to like independent underlings, yet many studies have shown that autocratic leadership only makes both boss and underlings more dependence-ridden.

The formal organization

We now turn from the picture of a developing self to the organization. What are its properties, and what impact can we expect these to make on the human personality we have just viewed? What reactions can we expect from this impact?

To begin, the most basic feature of a formal organization is that it is "rational"—that is, it has been "designed," and its parts are purposefully related within this design; it has pattern and is shaped by human minds to accomplish particular rational objectives. For instance, jobs within it must be clearly defined (in terms of rank, salary, and duties) so that the organization can have logical training, promotion, and resignation or retirement policies.

But most experts on such organizations are not content to point to, as Herbert Simon (1957) does, this "rational design"—they go on to say that this rationality, though an ideal that may have to be modified now and then, requires people in an organization to be very loyal to its formal structure if it is to work effectively. They have to "go by the rules." And the experts claim such design is "more human" in the long run than creating an organization haphazardly. It is senseless, cruel, wasteful, and inefficient, they argue, not to have a logical design. It is senseless to pay a man highly without clearly defining his position and its relation to the whole. It is cruel, because eventually people suffer when no structure exists. It is wasteful because without clearly pre-defined jobs it is impossible to plan a logical training or promotion or resignation or retirement policy. And it is inefficient because it allows the "personal touch" to dominate and this, in turn, is "playing politics."

In contrast to such experts, some human-relations researchers have unfortunately given the impression that formal structures are bad, and that individual needs should come first in creating and running an organization. These latter men, however, are swinging (as recent analysis of their research has shown) to recognize that an extreme emphasis on the individual's needs is not a very tenable position either, and that organizational rules can be well worth keeping.

Principles of design

What are the principles by which an organization is "rationally designed"? The traditionalists among experts in this field have singled out certain key assumptions about the best design for a formal organization. In our comments here these will be dealt with not as beyond question but only as the most useful and accurate so far offered. By accepting them to this extent, we can go on to look at the probable impact on human beings of an organization based on them.

As Gillespie (1948) suggests, these principles may be traced back to certain "principles of industrial economics," the most important of which is that "the concentration of effort on a limited field of endeavor increases quality and quantity of output." This principle leads to another: that the more similar the things that need doing, the more specialization will help to do them.

Specializing

The design-principle just mentioned carries three implications about human beings within organizations. First, that the human personality will behave more efficiently as the job gets more specialized. Second, that there can be found a one best way to define the job so it will be done faster. Third, that differences between human personalities may be ignored by transferring more skill and thought to machines.

But all these assumptions conflict sharply with the developmental needs or tendencies of human personality as a growing thing; a human being is always putting himself together, pushing himself into the future. How can we assume that this process can be choked off, or that the differences between individuals which result from the process can be ignored?

Besides, specialization requires a person to use only a few of his abilities, and the more specialized the task the simpler the ability involved. This goes directly counter to the human tendency to want more complex, more interesting jobs as he develops. Singing the same tune over and over is boring enough, but repeating the same note is absolutely maddening.

The chain of command

Mere efficiency of parts is not enough; an organization needs to have a pattern of parts, a chain of command. Thus, planners create "leadership," to control and coordinate. They assume that efficiency is increased by a fixed hierarchy of authority. The man at the top is given formal power to hire and fire, reward and penalize, so that employees will work for the organization's objectives.

The impact of this design-feature on human personality is clearly to make the individuals dependent on, passive and subordinate to, the leader. The results are obviously to lessen their self-control and shorten their time-perspective. It would seem, then, that the design-feature of hierarchic structure works against four of the growth-lines, pushing individuals back from active toward passive, from equal toward subordinate, from self-controlled toward dependent, from being aware of long time-perspectives toward having only a short time-perspective. In all these four ways, the result is to move employees back from adulthood toward immaturity.

Planners have tried to cushion this impact in several ways. First, they see to it that those who perform well in the hierarchy are rewarded. But the trouble with this is that the reward ought to be psychological as well as material—and yet, because of the job-specialization which simplifies and does not satisfy a worker, few psychological rewards are possible. So the material reward has to seem more important, and has to be increased. To do this, however, means that one does nothing about the on-the-job situation that is causing the trouble, but instead pays the employee for the dissatisfaction he experiences. Obviously, management in doing this leaves an employee to feel that basic causes of dissatisfaction are built into industrial life, that the rewards received are wages for dissatisfaction, and that any satisfaction to be gained must be looked for outside the organization.

Other things are wrong with raising wages to make up for dissatisfaction. For it assumes that the worker can so split himself up that he can be quite satisfied with the anomalous situation we have just described him as being in. Second, it assumes he is mainly interested in what money can get. And third, it assumes he is best rewarded as an individual producer, without regard to the work group in which he belongs. This may well mean that a worker whose group informally sanctions holding production down will therefore have to choose between pleasing the boss and getting paid more, or pleasing his fellows and getting paid less.

Keeping personalities out

A second "solution" has been suggested by planners: to have very good bosses. The leaders, that is, should be objective, rational, and personify the reasonableness of the organizational structure. To do this means they keep from getting emotionally involved; as one executive states, "We must try to keep our personalities out of the job." Evaluating others, he sets aside his own feelings. And, of course, he must be loyal to the organization.

But this solution too violates some of the basic properties of personality. To split what one does from what one is, or to ask others to do it, is to violate one's self-integrity, and the same goes for the effort to keep personality out of the job. (As for impartiality, as May (1953) has pointed out, the best way to be impartial is to be as partial as one's needs require but stay aware of this partiality so as to "correct" for it at the moment of decision.)

One other solution has been offered: to encourage competition among employees, so as to get them to show initiative and creativity. Competing for promotions, this "rabble hypothesis" suggests, will increase the efficiency of the competitors.

Williams (1956), however, conducting some controlled experiments, shows that this assumption is not necessarily valid for people placed in competitive situations. Deutsch (1949) supports Williams's results with extensive controlled research, and goes much further, suggesting that competitive situations make for so much tension that they lessen efficiency. Levy and Freedman (1956) confirm Deutsch's work and go on to relate competition to psychoneurosis.

Unity of direction

We have looked at the design-features of job-specialization and hierarchic structure. A final principle of design is *unity of direction:* efficiency is supposed to increase if each administrative unit has a single activity planned and directed by a single leader. The implication is that this leader sets the goal, the conditions for meeting the goal, and the path toward it, for all his employees. If, because of job-specialization, the workers are not personally interested in the work-goal, then unity of direction creates the ideal conditions for psychological failure. For each individual basically (as we have said) aims at psychological success, which comes only when he defines his own goals, in relation to his personal needs and to the difficulties of reaching the goals.

Human needs vs. organizational requirements

What we have seen is that if we use the principles of formal organization as ideally defined, employees will be working in an environment where (1) they have little or no control over their workaday world; (2) they are expected to be passive, dependent, and subordinate; (3) they are expected to have a short time-perspective; (4) job-specialization asks them to perfect and value only a few of their simplest abilities; and (5) they are asked to produce under conditions (imposed by the principle of unity of direction) ideal for psychological failure.

Since behavior in these ways is more childish than adult, it appears that formal organizations are willing to pay high wages and provide adequate seniority if mature adults will, for eight hours a day, behave like children. It is obvious that such behavior is incompatible with the human need to develop and "grow up." And it appears that the incongruency increases as (1) the employee is of greater maturity; (2) the formal structure is tightened in search of efficiency; (3) one goes down the line of command; (4) jobs become more mechanized.

That such incongruency will result in frustration, failure, short time-perspective and conflict hardly needs demonstration. How, in the face of all this, will the employee be able to maintain a sense of his own integrity? He will react in part like a turtle and in part like a porcupine: by leaving, by "ladder-climbing" within the organization, by such defense reactions as daydreaming, aggression, ambivalence, regression, projection, and so on; or by becoming apathetic toward the organization's makeup and goals. If this occurs, he will be apt to start "goldbricking" or even cheating. He may create informal groups who agree that it is right to be apathetic and uninvolved, and these informal groups may become formalized—instead of just gathering to gripe they will hold meetings and pass resolutions. Or he may take the view that money and "what's in it for me" have become the really important things about his work, and the "psychological rewards" are just malarkey. And he will end up by indoctrinating the new employees so that they will see the organization through the same mud-colored glasses as he does.

What to do?

There is only one real way to improve the sad picture described above: by *decreasing* the dependency, decreasing the subordination, and decreasing the submissiveness expected of employees. It can be shown that making a job "bigger"—not more specialized and small—will help do these things; and that employee-centered (or democratic or participative) leadership also will improve the situation.

Yet, these remedies are limited, for they require employees who are already highly interested in the organization. And the situation which makes them needed is one in which employees are anything but interested. In such a situation, strongly directive leadership is almost necessary to get the apathetic employee to move at all. This, in its own turn, helps to create the very problem it is trying to solve!

An unresolved dilemma

The dilemma, then, is basic and is a continuing challenge to the social scientist and the leader in an organization. They may well begin their efforts to work for a solution—one in which the organization will be as efficient as possible, while the people in it will be as free and strongly developing as possible —by considering two facts. The first is that no organization can be maximally efficient that stunts its own vital parts. And the second is that our culture and each of its institutions, from family through nations and beyond, are one vast interlocking set of organizations.

60 An overview of new patterns of management

RENSIS LIKERT

Based upon the principles and practices of the managers who are achieving the best results, a newer theory of organization and management can be stated. An attempt will be made here to present briefly some of the over-all characteristics of such a theory and to formulate a general integrating principle which can be useful in attempts to apply it.

Research findings indicate that the general pattern of operations of the highest-producing managers tends to differ from that of the managers of mediocre and low-producing units by more often showing the following characteristics:

> A preponderance of favorable attitudes on the part of each member of the organization toward all the other members, toward superiors, toward the work, toward the organization—toward all aspects of the job. These favorable attitudes toward others reflect a high level of mutual confidence and trust throughout the organization. The favorable attitudes toward the organization and the work are not those of easy complacency, but are the attitudes of identification with the organization and its objectives and a high sense of involvement in achieving them. As a consequence, the performance goals are high and dissatisfaction may occur whenever achievement falls short of the goals set.

This highly motivated, cooperative orientation toward the organization and its objectives is achieved by harnessing effectively all the major motivational forces which can exercise significant influence in an organizational setting and which, potentially, can be accompanied by cooperative and favorable attitudes. Reliance is not placed solely or fundamentally on the economic motive of buying a man's time and using control and authority as the organizing and coordinating principle of the organization. On the contrary, the following motives are all used fully and in such a way that they function in a cumulative and reinforcing manner and yield favorable attitudes:

> The ego motives. These are referred to throughout this volume as the desire to achieve and maintain a sense of personal worth and importance. This desire manifests itself in many forms, depending upon the norms and values of the persons and groups involved. Thus, it is responsible for such motivational forces as the desire for growth and significant achievement in terms of one's own values and goals, i.e., self-fulfillment, as well as the desire for status, recog-

Abridged from Chapter 8 of **New Patterns of Management**, New York: McGraw-Hill, 1961, pp. 97–118, with permission of the author and the publisher.

nition, approval, acceptance, and power and the desire to undertake significant and important tasks.

The security motives.

Curiosity, creativity, and the desire for new experiences.

The economic motives.

By tapping all the motives which yield favorable and cooperative attitudes, maximum motivation oriented toward realizing the organization's goals as well as the needs of each member of the organization is achieved. The substantial decrements in motivational forces which occur when powerful motives are pulling in opposite directions are thereby avoided. These conflicting forces exist, of course, when hostile and resentful attitudes are present.

The organization consists of a tightly knit, effectively functioning social system. This social system is made up of interlocking work groups with a high degree of group loyalty among the members and favorable attitudes and trust between superiors and subordinates. Sensitivity to others and relatively high levels of skill in personal interaction and the functioning of groups are also present. These skills permit effective participation in decisions on common problems. Participation is used, for example, to establish organizational objectives which are a satisfactory integration of the needs and desires of all members of the organization and of persons functionally related to it. High levels of reciprocal influence occur, and high levels of total coordinated influence are achieved in the organization. Communication is efficient and effective. There is a flow from one part of the organization to another of all the relevant information important for each decision and action. The leadership in the organization has developed what might well be called a highly effective social system for interaction and mutual influence.

Measurements of organizational performance are used primarily for self-guidance rather than for superimposed control. To tap the motives which bring cooperative and favorable rather than hostile attitudes, participation and involvement in decisions is a habitual part of the leadership processes. This kind of decision-making, of course, calls for the full sharing of available measurements and information. Moreover, as it becomes evident in the decision-making process that additional information or measurements are needed, steps are taken to obtain them.

In achieving operations which are more often characterized by the above pattern of highly cooperative, well-coordinated activity, the highest producing managers use all the technical resources of the classical theories of management, such as time-and-motion study, budgeting, and financial controls. They use these resources at least as completely as do the low-producing managers, but in quite different ways. This difference in use arises from the differences in the motives which the high-producing, in contrast to the low-producing, managers believe are important in influencing human behavior.

The low-producing managers, in keeping with traditional practice, feel that the way to motivate and direct behavior is to exercise control through authority. Jobs are organized, methods are prescribed, standards are set, performance goals and budgets are established. Compliance with them is sought through the use of hierarchical and economic pressures.

Widespread use of participation is one of the more important approaches employed by the high-producing managers in their efforts to get full benefit from the technical resources of the classical theories of management coupled with high levels of reinforcing motivation. This use of participation applies to all aspects of the job and work, as, for example, in setting work goals and budgets, controlling costs, organizing the work, etc. The high-producing managers have developed their organizations into highly coordinated, highly motivated, cooperative social systems. Under their leadership, the different motivational forces in each member of the organization have coalesced into a strong force aimed at accomplishing the mutually established objectives of the organization. This general pattern of highly motivated, cooperative members seems to be a central characteristic of the newer management system being developed by the highest-producing managers.

How do these high-producing managers build organizations which display this central characteristic? The research findings show, for example, that those supervisors and managers whose pattern of leadership yields consistently favorable attitudes more often think of employees as "human beings rather than just as persons to get the work done." Consistently, in study after study, the data show that treating people as "human beings" rather than as "cogs in a machine" is a variable highly related to the attitudes and motivation of the subordinate at every level in the organization.

The superiors who have the most favorable and cooperative attitudes in their work groups display the following characteristics:

> The attitude and behavior of the superior toward the subordinate as a person, *as perceived by the subordinate*, is as follows:
>
> He is supportive, friendly, and helpful rather than hostile. He is kind but firm, never threatening, genuinely interested in the wellbeing of subordinates and endeavors to treat people in a sensitive, considerate way. He is just, if not generous. He endeavors to serve the best interests of his employees as well as of the company.
>
> He shows confidence in the integrity, ability, and motivations of subordinates rather than suspicion and distrust.
>
> His confidence in subordinates leads him to have high expectations as to their level of performance. With confidence that he will not be disappointed, he expects much, not little. (This, again, is fundamentally a supportive rather than a critical or hostile relationship.)
>
> He sees that each subordinate is well trained for his particular job. He endeavors also to help subordinates be promoted by training them for jobs at the next level. This involves giving them relevant experience and coaching whenever the opportunity offers.
>
> He coaches and assists employees whose performance is below standard. In the case of a subordinate who is clearly misplaced and unable to do his job satisfactorily, he

> endeavors to find a position well suited to that employee's abilities and arranges to have the employee transferred to it.

The behavior of the superior in directing the work is characterized by such activity as:

> Planning and scheduling the work to be done, training subordinates, supplying them with material and tools, initiating work activity, etc.
> Providing adequate technical competence, particularly in those situations where the work has not been highly standardized.

The leader develops his subordinates into a working team with high group loyalty by using participation and other kinds of group-leadership practices.

The integrating principle

These results and similar data from other studies (Argyris, 1957; March & Simon, 1958; Viteles, 1953) show that subordinates react favorably to experiences which they feel are supportive and contribute to their sense of importance and personal worth. Similarly, persons react unfavorably to experiences which are threatening and decrease or minimize their sense of dignity and personal worth. These findings are supported also by substantial research on personality development (Argyris, 1957; Rogers, 1942; Rogers, 1951) and group behavior (Cartwright & Zander, 1960). Each of us wants appreciation, recognition, influence, a feeling of accomplishment, and a feeling that people who are important to us believe in us and respect us. We want to feel that we have a place in the world.

This provides the basis for stating the general principle which the high-producing managers seem to be using and which will be referred to as the *principle of supportive relationships.* This principle, which provides an invaluable guide in any attempt to apply the newer theory of management in a specific plant or organization, can be briefly stated: *The leadership and other processes of the organization must be such as to ensure a maximum probability that in all interactions and all relationships with the organization each member will, in the light of his background, values, and expectations, view the experience as supportive and one which builds and maintains his sense of personal worth and importance.*

The central role of the work group

An important theoretical derivation can be made from the principle of supportive relationships. This derivation is based directly on the desire to achieve and maintain a sense of personal worth, which is a central concept of the principle. The most important source of satisfaction for this desire is the response we get from the people we are close to, in whom we are interested, and whose approval and support we are eager to have. The face-to-face groups with whom we spend the bulk of our time are, consequently, the most important to us. Our work group is one in which we spend much of our time and one in which we are particularly eager to achieve and maintain a sense of personal worth. As a consequence, most persons are highly motivated to behave in ways consistent with the goals and values of their work group in order to obtain recognition, support, security, and favorable reactions from this group. It can be concluded, therefore, that *management will make full use of the potential capacities of its human resources only when each person in an organization is a member of one or more effectively functioning work groups that have a high degree of group loyalty, effective skills of interaction, and high performance goals.*

The full significance of this derivation becomes more evident when we examine the research findings that show how groups function when they are well knit and have effective interaction skills. Research shows, for example, that the greater the attraction and loyalty to the group, the more the individual is motivated (1) to accept the goals and decisions of the group; (2) to seek to influence the goals and decisions of the group so that they are consistent with his own experience and his own goals; (3) to communicate fully to the members of the group; (4) to welcome communication and influence attempts from the other members; (5) to behave so as to help implement the goals and decisions that are seen as most important to the group; and (6) to behave in ways calculated to receive support and favorable recognition from members of the group and especially from those who the individual feels are the more powerful and higher-status members (Cartwright & Zander, 1960).

As our theoretical derivation has indicated, an organization will function best when its personnel function not as individuals but as members of highly effective work groups with high performance goals. Consequently, management should deliberately endeavor to build these effective groups, linking them into an over-all organization by means of people who hold overlapping group membership. The superior in one group is a subordinate in the next group, and so on through the organization. If the work groups at each hierarchical level are well knit and effective, the linking process will be accomplished well.

An effectively functioning group pressing for solutions in the best interest of *all* the members and refusing to accept solutions which unduly favor a particular member or segment of the group is an important characteristic of the group pattern of organization. It also provides the president, or the superior at any level in an organization, with a powerful managerial tool for dealing with special requests or favors from subordinates. Often the subordinate may feel that the request is legitimate even though it may not be in the best interest of the organization. In the man-to-man operation the chief sometimes finds it difficult to turn down such requests. With the group pattern of operation, however, the superior can suggest that the subordinate submit his proposal to the group at their next staff meeting. If the request is legitimate and in the best interest of the organization, the group will grant the request. If the request is unreasonable, an effectively functioning group can skillfully turn it down by analyzing it in relation to what is best for the entire organization. Subordinates in this situation soon find they cannot get special favors or preferred treatment from the chief. This leads to a tradition that one does not ask for any treatment or decision which is recognized as unfair to one's colleagues.

Group decision-making

With the group model of organization, persons reporting to the president, such as vice presidents for sales, research, and manufacturing, contribute their technical knowledge in the decision-making process. They also make other contributions. One member of the group, for example, may be an imaginative person who comes up rapidly with many stimulating and original ideas. Others, such as the general counsel or the head of research, may make the group do a rigorous job of sifting ideas. In this way, the different contributions required for a competent job of thinking and decision-making are introduced.

In addition, these people become experienced in effective group functioning. They know what leadership involves. If the president grows absorbed in some detail and fails to keep the group focused on the topic for discussion, the members will help by performing appropriate leadership functions, such as asking, "Where are we? What have we decided so far? Why don't we summarize?"

There are other advantages to this sort of group action. The motivation is high to communicate accurately all relevant and important information. If any one of these men holds back important facts affecting the company so that he can take it to the president later, the president is likely to ask him why he withheld the information and request him to report it to the group at the next session. The group also is apt to be hard on any member who withholds important information from them. Moreover, the group can get ideas across to the boss that no subordinate dares tell him. As a consequence, there is better communication, which brings a better awareness of problems, and better decision-making than with the man-to-man system.

Another important advantage of effective group action is the high degree of motivation on the part of each member to do his best to implement decisions and to achieve the group goals. Since the goals of the group are arrived at through group decisions, each individual group member tends to have a high level of ego identification with the goals because of his involvement in the decisions.

Finally, there are indications that an organization operating in this way can be staffed for less than peak loads at each point. When one man is overburdened, some of his colleagues can pick up part of the load temporarily. This is possible with group methods of supervision because the struggle for power and status is less. Everybody recognizes his broad area of responsibility and is not alarmed by occasional shifts in one direction or the other. Moreover, he knows that his chances for promotion depend not upon the width of his responsibility, but upon his total performance, of which his work in the group is an important part. The group, including the president, comes to know the strengths and weaknesses of each member well as a result of working closely with him.

The "linking pin" function

The preceding discussion has been concerned with the group pattern of organization at the very top of a company. Our theoretical derivation indicates, however, that this pattern is equally applicable at all levels of an organization. If an organization is to apply this system effectively at all organizational levels, an important linking function must be performed.

The concept of the "linking pin" is shown by the arrows in Figure 1.

The linking pin function requires effective group processes and points to the following:

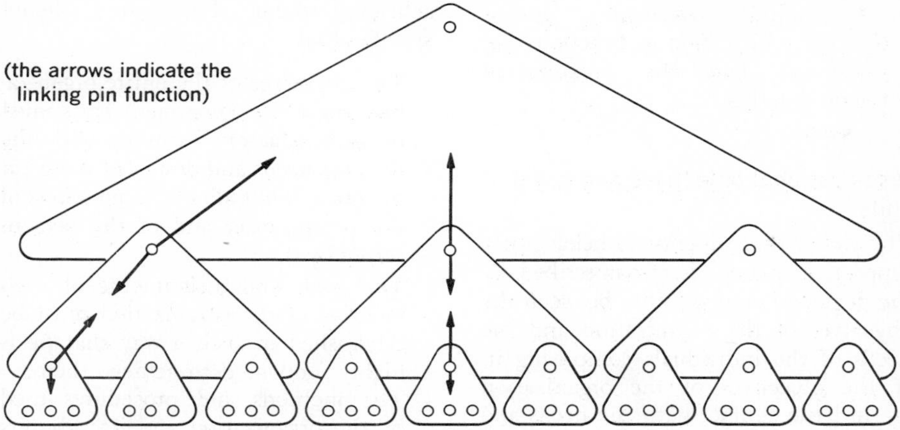
(the arrows indicate the
linking pin function)

Figure 1. The linking pin.

An organization will not derive the full benefit from its highly effective groups unless they are linked to the total organization by means of equally effective overlapping groups. The use of highly effective groups in only one part or in scattered portions of an organization will fail, therefore, to achieve the full potential value of such groups.

The potential power of the overlapping group form of organization will not be approached until all the groups in the organization are functioning reasonably well. The failure of any group will adversely affect the performance of the total organization. The higher an ineffective group is in the hierarchy, the greater is the adverse effect of its failure on the performance of the organization. The linking process is more important at high levels in an organization than at low because the policies and problems dealt with are more important to the total organization and affect more people.

To help maintain an effective organization, it is desirable for superiors not only to hold group meetings of their own subordinates, but also to have occasional meetings over two hierarchical levels. This enables the superior to observe any breakdown in the linking pin process as performed by the subordinates reporting to him. If in such meetings the subordinates under one of his subordinates are reluctant to talk, never question any procedure or policy, or give other evidence of fear, the superior can conclude that he has a coaching job to do with his own subordinate, who is failing both as a leader and in his performance of the linking pin function. This subordinate needs help in learning how to build his own subordinates into a work group with high group loyalty and with confidence and trust in their supervisor.

An organization takes a serious risk when it relies on a single linking pin or single linking process to tie the organization together. An organization is strengthened by having staff groups and *ad hoc* committees provide multiple overlapping groups through which linking functions are performed and the organization bound together.

Organizational objectives and goals of units

The ability of a superior to behave in a supportive manner is circumscribed by the degree of compatibility between the objectives of the organization and the needs of the individuals comprising it. If the objectives of the organization are in basic conflict with the needs and desires of the individual members, it is virtually impossible for the superior to be supportive to subordinates and at the same time serve the objectives of the organization. The principle of supportive relationships, consequently, points to the necessity for an adequate degree of harmony between organizational objectives and the needs and desires of its individual members.

Neither the needs and desires of individuals nor the objectives of organizations are stable and unchanging. The desires of individuals grow and change as people interact with other people. Similarly, the objectives of organizations must change continuously to meet the requirements of changed technologies, changed conditions, and the changes in needs and desires of those involved in the organization or served by it. The interaction process of the organization must be capable of dealing effectively with these requirements for continuous change.

In every healthy organization there is, consequently, an unending process of examining and modifying individual goals and organizational objectives as well as consideration of the methods for achieving them. The newer theory specifies that:

> The objectives of the entire organization and of its component parts must be in satisfactory harmony with the relevant needs and desires of the great majority, if not all, of the members of the organization and of the persons served by it.
>
> The goals and assignments of each member of the organization must be established in such a way that he is highly motivated to achieve them.
>
> The methods and procedures used by the organization and its subunits to achieve the agreed-upon objectives must be developed and adopted in such a way that the members are highly motivated to use these methods to their maximum potentiality.
>
> The members of the organization and the persons related to it must feel that the reward system of the organization—salaries, wages, bonuses, dividends, interest payments—yields them equitable compensation for their efforts and contributions.

The overlapping group form of organization offers a structure which, in conjunction with a high level of group interactional skills, is particularly effective in performing the processes necessary to meet these requirements.

Constructive use of conflict

An organization operating under the newer theory is not free from conflict. Conflict and differences of opinion always exist in a healthy, virile organization, for it is usually from such differences that new and better objectives and methods emerge. Differences are essential to progress, but bitter, unresolved differences can immobilize an organization. The central problem, consequently, becomes not how to reduce or eliminate conflict, but how to deal constructively with it. Effective organizations have extraordinary capacity to handle conflict. Their success is due to three very important characteristics:

1. They possess the machinery to deal constructively with conflict. They have an organizational structure which facilitates constructive interaction between individuals and between work groups.

2. The personnel of the organization is skilled in the processes of effective interaction and mutual influence.

3. There is high confidence and trust among the members of the organization in each other, high loyalty to the work group and to the organization, and high motivation to achieve the organization's objectives. Confidence, loyalty, and cooperative motivation produce earnest, sincere, and determined efforts to find solutions to conflict. There is greater motivation to find a constructive solution than to maintain an irreconcilable conflict. The solutions reached are often highly creative and represent a far better solution than any initially proposed by the conflicting interests (Metcalf & Urwick, 1940).

The discussion in this chapter has deliberately focused on and emphasized the group aspects of organization and management. This has been done to make clear some of the major differences between the classical and the newer theories of management. It should also sharpen the awareness of the kind of changes needed to start applying the newer theory.

Any organization which bases its operation on this theory will necessarily make use of individual counseling and coaching by superiors of subordinates. There is need in every situation for a balanced use of both procedures, individual and group. Here, as with other aspects of supervision, the balance which will be most appropriate and work best will depend upon the experience, expectations, and skills of the people involved.

X INTERGROUP RELATIONS

Of the several areas of social psychology that we have touched on, intergroup relations constitutes one of especially pressing concern to everyday life. Whether distinctions are made in terms of the multifarious groups which comprise a society, or in terms of international relations, the problem of hostility and conflict between such social entities is much in evidence.

Fundamentally, intergroup conflict stems from the identification of individuals with groups in terms of an "in-group" versus "out-group" distinction. The perceptual discrimination that this involves is quite common and by itself need not be destructive. However, it may lead to socially disruptive consequences because of the introduction of a value judgment between "we" and "they." Through the oversimplified mechanism of "stereotypes," it is all too easy to see all virtue residing in one's own group and all evil residing in others.

Sharp demarcations of this kind, especially where they are heavily overladen with this evaluative quality, impede effective communication and lead to a breakdown of understanding and cooperation. Furthermore, they are unrealistic in terms of their singlemindedness. As Allport indicates here, loyalties can be concentric, with the larger ones containing the smaller, and no exclusions implied. Thus, whatever distinctions are made in segmenting the populace in various ways, all people share certain common interests as residents of a neighborhood, or a city, or a nation, or the planet. Growing interest in air and water pollution, the conservation of natural resources, and the battle against disease, reflect human concerns which go beyond the various group distinctions which we make in our everyday thinking and actions. Yet, intergroup conflict poses a constant hazard to the preservation of society and indeed to the world, as a scanning of the daily paper reveals.

Social psychologists have long been concerned with understanding the processes underlying such conflicts, especially in terms of prejudice. Among those who have done significant work in this area, Gordon Allport and his colleagues have been in the forefront. His book, *The Nature of Prejudice* (1958), from which the selection here is drawn, is a landmark in understanding the processes and effects of prejudice.

Essentially, prejudice is an intergroup phenomenon that involves a negative attitude, a prejudgment, regarding other individuals in terms of their perceived group affiliations. Thus, sharp distinctions between in-group and out-group are the wellsprings of prejudice. The difficulty in overcoming prejudice stems from the combination of psychological and social factors which serve to bolster it. Features of the social structure, such as class distinctions, employment and residential patterns, are structural elements sustaining prejudice. Allport indicates that there is an equally potent psychological structure which may breed and maintain prejudice. The basis for prejudice often resides in individual attitudes which are functionally related to the ego needs discussed by Katz in Section VI. As Allport aptly notes, both perspectives on prejudice tell us that the problem ". . . is stitched into the fabric of social living." Yet, he advises caution lest we be falsely pessimistic about the prospects for change. Environmental supports for prejudice can be and are altered. Concern that people will not *accept* such change usually proves misplaced, especially where change is backed by law. Thus, studies of integration in the military services and in public housing demonstrate the effectiveness of legal supports in smoothing such change (e.g., Stouffer, *et al.*, 1949, Vol. I, Ch. 10; Deutsch & Collins, 1951).

Allport's positive principles for dealing with prejudice are a useful summary of what is known about coping with intergroup relationships of this kind. Among his more noteworthy points, he argues against any single approach, and especially one which fails to accept cultural pluralism (see Gordon and Shibutani, Section II). While Allport favors open communication and the publishing of scientifically sound information, he stresses that educational programs are not a panacea since they have only limited utility by themselves. Because so much of prejudice is rationalized, campaigns of this kind can be equally well rationalized, as Bauer's paper in Section VI indicates, at least by implication.

In overcoming prejudice, Allport mainly urges active involvement through action programs that do something, apart from preaching and exhortation. On the other hand, Allport is encouraging about the long-range effectiveness of teaching children about prejudice and its nature as part of intercultural education.

Bound into the problem of prejudice is the distinctive quality possessed by the various subcultures within a society. In Section II Pettigrew presents a picture of the effect of prejudice in producing a quality of life for the Negro which is at variance with the modal cultural pattern of American Society. This differential is made more acute by the inordinate number of Negroes who are represented among America's poor (see Harrington, 1963). In his paper here, Lewis briefly reviews the qualities he discerns in the "culture of poverty." His widely read book, *The Children of Sanchez* (1961), is a poignant account of the life of a typical family in the poorer stratum of Mexican society.

What Lewis has to say here about poverty, however, takes on a significance that transcends any given country or skin color. The marginality and alienation from organized society that he reports constitutes a worldwide intergroup problem. A fair share of the world's population lives in the culture of poverty and this stands as a potent fact of life, with strong ideological overtones, which is not likely to diminish even with a broad program of social assistance for the satisfaction of physical survival needs. Indeed, the central idea that Lewis conveys is that poverty is as much a psychological state, with reference group features, as a state of want. In proposing and implementing programs to aid those who are poor, his point is that we recognize that cultural change is what is at stake (see Cartwright in Section VIII). The potentialities inherent in a miscarriage of this social process, in terms of intergroup conflict, are, to say the least, considerable.

When groups are in conflict, the problem of prejudice acquires a dimension that can produce violent results. One's own group is seen as noble in its aspirations and entirely justified in the actions it takes. The adversary is painted in precisely opposite terms. In open conflicts, such as warfare, each side asserts its determination not to compromise but to fight harder in the face of a setback. Where ideologies—in the sense of strongly held beliefs—are involved, force often produces the opposite effect from that intended. Group ties are intensified and willing sacrifice becomes increasingly normative.

Muzafer Sherif has conducted extensive studies in the area of intergroup conflict. In two field experiments that he describes in his paper here, he was able to study the development of such hostility within groups of boys drawn from homogeneous backgrounds and then to determine the factors which led to the resolution of such conflict. As he indicates, the major device that appears to have a significant salutary effect is the invocation of superordinate goals that have an appeal to both groups in the conflict. The analogue in the sphere of international relations is to be seen when two countries enter into an agreement, exemplified by many international treaties, because of the mutual advantage of a higher level goal to both parties.

One of the most striking findings in Sherif's work is the degree to which leadership is constrained by the group member's attitudes of hostility toward the competitive group. It thus becomes more difficult for a leader to reach an accommodation with the other group lest he be seen as violating his group's position. The implications for this in terms of bargaining and negotiation are readily observed in such a crisis as a strike, where entrenched positions are held at least partly because of the heavy weight of prior attitudinal commitments within the contending groups. As Sherif observes, it does little good to open discussions in such an atmosphere. If contact between leaders takes place in a context of hostility, and without the perception of superordinate goals to be achieved, then communication only serves as a medium for further accusations and recriminations.

On the international scene, parallel patterns may be found though in more intensified form. Nations are political-geographical entities, but they also carry considerable psychological commitment for their citizenry. Manifestations of international conflict take on a particularly acute intensity with regard to shared attitudes of hostility or fear. Bronfenbrenner reports his observations of this phenomenon here from his background as an

American social psychologist who speaks Russian and has encountered the Soviet Union at close hand.

The essential feature of Bronfenbrenner's report is the idea that the Soviet citizen's view of America, encouraged by the government and the media at its disposal, is a "mirror image" of the American's view of the Soviet Union. The interrelated ideas that America is aggressive, that its people are exploited, deluded, and not really sympathetic to their government, that it is untrustworthy and that its policies verge on madness, are all counterparts of our views of the Soviet Union, says Bronfenbrenner.

Drawing upon concepts of cognitive balance (see Heider in Section V, and Festinger and Osgood in Section VI), Bronfenbrenner points up the heavy evaluative distortions in the views held on both sides. In effect, he says we are dealing with a human response to threat which is neither distinctively Soviet nor American. What particularly concerns him is that these projections are not likely to encourage the reduction of conflict and threat. If, as he says, our hope is to bring an end to the cold war, the real danger is that such attitudes will be self-confirming. Thus, in line with what is known about social interaction, both parties may react to the expectancies of the other.

The awesome challenge of breaking through the distortions that may precipitate unintentional outcomes is of the utmost importance in Bronfenbrenner's concluding comments. He emphasizes the need for positive programs of contact and communication to provide more realistic views of the joint predicament in which these two major powers find themselves. In a related vein, Deutsch is concerned here with the broader policy questions surrounding the development of "mutual trust" to replace "mutual terror."

The nub of the matter, from Deutsch's viewpoint, is that several kinds of psychological processes encourage trust, including a positive orientation to mutual welfare and signs of trustworthiness. He raises doubts about whether national policies aimed at military superiority and stable deterence can, in and of themselves, induce a reduction of hostility and a movement toward trust. Thus, he notes among other points the endlessly regressive arms race quality of the former, and the built-in hazards of the latter. In particular, he points to the irrational elements that pervade these approaches and which make them fragile structures on which to rely. The alternatives he offers, from a social psychological perspective, emphasize rationality with a concomitant weakening of conditions leading to disorder and a strengthening of those conditions which are likely to maintain order.

Various proposals from social psychologists and other social scientists have been put forth along the same line recently. The growth of this interest is attested to in such books as Osgood (1962), Wright, Evan and Deutsch (1962), Kelman (1965), and McNeil (1965). Research on international systems, through "internation simulation" techniques, has also been pursued with promising results for the understanding of social psychological factors in international relations (see Guetzkow, *et al.*, 1963).

It is evident that social psychology has the potential to make distinct contributions to both the theoretical and practical side of intergroup and international relations, though it does not have all the answers, by any means. There are quite obviously economic and political factors at work which are of great importance. But such factors have long been foci of attention, often at the expense of the distinctly "human element" represented in social psychology's interest in the individual's construction of his world as it is influenced by his social milieu, especially cultural and group-based attachments. There is, therefore, considerable promise in the further extension of social psychological concepts and research methods beyond the present frontier of this vital area.

61 On reducing prejudice

GORDON W. ALLPORT

Special obstacles

Anyone who works in the field of intercultural relations knows how often in his community he hears the remark, "There is no problem." Parents, teachers, public officials, police, community leaders seem unaware of the undercurrents of friction and hostility. Until or unless violence breaks out "there is no problem" (see G. Watson, 1947).

We spoke earlier of the "mechanism of denial," of the tendency for the ego to defend itself when conflict threatens to upset its equilibrium. The strategy of denial is a quick reflex against disturbing thoughts.

Sometimes the denial is not so deeply bedded, but rests upon sheer habituation to the status quo. People are so accustomed to the prevailing system of caste and discrimination that they think it eternally fixed and entirely satisfactory to all concerned. We have mentioned the finding that most American whites believe that American Negroes are on the whole well satisfied with conditions as they are, an assumption woefully contrary to fact. But even conceding that honest ignorance and sheer habituation account for some of the denial, we must also grant that the deeper mechanism is often at work. We have previously seen that those who are deeply prejudiced are inclined to deny that they are prejudiced. Lacking personal insight, they are unable to take an objective view of conditions in their community. Even a citizen without prejudices of his own is likely to blind himself to injustices and tensions which, if acknowledged, could only upset the even tenor of his life.

One encounters this obstacle widely in school systems, where principals, teachers, and parents often oppose the introduction of intercultural education. Even in communities seething with prejudice we hear, "There is no problem; aren't we all Americans?" "Why put ideas into children's heads?" The attitude reminds us of the resistance shown by many parents, schools, and churches to sex education on the grounds that children might think taboo thoughts (that are surely already in their minds in a muddled fashion).

Some people have the tendency, through ignorance or through maliciousness, to identify all advocates of civil rights and all workers in behalf of ethnic relations as "subversive" elements. McCarthyism is a specter that haunts every worker in the field. While the victim himself sees through the irrationality of the name-calling, most citizens do not. They are led to perceive the worker and his program as vaguely allied to communism. How to combat this irrational overcategorization is a baffling problem. The realistic conflict between east-west ideologies spreads out to include total irrelevancies.

Excerpted from Chapter 31 of The Nature of Prejudice, Garden City: Doubleday-Anchor, 1958, pp. 463–75, with permission of the author and the copyright owners, Addison-Wesley Publishing Company, Incorporated.

All of these obstacles are profoundly serious, representing as they do the most firmly entrenched aspects of irrationalism in people and in social systems. But no one has thought that the task of improving group relations is an easy one.

The social system

The sociologist correctly points out that all of us are confined within one or more social systems. While these systems have some variability, they are not infinitely plastic. Within each system there will be inevitable tensions between groups, due to economic rivalry, crowded housing or transportation facilities, or to traditions of conflict. To meet the strain, the society accords certain groups a superior, and other groups an inferior, position. Custom regulates the distribution of limited privileges, goods, and prestige. Vested interests are pivots within the system, and these in particular resist any attempts at basic change. Further, tradition earmarks certain groups as legitimate scapegoats within the system. Hostility is taken for granted. For example, minor ethnic riots may be tolerated as by-products of the existing strain. Chiefs of police may wink at ethnic gang fights, declaring them normal and natural "kid stuff." To be sure, if the disruption goes too far, the riot squad is called for, or reformers press for legislative relief of the excess tension. But this relief is only sufficient to restore the uneasy equilibrium. If relief went too far it also would destroy the system.

The point of view of the economic determinist is similar. He argues that all theories of individual causation are eyewash. A basic structure exists wherein people with higher socioeconomic status cannot, and will not, tolerate equality between laborers, immigrants, Negroes, and other needed peons, and themselves. Prejudice is merely an invention to justify economic self-interest. Until some drastic reform brings true industrial democracy, there can be no effective alteration in the basic social foundations upon which all prejudice rests.

You and I are not normally aware of the extent to which our behavior is constrained and regulated by such features of the social system. We ought not to expect a few detached hours of intercultural education to offset the total press of the environment. People who see a pro-tolerance film will view it as a specific episode and not allow it to threaten the foundations of the system they live in.

The theory holds further that one cannot change segregation, employment customs, or immigration without letting off a chain of effects that would cumulate to produce threatening fractures in the total structure. Each folkway is an ally of every other. If too strong an initial push is allowed it might lead to an acceleration of forces that would destroy the whole system, and therewith our sense of security. Such is the structural view of the sociologist.

The psychologist, too, it will be recalled, has a structural argument. A prejudiced attitude is not like a cinder in the eye that can be extracted without disturbing the integrity of the organism as a whole. On the contrary, prejudice is often so deeply embedded in character-structure that it cannot be changed unless the entire inner economy of the life is overhauled. Such embeddedness occurs whenever attitudes have "functional significance" for the organism. You cannot expect to change the part without changing the whole.

And it is never easy to remake the whole of a personality.

Some authors stress the interlocking dependence of both the personal and the social system. They say that one must attack an attitude with due regard to both kinds of systems, which, in combination, hold the attitude embedded in a structural matrix (cf. Vallance, 1951). Newcomb states the case as follows: "Attitudes tend to be persistent (relatively unchanged) when the individual continues to perceive objects in a more or less stable frame of reference" (1950, p. 233). A stable frame of reference may be anchored in the social environment. (All immigrants live on one side of the tracks, all native Americans on the other.) Or it may be an *inner* frame of reference (I am threatened by any alien). Or it may be both. This combined structural view would insist that a shift in the relevant frames of reference must precede change in attitude.

Critique. Whether sociological, psychological, or both, the structural point of view has great merit. It explains why piecemeal efforts are not more effective than they are. It tells us that our problem is stitched into the fabric of social living. It convinces us that the cinder-in-the-eye theory is too simple.

Yet, if we are not careful, the structural view may lead both to false psychology and to false pessimism. It really is not sensible to say that before we change personal attitudes we must change total structure; for in part, at least, the structure is the product of the attitudes of many single people. Change must begin somewhere. Indeed, according to the structural theory, it may start *anywhere,* for every system is to some extent altered by the change in any of its parts. A social or a psychological system is an equilibrium of forces, but it is an unstable equilibrium. The "American dilemma," for example, as Myrdal (1962) shows, is a case of such instability. All our official definitions of the social system call for equality, while many (not all) of the informal features of this system call for inequality. There is thus a state of "unstructuredness" in even our most structured systems. And while your personality or mine is certainly a system, can we say that it is impervious to change, or that alteration in the whole must *precede* alteration of parts? Such a view would be absurd.

Granted that America possesses a fairly stable class system wherein ethnic groups have an ascribed status, with prejudice as an accompaniment, still there are also in the American system factors that make for constant change. Americans, for example, seem to have great faith in the changeability of attitudes. The goliath of advertising in this country is erected on this faith; and we are equally confident in the power of education. Our system itself rejects the belief that "you can't change human nature." While this faith may not be entirely justified, the point is that the faith itself is a factor of prime importance. If everyone expects attitudes to change through education, publicity, therapy, then of course they are *more likely* to do so than if no one expects them to change. Our very gusto for change may bring it about, if anything can. A social system does not necessarily retard change; sometimes it encourages it.

Positive principles

We are not rejecting the structural argument, but rather pointing out that it cannot be used to justify total pessimism. It calls attention forcefully to limitations that exist, but does not deny that new horizons in human relationships are opening.

It is, for example, a perfectly sensible question to ask where, in order to alter social structure or personality structure, change may best begin. The following principles seem particularly germane.

1. Since the problem is many-sided, there can be no sovereign formula. The wisest thing to do is to attack all fronts simultaneously. If no single attack has large effect, yet many small attacks from many directions can have large cumulative results. They may even give the total system a push that will lead to accelerated change until a new and more agreeable equilibrium is attained.

2. Meliorism should be our guide. People who talk in terms of the ultimate assimilation of all minority groups into one ethnic stock are speaking of a distant Utopia. To be sure, there would be no minority-group problems in a homogeneous society, but it seems probable that in the United States our loss would be greater than our gain. In any case, it is certain that artificial attempts to hasten assimilation will not succeed. We shall improve human relations only by learning to live with racial and cultural pluralism for a long time to come.

3. It is reasonable to expect that our efforts will have some unsettling effects. The attack on a system always has. Thus a person who has been exposed to the intercultural education, to tolerance propaganda, to role-playing, may show greater inconsistency of behavior than before. But from the point of view of attitude change, this state of "unstructuredness" is a necessary stage. A wedge has been driven. While the individual may be more uncomfortable than before, he has at least a chance of recentering his outlook in a more tolerant manner. Investigation shows that people who are aware of, and ashamed of, their prejudices are well on the road to eliminating them (cf. G. W. Allport & Kramer, 1946).

4. Occasionally there may be a "boomerang effect." Efforts may serve only to stiffen opposition in defense of existing attitudes, or offer people unintended support for their hostile opinions (Hovland, *et al.*, 1949, pp. 46–50). Such evidence as we have indicates that this effect is relatively slight. It also is a question whether the effect may not be temporary, for any strategy sufficiently effective to arouse defensiveness may at the same time plant seeds of misgiving.

5. From what we know of mass media, it seems wise not to expect marked results from this method alone. Relatively few people are in the precise stage of "unstructuredness," and in precisely the right frame of mind, to admit the message. Further, it seems well, on the basis of existing evidence, to focus mass propaganda on specific issues rather than upon vague appeals that may not be understood.

6. The teaching and publishing of scientifically sound information concerning the history and characteristics of groups, and about the nature of prejudice, certainly does no harm. Yet it is not the panacea that many educators like to believe. The outpouring of information probably has three benign effects: (a) It sustains the confidence of minorities to see an effort being made to blanket prejudice with truth. (b) It encourages and reinforces tolerant people by integrating their attitudes with knowledge. (c) It tends to undermine

the rationalization of bigots. Belief in the biological inferiority of the Negro, for example, is wavering under the impact of scientific fact; racist doctrines today are on the defensive. Erroneous ideas, Spinoza observed, lead to passion —for they are so confused that no one can use them as a basis for realistic adjustment. Correct and adequate ideas, by contrast, pave the way for a true assessment of life's problems. While not everyone will admit correct ideas when they are offered, it is well to make them available.

7. Action is ordinarily better than mere information. Programs do well therefore to involve the individual in some project, perhaps a community self-survey or a neighborhood festival. When he *does* something, he *becomes* something. The deeper the acquaintance and the more realistic the contacts, the better the results.

By working in the community, for example, the individual may learn that neither his self-esteem nor his attachments are actually threatened by Negro neighbors. He may learn that his own security as a citizen is strengthened when social conditions improve. While preaching and exhortation may play a part in the process, the lesson will not be learned at the verbal level alone. It will be learned in muscle, nerve, and gland best through participation.

8. None of our commonly used methods is likely to work with bigots whose character structure is so inaccessible that it demands the exclusion of out-groups as a condition of life. Yet even for the rigid person there is left the possibility of individual therapy—an expensive method and one that is sure to be resisted; but in principle at least, we need not yet despair completely of the extreme case, especially if tackled young, perhaps in clinics of child guidance, or by wise teachers.

9. While there is no relevant research on the point, it seems likely that ridicule and humor help to prick the pomposity and irrational appeal of rabble-rousers. Laughter is a weapon against bigotry. It too often lies rusty while reformers grow unnecessarily solemn and heavy-handed.

10. Turning now to social programs (the social system), there is first of all considerable agreement that it is wiser to attack segregation and discrimination than to attack prejudice directly. For even if one dents the attitudes of the individual in isolation, he is still confronted by social norms that he cannot surmount. And until segregation is weakened, conditions will not exist that permit equal-status contacts in pursuit of common objectives.

11. It would seem intelligent to take advantage of the vulnerable points where social change is most likely to occur. As Saenger says, "Concentrate on the areas of least resistance." Gains in housing and economic opportunities are, on the whole, the easiest to achieve. Fortunately, it is these very gains that minorities most urgently desire.

12. Generally speaking, a *fait accompli* that fits in with our democratic creed is accepted with little more than an initial flurry of protest. Cities that introduce Negroes into public jobs find that the change soon ceases to attract attention. Sound legislation is similarly accepted. Official policies once established are hard to revoke. They set models that, once accepted, create habits and conditions favorable to their maintenance.

Administrators, more than they realize, have the power to establish desirable changes by executive order in industry, government, and schools. In 1848 a Negro applied for admission to Harvard College. There were loud protests. Edward Everett, then President, replied, "If this boy passes the examinations he will be admitted and, if the white students choose to withdraw, all the income of the college will be devoted to his education" (Frothingham, 1925, p. 299). Needless to say, no one withdrew, and the opposition quickly subsided. The College lost neither income nor prestige, though both at first seemed threatened. Clean-cut administrative decisions that brook no further argument are accepted when such decisions are in keeping with the voice of conscience.

13. The role of the militant reformer must not be forgotten. It is the noisy demands of crusading liberals that have been a decisive factor in many of the gains thus far made.

These conclusions represent some of the positive principles that derive from research and theory. They are not intended as a complete blueprint—such would be pretentious. The points represent rather certain wedges which if driven with skill might be expected to crack the crust of prejudice and discrimination.

Imperatives of intercultural education

Without prolonging our discussion of programs unduly, we wish to call attention once more to the role of the school. We do so partly because of the characteristic faith that Americans have in education, and partly because it is easier to install remedial programs in the school than in the home. School children comprise a vast captive audience; they study what is set before them. While school boards, principals, and teachers may resist the introduction of intercultural education, yet it is increasingly included in the curriculum.

Learning prejudice and learning tolerance are subtle and complex processes. The home is undoubtedly more important than the school. And the *atmosphere* of the home is as important, perhaps more important, than the parents' specific teaching concerning minority groups.

It is probably too much to expect teachers to offset the home environment, and yet, as the evaluative studies cited [see G. W. Allport, 1958. Ch. 30] show, a good deal can be accomplished. The school, like the church and the laws of the land, can set before the child a higher code than is learned at home, and may create a conscience and a healthful conflict even if the prejudiced teachings of the home are not entirely overcome.

As in the home, the atmosphere that surrounds the child at school is exceedingly important. If segregation of the sexes or races prevails, if authoritarianism and hierarchy dominate the system, the child cannot help but learn that power and status are the dominant factors in human relationships. If, on the other hand, the school system is democratic, if the teacher and child are each respected units, the lesson of respect for the person will easily register. As in society at large the *structure* of the pedagogical system will blanket, and may negate, the specific intercultural lessons taught (Brameld, 1946).

We have seen that instruction of the sort that involves the whole child in intercultural activities is probably more effective than merely verbal learning or exhortation. While information is likewise essential, facts stick best when embedded in the soil of interested activity.

Granted these points, the question remains as to what concrete lessons the child or adolescent should learn in the course of his school training. What should be the *content* of intercultural education? Here, as before, we cannot claim that all evidence is in. But we may suggest a few of the imperatives for intergroup education.

The age at which these lessons should be taught need not worry us. If taught in a simple fashion all the points can be made intelligible to younger children and, in a more fully developed way, they can be presented to older students in high school or college. In fact, at different levels of advancement, through "graded lessons," the same content can, and should, be offered year after year.

(1) *Meaning of race.* Various films, filmstrips, and pamphlets are available for school use; these present anthropological facts in as much detail as the child can absorb. The child should certainly learn the confusion that occurs between genetic and social definitions of race. For example, he should understand that many "colored" people are racially as much Caucasian as Negro, but that a caste definition obscures this biological fact. The misconceptions of racism in its various forms, and the psychology underlying racist myths, can be made clear to older children.

(2) *Customs and their significance in various ethnic groups.* Schools have traditionally taught this lesson, but in a dubious way. Modern exhibits and festivals give a more adequate impression, as do reports in the classroom from children who come from diverse ethnic backgrounds. Especially needed are sympathetic accounts of linguistic and religious backgrounds, with particular reference to the significance of religious holy days. Visits to places of worship in the community help anchor the lesson.

(3) *Nature of group differences.* Less easy to teach, but needed for the purpose of generalizing the two preceding lessons, is a sound understanding of the ways in which human groups differ and do not differ. It is here that fallacious stereotypes can be combatted, likewise "belief in essence." The fact that some differences are merely imaginary, some fall on overlapping normal curves, and some follow a *J*-curve distribution, can be taught in a simplified way. A child who understands the precise nature of group differences is less likely to form overbroad categories. The lesson should likewise include a restatement of the role of biological and social factors in producing these differences.

(4) *Nature of tabloid thinking.* Fairly early, children can be made critical of their own too simple categories. They can learn that Foreigner 1 is not the same as Foreigner 2. They can be shown how the law of linguistic precedence in learning creates dangers for them, particularly in the form of derogatory epithets such as "nigger" and "wop." Simple lessons in semantics and in elementary psychology are neither dull nor incomprehensible to children.

(5) *The scapegoating mechanism.* Even a seven-year-old can understand the displacement of guilt and aggression. As children grow older they can see the relevance of this principle to the persecution of minority groups throughout the ages.

(6) *Traits sometimes resulting from victimization.* The way in which ego defenses develop as a result of persecution is not hard to understand—though it is a delicate lesson to teach. The danger lies in creating a stereotype to the effect that *all* Jews are ambitious and aggressive in order to compensate for their handicaps; or that all Negroes are inclined to sullen hate or petty thieving.

The lesson can, however, be taught without primary reference to minority groups. It is essentially a lesson in mental hygiene. Through fiction, to start with, a youngster may learn of the compensations a handicapped (perhaps crippled) child develops. He may go from that point to a discussion of hypothetical cases in class. Through role-playing he may gain insight into the operation of ego defenses. By the age of fourteen the adolescent may be led to see that his own insecurity is due to his lack of firm ground: he is sometimes expected to act like a child, sometimes like an adult. He wants to be an adult, but the conduct of others makes him unsure of whether he belongs to the world of childhood or of adulthood. The teacher may point out that the predicament of the adolescent resembles the permanent uncertainty under which many minority groups have to live. Like adolescents, they sometimes show restlessness, tension, ego defensiveness, which occasionally lead to objectionable behavior. It is far better for the young person to learn the grounds for ego-defensive behavior than for him to be left with the idea that objectionable traits are inherent in certain groups of mankind.

(7) *Facts concerning discrimination and prejudice.* Pupils should not be kept ignorant of the blemishes of the society in which they live. They should know that the American Creed demands more equality than has been achieved. Children should know about the inequalities of housing and educational and job opportunities. They should know how Negroes and other minorities feel about their situation; what it is they especially resent; what hurts their feelings; and what elementary courtesies are in order. Films may be used in this connection, so too the "literature of protest," especially biographical accounts of young American Negroes, such as Richard Wright's *Black Boy.*

(8) *Multiple loyalties are possible.* Schools have always inculcated patriotism, but the terms of allegiance are often narrowly conceived The fact that loyalty to the nation requires loyalty to all subgroups within the nation is seldom pointed out. The institutional patriot, the superpatriotic nationalist, is more often than not a thoroughgoing bigot. The teaching of exclusive loyalty—whether to nation, school, fraternity, or family—is a method of instilling prejudice. The child may be brought up to see that loyalties are concentric, the larger may contain the smaller, with no exclusion implied.

62 The culture of poverty

OSCAR LEWIS

I want to take this opportunity to clear up some possible misunderstanding concerning the idea of a "culture of poverty." I would distinguish sharply between impoverishment and the culture of poverty. Not all people who are poor necessarily live in or develop a culture of poverty. For example, middle class people who become impoverished do not automatically become members of the culture of poverty, even though they may have to live in the slums for a while. Similarly, the Jews who lived in poverty in eastern Europe did not develop a culture of poverty because their tradition of literacy and their religion gave them a sense of identification with Jews all over the world. It gave them a sense of belonging to a community which was united by a common heritage and common religious beliefs.

In the introduction to *The Children of Sanchez* (Lewis, 1961), I listed approximately fifty traits which constitute what I call the culture of poverty. Although poverty is only one of the many traits which, in my judgment, go together, I have used it to name the total system because I consider it terribly important. However, the other traits, and especially the psychological and ideological ones, are also important and I should like to elaborate on this a bit.

The helpless and the homeless

The people in the culture of poverty have a strong feeling of marginality, of helplessness, of dependency, of not belonging. They are like aliens in their own country, convinced that the existing institutions do not serve their interests and needs. Along with this feeling of powerlessness is a widespread feeling of inferiority, of personal unworthiness. This is true of the slum dwellers of Mexico City, who do not constitute a distinct ethnic or racial group and do not suffer from racial discrimination. In the United States the culture of poverty of the Negroes has the additional disadvantage of racial discrimination.

People with a culture of poverty have very little sense of history. They are a marginal people who know only their own troubles, their own local conditions, their own neighborhood, their own way of life. Usually, they have neither the knowledge, the vision nor the ideology to see the similarities between their problems and those of others like themselves elsewhere in the world. In other words, they are not class conscious, although they are very sensitive indeed to status distinctions. When the poor become class conscious or members of trade union organizations, or when they adopt an internationalist outlook on the world they are, in my view, no longer part of the culture of poverty although they may still be desperately poor.

Is it all bad?

The idea of a culture of poverty that cuts across different societies enables us

Reprinted from **Trans-action**, 1963, 1, 17–19, with permission of the author and the publisher.

to see that many of the problems we think of as distinctively our own or distinctively Negro problems (or that of any other special racial or ethnic group), also exist in countries where there are no ethnic groups involved. It also suggests that the elimination of physical poverty as such may not be enough to eliminate the culture of poverty which is a whole way of life. One can speak readily about wiping out poverty; but to wipe out a culture or sub-culture is quite a different matter, for it raises the basic question of our respect for cultural differences.

Middle class people, and this certainly includes most social scientists, tend to concentrate on the negative aspects of the culture of poverty; they tend to have negative feelings about traits such as an emphasis on the present and a neglect of the future, or on concrete as against abstract orientations. I do not intend to idealize or romanticize the culture of poverty. As someone has said, "It is easier to praise poverty than to live it." However, we must not overlook some of the positive aspects that may flow from these traits. Living immersed in the present may develop a capacity for spontaneity, for the enjoyment of the sensual, the indulgence of impulse, which is too often blunted in our middle class future-oriented man. Perhaps it is this reality of the moment that middle class existentialist writers are so desperately trying to recapture, but which the culture of poverty experiences as a natural, everyday phenomenon. The frequent use of violence certainly provides a ready outlet for hostility, so that people in the culture of poverty suffer less from repression than does the middle class.

In this connection, I should also like to take exception to the trend in some studies to identify the lower class almost exclusively with vice, crime and juvenile delinquency, as if most poor people were thieves, beggars, ruffians, murderers or prostitutes. Certainly, in my own experience in Mexico, I found most of the poor decent, upright, courageous and lovable human beings. I believe it was the novelist Fielding who wrote, "The sufferings of the poor are indeed less observed than their misdeeds."

It is interesting that much the same ambivalence in the evaluation of the poor is reflected in proverbs and in literature. Some see the poor as virtuous, upright, serene, independent, honest, secure, kind, simple and happy, while others see them as evil, mean, violent, sordid and criminal.

Most people in the United States find it difficult to think of poverty as a stable, persistent, ever present phenomenon, because our expanding economy and the specially favorable circumstances of our history have led to an optimism which makes us think that poverty is transitory. As a matter of fact, the culture of poverty in the United States is indeed of *relatively* limited scope; but as Michael Harrington (1963) and others show, it is probably more widespread than has been generally recognized.

Poverty here and abroad

In considering what can be done about the culture of poverty, we must make a sharp distinction between those countries in which it involves a relatively small segment of the population, and those in which it constitutes a very large section. Obviously, the solutions will have to differ in these two areas.

In the United States, the major solution proposed by planners and social workers for dealing with what are called "multiple problem families," the "undeserving poor," and the "hard core of poverty," is slowly to raise their level of living and eventually incorporate them into the middle class. And, wherever possible, there is some reliance upon psychiatric treatment in an effort to imbue these "shiftless, lazy, unambitious people" with the higher middle class aspirations.

In the undeveloped countries, where great masses of people share in the culture of poverty, I doubt that social work solutions are feasible. Nor can psychiatrists begin to cope with the magnitude of the problem. They have all they can do to deal with the growing middle class.

In the United States, delinquency, vice and violence represent the major threats to the middle class from the culture of poverty. In our country there is no threat of revolution. In the less developed countries of the world, however, the people who live in the culture of poverty may one day become organized into political movements that seek fundamental revolutionary changes and that is one reason why their existence poses terribly urgent problems.

If my brief outline of the basic psychological aspects of the culture of poverty is essentially sound, then it may be more important to offer the poor of the world's countries a genuinely revolutionary ideology rather than the promise of material goods or a quick rise in the standards of living.

It is conceivable that some countries can eliminate the culture of poverty (at least in the early stages of their industrial revolution) without at first eliminating impoverishment, by changing the value systems and attitudes of the people so they no longer feel helpless and homeless—so they begin to feel that they are living in their own country, with their institutions, their government and their leadership.

63 Superordinate goals in the reduction of intergroup conflict

MUZAFER SHERIF

In the past, measures to combat the problems of intergroup conflicts, proposed by social scientists as well as by such people as administrators, policy-makers, municipal officials, and educators, have included the following: introduction of legal sanctions; creation of opportunities for social and other contacts among members of conflicting groups; dissemination of correct information to break down false prejudices and unfavorable stereotypes; appeals to the moral ideals of fair play and brotherhood; and even the introduction of rigorous physical activity to produce catharsis by releasing pent-up frustrations and aggressive complexes in the unconscious. Other measures proposed include the encouragement of co-operative habits in one's own community, and bringing together in the cozy atmosphere of a meeting room the leaders of antagonistic groups.

Many of these measures may have some value in the reduction of intergroup conflicts, but, to date, very few generalizations have been established concerning the circumstances and kinds of intergroup conflict in which these measures are effective. Today measures are applied in a somewhat trial-and-error fashion. Finding measures that have wide validity in practice can come only through clarification of the nature of intergroup conflict and analysis of the factors conducive to harmony and conflict between groups under given conditions.

The task of defining and analyzing the nature of the problem was undertaken in a previous publication (Sherif & Sherif, 1953). One of our major statements was the effectiveness of superordinate goals for the reduction of intergroup conflict. "Superordinate goals" we defined as goals which are compelling and highly appealing to members of two or more groups in conflict but which cannot be attained by the resources and energies of the groups separately. In effect, they are goals attained only when groups pull together.

Intergroup relations and the behavior of group members

Not every friendly or unfriendly act toward another person is related to the group membership of the individuals involved. Accordingly, we must select those actions relevant to relations between groups.

Let us start by defining the main concepts involved. Obviously, we must begin with an adequate conception of the key term—"group." A group is a social unit (1) which consists of a number of individuals who, at a given time, stand in more or less definite interdependent status and role relationships

Reprinted from the **American Journal of Sociology,** 1958, 63, 349–58, with permission of the author and the University of Chicago Press.

with one another and (2) which explicitly or implicitly possesses a set of values or norms regulating the behavior of individual members, at least in matters of consequence to the group. Thus, shared attitudes, sentiments, aspirations, and goals are related to and implicit in the common values or norms of the group.

The term "intergroup relations" refers to the relations between two or more groups and their respective members. In the present context we are interested in the acts that occur when individuals belonging to one group interact, collectively or individually, with members of another in terms of their group identification. The appropriate frame of reference for studying such behavior includes the functional relations between the groups. Intergroup situations are not voids. Though not independent of relationships within the groups in question, *the characteristics of relations between groups cannot be deduced or extrapolated from the properties of ingroup relations.*

Prevalent modes of behavior within a group, in the way of co-operativeness and solidarity or competitiveness and rivalry among members, need not be typical of actions involving members of an out-group. At times, hostility toward out-groups may be proportional to the degree of solidarity within the group. In this connection, results presented by the British statistician L. F. Richardson are instructive. His analysis of the number of wars conducted by the major nations of the world from 1850 to 1941 reveals that Great Britain heads the list with twenty wars—more than the Japanese (nine wars), the Germans (eight wars), or the United States (seven wars). We think that this significantly larger number of wars engaged in by a leading European democracy has more to do with the intergroup relations involved in perpetuating a far-flung empire than with dominant practices at home or with personal frustrations of individual Britishers who participated in these wars.

In recent years relationships between groups have sometimes been explained through analysis of individuals who have endured unusual degrees of frustration or extensive authoritarian treatment in their life-histories. There is good reason to believe that some people growing up in unfortunate life-circumstances may become more intense in their prejudices and hostilities. But at best these cases explain the intensity of behavior in a given dimension. In a conflict between two groups—a strike or a war—opinion within the groups is crystallized, slogans are formulated, and effective measures are organized by members recognized as the most responsible in their respective groups. The prejudice scale and the slogans are not usually imposed on the others by the deviate or neurotic members. Such individuals ordinarily exhibit their intense reactions within the reference scales of prejudice, hostility, or sacrifice established in their respective settings.

The behavior by members of any group toward another group is not primarily a problem of deviate behavior. If it were, intergroup behavior would not be the issue of vital consequence that it is today. The crux of the problem is the participation by group members in established practices and social-distance norms of their group and their response to new trends developing in relationships between their own group and other groups.

On the basis of his UNESCO studies in India, Gardner Murphy concludes that to be a good Hindu or a good Moslem implies belief in all the nasty qualities and practices attributed by one's own group—Hindu or Moslem—to the other. Good members remain deaf and dumb to favorable information concerning the adversary. Social contacts and avenues of communication serve, on the whole, as vehicles for further conflicts not merely for neurotic individuals but for the bulk of the membership.

In the process of interaction among members, an in-group is endowed with positive qualities which tend to be praiseworthy, self-justifying, and even self-glorifying. Individual members tend to develop these qualities through internalizing group norms and through example by high-status members, verbal dicta, and a set of correctives standardized to deal with cases of deviation. Hence, possession of these qualities, which reflect their particular brand of ethnocentrism, is not essentially a problem of deviation or personal frustration. It is a question of participation in in-group values and trends by good members, who constitute the majority of membership as long as group solidarity and morale are maintained.

To out-groups and their respective members are attributed positive or negative qualities, depending on the nature of functional relations between the groups in question. The character of functional relations between groups may result from actual harmony and interdependence or from actual incompatibility between the aspirations and directions of the groups. A number of field studies and experiments indicate that, if the functional relations between groups are positive, favorable attitudes are formed toward the out-group. If the functional relations between groups are negative, they give rise to hostile attitudes and unfavorable stereotypes in relation to the out-group. Of course, in large group units the picture of the out-group and relations with it depend very heavily on communication, particularly from the mass media.

Examples of these processes are recurrent in studies of small groups. For example, when a gang "appropriates" certain blocks in a city, it is considered "indecent" and a violation of its "rights" for another group to carry on its feats in that area. Intrusion by another group is conducive to conflict, at times with grim consequences, as Thrasher showed over three decades ago.

When a workers' group declares a strike, existing group lines are drawn more sharply. Those who are not actually for the strike are regarded as against it. There is no creature more lowly than the man who works while the strike is on. The same type of behavior is found in management groups under similar circumstances.

In time, the adjectives attributed to out-groups take their places in the repertory of group norms. The lasting, derogatory stereotypes attributed to groups low on the social-distance scale are particular cases of group norms pertaining to out-groups.

As studies by Bogardus show, the social-distance scale of a group, once established, continues over generations, despite changes of constituent individuals, who can hardly be said to have prejudices because of the same severe personal frustrations or authoritarian treatment.

Literature on the formation of prejudice by growing children shows that it is not even necessary for the individual to have actual unfavorable experiences with out-groups to form attitudes of prejudice toward them. In the very process of becoming an in-group member, the intergroup delineations and corresponding norms prevailing in the group are internalized by the individual.

A research program

A program of research has been under way since 1948 to test experimentally some hypotheses derived from the literature of intergroup relations. The first large-scale intergroup experiment was carried out in 1949, the second in 1953, and the third in 1954. The conclusions reported here briefly are based on the 1949 and 1954 experiments and on a series of laboratory studies carried out as co-ordinate parts of the program.

The methodology, techniques, and criteria for subject selection in the experiments must be summarized here very briefly. The experiments were carried out in successive stages: (1) groups were formed experimentally; (2) tension and conflict were produced between these groups by introducing conditions conducive to competitive and reciprocally frustrating relations between them; and (3) the attempt was made toward reduction of the intergroup conflict. This stage of reducing tension through introduction of superordinate goals was attempted in the 1954 study on the basis of lessons learned in the two previous studies.

At every stage the subjects interacted in activities which appeared natural to them at a specially arranged camp site completely under our experimental control. They were not aware of the fact that their behavior was under observation. No observation or recording was made in the subjects' presence in a way likely to arouse the suspicion that they were being observed. There is empirical and experimental evidence contrary to the contention that individuals cease to be mindful when they know they are being observed and that their words are being recorded.

In order to insure validity of conclusions, results obtained through observational methods were cross-checked with results obtained through sociometric technique, stereotype rating of in-groups and out-groups, and through data obtained by techniques adapted from the laboratory. Unfortunately, these procedures cannot be elaborated here. The conclusions summarized briefly are based on results cross-checked by two or more techniques.

The production of groups, the production of conflict between them, and the reduction of conflict in successive stages were brought about through the introduction of problem situations that were real and could not be ignored by individuals in the situation. Special "lecture methods" or "discussion methods" were not used. For example, the problem of getting a meal through their own initiative and planning was introduced when participating individuals were hungry.

Facing a problem situation which is immediate and compelling and which embodies a goal that cannot be ignored, group members *do* initiate discussion and *do* plan and carry through these plans until the objective is achieved. In this process the discussion becomes *their* discussion, the plan *their* plan, the action *their* action. In this process discussion, planning, and action have their place, and, when occasion arises, lecture or information has its place, too. The sequence of these related activities need not be the same in all cases.

The subjects were selected by rigorous criteria. They were healthy, normal boys around the age of eleven and twelve, socially well adjusted in school and neighborhood, and academically successful. They came from a homogeneous sociocultural background and from settled, well-adjusted families of middle or lower-middle class and Protestant affiliations. No subject came from a broken home. The mean I.Q. was above average. The subjects were not personally acquainted with one another prior to the experiment. Thus, explanation of results on the basis of background differences, social maladjustment, undue childhood frustrations, or previous interpersonal relations was ruled out at the beginning by the criteria for selecting subjects.

The first stage of the experiments was designed to produce groups with distinct structure (organization) and a set of norms which could be confronted with intergroup problems. The method for producing groups from unacquainted individuals with similar background was to introduce problem situations in which the attainment of the goal depended on the co-ordinated activity of all individuals. After a series of such activities, definite group structures or organizations developed.

The results warrant the following conclusions for the stage of group formation: When individuals interact in a series of situations toward goals which appeal to all and which require that they co-ordinate their activities, group structures arise having hierarchical status arrangements and a set of norms regulating behavior in matters of consequence to the activities of the group.

Once we had groups that satisfied our definition of "group," relations between groups could be studied. Specified conditions conducive to friction or conflict between groups were introduced. This negative aspect was deliberately undertaken because the major problem in intergroup relations today is the reduction of existing intergroup frictions. (Increasingly, friendly relations between groups is not nearly so great an issue.) The factors conducive to intergroup conflict give us realistic leads for reducing conflict.

A series of situations was introduced in which one group could achieve its goal only at the expense of the other group—through a tournament of competitive events with desirable prizes for the winning group. The results of the stage of intergroup conflict supported our main hypotheses. During interaction between groups in experimentally introduced activities which were competitive and mutually frustrating, members of each group developed hostile attitudes and highly unfavorable stereotypes toward the other group and its members. In fact, attitudes of social distance between the groups became so definite that they wanted to have nothing further to do with each other. This we take as a case of experimentally produced "social distance" in miniature. Conflict was manifested in derogatory name-calling and invectives, flare-ups of physical conflict, and raids on each other's cabins and territory. Over a period of time, negative stereotypes and unfavorable attitudes developed.

At the same time there was an increase in in-group solidarity and co-operativeness. This finding indicates that co-operation and democracy within groups do not necessarily lead to democracy and co-operation with out-groups, if the directions and interests of the groups are conflicting.

Increased solidarity forged in hostile encounters, in rallies from defeat, and in victories over the out-group is one instance of a more general finding: Intergroup relations, both conflicting and harmonious, *affected the nature of relations within the groups involved.* Altered relations between groups pro duced significant changes in the status arrangements *within* groups, in some instances resulting in shifts at the upper status levels or even a change in leadership. Always, consequential intergroup relations were reflected in new group values or norms which signified changes in practice, word, and deed within the group. Counterparts of this finding are not difficult to see in actual and consequential human relations. Probably many of our major preoccupations, anxieties, and activities in the past decade are incomprehensible without reference to the problems created by the prevailing "cold war" on an international scale.

Reduction of intergroup friction

A number of the measures proposed today for reducing intergroup friction could have been tried in this third stage. A few will be mentioned here, with a brief explanation of why they were discarded or were included in our experimental design.

1. Disseminating favorable information in regard to the out-group was not included. Information that is not related to the goals currently in focus in the activities of groups is relatively ineffective, as many studies on attitude change have shown.

2. In small groups it is possible to devise sufficiently attractive rewards to make individual achievement supreme. This may reduce tension between groups by splitting the membership on an "every-man-for-himself" basis. However, this measure has little relevance for actual intergroup tensions, which are in terms of group membership and group alignments.

3. The resolution of conflict through leaders alone was not utilized. Even when group leaders meet apart from their groups around a conference table, they cannot be considered independent of the dominant trends and prevailing attitudes of their membership. If a leader is too much out of step in his negotiations and agreements with outgroups, he will cease to be followed. It seemed more realistic, therefore, to study the influence of leadership within the framework of prevailing trends in the groups involved. Such results will give us leads concerning the conditions under which leadership can be effective in reducing intergroup tensions.

4. The "common-enemy" approach is effective in pulling two or more groups together against another group. This approach was utilized in the 1949 experiment as an expedient measure and yielded effective results. But bringing some groups together against others means larger and more devastating conflicts in the long run. For this reason, the measure was not used in the 1954 experiment.

5. Another measure, advanced both in theoretical and in practical work, centers around social contacts among members of antagonistic groups in activities which are pleasant in themselves. This measure was tried out in 1954 in the first phase of the integration stage.

6. As the second phase of the integration stage, we introduced a series of superordinate goals which necessitated co-operative interaction between groups.

The social contact situations consisted of activities which were satisfying in themselves—eating together in the same dining room, watching a movie in the same hall, or engaging in an entertainment in close physical proximity. These activities, which were satisfying to each group, but which did not involve a state of interdependence and co-operation for the attainment of goals, were not effective in reducing intergroup tension. On the contrary, such occasions of contact were utilized as opportunities to engage in name-calling and in abuse of each other to the point of physical manifestations of hostility.

The ineffective, even deleterious, results of intergroup contact without superordinate goals have implications for certain contemporary learning theories and for practice in intergroup relations. Contiguity in pleasant activities with members of an out-group does not necessarily lead to a pleasurable image of the out-group if relations between the groups are unfriendly. Intergroup contact without superordinate goals is not likely to produce lasting reduction of intergroup hostility. John Gunther, for instance, in his survey of contemporary Africa, concluded that, when the intergroup relationship is exploitation of one group by a "superior" group, intergroup contact inevitably breeds hostility and conflict.

Introduction of superordinate goals

After establishing the ineffectiveness, even the harm, in intergroup contacts which did not involve superordinate goals, we introduced a series of superordinate goals. Since the characteristics of the problem situations used as superordinate goals are implicit in the two main hypotheses for this stage, we shall present these hypotheses:

1. When groups in a state of conflict are brought into contact under conditions embodying superordinate goals, which are compelling but cannot be achieved by the efforts of one group alone, they will tend to co-operate toward the common goals.

2. Co-operation between groups, necessitated by a series of situations embodying superordinate goals, will have a cumulative effect in the direction of reducing existing conflict between groups.

The problem situations were varied in nature, but all had an essential feature in common—they involved goals that could not be attained by the efforts and energies of one group alone and thus created a state of interdependence between groups: combating a water shortage that affected all and could not help being "compelling"; securing a much-desired film, which could not be obtained by either group alone but required putting their resources together; putting into working shape, when everyone was hungry and the food was some distance away, the only means of transportation available to carry food.

The introduction of a series of such superordinate goals was indeed effective in reducing intergroup conflict: (1) when the groups in a state of friction interacted in conditions involving superordinate goals, they did co-operate in activities leading toward the common goal and (2) a series of joint activities leading toward superordinate goals had the cumulative effect of reducing the prevailing friction between groups and unfavorable stereotypes toward the out-group.

These major conclusions were reached on the basis of observational data and were confirmed by sociometric choices and stereotype ratings administered first during intergroup conflict and again after the introduction of a series of superordinate goals. Comparison of the sociometric choices during intergroup conflict and following the series of superordinate goals shows clearly the changed attitudes toward members of the out-group. Friendship preferences shifted from almost exclusive preference for in-group members toward increased inclusion of members from the "antagonists." Since the groups were still intact following co-operative efforts to gain superordinate goals, friends were found largely within one's group. However, choices of out-group members grew, in one group, from practically none during intergroup conflict to 23 per cent. Using chi square, this difference is significant ($P < .05$). In the other group, choices of the out-group increased to 36 per cent, and the difference is significant ($P < .001$). The findings confirm observations that the series of superordinate goals produced increasingly friendly associations and attitudes pertaining to out-group members.

Observations made after several superordinate goals were introduced showed a sharp decrease in the name-calling and derogation of the out-group common during intergroup friction and in the contact situations without superordinate goals. At the same time the blatant glorification and bragging about the in-group, observed during the period of conflict, diminished. These observations were confirmed by comparison of ratings of stereotypes (adjectives) the subjects had actually used in referring to their own group and the out-group during conflict with ratings made after the series of superordinate goals. Ratings of the out-group changed significantly from largely unfavorable ratings to largely favorable ratings. The proportions of the most unfavorable ratings found appropriate for the out-group—that is, the categorical verdicts that "all of them are stinkers" or ". . . smart alecks" or ". . . sneaky"—fell, in one group, from 21 per cent at the end of the friction stage to 1.5 per cent after interaction oriented toward superordinate goals. The corresponding reduction in these highly unfavorable verdicts by the other group was from 36.5 to 6 per cent. The over-all differences between the frequencies of stereotype rating made in relation to the out-group during intergroup conflict and following the series of superordinate goals are significant for both groups at the .001 level (using chi-square test).

Ratings of the in-group were not so exclusively favorable, in line with observed decreases in self-glorification. But the differences in ratings of the in-group were not statistically significant, as were the differences in rating of the out-group.

Our findings demonstrate the effectiveness of a series of superordinate goals in the reduction of intergroup conflict, hostility, and their by-products. They also have implications for other measures proposed for reducing intergroup tensions.

It is true that lines of communication between groups must be opened before prevailing hostility can be reduced. But, if contact between hostile groups takes place without superordinate goals, the communication channels serve as media for further accusations and recriminations. When contact situations involve superordinate goals, communication is utilized in the direction of reducing conflict in order to attain the common goals.

Favorable information about a disliked out-group tends to be ignored, rejected, or reinterpreted to fit prevailing stereotypes. But, when groups are pulling together toward superordinate goals, true and even favorable information about the out-group is seen in a new light. The probability of information being effective in eliminating unfavorable stereotypes is enormously enhanced.

When groups co-operate in the attainment of superordinate goals, leaders are in a position to take bolder steps toward bringing about understanding and harmonious relations. When groups are directed toward incompatible goals, genuine moves by a leader to reduce intergroup tension may be seen by the membership as out of step and ill advised. The leader may be subjected to severe criticism and even loss of faith and status in his own group. When compelling superordinate goals are introduced, the leader can make moves to further co-operative efforts, and his decisions receive support from other group members.

In short, various measures suggested for the reduction of intergroup conflict —disseminating information, increasing social contact, conferences of leaders—acquire new significance and effectiveness when they become part and parcel of interaction processes between groups oriented toward superordinate goals which have real and compelling value for all groups concerned.

64 The mirror image in Soviet-American relations

URIE BRONFENBRENNER

I should explain by way of introduction that I was in the Soviet Union during the summer of 1960, about a month after the U2 incident. The primary purpose of my trip was to become acquainted with scientific developments in my field, which is social psychology. But in addition to visting laboratories at universities and institutes, I wanted also to become acquainted with *living* social psychology—the Soviet people themselves. It was my good fortune to be able to speak Russian. I was traveling with a tourist visa on a new plan which permitted me to go about alone without a guide. Accordingly, after spending the first two or three days of my visit in a particular city at scientific centers, I would devote the remaining days to walking about the town and striking up conversations with people in public conveyances, parks, stores, restaurants, or just on the street. Since foreigners are a curiosity, and I was obviously a for-

Reprinted from the **Journal of Social Issues,** 1961, 17, 45–56, with permission of the author and the Society for the Psychological Study of Social Issues.

eigner (though, I quickly learned, not obviously an American), people were eager to talk. But I also went out of my way to strike up conversations with people who weren't taking the initiative —with fellow passengers who were remaining silent, with strollers in the park, with children and old people. Or I would enter a restaurant deciding in advance to sit at the third table on the left with whoever should turn out to be there. (In Soviet restaurants it is not uncommon to share a table with strangers.)

These conversations convinced me that the great majority of Russians feel a genuine pride in the accomplishments of their system and a conviction that communism is the way of the future not only for themselves but for the rest of the world as well. For several reasons my Soviet journey was a deeply disturbing experience. But what frightened me was not so much the facts of Soviet reality as the discrepancy between the real and the perceived. At first I was troubled only by the strange irrationality of the Soviet view of the world—especially their gross distortion of American society and American foreign policy as I knew them to be. But then, gradually, there came an even more disquieting awareness—an awareness which I resisted and still resist. Slowly and painfully, it forced itself upon me that *the Russian's distorted picture of us was curiously similar to our view of them—a mirror image*. But of course our image was real. Or could it be that our views too were distorted and irrational—a mirror image in a twisted glass?

It was—and is—a frightening prospect. For if such reciprocal distortion exists, it is a psychological phenomenon without parallel in the gravity of its consequences. For this reason, the possibility deserves serious consideration.

The mirror image magnified

Let us then briefly examine the common features in the American and Soviet view of each other's societies. For the Russian's image I drew mainly not on official government pronouncements but on what was said to me by Soviet citizens in the course of our conversations. Five major themes stand out.

1. *They* are the aggressors.

The American view: Russia is the warmonger bent on imposing its system on the rest of the world. Witness Czechoslovakia, Berlin, Hungary, and now Cuba and the Congo. The Soviet Union consistently blocks Western proposals for disarmament by refusing necessary inspection controls.

The Soviet view: America is the warmonger bent on imposing its power on the rest of the world and on the Soviet Union itself. Witness American intervention in 1918, Western encirclement after World War II with American troops and bases on every border of the USSR (West Germany, Norway, Turkey, Korea, Japan), intransigence over proposals to make Berlin a free city, intervention in Korea, Taiwan, Lebanon, Guatemala, Cuba. America has repeatedly rejected Soviet disarmament proposals while demanding the right to inspect within Soviet territory—finally attempting to take the right by force through deep penetration of Soviet air space.

2. Their government exploits and deludes the people.

The American view: Convinced communists, who form but a small proportion of Russia's population, control the government and exploit the society and its resources in their own interest. To justify their power and expansionist policies they have to perpetuate a war atmosphere and a fear of Western aggression. Russian elections are a travesty since only one party appears on the ballot. The Russian people are kept from knowing the truth through a controlled radio and press and conformity is insured through stringent economic and political sanctions against deviant individuals or groups.

The Soviet view: A capitalistic-militaristic clique controls the American government, the nation's economic resources, and its media of communication. This group exploits the society and its resources. It is in their economic and political interest to maintain a war atmosphere and engage in militaristic expansion. Voting in America is a farce since candidates for both parties are selected by the same powerful interests leaving nothing to chose between. The American people are kept from knowing the truth through a controlled radio and press and through economic and political sanctions against liberal elements.

3. *The mass of their people are not really sympathetic to the regime.*

The American view: In spite of the propaganda, the Soviet people are not really behind their government. Their praise of the government and the party is largely perfunctory, a necessary concession for getting along. They do not trust their own sources of information and have learned to read between the lines. Most of them would prefer to live under our system of government if they only could.

The Soviet view: Unlike their government, the bulk of the American people want peace. Thus, the majority disapproved of American aggression in Korea, the support of Chiang Kai Shek, and, above all, of the sending of U2. But of course they could do nothing since their welfare is completely under the control of the ruling financier-militaristic clique. If the American people were allowed to become acquainted with communism as it exists in the USSR, they would unquestionably choose it as their form of government. ("You Americans are such a nice people; it is a pity you have such a terrible government.")

4. *They* cannot be trusted.

The American view: The Soviets do not keep promises and they do not mean what they say. Thus while they claim to have discontinued all nuclear testing, they are probably carrying out secret underground explosions in order to gain an advantage over us. Their talk of peace is but a propaganda maneuver. Everything they do is to be viewed with suspicion since it is all part of a single coordinated scheme to further aggressive communist aims.

The Soviet view: The Americans do not keep promises and they do not mean what they say. Thus they insist on inspection only so that they can look at Soviet defenses; they have no real intention of disarming. Everything the Americans do is to be viewed with suspicion (e.g., they take advantage of Soviet hospitality by sending in spies as tourists).

5. *Their* policy verges on madness.

The American view: Soviet demands on such crucial problems as disarmament, Berlin, and unification are completely unrealistic. Disarmament without adequate inspection is meaningless, a "free Berlin" would be equivalent to a Soviet Berlin, and a united Germany without free elections is an impossibility. In pursuit of their irresponsible policies the Soviets do not hesitate to run the risk of war itself. Thus it is only due to the restraint and coordinated action of the Western alliance that Soviet provocations over Berlin did not precipitate World War III.

The Soviet view: The American position on such crucial problems as disarmament, East Germany, and China is completely unrealistic. They demand to know our secrets before they disarm; in Germany they insist on a policy which risks the resurgence of a fascist Reich; and as for China, they try to act as if it did not exist while at the same time supporting an aggressive puppet regime just off the Chinese mainland. And in pursuit of their irresponsible policies, the Americans do not hesitate to run the risk of war itself. Were it not for Soviet prudence and restraint, the sending of U2 deep into Russian territory could easily have precipitated World War III.

It is easy to recognize the gross distortions in the Soviet views summarized above. But is our own outlook completely realistic? Are we correct, for example, in thinking that the mass of the Soviet people would really prefer our way of life and are unenthusiastic about their own? Certainly the tone and tenor of my conversations with Soviet citizens hardly support this belief.

But, you may ask, why it is that other Western observers do not report the enthusiasm and commitment which I encountered?

I asked this very question of newspaper men and embassy officials in Moscow. Their answers were revealing. Thus one reporter replied somewhat dryly, "Sure, I know, but when a communist acts like a communist, it isn't news. If I want to be sure that it will be printed back home, I have to write about what's wrong with the system, not its successes." Others voiced an opinion expressed most clearly by representatives at our embassy. When I reported to them the gist of my Soviet conversations, they were grateful but skeptical: "Professor, you underestimate the effect of the police state. When these people talk to a stranger, especially an American, they *have* to say the right thing."

The argument is persuasive, and comforting to hear. But perhaps these very features should arouse our critical judgment. Indeed, it is instructive to view this argument against the background of its predecessor voiced by the newspaperman. To put it bluntly, what he was saying was that he could be sure of getting published only the material that the *American people wanted to hear*. But notice that the second argument also fulfills this objective, and it does so in a much more satisfactory and sophisticated way. The realization that "Soviet citizens *have* to say the right thing" enables the Western observer not only to discount most of what he hears, but even to interpret it as evidence in direct support of the West's accepted picture of the Soviet Union as a police state.

It should be clear that I am in no sense here suggesting that Western reporters and embassy officials deliberately misrepresent what they know to be the facts. Rather I am but calling attention to the operation, in a specific and critical context, of a phenomenon well known to psychologists—the tendency to assimilate new perceptions to old, and unconsciously to distort what one sees in such a way as to minimize a clash with previous expectations. In recent years, a number of leading social psychologists, notably Heider (1958), Festinger (1957), and Osgood (1960), have emphasized that this "strain toward consistency" is especially powerful in the sphere of social relations—that is, in our perceptions of the motives, attitudes, and actions of other persons or groups. Specifically, we strive to keep our views of other human beings compatible with each other. In the face of complex social reality, such consistency is typically accomplished by obliterating distinctions and organizing the world in terms of artificially-simplified frames of reference. One of the simplest of these, and hence one of the most inviting, is the dichotomy of good and bad. Hence we often perceive others, be they individuals, groups, or even whole societies, as simply "good" or "bad." Once this fateful decision is made, the rest is easy, for the "good" person or group can have only desirable social characteristics and the "bad" can have only reprehensible traits. And once such evaluative stability of social perception is established, it is extremely difficult to alter. Contradictory stimuli arouse only anxiety and resistance. When confronted with a desirable characteristic of something already known to be "bad," the observer will either just not "see" it, or will reorganize his perception of it so that it can be perceived as "bad." Finally, this tendency to regress to simple categories of perception is especially strong under conditions of emotional stress and external threat. Witness our readiness in times of war to exalt the virtues of our own side and to see the enemy as thoroughly evil.

Still one other social psychological phenomenon has direct relevance for the present discussion. I refer to a process demonstrated most dramatically and comprehensively in the experiments of Solomon Asch (1956), and known thereby as the "Asch phenomenon." In these experiments, the subject finds himself in a group of six or eight of his peers all of whom are asked to make comparative judgments of certain stimuli presented to them, for example, identifying the longer of two lines. At first the task seems simple enough; the subject hears others make their judgments and then makes his own. In the beginning he is usually in agreement, but then gradually he notices that more and more often his judgments differ from those of the rest of the group. Actually, the experiment is rigged. All the other group members have been instructed to give false responses on a predetermined schedule. In any event, the effect on our subject is dramatic. At first he is puzzled, then upset. Soon he begins to have serious doubts about his own judgment, and in an appreciable number of cases, he begins to "see" the stimuli as they are described by his fellows.

What I am suggesting, of course, is that the Asch phenomenon operates even more forcefully outside the laboratory where the game of social perception is being played for keeps. *Specifically, I am proposing that the mechanisms here described contribute substantially to producing and maintaining serious distortions in the reciprocal images of the Soviet Union and the United States.*

My suggestion springs from more than abstract theoretical inference. I call attention to the possible operation of the Asch phenomenon in the Soviet-American context for a very concrete reason: I had the distressing experience of being its victim. While in the Soviet Union I deliberately sought to minimize association with other Westerners and to spend as much time as I could with Soviet citizens. This was not easy to do. It was no pleasant experience to hear one's own country severely criticized and to be constantly out-debated in the bargain. I looked forward to the next chance meeting with a fellow Westerner so that I could get much-needed moral support and enjoy an evening's invective at the expense of Intourist and the "worker's paradise." But though I occasionally yielded to temptation, for the most part I kept true to my resolve and spent many hours in a completely Soviet environment. It was difficult, but interesting. I liked many of the people I met. Some of them apparently liked me. Though mistaken, they were obviously sincere. They wanted me to agree with them. The days went on, and strange things began to happen. I remember picking up a Soviet newspaper which featured an account of American activities in the Near East. "Oh, what are they doing now!" I asked myself, and stopped short; for I had thought in terms of "they," and it was my own country. Or I would become aware that I had been nodding to the points being made by my Soviet companion where before I had always taken issue. In short, when all around me saw the world in one way, I too found myself wanting to believe and belong.

And once I crossed the Soviet border on my way home, the process began to reverse itself. The more I talked with fellow Westerners, especially fellow Americans, the more I began to doubt the validity of my original impressions. "What would you expect them to say to an American?" my friends would ask. "How do you know that the person talking to you was not a trained agitator?" "Did you ever catch sight of them following you?" I never did. Perhaps I was naive. But, then, recently I reread a letter written to a friend during the last week of my stay. "I feel it is important," it begins, "to try to write to you in detail while I am still in it, for just as I could never have conceived of what I am now experiencing, so, I suspect, it will seem unreal and intangible once I am back in the West." The rest of the letter, and others like it, contain the record of the experiences reported in this account.

In sum, I take my stand on the view that there *is* a mirror image in Soviet and American perceptions of each other and that this image represents serious distortions by *both* parties of realities on either side.

The mirror image projected

And if so, what then? Do not distortions have adaptive functions? Especially in war is it not psychologically necessary to see the enemy as thoroughly evil and to enhance one's self image? And are we not engaged in a war, albeit a cold war, with the Soviet Union?

But is not our hope to bring an end to the cold war and, above all, to avoid the holocaust of a hot one? And herein lies the terrible danger of the distorted mirror image, for *it is characteristic of such images that they are self-confirming;* that is, each party, often against its own wishes, is increasingly driven to behave in a manner which fulfills the expectations of the other. As revealed in social psychological studies, the mechanism is a simple one: if A expects B to be friendly and acts accordingly, B responds with friendly advances; these in turn evoke additional positive actions from A, and thus a benign circle is set in motion. Conversely, where A's anticipations of B are unfavorable, it is the vicious circle which develops at an accelerating pace. And as tensions rise, perceptions become more primitive and still further removed from reality. Seen from this perspective, the primary danger of the Soviet-American mirror image is that it impels each nation to act in a manner which confirms and enhances the fear of the other to the point that even deliberate efforts to reverse the process are reinterpreted as evidences of confirmation.

Manifestations of this mechanism in Soviet-American relations are not difficult to find. A case in point is our policy of restricting the travel of Soviet nationals in the United States by designating as "closed areas" localities that correspond as closely as possible to those initially selected by Soviet authorities as "'off limits" to Americans in the USSR. As was brought home to me in conversations with Soviet scientists who had visited the United States, one of the effects of this policy is to neutralize substantially any favorable impressions the visitor might otherwise get of American freedoms.

To take another example in a more consequential area: in a recent issue of *Atlantic Monthly* (August 1960), Dr. Hans Bethe, an American physicist who participated in negotiations at the Geneva Conference on nuclear testing, reports that our tendency to expect trickery from the Soviets led us into spending considerable time and energy to discover scientific loopholes in their proposals which could have permitted them to continue nuclear tests undetected. As a result, our scientists did succeed in finding a theoretical basis for questioning the effectiveness of the Soviet plan. It seems that if the Soviets could dig a hole big enough, they could detonate underground explosions without being detected. Says Dr. Bethe:

> I had the doubtful honor of presenting the theory of the big hole to the Russians in Geneva in November 1959. I felt deeply embarrassed in so doing, because it implied that we considered the Russians capable of cheating on a massive scale. I think they would have been quite justified if they had considered this an insult and walked out of the negotiations in disgust.
>
> The Russians seemed stunned by the theory of the big hole. In private, they took Americans to task for having spent the last year inventing methods to cheat on a nuclear test cessation agreement. Officially, they spent considerable effort in trying to disprove the theory of the big hole. This is not the reaction of a country that is bent on cheating.

But the most frightful potential consequence of the mirror image lies in the possibility that it may confirm itself out of existence. For if it is possible for either side to interpret concessions as signs of treachery, it should not be difficult to recognize an off-course satellite as a missile on its way. After all, we, or they, would be expecting it.

But it is only in the final catastrophe that the mirror image is impartial in its effects. Short of doomsday, we have even more to lose from the accelerating vicious circle than do the Soviets. Internally, the communist system can justify itself to the Soviet people far more easily in the face of external threat than in times of peace. And in the international arena, the more the United States becomes committed to massive retaliation and preventive intervention abroad the more difficult it becomes for uncommitted or even friendly nations to perceive a real difference in the foreign policies of East and West.

The last point calls attention to still another weakness of the stance of the West in the hall of twisted mirrors. In the progressive exchange of moves and countermoves, it is the Soviet Union that has taken the initiative. It is they who choose the time, the place, and the weapons; and pressed by the anxiety of being a move behind, we hasten to retaliate, almost invariably on the terms of their choosing. They act, and we react. The result is often a greater gain for them than for us.

Finally, we should take note of another debilitating effect of the mirror image; it not only preoccupies us with a false reality but blinds us to the true one. Thus so long as we remain victims of the reassuring belief that the Soviet Union can acquire adherents only by force, *we are likely to underestimate the positive appeal, especially to economically backward countries, of communism not only as an ideology but as a technology that seems to work.* The Soviets themselves are certainly not blind to the effectiveness of this appeal and use it to considerable advantage. But because of our own deprecatory image of the constructive potential of communist ideas and methods, and our lack of any missionary zeal of our own, we are slow even to retaliate in this peaceful sphere of competition between systems. Rather we continue to concentrate our efforts on bigger and better nuclear weapons. In our anxiety to be prepared for the hot war, we risk losing the cold war and finding ourselves a minority in a world dominated by communism ideologically and economically.

Breaking the mirror image

How can we avoid such awesome consequences? One step seems clearly indicated: we must do everything we can to break down the psychological barrier that prevents both us and the Russians from seeing each other and ourselves as we really are. If we can succeed in dispelling the Soviet Union's bogeyman picture of America, we stand to gain, for to the same degree that militant communism thrives in a context of external threat, it is weakened as this threat is reduced. And as the *raison d'être* for sacrifice, surveillance, and submission disappears there arises opportunity for the expression of such potential for liberalization as may still exist in Russian society.

But we rejoice too soon. Before we can hope to make any progress in changing the views of the Russians, we must learn to see reality ourselves. And here the first requirement is *exposure*. We must be willing and eager to look. And so long as the Soviets continue to encourage American tourism and exchange, such looking remains possible on a grand scale; estimates of the number of American tourists in the Soviet Union last summer range from 8000 to 15,000.

But mere looking is not enough. One must be able to see what is there. Many a traveler returns from the USSR with little beyond confirmations of his prior expectations of black or white, as the case may be. How can we enhance the possibility of seeing something else besides the expected when it is there? One possibility is to encourage travel on an even larger scale by persons who have a legitimate basis for interacting and finding common ground with the Russians on ideologically neutral matters—in science, culture, industry and commerce. In the course of such interactions it should be easier for us to become aware of the actual realities of Soviet life—both good and bad. And in selecting persons for such exposure, we should pick those who have status and influence back home so that their accounts cannot be readily dismissed as the irresponsible ramblings of incompetents and fellow travelers.

But, you may say, all this is obvious, and hardly requires any radical reorientation of American policy. True, but this is only the first step, and the next step may not be so easy. For, if we are truly serious about exposing ourselves to the realities of the Soviet society and its people, then we must be willing to go much further than we have in permitting and encouraging Soviet citizens to travel in the United States. We should, for example, revise our immigration and travel restrictions, even in the absence of reciprocal concessions by the USSR. Indeed, to compete with the Soviets in this sphere, we would have to provide interpreters, set up conferences with opposite numbers, make travel arrangements. It would be a major enterprise.

And would it be worth it, since the Soviet Government permits only a small number to come, and only convinced communists at that? But is it not precisely these from whom we have the most to learn and whom it is most important for us to influence?

And here we come face to face with the even more challenging problem of bringing about a more realistic view of America in the Soviet Union. Despite the formidable barriers, opportunities for communication do exist. One of my many surprises in the Soviet Union was the fact that over half of the people with whom I talked mentioned having heard Russian language broadcasts from the West. But along with this encouraging discovery came a disturbing one, for I learned that the Russians' distorted views were a product not only of their propaganda but, ironically, also our own. For, in line with the mirror image psychology, our broadcasts to Russia apparently present a distorted, one-sided picture of ourselves. Thus the comments I heard about our foreign language programs—even from persons favorably disposed toward the United States—were hardly reassuring. Our reporting, they said, was much less objective than that of the BBC. In our presentations, America was always good; the Soviet Union always bad. Beyond that, many of our broadcasts seemed to have as their objective not furthering understanding of America but fomenting revolution in the USSR. And we kept emphasizing our military might and our determination to further American interests around the world.

Since I heard no broadcasts myself, I am in no position to judge to what extent these descriptions may be exaggerated. But to the extent that they are true at all, they illustrate the reality of the mirror image phenomenon and the dangers it entails. *For so long as our foreign broadcasts, diplomatic pronouncements and overt acts in the international arena give one-sided emphasis to our nuclear prowess, our readiness for massive retaliation, and our determination to defend American interests wherever they may be, we only confirm the image of aggressive intransigence in the eyes not only of the communist world—but what is perhaps more important—the non-committed nations as well.*

Let me be absolutely clear about what I am saying. I am *not* arguing against military preparedness. On the contrary, it is essential that we be strong, and that the Russians know it. Nor do I deny that we are contributing a great deal in the interests of peace and of the welfare of other nations of the world. I believe we should do much more, but even this is not my main concern. What I wish to express most forcefully, and here I speak as a psychologist, is my fear that *we are being incredibly naive in the one-sided picture we present of ourselves to the outside world—naive to the point that we further the cause of our adversary and run the risk of driving the uncommitted world into the communist camp.* We accomplish this awesome irony by dramatizing our aggressive stance and underplaying and even bungling opportunities to present ourselves as a nation committed to peace, human values, and the economic and social welfare of the world. Passing over our tragic ineptness in the handling of the U2 incident, consider the more recent examples of the fanfare with which we announced our launching of a nuclear missile submarine. Proudly we beamed to the whole world the official statement that this single vessel could release more destruction than was represented by the combined explosive power of all the munitions fired by both sides in World War II. Surely we could do little more to confirm to the Russian people (and other nations as well) what the Soviet government has been telling them for years about American aggressiveness.

But our greatest error is one of omission. For we fail to recognize the importance of giving not just equal but even greater prominence to events expressing our concern for human welfare, justice, and peace. Consider, for example, the psychological impact abroad of a public statement by the President, also made with great fanfare, that the United States, in the interests of furthering peaceful relations between nations, has unilaterally waived all restrictions on the travel of Soviet and satellite nationals within our borders. Other possibilities come to mind at a more consequential level. We could be making a great deal more, for example, of the closing down of some of our overseas bases. Suppose that we were to announce to the world, again with all the magnificent hoop-la at our command, that in the interests of decreasing world tensions, we were not only abolishing these bases but, to preserve the economy of the host countries, were turning the installations over to the United Nations for use as centers for exploring peaceful uses of atomic energy, international universities, and the like.

Of course the Soviets would immediately denounce such measures as obvious propaganda gestures. But if we really did what we said, the Soviet leaders would know it. And what is more, the pressure would now be on the Soviet Union to match our initiative. And in this manner, the way is opened to transforming the vicious circle into a benign one.

Finally, there remains the most risky possibility of all: taking the Russians at their word in selected instances. This would have to be done with the greatest caution and with careful weighing of alternative consequences. Nevertheless, our analysis argues the wisdom of moving even in this dangerous direction. For if our theory of the distorted mirror image is correct, it follows that proposals that seem, *and actually are,* genuine concessions for one side, will not appear to be genuine concessions to the other, and vice versa. In short, meeting the other party half way will never be enough. The only way to break the impasse is for one party or the other to be willing to take what it views as a calculated risk.

But one thing should be clear. Dispelling the image of the Soviet bogeyman will not dispel the Soviet danger. On the contrary, disabused of our delusions, we should be able to see the danger more clearly. The competition and conflict with the communist world will continue. But at least the battle will be over differences that are real, and hence less likely to propel us toward mutual annihilation.

65 Some considerations relevant to national policy

MORTON DEUTSCH

Peace is currently maintained by a delicate balance of terror. The delicacy of the balance has justifiably alarmed many of those who are aware of the awesome destructive power of nuclear weapons. A common response of intellectuals, military strategists, and statesmen alike to this alarm has been to focus their attention upon the problem of making the balance steadier and more durable. The interest in "arms control" and in the concept of "stable deterrence" reflects this focus. Although efforts to reduce the military insecurities of East and West are obviously laudable, I believe that the current emphasis on methods of stabilizing the mutual terror should be viewed as, at best, dealing with stopgap measures. The "hostile peace" of stabilized mutual terror and of institutionalized mutual suspicion is intrinsically vulnerable to the social and psychological maladies that breed in an atmosphere of tension and suspicion. We must begin to find roads to a peace rooted in mutual interests and mutual respect.

Thus, the basic theme of my paper centers on the question: How do we move from a peace of mutual terror to a peace of mutual trust? This question proliferates into many other, related questions, e.g.: What should our military policy be; what steps can we take to strengthen existing elements of international order; how can mutual suspicions be reduced; how can we learn to communicate with one another more effectively; what non-violent techniques for resolving international conflicts can be developed; how can the problems of a disarmed world be coped with? These are some of the difficult questions to which the social sciences must address

Reprinted from the **Journal of Social Issues**, 1961, 17, 57–68, with permission of the author and the Society for the Psychological Study of Social Issues.

themselves if civilization is to survive. Here, I cannot hope to do more than deal with some limited aspects of our military and international policy. For a fuller discussion of these matters see Wright, Evan, and Deutsch (1962).

Let me indicate in a brief, summary fashion some of the basic psychological assumptions underlying my discussion of national policy in this paper: assumptions which come from theoretical and experimental research that I have been doing on interpersonal trust and suspicion and interpersonal bargaining (Deutsch, 1949; 1958; 1960a; 1960b; 1961; Deutsch and Krauss, 1960).

1. There are social situations which do not allow the possibility of "rational" behavior so long as the conditions for mutual trust do not exist. I believe our current international situation is a situation of this kind. A characteristic symptom of such "nonrational situations" is that any attempt on the part of any individual or nation to increase its own welfare or security (without regard to the security or welfare of others) is self-defeating. Thus, for example, if the Soviet Union attempts to increase its security by taking over Berlin, it will decrease its real security by increasing the likelihood of nuclear war. In such situations the only way that an individual or nation can avoid being trapped in a mutually reinforcing, self-defeating cycle is to attempt to change the situation so that a basis of mutual trust can develop.

2. Mutual trust is most likely to occur when people are positively oriented to each other's welfare—i.e., when each has a stake in the other's doing well rather than poorly. Unfortunately, the East and West, at present, appear to have a stake in each other's defects and difficulties rather than in each other's welfare. Thus the Communists gloat over our racial problems and our unemployment and we do likewise over their agricultural failures and their lack of civil liberties.

3. To induce a mutual welfare orientation in another, you have to demonstrate toward the other that your own behavior is based upon such a premise and that he cannot improve his welfare by violation of it.

4. Another person is likely to be convinced that your behavior is guided by a mutual welfare orientation (i.e., is more likely to be *trusting*) as a function of such factors as: the amount and frequency of the benefits he receives from your behavior; the confidence he has that your behavior has no other purpose than to provide mutual benefit. The other is most likely to perceive that your behavior is not guided by ulterior purpose if it does not result in disproportionate gain or loss for yourself and if your behavior is not seen to be determined by weakness, insanity, or inanity.

5. Another person is less likely to violate a mutual welfare orientation (i.e., is more likely to be *trustworthy*) if he can trust you; if he knows what you consider to be a violation; and if he knows that you will neither condone a violation nor use an apparent one as an excuse for destructive retaliation but will, instead, attempt to restore cooperation without allowing yourself to be, or remain disadvantaged, by it.

6. Mutual trust can occur even under circumstances where the parties involved are unconcerned with each other's welfare. The presence of third parties who are "neutral" or who are valued in the same way (either favorably or unfavorably) may enable the development of limited forms of mutual trust. Thus, neutral nations, if they

were sufficiently united and uncommitted, might facilitate communication or mediate conflicts between the East and West.

Military policy

I shall discuss briefly two concepts: military superiority and stable deterrence.

MILITARY SUPERIORITY

A public opinion poll would, undoubtedly, show that most Americans accept the traditional view that the security of the United States would be enhanced if we had a clear-cut military superiority over the Soviet Union. However, in the age of hydrogen bombs and missiles, the quest for military superiority is dangerous, provocative, and enhances the possibility of war. The basic axiom of military doctrine for *both* the United States and the Soviet Union in the missile age must be the recognition that *military actions should only be taken which increase the military security of both sides; military actions which give a military superiority to one side or the other should be avoided.* We should recognize that we have a positive interest in the other side's military security as well as in our own. The military forces of both sides should be viewed as having the common primary aim of preventing *either* side (one's own or the other side) from starting a deliberate or accidental war. Possibly, periodic meeting of military leaders from East and West might foster the mutual awareness of common concerns.

The assumption here, as I see it, is very simple: neither the United States nor the Soviet Union will allow itself to be intimidated by the other on a vital matter. If one side envisages that the other may achieve a temporary military superiority, it may be frightened into rash actions to prevent this from occurring. If one side feels it has achieved a temporary military superiority it may be emboldened to attempt to intimidate the other before the seesaw shifts its balance. We must recognize that just as military inferiority is dangerous, so is military "superiority"; we neither want to *tempt* nor *frighten* a potential enemy into military action.

STABLE DETERRENCE

The recognition that none of the participants in a nuclear war are likely to be victorious has led to the concept of *stable deterrence* through a balance of mutual terror. The essential idea is that if each side has a nuclear retaliatory capacity which has a high degree of invulnerability (i.e., a capacity to inflict "unacceptable damage" on the other side which is unlikely to be destroyed by a surprise attack), neither side would dare to initiate a nuclear war against the other.

The proponents of the theory of stable deterrence have made a very valuable analysis of the delicacy of the present balance of terror and have presented important suggestions for making the balance steadier. However, some of the sources of instability are inherent even in "stable deterrents," others inhere in the atmosphere of tension and suspicion of the present "hostile peace." These latter sources of instability lead even some proponents of the doctrine of stable deterrence to neglect the *mutuality* of interest of both sides (i.e., that the weapon systems of the Soviet Union as well as those of the United States be equally invulnerable to surprise attack) which is implicit in the doctrine; it leads others who are not fully aware of the implications of the theory of stable deterrence to support such unstabilizing viewpoints as the doctrine of "massive retaliation" and the doctrine of "instantaneous, automatic retaliation."

Below, we examine some of the assumptions involved in the concept of "stable deterrence" and indicate some of the instabilities which plague it. A stable balance of terror implies (at the minimum): (1) the *mutual invulnerability* of nuclear weapon systems; (2) the *mutual vulnerability* of civilian populations; (3) *rational, responsible control* over the use of the weapon systems including the ability to prevent accident, misunderstanding, insanity, or local decision as the basis for use of the weapons; (4) an *unnervous* self-confidence in the face of potential attack or of an undeliberate attack. Moreover, for the "balance of terror" to serve as a deterrent to an attack, it is implied that: (5) the threat of retaliation is *credible* to the potential attacker; (6) the threat is *unprovocative* (i.e., does not stimulate what it is attempting to deter) and is appropriate rather than unjust; (7) the potential attacker is neither masochistic (i.e., is not self-destructive) nor irrational (e.g., has grandiose delusions of invulnerability); (8) the attacker can be correctly identified. In addition, any doctrine which is concerned with stability should provide some compensating mechanism to restore stability when it is threatened or disrupted, e.g., to prevent a vicious spiral of mutual misunderstandings about whether a deliberate attack is taking place.

Let us now consider the implicit assumptions we have listed above to see how likely they are to be realized and to see if some assumptions don't inherently conflict with others.

1. *Mutual invulnerability of weapon systems.* As Herman Kahn (1960) has pointed out, if the present level of expenditure on research relating to military weapons continues, one can be reasonably certain that new, surprising weapons will be developed. Weapons which are now considered to be relatively invulnerable will become relatively vulnerable. Recognition of this possibility has led military theorists to the view that it would be dangerous to "place all their eggs in one basket"—i.e., to rely on one weapons system (e.g., the Polaris submarine) rather than upon a mixture of different weapons systems. However, without an effective agreement to limit and control weapons development, one may expect that, sooner or later, unpredictable research developments will make the balance of mutual terror teeter to one side or the other. Pessimistically, one may even say that an agreement which limits and controls weapons and their development, even if "fully-inspected," might not prevent an imbalance from developing unless the agreement expresses or produces the intention not to violate it. This is possible because the technology of inspection *evasion* could, under some circumstances, develop more rapidly than the technology of detecting incipient evasions.

2. *Mutual vulnerability of populations.* The "balance of terror" doctrine not only assumes that the nuclear weapons are mutually invulnerable but also that they are mutually effective. Anything which *one-sidedly* limits the destructiveness of the other side's weapons disturbs the balance. Thus, if one side begins to develop a large-scale civil defense program, the other side may feel

that it will lose its ability to deter an attack since its retaliation will not be so fearsome. Yet it is evident that there are strong pressures for a *unilateral* development of civil defense. Some of these pressures, oddly enough, originate in strong proponents of the doctrine of stable deterrence: they warn of the dangerous implications for world peace were the Soviet Union to initiate unilaterally a civil defense program against nuclear attack, but advocate that we do so unilaterally (Rand Corporation Study, 1958). Perhaps their recommendations are based upon the assumption that the Soviet Union has already initiated such a program; if so, this basis for our action should be clearly stated. My criticism here is not of defensive measures (whether they be anti-missile or civil defense) *per se* but rather of measures which are not *mutual* in orientation.

3. *Rational, responsible control of the decision to use the weapons.* One of the greatest sources of instability arises from the possibility that one side or the other will use nuclear weapons without having made a responsible decision to use them or will use them because of misinformation or misunderstanding concerning the other side. The fact is that the facilities for gathering and processing information, the communication network, the governmental decision-making apparatus, and the military command and control techniques required to make a quick decision to use nuclear weapons are extremely complex. It is very unlikely that any nation has the capabilities necessary to make such a decision, which would not, in all likelihood, be regretted after the fact. Moreover, there is always the possibility that the decision to use the bomb would be made by an irresponsible local unit—by a "mischievous" missile squad, a "grandiose" bomber crew, a "paranoid" submarine crew—which could carry out its own decision. As a social psychologist, I do not minimize the possibility of something which may be described as "collective madness" in times of acute international crisis. For reports of some studies of social behavior in situations of stress see Maccoby, Newcomb, and Hartley (1958).

4. *Nervousness, the need to respond quickly because of the fear that one will lose either the desire or ability to respond, enhances the likelihood that a response will be triggered off by an insufficient stimulus and, thus, makes for instability.* The proponents of "stable deterrence," of course, strongly oppose reliance on retaliatory forces which would be destroyed if not used quickly. Some of the "nervousness" in military circles arises, however, from the fear of loss of a desire to retaliate if deterrence has failed.

5. *For a military threat of retaliation to deter, it must, at the minimum, have some credibility.* The doctrine of massive nuclear retaliation in relation to non-nuclear aggressions lost much of its credibility after the Soviet Union acquired nuclear weapons systems. Of course, both the Soviet Union and the United States in contemplating the use of conventional military weapons also have to contemplate the dangerous possibility that a conventional war, out of its own dynamism, will mushroom into a nuclear war. However, neither we nor our Allies now believe that we would initiate an all-out nuclear war unless the facts showed we were in danger of all-out devastation ourselves. (See Kahn, 1960a.)

The implication of the foregoing is

that, in the present situation, the threat of massive retaliation is itself largely deterred by the counter-threat of massive retaliation: deterrence is deterred. In a similar manner, one can argue that if one side has launched a surprise attack but has failed to wipe out the other side's nuclear striking force and has not done intolerable damage to its civilian population, the attacked nation would be deterred from a massive retaliation directed at their opponent's civilian population because of fear of counter-retaliation directed at its own population. Possibly thoughts such as those advanced in the preceding sentence have led to the doctrine of instant, automatic massive retaliation in relation to any nuclear attack: a doctrine seriously advanced by high ranking military leaders to insure the "credibility" of the threat. It is not necessary to dwell upon the great moral and physical dangers of being "nervous" and over-ready to kill 100 million or more people. Apart from the dangerous provocation and lack of control implicit in the concept of immediate and automatic retaliation, if attack and counterattack by missiles are not separated in time, how could the survivors know who started the war?

If we take the theory of stable deterrence seriously, the doctrine of retaliatory response to a nuclear attack should be a doctrine calling for an unanxious, deliberate, delayed response which permits the nuclear aggressor to be identified unambiguously before the world and before its own people. Such a doctrine might encompass the threat of limited retaliation (of *no more* than an eye for an eye) to induce the people of the aggressor nation to overthrow their government and to surrender to the U.N. The threat of limited retaliation in relation to limited aggression, in addition to being more justifiable (i.e., less provocative) and less likely to result in unlimited catastrophe, is also probably more credible than the threat of massive retaliation in relation to limited destruction.

6. *An effective threat does not provoke the events which it is trying to deter.* Psychologists, sociologists, and psychiatrists, who have long been concerned with the prevention and control of antisocial behavior, would undoubtedly agree that one of the great dangers in the threat of force (in a "get tough" policy) is that it often incites the behavior it is attempting to prevent. There are several common reasons why threats provoke rather than deter: (a) the threat of using force is perceived to be an expression of an underlying intent to injure, rather than of self-defense (e.g., if a military leader boasts of his nation's ability to destroy an attacker, the statement is more likely to be seen as aggressive "rocket rattling" than as peaceful in purpose); (b) the threat of force is perceived to be an attempt unjustly to restrain actions which the threatened party feels entitled to engage in; (c) the threatened party has desire to be a "martyr" or to be punished; (d) the threatener is perceived to be bluffing; and (e) the threatener is perceived to be so irresponsible or incompetent that he can not control the use or non-use of his threatened force and, hence, the only way to control him is to destroy his capacity to threaten.

If we examine our recent and current policies to see whether they provoke or deter, we must conclude that some of our policies are not unprovocative. The placement of vulnerable nuclear weapons and missiles in Europe and the use of vulnerable overseas bases by bombers carrying nuclear weapons are highly provocative, because the weapons and bases would not survive a nuclear attack and, hence, could not be used as a retaliatory force: their only feasible use is to initiate attack. Brinkmanship, the reliance on the perceived possibility that limited conflicts (e.g., over Berlin and over Quemoy) might escalate to all-out nuclear war as a means of deterring limited war, and the search for information which would make the other side's retaliatory force vulnerable to surprise attack are two examples of provocative policy. To be sure, military provocativeness is not limited to one side.

7. *The theory of stable deterrence assumes that the potential attacker is rational in the economic sense that he will not attack if the expected gain resulting from the attack is smaller than the expected loss and if the expected loss from not attacking is less than that from attacking.* Moreover, it assumes that the potential retaliator has a reasonably accurate conception of the nature of the potential attacker's complex system of values and disvalues. Both assumptions seem to be rather dubious. Behavior, particularly in a time of high tension and crisis, is more likely to be determined by anxiety, stereotypes, self-esteem defensive maneuvers, and social conformity pressures than by simple rational estimates of "economic" gain and loss. Further, there is little evidence to suggest that the Russians really understand us (or themselves) or that we understand them (or ourselves); certainly the Voice of America's conception of the Soviets is rejected by the Soviet citizens as is *Pravda*'s conception of America rejected by us.

8. *The theory of stable deterrence is a two-country theory.* No one appears to have been able to think through what happens when nuclear weapons become an "N-country" problem. That is, the diffusion of nuclear weapons creates extremely complex problems for such concepts as stability and deterrence, problems which have not been solved. What would represent a stable distribution of nuclear weapons? Whom to deter?

The point of my discussion of the theory of stable deterrence is: the notion that invulnerable nuclear weapons, in themselves, produce *stability* is a dangerously misleading notion. They do not. Stability depends also on many considerations. Do not misunderstand me, however; my view is that if nuclear weapons are to be maintained, it is better that these weapons be invulnerable to surprise attack.

Let me summarize my discussion of military policy by stating that: the central point which we must grasp is that *there is no rational solution possible to our problems of security in a nonrational world except to make the world more rational.* We are in a type of international situation which is similar to that of a panicky crowd in a theatre when there is a fire. By attempting to achieve individual safety without regard for the safety of others, a person enhances the danger for all. In such a situation, the only reasonable course of action that will avert catastrophe is to take the initiative in *creating order* by persuasively suggesting rules and procedures which will permit an organized exit from the situation before the fire rages out of control.

Some suggestions for international policy

But how does one create order out of

potential chaos? How does one take the initiative in such an attempt? What rules and procedures should be developed? How can one be confident that the rules will be followed? These are difficult questions, but I venture to sketch an answer in the following paragraphs. It is self-evident that to facilitate the development of order and justice in international relations we must weaken the conditions which promote disorder and injustice and strengthen the conditions which promote the opposite state of affairs.

WEAKENING THE CONDITIONS LEADING TO DISORDER

The major conditions leading to disorder in the present international scene are:

1. *The revolution in military technology and the arms race.* To overcome the dangers inherent in this situation we need to: (a) develop a counter-revolution in disarmament technology; (b) negotiate agreements and take steps unilaterally which will decrease military instability by preventing the diffusion of nuclear weapons, by reducing fear of surprise attacks, and by reducing the likelihood of devastating incidents through accident, misunderstanding, or insanity; and (c) move toward disarmament theory and technology which permits a reliable disarmament. It seems to me unlikely that substantial disarmament will be feasible before a marked change has occurred in the international atmosphere. Consider only the unrealism of disarmament negotiations without the participation of Communist China.

2. *The widening gap in standards of living between the rich countries of Europe and North America and the poor countries of Asia, Africa, and Latin America, coupled with the increasing awareness of this difference and a rising "revolution of expectations."* It is obvious that the rich countries have to spend much more organized, research-tutored effort in the attempt to assist the people in the "underdeveloped" countries to acquire the educational, economic, and political skills and resources to become *independent*, thriving nations. I stress "independent" to emphasize the importance of not involving these underdeveloped nations in the cold war, the importance of allowing them to develop in ways which do not pressure them to be committed to one "bloc" or the other.

3. *The existence of two organized crusading ideologies, one centered in the U.S. and the other in the Soviet Union, which emphasize their antagonistic interests while neglecting their mutually cooperative interests.* I think it is the special duty of the social scientists in each "bloc" to expose the mythologies of each system, to accurately describe and analyze the complexities of each society, and to point out the similarities as well as the differences. Our analysis can not be content with such ideologically determined categories as "free enterprise system," "Communism," "Democratic," "totalitarian." This is not to deny that there are real and important differences between the United States and the Soviet Union, but we should attempt to understand these differences by objective analysis and description rather than by using political slogans as labels for very complex social systems. An objective analysis would see each society in an appropriate historical perspective in terms of the conditions which have given rise to and which maintain its particular institutions. In addition, such an analysis would point

to the future by understanding the implications of the revolutionary changes in education, communications, industrial technology, and standards of living occurring in each society (see, for example, Rostow, 1960). Moreover, such an analysis would avoid the mythological tendencies which lead to the identification of oneself with the "angels" and the others with the "devils." It is interesting to note that in the mythology of each nation, the other nation is essentially characterized as a social system in which "the many are involuntarily exploited by the few," "the mass of the people are not really sympathetic to the regime," "the government is dominated by groups who will attempt to impose their views upon the rest of the world, by force if necessary" (Bronfenbrenner, 1961).

STRENGTHENING THE ELEMENTS OF ORDER

International order presupposes rules which effectively regulate the interaction among nations. Until there is a world government with sufficient power to coerce compliance with international rules, it is evident that powerful governments will comply with rules, whether they are formalized in treaties or not, only so long as they perceive that compliance is more beneficial than detrimental to their enlightened over-all self-interests. Any system of rules which is supported primarily through voluntary compliance is likely to be initiated and maintained only if sufficient communication among the potential participants in the system of rules is also maintained so that: (a) they can recognize that they hold certain values in common; (b) rules can be articulated which fairly represent the shared values, without systematically disadvantaging a given participant; (c) they can be reasonably certain that compliance is mutual; and (d) they can agree on procedures to resolve the misunderstanding and disputes about compliance which will inevitably occur. The ability of a system of rules to weather disputes and short-run disadvantages to a given participant is a function of the strength of the internal commitment to the system of rules and of the strength of the co-operative bonds that exist among the participants.

I shall employ this rather condensed presentation of "the conditions of normative order" to make some proposals for our international policy.

1. *We must be unremitting in our attempt to communicate with members of the Communist bloc in such a way that the mutual recognition of our sharing many values in common (e.g., peace, technological advance, prosperity, science, health, education, cultural progress) is fostered.* We should neither *initiate nor reciprocate* barriers to communication. Clearly our policy of non-communication with Communist China makes no sense if we ever expect them to participate in arms control or disarmament agreements.

2. *To develop a system of rules, our course of conduct in international affairs should exemplify supra-nationalistic or universalistic values; it should constantly indicate our willingness to live up to the values that we expect other to adhere to.* We must give up the doctrine of "special privilege" and the "double standard" in judging our own conduct and that of the Communist nations. In my view, only a double standard would suggest that Communist China is aggressive toward us, but that we have not been so toward them; that the use

of military force to maintain the status-quo is peace-preserving while the use of force to change it is aggressive; that Communist bases near the United States are menacing while United States bases adjacent to the Soviet Union are peaceful, etc.

3. *To cut through the atmosphere of basic mistrust which exists, the United States should engage in a sustained policy of attempting to establish co-operative bonds with the Communist block.* I emphasize "sustained" to indicate that the policy should not be withdrawn in the face of initial rebuffs, which may be expected. Our policy should be to avoid the reciprocation of hostility and to always leave open the possibility of mutual cooperation despite prior rebuff. This means that we should have a positive interest in helping people in the Communist nations toward a higher standard of living and our trade policies should reflect this. It means that we should have an active interest in reducing their fears that they may be the victims of military aggression. It means, basically, that we should attempt to relate to them as though they were human. Relating to them as though they are devils, or some inhuman horde, will only help to confirm our nightmares.

The thesis of this paper has been that an orientation to the other's welfare, *as well as to one's own,* is a basic prerequisite to a peace sustained by mutual confidence rather than by mutual terror. "As well as to one's own welfare" is underlined here to emphasize that loss of self-identity is a poor foundation for cooperation in international as well as in interpersonal relations. Thriving societies that are coping successfully with their own internal problems have less ground for the fears and less need for the hostilities that interfere with the international cooperation necessary to construct a civilized world for the genus man.

Bibliography

Abelson, R. P. Modes of resolution of belief dilemmas. Paper read at Western Psychological Association, Monterey, California, April, 1958.

Abelson, R. P., & Rosenberg, M. J. Symbolic psycho-logic: A model of attitudinal cognition. *Behavioral Sci.*, 1958, *3*, 1–13.

Aberle, D. F. Culture and socialization. In F. L. K. Hsu (Ed.), *Psychological anthropology*. Homewood, Ill.: Dorsey, 1961. Pp. 381–400.

Ackerman, W. I. Teacher competence and pupil change. *Harvard Educ. Rev.*, 1954, *24*, 273–289.

Adorno, T. W., Frenkel-Brunswik, Else, Levinson, D. J., & Sanford, R. N. *The authoritarian personality*. New York: Harper, 1950.

Allen, L. A. *Management and organization*. New York: McGraw-Hill, 1958.

Allport, F. H. The influence of the group upon association and thought. *J. exp. Psychol.*, 1920, *3*, 159–182.

Allport, F. H. *Social psychology*. Boston: Houghton Mifflin, 1924.

Allport, F. H. The J-curve hypothesis of conforming behavior. *J. soc. Psychol.*, 1934, *5*, 141–183.

Allport, F. H. *Theories of perception and the concept of structure*. New York: Wiley, 1955.

Allport, F. H. The contemporary appraisal of an old problem. *Contemp. Psychol.*, 1961, *6*, 195–197.

Allport, F. H. A structuronomic conception of behavior: Individual and collective. I. Structural theory and the master problem of social psychology. *J. abnorm. soc. Psychol.*, 1962, *64*, 3–30.

Allport, G. W. Attitudes. In C. Murchison (Ed.), *A handbook of social psychology*. Worcester: Clark Univer. Press, 1935. Pp. 798–844.

Allport, G. W. *Personality, a psychological interpretation*. New York: Holt, 1937.

Allport, G. W. Effect. A secondary principle of learning. *Psychol. Rev.*, 1946, *53*, 335–347.

Allport, G. W. *Becoming: Basic considerations for a psychology of personality*. New Haven: Yale Univer. Press, 1954a.

Allport, G. W. *The nature of prejudice*. Cambridge, Mass.: Addison-Wesley, 1954b. (Paperback edition by Doubleday Anchor, 1958).

Allport, G. W. The open system in personality theory. *J. abnorm. soc. Psychol.*, 1960, *61*, 301–311.

Allport, G. W. *Pattern and growth in personality*. New York: Holt, Rinehart, & Winston, 1961.

Allport, G. W. Traits revisited. *Amer. Psychologist*, 1966, *21*, 1–10.

Allport, G. W., & Kramer, B. M. Some roots of prejudice. *J. Psychol.*, 1946, *22*, 9–39.

Allport, G. W., & Postman, L. J. *The psychology of rumor*. New York: Henry Holt, 1943.

Angelini, A. L. Um novo método para avaliar a motivacão humana. Doctoral dissertation, São Paulo, Brazil: Universidade de São Paulo, 1955.

Angyal, A. *Foundations for a science of personality*. New York: Commonwealth Fund, 1941.

Argyris, C. *Personality and organization*. New York: Harper, 1957.

Argyris, C. Being human and being organized. *Trans-action*, 1964a, *1*, 3–6.

Argyris, C. *Integrating the individual and the organization*. New York: Wiley, 1964b.

Asch, S. E. *Social psychology*. New York: Prentice-Hall, 1952.

Asch, S. E. Studies of independence and conformity: A minority of one against a unanimous majority. *Psychol. Monogr.*, 1956, *70*, No. 9 (Whole No. 416).

Asch, S. A perspective on social psychology. In S. Koch (Ed.), *Psychology: A study of a science*. Vol. 3. New York: McGraw-Hill, 1959. Pp. 363–384.

Ashby, W. R. *An introduction to cybernetics*. New York: Wiley, 1956.

Atkinson, J. W. (Ed.) *Motives in fantasy, action, and society*. Princeton, N.J.: Van Nostrand, 1958.

Atkinson, J. W., & Reitman, W. R. Performance as a function of motive strength and expectancy of goal-attainment. *J. abnorm. soc. Psychol.*, 1956, 53, 361–366.

Bach, G. R. Father-fantasies and father-typing in father-separated children. *Child Develpm.*, 1946, 17, 63–79.

Back, K. W. The exertion of influence through social communication. In L. Festinger, K. Back, S. Schachter, H. H. Kelley, & J. Thibaut (Eds.), *Theory and experiment in social communication.* Ann Arbor: Institute for Social Research, Univer. of Michigan, 1950. Pp. 21–36.

Back, K. W. Influence through social communication. *J. abnorm. soc. Psychol.*, 1951, 46, 9–23.

Back, K. W., Festinger, L., Hymovitch, B., Kelley, H. H., Schachter, S., & Thibaut, J. The methodological problems of studying rumor transmission. *Hum. Relat.*, 1950, 3, 307–313.

Bagby, J. A cross cultural study of perceptual predominance in binocular rivalry. *J. abnorm. soc. Psychol.*, 1957, 54, 331–334.

Bakke, E. W. Concept of the social organization. In M. Haire (Ed.), *Modern organization theory.* New York: Wiley, 1959. Pp. 60–61.

Baldwin, A. L. Socialization and the parent-child relationship. *Child Develpm.*, 1948, 19, 127–136.

Baldwin, A. L., Kalhorn, J., & Breese, F. H. The appraisal of parent behavior. *Psychol. Monogr.*, 1945, 58, No. 3 (Whole No. 268).

Baldwin, J. *Notes of a native son.* Boston: Beacon Press, 1955.

Ball, W. W. Calculating prodigies. In J. R. Newman (Ed.), *The world of mathematics.* New York: Simon & Schuster, 1956.

Bandura, A., & Walters, R. H. *Adolescent aggression.* New York: Ronald, 1959.

Bandura, A., & Walters, R. H. *Social learning and personality development.* New York: Holt, Rinehart, & Winston, 1963.

Barker, R. G. Ecology and motivation. In M. R. Jones (Ed.), *Nebraska symposium on motivation.* Lincoln: Univer. Nebraska Press, 1960. Pp. 1-49.

Barker, R. G. On the nature of the environment. *J. soc. Issues,* 1963a, 19, 17–38.

Barker, R. G. (Ed.) *The stream of behavior.* New York: Appleton-Century-Crofts, 1963b.

Barker, R. G., & Barker, Louise S. Behavior units for the comparative study of cultures. In B. Kaplan (Ed.), *Studying personality cross-culturally.* New York: Harper & Row, 1961. Pp. 457–476.

Barker, R. G., & Wright, H. F. *Midwest and its children.* New York: Harper & Row, 1955.

Barker, R. G., Wright, H. F., Barker, Louise S., & Schoggen, Maxine F. *Specimen records of American and English children.* Lawrence, Kansas: Univer. Kansas Press, 1961.

Bass, B. M. *Leadership, psychology, and organizational behavior.* New York: Harper, 1960.

Bastide, R. *Sociologie et psychanalyse.* Paris: Presses Univer. de France, 1950.

Bates, F. L. Position, role and status: A reformulation of concepts. *Soc. Forces,* 1956, 34, 313–321.

Bauer, R. A. Risk handling in drug adoption: The role of company preference. *Publ. Opin. Quart.*, 1961, 25, 546–559.

Bauer, R. A. The initiative of the audience. Paper read at New England Psychological Association, Boston, November, 1962.

Bauer, R. A. The obstinate audience: The influence process from the point of view of social communication. *Amer. Psychologist,* 1964, 19, 319–328.

Bauer, R. A., Pool, I. de Sola., & Dexter, L. A. *American business and public policy.* New York: Atherton Press, 1963.

Bavelas, A. Leadership: Man and function. *Admin. Sci. Quart.*, 1960, 4, 491–498.

Bayer, E. Beiträge zur Zweikomponententheorie des Hungers. *Zeitschrift für Psychol.*, 1929, 112, 1–54.

Beach, F. A. The neural basis of innate behavior. I. Effects of cortical lesions upon the maternal behavior pattern in the rat. *J. comp. Psychol.*, 1937, 24, 393–436.

Beach, F. A. Current concepts of play in animals. *Amer. Natur.*, 1945, 79, 523–541.

Beach, F. A. The descent of instinct. *Psychol. Rev.*, 1955, 62, 401–410.

Beer, S. *Cybernetics and management.* New York: Wiley, 1959.

Bell, G. B., & Hall, H. E. The relationship between leadership and socioempathy. *J. abnorm. soc. Psychol.*, 1954, 49, 156–157.

Beloff, Halla. Two forms of social conformity: Acquiescence and conventionality. *J. abnorm. soc. Psychol.*, 1958, *56*, 99–103.
Bender, I. E., & Hastorf, A. H. On measuring generalized empathic ability (social sensitivity). *J. abnorm. soc. Psychol.*, 1953, *48*, 503–506.
Bendix, R. *Max Weber: An intellectual portrait*. New York: Doubleday, 1960.
Bennis, W. G. Beyond bureaucracy. *Transaction*, 1965, *2*, 31–35.
Bennis, W. G. *Changing organizations*. New York: McGraw-Hill, 1966.
Berelson, B. What missing the newspaper means. In P. F. Lazarsfeld & F. N. Stanton (Eds.), *Communications research, 1948–1949*. New York: Harper, 1949. Pp. 111–129.
Berelson, B. R., Lazarsfeld, P. F., & McPhee, W. N. *Voting: A study of opinion formation in a presidential campaign*. Chicago: Univer. Chicago Press, 1954.
Berelson, B., & Salter, Patricia J. Majority and minority Americans: An analysis of magazine fiction. *Publ. Opin. Quart.*, 1946, *10*, 168–190.
Berlyne, D. E. *Conflict, arousal, and curiosity*. New York: McGraw-Hill, 1960.
Bexton, W. H., Heron, W., & Scott, T. H. Effects of decreased variation in the sensory environment. *Canad. J. Psychol.*, 1954, *8*, 70–76.
Binder, A. A statistical model for the process of visual recognition. *Psychol. Rev.*, 1955, *62*, 119–129.
Blake, R. R., & Mouton, Jane S. *The managerial grid*. Houston, Texas: Gulf Publishing, 1964.
Blau, P. *The dynamics of bureaucracy*. Chicago: Univer. Chicago Press, 1955.
Bliss, E. L., Sandberg, A. A., Nelson, D. H., & Eik-Nes, K. The normal levels of 17-hydrocorticosteroids in the peripheral blood of man. *J. clin. Invest.*, 1953, *32*, 9.
Block, B., & Trager, G. L. *Outline of linguistic analysis*. Baltimore: Waverly Press, 1942.
Bloomfield, L. *Language*. New York: Henry Holt, 1933.
Board, F., Persky, H., & Hamburg, D. A. Psychological stress and endocrine functions. *Psychosom. Med.*, 1956, *18*, 324-333.
Boder, D. P. The adjective-verb quotient: A contribution to the psychology of language. *Psychol. Rev.*, 1940, *3*, 310–343.
Bogardus, E. S. Changes in racial distances. *Int. J. Opin. Att. Res.*, 1947, *1*, 55–62.
Bogart, L. Adult talk about newspaper comics. *Amer. J. Sociol.*, 1955, *61*, 26–30.
Bossard, J. H. S. Residential propinquity as a factor in marriage selection. *Amer. J. Sociol.*, 1932, *38*, 219–224.
Boulding, K. E. General system theory—The skeleton of a science. *Mgmt. Sci.*, 1956, *2*, 197–208.
Bousfield, W. A. An empirical study of the production of affectively toned items. *J. gen. Psychol.*, 1944, *30*, 205–215.
Bousfield, W. A. The relationship between mood and the production of affectively toned associates. *J. gen. Psychol.*, 1950, *42*, 67–85.
Bousfield, W. A., & Barclay, W. D. The relationship between order and frequency of occurrence of restricted associative responses. *J. exp. Psychol.*, 1950, *40*, 643–647.
Bousfield, W. A., & Barry, H., Jr. Quantitative correlates of euphoria. *J. exp. Psychol.*, 1937, *21*, 218–222.
Bousfield, W. A., & Sedgwick, C. H. W. An analysis of sequences of restricted associative responses. *J. gen. Psychol.*, 1944, *30*, 149–165.
Bovard, E. W. Conformity to social norms and attraction to the group. *Science*, 1953, *118*, 598–599.
Bovard, E. W. The effects of social stimuli on the response to stress. *Psychol. Rev.*, 1959, *66*, 267–277.
Braithwaite, R. B. *Scientific explanation*. Cambridge, England: Cambridge Univer. Press, 1953.
Brameld, T. *Minority problems in the public schools*. New York: Harper, 1946.
Brech, E. F. L. *Organization*. London: Longmans, Green & Co., 1957.
Bredemeier, H. C., & Stephenson, R. M. *The analysis of social systems*. New York: Holt, Rinehart, & Winston, 1962.
Brehm, J. W. Post-decision changes in desirability of alternatives. *J. abnorm. soc. Psychol.*, 1956, *46*, 384–389.
Brehm, J. W., & Cohen, A. R. Re-evaluation of choice alternatives as a function of their number and qualitative similarity. *J. abnorm. soc. Psychol.*, 1959, *58*, 373–378.
Brehm, J. W., & Cohen, A. R. *Explorations in cognitive dissonance*. New York: Wiley, 1962.

Bridgman, P. W. *The way things are*. Cambridge, Mass.: Harvard Univer. Press, 1959.

Bronfenbrenner, U. Socialization and social class through time and space. In E. E. Maccoby, T. M. Newcomb, & E. L. Hartley (Eds.), *Readings in social psychology*. New York: Henry Holt, 1958. Pp. 400–425.

Bronfenbrenner, U. Some Freudian theories of identification and their derivatives. *Child Developm.*, 1960, *31*, 15–40.

Bronfenbrenner, U. Some familial antecedents of responsibility and leadership in adolescents. In L. Petrullo & B. M. Bass (Eds.), *Leadership and interpersonal behavior*. New York: Holt, Rinehart, and Winston, 1961a.

Bronfenbrenner, U. The changing American child—a speculative analysis. *J. soc. Issues*, 1961b, 17, 6–18.

Bronfenbrenner, U. The mirror image in Soviet-American relations: A social psychologist's report. *J. soc. Issues*, 1961c, 17, 45–56.

Bronson, W. C., Katten, E. S., & Livson, N. Patterns of authority and affection in two generations. *J. abnorm. soc. Psychol.*, 1959, 58, 143–152.

Brown, R. How shall a thing be called? *Psychol. Rev.*, 1958a, *65*, 14–22.

Brown, R. *Words and things*. Glencoe, Ill.: Free Press, 1958b.

Brown, R. Models of attitude change. In R. Brown, E. Galanter, E. H. Hess, & G. Mandler, *New directions in psychology*. New York: Holt, Rinehart & Winston, 1962.

Bruce, D. Effects of context upon the intelligibility of heard speech. In C. Cherry (Ed.), *Information theory*. London: Butterworths, 1956. Pp. 245–252.

Bruner, J. S., Goodnow, Jacqueline J., & Austin, G. A. *A study of thinking*. New York: Wiley, 1956.

Bruner, J. S. On perceptual readiness. *Psychol. Rev.*, 1957, *64*, 123–152.

Bruner, J. S., & Tagiuri, R. The perception of people. In G. Lindzey (Ed.), *Handbook of social psychology*. Vol. 2. Cambridge, Mass.: Addison-Wesley, 1954.

Bruner, J. S., Matter, J., & Papanek, M. L. Breadth of learning as a function of drive level and mechanization. *Psychol. Rev.*, 1955, 62, 1–10.

Brunswik, E. *Wahrnehmung und Gegenstandswelt*. Leipzig and Vienna: Deuticke, 1934.

Brunswik, E. The conceptual framework of psychology. In *International encyclopedia of unified science*. Vol. I. Chicago: Univer. of Chicago Press, 1952.

Brunswik, E. Representative design and probabilistic theory. *Psychol. Rev.*, 1955, 62, 193–217.

Brunswik, E. Scope and aspects of the cognitive problem. In H. Gruber, R. Jessor, & K. Hammond (Eds.), *Cognition: The Colorado Symposium*. Cambridge, Mass.: Harvard Univer. Press, 1957. Pp. 5–31.

Buchanan, W., & Cantril, H. *How nations see each other*. Urbana, Ill.: Univer. Ill. Press, 1953.

Bühler, K. Displeasure and pleasure in relation to activity. In M. L. Reymert (Ed.), *Feelings and emotions: The Wittenberg symposium*. Worcester, Mass.: Clark Univer. Press, 1928. Ch. 14, pp. 195–199.

Bühler, K. *Die Krise der Psychologie*. Jena: G. Fischer, 1929.

Burton, R. V., & Whiting, J. W. M. The absent father and cross-sex identity. *Merrill-Palmer Quart.*, 1961, 7, 85–95.

Butler, R. A. Discrimination learning by rhesus monkeys to visual exploration motivation. *J. comp. physiol. Psychol.*, 1953, 46, 95–98.

Cadwallader, M. L. The cybernetic analysis of change in complex social organizations. *Amer. J. Sociol.*, 1959, 60, 156–157.

Calhoun, J. B. A comparative study of the social behavior of two inbred strains of house mice. *Ecological Monogr.*, 1956, 26, 81–103.

Calhoun, J. B. Population density and social pathology. In L. Duhl (Ed.), *The urban condition*. New York: Basic Books, 1963. Pp. 33–43.

Campbell, D. T. Ohio State University, Personnel Research Board. *Studies in naval leadership*. Columbus: Ohio State Univer. Research Foundation, 1949.

Campbell, D. T. Social attitudes and other acquired behavioral dispositions. In S. Koch (Ed.), *Psychology: A study of a science*. Vol. 6. New York: McGraw-Hill, 1963. Pp. 94–172.

Campbell, W. D. The importance of occupation, as compared with age and resi-

dence, in marital selection. Unpublished master's thesis, Univer. of Michigan, 1939.
Cannon, W. B. *Bodily changes in pain, hunger, fear, and rage.* New York: Appleton, 1929.
Cannon, W. B. *The wisdom of the body.* New York: Norton, 1932.
Cantril, H. Perception and interpersonal relations. *Amer. J. Psychiat.*, 1957, *113*, 119–127.
Cantril, H. The human design. *J. ind. Psychol.*, 1964, *20*, 129–136.
Cantril, H. *The pattern of human concerns.* New Brunswick, N.J.: Rutgers Univer. Press, 1965.
Cantril, H., & Livingson, W. K. The concept of transaction in psychology and neurology. *J. indiv. Psychol.*, 1963, *19*, 3–16.
Carmichael, L. The development of behavior in vertebrates experimentally removed from the influence of external stimulation. *Psychol. Rev.*, 1927, *34*, 34–47.
Carmichael, L. The growth of sensory control of behavior before birth. *Psychol. Rev.*, 1947, *54*, 316–324.
Carroll, J. B. Diversity of vocabulary and the harmonic series law of word-frequency distribution. *Psychol. Rec.*, 1938, *2*, 379–386.
Carroll, J. B. The analysis of verbal behavior. *Psychol. Rev.*, 1944, *51*, 102–119.
Carroll, J. B. *The study of language.* Cambridge, Mass.: Harvard Univer. Press, 1955.
Cartwright, D. Some principles of mass persuasion: Selected findings of research on the sale of United States War Bonds. *Hum. Relat.*, 1949, *2*, 253–267.
Cartwright, D. *The Research Center for Group Dynamics: A report of five years' activities and a view of future needs.* Ann Arbor: Institute for Social Research, 1950.
Cartwright, D. Achieving change in people: Some applications of group dynamics theory. *Hum. Relat.*, 1951, *4*, 381–393.
Cartwright, D. (Ed.) *Studies in social power.* Ann Arbor: Institute for Social Research, 1959.
Cartwright, D., & Harary, F. Structural balance: A generalization of Heider's theory. *Psychol. Rev.*, 1956, *63*, 277–293.
Cartwright, D., & Zander, A. (Eds.) *Group dynamics.* Evanston, Ill.: Row, Peterson, 1953 (2nd ed., 1960).
Cason, H., & Cason, E. B. Association tendencies and learning ability. *J. exp. Psychol.*, 1925, *8*, 167–189.
Cattell, R. B. *Personality: A systematic, theoretical, and factual study.* New York: McGraw-Hill, 1950.
Cattell, R. B. *Personality and motivation structure and measurement.* New York: World Book, 1957.
Cayton, H. R. The psychology of the Negro under discrimination. In A. Rose (ed.), *Race prejudice and discrimination.* New York: Knopf, 1951. Pp. 276–290.
Chang, H. T. The repetitive discharge of corticothalamic reverberating circuit. *J. Neurophysiol.*, 1950, *13*, 235–257.
Chapman, D. W., & Volkmann, J. A social determinant of the level of aspiration. *J. abnorm. soc. Psychol.*, 1939, *34*, 225–238.
Chen, S. C. Social modification of the activity of ants in nest-building. *Physiol. Zool.*, 1937, *10*, 420–436.
Child, I. Socialization. In G. Lindzey (Ed.), *Handbook of social psychology.* Vol. 2. Cambridge, Mass.: Addison-Wesley, 1954. Pp. 655–692.
Chomsky, N. *Syntactic structures.* The Hague: Mouton, 1957.
Chomsky, N. Explanatory models in linguistics. In E. Wagel, P. Suppes, & A. Tarski (Eds.), *Logic, methodology, and philosophy of science.* Calif.: Stanford Univer. Press, 1962. Pp. 528–550.
Chotlos, J. W. Studies in language behavior: IV. A statistical and comparative analysis of individual written language samples. *Psychol. Monogr.*, 1944, *56*, No. 2 (Whole No. 255), 75–111.
Chowdhry, Kamla, & Newcomb, T. M. The relative abilities of leaders and non-leaders to estimate opinions of their own groups. *J. abnorm. soc. Psychol.*, 1952, *47*, 51–57.
Clark, K. B. *Prejudice and your child.* (2nd ed.) Boston, Mass.: Beacon Press, 1963.
Clark, K. B., & Clark, Mamie P. Racial identification and preference in Negro children. In T. M. Newcomb & E. L. Hartley (Eds.), *Readings in social psychology.* (1st ed.) New York: Holt, 1947. Pp. 169–178.
Clinard, M. B. *Sociology of deviant behavior.* (Rev. ed.) New York: Holt, Rinehart, & Winston, 1963.
Coch, L., & French, J. R. P., Jr. Overcoming resistance to change. *Hum. Relat.*,

1948, *1*, 512–532. Reprinted in S. D. Hoslett (Ed.), *Human factors in management*. New York: Harper, 1951. Pp. 242–268.

Cohen, A. R. Some implications of self-esteem for social influence. In C. I. Hovland & I. L. Janis (Eds.), *Personality and persuasibility*. New Haven: Yale Univer. Press, 1959. Pp. 102–120.

Coleman, J., Katz, E., & Menzel, H. The diffusion of an innovation among physicians. *Sociometry*, 1957, *20*, 253–270.

Coleman, J., Menzel, H., & Katz, E. Social processes in physicians' adoption of a new drug. *J. chron. Dis.*, 1959, *9*, 1–19.

Combs, A. W., & Snygg, D. *Individual behavior: A perceptual approach to behavior*. New York: Harper, 1959.

Conant, J. B. *On understanding science*. New York: New American Library (Mentor No. 68), 1951.

Cooley, C. H. *Human nature and the social order*. New York: Scribner's, 1902 (Rev. edition, 1922).

Cottrell, L. S. The analysis of situational fields in social psychology. *Amer. sociol. Rev.*, 1942, *7*, 370–382.

Cottrell, L. S., & Dymond, Rosalind. The empathic responses: A neglected field for research. *Psychiatry*, 1949, *12*, 355–359.

Cottrell, W. F. *The railroader*. Palo Alto, Calif.: Stanford Univer. Press, 1940.

Cox, D. F. Information and uncertainty: Their effects on consumers' product evaluations. Unpublished doctoral dissertation, Harvard Univer., Graduate School of Bus. Admin., 1962.

Croner, M. D., & Willis, R. H. Perceived differences in task competency and asymmetry of dyadic influence. *J. abnorm. soc. Psychol.*, 1961, *62*, 705–708.

Crossman, R. *The god that failed*. New York: Harper, 1949.

Crutchfield, R. S. Conformity and character. *Amer. Psychologist*, 1955, *10*, 191–198.

Cunnison, I. *The gift*. Glencoe, Ill.: Free Press, 1954.

Dalton, M. Conflicts between staff and line managerial officers. *Amer. sociol. Rev.*, 1950, *15*, 342–351.

Dashiell, J. F. An experimental analysis of some group effects. *J. abnorm. soc. Psychol.*, 1930, *25*, 190–199.

Davie, M. *Negroes in American society*. New York: McGraw-Hill, 1949.

Davie, M. R., & Reeves, R. J. Propinquity of residence before marriage. *Amer. J. Sociol.*, 1939, *44*, 510–517.

Davis, K. *Human society*. New York: Macmillan, 1949.

Davis, K. *Human relations in business*. New York: McGraw-Hill, 1957.

Davis, R. C. *The fundamentals of top management*. New York: Harper, 1951.

Davison, W. P. On the effects of communication. *Publ. Opin. Quart.*, 1959, *23*, 343–360.

Davitz, J. R., & Mason, D. J. Socially facilitated reduction of a fear response in rats. *J. comp. Physiol. Psychol.*, 1955, *48*, 149–151.

DeLaguna, Grace. *Speech: its functions and development*. New Haven: Yale Univer. Press, 1927.

Dembo, Tamara, Leviton, Gloria L., & Wright, Beatrice A. Adjustment to misfortune—a problem of social psychological rehabilitation. *Artificial Limbs*, 1956, *3*, 4–62.

Dennenberg, V. H. The effects of early experience. In E. S. E. Hafez (Ed.), *The behavior of domestic animals*. London: Balliere, Tindall, & Cox, 1962. Ch. 6.

Dennis, W. Infant development under conditions of restricted practice. *Genet. psychol. Monogr.*, 1941, *23*, 143–189.

Dennis, W. Causes of retardation among institutional children: Iran. *J. genet. Psychol.*, 1960, *96*, 47–59.

Deutsch, K. W. On communication models in the social sciences. *Publ. Opin. Quart.*, 1952, *16*, 356–380.

Deutsch, M. An experimental study of the effects of cooperation and competition upon group processes. *Hum. Relat.*, 1949a, *2*, 199–232.

Deutsch, M. A theory of cooperation and competition. *Hum. Relat.*, 1949b, *2*, 129–152.

Deutsch, M. Trust and suspicion. *J. Conflict Resolution*, 1958, *2*, 265–279.

Deutsch, M. The effect of motivational orientation upon trust and suspicion. *Hum. Relat.*, 1960a, *13*, 123–140.

Deutsch, M. Trust, trustworthiness, and the F scale. *J. abnorm. soc. Psychol.*, 1960b, *61*, 138–140.

Deutsch, M. The face of bargaining. Paper presented at the Nineteenth Annual

Meetings of the Operations Research Society of America, Chicago, May 25, 1961a.
Deutsch, M. Some considerations relevant to national policy. *J. soc. Issues,* 1961b, *17,* 57–68.
Deutsch, M., & Collins, M. E. *Interracial housing: A psychological evaluation of a social experiment.* Minneapolis: Univer. Minnesota Press, 1951.
Deutsch, M., & Gerard, H. B. A study of normative and informational influences upon individual judgment. *J. abnorm. soc. Psychol.,* 1955, *51,* 629–636.
Deutsch, M., & Krauss, R. M. The effect of threat upon interpersonal bargaining. *J. abnorm. soc. Psychol.,* 1960, *61,* 181–189.
Deutsch, M., & Krauss, R. M. *Theories in social psychology.* New York: Basic Books, 1965.
Dewey, J. *How we think.* New York: Macmillan, 1910.
Dewey, J. *Human nature and conduct.* New York: Henry Holt, 1922.
Diamond, S. A neglected aspect of motivation. *Sociometry,* 1939, *2,* 77–85.
Dickman, H. The perception of behavioral units. In R. Barker (Ed.), *The stream of behavior.* New York: Appleton-Century-Crofts, 1963. Pp. 23–41.
Dickoff, Hilda. Reactions to evaluations by another person as a function of self-evaluation and the interaction context. Unpublished doctoral dissertation, Duke Univer., 1961.
Dittes, J. E., & Kelley, H. H. Effects of different conditions of acceptance upon conformity to group norms. *J. abnorm. soc. Psychol.,* 1956, *53,* 100–107.
Dodds, E. R. *The Greeks and the irrational.* Boston: Beacon Press, 1957. P. 246.
Dollard, J., Doob, L. W., Miller, N. E., Mowrer, O. H., & Sears, R. R. *Frustration and aggression.* New Haven, Conn.: Yale Univer. Press, 1939.
Dufy, E. *Activation and behavior.* New York: Wiley, 1962.
Dunlap, K. Are there any instincts? *J. abnorm. Psychol.,* 1919–20, *14,* 35–50.
Durkheim, E. *The division of labor in society.* (Trans. by George Simpson.) Glencoe, Ill.: Free Press, 1950.
Dymond, Rosalind. The relation of accuracy of perception of the spouse and marital happiness. *Amer. Psychologist,* 1953, *8,* 344. (Abstract)
Easton, D. Limits of the equilibrium model in social research. In *Profits and problems of homeostatic models in the behavioral sciences.* Publication I, Chicago Behavioral Sciences, 1953, p. 39.
Eckblad, G. The attractiveness of uncertainty. *Scand. J. Psychol.,* 1963, *4,* 1–13.
Edwards, A. L. *Techniques of attitude scale construction.* New York: Appleton-Century-Crofts, 1957.
Elkins, S. *Slavery.* Chicago: Univer. of Chicago Press, 1959.
Emerson, A. E. Ecology, evolution and society. *Amer. Nat.,* 1943, *77,* 97–118.
Endler, N. S., & Hunt, J. McV. Sources of variance in reported anxiousness as measured by the S-R Inventory. (Mimeographed publication, Psychology Dept., University of Illinois, 1964.)
Endler, N. S., Hunt, J. McV., & Rosenstein, A. J. An S-R Inventory of anxiousness. *Psychol. Monogr.,* 1962, *76,* No. 17, 1–33.
Engel, E. The role of content in binocular resolution. *Amer. J. Psychol.,* 1956, *69,* 87–91.
Epstein, W. The influence of syntactical structure on learning. *Amer. J. Psychol.,* 1961, *74,* 80–85.
Erikson, E. H. The problem of ego identity. *J. Amer. psychoanal. Assn.,* 1956, *4,* 56.
Etzioni, A. *A comparative analysis of complex organizations.* New York: Free Press, 1961.
Etzioni, A. *Modern organizations.* Englewood Cliffs, N.J.: Prentice-Hall, 1964.
Eysenck, H. J. *The structure of human personality.* New York: Wiley, 1953.
Eysenck, H. J. The science of personality: Nomothetic! *Psychol. Rev.,* 1954, *61,* 339–343.

Farber, I. E. Response fixation under anxiety and non-anxiety conditions. *J. Exp. Psychol.,* 1948, *38,* 111–131.
Feigl, H. Philosophical embarrassments of psychology. *Amer. Psychologist,* 1959, *14,* 115–128.
Festinger, L. Informal social communication. *Psychol. Rev.,* 1950, *57,* 271–282.
Festinger, L. An analysis of compliant behavior. In M. Sherif & M. O. Wilson (Eds.), *Group relations at the crossroads.* New York: Harper, 1953. Pp. 232–256.

Festinger, L. A *theory of cognitive dissonance*. Evanston, Ill.: Row, Peterson, 1957.

Festinger, L., Back, K., Schachter, S., Kelley, H. H., & Thibaut, J. *Theory and experiment in social communication*. Ann Arbor: Institute for Social Research, Univer. of Michigan, 1950.

Festinger, L., & Carlsmith, J. Cognitive consequences of forced compliance. *J. abnorm. soc. Psychol.*, 1959, 58, 203–210.

Festinger, L., Cartwright, D., *et al.* A study of a rumor: Its origin and spread. *Hum. Relat.*, 1948, 1, 464–486.

Festinger, L., Gerard, H. B., Hymovitch, B., Kelley, H. H., & Raven, B. The influence process in the presence of extreme deviates. *Hum. Relat.*, 1952, 5, 327–346.

Festinger, L., & Katz, D. (Eds.) *Research methods in the behavioral sciences*. New York: Dryden, 1953.

Festinger, L., Schachter, S., & Back, K. *Social pressures in informal groups: A study of a housing project*. New York: Harper, 1950.

Festinger, L., Schachter, S., & Back, K. The operation of group standards. In D. Cartwright & A. Zander, *Group dynamics: Research and theory*. Evanston, Ill.: Row, Peterson, 1953. Pp. 204–223.

Festinger, L., & Thibaut, J. Interpersonal communication in small groups. *J. abnorm. soc. Psychol.*, 1951, 46, 92–99.

Fiedler, F. E. Assumed similarity measures as predictors of team effectiveness. *J. abnorm. soc. Psychol.*, 1954, 49, 381–388.

Fiedler, F. E. Engineer the job to fit the manager. *Harvard Bus. Rev.*, 1965, 43, 115–122.

Fiedler, F. E., Warrington, W. G., & Blaisdell, F. J. Unconscious attitudes as correlates of sociometric choice in a social group. *J. abnorm. soc. Psychol.*, 1952, 47, 790–796.

Fishman, J. A. Childhood indoctrination for minority-group membership. *Daedalus: The Journal of the American Academy of Arts and Sciences*, 1961, 90, 329–349.

Forgays, D. G., & Forgays, Janet W. The nature of the effect of free environmental experience in the rat. *J. comp. physiol. Psychol.*, 1952, 45, 322–328.

Forgus, R. H. The effect of early perceptual learning on the behavioral organization of adult rats. *J. comp. physiol. Psychol.*, 1954, 47, 331–336.

Forgus, R. H. Influence of early experience on maze-learning with and without visual cues. *Canad. J. Psychol.*, 1955a, 9, 207–214.

Forgus, R. H. Early visual and motor experience as determiners of complex maze-learning ability under high and reduced stimulation. *J. comp. physiol. Psychol.*, 1955b, 48, 215–220.

Frank, J. D. Experimental studies of personal pressure and resistance: II. Methods of overcoming resistance. *J. gen. Psychol.*, 1944, 30, 43–46.

Frank, L. K. Time perspectives. *J. soc. Phil.*, 1939, 4, 293–312.

Frazier, E. F. *The Negro in the United States*. (Rev. edition.) New York: Macmillan, 1957.

French, Elizabeth G. Some characteristics of achievement motivation. *J. exp. Psychol.*, 1955, 50, 232–236.

French, J. R. P., Jr., Israel, Joachim, & Ås, Dagfinn. Arbeidernes medvirkning i industribedriften. En eksperimentell undersøkelse. Oslo: Institute for Social Research, 1957.

French, J. R. P., Jr., Morrison, H. W., & Levinger, G. Coercive power and forces affecting conformity. *J. abnorm. soc. Psychol.*, 1960, 61, 93–101.

French, J. R. P., Jr., & Raven, B. The bases of social power. In D. Cartwright (Ed.), *Studies in social power*. Ann Arbor: Institute for Social Research, 1959. Ch. 9.

Freud, Anna, & Burlingham, Dorothy. *Infants without families*. New York: International Universities Press, 1944.

Freud, Anna. *The ego and the mechanisms of defense*. (Trans. by C. Baines.) New York: International Universities Press, 1946.

Freud, S. *General introduction to psychoanalysis*. New York: Boni & Liveright, 1920.

Freud, S. Instincts and their vicissitudes. *Collected Papers*, 4, 60–83. London: Hogarth, 1927.

Freud, S. *Hemmung, Symptom und Angst*. (Trans. as *The problem of anxiety* by H. A. Bunker.) New York: Norton, 1936.

Freud, S. The interpretation of dreams. In A. A. Brill (Trans. & Ed.), *The basic writings of Sigmund Freud*. New York: Modern Library, 1938a.

Freud, S. Three contributions to the theory of sex. In A. A. Brill (Trans. & Ed.), *The basic writings of Sigmund Freud.* New York: Modern Library, 1938b.

Fries, C. C. *The structure of English.* New York: Harcourt Brace, 1952.

Fromm, E. *Escape from freedom.* New York: Rinehart, 1941.

Fromm, E. *Man for himself.* New York: Rinehart, 1947.

Frothingham, P. R. *Edward Everett, orator and statesman.* Boston: Houghton Mifflin, 1925.

Frumkin, R. M. Occupation and major mental disorders. In A. Rose (Ed.), *Mental health and mental disorder.* New York: Norton, 1955. Pp. 136–160.

Fuller, J. L., & Scott, J. P. Heredity and learning ability in infrahuman animals. *Eugenics Quart.*, 1954, *1*, 28–43.

Gage, N. L. Judging interests from expressive behavior. *Psychol. Monogr.*, 1952, 66, No. 18 (Whole No. 350).

Gage, N. L., & Suci, G. J. Social perception and teacher-pupil relationships. *J. educ. Psychol.*, 1951, *42*, 144–152.

Gardner, B. B., & Moore, D. G. *Human relations in industry.* Homewood, Ill.: Irwin, 1955.

Gardner, J. W. *Self-renewal: The individual and the innovative society.* New York: Harper, 1963.

Gerard, H. B. The anchorage of opinions in face-to-face groups. *Hum. Relat.*, 1954, 7, 313–325.

Gerth, H. H., & Mills, C. W. (Eds.) *From Max Weber: Essays in sociology.* New York: Oxford Univer. Press, 1946.

Gibb, C. A. Leadership. In G. Lindzey (Ed.), *Handbook of social psychology.* Vol. 2. Cambridge, Mass.: Addison-Wesley, 1954. Pp. 877–920.

Gibson, J. J. *The perception of the visual world.* Boston: Houghton Mifflin, 1950.

Gibson, J. J., & Gibson, Eleanor J. Perceptual learning: Differentiation or enrichment? *Psychol. Rev.*, 1955, *62*, 32–41.

Gillespie, J. J. *Free expression in industry.* London: Pilot Press, 1948.

Ginsburg, B. E., & Hovda, R. B. On the physiology of gene controlled audiogenic seizures in mice. *Anat. Rec.*, 1947, *99*, 65–66.

Gleason, H. A. *An introduction to descriptive linguistics.* New York: Henry Holt, 1961.

Gleser, Goldine C., Cronbach, L. J., & Rajaratnam, N. Generalizability of scores influenced by multiple sources of variance. Mimeographed Tech. Rep., Bureau of Educat. Res., Univer. Ill., 1961.

Goffman, E. *The presentation of self in everyday life.* Garden City, New York: Doubleday Anchor, 1959.

Goffman, E. *Encounters.* Indianapolis, Ind.: Bobbs-Merrill, 1961.

Goffman, E. *Behavior in public places.* New York: The Free Press of Glencoe, 1963.

Gold, M., & Slater, Carol. Office, factory, store—and family: A study of integration setting. *Amer. sociol. Rev.*, 1958, *23*, 64–74.

Goldfarb, W. Emotional and intellectual consequences of psychological deprivation in infancy: A re-evaluation. In P. H. Hoch & J. Zubin (Eds.), *Psychopathology of childhood.* New York: Grune & Stratton, 1955. Pp. 105–119.

Goldhammer, H., & Shils, E. A. Types of power and status. *Amer. J. Sociol.*, 1939, *45*, 171–178.

Goldman, Jacquelin R. The effects of handling and shocking in infancy upon adult behavior in the albino rat. *J. genet. Psychol.*, 1964, *104*, 301–310.

Goldstein, K. *Human nature in the light of psychotherapy.* Cambridge, Mass.: Harvard Univer. Press, 1940.

Gooddy, W. Two directions of memory. *J. indiv. Psychol.*, 1959, *15*, 83–88.

Goodman, Mary E. *Race awareness in young children.* Cambridge, Mass.: Addison-Wesley, 1952.

Gordon, M. M. *Assimilation in American life: The role of race, religion, and national origins.* New York: Oxford Univer. Press, 1964.

Gough, H. G. *Reference handbook for the Gough Adjective Checklist.* Berkeley: Inst. Personality Assessment and Research, Univer. of California, 1955. (Mimeographed)

Gouldner, A. Organizational analysis. In R. K. Merton, L. Broom, & L. S. Cottrell (Eds.), *Sociology today.* New York: Basic Books, 1959a. Pp. 400–429.

Gouldner, A. W. Reciprocity and autonomy in functional theory. In L. Gross (Ed.), *Symposium on sociological theory.* Evanston, Ill.: Row, Peterson, 1959b.

Gouldner, A. W. The norm of reciprocity: A preliminary statement. *Amer. sociol. Rev.*, 1960, *25*, 161–179.

Graicunas, V. A. Relationships in organization. *Papers on the science of administration.* New York: Columbia Univer. Press, 1937.

Green, A. The middle class male child and neurosis. *Amer. sociol. Rev.*, 1946, *11*, 31–41.

Green, A. W. *Sociology: An analysis of life in a modern society.* New York: McGraw-Hill, 1956.

Greenberg, J. (Ed.) *Universals of language.* Cambridge, Mass.: MIT Press, 1963.

Greer, F. L., Galanter, E. H., & Nordlie, P. G. Interpersonal knowledge and individual and group effectiveness. *J. abnorm. soc. Psychol.*, 1954, *49*, 411–414.

Griffiths, W. J., Jr. Effects of isolation and stress on escape thresholds of albino rats. *Psychol. Rep.*, 1960, *6*, 623–629.

Grinker, R. R., & Spiegel, J. P. *Men under stress.* Philadelphia: Blakiston, 1945.

Gross, L. Hierarchical authority in educational institutions. In H. J. Hartley & G. E. Holloway (Eds.), *Focus on change and the school administrator.* Buffalo, N.Y.: School of Education, State Univer. of New York, 1965. Pp. 23–37.

Gross, N., Mason, W. S., & McEachern, A. W. *Explorations in role analysis.* New York: Wiley, 1958.

Guetzkow, H., Alger, C. F., Brody, R. A., Noel, R. C., & Snyder, R. C. *Simulation in international relations: Developments for research and teaching.* Englewood Cliffs, N.J.: Prentice-Hall, 1963.

Gump, P. V., & Friesen, W. V. Participation of large and small school juniors in the nonclass settings of school. In R. G. Barker & P. V. Gump, *Big school, small school.* Calif.: Stanford Univer. Press, 1964a.

Gump, P. V., & Friesen, W. V. Satisfactions derived by juniors from nonclass settings of large and small high schools. In R. G. Barker & P. V. Gump, *Big school, small school.* Calif.: Stanford Univer. Press, 1964b.

Gump, P., & Sutton-Smith, B. The it role in children's games. *The Group*, 1955, *17*, 3–8.

Gump, P., Schoggen, P., & Redl, F. The camp milieu and its immediate effects. *J. soc. Issues*, 1957, *13*, 40–46.

Gump, P. V., Schoggen, P., & Redl, F. The behavior of the same child in different milieus. In R. Barker (Ed.), *The stream of behavior.* New York: Appleton-Century-Crofts, 1963. Pp. 169–202.

Gunther, J. *Inside Africa.* New York: Harper, 1955.

Gurnee, H. Effect of collective learning upon the individual participants. *J. abnorm. soc. Psychol.*, 1939, *34*, 529–532.

Gursslin, O., Hunt, R. G., & Roach, J. Social class and the mental health movement. *Soc. Probl.*, 1959, *7*, 210–218.

Haggard, E. A. Socialization, personality, and academic achievement in gifted children. *The School Rev.*, 1957, *65*, 388–414.

Haire, M. (Ed.) *Modern organization theory.* New York: Wiley, 1959a.

Haire, M. Psychology and the study of business: Joint behavioral sciences. In *Social science research on business: Product and potential.* New York: Columbia Univer. Press, 1959b. Pp. 53–59.

Hall, C. S. Emotional behavior in the rat. I. Defecation and urination as measures of individual differences in emotionality. *J. comp. Psychol.*, 1934, *18*, 385–403.

Hall, C. S. The inheritance of emotionability. *Sigma Xi Quart.*, 1938, *26*, 17–27.

Hall, C. S. Genetic differences in fatal audiogenic seizures between two inbred strains of house mice. *J. Hered.*, 1947, *38*, 2–6.

Hall, C. S. The genetics of behavior. In S. S. Stevens (Ed.), *Handbook of experimental psychology.* New York: Wiley, 1951.

Hall, C. S., & Lindzey, G. *Theories of personality.* New York: Wiley, 1957.

Hall, E. T. *The silent language.* Garden City, N.Y.: Doubleday, 1959.

Hall, R. H. The concept of bureaucracy: An empirical assessment. *Amer. J. Sociol.*, 1963, *69*, 32–40.

Halle, M., & Stevens, K. N. Speech recognition: A model and a program for research. *IRE Transactions on Information Theory*, 1962, *8*, 155–159.

Hamilton, G. V. *Objective psychopathology.* St. Louis: C. V. Mosby, 1925.

Hand, Learned. *The spirit of liberty.* New York: Knopf, 1952.

Handlin, O., & Handlin, Mary F. The United States. In *The positive contribution by immigrants.* Paris: UNESCO, 1955, Ch. 1.

Hanfmann, E. Social perception in Russian displaced persons and an American comparison group. *Psychiatry*, 1957, 20, 131–149.

Harary, F. On the measurement of structural balance. *Behav. Sci.*, 1959, 4, 316–323.

Hare, A. P. *Handbook of small group research*. New York: Free Press, 1961.

Hare, A. P., Borgatta, E. F., & Bales, R. F. *Small groups*. New York: Knopf, 1955 (2nd edition, 1965).

Harlow, H. F. Social facilitation of feeding in the albino rat. *J. genet. Psychol.*, 1932, 43, 211–221.

Harlow, H. F. Learning and satiation of response in intrinsically motivated complex puzzle performance by monkeys. *J. comp. physiol. Psychol.*, 1950, 43, 289–294.

Harlow, H. F. The nature of love. *Amer. Psychologist*, 1958, 13, 673–685.

Harlow, H. F., Harlow, M. K., & Meyer, D. R. Learning motivated by a manipulation drive. *J. exp. Psychol.*, 1950, 40, 228–234.

Harper, R. S., & Boring, E. G. Cues. *Amer. J. Psychol.*, 1948, 61, 119–123.

Harrington, M. *The other America*. Baltimore, Md.: Penguin Books, 1963.

Hayakawa, S. I. *Language in thought and action*. New York: Harcourt Brace, 1951 (2nd edition, 1964).

Hayek, F. A. *The sensory order*. Chicago: Univer. Chicago Press, 1952.

Hebb, D. O. On the nature of fear. *Psychol. Rev.*, 1946, 53, 259–276.

Hebb, D. O. The effects of early experience on problem-solving at maturity. *Amer. Psychologist*, 1947, 2, 306–307. (Abstract)

Hebb, D. O. *The organization of behavior*. New York: Wiley, 1949.

Hebb, D. O. The mammal and his environment. *Amer. J. Psychol.*, 1955, 111, 826–831.

Hebb, D. O., & Williams, K. A method of rating animal intelligence. *J. genet. Psychol.*, 1946, 34, 59–65.

Heider, F. Social perception and phenomenal causality. *Psychol. Rev.*, 1944, 51, 358–374.

Heider, F. Attitudes and cognitive organization. *J. Psychol.*, 1946, 21, 107–112.

Heider, F. *The psychology of interpersonal relations*. New York: Wiley, 1958.

Heider, F., & Simmel, Marianne. An experimental study of apparent behavior. *Amer. J. Psychol.*, 1944, 57, 243–259.

Heinroth, O. Beiträge zur Biologie, namentlich Ethnologie und Physiologie der Anatiden. *Verhl. Internat. Ornith. Congr.*, 1910, 5, 589–702.

Helson, H. Adaptation-level as a basis for a quantitative theory of frames of reference. *Psychol. Rev.*, 1948, 55, 297–313.

Helson, H. Adaptation level theory. In S. Koch (Ed.), *Psychology: A study of a science. Vol. I. Sensory, perceptual, and physiological formulations*. New York: McGraw-Hill, 1959. Pp. 565–621.

Hemphill, J. K. Relations between the size of the group and the behavior of "superior" leaders. *J. soc. Psychol.*, 1950, 32, 11–22.

Hemphill, J. K. Administration as problem-solving. In A. W. Halpin (Ed.), *Administrative theory in education*. Chicago: Midwest Administration Center, 1958.

Hemphill, J. K. Why people attempt to lead. In L. Petrullo & B. M. Bass (Eds.), *Leadership and interpersonal behavior*. New York: Holt, Rinehart, & Winston, 1961.

Henderson, L. J. *Pareto's general sociology*. Cambridge, Mass.: Harvard Univer. Press, 1935.

Hendrick, I. The discussion of the "instinct to master." *Psychoanal. Quart.*, 1943, 12, 561–565.

Herberg, W. *Protestant-Catholic-Jew*. New York: Doubleday, 1955.

Herbst, P. G. Analysis and measurement of a situation. *Hum. Relat.*, 1953, 2, 113–140.

Heron, W. T. The inheritance of maze learning ability in rats. *J. comp. Psychology*, 1935, 19, 77–89.

Herter, K. Die Beziehungen zwischen Vorzugstemperatur und Hautbeschaffenheit bei Mausen. *Zool. Anz. Suppl.*, 1938, 11, 48–55.

Herzog, Herta. What do we really know about daytime serial listeners? In P. F. Lazarsfeld & F. N. Stanton (Eds.), *Radio research, 1942–1943*. New York: Duell, Sloan & Pearce, 1944. Pp. 3–33.

Hilgard, E. R. Human motives and the concept of the self. *Amer. Psychologist*, 1949, 4, 374–382.

Hiller, E. T. *The strike*. Chicago: Univer. Chicago Press, 1928.

Hiller, E. T. *Social relations and structure.* New York: Harper, 1947.

Himmelstrand, U. Verbal attitudes and behavior. *Public opin. Quart.*, 1960, *24*, 224–250.

Himmelweit, Hilde T. Socio-economic background and personality. *Int. soc. Sci. Bull.*, 1955, 7, 29–35.

Hochbaum, G. M. Self-confidence and reactions to group pressures. *Amer. soc. Rev.*, 1954, *19*, 678–687.

Hodgson, R. E. An eight generation experiment in inbreeding swine. *J. Hered.*, 1935, 26, 209–217.

Hoffer, E. *The true believer.* New York: Harper, 1951.

Hollander, E. P. Conformity, status, and idiosyncrasy credit. *Psychol. Rev.*, 1958, 65, 117–127.

Hollander, E. P. Competence and conformity in the acceptance of influence. *J. abnorm. soc. Psychol.*, 1960a, *61*, 361–365.

Hollander, E. P. Reconsidering the issue of conformity in personality. Chapter XI in H. P. David and J. C. Brengelmann (Eds.), *Perspectives in personality research.* New York: Springer, 1960b.

Hollander, E. P. Emergent leadership and social influence. In L. Petrullo & B. M. Bass (Eds.), *Leadership and interpersonal behavior.* New York: Holt, Rinehart, & Winston, 1961. Pp. 30–47.

Hollander, E. P. *Leaders, groups, and influence.* New York: Oxford Univer. Press, 1964.

Hollander, E. P., & Webb, W. B. Leadership, followership, and friendship: An analysis of peer nominations. *J. abnorm. soc. Psychol.*, 1955, 50, 163–167.

Hollingshead, A. B. Trends in social stratification: A case study. *Amer. sociol. Rev.*, 1952, 17, 685.

Hollingshead, A. B., & Redlich, F. C. *Social class and mental illness.* New York: Wiley, 1958.

Holmes, Frances B. An experimental study of children's fears. In A. T. Jersild & Frances B. Holmes (Eds.), *Children's fears.* New York: Teachers College, Columbia Univer., 1935. (*Child Developm. Monogr.*, 20.)

Homans, G. C. *The human group.* New York: Harcourt Brace, 1950.

Homans, G. C. Status among clerical workers. *Hum. Organiz.*, 1953, *12*, 5–10.

Homans, G. C. Social behavior as exchange. *Amer. J. Sociol.*, 1958, *63*, 597–606.

Homans, G. C. *Social behavior: Its elementary forms.* New York: Harcourt Brace, 1961.

Hood, W. R., & Sherif, M. Personality oriented approaches to prejudice. *Sociol. soc. Res.*, 1955, *40*, 79–85.

Horowitz, E. L. Race attitudes. In O. Klineberg (Ed.), *Characteristics of the American Negro, part 4.* New York: Harper & Row, 1944.

Hovland, C. I. Reconciling conflicting results derived from experimental and survey studies of attitude change. *Amer. Psychologist*, 1959, *14*, 8–17.

Hovland, C. I., & Janis, I. L. (Eds.) *Personality and persuasibility.* New Haven, Conn.: Yale Univer. Press, 1959.

Hovland, C. I., Janis, I. L., & Kelley, H. H. *Communication and persuasion.* New Haven: Yale Univer. Press, 1953.

Hovland, C. I., Lumsdaine, A. A., & Sheffield, F. D. *Experiments on mass communication.* Princeton: Princeton Univer. Press, 1949.

Hovland, C. I., Mandell, W., Campbell, Enid H., Brock, T., Luchins, A. S., Cohen, A. R., McGuire, W. J., Janis, I. L., Feierabend, Rosalind L., & Anderson, N. H. *The order of presentation in persuasion.* New Haven: Yale Univer. Press, 1957.

Hovland, C. I., & Sherif, M. Judgmental phenomena and scales of attitude measurement: Item displacement in Thurstone scales. *J. abnorm. soc. Psychol.*, 1952, 47, 822–832.

Hovland, C. I., & Weiss, W. The influence of source credibility on communication effectiveness. *Publ. Opin. Quart.*, 1951, 15, 635–650.

Hsu, F. L. K. (Ed.) *Psychological anthropology: Approaches to culture and personality.* Homewood, Ill.: Dorsey, 1961.

Hughes, E. C. Dilemmas and contradictions of status. *Amer. J. Sociol.* 1945, *50*, 353–359.

Hull, C. L. Goal attraction and directing ideas conceived as habit phenomena. *Psychol. Rev.*, 1931, 38, 487–506.

Hull, C. L. *Principles of behavior: An introduction to behavior theory.* New York: Appleton-Century, 1943.

Hunt, J. McV. The effects of infantile

feeding-frustration upon adult hoarding in the albino rat. *J. abnorm. soc. Psychol.*, 1941, 36, 338–360.
Hunt, J. McV. Experimental psychoanalysis. In P. L. Harriman (Ed.), *Encyclopedia of psychology*. New York: Philosophical Library, 1946.
Hunt, J. McV. Experience and the development of motivation: Some reinterpretations. *Child Develpm.*, 1960, 31, 489–504.
Hunt, J. McV. *Intelligence and experience*. New York: Ronald, 1961.
Hunt, J. McV. Motivation inherent in information processing and action. In O. J. Harvey (Ed.), *Motivation and social interaction: The cognitive determinants*. New York: Ronald Press, 1963a. Ch. 3.
Hunt, J. McV. Piaget's observations as a source of hypotheses concerning motivation. *Merrill-Palmer Quart.*, 1963b, 9, 263–275.
Hunt, J. McV. Traditional personality theory in the light of recent evidence. *Amer. Scientist*, 1965, 53, 80–96.
Hunt, J. McV. Psychosexual development: The infant disciplines. Mimeographed paper written as a chapter for *Behavioral science and child rearing*, as yet unpublished, 1966.
Hunt, J. McV., Schlosberg, H., Solomon, R. L., & Stellab, E. Studies of the effects of infantile experience on adult behavior in rats. I. Effects of infantile feeding-frustration on adult hoarding. *J. comp. physiol. Psychol.*, 1947, 40, 291–304.
Hunt, J. McV., & Uzgiris, Ina C. Cathexis from recognitive familiarity: An exploratory study. In P. R. Merrifield (Ed.), *Personality and intelligence: Papers honoring J. P. Guilford*. Ohio: Kent State Univer. Press, 1966.
Hunt, R. G. Role and role conflict. In H. J. Hartley & G. E. Holloway, Jr. (Eds.), *Focus on change and the school administrator*. New York: State Univer. of New York, School of Educat., 1965. Pp. 37–46.
Hunt, R. G. & Winokur, G. Some generalities concerning parent attitudes and child behavior with special reference to changing them. In J. Glidewell (Ed.), *Parent attitudes and child behavior*. Springfield, Ill.: C. C. Thomas, 1961. Pp. 174-183.
Hurst, C. C. *Experiments in genetics*. Cambridge, England: Cambridge Univer. Press, 1925.
Husband, R. W. Analysis of methods in human maze learning. *J. genet. Psychol.*, 1931, 39, 258–278.
Hyman, H. H. The psychology of status. *Arch. Psychol.*, 1942, 38, 15.
Hyman, H. H. *Survey design and analysis*. Glencoe, Ill.: Free Press, 1955.
Hyman, H. H., & Sheatsley, P. B. Some reasons why information campaigns fail. *Publ. opin. Quart.*, 1947, 11, 412–423.
Hyman, H. H., & Sheatsley, P. B. The authoritarian personality: A methodological critique. In R. Christie & M. Jahoda (Eds.), *Studies in the scope and method of the authoritarian personality*. Glencoe, Ill.: Free Press, 1954.
Hymovitch, B. The effects of experimental variations in early experience on problem-solving in the rat. *J. comp. physiol. Psychol.*, 1952, 45, 313–321.

Ichheiser, G. Misunderstandings in human relations. *Amer. J. Sociol.*, 1949, 55, 2, Part 2.
Ihrig, H. Literalism and animism in schizophrenia. Unpublished doctoral dissertation, Univer. of Kansas, 1953.
Imms, A. D. *Recent advances in entymology*. Philadelphia: Blakiston's Sons, 1931.
Inkeles, A., & Bauer, R. A. *The Soviet citizen*. Cambridge, Mass.: Harvard Univer. Press, 1959.
International Kindergarten Union. A *study of the vocabulary of children before entering the first grade*. Baltimore: Williams & Wilkins, 1928.

Jackson, J. M., & Saltzstein, H. D. *Group membership and conformity processes*. Ann Arbor: Research Center for Group Dynamics, 1956.
Jackson, J. M., & Saltzstein, H. D. The effect of person-group relationships on conformity processes. *J. abnorm. soc. Psychol.*, 1958, 57, 17–24.
Jahoda, Marie. Conformity and independence: A psychological analysis. *Hum. Relat.*, 1959, 12, 99–120.
Jahoda, Marie, Deutsch, M., & Cook, S. W. *Research methods in social relations*. New York: Dryden, 1951. 2 vols.
James, W. *Principles of psychology*. New York: Henry Holt, 1890. 2 vols.

James, W. *Psychology: Briefer course.* New York: Henry Holt, 1892.

James, W. T. The development of social facilitation of eating in puppies. *J. genet. Psychol.*, 1960, *96*, 123–127.

James, W. T. Social facilitation of eating behavior in puppies after satiation. *J. comp. physiol. Psychol.*, 1953, *46*, 427–428.

James, W. T., & Cannon, D. J. Variation in social facilitation of eating behavior in puppies. *J. genet. Psychol.*, 1956, *87*, 225–228.

Janis, I. L. Personality correlates of susceptibility to persuasion. *J. Pers.*, 1954, *22*, 504–518.

Jenkins, W. O., & Stanley, J. C. Partial reinforcement: A review and critique. *Psychol. Bulletin*, 1950, *47*, 193–234.

Jennings, Helen H. *Leadership and isolation.* New York: Longmans, 1943 (2nd ed., 1950).

Jennings, Helen H. Sociometry of leadership. *Sociometry Monogr.*, 1947, *14*, 12–24.

Jespersen, O. *The philosophy of grammar.* London: Allen & Unwin, 1924.

Johnson, C. S. *Growing up in the black belt.* Washington, D.C.: American Council on Education, 1941.

Johnson, E. A. The executive, the organization, and operations research. In J. F. McCloskey & Florence H. Trefethen, *Operations research for management.* Baltimore: Johns Hopkins Press, 1954. Pp. xi–xxiv.

Johnson, E. E. The role of motivational strength in latent learning. *J. comp. physiol. Psychol.*, 1953, *45*, 526–530.

Johnson, W. Studies in language behavior: I. A program of research. *Psychol. Monogr.*, 1944, *56, No. 2* (Whole No. 255), 1–15.

Jones, E. E. *Ingratiation.* New York: Appleton-Century-Crofts, 1964.

Jones, E. E. Conformity as a tactic of ingratiation. *Science*, 1965, *149*, 144–150.

Jones, E. E., & deCharms, R. Changes in social perception as a function of the personal relevance of behavior. *Sociometry*, 1957, *20*, 75–85.

Jones, E. E., Jones, R. G., & Gergen, K. J. Some conditions affecting the evaluation of a conformist. *J. Pers.*, 1963, *31*, 270–288.

Jones, E. E., Gergen, K. J., & Jones, R. G. Tactics of ingratiation among leaders and subordinates in a status hierarchy. *Psychol. Monogr.*, 1963, *77* (Whole No. 566).

Jones, F. N., & Arrington, M. G. The explanations of physical phenomena given by white and Negro children. *Comp. Psychology Monogr.*, 1945, *18* (5), 1–43.

Jordan, N. Behavioral forces that are a function of attitudes and of cognitive organization. *Hum. Relat.*, 1953, *6*, 273–287.

Jordan, N. Some formal characteristics of the behavior of two disturbed boys. In R. Barker (Ed.), *The stream of behavior.* New York: Appleton-Century-Crofts, 1963. Pp. 203–218.

Juran, J. M. Improving the relationship between staff and line: An assist from the anthropologists. *Personnel,* 1956, *32*, 515–524.

Kahn, H. The arms race and some of its hazards. *Daedalus,* 1960a, *89*, 744–781.

Kahn, H. The nature and feasibility of war and deterrence. Rand Corporation Report P-1888-RC, Jan. 20, 1960b.

Kahn, R. L., Wolfe, D. M., Quinn, R. P., Snock, J. D., & Rosenthal, R. A. *Organizational stress.* New York: Wiley, 1964.

Kardiner, A. *The individual and his society.* New York: Columbia Univer. Press, 1939.

Kardiner, A., Linton, R., DuBois, C., & West, J. *The psychological frontiers of society.* New York: Columbia Univer. Press, 1945.

Katz, D. (Ed.) Attitude change. *Publ. Opin. Quart.*, spec. issue, 1960a, *14*, No. 2, i–365.

Katz, D. The functional approach to the study of attitudes. *Publ. opin. Quart.*, 1960b, *24*, 163–204.

Katz, D. Human interrelationships and organizational behavior. In S. Mailick & E. H. Van Ness (Eds.), *Concepts and issues in administrative behavior.* New York: Prentice-Hall, 1962. Pp. 166–186.

Katz, D. The motivational basis of organizational behavior. *Behav. Sci.*, 1964, *9*, 131–146.

Katz, D., & Eldersveld, S. J. The impact of local party activity upon the electorate. *Publ. opin. Quart.*, 1961, *25*, 1–24.

Katz, D., & Kahn, R. L. *The social psychology of organizations.* New York: Wiley, 1966.

Katz, D., Maccoby, N., & Morse, Nancy.

Productivity, supervision and morale in an office situation. Ann Arbor: Institute for Social Research, Univer. of Michigan, 1950.

Katz, D., & Stotland, E. A preliminary statement to a theory of attitude structure and change. In S. Koch (Ed.), *Psychology: A study of a science*. Vol. 3. New York: McGraw-Hill, 1959. Pp. 423-475.

Katz, E. The two-step flow of communication: An up-to-date report on an hypothesis. *Publ. opin. Quart.*, 1957, *21*, 61–78.

Katz, E., & Lazarsfeld, P. F. *Personal influence*. Glencoe, Ill.: Free Press, 1955.

Katz, I., & Benjamin, L. Effects of white authoritarianism in biracial work groups. *J. abnorm. soc. Psychol.*, 1960, *61*, 448–456.

Katz, J. J., & Fodor, J. A. The structure of semantic theory. *Language*, 1963, *34*, 170–210.

Keeler, C. E., & King, H. D. Multiple effects of coat color genes in the Norway rat, with special reference to temperature and domestication. *J. comp. Psychol.*, 1942, 34, 241–250.

Kelley, H. H. Communication in experimentally created hierarchies. *Hum. Relat.*, 1951, 4, 39–56.

Kelley, H. H. Two functions of reference groups. In G. E. Swanson, T. M. Newcomb, & E. L. Hartley, *Readings in social psychology*. New York: Holt, 1952. Pp. 410–414.

Kelley, H. H., & Volkart, E. H. The resistance to change of group-anchored attitudes. *Amer. sociol. Rev.*, 1952, 17, 453–465.

Kelly, G. A. *The psychology of personal constructs*. New York: Norton, 1955. 2 vols.

Kelly, G. A. A *theory of personality: The psychology of personal constructs* (Norton Library Edition). New York: Norton, 1963.

Kelman, H. C. Attitude change as a function of response restriction. *Hum. Relat.*, 1953, 6, 185–214.

Kelman, H. C. Processes of opinion change. *Publ. opin. Quart.*, 1961, 25, 57–78.

Kelman, H. C. (Ed.) *International behavior: A social-psychological analysis*. New York: Holt, Rinehart, & Winston, 1965.

Kelman, H. C., & Hovland, C. I. "Reinstatement" of the communicator in delayed measurement of opinion change. *J. abnorm. soc. Psychol.*, 1953, *48*, 327–335.

Kerr, C., Dunlop, J. T., Harbison, F., & Myers, C. *Industrialism and industrial man*. Cambridge, Mass.: Harvard Univer. Press, 1960.

Kerrick, J. S. News pictures, captions and the point of resolution. *Journalism Quart.*, 1959a, 36, 183–188.

Kerrick, J. S. The weekly newspaper as a source: Prediction of an editorial's effectiveness. Unpublished paper, 1959b.

Kierkegaard, S. "That individual": Two "notes" concerning my work as an author, 1859. In S. Kierkegaard, *The point of view*. (Translated by W. Lowrie.) New York: Oxford Univer. Press, 1939. P. 115.

Kilpatrick, F. P. Two processes in perceptual learning. *J. exp. Psychol.*, 1954, *47*, 362–370.

Kimball, P. People without papers. *Publ. Opin. Quart.*, 1959, 23, 389–398.

Klapper, J. *The effects of mass communication*. Glencoe, Ill.: Free Press, 1960.

Klein, G. The personal world through perception. In R. R. Blake & G. V. Ramsey (Eds.), *Perception: An approach to personality*. New York: Ronald, 1951.

Klineberg, O. *Social psychology*. (Rev. ed.) New York: Holt, 1954.

Kluckhohn, C. Culture and behavior. In G. Lindzey (Ed.), *Handbook of social psychology*. Vol. I. Cambridge, Mass.: Addison-Wesley, 1954.

Kluckhohn, C., & Mowrer, O. H. Culture and personality: A conceptual scheme. *Amer. Anthropologist*, 1944, *46*, 4.

Kluckhohn, C., Murray, H. A., & Schneider, D. *Personality in nature, society, and culture*. (2nd ed.) New York: Knopf, 1953.

Koch, Helen L. The social distance between certain racial, nationality, and skin pigmentation groups in selected populations of American school children. *J. genet. Psychol.*, 1946, 68, 63–95.

Koch, S. Clark L. Hull. In W. K. Estes, *et al.* (Eds.), *Modern learning theory: a critical analysis of five examples*. New York: Appleton-Century-Crofts, 1954. Pp. 1-76.

Köhler, W. *Gestalt psychology*. New York: Liveright, 1929.

Kohn, M. L. Social class and parental values. *Amer. J. Sociol.*, 1959, *44*, 337–351.

Kohn, M. L., & Clausen, J. A. Parental authority behavior and schizophrenia. *Amer. J. Orthopsychiat.*, 1956, *26*, 297–313.

Koontz, H., & O'Donnell, C. *Principles of management*. New York: McGraw-Hill, 1959.

Korzybski, A. *Science and sanity; an introduction to non-Aristotelian systems and general semantics*. (Rev. ed.) Lancaster, Pa.: Science Press, 1941.

Kounin, J. The meaning of rigidity: A reply to Heinz Werner. *Psychol. Rev.*, 1948, *55*, 157–166.

Krech, D. Notes toward a psychological theory. *J. Pers.*, 1949, *18*, 66–87.

Krech, D. Psychological theory and social psychology. In H. Helson (Ed.), *Theoretical foundations of psychology*. New York: D. Van Nostrand, 1951.

Krech, D., & Crutchfield, R. S. *Theory and problems of social psychology*. New York: McGraw-Hill, 1948.

Krech, D., Crutchfield, R. S., & Ballachey, E. L. *Individual in society: A textbook of social psychology*. New York: McGraw-Hill, 1962.

Kroeber, A. L. (Ed.) *Anthropology today*. Chicago: Univer. Chicago Press, 1953.

Kuo, Z. Y. A psychology without heredity. *Psychol. Rev.*, 1924, *31*, 427–451.

Landgrebe, L. The world as a phenomenological problem. *Phil. Phenomenol. Res.*, 1940, *1*, 38–58.

Landreth, Catherine, & Johnson, Barbara C. Young children's responses to a picture and inset test designed to reveal reactions to persons of different skin color. *Child Develpm.*, 1953, *24*, 63–80.

Lasagna, L., & McCann, W. P. Effect of "tranquilizing" drugs on amphetamine toxicity in aggregated mice. *Science*, 1957, *125*, 1241–1242.

Lashley, K. S. Experimental analysis of instinctive behavior. *Psychol. Rev.*, 1938, *45*, 445–471.

Lashley, K. S. The problem of cerebral organization in vision. In H. Klüver, *Visual mechanisms*. Lancaster, Pa.: Jacques Cattell, 1942. Pp. 301–322.

Lashley, K. S., & Wade, Marjorie. The Pavlovian theory of generalization. *Psychol. Rev.*, 1946, *53*, 72–87.

Lazarsfeld, P. F., Berelson, B., & Gaudet, Hazel. *The people's choice*. (2nd ed.) New York: Columbia Univer. Press, 1948.

Lazarsfeld, P. F., & Rosenberg, M. (Eds.) *The language of social research*. Glencoe, Ill.: Free Press, 1955.

Leavitt, H. J. Unhuman organizations. In *Readings in managerial psychology*. Chicago: Univer. of Chicago Press, 1964. Pp. 542–556.

Lederer, W. J., & Burdick, E. *The ugly American*. New York: Norton, 1958.

Lenneberg, E. Language, evolution and purposive behavior. In *Culture in history: Essays in honor of Paul Radin*. New York: Columbia Univer. Press, 1960.

Lenneberg, E. Understanding language without ability to speak: A case report. *J. abnorm. soc. Psychol.*, 1962, *65*, 419–425.

Lenneberg, E., Nichols, I. A., & Rosenberger, E. R. Primitive stages of language development in mongolism. In *Proceedings*, 42nd Annual Meeting, Association for Research in Nervous and Mental Diseases, 1962.

Lerner, D. *The passing of traditional society*. Glencoe, Ill.: Free Press, 1958. P. 148.

Levine, S. The effects of differential infantile stimulation on emotionality at weaning. *Canad. J. Psychol.*, 1959, *13*, 243–247.

Levine, S. Psychophysiological effects of early stimulation. In E. Bliss (Ed.), *Roots of behavior*. New York: Hoeber, 1961.

Levy, S., & Freedman, L. Z. Psychoneurosis and economic life. *Soc. Problems*, 1956, *4*, 55–67.

Lewin, K. *A dynamic theory of personality*. New York: McGraw-Hill, 1935.

Lewin, K. Formalization and progress in psychology. In *Studies in topological and vector psychology*. I., *Univ. Ia. Stud. Child Welf.*, 1940, *16*, No. 3.

Lewin, K. Time perspective and morale. In G. Watson (Ed.), *Civilian morale*. Boston: Houghton Mifflin, 1942.

Lewin, K. Constructs in psychology and psychological ecology. *Univ. Ia. Stud. Child Welf.*, 1944, *20*, 1–29.

Lewin, K. Frontiers in group dynamics. *Hum. Relat.*, 1947, *1*, 5–41.

Lewin, K. *Resolving social conflicts*. New York: Harper, 1948.

Lewin, K. *Field theory in social science*. New York: Harper, 1951.

Lewin, K., Lippitt, R., & White, R. K. Patterns of aggressive behavior in experimentally created "social climates." *J. soc. Psychol.*, 1939, 10, 271–299.

Lewis, O. *The children of Sanchez.* New York: Random House, 1961.

Lewis, O. The culture of poverty. *Transaction*, 1963, 1, 17–19.

Lifton, R. J. "Thought reform" of Western civilians in Chinese Communist prisons. *Psychiatry*, 1956, 19, 173–195.

Likert, R. *New patterns of management.* New York: McGraw-Hill, 1961.

Lindzey, G. (Ed.) *Handbook of social psychology.* Cambridge, Mass.: Addison-Wesley, 1954. 2 vols.

Lindzey G., Lykken, D. T., & Winston, H. C. Infantile trauma, genetic factors, and adult temperament. *J. abnorm. soc. Psychol.*, 1960, 61, 7–14.

Linton, R. *The cultural background of personality.* New York: Appleton-Century-Crofts, 1945.

Lippitt, R. *Training in community relations.* New York: Harper, 1949.

Lippitt, R., Polansky, N., Redl, F., & Rosen, S. The dynamics of power. *Hum. Relat.*, 1952, 5, 37–64.

Lippitt, R., Watson, J., & Westley, B. *The dynamics of planned change.* New York: Harcourt Brace, 1958.

Lippmann, W. *Public opinion.* New York: Macmillan, 1922.

Logan, R. *The negro in American life and thought: The Nadir,* 1877–1901. New York: Dial, 1954.

Lorenz, K. Der Kumpan in der Umwelt des Vögels. *J. Ornith.*, 1935, 83, 137–214, 289–413. (Cited by W. H. Thorpe, Jr. in *Learning and instinct in animals.* London: Methuen, 1956.)

Luce, R. D., Bush, R. R., & Galanter, E. *Handbook of mathematical psychology.* New York: Wiley, 1963,

Lynn, D. B., & Sawrey, W. L. The effects of father-absence on Norwegian boys and girls. *J. abnorm. soc. Psychol.*, 1959, 59, 258–262.

MacBeath, A. *Experiments in living.* London: Macmillan, 1952.

McCarthy, Dorothea. Language development in children. In L. Carmichael (Ed.), *Manual of child psychology.* New York: Wiley, 1946. Pp. 477–581.

McClelland, D. C. The psychology of mental content reconsidered. *Psychol. Rev.*, 1955, 62, 297–302.

McClelland, D. C. *The achieving society.* Princeton, N. J.: Van Nostrand, 1961.

McClelland, D. C., Atkinson, J. W., Clark, R. A., & Lowell, E. L. *The achievement motive.* New York: Appleton-Century-Crofts, 1953.

McDougall, W. *An introduction to social psychology.* London: Methuen, 1908.

McDougall, W. *Outline of psychology.* New York: Scribner's, 1923.

McDougall, W. Tendencies as indispensable postulates of all psychology. *Proc. XIth Int. Congr. Psychol.*, Paris, 1937. Pp. 157–170.

McGrath, J. E., & Altman, I. *Small group research: A synthesis and critique of the field.* New York: Holt, Rinehart, & Winston, 1966.

McGregor, D. *The human side of enterprise.* New York: McGraw-Hill, 1960.

MacIver, R. M. *The more perfect union.* New York: Macmillan, 1948.

MacIver, R. M., & Page, C. H. *Society: An introductory analysis.* New York: Rinehart, 1949.

McKelvey, R. K., & Marx, M. H. Effects of infantile food and water deprivation on adult hoarding in the rat. *J. comp. physiol. Psychol.*, 1951, 44, 423–430.

MacLeod, R. B. The place of phenomenological analysis in social psychological theory. In J. Rohrer & M. Sherif (Eds.), *Social psychology at the crossroads.* New York: Harper-Row, 1951. Pp. 215–241.

Macmurray, J. *The self as agent.* New York: Harper, 1957.

Macmurray, J. *Persons in relation.* London: Faber & Faber, 1961.

McNeil, E. B. (Ed.) *The nature of human conflict.* Englewood Cliffs, N.J.: Prentice-Hall, 1965.

McQuown, N. A. Analysis of the cultural content of language materials. In H. Hoijer (Ed.), *Language in culture.* Chicago: Univer. Chicago Press, 1954.

McQuown, N. A. Linguistic transcription and specification of psychiatric interview materials. *Psychiatry*, 1957, 20, 79–86.

Maccoby, Eleanor E. Why do children watch TV? *Publ. Opin. Quart.*, 1954, 18, 239–244.

Maccoby, Eleanor E., Newcomb, T., &

Hartley, E. (Eds.), *Readings in social psychology*. New York: Henry Holt, 1958.

Maccoby, N., & Maccoby, Eleanor E. Homeostatic theory in attitude change. *Publ. Opin. Quart.*, 1961, *25*, 535–545.

Malinowski, B. *Crime and custom in savage society*. London: Paul, Trench, Trubner, 1932.

Mandelbaum, D. G. (Ed.) *The selected writings of Edward Sapir in language, culture and personality*. Berkeley: Univer. California Press, 1949.

Mann, F. C., & Baumgartel, H. J. *Absences and employee attitudes in an electric power company*. Ann Arbor, Mich.: Institute for Social Research, Univer. of Michigan, 1953.

Mann, F. C., & Hoffman, R. L. *Automation and the worker*. New York: Holt, Rinehart, & Winston, 1960.

Mann, R. D. A review of the relationships between personality and performance in small groups. *Psychol. Bull.*, 1959, *56*, 241–270.

March, J. G. Group norms and the active minority. *Amer. sociol. Rev.*, 1954, *19*, 733–741.

March, J. G. (Ed.) *Handbook of organizations*. Chicago, Ill.: Rand-McNally, 1964.

March, J. G., & Simon, H. *Organizations*. New York: Wiley, 1958.

Marcuse, H. *Eros and civilization*. Boston: Beacon Press, 1955.

Marrow, A. J., & French, J. R. P., Jr. Changing a stereotype in industry. *J. soc. Issues*, 1945, *1*, 33–37.

Marschak, J. Efficient and viable organizational forms. In M. Haire (Ed.), *Modern organization theory*. New York: Wiley, 1959. Pp. 307–320.

Maruyama, M. The second cybernetics: deviation-amplifying mutual causal processes. *Amer. Scientist*, 1963, *51*, 164–179.

Marx, M. H. Infantile deprivation and adult behavior in the rat: Retention of increased rate of eating. *J. comp. physiol. Psychol.*, 1952, *45*, 43–49.

Maslow, A. H. *Motivation and personality*. New York: Harper, 1954.

Mason, J. W., & Brady, J. V. The sensitivity of psychoendocrine systems to social and physical environment. In P. H. Leiderman & D. Shapiro (Eds.), *Psychobiological approaches to social behavior*. Stanford, Calif.: Stanford Univer. Press, 1964. Pp. 4–23.

Matthews, D. R. United States Senators: A study of the recruitment of political leaders. Unpublished Ph.D. dissertation, Princeton, 1953.

May, R. Historical and philosophical presuppositions for understanding therapy. In O. H. Mowrer (Ed.), *Psychotherapy: Theory and research*. New York: Ronald Press, 1953, Pp. 9–43.

Mayo, E. *The social problems of an industrial civilization*. Boston: Harvard Univer. Press, 1945.

Mayo, E. *The human problems of an industrial civilization*. Cambridge, Mass.: Harvard Univer. Press, 1946.

Mayo, E., & Lombard, G. *Teamwork and labor turnover in the aircraft industry of Southern California. Business Res. Studies No.* 32. Cambridge, Mass.: Harvard Univer., 1944.

Mead, G. H. The genesis of the self and social control. *Int. J. Ethics*, 1925, *35*, 251–277.

Mead, G. H. *Mind, self, and society*. Chicago: Univer. Chicago Press, 1934.

Mead, G. H. *The philosophy of the act*. Chicago: Univer. Chicago Press, 1938.

Menzel, H., & Katz, E. Social relations and innovations in the medical profession: The epidemiology of a new drug. *Publ. Opin. Quart.*, 1955, *19*, 337–352.

Merton, R. K. Bureaucratic structure and personality. *Soc. Forces*, 1940, *18*, 560–568.

Merton, R. K. The social psychology of housing. In W. Dennis, *et al.*, *Current trends in social psychology*. Pittsburgh: Univer. Pittsburgh Press, 1948. Pp. 163–217.

Merton, R. K. Discrimination and the American creed. In R. M. MacIver (Ed.), *Discrimination and national welfare*. New York: Harper, 1949.

Merton, R. K. *Social theory and social structure*. Glencoe, Ill.: Free Press, 1957.

Merton, R. K., & Kitt, A. Contributions to the theory of reference group behavior. In R. K. Merton & P. F. Lazarsfeld (Eds.), *Studies in the scope and method of "The American soldier."* Glencoe, Ill.: Free Press, 1950.

Metcalf, H. C., & Urwick, L. (Eds.) *Dynamic administration: The collected works of Mary Parker Follett*. New York: Harper, 1940.

Mierke, K. Über die Objectionsfähigkeit

und ihre Bedeutung für die Typenlehre. *Arch. gest. Psychol.*, 1933, 89, 1–108.

Miles, M. B. On temporary system. In M. B. Miles (Ed.), *Innovation in education*. New York: Bureau of Publications, Teachers College, Columbia Univer., 1964. Pp. 437–490.

Miller, D. C., & Form, W. H. *Industrial sociology*. New York: Harper, 1951.

Miller, D. R. The study of social relationships: Situation, identity, and social interaction. In S. Koch (Ed.), *Psychology: A study of a science*. Vol. 5. New York: McGraw-Hill, 1963. Pp. 639–738.

Miller, D. R., & Swanson, G. E. *The changing American parent*. New York: Wiley, 1958.

Miller, D. R., & Swanson, G. E. *Inner conflict and defense*. New York: Henry Holt, 1960.

Miller, F. B. "Resistentialism" in applied social research. *Hum. Org.*, 1954, 12, 5–8.

Miller, G. A. *Language and communication*. New York: McGraw-Hill, 1951.

Miller, G. A. What is information measurement? *Amer. Psychologist*, 1953, 8, 3–12.

Miller, G. A. The psycholinguists. *Encounter*, 1964, 23, 29–37.

Miller, G. A., & Isard, S. Some perceptual consequences of linguistic rules. *J. verbal Learn. verbal Behav.*, 1963, 2, 217–228.

Miller, N. E. Theory and experiment relating psychoanalytic displacement to stimulus-response generalization. *J. abnorm. soc. Psychol.*, 1948, 43, 155–178.

Miller, N. E., & Dollard, J. *Social learning and imitation*. New Haven: Yale Univer. Press, 1941.

Milner, Esther. Some hypotheses concerning the influence of segregation on Negro personality development. *Psychiatry*, 1953, 16, 291–297.

Mischel, W. Preference for delayed reinforcement and social responsibility. *J. abnorm. soc. Psychol.*, 1961a, 62, 1–7.

Mischel, W. Delay of gratification, need for achievement, and acquiescence in another culture. *J. abnorm. soc. Psychol.*, 1961b, 62, 543–552.

Mischel, W. Father-absence and delay of gratification: Cross-cultural comparisons. *J. abnorm. soc. Psychol.*, 1961c, 63, 116–124.

Montaigne, M. E. *Essais* (Maurice Rat, Ed.). Paris: Classiques Garnier, 3 vols., 1948.

Montgomery, K. C. Exploratory behavior as a function of 'similarity' of stimulus situations. *J. comp. physiol. Psychol.*, 1953, 46, 129–133.

Montgomery, K. C. The relation between fear induced by novel stimulation and exploratory behavior. *J. comp. physiol. Psychol.*, 1955, 48, 254–260.

Mooney, J. D., & Reiley, A. C. *Onward industry*. New York: Harper & Bros., 1931.

Moore, H. T. The comparative influence of majority and expert opinion. *Amer. J. Psychol.*, 1921, 32, 16–20.

Morgan, C. T. The hoarding instinct. *Psychol. Rev.*, 1947, 54, 335–341.

Morland, J. K. Racial recognition by nursery school children in Lynchburg, Virginia. *Soc. Forces*, 1958, 37, 132–137.

Morris, C. *Foundations of the theory of signs*. Internat. Encycl. Unif. Sci., Vol. 1, No. 2. Chicago: Univer. Chicago Press, 1938.

Morris, C. *Signs, language and behavior*. New York: Prentice-Hall, 1946.

Morse, Nancy. *Satisfactions in the white collar job*. Ann Arbor: Institute for Social Research, Univer. of Michigan, 1953.

Mowrer, O. H. A cognitive theory of dynamics. Review of R. S. Woodworth, *Dynamics of behavior*. *Contemp. Psychol.*, 1959, 4, 129–133.

Mowrer, O. H. *Learning theory and behavior*. New York: Wiley, 1960.

Mowrer, O. H., & Ullman, A. D. Time as a determinant in integrative learning. *Psychol. Rev.*, 1945, 52, 61–90.

Muller, H. J. *The uses of the past*. New York: Mentor, 1954.

Munn, N. *Psychological development*. Boston: Houghton Mifflin, 1938.

Munsinger, H. L., & Kessen, W. Uncertainty, structure, and preference. Unpublished manuscript, 1964.

Munsterberg, H. *Psychology and industrial efficiency*. Boston: Houghton Mifflin, 1913.

Murdock, G. P. How culture changes. In H. L. Shapiro (Ed.), *Man, culture, and society*. New York: Oxford Univer. Press, 1956. Pp. 247–260.

Murphy, G. *Personality: A biosocial approach to origins and structure*. New York: Harper, 1947.

Murphy, G. *In the minds of men*. New York: Basic Books, 1953.
Murphy, G. *Human potentialities*. New York: Basic Books, 1958.
Murray, H. A. *Explorations in personality*. New York: Oxford Univer. Press, 1938.
Mussen, P. H., & Conger, J. J. *Child development and personality*. New York: Harper, 1956.
Mussen, P. H., & Distler, L. Masculinity, identification, and father-son relationships. *J. abnorm. soc. Psychol.*, 1959, *59*, 350–356.
Myrdal, G. *An American dilemma*. New York: Harper, 1944 (Rev. Edition, 1962).

Nelson, D. H., & Samuels, L. T. A method for the determination of 17-hydroxycorticosteroids in blood: 17-hydroxycorticosterone in the peripheral circulation. *J. clin. Endocrin.*, 1952, *12*, 519–526.
Newcomb, T. M. *Personality and social change*. New York: Holt, Rinehart, & Winston, 1943.
Newcomb, T. M. Autistic hostility and social reality. *Hum. Relat.*, 1947, *1*, 69–86.
Newcomb, T. M. *Social psychology*. New York: Dryden, 1950.
Newcomb, T. M. An approach to the study of communicative acts. *Psychol. Rev.*, 1953, *60*, 393–404.
Newcomb, T. M. The prediction of interpersonal attraction. *Amer. Psychologist*, 1956, *11*, 575–586.
Newcomb, T. M. Individual systems of orientation. In S. Koch (Ed.), *Psychology: A study of a science*. Vol. 3. New York: McGraw-Hill, 1959.
Newcomb, T. M. *The acquaintance process*. New York: Holt, Rinehart, and Winston, 1961.
Newcomb, T. M. The persistence and regression of changed attitudes. *J. soc. Issues*, 1963, *19*, 3–14.
Newman, W. H. *Administrative action*. Englewood Cliffs, N.J.: Prentice-Hall, 1951.
Newsweek editors. How whites feel about Negroes: A painful American dilemma. *Newsweek*, October 21, 1963, *62*, 44–57.
Nida, E. A. *Morphology*. Ann Arbor: Univer. Michigan Press, 1943.
Nissen, H. W. A study of exploratory behavior in the white rat by means of the obstruction method. *J. genet. Psychol.*, 1930, *37*, 361–376.
Norman, R. D. The interrelationships among acceptance-rejection, self-other identity, insight into self, and realistic perception of others. *J. soc. Psychol.*, 1953, *37*, 205–235.
Nowlis, H. H. The influence of success and failure on the resumption of an interrupted task. *J. exp. Psychol.*, 1941, *28*, 304–325.

Ogden, C. K., & Richards, I. A. *The meaning of meaning*. London: Kegan Paul, 1923.
Olds, J., & Milner, P. Positive reinforcement produced by electrical stimulation of septal area and other regions of rat brain. *J. comp. physiol. Psychol.*, 1954, *47*, 419–427.
Olmsted, M. S. *The small group*. New York: Random House, 1959.
Orlansky, H. Infant care and personality. *Psychol. Bull.*, 1949, *46*, 1–48.
Orwell, G. *1984*. New York: New American Library, 1951.
Osborn, A. F. *Applied imagination*. New York: Charles Scribner's Sons, 1953.
Osgood, C. E. The nature and measurement of meaning. *Psychol. Bull.*, 1952, *49*, 197–237.
Osgood, C. E. *Method and theory in experimental psychology*. New York: Oxford Univer. Press, 1953.
Osgood, C. E. Cognitive dynamics in the conduct of human affairs. *Publ. opin. Quart.*, 1960a, *24*, 341–365.
Osgood, C. E. *Graduated reciprocation in tension reduction*. Urbana: Univer. of Ill., Institute of Communications Research, 1960b.
Osgood, C. E. *An alternative to war or surrender*. Urbana: Univer. Ill. Press, 1962.
Osgood, C. E. Psycholinguistics. In S. Koch (Ed.), *Psychology: A study of a science*. Vol. 6. New York: McGraw-Hill, 1963. Pp. 244–317.
Osgood, C. E., Saporta, S., & Nunnally, J. C. Evaluative assertion analysis. *Litera.*, 1956, *3*, 47–102.
Osgood, C. E., & Sebeok, T. Psycholinguistics: A survey of theory and research problems. *J. abnorm. soc. Psychol.* (Supple.), 1954, *49*, No. 4, Part 2.
Osgood, C. E., Suci, G. J., & Tannenbaum,

P. H. *The measurement of meaning.* Urbana: Univer. Illinois Press, 1957.

Osgood, C. E., & Tannenbaum, P. H. The principle of congruity in the prediction of attitude change. *Psychol. Rev.*, 1955, *62*, 42–55.

Paget, R. *Human Speech.* New York: Harcourt Brace, 1930.

Papanek, Miriam. Authority and interpersonal relations in the family. Unpublished doctoral dissertation, Radcliffe College, 1957.

Parsons, T. *The social system.* Glencoe, Ill.: Free Press, 1951.

Parsons, T. The superego and the theory of social systems. *Psychiatry*, 1952, *15*, 15–25.

Parsons, T. An approach to psychological theory in terms of the theory of action. In S. Koch (Ed.), *Psychology: A study of a science.* Vol. 3. New York: McGraw-Hill, 1959.

Parsons, T., & Shils, E. A. (Eds.) *Toward a general theory of action.* Cambridge, Mass.: Harvard Univer. Press, 1951.

Pear, T. H. *Psychological factors of peace and war.* New York: Philosophical Librarv, 1950.

Peirce, C. S. How to make our ideas clear. *Pop. Sci. Mon.*, 1878, *12*, 286–302.

Pepinsky, Pauline N. Social exceptions that prove the rule. In I. A. Berg & B. M. Bass (Eds.), *Conformity and deviation.* New York: Harper, 1961. Pp. 380–411.

Pepinsky, Pauline, Hemphill, J. K., & Shevitz, R. N. Attempts to lead, group productivity, and morale under conditions of acceptance and rejection. *J. abnorm. soc. Psychol.*, 1958, *57*, 47–54.

Pessin, J. The comparative effects of social and mechanical stimulation on memorizing. *Amer. J. Psychol.*, 1933, *45*, 263–270.

Pessin, J., & Husband, R. W. Effects of social stimulation on human maze learning. *J. abnorm. soc. Psychol.*, 1933, *28*, 148–154.

Petegorsky, D. W. On combating racism. In A. Rose (Ed.), *Race prejudice and discrimination.* New York: Knopf, 1951.

Pettigrew, T. F. *A profile of the Negro American.* Princeton, N.J.: Van Nostrand, 1964.

Piaget, J. *The origins of intelligence in childhood.* New York: Norton, 1951.

Piaget, J. *The origins of intelligence in children.* (Trans. by M. Cook.) New York: International Univer. Press, 1952.

Pike, K. L. *Phonetics.* Ann Arbor: Univer. Michigan Press, 1943.

Pittenger, R. E., & Smith, H. L. A basis for some contributions of linguistics to psychiatry. *Psychiatry*, 1957, *20*, 61–78.

Polansky, N., Lippitt, R., & Redl, F. An investigation of behavioral contagion in groups. *Hum. Relat.*, 1950, *3*, 319–348.

Postman, L. Toward a general theory of cognition. In J. H. Rohrer & M. Sherif (Eds.), *Social psychology at the crossroads.* New York: Harper, 1951. Pp. 242–272.

Postman, L., Bruner, J. S., & McGinnies, E. Personal values as selective factors in perception. *J. abnorm. soc. Psychol.*, 1948, *43*, 142–154.

Pratt, C. C. The role of past experience in visual perception. *J. Psychol.*, 1950, *30*, 85–107.

Prentice, W. C. H. Paper read at Sympos. on Conceptual Trends in Psychology, at Amer. Psychol. Assoc., New York: September, 1954.

Preston, M. G., & Heintz, R. K. Effects of participatory vs. supervisory leadership on group judgment. *J. abnorm. soc. Psychol.*, 1949, *44*, 345–355.

Preston, M. G., Peltz, W. L., Mudd, E. H., & Froscher, H. B. Impressions of personality as a function of marital conflict. *J. abnorm. soc. Psychol.*, 1952, *47*, 326–336.

Pudovkin, V. I. *Film technique and film acting.* London: Vision, 1954.

Pumpian-Mindlin, E. Propositions concerning energetic-economic aspects of libido theory. *Ann. N.Y. Acad. Sci.*, 1959, *76*, 1038–1052.

RAND Corporation Study, Report on a study of non-military defenses. July 1, 1958. *Hearings before the Subcommittee on National Policy Machinery of the Committee on Governmental Operations United States Senate, Eighty-sixth Congress, Second Session, February 23, 24, and 25, 1960. Part 120.* Washington, D.C.: U. S. Government Printing Office, 1960.

Raush, H. L., Dittmann, A. T., & Taylor, T. J. The interpersonal behavior of children in residential treatment. *J. abnorm. soc. Psychol.*, 1959a, *58*, 9–27.

Raush, H. L., Dittmann, A. T., & Taylor, T. J. Person, setting, and change in social interaction. *Human Relat.*, 1959b, *12*, No. 4, 361–378.

Raush, H. L., Dittmann, A. T., & Taylor, T. J. Person, setting, and change in social interaction: II. A normal control study. *Human Relat.*, 1960, *13*, No. 4, 305–332.

Raven, B. H., & French, J. R. P., Jr. Group support, legitimate power, and social influence. *J. Pers.*, 1958a, *26*, 400–409.

Raven, B. H., & French, J. R. P., Jr. Legitimate power, coercive power, and observability in social influence. *Sociometry*, 1958b, *21*, 83–97.

Razran, G. H. S. Conditioning away social bias by the luncheon technique. *Psychol. Bull.*, 1938a, *35*, 693.

Razran, G. H. S. Music, art, and the conditioned response. Paper read at Eastern Psychol. Assoc., April, 1938b.

Redfield, R. *The folk culture of Yucatan*. Chicago: Univer. Chicago Press, 1941.

Riecken, H. W. The effect of talkativeness on ability to influence group solutions to problems. *Sociometry*, 1958, *21*, 309–321.

Riecken, H. W., & Homans, G. C. Psychological aspects of social structure. In G. Lindzey (Ed.), *Handbook of social psychology*. Vol. 2. Cambridge, Mass.: Addison-Wesley, 1954.

Riess, B. F. The isolation of factors of learning and native behavior in field and laboratory studies. *Ann. N. Y. Acad. Sci.*, 1950, *51*, 1093–1102.

Riezler, K. *Man: Mutable and immutable*. Chicago: Henry Regnery, 1950.

Roby, T. B. An opinion on the construction of behavior theory. *Amer. Psychologist*, 1959, *14*, 127–134.

Roche, J. P., & Gordon, M. M. Can morality be legislated? In M. L. Barron (Ed.), *American minorities*. New York: Knopf, 1957.

Roethlisberger, F. J., & Dickson, W. J. *Management and the worker*. Cambridge, Mass.: Harvard Univer. Press, 1939.

Rogers, C. R. *Counseling and psychotherapy*. Boston: Houghton Mifflin, 1942.

Rogers, C. R. *Client-centered therapy: Its current practice, implications, and theory*. Boston: Houghton Mifflin, 1951.

Rogers, C. R. A theory of therapy, personality, and interpersonal relationships, as developed in the client-centered framework. In S. Koch (Ed.), *Psychology: A study of a science*, Vol. 3. New York: McGraw-Hill, 1959. Pp. 184–256.

Rogers, E. M. *Diffusion of innovations*. Glencoe, Ill.: Free Press, 1962.

Rokeach, M. Generalized mental rigidity as a factor in ethnocentrism. *J. abnorm. soc. Psychol.*, 1948, *43*, 259–278.

Rokeach, M. A method for studying individual differences in "narrow-mindedness." *J. Pers.*, 1951a, *20*, 219–233.

Rokeach, M. Toward the scientific evaluation of social attitudes and ideologies. *J. Psychol.*, 1951b, *31*, 97–104.

Rokeach, M. Dogmatism and opinionation on the left and on the right. *Amer. Psychologist*, 1952, *7*, 310. (Abstract)

Rokeach, M. The nature and meaning of dogmatism. *Psychol. Rev.*, 1954, *61*, 194–205.

Rokeach, M. *The open and closed mind*. New York: Basic Books, 1960.

Rokeach, M. The organization and modification of beliefs. *Centennial Rev.*, 1963, *7*, 375–395.

Rokeach, M. *The three Christs of Ypsilanti*. New York: Knopf, 1964.

Rommetveit, R. *Social norms and roles*. Minneapolis: Univer. Minnesota Press, 1954.

Rose, A. The influence of legislation on prejudice. In A. Rose (Ed.), *Race prejudice and discrimination*. New York: Knopf, 1951.

Rose, A. (Ed.) *Human behavior and social processes*. Boston: Houghton Mifflin, 1962.

Rosen, B. L., & D'Andrade, R. The psychosocial origins of achievement motivation. *Sociometry*, 1959, *22*, 185–217.

Rosenberg, M. J. Cognitive structure and attitudinal affect. *J. abnorm. soc. Psychol.*, 1956, *53*, 367–372.

Rosenberg, M. J. A structural theory of attitude dynamics. *Publ. opin. Quart.*, 1960, *24*, 319–340.

Rosenzweig, S. Preferences in the repetition of successful and unsuccessful activities as a function of age and personality. *J. genet. Psychol.*, 1933, *42*, 423–441.

Rosenzweig, S. The place of the individual and of idiodynamics in psychology: A dialogue. *J. indiv. Psychol.*, 1958, *14*, 3–21.

Ross, E. A. *Social psychology*. New York: Macmillan, 1908.

Rostow, W. W. *The stages of economic growth*. New York: Cambridge Univer. Press, 1960.

Rundquist, E. A. The inheritance of spontaneous activity in rats. *J. comp. Psychol.*, 1933, *16*, 415–438.

Ryan, B., & Gross, N. The diffusion of hybrid seed corn in two Iowa communities. *Rural Sociol.*, 1942, *8*, 15–24.

Salama, A. A. Fixation in the rat as a function of infantile shocking, handling, and gentling. Unpublished doctoral dissertation, Univer. Ill., 1962.

Salama, A. A., & Hunt, J. McV. Fixation in the rat as a function of infantile shocking, handling, and gentling. *J. genet. Psychol.*, 1964, *105*, 131–262.

Saltonstall, R. *Human relations in administration*. New York: McGraw-Hill, 1959.

Sanford, N. Personality: Its place in psychology. In S. Koch (Ed.), *Psychology: A study of a science*. Vol. 5. New York: McGraw-Hill, 1963. Pp. 488–593.

Sarbin, T. R. Role theory. In G. Lindzey (Ed.), *Handbook of social psychology*. Vol. I. Cambridge, Mass.: Addison-Wesley, 1954. Pp. 223–258.

Sarnoff, I. Psychoanalytic theory and social attitudes. *Publ. opin. Quart.*, 1960, *24*, 251–279.

Sarnoff, I., & Katz, D. The motivational bases of attitude change. *J. abnorm. soc. Psychol.*, 1954, *49*, 115–124.

Schachtel, E. G. The development of focal attention and the emergence of reality. *Psychiatry*, 1954, *17*, 309–324.

Schachter, S. Deviation, rejection, and communication. *J. abnorm. soc. Psychol.*, 1951, *46*, 190–207.

Schachter, S. *The psychology of affiliation*. Palo Alto: Stanford Univer. Press, 1959.

Schachter, S., Ellertson, N., McBride, Dorothy, & Gregory, Doris. An experimental study of cohesiveness and productivity. *Hum. Relat.*, 1951, *4*, 220–238.

Schelling, T. C. An essay on bargaining. *Amer. Econ. Rev.*, 1956, *46*, 281–306.

Schuetz, A. The stranger: An essay in social psychology. *Amer. J. Sociol.*, 1944, *44*, 499–507.

Scott, J. P. Genetic differences in the social behavior of inbred strains of mice. *J. Hered.*, 1942, *33*, 11–15.

Scott, W. A. Rationality and non-rationality of international attitudes. *J. Conflict Resolution*, 1958, *2*, 9–16.

Scott, W. G. Organization theory: An overview and an appraisal. *J. Acad. Management*, 1961, *4*, 7–27.

Scott, W. R. Theory of organizations. In R. E. L. Faris (Ed.), *Handbook of modern sociology*. Chicago, Ill.: Rand-McNally, 1964. Pp. 485–530.

Sears, R. R. Personality development in contemporary culture. *Proc. Amer. Philos., Soc.*, 1948, *92*, 363–370.

Sears, R. R. Relation of fantasy aggression to interpersonal aggression. *Child Developm.*, 1950, *21*, 5–6.

Sears, R. R. A theoretical framework for personality and social behavior. *Amer. Psychologist*, 1951a, *6*, 476–483.

Sears, R. R. Effects of frustration and anxiety on fantasy aggression. *Amer. J. Orthopsychiat.*, 1951b, *21*, 498–505.

Sears, R. R., Maccoby, Eleanor, & Levin, H. *Patterns of child-rearing*. Evanston, Ill.: Row, Peterson, 1957.

Sears, R. R., Pintler, M. H., & Sears, P. S. Effects of father-separation on preschool children's doll play aggression. *Child Develpm.*, 1946, *17*, 219–243.

Seashore, S. *Group cohesiveness in the industrial work group*. Ann Arbor, Mich.: Institute for Social Research, Univer. of Michigan, 1954.

Secord, P. F., & Backman, C. W. Personality theory and the problem of stability and change in individual behavior: An interpersonal approach. *Psychol. Rev.*, 1961, *68*, 21–33.

Seeman, M. A situational approach to intragroup negro attitudes. *Sociometry*, 1946, *9*, 199–206.

Seidenburg, R. *Post historic man*. Boston: Beacon Press, 1951.

Seidenfeld, M. A. Consumer psychology in public service and government. In R. W. Seaton (Chm.), *Consumer psychology: The growth of a movement*. Symposium presented at Amer. Psychol. Assn., New York, Sept., 1961.

Sells, S. B. (Ed.) *The stimulus determinants of behavior*. New York: Ronald Press, 1963.

Selltiz, Claire, Jahoda, Marie, Deutsch, M., & Cook, S. W. *Research methods in social relations*. (Rev. ed.) New York: Henry Holt, 1959.

Selye, H. The general adaptation syndrome and the diseases of adaptation. *J. clin. Endocrin.*, 1946, *6*, 117–230.

Selye, H. *Stress.* Montreal: Acta, 1950.

Shannon, C., & Weaver, W. *The mathematical theory of communication.* Urbana, Ill.: Univer. Illinois Press, 1949.

Sherif, Carolyn W., Sherif, M., & Nebergall, R. E. *Attitude and attitude change: The social judgment-involvement approach.* Philadelphia: W. B. Saunders Co., 1965.

Sherif, M. A study of some social factors in perception. *Arch. Psychol.*, 1935, *27*, No. 187.

Sherif, M. *The psychology of social norms.* New York: Harper, 1936.

Sherif, M. The concept of reference groups in human relations. In M. Sherif & M. O. Wilson (Eds.), *Group relations at the crossroads.* New York: Harper, 1953. Pp. 203–231.

Sherif, M. Integrating field work and laboratory in small group research. *Amer. sociol. Rev.*, 1954, *19*, 759–771.

Sherif, M. Superordinate goals in the reduction of intergroup conflict. *Amer. J. Sociol.*, 1958, *63*, 349–358.

Sherif, M., & Hovland, C. I. Judgmental phenomena and scales of attitude measurement: Placement of items with individual choice of number of categories. *J. abnorm. soc. Psychol.*, 1953, *48*, 135–141.

Sherif, M., & Hovland, C. I. *Social judgment.* New Haven: Yale Univer. Press, 1961.

Sherif, M., & Sherif, Carolyn W. *Groups in harmony and tension.* New York: Harper & Row, 1953.

Sherif, M., & Sherif, Carolyn W. *An outline of social psychology.* (Rev. ed.) New York: Harper & Row, 1956.

Sherif, M., Harvey, O. J., White, B. J., Hood, W. R., & Sherif, Carolyn W. *Experimental study of positive and negative intergroup attitudes between experimentally produced groups: Robbers cave study.* Norman: Univer. Oklahoma, 1954. (Multilithed.)

Sherif, M., White, B. J., & Harvey, O. J. Status in experimentally produced groups. *Amer. J. Sociol.*, 1955, *60*, 370–379.

Shibutani, T. Reference groups as perspectives. *Amer. J. Soc.*, 1955, *60*, 562–570.

Shibutani, T. *Society and personality.* New York: Prentice-Hall, 1961.

Shibutani, T. Reference groups and social control. In A. M. Rose (Ed.), *Human behavior and social processes.* Boston: Houghton Mifflin, 1962. Pp. 128–147.

Shils, E. A., & Janowitz, M. Cohesion and disintegration in the Wehrmacht in World War II. *Publ. opin. Quart.*, 1948, *12*, 280–315.

Shuey, Audrey, King, Nancy, & Griffith, Barbara. Stereotyping of negroes and whites: An analysis of magazine pictures. *Publ. Opin. Quart.*, 1953, *17*, 281–287.

Simmel, G. The number of members as determining the sociological form of the group. *Amer. J. Sociol.*, 1902–03, *8*, 19n.

Simmel, G. *The sociology of Georg Simmel.* (Trans. and edited by K. H. Wolff.) Glencoe, Ill.: Free Press, 1950.

Simon, H. *Administrative behavior.* (2nd ed.) New York: Macmillan, 1957.

Skinner, B. F. The distribution of associated words. *Psychol. Rec.*, 1937, *1*, 69–76.

Skinner, B. F. *The behavior of organisms.* New York: Appleton-Century, 1938.

Skinner, B. F. *Science and human behavior.* New York: Macmillan, 1953.

Skinner, B. F. *Verbal behavior.* New York: Appleton-Century-Crofts, 1957.

Smith, B. L., Lasswell, H. D., & Casey, R. D. *Propaganda, communication and public opinion.* Princeton: Princeton Univer. Press, 1946.

Smith, H. *The religions of man.* New York: Harper, 1958. (Mentor Book ed., 1959.)

Smith, M. B. The personal setting of public opinions: A study of attitudes toward Russia. *Publ. Opin. Quart.*, 1947, *11*, 507–523.

Smith, M. B., Bruner, J. S., & White, R. W. *Opinions and personality.* New York: Wiley, 1956.

Smith, M. E. An investigation of the development of the sentence and the extent of vocabulary in young children. *Univer. Iowa Stud. Child Welfare,* 1926, 3, No. 5.

Sontag, L. W. The genetics of difference in psychosomatic patterns in childhood. *Amer. J. Orthopsychiat.*, 1950, *20*, 479–489.

Soskin, W., & John, Vera P. The study of spontaneous talk. In R. Barker (Ed.), *The stream of behavior.* New York: Appleton-Century-Crofts, 1963. Pp. 228–282.

Spence, K. W. *Behavior theory and condi-*

tioning. New Haven, Conn.: Yale Univer. Press, 1956.

Spier, Leslie. Inventions and human society. In H. L. Shapiro (Ed.), *Man, culture and society*. New York: Oxford Univer. Press, 1956. Pp. 224–246.

Spitz, R. A. The smiling response: A contribution to the ontogenesis of social relations. *Genet. Psychol. Monogr.*, 1946, 34, 67–125.

Spock, B. *The pocket book of baby and child care*. New York: Pocket Books, 1949. Originally published under the title of *The commonsense book of baby and child care*. New York: Duell, Sloan, & Pearce, 1946.

Sprunger, J. A. Relationship of a test of ability to estimate group opinion to other variables. Unpublished master's thesis, Ohio State Univer., 1949.

Stagner, R. Homeostasis as a unifying concept in personality theory. *Psychol. Rev.*, 1951, 58, 5–18.

Steiner, I. D. Interpersonal behavior as influenced by accuracy of social perception. *Psychol. Rev.*, 1955, 62, 268–274.

Stern, Clara, & Stern, W. *Die Kindersprache*. Leipzig: Barth, 1920.

Stevenson, H. W., & Stewart, E. C. A developmental study of racial awareness in young children. *Child Develpm.*, 1958, 29, 399–409.

Stewart, G. R. *American ways of life*. New York: Doubleday, 1954.

Stigler, G. J. *The theory of price*. (Rev. ed.) New York: Macmillan, 1952.

Stonequist, E. V. *The marginal man*. New York: Scribner's, 1937.

Stouffer, S. A. An analysis of conflicting social norms. *Amer. sociol. Rev.*, 1949, 14, 707–717.

Stouffer, S. A., Suchman, E. A., DeVinney, L. C., Star, Shirley, & Williams, Jr., R. M. *The American soldier: Adjustment during army life*. Vol. I. Princeton: Princeton Univer. Press, 1949.

Strodtbeck, F. L. Family interaction, values, and achievement. In D. C. McClelland, A. L. Baldwin, U. Bronfenbrenner, & F. L. Strodtbeck, *Talent and society*. Princeton, N.J.: Van Nostrand, 1958. Pp. 135–194.

Sullivan, H. S. *Conceptions of modern psychiatry*. Washington: W. H. White Psychiatric Foundation, 1947.

Sullivan, H. S. *The interpersonal theory of psychiatry*. New York: Norton, 1953.

Tagiuri, R. Relational analysis: An extension of sociometric method with emphasis upon social perception. *Sociometry*, 1952, 15, 91–104.

Tagiuri, R. Perceptual sociometry: Introduction. In J. L. Moreno, *et al.* (Eds.), *The Sociometry Reader*. Glencoe, Ill.: Free Press, 1960.

Tagiuri, R., & Petrullo, L. (Eds.) *Person perception and interpersonal behavior*. Stanford: Stanford Univer. Press, 1958.

Talland, G. A. The assessment of group opinion by leaders, and their influence on its formation. *J. abnorm. soc. Psychol.*, 1954, 49, 431–434.

Tannenbaum, F. *Slave and citizen: The negro in the Americas*. New York: Knopf, 1947.

Tannenbaum, P. H. Attitudes toward source and concept as factors in attitude change through communications. Unpublished doctoral dissertation, Univer. Ill., 1953.

Taylor, J. G. Experimental design: A cloak for intellectual sterility. *Brit. J. Psychol.*, 1958, 49, 106–116.

Thibaut, J. W. An experimental study of the cohesiveness of underprivileged groups. *Hum. Relat.*, 1950, 3, 251–278.

Thibaut, J. W., & Kelley, H. H. *The social psychology of groups*. New York: Wiley, 1959.

Thibaut, J. W., & Strickland, L. H. Psychological set and social conformity. *J. Pers.*, 1956, 25, 115–129.

Thiessen, D. D. Population density, mouse genotype, and endocrine function in behavior. *J. comp. physiol. Psychol.*, 1964, 57, 412–416.

Thompson, W. R. The inheritance of behavior: Behavioral differences in fifteen mouse strains. *Canad. J. Psychol.*, 1953, 7, 145–155.

Thompson, W. R., & Heron, W. The effects of restricting early experience on the problem-solving capacity of dogs. *Canad. J. Psychol.*, 1954, 8, 17–31.

Thorndike, E. L. *The teacher's word book*. New York: Teachers Coll., Columbia Univer., 1921.

Thorndike, E. L., & Lorge, I. *The teacher's word book of 30,000 words*. New York: Teachers Coll., Columbia Univer., 1944.

Thorpe, W. H., Jr. Some problems of animal learning. *Proc. Linn. Soc. Lond.*, 1944, 156, 70–83.

Thrasher, F. M. *The gang*. Chicago: Univer. of Chicago Press, 1927.

Thumb, A., & Marbe, K. *Experimentelle Untersuchungen über die psychologischen Grundlagen der sprachlichen Analogiebildung*. Leipzig: W. Engelmann, 1901.

Thurnwald, R. *Economics in primitive communities*. London: Oxford Univer. Press, 1932.

Thurstone, L. L. Theory of attitude measurement. *Psychol. Rev.*, 1929, 36, 222–241.

Tiller, P. O. Father-absence and personality development of children in sailor families. *Nordisk Psykologis Monogr. Series*, 1958, 9.

Tillich, P. *The courage to be*. New Haven, Conn.: Yale Univer. Press, 1952.

Tinbergen, N. *The study of instinct*. London: Oxford Univer. Press, 1951.

Titchener, E. B. *A beginner's psychology*. New York: Macmillan, 1916.

Titus, H. E., & Hollander, E. P. The California F scale in psychological research: 1950–1955. *Psychol. Bull.*, 1957, 54, 47–65.

Toch, H. H., & Hastorf, A. H. Homeostasis in psychology. *Psychiatry*, 1955, 18, 81–91.

Toda, M. Information-receiving behavior of man. *Psychol. Rev.*, 1956, 63, 204–213.

Tolman, C. W., & Wilson, G. F. Social feeding in domestic chicks. *Animal Behaviour*, 1965, 13, 134–142.

Tolman, E. C. Cognitive maps of rats and men. *Psychol. Rev.*, 1948, 55, 189–208.

Torrance, E. P., & Mason, R. Instructor effort to influence: An experimental evaluation of six approaches. Paper presented at USAF–NRC Symposium on Personnel, Training, and Human Engineering, Washington, D. C., 1956.

Trager, G. L. Paralanguage: A first approximation. *Studies in Linguistics*, 1958, 13, 1–12.

Trager, G. L., & Smith, H. L. *An outline of English structure*. Washington, D. C.: American Council of Learned Societies, 1951.

Trager, Helen G., & Yarrow, Marian R. *They live what they learn*. New York: Harper, 1952.

Travis, L. E. The effect of a small audience upon eye-hand coordination. *J. abnorm. soc. Psychol.*, 1925, 20, 142–146.

Triplett, N. The dynamogenic factors in pacemaking and competition. *Amer. J. Psychol.*, 1897, 9, 507–533.

Trist, E., & Bamforth, K. W. Some social and psychological consequences of the long wall method of coal-getting. *Hum. Relat.*, 1951, 4, 3–38.

Tryon, R. C. Genetics of learning ability in rats. *Univer. Calif. Publ. Psychol.*, 1929, 4, 71–89.

Ullman, A. D. *Sociocultural foundations of personality*. Boston: Houghton Mifflin, 1965.

United States Bureau of the Census, *U.S. Census of population. General social and economic characteristics, United States summary*. Final Report PC (1)—IC. Washington, D. C.: U.S. Gov. Printing Office, 1962.

Vallance, T. R. Methodology in propaganda research. *Psychol. Bull.*, 1951, 48, 32–61.

Vickery, W. E., & Cole, S. G. *Intercultural education in American schools*. New York: Harper, 1943.

Viteles, M. S. *Motivation and morale in industry*. New York: Norton, 1953.

Volkart, E. H. *Social behavior and personality: The contributions of W. I. Thomas to theory and social research*. New York: Social Science Research Council, 1951.

von Bertalanffy, L. *Problems of life*. (Trans. of *Das biologische Weltbild*, 1949.) New York: Wiley, 1952a.

von Bertalanffy, L. Theoretical models in biology and psychology. In D. Krech & G. S. Klein (Eds.), *Theoretical models and personality theory*. Durham: Duke Univer. Press, 1952b.

von Frisch, K. *Bees, their vision, chemical senses, and language*. Ithaca, N.Y.: Cornell Univer. Press, 1950.

von Hornbostel, E. M. Die Einheit der Sinne. *Melos*, 1925, 4, 290–298.

von Hornbostel, E. M. Unity of the senses. *Psyche*, 1926, 7, 83–89.

von Neumann, J. The general and logical theory of automata. In L. A. Jeffress (Ed.), *Cerebral mechanisms in behavior*. New York: Wiley, 1951.

von Neumann, J., & Morgenstern, O. *The theory of games and economic behavior.* (2nd ed.) Princeton: Princeton Univer. Press, 1947.

Waddell, D. Hoarding behavior in the Golden Hamster. *J. comp. physiol. Psychol.*, 1951, *44*, 383–388.

Wallach, H. Some considerations concerning the relation between perception and cognition. *J. Pers.*, 1949, *18*, 6–13.

Waller, W., and Hill, R. *The family, a dynamic interpretation.* New York: Dryden, 1951.

Wapner, S., & Alper, T. G. The effect of an audience on behavior in a choice situation. *J. abnorm. soc. Psychol.*, 1952, *47*, 222–229.

Warner, W. L., & Henry, W. E. The radio daytime serial: A symbolic analysis. *Genet. Psychol. Monogr.*, 1948, *37*, 3–71.

Watson, G. *Action for unity.* New York: Harper, 1947.

Weber, M. *Essays in sociology.* (Edited by H. H. Gerth & C. W. Mills.) New York: Oxford Univer. Press, 1946.

Weber, M. *Theory of social and economic organization.* (Trans. by A. M. Henderson & T. Parsons.) New York: Oxford Univer. Press, 1947.

Welty, J. C. Experiments in group behavior of fishes. *Physiol. Zool.*, 1934, *7*, 85–128.

Werner, H. *Comparative psychology of mental development.* (Rev. ed.) Chicago: Follett, 1948.

Westermarck, E. *The origin and development of the moral ideas.* Vol. 2. London: Macmillan, 1908.

White, L. A. *The science of culture.* New York: Grove, 1949.

White, L. A. The concept of culture. *Amer. Anthropologist*, 1959, *61*, 227–252.

White, M. *The age of analysis.* New York: New American Library, 1955.

White, R. W. Motivation reconsidered: The concept of competence. *Psychol. Rev.*, 1959, *66*, 297–333.

Whitehead, A. N. *Process and reality.* New York: Macmillan, 1929.

Whitehead, A. N. *Modes of thought.* New York: Macmillan, 1938.

Whiting, J. Sorcery, sin, and the superego. In M. R. Jones (Ed.), *Nebraska symposium on motivation.* Lincoln, Nebr.: Univer. Nebr. Press, 1959.

Whiting, J. Socialization process and personality. In F. L. K. Hsu (Ed.), *Psychological anthropology.* Homewood, Ill.: Dorsey, 1961. Pp. 355–381.

Whiting, J., & Child, I. *Child training and personality.* New Haven: Yale Univer. Press, 1953.

Whitney, L. F. Heredity of trail barking propensity of dogs. *J. Hered.*, 1929, *20*, 561–562.

Whorf, B. L. *Language, thought, and reality.* New York: Wiley, 1956.

Whyte, W. F. *Street corner society.* Chicago: Univer. Chicago Press, 1943.

Whyte, W. F. When workers and customers meet. In W. F. Whyte (Ed.), *Industry and society.* New York: McGraw-Hill, 1946. Pp. 132–133.

Whyte, W. H. *The organization man.* New York: Simon & Schuster, 1956.

Willems, E. P. Review of research. In R. G. Barker & P. V. Gump, *Big school, small school.* Calif.: Stanford Univer. Press, 1964a.

Willems, E. P. Forces toward participation in behavior settings of small and large schools. In R. G. Barker & P. V. Gump, *Big school, small school.* Calif.: Stanford Univer. Press, 1964b.

Williams, D. Effects of competition between groups in a training situation. *Occupational Psychology*, 1956, *30*, 85–93.

Williams, K. A. The reward value of a conditioned stimulus. *Univer. Calif. Publ. Psychol.*, 1929, *4*, 31–55.

Williams, R. M. The reduction of intergroup tensions. *Soc. Sci. Res. Coun. Bull.* 57, New York, 1947.

Williams, S. B., & Williams, E. Barrier-frustration and extinction in instrumental learning. *Amer. J. Psychol.*, 1943, *56*, 247–261.

Willis, R. H. Social influence and conformity—some research perspectives. *Acta Sociologica*, 1961, *5*, 100–114.

Willis, R. H. Two dimensions of conformity-non-conformity. *Sociometry*, 1963, *26*, 499–513.

Willis, R. H. Conformity, independence, and anticonformity. *Hum. Relat.*, 1965, *18*, 373–388.

Willis, R. H., & Hollander, E. P. An experimental study of three response modes in social influence situations. *J. abnorm. soc. Psychol.*, 1964, 69, 150–156.

Winch, R. F., Ktsanes, T., & Ktsanes, Virginia. Empirical elaboration of the theory of complementary needs in mate-selection. *J. abnorm. soc. Psychol.*, 1955, 51, 508–513.

Winch, R. F., & More, D. M. Quantitative analysis of qualitative data in the assessment of motivation: Reliability, congruence, and validity. *Amer. J. Sociol.*, 1956, 61, 445–452.

Winick, C. Teenagers, satire and *Mad. Merrill-Palmer Quart.*, 1962, 8, 183–203.

Winterbottom, M. R. The relation of need achievement to learning experience in independence and mastery. In J. W. Atkinson (Ed.), *Motives in fantasy, action, and society.* Princeton, N.J.: Van Nostrand, 1958. Pp. 453–494.

Wispe, L. G., & Lloyd, K. E. Some situational and psychological determinants of the desire for structural interpersonal relations. *J. abnorm. soc. Psychol.*, 1955, 51, 57–60.

Wittreich, W. J. The Honi phenomenon: A case of selective perceptual distortion. *J. abnorm. soc. Psychol.*, 1952, 47, 705–712.

Wood, H. An analysis of social sensitivity. Unpublished doctoral dissertation, Yale Univer., 1948.

Woodworth, R. S. *Dynamics of behavior.* New York: Henry Holt, 1958.

Wright, Q., Evan, W. M., & Deutsch, M. (Eds.) *Preventing World War III: Some proposals.* New York: Simon & Schuster, 1962.

Writers' War Board. *How writers perpetuate stereotypes.* New York: Writers' War Board, 1945.

Yarrow, Marian R. (Ed.) Interpersonal dynamics in a desegregation process. *J. soc. Issues*, 1958, 14, 3–63.

Yerkes, R. M. The heredity of savageness and wildness in rats. *J. anim. Behav.*, 1913, 3, 286–296.

Yerkes, R. M., & Dodson, J. D. The relation of strength of stimulus to rapidity of habit-formation. *J. comp. Neurol.*, 1908, 18, 459–482.

Zajonc, R. Social facilitation. *Science*, 1965, 149, 269–274.

Zajonc, R. B., & Nieuwenhuyse, B. Relationship between word frequency and recognition: Perceptual process or response bias? *J. exp. Psychol.*, 1964, 67, 276–285.

Zimmerman, Claire, & Bauer, R. A. The effects of an audience on what is remembered. *Publ. Opin. Quart.*, 1956, 20, 238–248.

Zipf, G. K. *The psycho-biology of language.* Boston: Houghton Mifflin, 1935.

Zipf, G. K. *Human behavior and the principle of least effort.* Cambridge, Mass.: Addison-Wesley, 1949.

Name Index

Subject Index